RETHINKING THE LAWYERS' MONOPOLY

For decades, American lawyers have enjoyed a monopoly over legal services, built upon strict unauthorized practice of law rules and prohibitions on nonlawyer ownership of law firms. Now, though, this monopoly is under threat – challenged by the one-two punch of new artificial intelligence (AI)-driven technologies and a staggering access-to-justice crisis, which sees most Americans priced out of the market for legal services. At this pivotal moment, this volume brings together leading legal scholars and practitioners to propose new conceptual frameworks for reform, drawing lessons from other professions, industries, and places, both within the United States and across the world. With critical insights and thoughtful assessments, *Rethinking the Lawyers' Monopoly* seeks to help shape and steer the coming revolution in the legal services marketplace. This title is also available as open access on Cambridge Core.

David Freeman Engstrom is the LSVF Professor in Law and Co-Director of the Deborah L. Rhode Center on the Legal Profession at Stanford University. An award-winning scholar, longtime litigator, and nationally recognized expert on procedure and law and technology, Engstrom is a member of the American Law Institute, where he serves as Reporter for Principles of the Law, High-Volume Civil Adjudication, a member of the Administrative Conference of the United States, and a faculty affiliate at the Stanford Institute for Human-Centered Artificial Intelligence.

Nora Freeman Engstrom is the Ernest W. McFarland Professor of Law and Co-Director of the Deborah L. Rhode Center on the Legal Profession at Stanford University, and she also holds the R. Ammi Cutter Reporter's Chair of the American Law Institute. A nationally recognized authority on tort law, professional responsibility, and complex litigation, she is the author of numerous award-winning scholarly articles, the co-author of two leading casebooks, and Reporter for two Third Restatement of Torts projects.

Rethinking the Lawyers' Monopoly

ACCESS TO JUSTICE AND THE FUTURE OF LEGAL SERVICES

Edited by

DAVID FREEMAN ENGSTROM

Stanford University

NORA FREEMAN ENGSTROM

Stanford University

CAMBRIDGE
UNIVERSITY PRESS

CAMBRIDGE
UNIVERSITY PRESS

Shaftesbury Road, Cambridge CB2 8EA, United Kingdom

One Liberty Plaza, 20th Floor, New York, NY 10006, USA

477 Williamstown Road, Port Melbourne, VIC 3207, Australia

314–321, 3rd Floor, Plot 3, Splendor Forum, Jasola District Centre, New Delhi – 110025, India

103 Penang Road, #05-06/07, Visioncrest Commercial, Singapore 238467

Cambridge University Press is part of Cambridge University Press & Assessment, a department of the University of Cambridge.

We share the University's mission to contribute to society through the pursuit of education, learning and research at the highest international levels of excellence.

www.cambridge.org
Information on this title: www.cambridge.org/9781009528559

DOI: 10.1017/9781009528535

Cover art by Clive Elliott

When citing this work, please include a reference to the DOI 10.1017/9781009528535

First published 2025

A catalogue record for this publication is available from the British Library

A Cataloging-in-Publication data record for this book is available from the Library of Congress

ISBN 978-1-009-52855-9 Hardback
ISBN 978-1-009-52854-2 Paperback

For Deborah L. Rhode

Mentor, teacher, friend, inspiration, and pioneer.

Contents

Figures

Tables

Contributors

Rebecca Haw Allensworth, the David Daniels Allen Professor of Law at Vanderbilt Law School, studies antitrust and professional licensing. Her work on antitrust focuses on how to adapt competition policy to address competition problems posed by tech platforms, and her research on professional licensing explores how lawmakers should balance the need for expertise in regulating the professions with the problems that can arise from self-regulation. Her book, *The Licensing Racket: How We Decide Who Is Allowed to Work and Why It Goes Wrong*, was published by Harvard University Press in 2025.

Rebecca Aviel is a professor and Maxine Kurtz Faculty Research Scholar at the University of Denver Sturm College of Law. Her research and teaching interests include legal ethics and professional responsibility, family law, and constitutional law, with a scholarly focus on the opportunities for insight where these fields intersect. Her current research examines the role of lawyers in a constitutional democracy, the constitutional implications of professional regulation, and innovation in the delivery of legal services to litigants in family court.

Matthew Burnett is Senior Program Officer for the Access to Justice Research Initiative at the American Bar Foundation (ABF), a visiting scholar with the Justice Futures Project at Arizona State University, and an adjunct professor of law at Georgetown University Law Center. Burnett's writing on access to justice and legal empowerment has appeared in more than twenty publications, and he has given more than eighty presentations and workshops around the world. His research has been funded by the National Science Foundation, the U.S. Department of Justice Bureau of Justice Statistics, the World Bank, and the International Development Research Centre. He serves as an advisor to the National Center for Access to Justice and is co-founder of Frontline Justice.

Natalie Byrom is a UK-based researcher and policy adviser with expertise in justice system reform, data-driven technologies, and data governance. She has a track record of leading high-quality research and translating this into meaningful policy impact. Between 2018 and 2020, Dr. Byrom was seconded to the UK Ministry of Justice as expert adviser on data in the context of an ongoing £1 billion program of digital court reform. She is part of the BBC Expert Women Network and currently holds a number of public appointments, membership of the Ministry of Justice's Senior Data Governance Panel, and the Civil Justice Council, where she was appointed in 2022 as member for information architecture and econometrics.

Samantha DiDomenico is a senior manager at Stout Risius Ross, LLC, and has nearly ten years of experience providing consulting services to for-profit and non-profit clients in a variety of industries. She has expertise in understanding large, complex systems and data sets and their intersection with business and social issues. Her work often includes conducting economic impact assessments and program evaluations, conducting independent research, interpreting and analyzing voluminous data sets, and developing transformative change strategies for her clients.

David Freeman Engstrom is the LSVF Professor in Law and Co-Director of the Deborah L. Rhode Center on the Legal Profession at Stanford University. An award-winning scholar, longtime litigator, and nationally recognized expert on procedure and law and technology, Engstrom is a member of the American Law Institute, where he serves as the Reporter for Principles of the Law, High-Volume Civil Adjudication, a member of the Administrative Conference of the United States, and a faculty affiliate at the Stanford Institute for Human-Centered Artificial Intelligence.

Allison K. Hoffman is a professor at the University of Pennsylvania Carey Law School. She is an expert on health care law and policy, and examines some of the most important legal and social issues of our time, including health insurance regulation, the Affordable Care Act, Medicare and retiree health care expenses, and long-term care. Her research aims to bring greater descriptive and analytical clarity to the purposes of health care and health insurance regulation and policy design. She co-edited the *Oxford Handbook of U.S. Health Law* (2017), with I. Glenn Cohen and William M. Sage, which offers the most comprehensive review of US health law in the post-Affordable Care Act (ACA) era.

Samuel Issacharoff is the Bonnie and Richard Reiss Professor of Constitutional Law at NYU School of Law. He is a leading figure in the study of democracy, constitutions, and the courts, and is the author of *Fragile Democracies: Contested Power in the Era of Constitutional Courts* (2015) and, more recently, *Democracy Unmoored: Populism and the Corruption of Popular Sovereignty* (2023). He served as a senior legal advisor to the presidential campaigns of Barack Obama and has long experience as an appellate advocate in American courts.

Hon. Carolyn B. Kuhl presides in a Complex Civil Litigation Department of the Los Angeles Superior Court (LASC). She previously served as the Presiding Judge of the LASC in 2015 and 2016, Assistant Presiding Judge in 2013 and 2014, and Supervising Judge of the Civil Departments from 2011 to 2012 and from 2003 to 2004. A leader in the reform of civil litigation and case management, Judge Kuhl is the co-author of "Toward Fairer, Quicker, Cheaper Litigation: A Unified Theory of Civil Case Management," published in *Judicature* in 2023. Judge Kuhl is a member of the American Law Institute's Council.

Genevieve Lakier is a professor of law and a Herbert and Marjorie Fried Teaching Scholar at the University of Chicago Law School. She teaches and writes about freedom of speech and American constitutional law. Her work examines the changing meaning of freedom of speech in the United States, the role that legislatures play in safeguarding free speech values, and the fight over freedom of speech on social media platforms.

Brian Libgober is an assistant professor of political science and law at Northwestern University. His research focuses on the political economy of American institutions, with a special emphasis on the making of regulations by executive agencies. Thematically, he is interested in the relationship between economic inequality, interest group power, and the design of legal institutions. Methodologically, his work combines a variety of approaches, including formal models, quantitative empirics, and case studies.

Jess X. Lu graduated from Stanford Law School in June of 2024. She is a graduate of Dartmouth College and, prior to law school, worked as a senior associate consultant in Bain & Company's Boston office. In the fall of 2024, Lu began working as an associate at Williams & Connolly LLP in Washington, DC. She will then clerk for Chief Judge Laura Taylor Swain on the US District Court for the Southern District of New York in 2025.

Beverly B. Martin is the Director of NYU School of Law's Center on Civil Justice. From 2010 through 2021, she served as a judge on the U.S. Court of Appeals for the Eleventh Circuit. Prior to joining the Court of Appeals, Judge Martin sat for nearly a decade as a US District Judge for the Northern District of Georgia. She also serves on the boards of the Southern Center for Human Rights and the Campaign Legal Center.

Jamila Michener is an associate professor in Cornell University's Department of Government and School of Public Policy. Her research focuses on poverty, racial inequality, and public policy in the United States. Her recent book, *Fragmented Democracy: Medicaid, Federalism and Unequal Politics* (2018), examines how Medicaid – the nation's public health insurance program for people with low income – affects democratic citizenship, and assesses American political life from the vantage points of those who are living in or near poverty, are (disproportionately) Black or Latino, and are reliant on a federated government for vital resources. Her next book (with Mallory SoRelle), *Uncivil Democracy: Power, Politics, and Access to Justice*, explores how civil legal institutions influence the political lives of racially and economically marginalized people.

Philip G. Peters is the Ruth L. Hulston Professor Emeritus of Law at the University of Missouri School of Law. He is an expert in medical malpractice law and medical malpractice reform. In that capacity, he currently serves as an advisor to the drafters of medical malpractice provisions of the Restatement Third of Torts. His other area of scholarly interest is the identification of educational reforms with the greatest potential to reduce racial achievement disparities.

Daniel B. Rodriguez is the Harold Washington Professor at Northwestern Pritzker School of Law, where he served as Dean from 2012 to 2018. His principal academic work is in the areas of administrative law, local government law, statutory interpretation, federal and state constitutional law, and the law-business-technology interface. He is a member of the American Law Institute's Council.

Giesela Rühl is a professor at Humboldt University Berlin (Germany) and a director of the Humboldt Center for the Legal Profession. Her current research focuses on the opportunities and risks that digitalization poses for the enforcement of (consumer) rights. She investigates how (state) court proceedings can benefit from digitalization processes – and what the (German) judiciary can learn from other countries and from legal tech companies. Rühl is an (elected) member of the European Law Institute, the International Academy of Comparative Law, and the European Academy of Sciences and Arts. She is also the Secretary General of the European Association of Private International Law and a member of the Advisory Board of the German Legal Tech Association.

Rebecca L. Sandefur is a professor in, and director of, the Sanford School of Social and Family Dynamics at Arizona State University (ASU). She investigates access to civil justice from every angle – from how legal services are delivered and consumed, to how civil legal aid is organized around the nation, to the role of pro bono, to the relative efficacy of lawyers, nonlawyers, and digital tools as advisers and representatives, to how ordinary people think about their justice problems and try to resolve them. In addition to her appointment at ASU, Sandefur is Faculty Fellow at the American Bar Foundation, where she founded and leads the Access to Justice Research Initiative.

Lauren van Schilfgaarde is an assistant professor at UCLA School of Law. Her research focuses on Tribal sovereignty and federal Indian law. She previously was the San Manuel Band of Mission Indians Tribal Legal Development Clinic Director at UCLA Law wherein she supervised live-client projects concerning tribal governance and justice systems, ethics, cultural resource protection, voting, child welfare, and more. She currently serves as co-chair for the Native American Concerns Committee of the American Bar Association and as a board member of the Wishtoyo Chumash Foundation, Pukúu Cultural Community Services, and the American Association of Law Schools (AALS) Section on Indian Nations & Indigenous Peoples.

Neil Steinkamp is a managing director at Stout Risius Ross, LLC, and is a well-recognized expert and consultant on a broad range of strategic, organizational, compliance, and financial issues to government, business, courts, and community leaders and their advisors. He has over twenty years of experience covering many industries and matter types and has particular expertise in transformative change strategies, complex structured and unstructured data analysis and assessment, multi-stakeholder collaboration and coordination, the development of pathways to compliance and iterative change strategies, financial and fiscal impact analyses, and other complex topics. He also leads Stout's pro bono practice.

W. Bradley Wendel is the Edwin H. Woodruff Professor of Law at Cornell Law School. His teaching interests are in the regulation of the legal profession and torts, and his research focuses on the application of moral and political philosophy to problems of legal ethics. He previously served as a co-reporter for the American Bar Association's Ethics 20/20 Commission and as co-chair of the New York State Judicial Task Force on Attorney Discipline. He has been a member of the Multistate Professional Responsibility Exam drafting committee since 2007.

Acknowledgments

This book volume was a true team effort, and we have gratitude galore. We are grateful, first and foremost, to the many authors who contributed chapters to this volume. Their words, quite literally, make this monograph. Next, we are indebted to Larry Kramer and to the Hewlett Foundation for supporting both this volume and the spring 2023 convening at Stanford Law School, where many of the ideas that appear here were first discussed. We additionally want to convey our thanks to all of the 2023–24 Rhode Center Civil Justice Fellows who contributed their time and talent to this project, and particularly to Jess Lu and Graham Ambrose. Next, Brianne Holland-Stergar and Todd Venook were instrumental in turning these chapters into a coherent whole. And, last but certainly not least: We are ever grateful to the indefatigable Lucy Ricca, who runs the Rhode Center and is key to the Center's output and success.

Introduction

Envisioning the Future of Legal Services

David Freeman Engstrom and Nora Freeman Engstrom

The legal services marketplace sits on the cusp of a revolution. For nearly a century, American lawyers have enjoyed a monopoly over the provision of legal services. Sweeping unauthorized practice of law (UPL) laws have prohibited (and in some cases, criminalized) the practice of law by anyone other than a licensed attorney – and these rules have further mandated that lawyers work as solo practitioners or in lawyer-owned law firms.[1] This one-two punch has meant that only lawyers can provide legal advice and that even lawyers can't practice law in nonlawyer-owned entities.[2]

Yet, that monopoly is increasingly under threat, as more and more stakeholders have begun to question lawyers' stranglehold over the delivery of legal services.[3] Is it really the case that *only* a licensed attorney possesses the expertise necessary to advise an individual on *every* aspect of a case? Does one *really* need a J.D. to help an unrepresented person fill out a form answer to avoid default in a debt collection or eviction proceeding? Should UPL laws prevent legal tech companies from leveraging new technologies, particularly artificial intelligence (AI), to create user-friendly products that help individuals write wills, navigate court processes, and settle claims? Is lawyers' professional independence really so tenuous that capital investment from nonlawyers must be banned? If we relax the lawyers' monopoly, will consumers actually suffer substantial and intolerable harm?

For a growing number of states, the answer to these questions is "no." Arizona and Utah have led the charge, rewriting the rules around UPL and law practice

1 For how lawyers developed this stranglehold, see generally Nora Freeman Engstrom & James Stone, *Auto Clubs and the Lost Origins of the Access-to-Justice Crisis*, 134 YALE L.J. 123 (Oct. 2024). There are a few exceptions to the latter rule, including if the lawyer is working for the government or a nonprofit or is offering legal services to the entity itself (i.e., an in-house lawyer). *See id.*

2 *See id.*

3 Jessica K. Steinberg et al., *Judges and the Deregulation of the Lawyer's Monopoly*, 89 FORDHAM L. REV. 1315, 1315 (2020).

ownership.[4] Other states have revised their regulatory frameworks to permit nonlawyer community justice workers to offer legal advice in at least certain circumstances.[5] Still others, including Colorado and Oregon, have changed their rules to permit licensed legal paraprofessionals to provide legal help.[6] And numerous other states, including Michigan, North Carolina, and Texas, are weighing whether to follow suit.[7] Put simply, after nearly a century of relative stasis, policymakers, legislatures, and lawyers are devoting serious attention to a dizzying array of reforms to liberalize – and, indeed, to rethink and remake – the legal services marketplace.[8]

Such a convulsive change to a billion-dollar legal services industry is hardly uncontroversial, and many are on record opposing these reforms. In 2022, for instance, the American Bar Association's (ABA) House of Delegates passed, by a landslide vote, a resolution discouraging states from permitting lawyers to share fees with nonlawyers.[9] Such fee-sharing, the ABA intoned, is "inconsistent with the core values of the legal profession."[10] The same year, the California legislature shuttered a working group that had been tasked with examining ways to liberalize regulations and expand categories of legal providers in the Golden State.[11] In Florida, a proposal to open law firm ownership to nonlawyers was quietly killed by the state's highest court.[12] And, leading lawyers have joined the chorus, offering unsparing criticism of

[4] *See generally* DAVID FREEMAN ENGSTROM ET AL., LEGAL INNOVATION AFTER REFORM: EVIDENCE FROM REGULATORY CHANGE (2022) (discussing recent regulatory reforms, including in Utah and Arizona).

[5] Stacy Rupprecht & Jane Balser Cayley, *The Diverse Landscape of Community-Based Justice Workers*, IAALS (Feb. 22, 2024) (explaining that five states, including Alaska, have established community justice worker programs).

[6] Maddie Hosack, *Colorado Supreme Court Approves Licensed Legal Paraprofessionals*, IAALS (Apr. 5, 2023) (listing five states that, as of April 2023, had created such schemes); *Colorado Supreme Court Approves Creation of Legal Paraprofessional License*, COLO. JUD. BRANCH (Mar. 27, 2023), https://www.mncourts.gov/About-The-Courts/NewsAndAnnouncements/ItemDetail.aspx?id=2332. In addition, Minnesota's Supreme Court is currently accepting public comments on whether to extend its legal paraprofessional pilot program. *See Supreme Court Accepting Public Comment on Legal Paraprofessional Pilot Project – Comment Period Deadline Extended*, MINN. JUD. BRANCH (Feb. 21, 2024), https://www.mncourts.gov/About-The-Courts/NewsAndAnnouncements/ItemDetail.aspx?id=2332.

[7] *See* Engstrom & Stone, *supra* note 1.

[8] For a recent catalog of reforms, see *id.*

[9] *See* Sam Skolnik, *ABA Sides against Opening Law Firms up to New Competition*, BLOOMBERG L. (Aug. 9, 2022).

[10] AM. BAR ASS'N, RESOLUTION 402 (Aug. 2022).

[11] *See* Joyce E. Cutler, *California Restrains State Bar from Expanding Nonlawyer Practice*, BLOOMBERG L. (Sept. 19, 2022); David Freeman Engstrom & Nora Freeman Engstrom, *Why Do Blue States Keep Prioritizing Lawyers over Low-Income Americans?*, SLATE (Oct. 17, 2022).

[12] *See* Letter of President Michael G. Tanner to The Honorable Charles T. Çanady, FLORIDA BAR (Dec. 29, 2021), https://www.floridabar.org/news/publications/publications002/special-committee-to-improve-the-delivery-of-legal-services/#reports [hereinafter Tanner Letter]; *see also* Lyle Moran, *Florida Supreme Court Rejects Bar Committee's Reform Proposals, Asks for Alternatives*, AM. BAR ASS'N J. (Mar. 22, 2022).

reforms under consideration in additional states.[13] There is, in short, little attorney appetite to change a regime that has given those with a J.D. nearly a century of unfettered control.

At the same time, *some* form of change now seems inevitable, given the collision of two powerful and cross-cutting forces. First is mounting public concern about what many rightly see as an accessibility crisis in the American civil justice system. Second is the rise of new tech-powered legal service delivery models that seem capable of ameliorating that crisis.

Start with the escalating access-to-justice crisis in the United States. After decades of neglect, access to justice has roared onto legal and political radars, fueled by a growing realization, first among lawyers but increasingly among the wider American public, that the civil justice system is nearing a breaking point. The best current evidence suggests that "as many as half of American households are experiencing at least one significant civil justice situation at any given time."[14] And many of these situations are serious, including eviction, wage theft, uninhabitable housing, domestic violence, harassment, or the unjustified denial of an insurance claim or public benefit.[15]

Yet, the vast majority of these issues go unaddressed. Most folks, even those with serious legal problems, "lump it."[16] They never so much as *try* to vindicate their rights.[17] Even when individuals are on the receiving end of litigation and are sued, rather than suing, many lawsuits end in a default judgment because the individual never appears.[18] Just as worrying, on those occasions when individuals defy the odds and actually make their way into court, they typically do so alone. In approximately

[13] *See, for example*, Stephen P. Younger, *The Pitfalls and False Promises of Nonlawyer Ownership of Law Firms*, 132 Yale L.J. Forum 259 (2022) (criticizing reforms that would permit nonlawyer ownership of law firms); Lynn LaRowe, *Texas Non-Atty Ownership Plan Fizzles as Justice Gap Fix*, Law360 Pulse (Jan. 1, 2024) (discussing various opponents of such reforms in Texas); Heather Linn Rosing, *California Lawyers Association ATILS Comment*, Cal. Laws.' Ass'n (Sept. 25, 2019), https://calawyers.org/california-lawyers-association/california-lawyers-association-atils-comment/ (opposing various regulatory reforms in California).

[14] Rebecca L. Sandefur, *What We Know and Need to Know about the Legal Needs of the Public*, 67 S.C. L. Rev. 443, 445 (2016); *see also* Legal Servs. Corp., The Justice Gap: the Unmet Civil Legal Needs of Low-Income Americans 18 (2022) ("[N]early three quarters (74 percent) of low-income households have experienced at least one civil legal problem in the past year.") [hereinafter LSC Report].

[15] *See* Rebecca L. Sandefur & Emily Denne, *Access to Justice and Legal Services Regulatory Reform*, 18 Ann. Rev. of L. & Soc. Sci. 27, 28 (2022); *see also* LSC Report, *supra* note 14, at 32–38 (cataloging common problems individuals confront).

[16] Nora Freeman Engstrom, *She Stood Up*, 74 Stan. L. Rev. Online 1, 8 (2021); *see* LSC Report, *supra* note 14, at 7 ("Low-income Americans do not get any or enough help for 92 percent of their substantial civil legal problems.").

[17] Sandefur, *supra* note 14, at 445.

[18] *See* Nora Freeman Engstrom & David Freeman Engstrom, *The Making of the A2J Crisis*, 75 Stan. L. Rev. Online 146, 149 (2024) (explaining that "in many jurisdictions and in certain litigation areas – again, most prominently debt collection actions – the *majority* of lawsuits *never draw a responsive pleading* and, as a result, end in default judgment").

three-quarters of the 20 million civil cases filed in state courts each year, at least one side proceeds pro se.[19]

Further, although it's long been reassuringly said that these pro se numbers reflect individual choice – individual litigants' stubborn distrust of lawyers or their plucky desire to go it alone – the evidence strongly suggests otherwise. When asked why they are proceeding pro se, individuals tend to indicate that they don't *want* to take on the baffling and byzantine civil litigation system entirely without assistance.[20] They are consigned to do so. Pro se litigants don't prefer to litigate pro se. They are, rather, condemned to that fate.

Why? The simple answer is there are simply too few attorneys to meet the needs of low- and moderate-income Americans. The Legal Services Corporation (LSC), the country's largest provider of legal aid funding, reports that LSC-funded organizations turn away half of all requests for legal assistance "due to limited resources."[21] In all, that means that LSC-funded organizations "are unable to provide any or enough legal help for an estimated 1.4 million civil legal problems ... that are brought to their doors" each year.[22]

Also clear: Simple and uncontroversial fixes to address that gap, such as a little more pro bono here or a redoubling of our investment in legal aid there, won't cut it. Attorneys in the United States would need to increase their pro bono work from an annual average of thirty hours each to over *nine hundred hours each* to "provide some measure of assistance to all households with legal needs."[23] Likewise, even a tripling or quadrupling of legal aid funding would barely be a drop in the bucket. If, as Deborah Rhode astutely observed two decades ago, "[w]hat Americans want is more justice, not more lawyering," it is incumbent on us to rethink how the current professional monopoly impacts the supply of necessary legal services.[24]

The other tectonic force fueling skepticism about the lawyers' monopoly is the coming of new technologies, particularly AI. AI has already disrupted numerous

[19] *See* Nat'l Ctr. for State Cts., The Landscape of Civil Litigation in State Courts, at iv (2015) (explaining that, in three-quarters of cases, at least one side proceeds pro se); Family Justice Initiative: The Landscape of Domestic Relations Cases in State Court, at ii (2018) (reporting that, in domestic relations cases, "the majority of cases (72 percent) involved at least one self-represented party") [hereinafter, Landscape of Domestic Relations]. Federal court statistics are only marginally better. *See* Judith Resnik, *Mature Aggregation and Angst: Reframing Complex Litigation by Echoing Francis McGovern's Early Insights into Remedial Innovation*, 84 Law & Contemp. Probs. 231, 238–39 (2021) ("Of some 260,000 civil cases filed annually [in the federal courts], about twenty-five percent are brought by people without lawyers, and more than half the cases before the federal appellate courts are brought by self-represented parties.").

[20] Engstrom & Engstrom, *supra* note 18, at 156–57.

[21] LSC Report, *supra* note 14, at 9.

[22] *Id.*

[23] Gillian K. Hadfield, *Innovating to Improve Access: Changing the Way Courts Regulate Legal Markets*, 143 Daedalus 83, 87 (2014).

[24] Deborah L. Rhode, Access to Justice 81 (2004).

aspects of American society, and the legal industry may well be next.[25] As some have commented, "the automation of the law is nigh."[26] Increasingly flush with venture capital funding, a growing "legal tech" industry is working to create new tools that will augment and even outright automate the delivery of legal services at all levels of the system.[27] Leveraging potent new forms of generative AI, legal tech tools can now perform a growing array of higher-order legal cognitions, supercharging how lawyers serve their clients. Generative AI is also sweeping into "direct to consumer" tools that serve litigants directly and, in important ways, double for the services that lawyers or other legal services providers might offer. Indeed, the advent of generative AI holds the promise that the millions who currently go without any legal help at all can enter plain language descriptions of a legal problem into a machine and receive back actionable information and advice. Courts, too, are fast-digitizing a suite of self-help mechanisms, from court "portals" to form-filing and filing tools they pioneered beginning in the 1990s as the pro se crisis initially took root.

The rapid emergence of these tech tools presents a challenge – even an existential threat – to the current regulatory regime. Should technologies that generate legal advice be reserved for use solely by attorneys, or can they be safely put directly into consumers' hands? Should courts themselves create generative AI-driven tools to assist self-represented litigants? In what circumstances does a legal tech tool, including a court-hosted one, run afoul of UPL laws?[28] And will lawyers be the ones to decide these questions, or will the regulatory monopoly shatter in the face of this highly disruptive force?

Important in their own right, these sorts of questions take on both moral and practical urgency, given the justice gap laid out above. If millions of Americans with serious legal needs are indeed condemned to navigate the civil justice system alone, can legal tech at least light the way? Or will these outmatched individuals be deprived of tech-powered help, too?

This collision – the access-to-justice crisis hitting up against the growing presence of legal tech, all on top of a creaky and restrictive regulatory regime built in an earlier, analog era – leaves the lawyers' monopoly on increasingly thin ice. The cries of those resisting reform are drowned out by the realization that *some* change is necessary and also inevitable. And if *change is coming*, one must then contemplate what that change will look like and how it can responsibly be ushered into existence.

[25] *See generally* David Freeman Engstrom, ed., Legal Tech and the Future of Civil Justice (2023).

[26] Michael Simon et al., *Lola v. Skadden and the Automation of the Legal Profession*, 20 Yale J.L. & Tech. 234, 257 (2018).

[27] Megan Ma et al., Generative AI Legal Landscape 2024, at 3 (2024) (noting a 30 percent rise in venture funding since 2021).

[28] *See, for example*, *id.* at 8 (explaining that UPL laws present an obstacle to putting legal tech products in the hands of consumers).

This volume aims to provide a sophisticated but accessible survey of this fast-changing landscape in order to inform, enrich, and expand mounting debate about the future of legal services regulation and access to justice. It identifies and diagnoses the effects of the lawyers' monopoly, proposes conceptual frameworks and perspectives as starting points for reform, and critically, proposes how best to shape and steer the coming revolution. By reframing the issues, infusing empirically minded expertise, and tapping a diverse array of stakeholders and disciplinary perspectives, the volume contributes to a growing and vital debate about what works, what doesn't, and what lies ahead in the next chapter of the civil justice system.

The chapters in this volume are grouped into four parts, each organized around a central, organizing question. Part I asks how best to frame the many issues at the intersection of legal services regulation and access to justice. From what angle should stakeholders analyze and evaluate the role of the lawyer and other legal service providers in a system that is not functioning as it should? Are current access woes best thought of as a regulatory problem, an economics problem, a political problem, or something else entirely, and what follows from each framing?

Part II focuses on the existing market for legal services and asks what might be learned from some of the reform efforts already undertaken. From initiatives by one of the nation's largest court systems to help self-represented litigants, to the role of grassroots organizing and data collection in support of "right to counsel" reforms, to the successes and failures of purveyors of direct-to-consumer (DTC) legal tech products, Part II offers reports from the field. Along the way, it tours some of the steps already taken to modernize the legal services market, and it calls on the profession to see the promise – and sometimes, the peril – of these multifaceted efforts.

Part III adopts a comparative lens. It interrogates the lessons that can be learned both from other jurisdictions that have grappled with a changing legal services market and also from law's sister profession – medicine – which has undergone substantial, and in many ways similar, reform.

Part IV closes the volume with a longer-term vantage, exploring new frontiers for thinking about the future of legal services regulation. Part of that task is to identify and explore key change vectors – like challenges to UPL laws on First Amendment grounds – that have begun to exert pressure on the current system. A second vital task is to better understand what more ambitious changes to the structure of American legal services regulation might look like, were there political will to entertain them. This culminating segment aims to help lawyers, judges, policymakers, scholars, and activists think about the benefits, risks, and tradeoffs of radical change – and also the dire consequences of continued inaction.

Throughout, this volume does not purport to provide any definitive "answer" to any single question posed above. Instead, it infuses the dialogue surrounding each with dynamic perspectives, grounded expertise, and passionate appeals to bring the legal services industry into a more effective and accessible era.

I.1 FRAMING THE ISSUE: CONCEPTUALIZING THE CHALLENGE OF ACCESS TO JUSTICE AND LEGAL SERVICES REGULATION

In order to bring structure and realism to any discussion of possible reform, it is useful to step back to consider how best to approach the weighty problems facing the legal profession. Part I presents a mix of conceptual perspectives that can serve to organize thinking about the current legal services market.

For decades, stakeholders viewed the market for legal services through a lawyer-centric lens – one that focused almost exclusively on lawyers as a panacea to society's legal woes. Through this lens, access-to-justice reformers focused on closing the justice gap by increasing attorney supply. For them, problems could be solved by upping lawyers' commitment to pro bono service, providing more funding to legal aid organizations, and cementing "civil *Gideon*," that is, establishing a right to counsel in civil matters akin to the guarantee of counsel to criminal defendants.[29]

But this framework has proved too simplistic. A steady increase in the number of available attorneys has not led to commensurate decreases in the need for legal services – far from it.[30] Nor do myopic, lawyer-centric perspectives permit the flexible thinking required to situate the legal profession in the tech-powered twenty-first century. It has become clear that *more* lawyers doing *more* work will not close the justice gap. Instead, stakeholders must embrace a more holistic and nuanced conception – a gaze that expands beyond the simple supply of lawyers and appreciates a market made up of a vast array of complex, interacting variables, which, in turn, are bound up in broad societal power structures and imbalances.

The four chapters in Part I embrace that reality, setting forth diverse analytical and conceptual frameworks to guide the volume's subsequent inquiry into a changing market for legal services.

First up is "Justice Futures: Access to Justice and the Future of Justice Work." In it, Professor Rebecca L. Sandefur, the dean of the access-to-justice field, and Matthew Burnett, a senior program officer at the American Bar Foundation, advance a framework that does away with "lawyer-centric" modes of thinking and instead centers debate on the individuals in need of legal advice. Empirical evidence, they point out, demonstrates that a vast number of individuals experience legal needs – and those needs are shaped by a range of factors, including gender, race, geography, and willingness to invoke or engage with law. But previous reforms, they point out, have largely ignored these realities, instead offering blanket, one-size-fits-all, lawyer-driven solutions – all destined to fail. A new generation of reform, they

[29] Hadfield, *supra* note 23, at 87.

[30] For the growth in the profession (some 30 percent since 2000), see *ABA Profile of the Legal Profession 2023 – Lawyer Demographics*, Am. Bar. Ass'n (2023), https://www.abalegalprofile.com/demographics.html (last accessed Apr. 5, 2024). For the fact that growth hasn't translated into a reduction in the justice gap, see *supra* notes 14–19 and accompanying text.

suggest, must be attuned to this history and complexity. And, just as critically, it must expand categories of legal service providers to include actors that can best respond to the particular identities, priorities, and preferences of individuals seeking assistance – including paraprofessionals, community justice workers, and Tribal lay advocates.

Professor Brian Libgober, a political scientist at Northwestern, takes a different tack, approaching the market for legal services from a political economy perspective. In "Race and the Political Economy of Civil Justice," he zooms in on the racial aspects of legal service regulation, dissecting the significant racial disparities in the civil justice system through a market-based lens. In so doing, Professor Libgober presents a strikingly original argument connecting bias in legal services markets – and resulting gaps in attorney availability – to restrictive regulations.

The chapter builds on Libgober's past work which has shown that racial bias pervades legal markets, making it harder for people of color to retain counsel. For instance, one of Libgober's past studies demonstrated that "those with [B]lack-sounding names receive only half the callbacks of those with white-sounding names in response to requests for legal representation."[31] Expanding on that insight, here, Libgober explains that lawyers are even *more* likely to discriminate in geographic markets where there is an inadequate supply of attorneys to meet demand. Lawyers can afford to be "choosy," as Libgober puts it, in a market where demand badly outstrips supply, and when lawyers are "choosy," persons of color lose out. Restrictive rules that artificially constrain supply, it follows, may exacerbate racial inequities – and may further skew the allocation of legal assistance. Libgober's distinctive political economy lens thus helps reveal how interventions designed to open up the legal services market to new types of providers can also make the civil justice system more inclusive.

In "The Hypocrisy of Attorney Licensing," Professor Rebecca Haw Allensworth, an antitrust expert from Vanderbilt, offers a very different regulatory perspective – and takes us deep into the deficiencies of the current state-level attorney disciplinary framework. Rather than focusing on how the legal profession *over*regulates the provision of legal services, she explores how the profession concomitantly engages in pernicious *under*regulation by too lightly disciplining attorneys who engage in misconduct. The system, in other words, is simultaneously too strong and too slack – in the latter case, because of a near-phobic resistance to permanent disbarment. In most states, permanent disbarment is a misnomer; even "permanently" disbarred attorneys can petition to return to practice.[32] Worse, permanent (but not truly permanent) disbarment is rare. Only some 500 lawyers, total, were disbarred nationwide in 2021, out of 1.4 million licensed practitioners.[33] As a result, the system – unwilling to impose the "ultimate penalty" – lets even bad apples keep practicing.

[31] Brian Libgober, *Getting a Lawyer While Black: A Field Experiment*, 24 Lewis & Clark Rev. 53, 53, 76 (2020).

[32] Ashley Merryman, *What Does It Take for an Attorney to Be Disbarred?*, U.S. News (Jan. 19, 2024).

[33] *Id.*

But, in a perverse twist, the system tends to relegate these bad apples to the outskirts of the profession, particularly into solo or court-appointed practice. There, on the profession's fringes, these bad apples are subject to little peer oversight and also are more likely to serve vulnerable individuals from underserved communities (which is to say, precisely those individuals who need protection most). This de facto system of retention-then-relegation, Allensworth convincingly concludes, is indefensible. It militates not only in favor of an overhaul of the disciplinary system – to beef it up – but also in favor of a relaxation of those rules that lock even high-quality nonlawyers out. This one-two adjustment, Allensworth explains, will facilitate greater access to quality representation.

Finally, W. Bradley Wendel of Cornell Law School – a renowned legal ethicist – closes out Part I with "The Case for Traditionalists." In it, he presents a framework centered on the need to uphold the norms and ideals of the legal profession. While acknowledging that reforms are necessary to bring the legal services market into a new era, such reforms, he insists, must be mindful of the "public side" of lawyer's duties: the duties of judgment and professionalism that lawyers owe not only their clients but also courts, the public, and their fellow attorneys. Using hypotheticals, Wendel illustrates how nonlawyer providers may struggle to fulfill the "public side" of lawyering, highlighting the need for reformers to account for the vital public-facing functions that lawyers – and, ideally, nonlawyer service providers that are welcomed into the system – can and must serve.

Three key conclusions cut through the diverse perspectives, frameworks, and approaches gathered in Part I. First, the chapters collectively reaffirm that the market for legal services is not only shaped by the lawyers who, until now, have dominated. The market is also shaped by the needs and identities of those who *require legal assistance*. As a corollary, class, power, race, gender, education, ethnicity, and other features of an individual's identity powerfully shape how an individual responds to legal problems and utilizes (or fails to utilize) legal services. For too long, the legal profession has mostly ignored the above realities. That inattention must end.

The second conclusion flows from the first: Once the focus shifts from the supply side to the demand side – from lawyers to the individuals in need of legal services – there is a corresponding need to expand the frame. A healthy, robust, and responsive legal services market can't be one-size-fits-all. Depending on the person or problem, legal paraprofessionals, community justice workers, or Tribal lay advocates may be far better suited to offer assistance and support.

Third, an expanded conception of legal services requires a corresponding expansion of the experts on whom the legal profession relies. The profession cannot continue to turn only to attorneys for their perspectives and knowledge but must instead embrace political economists, consultants, union organizers, and more. For much of the previous century, lawyers effectively boxed these actors out of the conversation. Part I's multifaceted contributions make clear that a wider mix of voices will be necessary to gain a dynamic, nuanced understanding of legal needs in this country, and accordingly, to design the interventions best equipped to respond to those needs.

I.2 LESSONS FROM THE FIELD: ON-THE-GROUND EFFORTS TO EFFECT POSITIVE CHANGE

Numerous reforms to the legal services market are already off and running. Arizona and Utah lead the pack, as they have enacted revolutionary reforms that open the legal profession to outside investment and permit nonlawyer provision of legal services.[34] But, while Arizona and Utah are blazing a trail, their reforms should not obscure other efforts to narrow the justice gap. For instance, courts across the country have implemented a wide range of self-help services to assist self-represented litigants.[35] Other reforms are geographically targeted: The Alaska Legal Services Corporation (ALSC), for example, has launched a first-of-its-kind community justice worker program, obtaining a regulatory waiver that permits ALSC to supervise and train local community members to provide legal advice to their fellow citizens in rural Alaska.[36] And still other efforts come from a growing cast of for-profit and nonprofit legal tech providers. Upsolve, to cite just one example, is a nonprofit dedicated to developing online tools to permit individuals to navigate the Chapter 7 bankruptcy process.[37]

This part canvasses a few of these efforts – and surfaces various lessons to help guide further experimentation.

First up, The Honorable Carolyn Kuhl, former Presiding Judge of the Los Angeles Superior Court (LASC) and a leading voice in the regulation of the legal profession, describes and critiques previous access-to-justice-minded reforms implemented in the nation's largest trial court. "What Can Legal Services Reformers Learn from Court Efforts to Assist Self-Represented Litigants?" first points out the growing number of unrepresented individuals bringing or defending cases in state courts – an onslaught that prompted numerous state courts, including LASC, to undertake measures to assist these individuals, while still maintaining their role as a neutral adjudicator. She catalogs and critically evaluates LASC's wide array of interventions aimed at assisting these pro se litigants, including educational services offered to self-represented family law litigants; online dispute resolution (ODR) platforms; and "Gina the Traffic Avatar," a computer-based chatbot that helps users gauge their options for paying or contesting traffic tickets. Her guidance offers

[34] *See* ENGSTROM ET AL., *supra* note 4, and accompanying discussion.

[35] NAT'L CTR. FOR STATE CTS. & MASS. APPLESEED CTR. FOR L. & JUST., COURT BASED SELF-HELP CENTERS 7 (2023) (reporting that courts in twenty-five of thirty-two states surveyed had implemented some form of self-help kiosk).

[36] Community Justice Worker Program, ALASKA L. SERVICES CORP., https://www.alsc-law.org/community-justice-worker-program/ (last accessed May 5, 2024).

[37] *How Upsolve Works*, UPSOLVE, https://upsolve.org/how-we-work/ (last accessed May 5, 2024).

critical insights for other court systems hoping to integrate similar reforms, and more broadly, infuses the ongoing dialogue regarding the future of the legal services market with real-world experience and candor.

Next, in "Civil [Justice] Engineering," Neil Steinkamp and Samantha DiDomenico, both of the global advisory firm Stout Risius Ross, LLC, offer lessons in reform efforts gleaned from their combined decades of experience directly working as strategic advisors on issues of social change. They focus on their efforts enacting limited "civil *Gideon*" in a number of jurisdictions – efforts that have minted a civil right to counsel in eviction proceedings akin to what criminal defendants have long enjoyed under the Sixth Amendment. Steinkamp and DiDomenico offer a step-by-step roadmap for building an empirically rigorous but politically potent movement toward regulatory reform. The result is a unique how-to guide for engaging courts and community stakeholders in generating the quantitative and qualitative data that drives reform efforts. Just as important, their chapter is a bracing reminder of the ways in which the current system remains stuck in a kind of stasis – and has historically been intractable to real and rigorous empiricism that might inform, and also drive, reform efforts.

Professor Jamila Michener of Cornell's Department of Government next takes us out of the courthouse, urging reformers to focus their efforts on correcting the societal power imbalances that lead to legal disputes in the first place. In "Beyond Access to Justice: Power, Organizing, and Civil Legal Inequality," she shares stories of community members and political organizers who have used tenants unions to attack legal problems at their root. Collective action, she says, can ameliorate the power structures that *create* legal problems, like predatory landlords, exploitative employers, and the insufficient availability of affordable housing. Tenants unions mobilize those so often harmed by such structural injustices, using collective power to improve harmful building conditions and expel notorious building management companies, thereby avoiding legal disputes and decreasing the demand for legal services in the first place. Professor Michener authoritatively argues that "supply-side" reforms (e.g., increasing access to attorneys and funding for legal aid organizations) must be complemented with demand-side interventions, such as legislation to promote and empower the political organizing necessary to address legal problems at their source.

Finally, Professor David Freeman Engstrom of Stanford and Jess X. Lu, a Stanford Law graduate and former management consultant, offer a different type of report from the field, and a less optimistic one, in their examination of how legal tech companies are navigating restrictive rules in their efforts to build sustainable business models that can also narrow the justice gap. In "The Puzzle of Anemic 'Legal Tech' and the Future of Legal Services," Engstrom and Lu question why rapid advances in technology, and especially AI, have not resulted in a robust DTC legal tech market. While restrictive UPL laws and antiquated court-run technology systems may provide a partial answer, Engstrom and Lu theorize that the better explanation is the challenging market economics of providing low- and middle-income Americans with tech-based services and the "lifetime value trap": The low revenue potential of a customer base that needs services only episodically and often only once and, in any event, has limited ability to pay for additional services or products. They conclude that, in order to build sustainable business models, DTC legal tech may need passive income streams and enterprise-level customers. Their analysis sheds new light on the role technology may play in the legal services market of the future, and it may even call into question reforms focused on liberalizing legal practice rules. Indeed, if those reforms will not yield a robust, competitive marketplace of DTC legal tech providers, then perhaps reform advocates should allocate scarce real and political capital to other potential solutions.

The chapters in Part II cover only a sliver of the many impactful efforts that have shaped the decades-long journey to improve the legal services market. But these examples hold broad-based lessons for those seeking to push the legal services market into its next phase. LASC's numerous efforts to improve services for pro se litigants – some of which were more successful than others – remind reformers to critically analyze interventions as they are put into place, always seeking to find room for improvement. Lessons from the consulting world prompt a focus on the stakeholder buy-in and empirical thinking that drives impactful interventions. The impact of political organizing calls on the reform movement to remember that the access-to-justice crisis did not arise solely from inadequate court systems or a constrained supply of legal services; instead, it finds its roots in the power imbalances that lead to legal disputes in the first place. And the successes and failures of various DTC legal tech products are a reminder that reformers cannot pin their hopes for solving the access-to-justice crisis solely on evolving technologies. Instead, careful consideration must be given to the market forces undergirding the industry if one expects legal tech to meaningfully change the game. At base, as reformers seek to usher the legal profession into its next era, the chapters in Part II remind them to remain mindful of the steps that have already been taken on that journey.

I.3 THE COMPARATIVE LENS: WHAT CAN BE LEARNED FROM OTHERS?

Part III turns outward. It applies a comparative lens to ask what the US legal profession of today can learn from other professions and places.

I.3.1 *Lessons from Medicine*

In many ways, medicine and law (the "sister professions," as the Supreme Court has put it) have proceeded along parallel evolutionary tracks.[38] Over the past century, both

[38] Bates v. State Bar of Arizona, 433 U.S. 350, 382 (1977) (dubbing medicine law's "sister profession").

have witnessed the decline of solo practitioners and attendant growth of large firms.[39] Both have increasingly seen providers shy away from generalist practices and drift to more specialized fields.[40] Both are in something of an access crisis, as the demand for at least certain kinds of medical and legal services outstrips supply.[41] And finally, both have grappled with deeply rooted historical prejudices – meaning that, at least in the highest echelons, both law and medicine remain stubbornly male and white.[42]

But, over the past forty years, law and medicine have diverged in at least two critical ways, and both are instructive for any serious effort to rethink the legal services marketplace. First, in recent years, most states have retained restrictions on nonlawyer ownership and investment, whereas medicine has accepted funding from outsiders, including from private equity.[43] In fact, in the medical arena, over the past ten years, private equity firms have invested nearly $1 trillion buying up everything from neighborhood primary care offices to fertility clinics, cardiology practices, nursing homes, hospitals, and even hospices.[44]

In medicine, the receipts on this private equity investment have started to come in – and they are deeply discouraging. A battery of recent studies indicate that private equity investment in health care is associated with both a drop in quality and a rise in cost.[45] As Dr. Ashish Jha, the dean of the Brown University School

[39] *See, for example*, Yashaswini Singh & Christopher Whaley, *Private Equity Is Buying up Health Care, but the Real Problem Is Why Doctors Are Selling*, Hill (Dec. 21, 2023) (reporting that "nearly 75 percent of physicians now work for a hospital or corporate owner"); Benjamin H. Barton, *Middle Class Lawyers Are a Dying Breed*, Bus. Insider (June 23, 2015) (reciting statistics showing the decline of solo practitioners in law, and the growth of law firms).

[40] Michael Ariens, *Top Ten Changes in the Legal Profession Since 1979, Part II*, Marquette U. L. School Faculty Blog (Feb. 19, 2012), https://law.marquette.edu/facultyblog/2010/01/top-ten-changes-in-the-legal-profession-since-1979-part-ii/ (last accessed Feb. 24, 2025) (noting the rise of legal specialization); James E. Dalen et al., *Where Have the Generalists Gone? They Became Specialists, Then Subspecialists*, 130 Am. J. Med. 766 (2017) (same, but for medicine).

[41] The discussion above outlines the access problem in law. For medicine, see Press Release, Am. Med. Ass'n, *AMA President Sounds Alarm on National Physician Shortage*, AMA (Oct. 24, 2023), https://www.ama-assn.org/press-center/press-releases/ama-president-sounds-alarm-national-physician-shortage (last accessed Feb. 24, 2025).

[42] Brian Dolan, The Medical Profession through History 39–42 (2021) (describing the roots of the lack of diversity in the medical profession); Allison Laffey & Allison Ng, *Diversity and Inclusion in the Law: Challenges and Initiatives*, Am. Bar Ass'n (May 2, 2018) (describing issues of diversity in the law).

[43] *See, for example*, Richard M. Scheffler et al., Monetizing Medicine: Private Equity and Competition in Physician Practice Markets (2023); Erin C. Fuse Brown & Mark A. Hall, *Private Equity and the Corporatization of Health Care*, 76 Stan. L. Rev. 527 (2024); Edward P. Hoffer, *Private Equity and Medicine: A Marriage Made in Hell*, 137 Am. J. Med. 5 (Jan. 2024).

[44] Singh & Whaley, *supra* note 39.

[45] For costs, see Scheffler et al., *supra* note 43, at 23–31 (finding that private equity acquisition of medical practices tends to be associated with significant price hikes and that increased prices "will eventually be paid by consumers in the form of higher health insurance premiums"); Singh & Whaley, *supra* note 39 ("[T]here is clear evidence that private equity ownership increases prices."). For quality, see Atul Gupta et al., *Owner Incentives and Performance in*

of Public Health, has put it, "there is a quality problem when private equity takes over."[46]

In "How Power Undermined the Medical Profession," Professor Allison K. Hoffman, an expert on health care law and policy at the University of Pennsylvania Carey Law School, catalogs this research regarding cost and quality, explores how corporate investment came to take over medicine, and plumbs both for relevant lessons for law reformers. Over the past century, Hoffman explains, the medical profession gained significant power and influence by setting stringent licensure laws, controlling the physician pipeline, and (for a time) restricting corporate practice. Yet, she says, those measures ultimately backfired – and unwittingly paved the way for corporate interests to take over, free from regulatory strictures or oversight. Sounding the alarm concerning the peril of private equity, Hoffman asks: As the legal profession considers whether to follow the medical profession in opening its doors to nonlawyer funding and ownership, can the pitfalls experienced by the medical profession be avoided?

The second way law and medicine have diverged concerns the use and acceptance of adjunct providers. Medicine has been welcoming of such providers to the point that, today, over half of primary care visits are performed by those without an M.D.[47] Physicians, it seems, at least grudgingly recognize that X-ray technicians, physician assistants, phlebotomists, and other professionals positively contribute to the overall patient experience.[48] Indeed, to give just one example, in most states, nurse practitioners have full practice authority – meaning that they can independently evaluate patients, diagnose conditions, order tests, furnish treatment, and prescribe medication, no physician supervision required.[49]

Not so in law. In most states, regulations *still* prevent nonlawyers from independently providing virtually *any* legal services. "The legal equivalents of physician assistants or nurse practitioners," as one expert recently put it, "do not exist."[50]

Healthcare: Private Equity Investment in Nursing Homes, 37 Rev. Fin. Stud. 1029 (2024) (reporting that patients at private-equity-owned nursing homes suffered an 11 percent increase in mortality, as compared to controls); Sneha Kannan et al., *Changes in Hospital Adverse Events and Patient Outcomes Associated with Private Equity Acquisition*, 330 JAMA 2366, 2366 (2023) (reporting that "private equity acquisition was associated with a 25.4 percent increase in hospital-acquired conditions," including falls and infections).

[46] Reed Abelson & Margot Sanger-Katz, *Serious Medical Errors Rose After Private Equity Firms Bought Hospitals*, N.Y. Times (Dec. 26, 2023).

[47] Anuradha Jetty et al., *How Primary Care Utilization Patterns Have Changed over the Decade*, 21 Annals Fam. Med. 5127 (2023).

[48] *See* Ben Barton, *A Comparison between the American Markets for Medical and Legal Services*, 67 Hastings L.J. 1331, 1358 (2016) (explaining that, unlike the ABA, which has kept nonlawyers out, the American Medical Association "has had to accept (often at the prompting of antitrust regulators or lawsuits) the presence of competitors, from chiropractors, osteopaths, or nurse practitioners, to Reiki healers and the many other types of individuals who sell what might broadly be called medical services").

[49] *See* Engstrom & Stone, *supra* note 1, at n.11 (collecting sources).

[50] Joan W. Howarth, Shaping the Bar: The Future of Attorney Licensing 12 (2023).

Rather, paralegals and other trained nonlawyer legal professionals cannot furnish legal advice and must, at all times, be directly supervised by an attorney. They cannot independently contribute their skills to meet the significant demand for legal help.[51]

In "Lessons from Medicine's Experiment with Nurse Practitioners and Physician Assistants," Professor Phillip G. Peters of the University of Missouri School of Law – a leading medical-legal scholar – traces this disjunction. He explains how medicine overcame initial resistance to accept these non-M.D. providers and catalogs recent evidence showing that nurse practitioners and physician assistants deliver cost-effective, high-quality care, often in rural communities. In his words, members of those professions provide care "at lower cost than physicians and in under-served areas where it is difficult to recruit physicians." In so doing, Peters offers a lucid, one-stop shop for those seeking to understand the spread of adjunct providers in medicine and what that evolution means for law-side reforms.

I.3.2 *Lessons from Other Legal Systems*

Just as there are lessons to be learned from other industries, there are also lessons to be learned from other places regarding both loosening restrictions on the legal services market and responding to the rise of new technology.

Restrictions on who can provide legal services vary greatly across the world. Some countries are similar to the United States – a full-fledged lawyer monopoly.[52] Others sit at the far end of the spectrum. Think Switzerland, where nonlawyers can provide almost all legal services, except for a small subset reserved solely for professional "Advokats."[53] Most other places, however, fall somewhere in the middle of the spectrum. Japan, for instance, imposes strong restrictions to prevent nonlawyers from, among other things, appearing in court but has a relatively robust subset of "legal advisors" that assist with more administrative tasks.[54] Likewise, in Canada, nonlawyers are permitted to provide legal assistance in a range of settings.[55] As one scholar explains: "Across Canada, the statutes that govern the legal profession contain both *exceptions* to the practice of law – activities that would otherwise

[51] *See, for example*, Am. Bar Ass'n, *Model Rules of Prof'l Conduct R.* 5.3 (2019) (requiring paralegals be supervised by an attorney at all times); *Information for Lawyers: How Paralegals Can Improve Your Practice*, AM. BAR ASS'N, https://www.americanbar.org/groups/paralegals/profession-information/information_for_lawyers_how_paralegals_can_improve_your_practice/ (last accessed Apr. 25, 2024) (paralegals "may not give legal advice to a client").

[52] Ivan Mitchell Merrow & Madeleine Dusseault, *Non-Lawyer Legal Services: An International Round-Up*, JUSTICE LAB (June 16, 2017).

[53] *Practical Guide for EU, EEA and Swiss Lawyers on Service and Establishment*, COUNCIL OF BARS AND L. SOCS. OF EUROPE, at ¶ 1.7 (2018).

[54] *Id.*

[55] *See* Lisa Trabucco, *Lawyers' Monopoly? Think Again: The Reality of Non-Lawyer Legal Service Provision in Canada*, 96 CAN. B. REV. 460 (2018).

constitute the practice of law but do not in certain circumstances – and *exemptions* that allow others to engage in practice-of-law activities. In addition, numerous other statutes in all jurisdictions authorize nonlawyer representation before courts and administrative tribunals."[56]

In "The Statutory Influence of Tribal Lay Advocates," Professor Lauren van Schilfgaarde, an expert in Tribal sovereignty and federal Indian law at University of California Los Angeles School of Law and a member of the Cochiti Pueblo Tribe, provides a first-of-its-kind analysis of the codification of Tribal lay advocates – nonlawyer legal services providers operating in Native American Tribal Courts. First, she highlights the exceptional nature of the nation's vast array of Tribal law and Tribal Courts, pointing out that Tribal law is not necessarily lawyer-centric: Nonlawyer experts and community members play key roles. Nor does Tribal law always rely on an adversarial, winner-take-all framework. Instead, it incorporates practices like peacemaking and restorative justice. After setting the table, van Schilfgaarde canvasses Tribal codes to evaluate how they embrace, codify, and regulate Tribal lay advocacy. This analysis reveals that Tribal lay advocates are not conceived of as a "gap-filler" for lawyers but are instead recognized as qualified, competent legal experts who are held to high ethical standards and are well-versed in the Tribe's community, law, and culture. The codification of the Tribal lay advocate, she says, may hold valuable insight for the access-to-justice movement outside of Indian Country.

Continuing the comparative theme, two further chapters consider how other jurisdictions are responding to the rapid rise of "legal tech," particularly new AI-based legal services delivery models.

Natalie Byrom, a UK-based expert in justice system reforms, takes us across the pond in "Necessary but Insufficient? Reforms to Legal Services Regulation, Technology, and the Role of the Courts in Increasing Access to Justice in England and Wales." Byrom first zeroes in on the UK's Legal Services Act of 2007. Enacted with great fanfare, the Act initially promised to leverage technology to increase competition and improve access to justice. But, as Byrom explains, the Legal Services Act failed to live up to these lofty expectations, leading the government to try, in fits and starts, to develop technological fixes that would allow individuals to more easily navigate the court system and resolve their disputes. But even those fixes mostly fizzled: By 2023, the program had spent most of its budget with only over half of the planned projects completed. Unbowed, the UK government recently announced a new vision for a digital justice system founded on public–private partnerships that integrate private-sector digital services into governmental court systems. Despite its laudable aim, that proposal, Byrom suggests, *also* raises a host of questions, including whether private entities are properly incentivized to participate in the anticipated partnerships, and whether the proposal will, in fact, deliver services in the areas of law with the most significant unmet need. All

[56] *Id.* at 469.

told, these misses, feints, and false starts, Byrom suggests, may hold important lessons for American reformers, helping them build on the UK's successes while avoiding its pitfalls.

Part III's final contribution comes from Professor Giesela Rühl of Humboldt University of Berlin. In "Legal Tech Companies and Access to Justice in Germany," Professor Rühl explains that, over the past twenty-five years, German courts have seen significant reductions in the number of small claims actions being filed. This reduction may stem from claimants forgoing legal action due to prohibitive costs or daunting procedural complexity. One solution to this issue, she suggests, could come from the growing number of legal tech companies in Germany that have leveraged digital technology to standardize and enforce small-scale consumer claims. These companies initially operated in a largely deregulated zone, with German courts broadly interpreting debt collection licensure statutes to accommodate the companies' business models. Eventually, the Legal Tech Act of 2021 was passed to introduce a new regulatory scheme for both lawyers and legal tech companies. But the Act, Ruhl says, failed to level the playing field between lawyers, who remain relatively tightly regulated, and legal tech companies, which continue to operate free from onerous requirements. The German experience could provide critical insights to stakeholders, considering how to strike the appropriate regulatory balance between lawyers and legal tech companies in the United States.

Read together, the comparative lens applied across the chapters in Part III reveals not only the shared challenges of adapting to a rapidly changing landscape but also the unique opportunities for learning and growth. The examples of nurse practitioners, physician assistants, and Tribal advocates showcase the promise of expanding the pool of individuals permitted to provide legal services; these examples also provide ideas for ensuring those individuals will provide high-quality services. Meanwhile, the story of private equity in medicine provides something of a cautionary tale. Then, accounts of reform efforts in the UK and Germany illustrate a growing consensus that legal tech could improve the delivery of, and access to, legal services – but only if regulation is properly calibrated. While the UK and German experiences of reform each suggest concrete dos and don'ts for American reformers, together, they encourage the legal profession to remember that getting to a regulatory sweet spot may take time and a willingness to course-correct.

I.4 NEW FRONTIERS: CHARTING THE FUTURE OF LEGAL SERVICES

The fourth and final part extends its focus beyond existing reforms, asking what the *future* of legal services will look like. The contours of that future are far from clear, and sketching them out requires one to grapple with a bevy of interrelated questions. Among them: Will reforms, when they come, be the product of careful policymaking? Or will they be the impulsive products of partisan politics – or will they perhaps come slashingly, from federal courts? Should reforms be transsubstantive (affecting all areas of law equally)? Or, should we pick and choose between substantive specialties – and if so, how? Who ought to drive and oversee reform efforts? And: Have the most effective reforms already been proposed, or is further imagination required?[57]

The Part's first two chapters address the question of *who* will drive reform. Will reforms emanate from within the existing regulatory structure, pushed forward by state bars and state supreme courts? Or will litigation drive change, with a judge issuing a single decision that radically reshapes the legal market? Will change come from the states? Or will the federal government lead the charge?

The first to tackle the *who* question is Professor Genevieve Lakier, a noted First Amendment scholar from the University of Chicago Law School, who outlines the implications of litigation-driven reforms. In "Professional Speech, the *Lochnerized* First Amendment, and the Unauthorized Practice of Law," Lakier explores *Upsolve, Inc. v. James*, a case currently winding its way through federal court. The case arose when Upsolve, a nonprofit that offers tech-based services to consumers who are facing financial trouble, sought to train nonlawyers to provide free legal advice to those hit with debt collection actions.[58] Recognizing that lay advice could violate New York's stringent UPL restrictions, Upsolve brought suit against the New York Attorney General seeking the court's assurance that it could follow through on its plans.[59] A court battle followed. Upsolve won the first round, as a trial court found that the training and advice provided by Upsolve's volunteers constituted protected speech under the First Amendment.[60] Though still on appeal, many have hailed the trial court's decision as a major win for access-to-justice advocates.[61] Yet, the trial court's decision, Lakier concludes, should be viewed cautiously. That's because, says

[57] Certainly, this volume is not the first to grapple with these questions. Part IV's chapters are situated within an already robust, ever-evolving spectrum of proposed reforms. At one end of this continuum, stakeholders have proposed relatively uncontroversial reforms, such as increasing legal aid and expanding pro bono. At the other end lie ambitious, industry-upheaving proposals, including the recognition of a constitutional right to civil council and a massive fortification of the welfare state to help low-income individuals avoid legal problems in the first instance. For the former, see Hon. Robert W. Sweet, *Civil Gideon and Confidence in a Just Society*, 17 YALE L. & POL'Y REV. 503 (1998). For the latter, see Juliet M. Brodie & Larisa G. Bowman, *Lawyers Aren't Rent*, 75 STAN. L. REV. ONLINE 132 (2023). Many other potential interventions (and there are many) are scattered along that continuum. *See* Engstrom & Engstrom, *supra* note 18, at 146–47 (cataloging reform ideas).

[58] Without assistance, the majority of alleged debtors never file a responsive pleading and are hit with a default judgment. Engstrom & Engstrom, *supra* note 18, at 149.

[59] For a discussion of the litigation, see Nora Freeman Engstrom, *UPL, Upsolve, and the Community Provision of Legal Advice*, LEGAL AGGREGATE (Jan. 27, 2022).

[60] 604 F. Supp. 3d 97, 104 (S.D.N.Y. 2022).

[61] *See, for example*, Thomas A. Berry, *Upsolve Wins the Right to Give Basic Legal Advice*, CATO INST. (June 1, 2022), https://www.cato.org/blog/upsolve-wins-right-give-basic-legal-advice (last accessed Feb. 24, 2025); Jack Karp, *The Cases That Most Affected Access to Justice in 2022*, LAW360 (Dec. 16, 2022).

Lakier, *Upsolve's* seemingly narrow holding plants seeds for broader decisions holding that *any* limitations on nonlawyer practice violate free speech rights – part of a sweeping "Lochnerization" of the First Amendment that could broadly deregulate the legal profession in ways that cause more harm than good. The genie, she argues, could be hard to get back into the bottle.

In "Our Bar Federalism" Professor David Freeman Engstrom and Professor Daniel B. Rodriguez of Northwestern Law posit that effective reform may necessarily require a shakeup of the current, state-centric regulatory regime – one that calls on the federal government to play a larger role. They argue that existing "Bar Federalism," with its state-by-state patchwork of regulations, is misaligned with the increasingly national and global nature of the legal profession and also discourages innovations that could help address the burgeoning access-to-justice crisis. In place of our current fifty-state regulatory regime, Engstrom and Rodriguez propose a "hybrid" federal-state regulatory model. In their envisioned system, state bars would maintain regulatory control over conventional, one-to-one legal services provided by lawyers and paraprofessionals. But a new federal regulatory authority would seize regulatory control of organizations and entities that furnish one-to-many services. This approach, the authors contend, would retain the benefits of state experimentation and local knowledge, while enabling a more unified and efficient regulatory structure for modern legal services delivery.

The part closes with a pair of chapters that explore *where* reforms should be targeted. Some reformers have set their sights on upending aspects of the legal profession that are common across all of its substantive areas: If nonlawyer investment were permitted, for instance, lawyers would be able to solicit outside investors regardless of whether they practiced housing law, art law, sports law, antitrust law, or any other substantive legal area. Other reform proposals are more surgical, targeting one discrete, substantive area of the law: What works in securities law may not be effective for a personal injury attorney. The Part's final two chapters take this second tack, exploring potential reforms targeted at discrete, substantive legal areas.

First, nationally acclaimed family law expert Rebecca J. Aviel, of the University of Denver (Sturm), zooms in on the family justice system in "Access to Advice as a Linchpin of Family Justice." There, she conducts a careful analysis of the access-to-justice challenges afflicting family law, where studies show that in roughly three-quarters of cases, at least one party is unrepresented.[62] She points out that, compared to other litigation areas, family law is distinctive in many respects. These include, for example: "divorcing spouses cannot resolve their affairs without beginning and ending in court"; many divorcing spouses have aligned, rather than adverse, interests; and "many families are better served by a system that does not run on the kind

[62] Landscape of Domestic Relations, *supra* note 19, at ii; Natalie Anne Knowlton et al., IAALS, Cases without Counsel: Research on Experiences of Self-representation in U.S. Family Court 1 (2016).

of individualized partisan advocacy that is taken to be the lawyer's stock-in-trade." Those distinctive attributes, Aviel posits, may require tailored interventions, including permitting joint representations, promoting early neutral evaluations, and permitting nonlawyer family law professionals to offer their services to divorcing spouses. Aviel's methodological exploration of the family law market for legal services – one that begins with an exploration of the substantive area of law at issue, followed by an identification of entry points for possible narrow-gauge reforms – presents a compelling model for stakeholders eager to jettison a transsubstantive framework and think through tailored reforms in other specific areas of the law.

Finally, Professor Samuel Issacharoff of New York University School of Law and the Honorable Beverly B. Martin (ret.), of the US Court of Appeals for the Eleventh Circuit, who also serves as the Director of the Center on Civil Justice at NYU Law, envision reforms that would address the issue of small value debt collection lawsuits flooding state courts in the United States. Most of these cases pit sophisticated, institutional debt collection agencies against unrepresented defendants that lack the knowledge and resources to vigorously litigate the matter, in what the authors call "asymmetric aggregation." They propose several reforms to rein in these problematic lawsuits, including expanding the pool of individuals able to provide legal advice to defendants in these actions, utilizing online dispute resolution platforms, and, most prominently, direct regulatory oversight by state or federal agencies, perhaps led by the Consumer Financial Protection Bureau. While each of these approaches has certain limitations, they say, a robust and multifaceted regulatory response is required to better respond to the lawsuits currently engulfing – and ravaging – court systems and individuals alike.

Part IV's contributions yield at least two key insights. First, they illustrate the sheer breadth and depth of the potential avenues for reforms. Whether reformers focus their efforts on shaking up existing regulatory structures, or on targeting discrete substantive legal areas, or on broader-based reforms, there exists a rich landscape for critical exploration and action. Put simply, the universe of potential visions for the legal services market is vast and diverse.

Certainly, the sheer number of potential interventions may at first glance seem overwhelming, but that's where the second insight comes in: The chapters in this part showcase the thoughtful analysis and ordered thinking required to effectively navigate the myriad potential routes for change. The considered diagnoses, thoughtful problem-solving, and innovative solutions presented in this part set a precedent for engaging in the dynamic dialogue currently shaping the path that will one day lead to the future of legal services delivery.

******

Our friend and colleague, Professor Deborah L. Rhode, once observed that the American legal profession's "success, and the structural forces that ensure it, have shielded the profession from the accountability and innovation that would best serve societal interests."[63] Today, in the face of a mounting access-to-justice crisis and booming legal tech industry, those shields have all but been shattered. A revolution in legal services regulation is upon us. The conversations that will shape that revolution are happening now in courthouses, state bar associations, law schools, legislatures, and Silicon Valley start-ups. This volume seeks to enrich and inform those conversations. And it ultimately seeks to guide the market for legal services into a new, more accessible era.

[63] Deborah L. Rhode, The Trouble with Lawyers 88 (2015).

PART I

Framing the Issue

Conceptualizing the Challenge of Access to Justice and Legal Services Regulation

1

Justice Futures

Access to Justice and the Future of Justice Work

Rebecca L. Sandefur and Matthew Burnett

The United States faces an access-to-justice crisis of extraordinary scale. Decades of efforts to respond demonstrate a robust track record of failure. Each year, Americans will experience 150 to 250 million new civil justice issues, many involving basic human needs like having a place to live, making a living, and caring for those who depend on them.[1] As many as 120 million of those problems will go unresolved, with consequences like eviction, homelessness, lost wages, separated families, and impaired health.[2] For many years in the United States, access to justice has been understood as access to courts and lawyers. Accordingly, access-to-justice efforts have focused on expanding access to lawyers by pushing for increased funding for civil legal aid, exhorting and incentivizing pro bono work, and advocating for a civil right to counsel.

Yet while the American legal profession has quadrupled in size over the past fifty years, all evidence suggests that this crisis has only deepened. The most recent study of poor people's civil justice experiences found that this group of Americans received legal help for less than 10 percent of their civil justice issues.[3] The estrangement of Americans from their own law is not just a problem of social welfare policy or justice service delivery; it is a failure of democracy. Without meaningful access to justice, it is impossible to achieve equal justice.

The access-to-justice crisis affects every group in society, entrenching poverty and inequality. Our collective failure to address this crisis fundamentally threatens core democratic principles. Investment in more lawyers and advances in technology have failed to stem the tide, which continues to overwhelm courts, legal aid

1 Inst. for the Advancement of the Am. L. Sys. (IAALS) & The Hague Inst. for Innovation of L. (HiiL), *Justice Needs and Satisfaction in the United States of America* (2021), https://iaals.du.edu/sites/default/files/documents/publications/justice-needs-and-satisfaction-us.pdf (last accessed Aug. 7, 2023) [hereinafter IAALS & HiiL]; Rebecca L. Sandefur & James Teufel, *Assessing America's Access to Civil Justice Crisis*, 11 U.C. Irvine L. Rev. 753 (2020).

2 IAALS, *supra* note 1.

3 L. Serv. Corp., *The Justice Gap: The Unmet Civil Legal Needs of Low-Income Americans* (2022), https://justicegap.lsc.gov/resource/2022-justice-gap-report/ (last accessed Aug. 7, 2023).

providers, and millions of everyday people with civil justice needs. The crisis is seemingly intractable.

While the crisis deepens, jurisdictions explore ways to re-regulate the delivery of legal services. Often justified by – though not necessarily motivated by – seeking to increase access to justice, reform projects follow two routes. One removes restrictions on who and what can practice law. The other permits people who are not lawyers and organizations that are not law firms to control or profit from law practice. The first route directly expands sources of meaningful legal assistance by increasing both the scale of the justice workforce and the scope of what justice workers are authorized to do. The impact of the second route would be indirect: Outside investment would permit law firms to expand into technology and take advantage of economies of scale to produce commodified legal services at reduced cost to consumers. Existing empirical evidence supports the first approach: Lawyerless legal services can and do expand access to justice. Evidence on the second is mixed at best.

These findings should inform our choice of strategies if the goal is actually to increase access to justice. The true good at stake is enabling poor and otherwise excluded people to use their rights under the law to act on problems that entrench their poverty and exclusion. Effective reform projects should begin with this end in mind. And they should design interventions based on what the evidence suggests will be effective in achieving it. Imagining justice futures, or a reality in which ordinary people have routine and meaningful access to justice, requires fundamentally reimagining the future of justice work.

This chapter outlines our approach to effective reform – one that responds to the call for new interventions by turning the conventional approach on its head. We start not with lawyers or courts but with ordinary people and the events in their lives that the civil law constitutes as "justiciable," or legally actionable and governed by authoritative legal norms.[4] In Section 1.1, we discuss what research teaches about peoples' legal needs and how they seek to resolve legal issues. Section 1.2 explains why traditional lawyer-centric models of legal services delivery fail. Section 1.3 offers examples of existing lawyerless access-to-justice interventions that meet people where they are. Section 1.4 calls for new research into effective access-to-justice solutions.

We highlight the need to toss out past orthodoxy as a guide for reform, and adopt approaches grounded in the growing body of empirical evidence about people's justice experiences and effective solutions to justice problems. And, most

[4] *See, for example*, Hazel Genn & Sarah Beinart, Paths to Justice: What People Do and Think about Going to Law (1999); Org. Econ. Cooperation & Dev. (OECD), *OECD Framework and Good Practice Principles for People-Centred Justice* (2021), https://www.oecd-ilibrary.org/governance/oecd-framework-and-good-practice-principles-for-people-centred-justice_cdc3bde7-en (last accessed Aug. 8, 2023).

importantly, we begin with the end – access to justice – in mind. Regulatory reform is simply one means to that end.

1.1 BEGIN WITH THE END IN MIND: REDEFINING ACCESS TO JUSTICE

The past two decades have seen an explosion of empirical research around the world that is transforming the way that access to justice is understood. The centerpiece is a wide range of "legal needs studies" from across the globe.[5] The central method of this work is population surveys in which ordinary people are asked about concrete events in their lives that are justiciable, or that have civil legal aspects or raise civil legal issues. In this people-centered method of understanding public experience, surveyed people do not need to understand the legal aspects of their issues at all. They simply need to report on whether they have encountered specific circumstances, such as an employer not paying them overtime pay; being one or more months behind on paying their rent or mortgage; or taking responsibility for the care of a grandchild. They do not need to diagnose, for example, that they are experiencing wage theft; that they are in breach of contract and at risk of eviction or foreclosure; or that they will need legal guardianship or power of attorney to take basic actions like enrolling a grandchild in school or getting them onto health insurance. In these surveys, people are typically asked how they responded to the situation, including where they sought help (if at all) and whether and how the problem was resolved. Some surveys also ask about "problem characterization" – how people understand their justiciable issues – for example as legal, moral, personal, or bureaucratic problems, or simply as bad luck.[6] This research has produced a range of transformative discoveries.

A key finding of this research is that civil justice problems are common and widespread, and affect every group in every studied society.[7] These problems fall in core areas of life and threaten basic human needs, like having a place to live, making a living, getting access to medical care, and caring for dependent children and adults. Justice issues are often clustered or cascading. For example, job loss can lead to application for unemployment insurance. Lost income from lost employment can lead to inability to pay rent and routine debts, resulting in other justice issues such as

[5] OECD & Open Soc'y Found., *Legal Needs Surveys and Access to Justice* (2019), https://www.oecd-ilibrary.org/governance/legal-needs-surveys-and-access-to-justice_g2g9a36c-en (last accessed Aug. 8, 2023).

[6] Pascoe Pleasence et al., *What Really Drives Advice Seeking Behaviour? Looking beyond the Subject of Legal Disputes*, 1 Oñati Socio-Legal Series 1 (2011).

[7] For the United States, see IAALS & HiiL, *supra* note 1; Rebecca L. Sandefur, *What We Know and Need to Know about the Legal Needs of the Public*, 67 S.C. L. Rev. 443 (2016). Globally, see World Just. Project, *Global Insights on Access to Justice* (2019), http://data.worldjusticeproject.org/accesstojustice (last accessed Aug. 9, 2023).

eviction and debt collection lawsuits.[8] Justice issues often have life-altering collateral consequences. For example, a study based on data collected shortly before the onset of the COVID-19 pandemic estimates that in 2019, 19.5 million Americans' civil justice problems resulted in impaired health and 18 million led to lost employment, income, or housing.[9]

When facing these issues, people show enormous creativity in their search for solutions and assistance. They reach widely, yet they rarely reach out to lawyers or courts.[10] Turning to law is only a small part of a richly textured terrain of experience with civil justice problems. People simply attempt to handle many of these issues on their own. Indeed, at times they do nothing at all to try to resolve some of the more significant civil justice issues.[11] And when they do seek help, their first and sometimes only stop is friends and family. They also reach out to a range of sources in their communities and beyond, such as religious and community organizations, physicians, or membership organizations like the AARP or trade unions.

The central reason why people seek assistance for legal issues outside the formal law is that they do not understand their issues to be legal, and thus do not see them as proper objects of legal action or help. Indeed, one study in the United States finds that the most common way in which people understand the justiciable events of their lives is as "bad luck" or "God's will for me."[12] Almost always, when people seek assistance with legal issues, they seek help from people who are not authorized to offer legal advice. All U.S. states prohibit the "unauthorized practice of law" (UPL) by people who are not licensed, and most actually criminalize it.[13] This inability to access meaningful help is a central reason that over 120 million civil justice problems go unresolved in the United States each year.[14] While the United States is not unique in these prohibitions, it affords lawyers a more robust and punitive monopoly on the law than is granted to lawyers in many other contexts, restricting not only rights of appearance but even the ability to offer legal advice. And, as we noted above, it in many instances criminalizes UPL.[15]

8 Pascoe Pleasence et al., *Multiple Justiciable Problems: Common Clusters and Their Social and Demographic Indicators*, 1 J. Empirical Legal Stud. 301 (2004).

9 Sandefur & Teufel, *supra* note 1.

10 Sandefur, *supra* note 7.

11 Genn & Beinart, *supra* note 4; Rebecca L. Sandefur, *The Importance of Doing Nothing: Everyday Problems and Responses of Inaction*, *in* Transforming Lives: Law and Social Process 112 (Pascoe Pleasence et al. eds., 2007).

12 Rebecca L. Sandefur, *Accessing Justice in the Contemporary USA: Findings from the Community Needs and Services Study* (2014), https://www.ssrn.com/abstract=2478040 (last accessed Aug. 8, 2023); Sandefur, *supra* note 7.

13 Nat'l Ctr. for Access to Just., *Working with Your Hands Tied behind Your Back: Non-Lawyer Perspectives on Legal Empowerment* (2021), https://ncaj.org/working-your-hands-tied-behind-your-back (last accessed Aug. 7, 2023).

14 IAALS & HiiL, *supra* note 1.

15 Laurel Terry, *Putting the Legal Profession's Monopoly on the Practice of Law in a Global Context*, 82 Fordham L. Rev. 2903 (2013).

But while justice issues are widespread and many people suffer from the lack of access to meaningful support, such issues and their consequences do not fall equally across the population. Poor people and people of color are more likely to experience civil justice problems than white people and people of higher incomes, and they are also more likely to experience negative impacts of those problems, such as lost wages or housing.[16] These dynamics entrench and expand existing inequalities, and calcify the exclusion of vulnerable and marginalized groups from law and justice.[17] In a context like the United States, emerging solutions – such as websites and software that may assist people in learning about or using the law – are difficult for people to find. They also require technical literacy, hardware, and broadband access that many low-income and rural people may not have.[18] Using these solutions also often requires both reading proficiency and English-language literacy that many people in a diverse polity simply do not have.[19]

Inequalities in both exposure to justice problems and the ability to act on them are even more richly textured than this review implies.[20] In some contexts, for example, Jordan, gender is a critical line of division in the experience of a wide range of civil justice problems, reflecting women's lesser social power and greater vulnerability.[21] In contexts like the United States, women are much more likely to be victims of domestic violence, and therefore to need access to orders of protection and, often, legal supports for child custody and income maintenance. To take another example, American jurisdictions offer tremendous linguistic diversity: For example, within the United States, Alaska recognizes twenty different indigenous languages spoken throughout the state[22] while over 200 distinct languages are

[16] Rebecca L. Sandefur, *Access to Civil Justice and Race, Class, and Gender Inequality*, 34 Ann. Rev. Sociol. 339 (2008).

[17] *Id.*

[18] Rebecca L. Sandefur, *Legal Tech for Non-Lawyers: Report of the Survey of U.S. Legal Technologies*, Am. Bar Found. (2019), https://www.americanbarfoundation.org/wp-content/uploads/2023/04/report_us_digital_legal_tech_for_nonlawyers.pdf (last accessed Feb. 24, 2025); Tanina Rostain, *Techno-Optimism and Access to the Legal System*, 148 Daedalus 93 (2019).

[19] Margaret Hagan, *The Supply and Demand of Legal Help on the Internet, in* Legal Tech and the Future of Civil Justice 199 (David Freeman Engstrom ed., 2023), https://www.cambridge.org/core/product/identifier/9781009255301%23CN-bp-9/type/book_part (last accessed Feb. 24, 2025); Rostain, *supra* note 18; Rebecca L. Sandefur, *Access to What*, 148 Daedalus 49 (2019).

[20] Pascoe Pleasence & Nigel J. Balmer, *Justice & the Capability to Function in Society*, 148 Daedalus 140 (2019).

[21] Paul Scott Prettitore, *The Justice Gap and Poverty: Learning from Household Surveys in Jordan and Colombia*, World Bank (2014).

[22] *Alaska Native Language Preservation & Advisory Council*, Alaska Dep't of Comm. (2023), https://www.commerce.alaska.gov/web/dcra/AKNativeLanguagePreservationAdvisoryCouncil/Languages.aspx#:~:text=The%20two%20groupings%20include%20Inuit,and%20documented%20Alaska's%20Native%20languages (last accessed Mar. 23, 2024).

spoken in the state of California.[23] Yet the language of the courts, for example, is often English-only.

Both who one is and where one is shape legal needs and capabilities. About one in five Americans lives in a rural area,[24] which presents distinctive challenges for access to justice. Lawyers are often not present in these communities, and challenges of distance and transportation may make it difficult for people to get to those lawyers who are available as well as to courthouses.[25] Providers in rural communities face distinctive pressures that arise from the critical importance of personal relationships and place in these small communities: "[P]eople may not wish to jeopardize important interpersonal relationships with family, friends, or business associates by assertive advocacy for a client, potential client's – or, indeed, their own – needs."[26]

Finally, different groups have different beliefs about the law and whether it is open, accessible, and fair for people like themselves. There are documented differences in the willingness of different groups of people to invoke or engage with the law.[27] Relationships between these beliefs and people's location on various axes of difference such as race, gender, income, or age are not straightforward. For example, social class shapes people's willingness to assert rights in hypothetical police encounters.[28] But the patterns are not that simple. To take a different example, a study of low-income African American women found that the behavior of calling the police reflects the dynamics of specific situations, such as whether they involve domestic violence, a child's addiction or mental health, or neighborhood illegal drug sales.[29] In contrast, a different study of poor women of color facing justice problems finds them expressing a sense of entitlement to help from the law and legal

[23] *The Most Spoken Languages in California*, WORLD ATLAS (2023), https://www.worldatlas.com/articles/the-most-spoken-languages-in-california.html (last accessed Aug. 9, 2023).

[24] America Counts Staff, U.S. Census Bureau, *One in Five Americans Live in Rural Areas*, CENSUS.GOV (Aug. 9, 2017), https://www.census.gov/library/stories/2017/08/rural-america.html (last accessed Feb. 24, 2025).

[25] Lisa R. Pruitt et al., *Legal Deserts: A Multi-State Perspective on Rural Access to Justice*, 13 HARV. L. & POL'Y REV. 15 (2018).

[26] Rebecca L. Sandefur & Matthew Burnett, *All Together Now: Building a Shared Access to Justice Research Framework for Theoretical Insight and Actionable Intelligence*, OÑATI SOCIO-L. SER. 1330, 1342 (July 28, 2024), https://opo.iisj.net/index.php/osls/article/view/1437 (last accessed Feb. 24, 2025); *see also* ROBERT C. ELLICKSON, ORDER WITHOUT LAW: HOW NEIGHBORS SETTLE DISPUTES (1991); David M. Engel, *The Oven Bird's Song: Insiders, Outsiders, and Personal Injuries in an American Community*, 18 LAW & SOC'Y REV. 551 (1984); Pruitt et al., *supra* note 25; Michele Statz, *On Shared Suffering: Judicial Intimacy in the Rural Northland*, 55 LAW & SOC'Y REV. 5 (2021).

[27] Sara Sternberg Greene, *Race, Class, and Access to Civil Justice*, 101 IOWA L. REV. 1234 (2016).

[28] Kathryne M. Young & Katie R. Billings, *Legal Consciousness and Cultural Capital*, 54 LAW & SOC'Y REV. 33 (2020).

[29] Monica C. Bell, *Situational Trust: How Disadvantaged Mothers Reconceive Legal Cynicism*, 50 LAW & SOC'Y REV. 314 (2016).

professionals.[30] Intersectional experiences of disability, sexual identity, income, and race, among other factors, all interact to shape justice experiences.[31]

While our understanding of the ways in which people's identities, capabilities, and place shape their experience of justice is still developing, some clear findings emerge. One is that systematic inequalities in experience of the civil law can entrench or widen existing social and economic inequalities. Another is that people have a range of needs, beliefs, and capabilities that affect their ability and willingness to access, engage with, and use different kinds of services for legal issues. A third is that the contexts in which people live shape both their experience of justice issues and their willingness and ability to respond with different types of solutions. The design of effective solutions requires keeping all of these variables – and more, as these are only illustrations – in mind. Recognizing this, we should pursue a distributed approach, enabling and supporting locally designed and culturally responsive solutions that are evidence-based and outcome-focused.

1.2 JUST SOLUTIONS AND THE REIMAGINATION OF JUSTICE WORK

The first step in crafting effective solutions is an accurate understanding of the problem to be solved. Lawyer-centric models of legal services delivery have failed to meet critical needs because they fail to recognize and respond to people's experience of the law and how they respond (or do not respond) to justice issues. Lawyer-centric models of legal services regulation fail to create an environment that enables effective and responsive models of people-centered service delivery. The practice of law has been defined essentially as the work that lawyers do, and it is this current definition that guides the authorization of legal practice in most of the United States. The status quo reflects a history of American lawyers' attempts to gain control of legal practice. In the late nineteenth century, American lawyers, like English lawyers, held rights of appearance but little else.[32] By the middle of the twentieth century, American lawyers had successfully captured most of the tasks that today constitute the practice of law, including negotiation and legal advice.[33] They had also clawed back control of how legal services may be delivered so that membership organizations and other groups, from unions to automobile clubs, could no longer employ lawyers to serve their constituencies and members.[34]

[30] Diana Hernández, *"I'm Gonna Call My Lawyer:" Shifting Legal Consciousness at the Intersection of Inequality*, 51 Interdisc. L. Stud.: The Next Generation (Special Issue) 95 (2010).

[31] Kathryne M. Young & Katie R. Billings, *An Intersectional Examination of U.S. Civil Justice Problems*, 2023 Utah L. Rev. 487 (2023).

[32] Richard L. Abel, American Lawyers (1989).

[33] *Id.*

[34] Laurel Rigertas, *Lobbying and Litigating against "Legal Bootleggers" – The Role of the Organized Bar in the Expansion of the Courts' Inherent Powers in the Early Twentieth Century*, 46 Cal. W. L. Rev. 65 (2009).

The capture of law by lawyers is not only a market monopoly but also a political capture that chills attempts to help people use their own law and relegates debate about solutions into narrow, unimaginative channels. What could be a thriving justice sector with a multiplicity of approaches to meeting people's justice needs where they are, through a variety of different kinds of service models, is instead a monolithic, money-seeking, and monopolistic guild that fails to meet even the basic justice needs of everyday Americans. Available evidence suggests that most complaints about UPL come not from aggrieved members of the public but rather from lawyers themselves.[35] By stopping people who are not lawyers from being able to assist, these complaints have been used as a tool to keep people from being *able* to take action on critical problems within the context of their rights, whether the issue is wage theft or environmental toxins.[36]

Attempts to make space for change have been largely lawyer-led and business-focused. For example, a marquee legal regulation event of the 1990s was the American Bar Association's dustup over multidisciplinary practice, one example of a model that would permit lawyers to share fees, profits, and investments with people who are not lawyers or organizations that are not lawyer-led. The traditionalists won that battle and continue to win. Since the 2000s, the rhetoric of change has been innovation, and again lawyer and business interests have crowded out meaningful access-to-justice reforms, arguing for outside investment in legal-services-producing organizations as a way to permit the kinds of capitalization that might allow for investments in technology, organizational growth, and economies of scale.[37] Evidence from jurisdictions where these kinds of "outside" investments are allowed is so far equivocal about impacts on access to justice; albeit, these experiments are in their early days.[38]

None of these activities, which focus on opening up who can make money from the practice of law, bear any necessary connection with the lives and needs of ordinary people who, in a democracy, are the final authors and true owners of the law. These attempts at reform by the legal profession reflect a long-standing pattern in how lawyers engage with justice. As the late Gary Bellow observed, lawyers, even passionate advocates for the poor and the otherwise disenfranchised, have had a

[35] Deborah L. Rhode & Lucy Buford Ricca, *Protecting the Profession or the Public? Rethinking Unauthorized-Practice Enforcement*, 82 FORDHAM L. REV. 2587 (2013).

[36] Rebecca L. Sandefur, *Legal Advice from Nonlawyers: Consumer Demand, Provider Quality, and Public Harms*, 16 STAN. J. C.R. & C.L. 283 (2020).

[37] Gillian K. Hadfield, *Higher Demand, Lower Supply? A Comparative Assessment of the Legal Resource Landscape for Ordinary Americans*, 37 FORDHAM URB. L.J. 129 (2010); Gillian K. Hadfield, *The Cost of Law: Promoting Access to Justice through the (Un)Corporate Practice of Law*, 38 INT'L REV. L. & ECON. 43 (2014).

[38] Rebecca L. Sandefur & Emily Denne, *Access to Justice and Legal Services Regulatory Reform*, 18 ANN. REV. L. & SOC. SCI. 27 (2022); DAVID FREEMAN ENGSTROM ET AL., *Legal Innovation after Reform: Evidence from Regulatory Change*, DEBORAH L. RHODE CENTER ON THE LEGAL PROFESSION (Sept. 2022).

strong tendency to design people's problems around the solutions that lawyers offer, rather than designing solutions around problems as people experience them.[39] By contrast, "just solutions," which are grounded in evidence and focused on the substantive outcomes achieved by people at the center of their own problems, decenter lawyers in an obvious way, privileging ordinary people's experiences and offering human alternatives in the form of other types of justice workers.[40] Perhaps this is why human examples of the "unauthorized practice of law" garner more opposition than law-practicing computer programs, which have already replaced much work that lawyers used to perform.

If the true goal is people being able to understand and engage with their own laws – access to justice – reform efforts should center that end, with the goal of creating just solutions. The evidence reviewed above makes clear that solutions designed around problems as people experience them would not be lawyer-centered; rather, they would be people-centered and designed to meet people where they are in order to address their everyday justice needs.

1.3 DISMANTLING BARRIERS TO EMPOWER EFFECTIVE JUSTICE WORK

An effective approach to regulating legal services for access to justice would change the terms of the conversation, dismantling conceptual, legal, and social barriers to justice work. The current model is such a robust failure that there is little point in tinkering with it around the edges; the magnitude of the problem requires wholesale change. The most basic need is to empower more people to provide more effective help. The current legal labor force is expensive to produce and maintain. It is also substantially less diverse than the people to whom it is supposed to be accountable. If we hope to make headway, it is imperative to reimagine fundamentally the future of justice work and the policy, program design, and implementation strategies required to realize justice futures.

American justice work has long been highly stratified. In the 1970s, lawyers were famously found to be divided into two "hemispheres" of roughly equal size, one serving personal clients and the other serving businesses and other large organizations.[41] The law schools, social backgrounds, and legal incomes of the lawyers working in each hemisphere were sharply different, with elite law schools,

[39] Gary Bellow, *Turning Solutions into Problems: The Legal Aid Experience*, 34 NLADA Briefcase 106 (1977).

[40] Matthew Burnett & Rebecca L. Sandefur, *Designing Just Solutions at Scale: Lawyerless Legal Services and Evidence-Based Regulation*, 19 Rev. Direito Público (2022), https://www.portaldeperiodicos.idp.edu.br/direitopublico/article/view/6604; Jeanne Charn, *Legal Services for All: Is the Profession Ready*, 42 Loy. L.A. L. Rev. 1021 (2008).

[41] John P. Heinz & Edward O. Laumann, Chicago Lawyers: The Social Structure of the Bar (1982).

elite backgrounds, and high pay much more strongly represented in the business half of the bar and lower prestige law schools, working-class, immigrant, and ethnic minority backgrounds, and lower pay more strongly represented among lawyers working for people.[42] A follow-up study twenty years later found the profession even more unequal in pay, with continued differences in who had access to elite law positions.[43] That study also found that the size of the personal client sector had dwindled: A minority of lawyers were working for people; the vast majority were working for businesses and other large organizations.[44] Though lawyers today are more diverse in gender, race, ethnicity, and social class background than those of fifty years ago, the profession remains far less diverse than the people it serves.

The stratification of justice work extends out from lawyers. American lawyers have long had subsidiary occupations working under their supervision, most notably paralegals.[45] This is a classic strategy of professional control of work: keeping alternative providers subordinate to the main profession.[46] Regulatory reforms of recent years have included the expansion of independent paralegal occupations, permitting paraprofessionals to engage in limited practice outside the supervision of fully licensed attorneys. The regulatory models for these occupations parallel those for lawyers, requiring multiple years of higher education, certification, and licensing, all typically designed and administered by state bars to whom state supreme courts have often delegated their regulatory authority. These paraprofessional licensing models also often embrace discriminatory "character and fitness" requirements similar to those for lawyers, replicating and entrenching the same barriers to entry, particularly for groups that suffer from disproportionate criminal enforcement and despite a lack of evidence that these requirements have any bearing on ethical practice.

These highly credentialed paraprofessional law occupations have been slow to grow. The first such program in the twenty-first century, Washington State's Limited License Legal Technicians, never had more than forty active licensed practitioners.[47] A 2021 survey found fewer than eighty practitioners total around the country.[48] By 2022, the number of programs and practitioners across four states (Washington, Utah, Arizona, and Michigan) had grown to only 166.[49] Like lawyers, allied legal

[42] *Id.*

[43] John P. Heinz et al., Urban Lawyers: The New Social Structure of the Bar (2005).

[44] *Id.*

[45] Hilary Sommerlad et al., *Paralegals and the Casualisation of Legal Labour Markets*, *in* Lawyers in 21st-Century Societies (R. L. Abel et al. eds., 2022).

[46] Andrew Abbott, The System of Professions: An Essay on the Division of Expert Labor (1988).

[47] Sandefur & Denne, *supra* note 38.

[48] *Id.*

[49] IAALS, *The Landscape of Allied Legal Professional Programs in the United States* (2022), https://iaals.du.edu/sites/default/files/documents/publications/landscape_allied_legal_professionals.pdf (last accessed Aug. 7, 2023).

professionals that are trained and certified in these traditional ways have difficulty scaling to meet the legal needs of a country of over 330 million people. And, as with lawyers, the many up-front barriers to entry into these paraprofessions may restrict access by those same groups currently locked out of the law.

Exceptions to these lawyer-centric models exist. Some have operated for many decades, yet rarely feature as examples of important access-to-justice solutions, in large part because they fall outside of these stratified norms and lawyer control. For example, the federal government permits individual representation by nonlawyers in a range of administrative hearings. In the context of both affirmative immigration filings and defensive cases, there are over 2,000 partially and fully accredited nonlawyer immigration representatives who represent clients in a wide range of complex matters, including in immigration court and before the Board of Immigration Appeals.[50] These justice workers are embedded in hundreds of nonprofit community and religious organizations across the country, authorized by the U.S. Executive Office for Immigration Review to offer legal advice and representation through nonlawyer staff and volunteers. Indeed, there exists a robust and well-coordinated network of nonprofit organizations that provide training and technical assistance to support these justice workers and programs. Similarly, the Social Security Administration clearly states that claimants have a right to representation in appealing determinations but does not require those representatives to be attorneys.[51] This is also true of other federal administrative agencies, ranging from the Veterans Administration to the Internal Revenue Service.

As discussed in Chapter 11,[52] another well-established yet underrecognized category of justice workers are Tribal lay advocates who work across the hundreds of Tribal courts in the United States, including as many as 300 trial courts and over 150 appellate courts.[53] They are required to meet the practice requirements of the tribes in which they practice, for example by taking a Tribal bar exam, and may handle both civil and criminal matters.[54] Tribal lay advocates are typically members of the same tribes in which they practice, which facilitates trust between providers and clients, and means that these advocates can offer critical cultural and linguistic expertise. For exactly these reasons, some legal aid providers serving Indian country

[50] Dep't of Just., *Recognized Organizations and Accredited Representatives Roster by State and City* (2023), https://www.justice.gov/eoir/recognized-organizations-and-accredited-representatives-roster-state-and-city (last accessed Aug. 9, 2023).

[51] *Your Right to Representation*, Soc. Sec. Admin (Sept. 2023), https://www.ssa.gov/pubs/EN-05-10075.pdf (last accessed Feb. 24, 2025).

[52] *See* Chapter 9 in this volume.

[53] Gregory D. Smith, *Native American Tribal Appellate Courts: Underestimated and Overlooked*, 19 J. App. Prac. & Process 25 (2018).

[54] Judith M. Stinson et al., *Trusting Tribal Courts: More Lawyers Is Not Always the Answer*, 14 L.J. Soc. Just. Ariz. St. U. 130 (2021).

have enthusiastically embraced Tribal lay advocates to provide culturally and linguistically competent services to their clients.[55]

Justice workers also represent individuals in some state courts. For example, both Delaware and Texas allow nonlawyer justice workers to represent both landlords and tenants in eviction proceedings.[56] For decades, domestic violence has been an area where advocates have called for expanded roles for nonlawyer victim advocates.[57] In 2020, the Arizona Supreme Court issued an administrative order authorizing a Licensed Legal Advocate program that allows domestic violence advocates to provide legal advice and support, including orders of protection and other related family law issues.[58]

In addition to these more targeted interventions, two states – Utah and Alaska – have made far more sweeping reforms to empower justice workers. Utah launched the first, and currently only, legal services regulatory sandbox in the United States in 2020. The Utah sandbox allows entities to seek waivers of existing blanket UPL prohibitions in favor of assessing applicants' risk of harming consumers and monitoring the impact of admitted entities' work on consumers.[59] These potential harms include: "achiev[ing] an inaccurate or inappropriate legal result," "fail[ing] to exercise legal rights through ignorance or bad advice," and "purchas[ing] an unnecessary or inappropriate legal service."[60] Each entity's risk of exposing consumers to these three harms is assessed when they apply to the sandbox, and entities are classified on a scale from low to high risk to consumers. The risk assessment affects the intensity of monitoring by the regulator, specifically the frequency and scope of the data about consumer experience that approved entities must submit for review and analysis. Consumers' outcomes from legal services received in the sandbox are monitored in more or less real time. Analysis of the data is published in a monthly Activity Report that includes information about the activities of admitted entities and an assessment of evidence that an entity's work is causing any of the three consumer harms. So far, across over 70,000 services, the Utah Office of Legal Services Innovation has received fewer than 10 complaints related to the

[55] *Tribal Advocacy Incubator Project*, MONT. L. SERV. ASS'N, https://www.mtlsa.org/tribal-advocate-incubator-project (last accessed Aug. 7, 2023); Annamarie Johnson, *Nevada Legal Services Tribal Court Advocate Training Project*, NEV. LAWYER 32 (2011).

[56] Del. S. Ct. R. 57.1; Tex. R. Civ. P. 500.4.

[57] *See, for example*, Catherine Klein & Leslye Orloff, *Providing Legal Protection for Battered Women: An Analysis of State Statutes and Case Law*, 21 HOFSTRA L. REV. 801 (1993); Margaret F. Brown, *Domestic Violence Advocates' Exposure to Liability for Engaging in the Unauthorized Practice of Law*, 34 COLUM. J.L. & SOC. PROBS. 279, 294 (2001); Suzanne Schmitz, *Whats the Harm?: Rethinking the Role of Domestic Violence Advocates and the Unauthorized Practice of Law*, 10 WM. & MARY J. RACE GENDER & SOC. JUST. 295 (2004).

[58] Ariz. S. Ct., Admin. Order No. 2020-84.

[59] Burnett & Sandefur, *supra* note 40.

[60] Utah Off. of Legal Servs. Innovation, *Innovation Office Manual 2024* 2–3 (updated Feb. 20, 2024), https://utahinnovationoffice.org/wp-content/uploads/2024/02/Innovation-Office-Manual.pdf (last accessed Feb. 24, 2025).

three harms, all of which have been investigated and resolved satisfactorily from the perspective of both the affected consumer and the regulator.[61] In the Utah sandbox, nonprofits currently engage justice workers to help the public with a range of civil justice issues, including medical debt, domestic violence protection orders, and expungement. They also deploy innovative models such as embedding domestic violence legal advocates within municipal and county law enforcement and government agencies.

In Alaska, the Supreme Court last year was the first in the country to authorize a UPL waiver that allows Community Justice Workers trained and supervised by Alaska Legal Services Corporation (ALSC) to provide limited-scope legal advice and representation without a law license.[62] As part of their training, each justice worker must handle a case under the supervision of an ALSC attorney. Currently, over 400 Community Justice Workers are at work or in training, helping their neighbors in over 40 communities across the vast and rural state, most of which are not connected by roads.[63] Hundreds of cases have been handled by Community Justice Workers, the majority of whom work in remote Alaska Native communities, where there are no lawyers. The program currently boasts a 100 percent client success rate.

As the examples from immigration, federal benefits, and Tribal justice show, justice workers are not new. At the same time, the recent sweeping reforms to UPL rules that now allow justice workers to serve low-income and marginalized communities constitute profound changes in the landscape of justice work. The evidence from both the United States and other countries is clear. Justice workers who have not attended law school and are not licensed attorneys can be competent and effective across a wide range of justice issues that people face, both inside courts and other fora and upstream in the development of people's justice issues. Research shows that justice workers do not increase consumer harm; in fact, they bring other critical strengths and skills uncommon among lawyers, including community trust, linguistic expertise, and cultural competency.[64] When justice workers are available, people go to them for help.[65] And in jurisdictions where they are permitted, they show themselves capable of scaling. For example, the United Kingdom has for over seventy years had a network of Citizens Advice bureaus, where trained community volunteers assist people in understanding and using the law; these now exist in

[61] Utah Off. of Legal Servs. Innovation, *Activity Report: March 2023* (Apr. 20, 2023), https://utahinnovationoffice.org/wp-content/uploads/2023/05/2023.3-Public-Report.pdf (last accessed Feb. 24, 2025).

[62] S. C. of Alaska, Order No. 1994 (2022), https://www.alsc-law.org/wp-content/uploads/2022/12/sc01994.pdf (last accessed Feb. 24, 2025) (adopting Alaska Bar Rule 43.5).

[63] Alaska L. Serv. Corp., *About Alaska Bar Rule* 43.5, https://www.alsc-law.org/wp-content/uploads/2022/12/Alaska-Bar-Rule-43.5.pdf (last accessed Mar. 29, 2024).

[64] IAALS, *supra* note 49; Sandefur, *supra* note 36.

[65] Rebecca L. Sandefur, *The Fulcrum Point of Equal Access to Justice: Legal and Nonlegal Institutions of Remedy*, 42 Loy. L.A. L. Rev. 949 (2009); Sandefur, *supra* note 36.

physical offices around the country and are available by internet and phone. In 2021 and 2022, Citizens Advice assisted over two and a half million people.[66]

1.4 DESIGNING JUSTICE FUTURES

Effectively designing justice futures requires incorporating three elements. The first is a solid understanding of people's lived experience of the law and the forces – including identity, capability, and place – that shape that experience. Responding to this richly textured experience requires an equally rich ecosystem of justice work and justice workers. To make that work possible, we must add the second element, the elimination of regulatory barriers to justice workers and justice work, just as other professions like education, psychology, and medicine have done. States like Alaska and Utah are leading the way, but reforms must go further, and be pursued with a greater sense of urgency.

The third critical element is a research agenda that looks beyond the effectiveness of services at achieving narrow goals. A growing body of evidence suggests that effective solutions have four qualities: (1) they are timely, in the sense that they are visible when people recognize that they have a problem; (2) they are targeted, in the sense that they are specific to the problem someone has and framed in terms that person understands; (3) they are trustworthy, in the sense that people believe the source of help is working for their good interest; and (4) they are transparent, in the sense that they make clear to people their decision points and the possible consequences of different courses of action.[67] If the ultimate goal is increasing people's capability to engage with their own law – or, legal empowerment – then research should explore whether these features actually support that objective.

In contexts where these experiments are underway, evidence to guide practice will come from a robust research program informed by a clear and shared agenda about two kinds of effectiveness: Effectiveness at solving people's problems, and effectiveness at changing people's relation to the law. For these solutions to increase access to justice in a country of over 330 million people, we must also understand the potential for sustainability and scalability of both justice workers and justice work.

The current lawyer-centric models have resulted in large numbers of people, and particularly people with low incomes and people of color, being systemically excluded, isolated, and estranged from their own law. Justice futures require an alternative vision of access to justice – a reimagining of access to justice – that

[66] *What We Do*, Citizens Advice, https://www.citizensadvice.org.uk/about-us/about-us1/introduction-to-the-citizens-advice-service/ (last accessed Aug. 7, 2023).

[67] Pascoe Pleasence et al., *Reshaping Legal Assistance Services: Building on the Evidence Base*, L. & Just. Found. of New South Wales (2014); Rebecca L. Sandefur, *Bridging the Gap: Rethinking Outreach for Greater Access to Justice*, 37 U. Ark. Little Rock L. Rev. 721 (2015).

focuses on empowerment, agency, and action. That future requires a diverse and emboldened field of justice workers and an expansive view of justice work.

We can no longer abide by the status quo. Reforms must cease replicating failed models that perpetuate exclusionary and discriminatory barriers to engaging with law. Instead, they must place access to justice – rather than the potential for profit or the past prerogatives of a profession – at the forefront. Meaningful progress in addressing the access-to-justice crisis requires experimentation and a commitment to evidence-based strategies. This approach is exemplified in the models currently operating in Utah and Alaska and bolstered by learnings from the critical work already happening in immigration and other federal agency proceedings. This new approach is grounded in deep commitment to addressing individual and community needs and to shedding existing orthodoxy that centers lawyers and courts. An expansive and richly diverse field of justice work and justice workers requires not only regulatory reforms but also empowered individual and community action. So long as everyday people continue to be systemically estranged from their own law, it is not only just solutions to common legal problems but democracy itself that is ultimately at stake.

2

Race and the Political Economy of Civil Justice

Brian Libgober

There are profound racial disparities in the U.S. civil justice system. According to best recent estimates, U.S. state courts handle over twenty million civil matters annually.[1] Some of the most common matters before these courts involve issues such as housing (roughly 15 percent of all cases), child custody, child support and child welfare (another 15 percent), and debt collection (roughly 5 percent).[2] These are all areas where scholarly literature has revealed dramatic overrepresentation of racial minorities and the poor among civil defendants.[3] The literature has also established that, in addressing such matters, courts frequently look, feel, and act in ways that are far removed from the model of courts described in law school lecture halls. Judges in these courts are pretty frequently not even lawyers, for example.[4] Even if they are lawyers, they may follow ad hoc procedures overseeing litigants who are often not even present. If they are present, they frequently lack a lawyer or other kind of legal adviser.[5]

1 Colleen F. Shanahan et al., *The Institutional Mismatch of State Civil Courts*, 122 COLUM. L. REV. 1471, 1486 (2022).

2 *Id.* at 1533–37.

3 On housing, see, for example, Peter Hepburn et al., *Racial and Gender Disparities among Evicted Americans*, 7 SOCIO. SCI. 649 (2020); Matthew Desmond, *Eviction and the Reproduction of Urban Poverty*, 118 AM. J. SOCIO. 88 (2012); MATTHEW DESMOND, EVICTED: POVERTY AND PROFIT IN THE AMERICAN CITY (2016). On child welfare, see, for example, DOROTHY ROBERTS, SHATTERED BONDS: THE COLOR OF CHILD WELFARE (2001); Tonya L. Brito et al., *"I Do for My Kids": Negotiating Race and Racial Inequality in Family Court*, 83 FORDHAM L. REV. 3027 (2015); DOROTHY ROBERTS, TORN APART: HOW THE CHILD WELFARE SYSTEM DESTROYS BLACK FAMILIES – AND HOW ABOLITION CAN BUILD A SAFER WORLD (2022). On debt collection, Paul Kiel & Annie Waldman, *The Color of Debt: How Collection Suits Squeeze Black Neighborhoods*, PROPUBLICA (Oct. 8, 2015), https://www.propublica.org/article/debt-collection-lawsuits-squeeze-black-neighborhoods; Dalie Jimenez, *Dirty Debts Sold Dirt Cheap*, 52 HARV. J. ON LEGIS. 41 (2015); Abbye Atkinson, *Borrowing Equality*, 120 COLUM. L. REV. 1403 (2020).

4 Sara Sternberg Greene & Kristen Renberg, *Judging without a J.D.*, 122 COLUM. L. REV. 1287 (2022).

5 Daniel Wilf-Townsend, *Assembly-Line Plaintiffs*, 135 HARV. L. REV. 1706 (2022); Greene & Renberg, *supra* note 4; Pamela K. Bookman & Colleen F. Shanahan, *A Tale of Two Civil Procedures*, 122 COLUM. L. REV. 1183 (2022).

The consequences of weak or nonexistent representation in these Kafkaesque courts are profound. A default judgment in such cases can lead to the loss of credit, one's home, or one's children. Worse, the civil justice gap confronting racial minorities likely extends far beyond what even these dismal statistics suggest. Many legal problems never become a case in a court docket.[6] Determining what happens to one's assets after death, starting a small business, getting the federal disability benefits to which one is entitled: These are common legal issues that state courts do not engage much, if ever. These are also issues where we can reasonably expect a strong relationship between race and problem resolution.[7]

At the same time as racial disparities in civil justice are troubling, civil justice is hardly the only public necessity that is under provided and distributed unequally according to race.[8] Indeed, we see similar issues in access to housing, education, banking, and still other areas.[9] Civil justice is also like these other necessities in the sense that contemporary political economies provide these goods through a coproduction of government and markets.[10] Notwithstanding the above-mentioned findings about how civil justice actually operates in the United States, at least theoretically civil justice is typically provided by lawyers in private practice. Lawyers are a professional class whose members are tightly connected to the government, not only through the kind of professional regulation that is typical of licensed professionals.[11] Indeed, lawyers are officers of the court who routinely participate in the process of the state authorizing pretty violent remedies such as taking a person's assets, even their kids – and that's just in U.S. civil courts.[12]

6 Catherine R. Albiston et al., *The Dispute Tree and the Legal Forest*, 10 Ann. Rev. L. & Soc. Sci. 105 (Nov. 3, 2014).

7 On racial gaps in small business formation, see, for example, Robert W. Fairlie et al., *Black and White: Access to Capital among Minority-Owned Start-Ups*, 68 Mgmt. Sci. 2377 (Apr. 2022); Aaron K. Chatterji et al., *The Impact of City Contracting Set-Asides on Black Self-Employment and Employment*, 32 J. Lab. & Econ. 507 (July 2014). On the relationship between wills, intestacy, and demographics, see, for example, Alyssa A. DiRusso, *Testacy and Intestacy: The Dynamics of Wills and Demographic Status*, 23 Quinnipiac Prob. L.J. 36 (2009); Reetu Pepoff, *The Intersection of Racial Inequities and Estate Planning*, 47 ACTEC L.J. 97 (2021). On the huge backlog in Social Security disability claims, see Jonah Gelbach & David Marcus, *Crushed: Social Security Legislation in the Federal Courts*, 101 Judicature 65 (2017), and on the racial incidence of disability status, see Alexa A. Hendley & Natasha F. Bilmoria, *Minorities and Social Security: An Analysis of Racial and Ethnic Differences in the Current Program*, 62 Soc. Sec. Bull. 59 (1999).

8 Chloe Thurston, *Racial Inequality, Market Inequality, and the American Political Economy*, *in* The American Political Economy 133 (Jacob S. Hacker et al. eds., 2021).

9 *Id.*

10 Peter A. Hall & David Soskice, Varieties of Capitalism: The Institutional Foundations of Comparative Advantage (2001).

11 Adam Bonica & Maya Sen, The Judicial Tug of War: How Lawyers, Politicians, and Ideological Incentives Shape the American Judiciary (2020).

12 Diane Redleaf, They Took the Kids Last Night: How the Child Protection System Puts Families at Risk (2018).

Because lawyers are not the only potential providers of solutions to civil justice problems,[13] any more than doctors are the only possible providers of medical care, I will typically try to refer to the private market for services addressing civil disputes and issues as the "market for civil justice." In the status quo, the market for civil justice and the legal market largely overlap, but how they overlap is a policy choice with profound consequences for both efficiency and distribution. While it is easy to imagine an (almost) fully private or (almost) fully public system for providing housing or banking, with civil justice it is harder to see how one could possibly disentangle government and markets from one another. But on reflection, there are robust markets for civil justice where government has little if any involvement, for example international commercial arbitration[14] or religious courts.[15] And it is not impossible to imagine a system where all civil litigants had representatives assigned by the court and paid through public funds.

While it is an interesting question how necessary coproduction by government and markets is for any of these goods, empirically at least, governments rarely attempt to provide these services wholly on their own. Instead, governments encourage and oversee private provision with various public backstops, although exactly how they encourage, oversee, and backstop varies tremendously across contexts.[16] Governments pursue such coproduction strategies because these goods are important. Private provision of essential goods through markets with the help and oversight of government is what builds more houses, nursing homes, and hospitals, while hopefully making sure they are of the right kinds. While one presumes that a mixed public-private strategy does provide more, or better, or more *of* better than pure strategies would, racial inequality often remains a stubborn issue in private markets, whether nurtured by the government or not.

While civil justice is certainly a fraught problem in race and political economy in the United States, I would argue it is one of the most important problems in any political economy. Civil justice is a piece of hardware that is needed to make other markets run.[17] When there are disputes about housing, credit, health care, and labor, courts are the problem-solver of last resort.[18] Or if not courts, some private entity or public non-court adjudicator that often emulates the manner and process

[13] *See* Albiston et al., *supra* note 6.

[14] Walter Mattli, *Private Justice in a Global Economy: From Litigation to Arbitration*, 55 INT'L ORG. 919 (2001).

[15] Rabea Benhalim, *Religious Courts in Secular Jurisdictions*, 84 BROOK. L. REV. 745 (2019).

[16] *See* HALL & SOSKICE, *supra* note 10.

[17] Daniel P. Kessler & Daniel L. Rubinfeld, *Chapter 5: Empirical Study of the Civil Justice System*, *in* HANDBOOK OF LAW AND ECONOMICS, vol. 1, 343 (A. Mitchell Polinsky & Steven Shavell eds., 2007).

[18] Austin Sarat & Joel B. Grossman, *Courts and Conflict Resolution: Problems in the Mobilization of Adjudication*, 69 AM. POL. SCI. REV. 1200 (1975).

of courts, and even at times has overlapping personnel.[19] The market for civil justice is so intimately connected to the basic operation of government that interventions in these markets inevitably change how government works, and are intensely political in the sense that they influence who gets, what, when, and why.

Despite the rich, thorny political economy problem that civil justice represents, it is only slightly exaggerating to say that political economists have ignored the civil justice system. The main reason I would qualify that statement is "political economy" is a big tent, after all. But it really is no exaggeration at all to say that civil justice is off the radar of political scientists who think about economic problems, and also of economists who think about politics and government.[20] One might hope that with increasing awareness about the deep problems in many areas touching civil justice (i.e., eviction, debt, fines, and fees), that will begin to change. Racial inequality that exists in the civil justice system is likely to reproduce and multiply in every market where governmental intervention is needed to ensure racial equality, and especially where private rights of action are a key enforcement strategy.[21]

To the limited extent that scholars working on civil justice have focused on race, they have not often done so by thinking *first* and *foremost* about market dynamics. Owing to the disciplinary background and methodological approaches of most academics working on access to justice, the prevailing research methodologies are largely qualitative and have involved ethnographic and survey-based approaches. These research strategies have yielded valuable insights into how and why minorities distrust civil justice institutions,[22] inequalities with respect to obtaining counsel and in quality of representation,[23] the role of overlapping and intersecting identities in shaping legal needs,[24] and many other important facets of race and access to justice.[25]

[19] Yarik Kryvoi, *Private or Public Adjudication? Procedure, Substance and Legitimacy*, 34 Leiden J. Int'l L. 681 (2021).

[20] Proving that no one in an area of scholarship is paying attention is difficult, but recent high-level publications addressing the topic by well-known authorities cite few, if any, political scientists or economists. *See, for example*, Rebecca L. Sandefur, *Access to What?*, 148 Daedalus 49 (Jan. 2019); Jamila Michener et al., *From the Margins to the Center: A Bottom-Up Approach to Welfare State Scholarship*, 20 Persp. Pol. 154 (Mar. 2022).

[21] Sean Farhang, The Litigation State: Public Regulations and Private Lawsuits in the U.S. (2010).

[22] Sara Sternberg Greene, *Race, Class, and Access to Civil Justice*, 101 Iowa L. Rev. 1263 (2015); Amy Myrick et al., *Race and Representation: Racial Disparities in Legal Representation for Employment Civil Rights Plaintiffs*, 15 N.Y.U. J. Legis. & Pub. Pol'y 705 (2012).

[23] *See, for example*, Colleen F. Shanahan & Anna E. Carpenter, *Simplified Courts Can't Solve Inequality* 148 Daedalus 128 (2019).

[24] Kathryne M. Young & Katie R. Billings, *An Intersectional Examination of U.S. Civil Justice Problems*, 3 Utah L. Rev. 487 (2023).

[25] Two useful references discussing the overall state of the race and access-to-justice literature are Rebecca L. Sandefur, *Access to Civil Justice and Race, Class, and Gender Inequality*, 34 Ann. Rev. Socio. 339 (Aug. 1, 2008), and Tonya L. Brito et al., *Racial Capitalism in the Civil Courts*, 122 Colum. L. Rev. 1243 (2022). It is unfortunately the case that both articles note that race has not had attention from the scholarly literature commensurate with its importance.

The importance of continuing to pursue research in these modalities and frameworks should go without saying. At the same time, the rational-choice perspective that political scientists and economists typically adopt also has great value for understanding why markets function or do not.[26] So too do the methods of causal identification that these disciplines typically favor. While civil justice scholarship has not exactly flourished in political science and economics departments, the study of race and markets truly has. There is much to gain in considering problems of race as problems of markets, and further in thinking about problems of civil justice as problems of markets.

My goal in this introduction has been to make the case for thinking like a political economist about civil justice in general and to see the dramatic racial inequality we see as an all too common, but uniquely important, market failure. Going forward, I wish to continue fleshing out what this perspective might entail. I must admit at the outset that all conclusions and recommendations are preliminary, because this line of inquiry is nascent. The ideas and proposals I offer are meant to provoke thought and debate. I will present findings that describe how severe the problem of racial discrimination is in legal markets and why it occurs. But I do not purport to offer here evidenced-based recommendations about what is to be done. In Section 2.1, which follows, I will introduce two key concepts that are important for contemporary debates in political economy about the causes of racial inequality in markets: racial preferences and statistical discrimination. I also discuss and explain why it is so important to distinguish between these two in thinking about policy solutions. Section 2.2 shows how recent work by myself and others has sought to document and explain the extent of racial disparities in legal markets. Section 2.3 discusses how and why broadening the base of legal service providers seems to be the key for ameliorating racial disparities in access to justice, and considers alternative paths to doing that, respectively through a civil right to counsel and loosening restrictions on alternative potential service providers, such as H&R Block.

2.1 UNTANGLING RACIAL PREFERENCES AND STATISTICAL DISCRIMINATION

The literature on discrimination in economics, both empirical and theoretical, has pursued questions of how race influences outcomes very directly. Its conceptual architecture for doing so is greatly indebted to the early mathematical models of Arrow and Becker.[27] These models distinguish *racial preferences*, which is when race

[26] Kenneth A. Shepsle, *Statistical Political Philosophy and Positive Political Theory*, 9 Critical Rev. 213 (Jan. 1995).

[27] Gary S. Becker, The Economics of Discrimination (1971); Kenneth J. Arrow, *The Theory of Discrimination*, *in* Discrimination in Labor Markets 3 (Orley Ashenfelter & Albert Rees eds., 1973); Kenneth J. Arrow, *What Has Economics to Say about Racial Discrimination?*, 12 J. Econ. Persp. 91 (May 1998).

directly influences an individual's enjoyment of a good or service, from *statistical discrimination*, which is when race is used to make inferences about the presence or absence of traits that influence enjoyment. For example, a widget-retailer exhibits a negative racial preference when he believes a black employee will sell as many widgets as a white employee, but nevertheless prefers to have the white employee to the black one simply because he likes white employees more. Equivalently, a widget-retailer who is willing to pay for the privilege of not working with a racial minority has negative racial preferences. By contrast, a widget-retailer *statistically* discriminates when she makes assumptions about the productivity of the workers based on what race they happen to be. This is to say, a widget-retailer who only cares about widget sales volume nevertheless may discriminate statistically if she has a belief structure enabling her discrimination (e.g., she believes minorities take too long to close a sale, believes minorities take off early on Fridays, whatever).

Racial preferences and *statistical discrimination* are not exclusive concepts. Indeed, evidence suggests that people with aversive racial preferences also tend to harbor racial stereotypes.[28] But because race marks so many aspects of American society especially, and because what is in people's heads is harder to see than what is written in an economist's equation, it is often very hard to determine whether disparities result from racial preferences or statistical discrimination. Why, then, does it help to distinguish between these two overlapping kinds of discrimination? Because the mechanisms of discrimination matter for why the discrimination happens and what would stop it. Potentially, problematic racial preferences require vastly different policy interventions than, say, problematic beliefs and inferences. An important, often implicit assumption of those operating from the economics perspective is that economically motivated agents are going to act according to the incentives determined by their beliefs. Particularly if those beliefs do have a strong empirical basis, changing behaviors implied by these beliefs will be tough or impossible.

As a more concrete illustration of why disentangling racial preferences from statistical discrimination matters for policymakers, I often gesture to the work of noted sociologist Devah Pager. Pager persuasively shows that in the absence of information, employers who hire low-skilled workers are more likely to assume that black male applicants have a criminal record than white male applicants.[29] Given the dismal statistics about criminal records in lower-income black versus white men, empirically their belief is well-justified. The upshot of Pager's observation is that well-intentioned policies that "ban the box" and prohibit employers from asking about criminal records in job applications or interviews risk hurting well-qualified minorities, who no longer have the opportunity to distinguish themselves from white

[28] Kyle Peyton & Gregory A. Huber, *Racial Resentment, Prejudice, and Discrimination*, 83 J. Pol. 1829 (Oct. 1, 2021).

[29] Devah Pager, *The Mark of a Criminal Record*, 108 Am. J. Socio. 937 (2003).

people with red flags in their background. Using the language of the economics literature, banning the box may encourage more statistical discrimination, not less, which could make racial disparities in hiring even worse.[30] Work such as Pager's illustrates why it is so important to ask *how exactly* race matters for the outcomes in question. If one does not consider the incentives of relevant actors in the system one wishes to reform, one may find one's solutions are counterproductive. Indeed, this is perhaps the real core of the economics perspective on race and discrimination. It is not simply about the introduction of terms like *racial preferences* and *statistical discrimination*, which are important but controversial in some quarters. Rather, an economics perspective is about disentangling *how* racial disparities emerge as a byproduct of some aspect of the strategic interaction between agents who follow the incentives determined by their beliefs but do not necessarily have the preferences and values we would hope that they would.

2.2 RACE, ACCESS TO JUSTICE, AND THE LEGAL SERVICE MARKET

Returning to the topic of access to justice, there are many entry points for thinking about the distinct role of race in an economics framework. We could think about the rational expectations and aversive preferences of judges, of juries, and of plaintiffs and defendants, both in the courtroom and also even earlier in the dispute resolution process. But perhaps the simplest and most direct way of relating these literatures is through the question of how race impacts the ability of a person with a legal problem to hire a lawyer. Getting a lawyer is a key step in the folk model of dispute settlement that naive and sophisticated commentators alike bring to the table.[31] It is also a step that an extraordinarily large number of self-represented or unrepresented minorities caught up in eviction, debt collection, and other matters have not taken, in many cases despite attempts to do so.[32] Two empirical questions, which I engage in much more detail in a law review article called *Getting a Lawyer while Black*,[33] are (a) whether race makes any difference in the ability of an individual to get a lawyer to help them solve their legal problem; and (b) if there is a difference, whether that difference is due to racial preferences or statistical discrimination. Greater details are available in the article, including greater

[30] *See also* John W. Patty & Elizabeth Maggie Penn, *Ban the Box? Information, Incentives, and Statistical Discrimination*, 18 Q. J. POL. SCI. 513 (2023).

[31] Young & Billings, *supra* note 24 (noting that until recently scholarship had typically conflated access to justice with access to lawyers, and supporting a broader perspective incorporating legal needs and justiciable events that overlap but do not subsume court cases).

[32] Tonya L. Brito, *The Right to Civil Counsel*, 148 DAEDALUS 56 (2019) (discussing the legal trouble of one Dearis Calahan who failed to appear in one case and represented himself in another after his attempts to secure a lawyer failed).

[33] Brian Libgober, *Getting a Lawyer while Black: A Field Experiment*, 24 LEWIS & CLARK L. REV. 96 (2020).

FROM: **{Latoya-Jackson@comcast.net;Laurie-McCarthy@comcast.net;Darnell-Jackson@comcast.net;Brad-McCarthy@comcast.net}**
SUBJECT: Looking for a lawyer

To Whom It May Concern,

My name is **{Latoya Jackson;Laurie McCarthy;Darnell Jackson; Brad McCarthy}** and I am a 34 year old medical sales representative (income around **{$40,000;$80,000}** per year). Two nights ago I was stopped for drunk driving by two policemen. I had my license suspended and my car towed. I had been drinking that night, but I did not feel I was too drunk to drive. If anything I was just tired. After I was pulled over they tried to give me a breathalyzer but I refused. Now they say I can't drive for a year, but that just can't work for me since my employer is located thirty-five minutes from my home and public transportation can't get me there. I am looking for a lawyer to overturn that suspension and get me back my license, and keep my record clean. Please let me know if you can take my case, and if so how we should go forward.

Best,
{Latoya;Laurie;Darnell;Brad}

FIGURE 2.1 Prospective client solicitation in the California experiment.

justifications and caveats than I have space for here; however, I focus here on the big picture conclusions.

To answer the question of whether race influences the ability of an individual to get a lawyer to help solve their problem, I rely on the popular audit study methodology.[34] Posing as a prospective client, I contacted California criminal attorneys in private practice via email asking whether they could help me regain my driver's license, which had been taken when I refused a breathalyzer. Figure 2.1 provides the email template used in the experiment. Crucial to the audit methodology, the email template varied several factors at random, including the name I pretended to have, as well as an off-handed description of my income. The names I used were Brad McCarthy, Laurie McCarthy, Darnell Jackson, and Latoya Jackson, each of which is strongly suggestive of an individual's race, both based on survey evidence and analysis of birth certificates. Figure 2.2 shows the difference that a name makes in an otherwise identical email. Laurie and Brad had a 40 percent chance of getting a reply to this email, while Darnell and Latoya had a 19 percent chance of getting a reply to the exact same email. Such a tremendous difference in response rates, with

[34] Marianne Bertrand & Sendhil Mullainathan, *Are Emily and Greg More Employable than Lakisha and Jamal? A Field Experiment on Labor Market Discrimination*, 94 AM. ECON. REV. 991 (2004); AUDIT STUDIES: BEHIND THE SCENES WITH THEORY, METHOD, AND NUANCE (S. Michael Gaddis ed., 2018).

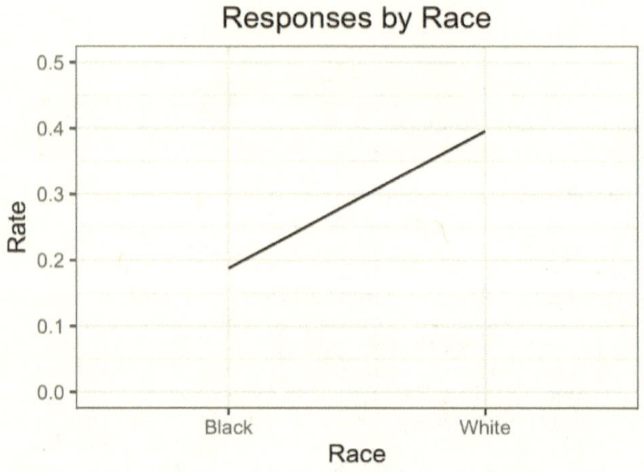

FIGURE 2.2 Response rate of California criminal lawyers based on likely race of prospective client.

white-named clients more than twice as likely to get a reply, was unlikely to be due to chance. Put differently, the estimates imply that the anticipated race of the client mattered to about 20 percent of the California criminal bar in choosing whether to reply to this solicitation. Unusually for social scientific research, this experiment was subject to a second and even third replication. The results were substantially similar each time, at least in California.

To begin to answer the question of *why* race seems to matter for one in five of the lawyers sampled, one can examine Figure 2.3, which shows the difference that claiming twice as much annual income makes. Surprisingly, response rates were slightly *lower* for individuals claiming to make more money. That said, the difference is quite small and could easily emerge if the self-represented income did not matter to lawyers one way or another. The fact that lawyers do not respond to explicit signals of income is evidence that racial preferences drive these results rather than statistical discrimination. This is not to say that statistical discrimination would never emerge in client selection. Indeed, it seems to me relatively likely that statistical discrimination would emerge in contexts where the ability to pay is truly in question, for example, bankruptcy, or the lawyer has a long running matter the client has to pay for entirely, for example, complex felonies. Yet for relatively simple, routine, and self-contained legal problems, one would not expect concerns about the ability to pay to dominate lawyers' thinking. And the evidence suggests they do not. Based on my own prior qualitative research in designing the study, lawyers who do this sort of work know exactly what they will charge and know that people with relatively modest incomes (for instance, even as little as $40,000 a year) will be able to find the cash to fund the work, especially when confronted with the much more economically damaging prospect of losing their ability to drive a car.

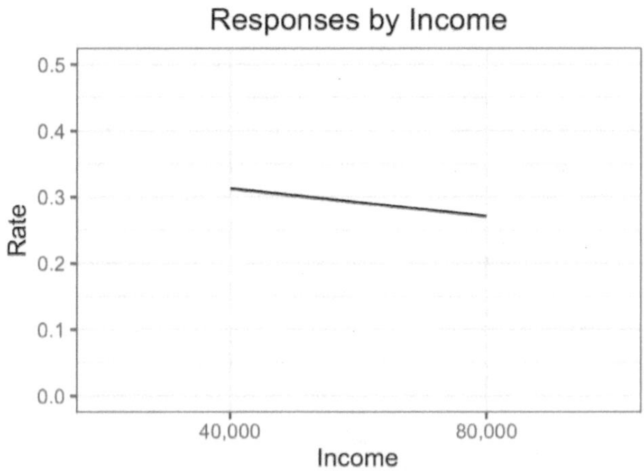

FIGURE 2.3 Response rates of California criminal lawyers based on self-described client income.

These findings present strong evidence that race sometimes influences the ease with which a prospective client finds a lawyer, and, particularly in routine legal matters, race has this influence to a substantial degree because of taste-based discrimination by lawyers, rather than some kind of economic stereotyping. Further, another recent study by Frankenreiter and Livermore in the *Journal of Legal Studies* that uses similar audit methods also finds that race often matters a great deal.[35] But in both their study and mine, the story gets a bit more complicated because it seems that *the degree of racial disparities varies greatly across legal markets*.

Figure 2.4 provides striking evidence that disparities vary geographically. This remarkable diagram, which is based on a full-color figure deep in the Online Appendix of Frankenreiter and Livermore's article, shows how the response rates vary by state among some 24,211 personal injury lawyers found on a commercial database. Darker areas are those where their audit study found greater preference for white-named clients. White areas are those where they found no preferences or preferences actually tilting toward minorities. While the California effects do appear more muted than in Libgober (2020), they are directionally similar, and Frankenreiter and Livermore do make equally strong findings of discrimination as I initially did in both the rural west (Montana, Utah) and the densely urban Northeast (Rhode Island). Because of differences in sample recruitment strategies (e.g., commercial database in their approach versus bar directory in mine), the effects found across the two studies are not directly comparable and should not be regarded as direct tests of replicability. Even so, the crazy quilt pattern of

[35] Jens Frankenreiter and Michael A. Livermore, *Are Lawyers' Case Selection Decisions Biased? A Field Experiment on Access to Justice*, 62 J. OF LEGAL STUDIES 273 (2023).

FIGURE 2.4 Size of treatment effects by state based on findings of Frankenreiter and Livermore (2023), reported originally as OA6 in their supplemental materials.
Source: *Are Lawyers' Case Selection Decisions Biased? A Field Experiment on Access to Justice*, 62 J. of Legal Studies 273 (2023).

discrimination is clearly evident in their figure. There are "red states" where no racial discrimination against minorities is detected through these methods, and "blue states" with intense discrimination against minorities found.

Frankenreiter and Livermore's work confirms the remarkable geographic variation in the degree of discrimination within the United States, which my earlier study too picked up on. Understanding some details of what I did previously is necessary to go forward and explain my proposed resolution. Returning then to the mid-2010s, after conducting my audit study in California, I sought to examine whether the very strong effect found in California was limited to criminal lawyers or if it was visible in other practice areas as well. In particular, the argument could be made, as I have above, that driving under the influence ("DUI") cases do not lend themselves to statistical discrimination. For this reason, I sought to examine further practice areas with different payment models to see if that mattered at all.

For technical reasons, the California bar directory at the time did not lend itself to these kinds of endeavors, so I made a switch to field a much larger follow-up experiment in Florida, where doing so was more practicable. At the time, I did not expect the state context to matter. If anything, I expected effects of potential clients' race would be larger in Florida. And yet, my results regarding personal injury, criminal, and divorce lawyers in Florida were remarkably in line with what Frankenreiter and Livermore later found about personal injury lawyers in Florida: practically *no discrimination* against prospective clients whose names suggest minority status. This geographic variation was difficult to believe, and for this reason

I undertook very extensive internal replication efforts described at greater length in Libgober (2020). These replication efforts confirmed that there were indeed huge disparities by race in California but not in Florida. If Florida and California are different, and if as Frankenreiter and Livermore later would find two states are often quite different, the main question is why.

In my prior study, I proposed several possibilities and tried as best I could with data on hand to offer answers. One possibility is that far fewer lawyers in Florida have aversive racial preferences than in California. For several reasons, I rejected that explanation, most importantly because both subtle and unsubtle methods of determining aversive racial preferences among the general public find that California is more racially progressive than Florida. If racial preferences among the bar were the only thing that mattered, we would see about the same or bigger effects in Florida than California, not the muted effects we do find there.

After puzzling through several alternatives, I eventually came to the view the best explanation for geographic variability in discrimination is the prevalence of lawyers and the profitability of legal practice. Put differently, it's not the state or geography *per se*, it's the fact that states in these studies represent different legal markets, and the market plays a large mediating role in the emergence of racial disparities. Florida and California appear quite different in both dimensions of lawyer prevalence and lawyer profitability. According to the Bureau of Economic Analysis, there are about 20 percent more lawyers per capita in Florida than in California.[36] Unsurprisingly, Florida lawyers make considerably less. The mean hourly wage for a Florida lawyer is $65 per hour, while in California it is $97 per hour.[37]

Why do lawyer prevalence and profitability matter? Because both speak to the supply constraints of the lawyers who participate in these audit studies. A lawyer who has the capacity to undertake additional work has strong incentive to do so, regardless of their race, while a lawyer who continuously works at or near capacity can act in a choosy fashion about their clientele. And if someone can be choosy, they are likely to do so for all sorts of idiosyncratic reasons. It would be very surprising if race were not occasionally an important factor for some. In California, it seems that race is an important factor for about 20 percent, while in Florida it is likely a similar percentage but because of economic incentives those individuals "get over it." A regression analysis within Florida counties provides some confirmatory evidence of this theory, with counties where lawyer pay is stronger observing *more* disparities in response to client solicitations. Frankenreiter and Livermore did not use their national set of data to do the same sort of regression analysis I did within Florida to test mechanisms, but perhaps future work can do so. Even so, racialized service rationing remains an intuitive interpretation for the surprising

[36] *Occupational Employment and Wages, May 2017: 23-1011 Lawyers*, Bureau of Lab. Stats., https://www.bls.gov/oes/current/oes231011.htm (last accessed Mar. 22, 2024).

[37] *Id.*

geographic patterns we see across audit studies, and an interpretation supported by limited observational evidence.

The argument that inadequate supply of lawyers is an important cause of access to justice issues is not new. Nor is the expectation that the burdens of inadequate supply will fall in disparate ways along racial lines. But the idea that when supply shortages are present it allows lawyers who would ration services along racial lines to do so is a novel point. It also raises the racial stakes on all sorts of questions about professional regulation and licensing reform, which is perhaps more useful politically. The point is not to solve the fundamental racial inequities in American (or other) societies. Rather, a more modest goal is to provide enough supply that the typical lawyer does not ration their services along racial lines. California does not need to try to achieve some utopian economic vision; they can simply try to make their legal market look more like Florida's. Whether the Bar will want to do that given the differentials in lawyer pay is another matter; however, racial justice is a powerful political angle that often does have traction in progressive political climates like California.

To summarize where these findings fit in the broader understanding of race and access to justice, we know from extensive research across the social sciences that race is conspicuously related to many varied civil justice problems. At the same time, it is questionable whether these are simply correlates of a racially inegalitarian society or more directly a consequence of racism by key intermediaries in the civil justice system (i.e., lawyers, judges, juries) or in parts of the broader world that have a tight connection with civil justice problems (i.e., landlords, credit rating agencies, social workers, and others). The stakes of answering this question are both practical and political. On the one hand, one wants an accurate diagnosis if one wants an effective cure. One imagines that interventions making access to justice more equitable will tend to benefit previously underserved demographic minorities more than white people, just as the expansion of health care access was disproportionately beneficial to racial minorities because their situation was previously the most precarious. But perhaps not, or perhaps not enough, unless the interventions do not pay attention to the key mediators.

On the other hand, political claims about racism are different from claims about economic disadvantage. In some cases, the argument that a system is racist or enables racism may prove more powerful and persuasive than claims that this system is disadvantageous to the poor.[38] The findings discussed above work on both levels. In some jurisdictions, the bar exhibits profound negative racial preferences over clients as distinct from favoring the affluent, who are perhaps less likely to come from minority backgrounds. But crucially, the legal market does seem to mediate these preferences, as political economists might suppose. If the market actually

[38] Jan E. Leighley, Strength in Numbers?: The Political Mobilization of Racial and Ethnic Minorities (2001).

makes lawyers pay the price for their racial preferences, most of those who would like to discriminate in client selection will decline to do so. The upshot is that in designing policy interventions about access to justice, the likely continuing presence of racism by large enough fractions of the bar must be considered.

Moreover, there is to my mind a powerful political argument here, that severe constraints on the number of attorneys that practice in a given field of law in a given legal market basically encourage and enable segments of the bar to be choosy over the race of their clients in a way that is at odds with the official, anti-racist sentiment expressed by all major legal professional associations.

2.3 IS ATTORNEY SUPPLY THE KEY TO DE-BIASING?

Having resituated my own research findings within the broader topic, I wish to turn and examine the policy implication. If the basic claim is that insufficient supply of attorneys creates conditions whereby racial discrimination against clients by lawyers becomes likely, then that obviously pours additional gasoline (as if that were needed) on previous arguments made by authors such as Deborah Rhode,[39] Herbert Kritzer,[40] and others going back many decades that liberalization of the professional monopoly is necessary to improve access to justice. Particularly in the large number of routine legal matters where underrepresentation is most acute, representational discrepancies appear to be more strongly rooted in racist preferences of sizable segments of the bar rather than background economic inequality or statistical discrimination. Greater liberalization of the professional monopoly implies more market discipline against racist preferences by legal service providers. At this point, I could continue to recapitulate arguments about the benefits of liberalizing the professional monopoly, but I will instead emphasize some perhaps more surprising connections that attention to race might imply.

2.3.1 *Rethinking the Rationale for Affirmative Action*

If we seek to increase attorney supply, we must also pay attention to the need to increase the supply of black and brown attorneys. In *Getting a Lawyer While Black*, for example, I explore the extent to which black lawyers behave differently than white lawyers in response to client solicitations.[41] There, I find evidence that black lawyers have a greater interest in serving black clients than white lawyers do.[42]

39 Deborah L. Rhode, *Policing the Professional Monopoly: A Constitutional and Empirical Analysis of Unauthorized Practice Prohibitions*, 34 STAN. L. REV. 1 (1981).

40 Herbert M. Kritzer, *Rethinking Barriers to Legal Practice: It Is Time to Repeal Unauthorized Practice of Law Statutes*, 81 JUDICATURE 100 (1997).

41 Libgober, *supra* note 33.

42 *Id.* at 99. In one branch of the experiment, 122 black criminal lawyers showed a 13.5 percent greater response rate to client solicitations using a distinctively black name than a distinctively

These findings factor into older (and perhaps once again new) debates about the use of affirmative action in admission to educational institutions. In particular, my findings support a governmental rationale for affirmative action already described in *Bakke* but not evaluated at great length.[43] In *Bakke*, the University of California system argued that having enough minority health care providers was necessary to guarantee essential services to minority communities. The court agreed that "in some situations, a State's interest in facilitating the health care of its citizens is sufficiently compelling to support the use of a suspect classification."[44] Apparently, however, the University of California did not present sufficient evidence to show that the university's policy advanced this interest, and the court dismissed the argument on the ground that the University had not shown that its admissions policy was narrowly tailored to advance that interest, while leaving the door open that in some cases, it might be.[45]

Today's access-to-justice crisis may be such a case. There is abundant evidence that minority communities are badly underserved in legal contexts, and also evidence that having more minority lawyers would improve access to lawyers for individuals of minority backgrounds. Enough evidence to survive strict scrutiny of a hostile court? In *Getting a Lawyer While Black*, I expressed some doubts about that. Today, when the court has all but eliminated affirmative action, I have even more doubt.[46] Still, whatever the constitutional situation, the important point is that as a *policy matter* one must understand why preserving and enhancing professional diversity is so important.

It is worth zeroing in on the meaning of "diversity" in this context. In discussing diversity, one often focuses on distribution or composition – for example what share of the profession comes from which racial, gender, or other background.[47] Yet it is hardly clear that distribution matters as much for access to justice as the overall number of providers. Most arguments about affirmative action address a fair or

white name, a borderline statistically significant difference ($p = 0.094$). This black lawyer for black client preference was not observed in other arms of the experiment, but equally there was no evidence against a small preference in any other arms. Overall, I regard the evidence as consistent with the view that black lawyers do sometimes exhibit substantial preferences for black clients, although that preference is context dependent and not likely to be overwhelming.

43 Regents of the Univ. of Cal. v. Bakke, 438 U.S. 265, 310 (1978).

44 *Id.*

45 *Id.* The Court endorsed the speculation of the lower court that there might be white applicants who had demonstrated and expressed an interest in serving minority communities would be even better for remediating shortages than an applicant who merely grew up in a poor minority community but would otherwise be preferred.

46 *See* Students for Fair Admissions v. Harvard, 600 U.S. 181 (2023).

47 *See, for example*, Am. Bar Ass'n, *Member Diversity, Equity, and Inclusion Plan* https://www.americanbar.org/content/dam/aba/administrative/diversity-inclusion-center/new-bog-approved-member-dei-plan.pdf (last accessed Feb. 13, 2025) ("We strive to strive to mirror population demographics of the United States and to represent the communities the ABA serves.").

desirable composition of, say, a matriculating class of students.[48] From the standpoint of access to justice for underserved communities, it is less clear why the composition of the bar matters. If one doubled the number of minority lawyers, while quintupling the overall number of lawyers, then the share of the profession of diverse backgrounds would decrease, but there would be more providers of minority backgrounds. Presumably, minorities would then have an easier time finding an attorney to help them with their legal issues. And if the market logic holds, the additional supply of nondiverse lawyers would also help remedy shortfalls.

In my view, this line of reasoning presents the biggest challenge to providing essential services to underserved communities as a rationale for affirmative action. What is the overwhelming governmental interest in keeping the profession's size fixed that justifies the consideration of otherwise and normally forbidden racial factors? Certainly, states have not fully explored methods for producing sufficient numbers of lawyers from every community background. For example, few states have an apprenticeship path to the bar,[49] even though that is a well-precedented approach that would at least marginally increase the size of the profession, potentially bringing in more providers of minority backgrounds.[50] States differ in the Uniform Bar Exam score they require for admission,[51] and although I am not aware of any specific studies, it is likely that lowering these requirements would have a demonstrably positive impact on lawyer supply and the number of lawyers from underrepresented backgrounds. The major conceptual argument against weaker *ex ante* controls like these is that the quality of legal services will suffer; however, the fascinating chapter by Rebecca Haw Allensworth (Chapter 3 in this volume) shows that the weak *ex post* oversight on known bad apples raises doubts about how necessary it is to have stringent *ex ante* controls.[52] Surely, there is a way to have tougher controls on the backend and looser controls on the front end, especially if it helps deal with the twin and as we now know related crises of insufficient racial diversity in the profession and disproportionate over participation by racial minorities in civil justice procedures.

In considering how to increase the number of diverse lawyers, without necessarily worrying too much about their relative abundance in the profession, it is important

48 *See, for example*, Grutter v. Bollinger, 539 U.S. 306 (2003) (contrasting affirmative action quotas based on percentages of the class with the similar, if squishier and for some time permissible, notion of a "critical mass" of minority students in a cohort).

49 *Advocating for Apprenticeship*, Center on the Legal Profession at Harvard Law School (Jan./Feb. 2024), https://clp.law.harvard.edu/knowledge-hub/magazine/issues/rethinking-licensure/advocating-for-apprenticeship/ (last accessed Mar. 22, 2024).

50 *See, for example*, *Case Studies*, ApprenticeshipUSA, https://www.apprenticeship.gov/case-studies (this webpage is no longer accessible) (describing numerous Department of Labor sanctioned apprenticeship programs, such as Building Pathways, Inc., that have outsized impacts on diversity).

51 *UBE Minimum Scores*, Nat'l Conf. Bar Examiners (undated), https://www.ncbex.org/exams/ube/ube-minimum-scores (last accessed Mar. 22, 2024).

52 See Chapter 3 in this volume.

to recognize that many of the profession's most obvious *ex ante* entry barriers, such as the bar exam, only bind lawyer supply in the short run. In the long run, it seems that there are other important reasons why lawyers are so few and far between. In 2010, 52,404 students started the first year of law school, but those numbers have declined precipitously. In 2022, for example, there were only 38,019.[53] As many lawyers have been trained in recent years as in the early 1970s, but today the overall U.S. population is 60 percent *larger*.[54] The fact that law schools a decade ago were training 40 percent more students, and absorbed a full 3,000 additional students in 2021 when the pandemic temporarily made law school a relatively attractive option, certainly suggests law schools have the capacity to train more students. The situation is not like medicine, where the limited number of residency placements discourages medical schools from creating more seats, in turn creating an extraordinarily competitive process for all seats available in U.S. medical schools.[55]

As the declining enrollment statistics reveal, the issue with U.S. law schools is really one of limited student demand. Why not get a law degree if one is a smart, hard-working, and ethical individual? Some of the obvious detractors: The law degree is expensive;[56] lawyer pay is relatively high, but jobs in finance, consulting, tech, and so forth may have wages that are competitive or higher;[57] and surveys indicate that lawyers are remarkably unhappy as a profession.[58]

Not all of these aspects are fully within the control of the legal profession, but the costs of getting a degree are very conspicuously a professional policy choice. The United States is virtually alone in requiring an additional three-year degree on top of the baccalaureate for individuals to practice law. Law school attendees are somewhat less racially diverse than college students, but the compositional differences are

53 *Law School Enrollment Trends*, 1963–2023, LAW SCH. TRANSPARENCY, https://www.lawschooltransparency.com/trends/enrollment/all (last accessed Mar. 22, 2024).

54 *See Population*, USAFACTS.ORG, https://usafacts.org/data/topics/people-society/population-and-demographics/population-data/population/ (last accessed Feb. 13, 2025) (line chart of census data showing US population at a little above 200 million in 1970 and at roughly 330 million in 2020).

55 Rebekah Bernard, *Match Day 2023 a Reminder of the Real Cause of the Physician Shortage: Not Enough Residency Positions*, MED. ECON. (Mar. 15, 2023), https://www.medicaleconomics.com/view/match-day-2023-a-reminder-of-the-real-cause-of-the-physician-shortage-not-enough-residency-positions (last accessed Feb. 13 2025).

56 Melanie Hanson, *Average Cost of Law School*, EDUCATIONDATA.ORG (Sept. 13, 2023), https://educationdata.org/average-cost-of-law-school (last accessed Feb. 13, 2025) (pegging average total cost of law school at $220,335).

57 Sarah Butcher, *Pay in Banking vs. Consulting vs. Tech vs. Medicine vs. Law*, EFINANCIALCAREERS.COM (Jan. 15, 2020), https://www.efinancialcareers.com/news/2020/01/pay-in-banking-vs-consulting-vs-tech-vs-medicine-vs-law (last accessed Feb. 25, 2024).

58 Yair Listokin & Raymond Noonan, *Measuring Lawyer Well-Being Systematically: Evidence from the National Health Interview Survey*, 18 J. EMPIRICAL LEGAL STUD. 4 (discussing the profession's reputation for unhappiness, while critiquing existing evidence and providing more credible evidence that is still somewhat mixed).

less dramatic than some might suppose.[59] Even so, the number of individuals attending college annually dwarfs the number of those attending law school (i.e., in 2010, there were twenty-one million college students[60]), and the number of bachelor degrees awarded in a *single* law-adjacent major like political science is roughly similar to the total number of JDs admitted from *many such* majors, for example, economics, history, sociology, and so forth.[61] There are a large number of law schools housed at flagship state schools, and from an outsider perspective it is hard to see why these law schools could not relatively quickly turn around and expand their services to educating undergraduates, with for example a five- or six-year BA/JD.[62] It is far from obvious that requiring a second educational institution and degree enhances the quality of individuals serving in the profession, although it greatly enhances the cost of getting a law degree, keeps the size of the profession small, and diminishes the number of diverse practitioners. While I do not see much reason to believe that addressing the educational barriers to entry would produce a bar that is more racially *representative*, it is almost inevitable that lowering these barriers would bring more diverse practitioners to the profession.

2.3.2 *Civil Gideon's Hidden Potential: Countering Professional Demoralization*

Besides cost, another important reason why fewer individuals enter the legal profession is the relatively limited prospects for having the kind of meaningful career that individuals want. While the true extent of unhappiness in the profession is debatable,[63] it is agreed that the "institutional glide path"[64] of many law schools is toward

59 ABA data from 2023 counts 2,969 black students admits to accredited law schools and 5,368 Hispanic admits against 37,886 total, implying 7.8 percent and 14.2 percent of admits are Black students or Hispanic, respectively. Am. Bar Ass'n, 2023 *First-Year Enrollment by Gender & Race/Ethnicity (Aggregate)*, https://www.americanbar.org/groups/legal_education/resources/statistics/ (last accessed Feb. 13, 2025). By contrast, 13.4 percent of college students are Black and 19.5 percent are Hispanic. Melanie Hanson, *College Enrollment & Student Demographic Statistics*, EDUCATIONDATA.ORG (Jan. 10, 2024), https://educationdata.org/college-enrollment-statistics (last accessed Feb. 13, 2025).

60 Hanson, *supra* note 56.

61 John Ishiyama, *Rethinking the Undergraduate Political Science Major*, POL. SCI. TODAY (Summer 2019), https://educate.apsanet.org/rethinking-the-undergraduate-political-science-majo (last accessed Feb. 13, 2025) (claiming there were 40,000 US political science majors in 2011–12 and that this number was around 34,000 in 2015–16). Other sources suggest there are far more political science BAs than law students, for example 2023 *Political Science & Government Degree Guide*, COLLEGE FACTUAL, https://www.collegefactual.com/majors/social-sciences/political-science-and-government/ (last accessed Apr. 23, 2024).

62 *See, for example, Accelerated Dual Degree BA or BS/JD*, QUINNIPIAC, https://law.qu.edu/programs/accelerated-dual-degree/ba-or-bs-jd/ (last accessed Mar. 22, 2024).

63 Listokin & Noonan, *supra* note 58.

64 NANCY LEVIT & DOUGLAS O. LINDER, THE HAPPY LAWYER: MAKING A GOOD LIFE IN THE LAW 138–40 (2010).

large law firms where lawyers, especially younger lawyers, are often miserable despite enviable pay.[65] It is in this context that I would view questions about the advisability of recent efforts to legislatively establish civil Gideon in particular settings, which it is hard to overlook as a potential solution to gaps in civil justice. To recapitulate this policy idea, the Supreme Court's decision in *Gideon v. Wainwright* established a right to counsel in criminal matters. In so doing, the Supreme Court issued an unfunded mandate that resulted in profound government subsidies for legal work that would otherwise have limited economic value – work representing the criminally accused and economically indigent.[66] While the Supreme Court declined to create a similar right in civil matters, several jurisdictions have started on the path to enshrining this right in certain very high stakes areas, such as housing or child welfare.[67] Unsurprisingly from a political economy perspective, the American Bar Association has also voiced strong support for civil Gideon.[68]

While it is easy to suppose that civil Gideon would help with the huge civil justice needs that fall disproportionately on minorities, it is questionable whether civil Gideon provides the best bang for the buck. Nor is it clear that civil Gideon would avoid the issues of the criminal public defender system, including chronic underfunding and, potentially, worse outcomes for criminal defendants represented by public defenders.[69] Moreover, I find myself substantially in agreement with Tonya Brito's claim that the right to civil counsel is fundamentally conceptualized in such a way as to be too little too late.[70] At the point at which a counsel is appointed to help with a civil problem, the issues will have gotten so out of hand that there is little to be done in terms of reconciliation or problem-prevention.[71] Indeed, evaluations of programs that provide free civil legal assistance have failed to find the anticipated benefit.[72]

65 Martin E. P. Seligman et al., *Why Lawyers Are Unhappy*, 23 Cardozo L. Rev. 33 (2001).

66 David Rudovsky, *Gideon and the Effective Assistance of Counsel: The Rhetoric and the Reality*, 32 Minn. J.L. & Ineq. 373 (2014) ("*Gideon* imposed an unfunded mandate on state and local governments, and criminal defendants are among the most disliked and politically powerless constituencies in our polity.").

67 Brito, *supra* note 32.

68 *See Civil Right to Counsel*, Am. Bar Ass'n, https://www.americanbar.org/groups/legal_aid_indigent_defense/civil_right_to_counsel1/ (last accessed Feb. 13, 2025) Am. Bar Ass'n, *ABA Toolkit for a Right to Counsel in Civil Proceedings* (2010), https://www.americanbar.org/content/dam/aba/administrative/legal_aid_indigent_defendants/ls_sclaid_toolkit_for_crtc.pdf (last accessed Feb. 13, 2025).

69 *See* Erwin Chemerinsky, *Lessons from Gideon*, 122 Yale L.J. 2678 (2013) (discussing correlative evidence suggesting that individuals represented by public defenders were more likely to be convicted than those with private attorneys, and suggesting that self-represented defendants may fare better than those represented by public defenders).

70 Brito, *supra* note 32.

71 Certainly, such findings and theories should not discourage yet-to-be-attempted access-to-justice reforms. But they should alert us to the fact that we lack abundant theories and evidence regarding what truly effective legal-assistance interventions might be.

72 D. James Greiner, *The New Legal Empiricism & Its Application to Access-to-Justice Inquiries*, 148 Daedalus 64 (Jan. 2019); D. James Greiner & Cassandra Wolos Pattanayak, *Randomized*

But regardless of debates around civil Gideon's potential efficacy, it may hold promise as a device for addressing the legal profession's dismal recruitment problems, and in particular, its inability to attract individuals in sufficient numbers and with sufficient diversity to address the legal needs of American society. Few individuals go to law school with an idea of what the Legal Services Corporation is,[73] but most presumably have an idea of what it is that a public defender does. And those who seek to do the kind of work that a public defender does know they must go to law school to do it.

That said, working with the criminally accused is not for everyone. There are likely many individuals potentially open to civil defense work on eviction, debt collection, family, and other civil law matters overwhelming our court system, but for various reasons less likely to want to work with the criminally accused.[74] Indeed, that public financing of legal services only is available for criminal defense work presents public-service-minded prospective lawyers with unfortunate tradeoffs. They have to choose between jobs where they will have to work defending criminals who are actually guilty of heinous crimes, or doing public interest work at all. "If I do not want to work as a public defender," many law students ask themselves, "what other kind of public interest work can I do?" The answer is frequently not clear, and the hydraulic pull of working on rich people's problems can become very strong.[75] To the extent that civil rights to counsel create visible pathways for law students to have stable careers that are readily understood as addressing the public's real legal needs, perhaps one might see increasing student demand, and especially minority student demand, for degrees and careers in law.

2.3.3 *Race and an Expanded Legal Services Marketplace*

In addition to civil Gideon, commentators often wonder whether other sorts of providers can play a greater role. Professor Kritzer, for example, looks to the United Kingdom and argues that their Citizens Advice Bureaus represent a potential (if somewhat expensive) model for what could get built in the United States.[76] But

Evaluation in Legal Assistance: What Difference Does Representation (Offer and Actual Use) Make?, 121 YALE L.J. 2118 (2012).

[73] The Legal Services Corporation is a government-run entity and is the nation's largest provider of funding for civil legal aid for low-income Americans. *See About*, LEGAL SERVS. CORP., https://www.lsc.gov/about-lsc (last accessed Mar. 24, 2024).

[74] Patrick C. Brayer, *The Power of the Public Defender Experience: Learning by Fighting for the Incarcerated and Poor*, 53 WASH. U. J.L. & POL'Y 105 (2017) ("The first and most predominant reaction from a student assigned to meet with a client in jail, alone, is fear.").

[75] Leeor Neta, *The Most Common Path to a Public Interest Career Is also the Least Discussed*, NALP BULL. (Jan. 2012), http://digitalcommons.law.ggu.edu/pubs/457 (last accessed Feb. 13, 2025) ("[M]ost future public interest lawyers. ... averse to jump ship to the private sector option.").

[76] Kritzer, *supra* note 40.

given the United States' political economy, it is reasonable to anticipate that black and brown communities underserved by existing civil infrastructure would also receive underwhelming services from a new public venture in the model of Citizens Advice Bureaus. This is not to say that supporters of racial equity in access to justice should reject such ideas. It is notable that advocates for postal banking often base their arguments in the fact that civil infrastructure like post offices are more accessible to underserved communities than most other mechanisms for delivering banking services. Still, it is important to recognize that, without special attention, public alternatives to service provision are unlikely to generate perfectly equitable solutions.

Rather than creating a new (and expensive) public venture, the United States has previously sought to deputize and expand existing private capacities for delivering services. The major issue here is that the private companies that tend to specialize in serving economically marginal communities also often take advantage of the marginal position of their clients. For example, the U.S. system for delivering the Earned Income Tax Credit (EITC) deputizes large numbers of private tax preparers to determine who is eligible for this very important public benefit. Collectively, private tax preparers earn billions of dollars in exchange for doing this work,[77] and some 98 percent of families with incomes below $30,000 receive assistance from a tax preparer.[78] Chain tax preparers such as Jackson-Hewitt and H&R Block have thousands of storefront locations that particularly concentrate in zip codes where EITC recipients live.[79] Historically, they have sold to these communities financial products that are essentially fast, often high-interest loans that use anticipated returns as collateral.[80] The American Prospect reported one typical case, where an individual expecting $9,697 from the Internal Revenue Service (IRS) paid their tax preparer $970 in total fees, or about 10 percent of the total refund.

Access-to-justice advocates are unlikely to receive warmly the idea of having private, storefront entities such as H&R Block providing for a fee the sort of services a government-funded Citizens Advice Bureau might offer for free. Indeed, it seems

[77] Alan Berube et al., *The Price of Paying Taxes: How Tax Preparations and Refund Loan Fees Erode the Benefits of the EITC*, Brookings (May 1, 2002), https://www.brookings.edu/articles/the-price-of-paying-taxes-how-tax-preparation-and-refund-loan-fees-erode-the-benefits-of-the-eitc/ (last accessed Feb. 13, 2025).

[78] Elain Maag, *Paying the Price? Low-Income Parents and the Use of Paid Tax Preparers*, Urban Inst. (Feb. 1, 2005), https://webarchive.urban.org/publications/411145.html (last accessed Feb. 13, 2025).

[79] Paul Weinstein & Beathany Patten, *The Price of Paying Taxes II: How Paid Tax Preparers Are Diminishing the Earned Income Tax Credit*, Prog. Pol. Inst. (Apr. 2016), https://www.progressivepolicy.org/publication/the-price-of-paying-taxes-ii-how-paid-tax-preparer-fees-are-diminishing-the-earned-income-tax-credit-eitc/ (last accessed Feb. 13, 2025).

[80] Berube et al., *supra* note 77.

likely that instead of private providers skimming billions off government benefit programs, one could fund directly a governmental entity to do this work for less. On the other hand, building programmatic capacity is tough. Through flipping the right combination of regulatory switches, the private sector can self-organize a system that works better than no system at all or a system that is so overworked it barely functions. Given the dismal situation in many state courts, especially for minorities, it is worth seriously considering regulatory changes that would allow entities already facilitating usually routine, possibly complex, legal issues the ability to do more. It is pretty easy to imagine that companies such as a tax prep chain might have a large comparative advantage in the development of software, as well as the training of personnel, necessary to provide many basic form and process services for which a lawyer may seem too expensive and self-service too confusing or difficult. It is in some sense outrageous to ask someone already struggling to make ends meet to fork over $29.95 to H&R Block to help them file a notice to appear with a court in an eviction matter, for example, when courts could without much difficulty provide defendants with a postcard to indicate whether they wish to defend the matter or not. But the hidden costs of requiring individuals to file at a courthouse or navigate confusing online resources, particularly those who are going through an eviction, are also high. The value to the consumer from having a legal solution at hand may certainly exceed that fee.

Of course, people with legal problems are in distress, and the risks of price gouging seem high.[81] Liberalization in this direction needs to consider those risks, for sure. But the costs for services can also be monitored and regulated, as other fees routinely are.[82] The EITC already effectively subsidizes a large amount of private administrative capacity in the form of these storefront tax preparers, which it so happens already do disproportionately congregate in minority communities. It is hard to avoid the expectation, however disagreeable, that allowing these kinds of entities to do more basic form filing would help close the racial justice gap.

A major reason why entities like H&R Block stay in their tax lane and do not expand into other legal and benefit services is the presence of laws criminalizing the unauthorized practice of law, which prohibit nonlawyers from providing legal advice. As discussed in much greater detail by Genevieve Lakier (Chapter 14 in this volume),[83] current challenges to such laws have been met with success, providing hope that nonlawyer service providers may be able to expand the services they can

[81] Annamaria Lusardi & Carlo De Bassa Scheresberg, *Financial Literacy and High-Cost Borrowing in the United States*, Nat'l Bureau of Econ. Rsch. (Apr. 2013).

[82] Brian Deese et al., *The President's Initiative on Junk Fees and Related Pricing Practices*, The White House (Oct. 26. 2022), https://www.whitehouse.gov/briefing-room/blog/2022/10/26/the-presidents-initiative-on-junk-fees-and-related-pricing-practices/ (this webpage is no longer accessible).

[83] See Chapter 12 in this volume.

provide, including to black and brown communities. From a 30,000-foot policy-view, it is strange for New York to insist on creating new programmatic capacities in already thinly stretched nonprofits, when it could leverage the thousands of existing storefront operations to assist with legal document preparation for a small fee.[84]

As one descends from 30,000 feet, the most pressing concern seems to be that, unless there are the right *ex ante* constraints on who gets to provide these services, exploitative outcomes are likely to result. And as the exploitative practices of tax preparers show, there are very real concerns about these storefront operations as well. But the status quo is also an exploitative one. Courts are not well-suited to designing entire regulatory regimes,[85] but that should not prevent other governmental actors from venturing to do so. They are not able to broadly examine how much specialization and background is really necessary to provide which service, nor what level of compensation is appropriate for particular services as opposed to exploitative. Still, the statement that courts are not going to design a good regime of alternative providers is no argument against the possibility of someone else designing such a regime. The fact that the United States provides so much financial assistance to document preparers involved with the tax system, and that these preparers have such a large footprint in the very underserved communities access-to-justice advocates want to reach, has to be taken seriously in thinking about reforms.

We may not like these kinds of entities. And in an ideal world, perhaps we would want someone else serving clients. But for the sake of argument, and following the estimates above, let's suppose a fifth of the bar is somewhat racist in the sense that, all else equal, they would prefer not to have minority clients. For the clients' sake, we would probably not want them to take minority clients either, in an ideal world. Yet ours is not an ideal world. Provided the right incentive and professional regulatory structure they can deliver helpful legal assistance, even to minorities. And, it seems, in some jurisdictions that problematic fifth of the bar does actually serve minorities, where in others it does not.

2.4 CONCLUSION

Perhaps the most important lesson of the political economy perspective on this topic is recognizing that eliminating racism is neither necessary nor sufficient to generate more racially just outcomes. We are not going to fix peoples' hearts overnight, or even over decades. Instead, we need to carefully think about why minorities *do* achieve justice outcomes on par with white people in cases where they do, in spite of

[84] *Number of H&R Block Locations in the United States in* 2024, ScrapeHero (Feb. 12, 2024), https://www.scrapehero.com/location-reports/H&R%20Block-USA/ (reporting 8,788 H&R Block locations in the United States, with 444 in New York).

[85] Richard A. Posner, *Regulation (Agencies) versus Litigation (Courts): An Analytical Framework*, *in* Regulation versus Litigation: Perspectives from Economics and Law (Daniel P. Kessler ed., 2010).

likely racism, and why they do not in other cases. To the extent that they do not achieve equal outcomes because of incentives facing providers of solutions to legal problems, it is politically and rhetorically useful to note that many individuals who claim to have good hearts nevertheless actively sustain and support incentive systems that enable racially disparate outcomes. There is a lot of letting perfection be the enemy of the better, particularly among those with the luxury of comfortably waiting for greater racial justice. The severity of the civil justice disparities belies that comfort and makes understanding its causes particularly urgent.

3

The Hypocrisy of Attorney Licensing

Rebecca Haw Allensworth

The attorney licensing system poorly serves those most in need of legal help. Some dimensions of this problem are relatively well-understood. Access-to-justice scholarship about professional licensing has revealed that state bars[1] create high entry barriers and perpetuate a monolithic definition of the practice of law, both of which contribute to a shortage of lawyers in America.[2] Attorney scarcity has, in turn, increased the cost of professional services, leaving out of the market the clients most desperately in need of a lawyer – the rural poor, indigent defendants, accident victims, children, older adults, and immigrants.[3] The Sixth Amendment right to criminal defense counsel and the court appointment process have tempered this effect for some clients. But for other clients – like immigrants and accident victims – there is no safety net at all. Yet in the face of these shortages, state bars have done little to reform licensure with an eye toward access.[4]

This conventional account of how the attorney licensing system fails needy clients is accurate but incomplete. In fact, the state of attorney licensure and access to justice is

[1] While in every state the supreme court holds the ultimate authority over the licensing and professional discipline of lawyers, the entities to which courts delegate the day-to-day regulation of the profession vary. In most states, the supreme court uses a nominally governmental agency (or agencies) – dominated by lawyers and heavily influenced by the private bar association – to review applications, administer the bar, and decide disciplinary matters. In a few states, some or all of these tasks are delegated directly to the state bar association. In this chapter, I use the terms "licensing authority" and "disciplinary authority" to refer to the bodies delegated the supreme court's authority to regulate the profession. Sometimes, as a shorthand, I refer to the regulator as the "state bar"; when I do this, I do not mean to invoke the state bar association in its capacity as a private membership association of the state's lawyers.

[2] For a discussion of how the bar exam contributes to lawyer scarcity and access-to-justice problems, see, for example, Milan Markovic, *Protecting the Guild or Protecting the Public? Bar Exams and the Diploma Privilege*, 35 Geo. J. Legal Ethics 163 (2022). For a discussion of how a vague and monolithic definition of the unlicensed practice of law does the same thing, see, for example, Ralph Baxter, *Dereliction of Duty: State-bar Inaction in Response to America's Access to Justice Crisis*, 132 Yale L.J. Forum 228 (2022).

[3] *See generally* Deborah L. Rhode, *Access to Justice: A Roadmap for Reform*, 41 Fordham Urb. L.J. 1227, 1228 (2014).

[4] *See, for example,* Baxter, *supra* note 2.

even worse than many scholars recognize because lawyer licensing is not only *over*-regulatory but *under*-regulatory in ways that also harm low-income clients. As strict as state bars are when it comes to entry requirements and ethics rules, they are lax when it comes to professional discipline. In this sense, the lawyer licensing system is hypocritical. In rulemaking, it appears to place attorney quality and public protection above all else, including access to justice. Yet when it comes to discipline, the system puts public protection in the back seat, content to leave unethical and incompetent lawyers in the profession and allow market forces to push them toward the neediest clients.

Every year, thousands of lawyers temporarily lose their ability to practice law or have it significantly curtailed because they have engaged in the unethical or incompetent practice of law.[5] This roster of problematic lawyers is underinclusive; professional discipline as meted out by licensing agencies is notoriously lax, slow, and opaque, and it likely only catches the worst of the worst in its net.[6] Thus, the records of public discipline reflect some of the most serious sins a lawyer can commit: conversion of client funds, exchanging sex for services, and severe client neglect. Yet only a fraction of these attorneys lose their ability to practice law.[7] Far more common are reprimands, probation, and suspensions that allow an attorney to return to practice, even for offenses that suggest that the offending lawyer's judgment or competency remains in serious doubt.

Where do those attorneys turn for work after having gotten in trouble for serious professional misconduct? The short answer is it's a mystery. Scholars have for years lamented the lack of data about which lawyers are disciplined and why.[8] This chapter, however, draws on the limited data available to assert the hypothesis that the disciplinary process drives the profession's most problematic providers into solo and court-appointed practice, where they are likely to serve the underserved. This chapter further argues that using the profession's bad apples to bridge the access-to-justice gap is problematic not only because it matches the unethical and incompetent with those least able to protect themselves or change attorneys, but also because solo and small-firm work – where supervision is virtually nonexistent – presents unique incentives and opportunities to behave unethically.

If, indeed, the most unethical and incompetent lawyers are being pushed by market forces toward the neediest of clients, the solution cannot be merely to tighten

5 Am. Bar Ass'n, ABA Profile of the Legal Profession 2022 (2022) ("In 2019, 2,308 lawyers were publicly disciplined for misconduct in 43 states and the District of Columbia, according to the 2019 ABA Survey on Lawyer Discipline Systems."). This figure is notably underinclusive; it does not include disciplinary actions from California, Massachusetts, New Jersey, South Carolina, South Dakota, Vermont, West Virginia, and part of New York.

6 *See generally* Leslie C. Levin, *The Emperor's Clothes and Other Tales about the Standards for Imposing Lawyer Discipline Sanctions*, 48 Am. U. L. Rev. 1 (1998).

7 *See* ABA Profile, *supra* note 5 (reporting that only 21 percent of public discipline against lawyers resulted in disbarment).

8 *See, for example*, Leslie C. Levin, *The Case for Less Secrecy in Lawyer Discipline*, 20 Geo. J. Legal Ethics 1 (2007).

up attorney discipline. This will further contribute to the attorney shortage problem for which indigent clients suffer the worst consequences. Rather, if the licensing system is to be reformed in a way that meaningfully improves access to justice in America, both problems – the ways in which it is over-regulatory and under-regulatory – need to be addressed simultaneously. Arguments for how to increase the supply of lawyers have been made elsewhere. This chapter concludes by sketching some reforms that would meaningfully ensure that supply remains free from providers who have shown themselves to be unfit.

3.1 TOO FEW LAWYERS

It is by now well-documented that the United States has a severe access-to-justice problem.[9] A 2022 report from the Legal Services Corporation found that low-income Americans do not get enough legal help for 92 percent of the civil justice issues that affect them.[10] In most civil cases in state court, at least one party has no lawyer;[11] in cases involving debt collection, family law, and landlord–tenant cases, well over 90 percent of cases involve at least one pro se litigant.[12] The rural poor are especially bad off. For example, in Georgia, where 70 percent of lawyers work in or near Atlanta, nearly half the state's counties have fewer than ten active lawyers. Five counties have none at all.[13]

Part of the problem lies with inadequate governmental assistance. The constitutional right to an attorney paid by the government only exists in the criminal context; federal and state funding for legal aid in civil matters is woefully inadequate,[14] and out of step with other developed countries.[15] Lack of free and reduced-fee services, however, is only half of the story. The other half of the problem lies with a regulatory

[9] *See* Legal Services Corporation, *The Justice Gap: Executive Summary*, LSC (2022).

[10] *Id.*; *see also* Rebecca L. Sandefur, *Money Isn't Everything: Understanding Moderate Income Households' Use of Lawyers' Services*, *in* Middle Income Access to Justice 5, 14 (Michael Trebilcock et al. eds., 2012).

[11] Paula Hannaford-Agor et al., *The Landscape of Civil Litigation in State Courts*, Nat'l Ctr. for State Cts. at iv (2015). *See also* Rhode, *supra* note 3, at 1231 n.23 (citing Russell Engler, *Connecting Self-Representation to Civil Gideon: What Existing Data Reveal about When Counsel Is Most Needed*, 37 Fordham Urb. L.J. 37, 41–43 (2010)).

[12] *See, for example*, Tyler Hubbard et al., *Getting to the Bottom of the Access-to-Justice Gap*, 33 Utah B.J. 15, 18 (2020) (discussing the low rate of representation in family law and debt collection cases); Report to the Chief Judge of the State of New York, *Task Force to Expand Access to Civ. Legal Servs. in N.Y.* 1 (Nov. 2010) (same).

[13] *See* Lisa R. Pruitt et al., *Legal Deserts: A Multi-State Perspective on Rural Access to Justice*, 13 Harv. L. & Pol'y Rev. 15, 69 (2018).

[14] The federal government spends a little over one dollar per person per year on providing legal help in civil cases, where free counsel is not guaranteed by the Constitution. Rhode, *supra* note 3, at 1229 n.7.

[15] *See* Gillian K. Hadfield, *Higher Demand, Lower Supply? A Comparative Assessment of the Legal Resource Landscape for Ordinary Americans*, 37 Fordham Urb. L.J. 129, 148 (2010); Deborah L. Rhode, In the Interests of Justice 7 (2000).

structure that creates a scarcity of legal services – and, in turn, increases the cost of services beyond reach of low- and middle-income clients. There are many jokes about America having too many lawyers, but in fact it would seem we have too few.

3.1.1 *The Bar Exam*

Scarcity of legal help is perpetuated by a regulatory system that erects high barriers to entry. For decades, the legal profession has controlled entry by requiring an extensive education – about two years longer than in similar countries – that can cost over $100,000. The bar has also held firm to a requirement that lawyers pass an exam that is so difficult that, in some states, passage rates do not rise above 50 percent. For many access-to-justice advocates, it is this examination requirement that represents the most serious and least justifiable barrier to entry into a profession that cannot keep up with demand.[16]

Bar exams restrict entry into the profession in obvious ways – by excluding from practice the 40 percent who fail any given administration.[17] But bar exams also restrict professional entry in a less observable way by acting as a deterrent to would-be lawyers who are risk averse and would prefer not to invest in an expensive legal education without knowing that they will ever be able to practice. It also acts as a deterrent to people who cannot afford the several thousands of dollars of test prep classes and to candidates who know they perform badly on tests but would otherwise make good lawyers. A disproportionate number of candidates failing the bar are non-white applicants and those from underprivileged backgrounds.[18] The possibility that the bar exam is racially exclusive is problematic in itself, but its effect on access to justice is particularly troubling because non-white lawyers and those from low- and middle-income backgrounds are especially likely to serve the underserved.[19]

For all these reasons, some access-to-justice advocates have been beating the drum for the elimination of the bar exam as a way of both increasing the supply of lawyers and diversifying that supply. These scholars point to evidence in Wisconsin, where graduates of in-state law schools can become licensed without taking an exam, showing that disciplinary rates between lawyers who entered the

16 *Cf.* Kyle Rozema, *How Do Occupational Licensing Requirements Affect the Size of the U.S. Legal Profession?* (June 10, 2023), SSRN: https://ssrn.com/abstract=4475434 (last. accessed Feb. 24, 2025) (finding that lenient exam standards create an 8 percent increase in labor supply and the strictest exam decreases labor supply by 14 percent).

17 Many, however, go on to retake the exam and eventually pass. *See* Markovic, *supra* note 2, at 177 (observing that "nearly ninety percent [of law school graduates] passed a bar exam within two years of graduation").

18 *See id.* at 166.

19 *Cf.* Am. Bar Ass'n, ABA Profile of the Legal Profession 44 (2020). For a discussion about the need for more data about the racial makeup of the pro bono bar, public defenders, and legal aid attorneys, see Atinuke O. Adediran & Shaun Ossei-Owusu, *The Racial Reckoning of Public Interest Law*, 12 Calif. L. Rev. Online 1 (2021).

profession with and without taking the bar are nearly identical.[20] Bar exam results are closely correlated with performance in law school, suggesting that the exam, as a predictor of future performance as a lawyer, offers no additional information beyond what is already known about the applicant.

3.1.2 *Unlicensed Practice of Law*

Another feature of legal professional regulation that contributes to the shortage of services is the capacious and vague definition of the "practice of law." The unauthorized practice of law (UPL) is a crime in most states,[21] yet licensing authorities do little to define it other than circularly, as "what lawyers do."[22] A definition must therefore be gleaned from cases finding nonlawyers-lia-ble for performing various tasks – such as telling someone the appropriate form to file or describing the current state of the law. The lack of clarity on what is and is not the practice of law has had a chilling effect on nonlawyers wanting to help someone with a legal issue. One scholar writes, "[a]t a time when we desperately need more people to deliver legal services to individuals and small businesses, the foundational rule of our legal system tells anyone who is not a lawyer: 'Don't you dare lend a hand.'"[23] The prohibition on UPL also deters members of related professions, like accountants and real estate professionals, from walking close to the line of legal practice in ways that make their services less efficient and effective. And sometimes these professionals are far more expert about the legal questions than a general practice lawyer would be.[24]

For low- and middle-income clients, the prohibition on UPL, vaguely defined, is especially unfortunate. Hybrid service models providing one-stop shops for clients seeking help with issues that cut across professional boundaries – like housing, immigration, debt, and personal injury (PI) – are innovative ways to reach clients who are otherwise forced to go without representation. Requiring advisors to have separate licenses in law, medicine, and accounting makes these models more expensive if not impossible. Even other legal professionals such as judges and court

20 *See, for example*, Markovic, *supra* note 2.

21 *See* Bruce A. Green, *Why State Courts Should Authorize Nonlawyers to Practice Law*, 91 FORDHAM L. REV. 1249, 1251 (2023) (citing Deborah L. Rhode, *Policing the Professional Monopoly: A Constitutional and Empirical Analysis of Unauthorized Practice Prohibitions*, 34 STAN. L. REV. 1, 8–9 (1981)).

22 *See* DEBORAH L. RHODE, THE TROUBLE WITH LAWYERS 41 (2015) ("Others take a circular approach: the practice of law is what lawyers do."); Baxter, *supra* note 2, at 243 ("The UPL statutes effectively treat all elements of service that implicate the law as the '*practice of law*.'").

23 Baxter, *supra* note 2, at 242.

24 A study from the United Kingdom showed that some paraprofessionals in certain contexts outperformed lawyers results and client satisfaction. *See* Richard Moorhead et al., *Contesting Professionalism: Legal Aid and Nonlawyers in England and Wales*, 37 LAW & SOC'Y REV. 765, 795 (2003) ("[I]t is specialization, not professional status, which appears to be the best predictor of quality.")

personnel, who may be especially well-positioned to help low-income clients, are forbidden from providing legal advice.[25] And a capacious definition of the practice of law is bad for low-income clients because it would seem to preclude online products that help pro se litigants represent themselves. For example, LegalZoom, a repository of forms and basic advice for clients representing themselves, has been sued in several states as violating UPL statutes. A similar problem is posed by rules that prohibit lawyers from working for nonlawyers and also allowing nonlawyers to share in the profits of their enterprise. Critics say this rule, ABA Model Rule 5.4, hinders promising new models for delivering legal services to needy clients.[26]

3.1.3 *Self-Regulation and the Scarcity of Legal Services*

For access-to-justice advocates, the cause behind these overly strict regulations that limit legal services is clear: state bars acting as self-regulators of the profession.[27] State supreme courts hold the authority to license lawyers, which they delegate either to the state bar association or to a nominal state agency that is, for all intents and purposes, an arm of the state bar association. These regulators sometimes include nonlawyer individuals on the panels, but they are never in the majority. Practice rules, canons of ethics, and entry criteria are promulgated by the state supreme court – in other words, by more lawyers. This regulatory structure has led critics to observe that law is the most intensely self-regulatory of all the professions.[28]

What do lawyers want for their own profession? They want rules that protect the public, both because they care about clients intrinsically and because bad lawyers erode public trust in the profession.[29] High entry barriers and restrictive practice rules protect the public by ensuring that lawyers are qualified and act in their clients' interests. But regulatory red tape is also good for the legal profession for reasons that have nothing to do with public protection. Strict rules protect incumbent lawyers from competition and contribute to the profession's prestige by ensuring that "not just anyone" can provide legal help. The downsides of too much regulation – attorney shortages and high prices for services – are less salient to incumbent professionals who *want* their profession to be exclusive and remunerative. Thus, attorneys picking their own entry barriers and ethics rules have an inherent conflict of interest between what's good for the public and what's good for the profession. In particular, we might expect lawyers regulating themselves to go too far in building

[25] *See* Lauren Sudeall, *The Overreach of Limits on "Legal Advice"*, 131 YALE L.J. FORUM 637, 646–47 (2022).

[26] *See* Baxter, *supra* note 2, at 235.

[27] *See id.* at 235.

[28] *See, for example*, RICHARD SUSSKIND & DANIEL SUSSKIND, THE FUTURE OF THE PROFESSIONS: HOW TECHNOLOGY WILL TRANSFORM THE WORK OF HUMAN EXPERTS (2015); RHODE, *supra* note 15, at 145–46.

[29] *See* Green, *supra* note 21, at 164.

barriers to entry and restricting competition. And that, it would seem, is exactly what has happened over more than a century of self-regulation.[30]

Antitrust law, because it prohibits competitors from colluding to suppress competition, theoretically presents a way to curb the regulatory excesses of professional self-regulation.[31] This idea was put on the table by the US Supreme Court in 2015, when it held in *FTC v. North Carolina Board of Dental Examiners*[32] that professional licensing boards must be "actively supervised" by the state to enjoy immunity from antitrust suits. In practice, however, *North Carolina Dental* has not led to widespread antitrust liability for professional boards, primarily because courts have been less-than-exacting in their tests for what qualifies as active supervision. And in law, antitrust liability is an even less useful tool to use against licensing authorities, where courts view bar regulatory activity as *per se* immune from suit. In *Hoover v. Ronwin*, for example, the Supreme Court held that law licensing decisions by state bars, agencies, and disciplinary authorities are actually, at bottom, decisions by that state's supreme court.[33] As such, they are acts of the sovereign and enjoy full antitrust immunity, even if they are created by a self-regulating board or bar that isn't supervised by the supreme court in any meaningful way.

Although antitrust law would see lawyers' interests in public and professional protection as conflicting, attorneys tend to emphasize the ways in which they are aligned. Specifically, they argue that strict entry requirements, strong UPL statutes, and the prohibition on revenue sharing protect the public.[34] In at least one of these categories, they have some evidence to point to: A study has shown that poor performance on the bar exam is correlated with subsequent professional discipline.[35] For the others, defenders of the strict regulation of lawyers make theoretical arguments. They say that only lawyers are qualified to give legal advice, and so strongly enforcing UPL statutes protects the public from uninformed and dangerous advisors. They also argue that bans on revenue sharing between lawyers and nonlawyers improve service quality by preserving attorneys' independent judgment.[36]

But critics of the excesses of self-regulation among lawyers point out that the empirical correlation between bar performance and future discipline is minimal,[37] and that the benefits of strong UPL statutes and prohibitions on revenue sharing

[30] *See* Benjamin H. Barton, *An Institutional Analysis of Lawyer Regulation: Who Should Control Lawyer Regulation-Courts, Legislatures, or the Market?*, 37 GA. L. REV. 1167, 1189 (2003).

[31] *See* Aaron Edlin & Rebecca Haw, *Cartels by Another Name: Should Licensed Occupations Face Antitrust Scrutiny?* 162 U. PA. L. REV. 1093 (2014).

[32] N. Carolina State Bd. of Dental Examiners v. F.T.C., 574 U.S. 494 (2015).

[33] 466 U.S. 558 (1984). *See also* Bates v. State Bar of Ariz., 433 U.S. 350, 350 (1977) (holding that the "Supreme Court of Arizona wielding the power of the State over the practice of law is not subject to attack under the Sherman Act").

[34] *Cf.* RHODE, *supra* note 15, at 136.

[35] Kyle Rozema, *Does the Bar Exam Protect the Public?* 18 J. EMPIRICAL LEGAL STUD. 801 (2021).

[36] *See, for example*, Stephen P. Younger, *The Pitfalls and False Promises of Nonlawyer Ownership of Law Firms*, 132 YALE L.J. FORUM 259, 261 (2022).

[37] *See* Markovic, *supra* note 2, at 202.

may theoretically benefit those who can afford lawyers, but they more concretely and demonstrably harm those who can't.[38] To these critics, attorney self-regulation has resulted in a balance of regulation that can only be justified as protecting the public if we define the public as those with financial means.

3.2 TOO LITTLE DISCIPLINE, TOO LIGHT

The professional regulatory system for lawyers also fails low-income clients in a way that is less familiar than these arguments about regulation gone too far. State licensing authorities justify the heavy hand they take in restricting entry to the profession as protecting the public from lawyers who are either incompetent or unethical, or as is all too common, both. Yet for all the measures these regulators take to prevent *theoretically* bad providers from practicing law, they do very little to remove *actually* bad providers from the profession.

3.2.1 *Procedural Defects of the Disciplinary System*

The disciplinary process goes wrong right from the beginning. The system relies entirely on complaints to initiate an investigation into attorney misconduct. Such a reactive system has serious drawbacks. Clients are unlikely to complain about lawyer misconduct for the simple reason that they do not know misconduct when they see it;[39] indeed the difficulty of knowing whether you are receiving good or bad legal advice is one of the justifications for licensing lawyers in the first place. Even clients who know their lawyer has engaged in misconduct have to feel unhappy about it to complain, leaving out clients whose lawyers have helped them commit fraud or lied to a court on their behalf.[40] Next, a client must know where to go to complain.[41] Not all licensing authorities make this transparent, and some actively discourage the filing of complaints by providing ominous warnings on the online complaint form, such as warning that clients often misunderstand what constitutes acceptable practice of law. Others go further by saying that filing a complaint may expose the complainant to a lawsuit.[42] Finally, complainants must be willing to confront a professional system that is elite, hierarchical, and inherently litigious.

[38] *Cf.* Baxter, *supra* note 2, at 248–50; RHODE, *supra* note 22, at 42.

[39] *See* David Adam Friedman, *Do We Need a Bar Exam . . . for Experienced Lawyers?*, 12 U.C. IRVINE L. REV. 1161, 1173 (2022).

[40] *See* David B. Wilkins, *Who Should Regulate Lawyers?* 105 HARV. L. REV. 799, 823 (1992).

[41] *Cf.* Nora Freeman Engstrom, *Sunlight and Settlement Mills*, 86 N.Y.U. L. REV. 805, 856 (2011) (explaining the defects in a complaint-based disciplinary system and observing that personal injury clients, for example, are unlikely to complain about unethical practice).

[42] *See, for example*, *Misconduct Complaints*, VA. ST. BAR ASS'N, https://www.vsb.org/Site/03_Legal-Help/misconduct-claim.aspx (last accessed Feb. 18, 2025) ("The confidentiality requirement will not protect you from a civil lawsuit by a lawyer who believes he or she has been wrongly accused.").

Relying on other lawyers to file complaints against their colleagues is a more promising avenue for catching bad practice in the sense that lawyers are better positioned to know malpractice when they see it and to know that the state bar exists and disciplines lawyers. But relying on tattling within a professional culture of closed ranks has not proved an effective way to detect misconduct, even with a bar-imposed ethical obligation to speak out against offending colleagues.[43]

The complaints a licensing board receives are therefore likely to understate the number of problematic providers and the depth of their misconduct. Yet even on the complaints the boards do receive, they are reluctant to take public disciplinary action. Only about 3 percent of complaints result in any disciplinary action whatsoever.[44] About two-thirds of these actions are private warnings to the attorney with no public record.[45]

Legal discipline, when it does happen, is slow. It is not uncommon for a licensing authority to take years between learning of misconduct and taking action against the attorney's license to practice.[46] This delay is in part because of the extraordinary legal protections that lawyers have built for themselves into the disciplinary process. A license to practice law is a property right, and it cannot be taken away without due process. But in the context of lawyers, the process "due" has come to mean protections beyond those typical in an administrative hearing and approaching (if not exceeding) those afforded criminal defendants.[47]

3.2.2 *Too Many Second Chances*

Thus, the lawyer disciplinary system takes action against too few lawyers, and too late. But when it comes to assuring access to quality lawyering for low-income clients, perhaps the most problematic feature of the legal disciplinary system is that it is too lenient, if inconsistently so,[48] even on providers it does manage to identify for professional discipline. Hard empirical data on the leniency of the legal disciplinary system is difficult to come by, but adding up the information we

[43] *See* Richard L. Abel, Lawyers in the Dock 501 (2008) (observing that some lawyers "remain silent by reason of collegiality").

[44] *See* Am. Bar Ass'n, Survey on Lawyer Discipline Systems 2019 (2019) (finding that in 2019, 2,308 disciplinary actions resulted from 69,716 complaints received).

[45] Levin, *supra* note 6, at 9 ("Private sanctions – the lightest form of discipline – are imposed almost twice as often as any other type of sanction."). *Cf.* Stephen Gillers, *Lowering the Bar: How Lawyer Discipline in New York Fails to Protect the Public*, 17 N.Y.U. J. Legis. & Pub. Pol'y 485, 541 (2014) (presenting a qualitative empirical study of New York state attorney discipline and lamenting the private nature of board action).

[46] Gillers, *supra* note 45, at 496.

[47] *See* Michael S. Frisch, *No Stone Left Unturned: The Failure of Attorney Self-Regulation in the District of Columbia*, 18 Geo. J. Legal Ethics 325, 331 (2005).

[48] For discussions of the inconsistency of discipline, see Rhode, *supra* note 15, at 160 and Levin, *supra* note 6, at 80.

have paints a picture of a system that is driven by attorney rehabilitation, generous with second chances, and more focused on attorney welfare than public protection.

State bars have kept in practice attorneys whose conduct has called into question their honesty and character, key issues when *applying* for a license. For example, bars have kept in practice attorneys who have cheated on their taxes,[49] lied to the government,[50] and been convicted of major federal crimes involving dishonesty.[51] Especially problematic for low-income clients, state bars take a forgiving stance toward neglect of client matters,[52] even when they have ignored repeated complaints from indigent defendants about their appointed counsel's refusal to communicate.[53]

Perhaps these are venial sins for lawyers. Yet even for one of the legal profession's cardinal sins – taking money from a client – second chances abound. For example, the state of Tennessee re-admitted Kevin Teets to the profession after he stole $5,454 from a nonprofit providing legal aid and other services to the homeless, for which he acted as treasurer. It took the disciplinary system four years to impose discipline, during which time Teets continued to practice. The Board of Professional Responsibility said his gambling addiction and remorse justified a light sanction in the form of a reprimand, but the Chancery Court imposed a brief suspension "to protect the integrity of the profession." He was allowed to return to practice in 2020.[54] Similarly, the District of Columbia allowed Harnan Arneja to return to practice after using a settlement earmarked for his client's hospital bills to pay his own bills and business operating expenses. The client, a Salvadoran refugee who spoke no English, received none of the settlement, nor did the hospital where he was treated for his injuries. The hospital later garnished the client's wages to cover the debt. The District of Columbia Court of Appeals

49 *See* Gillers, *supra* note 45, at 524–27 (collecting cases about lawyers cheating on their taxes). For an example, see *In re* Newman, 821 S.E.2d 689, 690–91 (S.C. 2018) (Supreme Court of South Carolina imposes six-month suspension of license, to apply retroactively, for a respondent who pled guilty to two counts of failing to file tax returns).

50 For two examples, see Gillers, *supra* note 45, at 521–24. *See also* Green, *supra* note 21, at 178 (describing a disciplinary case against a lawyer who "concealed and falsified information to extract a favorable settlement for a client" and then lied about it to a federal court investigating his misconduct).

51 *See* Levin, *supra* note 6, at 12–13.

52 *See, for example*, Frisch, *supra* note 47, at 325–26; ABEL, *supra* note 43 at 66. *See also* People v. Fagan, 423 P.3d 412, 417 (Office of Presiding Disciplinary Judge of the Sp. Ct. of Colo. 2018).

53 Paul Walwyn (Tenn. Bd. of Pro. Resp., Feb. 23, 2018) (reinstating the license of a lawyer who had been censured or suspended on five previous occasions for neglecting client matters and held in criminal contempt by a judge for missing filing deadlines).

54 Kevin Teets, BPR #029981 (Tenn. Bd. of Pro. Resp., Aug. 26, 2020), https://s3.amazonaws.com/membercentralcdn/sitedocuments/tnbar/tnbar/0448/2390448.pdf? (last accessed Feb. 13, 2025). For the Chancery Court's decision, see https://docs.tbpr.org/teets-2784-chancery-court-decision.pdf (last accessed Feb. 13, 2025).

allowed Arneja to return to practice after a year, without any showing of rehabilitation or remorse.[55]

Not even sexual abuse of a client is a guarantee of disbarment. For example, Oklahoma attorney Richard Stout was found to have asked one client for sexual photos of herself and sent sexually suggestive texts to another (and demanded that she delete them). Stout coerced a third client into having sex with him by offering her a reduced fee.[56] The client, a criminal defendant, reluctantly agreed because, as she told the board, she "was in a desperate situation." The disciplinary authorities allowed him to return to practice after a three-month suspension.[57]

The case of Ohio attorney Jason Allen Sarver presents an extreme case of licensing authority laxity in sex abuse cases. By the time Sarver's disciplinary case appeared before the licensing authority, Sarver had been criminally charged for repeatedly coercing sex from a defendant he was appointed to represent. The client had agreed to testify against him in exchange for a reduced plea offer for her own criminal charges, a fact that Sarver's disciplinary panel found mitigating. Its order stated: "[N]ot only was there no harm to the client but the client leveraged her relationship with [Sarver] to get a better plea deal." Although the Ohio Supreme Court criticized this reasoning, it adopted the panel's lenient stance by opting for a temporary suspension over disbarment.[58] A recent study of attorney discipline finds that cases like Sarver's and Stout's are not aberrations: "too many attorneys have sexually abused and harassed their clients with relative impunity and returned to the profession with little to no additional oversight, limitations, or safeguards against future abuses."[59]

There is plenty more anecdotal evidence of inappropriately lax disciplinary decisions about lawyer misconduct. And although more empirical research is badly needed, the few systematic studies that have been done on attorney discipline show the same thing. Professor Gillers' study of five years of disciplinary cases from New York revealed a system that was "deficient in design and operation."[60] He showed that its decisions were too light, often focusing on mitigating factors that might explain the behavior but not why it was unlikely to recur and harm clients. Likewise, Professor Michael Frisch studied the disciplinary decisions of the District of Columbia and found that the decisions were too light to protect the public.[61]

55 *See* Frisch, *supra* note 47, at 345–57.

56 Gillian R. Chadwick, *Time's Up for Attorney-Client Sexual Violence*, 22 U. Md. L.J. Race Relig. Gender & Class 76, 85 (2022).

57 *Id.* at 85–86.

58 *Id.* at 86–90.

59 *Id.* at 80 ("Indeed, case after case shows that lawyers have been allowed to sexually prey upon particularly vulnerable clients, even children, and continue practicing law after a brief – if any – suspension.").

60 Gillers, *supra* note 45, at 490.

61 Frisch, *supra* note 47, at 331.

Gillers' and Frisch's studies use a commonsense definition of "too light" discipline,[62] but we might also want a more rigorous and objective measure of whether attorney discipline is working for the public. Here, the limited information we have about how often disciplined attorneys reappear before the disciplinary authorities suggests that recidivism after bar discipline is high.[63] Somewhere between one-third and half of publicly disciplined attorneys go on to receive a second round of board discipline, and almost a quarter are eventually disbarred.[64] Put another way, a disciplined attorney is *thirty times* more likely to get in trouble with a licensing board in the five-year period following his or her initial discipline and *one-quarter* of all lawyers with a disciplinary history are on their way to losing their license altogether.[65] (Both Teets, who embezzled from the homeless, and Sarver, whose sexual abuse was "leveraged" by his client into a plea deal, went on to reoffend.) Even "capital punishment" for lawyers – disbarment – is temporary in most states and may present an opportunity to reoffend.[66] Rates of repeat discipline

62 For a discussion of what "too light" might mean in terms of promoting the goals of attorney discipline, see Levin, *supra* note 6.

63 *See* Levin, *supra* note 8, at 3. To be sure, the rate at which lawyers get repeat discipline is an imperfect proxy for recidivism. An attorney disciplined once is likely to stay on a licensing authority's radar, increasing their chance of getting caught for subsequent misconduct. And when a disciplined attorney does raise a second red flag, boards are almost certainly more likely to react with public discipline.

64 *See* Kyle Rozema, *Professional Discipline and the Labor Market: Evidence from Lawyers*, forthcoming, J. L. & Econ., at 16 ("Of lawyers who are not disbarred after a first disciplinary action, 48 percent reoffend and 24 percent are eventually disbarred."); Levin, *supra* note 8, at 3 n.10 (finding that in Michigan as much as one-third of disciplined attorneys have a history of prior trouble with the bar). *Cf.* Leslie C. Levin & Susan Saab Forney, Report to the Wisconsin Office of Lawyer Regulation: Analysis of Grievances Filed in Criminal and Family Matters from 2013–2016 (2020) (studying grievances concerning criminal and family matters finding that approximately 40 percent involved lawyers with previous "substantial interaction" with the disciplinary system).

65 Rozema, *supra* note 64, at 16.

66 Indeed, Professor Frisch calls disbarment in the District of Columbia "a five-year suspension" with a requirement to prove fitness. Frisch, *supra* note 47, at 344. For more information on the temporary nature of disbarment, see Ronald D. Rotunda & Mary M. Devlin, *Permanent Disbarment: A Market-Oriented Proposal*, 9(1) Prof. Law. 2 (1997). There is widely varying data about how often attorneys attempt and succeed in getting their license back after disbarment. For example, Professor Deborah Rhode notes that half of disbarred attorneys are reinstated. Rhode, *supra* note 15, at 161. And an old study of relicensure in Louisiana found that most lawyers who attempt to get their license back succeed, but of course not everyone tries. *See* Terry Carter, *Bounced from the Bar: Lawyers Who Lose Their Licenses for Fraud or Other Misconduct Can Win Reinstatement, if They Practice in the Right State*, 89 A.B.A. J. 56, 60 (2003) ("The [Louisiana] bar looked at disbarments over a 25-year period, 1975 to 2000, and found that 85 percent of the lawyers who applied for readmission succeeded and that 44 percent of them were disciplined again."). More recently, Kyle Rozema found that the vast majority of lawyers who are disbarred stay out of the profession. Rozema, *supra* note 64, at 19. This finding is consistent with an investigation of the Florida bar. *See* Gary Blankenship, *Few Disbarred Lawyers Ever Seek Readmission*, Fla. Bar News (June 15, 2009) (finding that from 1992 to 2008 only 2 percent successfully reapplied).

are so high that several states have had to implement a "three strikes" rule for its frequent flyers.[67]

3.2.3 *Self-Regulation and a Forgiving System of Discipline*

Again, self-regulation may be to blame for too-light discipline, as has been suggested by many scholars.[68] Why, exactly, might lawyers go easy on their peers? First, and most obviously, lawyers regulating themselves may identify with the accused. Lawyers, knowing that their own practice is far from perfect, may feel a bit of "there-but-for-the-grace-of-God-go-I" in making disciplinary decisions.[69] Here, self-regulating lawyers may apply a sort of "golden rule" and treat their peers as they would want to be treated when facing a wrongful accusation.

Second, lawyers may feel the need to protect their profession, as a general matter, from second-guessing by outside voices, even (or especially) if those voices are clients. Professor Frisch concluded that the disciplinary system evinced an "institutional hostility to both [the lawyers prosecuting disciplinary cases] and victims of lawyer misconduct."[70] Sociologists emphasize the importance of autonomy in establishing professional identity,[71] and governmental incursions on that, in the form of a licensure action, may be viewed as encroachments on the professional domain.

Finally, lawyers regulating themselves may be especially receptive to narratives about their peers' addiction and mental health struggles.[72] Indeed, self-regulating

[67] Levin, *supra* note 8, at 3 ("Indeed, in apparent recognition of this problem, some jurisdictions have instituted a 'three strikes' rule, which provides that if a lawyer receives three reprimands within five years, he will be presented to the court for more serious discipline."); *Rules for Enf't of Law. Conduct r.* 13.6 (WASH. STATE CT. RULES 2002) ("A lawyer may be subject to sanction or other remedy under rule 13.1 if the lawyer receives three admonitions within a five year period."); Lisa Siegel, *Lawyer Reprimand Not a Wrist Slap Anymore*, CONN. L. TRIB. (Feb. 13, 2006, 12:00 AM) ("The new rule, Practice Book § 2-47(d), requires an attorney who has been disciplined three times within the previous five years to be automatically presented to the Superior Court for discipline.").

[68] *See, for example*, Chadwick, *supra* note 56, at 108 (attributing the bar's reluctance to discipline sexually predatory lawyers to "the self-regulating nature of the legal profession"); Barton, *supra* note 30, at 1208–09 (arguing that, "[f]or obvious reasons, regulation of attorney discipline is a low priority for bar associations" and that "the regulatory preferences of lawyers are well-reflected in the actual processes"); Frisch, *supra* note 47, at 331 (concluding that the New York law disciplinary board "has reached interpretations of the rules of conduct that too often further the parochial and self-interested concerns of the legal profession").

[69] *See* Chadwick, *supra* note 56, at 108 (identifying "overidentification" between lawyers sitting on a disciplinary panel and the accused as a reason for leniency, noting that they likely "relate to attorney-respondents more than victimized clients").

[70] Frisch, *supra* note 47, at 331.

[71] ELIOT FREIDSON, PROFESSION OF MEDICINE: A STUDY OF THE SOCIOLOGY OF APPLIED KNOWLEDGE 368 (1970) (observing that in their quest for professional status, "[a]utonomy is the prize sought by virtually all occupational groups").

[72] *See, for example*, ABEL, *supra* note 43 at 202–03 (recounting of the case of Lawrence M. Furtzaig who blamed misconduct on mental health); Gillers, *supra* note 45, at 526–28 (describing the case of *In re Levitt*, where a court accepted a lawyer's argument that "two

boards and bars rely heavily on lawyer assistance programs in the disciplinary process, and many states exempt lawyers from the requirement that they report a colleague's misconduct if that colleague is already involved in a state assistance program.[73] Lawyers regulating themselves usually view addiction as a mitigating fact, and addiction was argued by the defense in both the Teets and Stout cases (Teets used the money he stole from the nonprofit to feed his gambling addiction; Stout was evidently addicted to sex). It is unclear, however, that an attorney who has stolen from or sexually abused his clients is a safer lawyer because he did so in the grips of addiction.[74] Disciplinary orders inspired by the idea that an attorney is sick, not unfit, sometimes miss larger issues of ethics and competence. For example, Oklahoma's condition that Stout not accept female clients overlooks the broader – and profound – lack of judgment it takes to trade your services for sex.

Ading it up, scholars of the profession are essentially unanimous in finding the self-regulatory legal disciplinary system lacking.[75] It doesnot detect or punish most wrongdoing at all, and when it does act, it is too little, too late. The system is set up to re-admit dangerous, unethical, and incompetent providers in the profession – the likes of which would probably never clear the bar for admission in the first place.

3.3 THE FALLEN LAWYER

What happens when an inadequate supply of professionals, containing a significant number of providers known to be incompetent or unethical, encounters a market for services where some clients are well-heeled, savvy, and able to choose – and others demonstrably aren't? Little is known for sure about how this labor market works, but all signs point to the conclusion that the profession's most problematic providers end up serving the country's neediest clients.

3.3.1 *Discipline and Small Practice Settings*

Public discipline can have severe consequences for an attorney's career. States vary in their systems of disclosure, but often disciplinary authorities publish their

mental disorders, obsessive-compulsive disorder and obsessive-compulsive personality disorder" caused him to commit a tax crime and then censured the attorney rather than suspending his license); Chadwick, *supra* note 56, at 85–86. ("The court seemed to weigh heavily Stout's claim that sex addiction caused him to harm his clients, even though Stout did not seek help for his alleged addiction until he was facing disciplinary consequences.")

73 *See* Levin, *supra* note 8, at 5 ("Diversion may include law office management assistance, lawyer assistance programs, counseling, monitoring, and legal education. . . . It appears that as many as 20%–35% of the cases that might otherwise result in discipline are being sent to diversion programs."); Nicholas D. Lawson, *To Be a Good Lawyer, One Has to Be a Healthy Lawyer: Lawyer Well-Being, Discrimination, and Discretionary Systems of Discipline*, 34 GEO. J. LEGAL ETHICS 65 (2021).

74 Professor Gillers argues that mental health issues, to the extent that they are likely to persist through and after the disciplinary process, may be better thought of as aggravating, not mitigating factors. *See* Gillers, *supra* note 45, at 523, 528.

75 *See, for example, id.* at 490; Frisch, *supra* note 47, at 331; Levin, *supra* note 6, at 80.

decisions in some form. The transparency of this system could be better – there is no easy-to-use, reliable, national repository of lawyer information, so employers and clients have to search state-by-state. Some states do not offer searchable databases where one might look up a lawyer's disciplinary history by name or bar number, rather one must sift through years of newsletters and press releases to find an attorney of interest. And public descriptions of the facts underlying discipline can be elliptical, to say the least.[76]

The transparency, such as it is, does seem to have an effect on an attorney's professional prospects, at least with employers like law firms. In a forthcoming study, economist and law professor Kyle Rozema studied the effect of public discipline on the likelihood that a lawyer would separate from his or her law firm.[77] He found that the rate of separation from law firms during an eight-year period was significantly higher for attorneys who received public discipline during that time. The effect was particularly strong for mid-career lawyers at mid-size and large firms, where disciplined lawyers left their firms at rates 81 percent and 76 percent higher than their non-disciplined peers. Relatedly, his study found that firms of more than one lawyer were net exporters of disciplined attorneys. Yet the study also found that discipline does not decrease the likelihood that lawyers are reemployed after separation. While public discipline changes your professional prospects, it does not end them.

Where do these lawyers go? The rest of Professor Rozema's analysis completes the picture of a disciplined lawyer's professional trajectory: Discipline makes it more likely that a lawyer will go on to start a solo practice. In fact, he found that 12 percent of solo practice lawyers with a disciplinary record moved into solo practice *after* discipline. He also found support for the idea that discipline makes it hard to get out of solo practice and join a firm. As for small firms (defined as fewer than ten lawyers), Rozema found that disciplined attorneys tended to cluster together in a subset of firms with a high tolerance for disciplinary records.

These new data enrich the existing statistics showing high rates of discipline among solo and small-firm practitioners (and correspondingly low numbers of disciplined attorneys at large firms). In the years 2000 and 2001, 78 percent of disciplinary decisions against attorneys in California were against solo practitioners, even though they accounted for only 23 percent of the state's attorneys. Similarly, in Texas, lawyers working alone or in firms with fewer than five partners accounted for 59 percent of all lawyers but made up 98 percent of disciplinary cases.[78] Data from the last decades show the same thing.[79]

[76] *See* Mary Pat Gunderson, *Gender and the Language of Judicial Opinion Writing*, 21 GEO. J. GENDER & L. 1 (2019).

[77] Rozema, *supra* note 64.

[78] *See, for example*, Leslie C. Levin, *The Ethical World of Solo and Small Firm Practitioners*, 41 HOUS. L. REV. 309, 312–14 (2004).

[79] Rozema, *supra* note 64, at 7 ("Solo practitioners make up 30 percent of the legal profession but receive 56 percent of disciplinary measures, and lawyers at large law firms make up 10 percent

How to interpret these statistics has long been disputed, because some of the reasons for high rates of discipline against solo and small-firm attorneys probably have nothing to do with attorney competence.[80] Licensing authorities may hold solo-practice bias, or, relatedly, large firms may have more leverage with the disciplinary authorities in disciplinary investigations. Additionally, clients of large law firms may be less likely to complain about their lawyers because they have the luxury of choice and may decide that firing their incompetent lawyer is punishment enough.[81] On the flip side of this argument, scholars have noted that the clients of solo practitioners, who tend to work in matters of great emotional importance, may be especially likely to complain to the bar.[82]

Of course, the possibility that firm lawyers actually are more competent and ethical cannot be ruled out as a factor contributing to the disparity. By showing that discipline pushes firm lawyers into small-practice settings and locks them in, Professor Rozema's study provides at least modest support for the idea that the bar's

of the profession but receive only 2 percent of disciplinary measures"). For recent data on individual states, see State Bar of California, Report on Disparities in the Discipline System 4–6 (Nov. 14, 2019) (describing lower proportions of complaints against firm-affiliated attorneys, and lower rates of disbarment against firm-affiliated attorneys when complaints were brought); Trisha Rich, *ARCD's Annual Report Sheds Light on Illinois Legal Industry*, CBA Rec. (July/Aug. 2022), at 50 (reporting that 70 percent of disciplined Illinois attorneys were solo practitioners); Karen L. Valihura et al., *Delaware's Access to Justice Commission: Progress of the Civil Committees*, 17 Del. L. Rev. 71, 86 (2018) (reporting that from 2013–15, the "majority" of disciplinary actions in Delaware were against solo practitioners).

80 There is significant controversy about whether solo and small-firm practitioners actually are less competent and ethical, and, if they are, about whether the economic realities of that practice setting are to blame. Some commentators say that because of high caseloads, solo practitioners must cut ethical corners. *Cf.* Emily Couric, *What Goes Wrong?*, 72 ABA J. 65, 67 (1986) (asserting that "[i]t is the solo and small-firm practitioner who is boxed in by the lethal combination of case overload, insufficient office support, financial pressure, and emotional isolation" and that this leads to unethical practice); Jennifer Gerarda Brown & Liana G. T. Wolf, *The Paradox and Promise of Restorative Attorney Discipline*, 12 Nev. L.J. 254–55, 282 (2012) (arguing that solo practitioners face economic pressure to maintain high client loads with minimal infrastructural support, causing unintentional harm especially as relates to the duty of communication); *but see* Levin, *supra* note 78, at 312–16 (challenging the assertion that overwork leads to unethical practice for solo practitioners). Others, however, attribute higher rates of discipline in solo and small-firm practice to large firms' enhanced resources, structural advantages, and client sophistication, which prevent complaints from being brought and discipline from being doled out against affiliated attorneys. *See also*, Couric, *supra* note 80, at 68 (arguing that large firms are more likely to handle misconduct internally and that firm clients are unlikely to complain).

81 *Cf.* Wilkins, *supra* note 40, at 824–29 (describing why corporate clients are unlikely to complain to disciplinary authorities); Nicole Leeper Piquero et al., *Exploring Lawyer Misconduct: An Examination of the Self-Regulation Process*, 37(5) Deviant Behav. 573 (2016).

82 *See* Levin, *supra* note 78 ([P]ractice specialties commonly found in small law offices produce the most complaints about lawyer conduct because they produce the most acrimonious disputes and charges generally.").

disciplinary focus on small-practice attorneys is rational – it's where the disciplinary system itself puts lawyers more likely to break the rules.[83]

3.3.2 *Solo Practitioners and the Underserved*

The mechanics of this sorting process by which disciplined providers are pushed into solo practice are not hard to imagine, although little is known empirically. Firms making employment decisions are likely to be savvier about researching an attorney's disciplinary history than an individual client hiring a solo practitioner. Indeed, most individual clients probably believe the fact of licensure is enough to ensure a lawyer's minimum competence and ethicality; law firms know better. There is another reason – one perhaps more troubling from an access-to-justice perspective – why the labor market may be tilted toward solo practice for disciplined attorneys. Solo practitioners tend to represent clients and work in areas of legal practice for which there is great unmet demand.

The idea that solo practitioners serve the underserved has been recited at least as far back as 1970, when a student note in the *Yale Law Journal* made the following observation after remarking that the income of a solo practitioner is less than half of that of firm lawyers: "It is this large group of solo practitioners that serves the poor and much of the middle class, and its failure to perform this function effectively has led to renewed interest in the problems of 'marginal practice.'"[84] Today, we know that solo practitioners are a diverse group, and some serve very sophisticated, high-paying clientele. But we also have data that suggest this kind of lawyer is not the modal solo or small-firm practitioner. When the practice of law is subdivided into twenty-three areas of practice, the four with the smallest average-sized firms are criminal, property, PI, and family law, all practice areas with limited access-to-justice and low-income clients. And there is evidence that a significant proportion of disciplined attorneys in these areas moved into them *after* receiving discipline. In contrast, some of the largest firms are those that handle intellectual property and antitrust matters, and these are among the biggest exporters of attorneys with professional discipline on their records.[85] These data are consistent with qualitative empirical work by Leslie Levin, who interviewed forty solo practitioners in the New York City area. She found that the most common areas of practice in her sample

[83] Whether that can account for the full disparity of discipline between solos and large firms is another question altogether. Many forces, including bias and clout, are likely in play. And although Rozema's data support the idea that a disciplined lawyer is thirty times more likely to get discipline within five years than someone without discipline, it is probably not fair to say that disciplined lawyers are thirty times more likely to offend than their counterparts with clean licenses. As discussed above, being "on the radar" of a law licensing board probably makes you more likely to be caught, not just more likely to reoffend.

[84] Note, Legal Ethics and Professionalism, 79 Yale L. J. 1179, 1181 (1970) (citing Jerome E. Carlin, Lawyers on Their Own: The Solo Practitioner in an Urban Setting (1962)).

[85] Rozema, *supra* noted 16, at 44, 52, 64.

were "personal plight" legal needs, including family law, PI, workers' compensation, and trusts and estates,[86] all areas lacking in adequate legal help.

Immigration law – where access to justice is particularly dire – has an extremely high proportion of solo- and small-firm practitioners. A study of immigration courts in New York state revealed that only 37 percent of immigrants secured representation in their removal proceedings, and 90 percent of those clients were represented by a solo or small-firm practitioner.[87] Immigration law may be an especially attractive practice area for attorneys with a disciplinary record not only because of the large unmet demand but also because foreign-born and non-English-speaking clients are especially unlikely to learn about their attorney's past bar discipline. Moreover, the overall quality of the immigration bar, as revealed by a survey of immigration judges, is deplorable.[88] The prevalence of attorneys with disciplinary histories, though still likely to be only a fraction of immigration attorneys, may contribute to this state of affairs.

Another area of practice that may be attractive to disciplined practitioners is PI. Like immigration lawyers, PI attorneys tend to serve unsophisticated, low-income clients who are not repeat players. We have only anecdotal evidence about the rate of discipline among PI lawyers[89] (and even that evidence concerns lawyers who received discipline because of their work in PI, not lawyers who turned to PI after discipline), but we do know they tend to work in solo or small-firm settings.[90] And PI law would seem to represent a financial opportunity to disciplined lawyers looking for clients who won't learn about their history, don't care, or don't feel they have a meaningful choice of attorney.[91]

Some clients literally have no choice at all. Courts will often appoint an attorney to represent a client unable to afford a private lawyer. Courts must do this for indigent criminal defendants in cases where there is no public defender's office, or where an existing public defender's office has a conflict of interest. Courts will also appoint lawyers for children, the mentally ill and incompetent, and respondents facing termination of parental rights. We know very little about the proportion of disciplined attorneys taking court appointments, but even without systematic data about appointed attorneys, we can make an educated guess about whether disciplined lawyers gravitate toward this work.

First, court-appointed lawyers are probably drawn disproportionately from solo and small-firm practice, a group especially likely to contain disciplined providers. Second, we know that courts have difficulty – sometimes extreme difficulty – finding attorneys who will take appointed cases because of the abysmally low

86 Levin, *supra* note 78, at 312–14.

87 Ingrid V. Eagly & Steven Shafer, *A National Study of Access to Counsel in Immigration Court*, 164 U. PA. L. REV. 1 (2015).

88 *Id.*

89 *See* Nora Freeman Engstrom, *Run of the Mill Justice*, 22 GEO. J. LEGAL ETHICS 1485 (2009).

90 Rozema, *supra* note 16, at 52.

91 *Cf.* Engstrom, *supra* note 89.

reimbursement rates,[92] implying that courts may need to scrape the bottom of the barrel. We also know that appointed criminal defense attorneys underperform salaried public defenders and private counsel.[93] The difference is particularly stark in capital defense, where defendants represented by an appointed attorney are twice as likely to be sentenced to death than those with private counsel.[94] Perhaps relatedly, several studies have shown that among lawyers whose clients were sent to death row, professional disciplinary rates are extremely high – in Texas, one in four.[95]

3.3.3 *Why It Matters*

If indeed lawyers with a disciplinary record gravitate toward the populations of clients who typically can't afford legal services, is that a problem? After all, the market for legal services is just that, and sorting providers and clients according to professional strength on the one hand, and ability to pay on the other, is inevitable in any market. According to Adam Smith's "invisible hand" theory, it's also efficient. As the saying goes, "you get what you pay for," in legal services and in everything else.[96]

It is true that any market will feature a sorting mechanism by which the most desirable providers go to the highest-paying clients. But professional licensure is supposed to blunt these forces of capitalism by creating a floor below which providers cannot pass, to assure any client, low-income or otherwise, that their lawyer meets a minimum standard. Incompetent lawyers can create significant harm, both to their clients and society at large.[97] The licensure system cannot have

[92] *See generally* Hannah Haksgaard, *Court Appointment Compensation and Rural Access to Justice*, 14 U. St. Thomas J.L. & Pub. Pol'y 88 (2020).

[93] *See* Dru Stevenson, *Monopsony Problems with Court-Appointed Counsel*, 99 Iowa L. Rev. 2273, 2293–97 (2014).

[94] See Galia Benson-Amram, *Protecting the Integrity of the Court: Trial Court Responsibility for Preventing Ineffective Assistance of Counsel in Criminal Cases*, 29 N.Y.U. Rev. L. & Soc. Change 425, 432, 431 (2004) (finding that "three-quarters of those convicted of capital murder while represented by court-appointed lawyers were sentenced to death, while only about one-third of those represented by private attorneys received the death penalty").

[95] See *id.* at 432 n.35 (collecting studies showing elevated rates of discipline among appointed capital defenders); Diane Jennings et al., *Defense Called Lacking for Death Row Indigents: But System Supporters Say Most Attorneys Effective*, Dallas Morning News (Sept. 10, 2000), at 1A. *But see* Justin A. Hinkley & Matt Mencarini, *Court-Appointed Attorneys Do Little Work, Records Show*, Detroit Free Press (Nov. 3, 2016).

[96] An exception to idea that you get what you pay for is the quality of pro bono, nonprofit, and law school clinic representation, which tends to be higher quality than private representation in at least some contexts. *See* Stacy Caplow et al., *Accessing Justice: The Availability and Adequacy of Counsel Removal Proceedings*, New York Immigration Representation Study Report 357, 364, 401–02 (2011).

[97] *See* Benjamin P. Edwards, *The Professional Prospectus: A Call for Effective Professional Disclosure*, 74 Wash. & Lee L. Rev. 1457, 1474–75 (2017). ("Markets that sustain substandard professionals may drive public costs. Consider the social costs created by incompetent

it both ways. State bars should not be allowed to use ethics and entry rules to fetter the market for legal services in the name of minimum competency, and then abandon their obligation to hold the line against unethical and incompetent providers and allow market forces to shunt these providers toward the clients most harmed by the very scarcity they created in the first place.

There are other reasons to condemn a system that pushes bad apples toward solo and appointed practice. First, the economics of solo practice may contribute to unethical practice, creating a vicious cycle.[98] Serving the underserved, especially as an appointed lawyer, means accepting relatively little money for each case. The most efficient way to make ends meet, therefore, is to run volume through your practice.

The most notable example of high-volume practice serving low-income clients can be found in PI,[99] but the phenomenon of the legal mill is not unique to PI. Similar incentives can be found wherever lawyers are effectively paid by the case, rather than an hourly rate. Many attorneys serving low-income clients price their services by the piece – $1,000 for a driving under the influence (DUI) defense; $595 for a divorce.[100] The same incentives may be present in appointed work, where caps on fees turn nominally hourly rates into a pay-by-the-case arrangement. For example, Tennessee caps the total an attorney appointed in a murder case can bill at $3,000.[101] The most lucrative way to make a living as a court-appointed lawyer is to run it like a settlement mill – to take on as many cases as possible, without performing extensive investigation or investing in much client interaction.[102] The twenty busiest court-appointed lawyers in Nashville, Tennessee, handle nearly 50 percent of the appointed work, each billing the courts, on average, for over two hundred matters a year. And at 10 percent, their rate of public discipline is several multiples of the average.[103] Putting attorneys who have shown themselves willing to

attorneys. Judges and attorneys may spend excessive amounts of time addressing frivolous or plainly meritless arguments, generating crowded dockets, and slowing the delivery of justice generally.")

98 *See* Couric, *supra* note 80.

99 *See* Engstrom, *supra* note 89.

100 "Cost Benefit of Hiring a DUI Lawyer," QuoteWizard (updated Mar. 30, 2022), https://quotewizard.com/auto-insurance/cost-benefit-of-hiring-a-dui-lawyer (last accessed Feb. 13, 2025) (reporting lawyers offering flat-fee DUI defenses for $1,000 to $5,000); "Uncontested Divorce," Tim W. Smith, Attorney at Law, https://tennesseeflatratedivorce.com/practice-areas/uncontested-flat-fee-divorce/ (offering uncontested divorces for $695 with children and $550 without) (last accessed Feb. 13, 2025).

101 Tenn. S. Ct. Rule 13 § 2(d)(5)(B). It is worth noting, however, that judges can increase this cap in extraordinary circumstances. *See id.* at § 2(e).

102 *Cf.* Haksgaard, *supra* note 92 (concluding that appointed attorneys sometimes "take on more than they can handle" and that "similar concerns arise for both prosecutors and defense attorneys hired after a competitive bidding process because the focus is on hiring the lowest bidder, not the best-qualified bidder").

103 Data from Davidson County public records request, provided to author by Dawn Deaner of The Choosing Justice Initiative, on file with author.

cut corners into a practice environment where cutting corners is virtually required by the system is a recipe for recidivism.

Second, solo and appointed practice presents sexually abusive attorneys with opportunities to take advantage of particularly vulnerable clients. Attorney sexual abuse of a client almost invariably involves a power dynamic that goes beyond the typical attorney–client relationship. In every case reviewed for this chapter where an attorney coerced a client into sex, either the attorney was appointed to represent the client (so the client could not walk away from the representation) or the victim faced dire personal consequences (like losing her children or freedom), or both.[104] In the areas of legal practice with the widest access-to-justice gap, a sexually abusive attorney will find the most vulnerable of clients.

The final reason to be worried about a system that pushes problematic providers toward solo and small-firm work is that it severs the troubled lawyer from whatever supervision and accountability he or she may have at a firm. In solo work there is no structured mentoring, case review, hours reporting, or conflict disclosures. Essentially, there is no one to regulate a lawyer's practice but the state bar itself, such as it is. Given the economic pressures, opportunities for abuse, and lack of supervision found outside of firm practice, it is not surprising that nearly half of disciplined lawyers find themselves back before the disciplinary authority that relegated them to solo practice in the first place.

3.4 CONCLUSION

In solving the problem of hypocrisy at the heart of lawyer licensing, the stakes are highest for those who have the least access to justice. As it stands, low- and middle-income clients suffer the most for a disciplinary system that keeps in practice dangerous, predatory, and incompetent lawyers. But single-minded reform aimed at cracking down on the profession's bad apples could also hurt those same clients, either through false positives or by chilling innovative ways of delivering legal services that may end up in the crosshairs of an overactive disciplinary system. Solutions, therefore, should be synthetic.

First, the fetters of legal practice need to be loosened to allow for more access to justice. State bars should promulgate a clear definition of the practice of law that allows non-licensed advisors and other professionals to walk up to the line of legal practice without fear of bar sanction or criminal prosecution. The definition should only include tasks for which an elaborate legal education is required; whatever can be handled competently by a social worker, accountant, paralegal,

[104] See the examples cited in Chadwick, *supra* note 56, at 85–86 and the case of Gerald Moothart, who was disbarred for sexually assaulting or harassing four clients, some of whom he was appointed to represent in high-stakes cases. Iowa Supreme Ct. Att'y Disciplinary Bd. v. Moothart, 860 N.W.2d 598, 602, 615–18 (Iowa 2015).

court clerk, or administrative assistant should be excluded. State bars should get out of the business of strictly regulating the corporate form of legal practice and allow for more novel business models to reach clients in need of legal help. Self-help tools, like online forms and algorithmic legal advice, should be allowed to help pro se litigants learn their rights and make their arguments clearly and persuasively. States should build on their progress in streamlining the bar exam across states, and perhaps revisit the need for a bar exam altogether. And states and municipalities should expand access to justice by guaranteeing appointed representation in more civil matters,[105] with a rate-of-pay that would attract not only the providers at the bottom of the barrel. If we are to bridge the access gap in law, the supply of legal services needs to be expanded.

Second, the disciplinary system should be overhauled to ensure that supply is reasonably free of unfit lawyers. I have made a detailed proposal for how to fix the professional disciplinary system for other professions,[106] and its lessons can be imported here. States need to promulgate and adhere to disciplinary rules and sanction guidelines aimed at public protection. Specifically, the rules should make clear that clients cannot consent to sex with their attorneys in the course of representation, misappropriating client funds creates a presumption of disbarment, and client neglect, especially where it results in prejudice, is a serious offense. Addiction and other mental health issues, when resulting in actual client harm, should be seen as aggravating, not mitigating factors, especially in cases of misconduct like exchanging services for sex or stealing money to support an addiction.

The disciplinary system should be more transparent, investigative agencies fully funded and pro active, and complaints easy to file and immune from suit. Information about disciplined lawyers, including anonymized complaint data, should be easily accessible and centralized at the national level. At the same time, it's also important to note that transparency can help only to the degree that someone has a choice of lawyer, which is often not the case for many clients with limited access to justice.

Above all, legal disciplinary authorities need to be more clear-eyed about the likelihood of recidivism and recognize that when a disciplined attorney reoffends,

[105] The movement to secure "Civil Gideon" through an appointment process, although unlikely to succeed as a federal constitutional matter, is already underway at the state and local levels. Take, for example, the guarantee of an attorney for tenants in eviction cases – three states (Connecticut, Maryland, and Washington) have adopted a legislative right to counsel, and many large cities have done the same (New York City, San Francisco, Newark, Philadelphia, Cleveland, Boulder, Baltimore, Seattle, Louisville, Denver, Toledo, Minneapolis, Kansas City, and New Orleans). The Supreme Court of Ohio also found a right to attorney in involuntary adoption cases. *See In the Matter of* Adoption of Y.E.F., 171 N.E.3d 302 (Ohio Dec. 22, 2020). We should demand more data about the pool of lawyers tapped for appointments and their rates of professional discipline and malpractice history as we expand these programs.

[106] Rebecca Haw Allensworth & Cathal T. Gallagher, *Doctors Playing Lawyers*, manuscript on file with the author. *See also* REBECCA HAW ALLENSWORTH, THE LICENSING RACKET: HOW WE DECIDE WHO IS ALLOWED TO WORK, AND WHY IT GOES WRONG (2025).

his victims are likely to be the rural poor, the mentally ill or incompetent, immigrants, and indigent defendants. To this end, the monopoly of lawyers over the disciplinary process should end, as self-regulation seems a likely contributor to lax professional discipline. Cases should be decided by panels that are not dominated by lawyers – other professionals and members of the community should have a say in defining competence and ethicality in the provision of legal services. This could be achieved by using a pool of hearing officers that are only one-third lawyers, who hear cases in panels reflecting that balance of expertise in law (one-third) and expertise in community and client legal needs (two-thirds). All hearing officers should be paid appropriately for their time and trained in the regulatory imperatives of the legal profession.

None of these ideas is especially radical, and most of them have been made before. Some have been on the table for many years. And yet little in the attorney disciplinary system has changed. On paper, most lawyers can agree that the system should protect the public from incompetence, abuse, and graft. Why, then, have we made little headway toward a fairer and safer system of attorney discipline? Because even the legal profession's most vocal critics – lawyers themselves – are unwilling to give up self-regulation. For the most part, reform proposals have gone to the substance of professional rules and the procedure of their enforcement. These proposals have had little impact without changes to the institutional structure of professional regulation in law. Only once we are prepared to be held accountable to someone other than another lawyer will we confront the fact that the legal licensing system is designed not to meet the country's overall demand for legal services but to meet the needs of the elite, and, above all else, the needs of the profession itself.

4

The Case for the Traditionalists

W. Bradley Wendel[*]

The legal profession remains strongly committed, politically and rhetorically, to core values of loyal client service, confidentiality, avoidance of conflicts of interest, and professional independence as the justification for opposing the provision of legal services by nonlawyers. As a result, the profession has been remarkably consistent over decades in its resistance to changing the form of regulating legal services. As an article from the Deborah L. Rhode Center on the Legal Profession at Stanford Law School notes, with an undertone of weariness,

> Opponents of reform stand by their usual arguments: allowing nonlawyer ownership or practice will undermine the ethical values and independence of the legal profession and result in lower quality legal services, leading to potentially significant consumer and societal harm.[1]

Given the magnitude of the problem of lack of access to legal services, it can be tiresome to listen to the "usual arguments" against loosening unauthorized practice of law (UPL) restrictions. The theme of this book volume, after all, is "rethinking the lawyer's monopoly." This chapter contends, however, that one of the usual arguments for prohibiting nonlawyers from providing legal services deserves to be taken seriously. The application of knowledge and training in law to the specific situation of another – the standard definition of the practice of law[2] – necessarily involves a style of judgment that depends on extensive training and experience in

[*] Special thanks to Nora Freeman Engstrom for her insightful critical response to a draft of this paper presented at the New Voices in Access to Justice Workshop, as well as the Workshop participants for a lively and useful debate. I gratefully acknowledge the research funding provided by the Judge Albert Conway Memorial Fund for Legal Research, established by the William C. and Joyce C. O'Neil Charitable Trust.

[1] Lucy Ricca & Graham Ambrose, *The High Highs and Low Lows of Legal Regulatory Reform*, Stan. L. Sch. (Oct. 17, 2022), https://law.stanford.edu/2022/10/17/the-high-highs-and-low-lows-of-legal-regulatory-reform-333/ (last accessed Feb. 14, 2025).

[2] *See, for example*, Jason v. LegalZoom, Inc., 802 F. Supp. 2d 1053, 1064 (W.D. Mo. 2011); *In re* Jackman, 761 A.2d 1103, 1106 (N.J. 2000); Birbrower v. Superior Ct., 949 P.2d 1, 5 (Cal. 1999).

the practice of law. Judgment is something that nonlawyers can develop, but any expansion of the rights of nonlawyers to provide legal services must ensure that the nonlawyer service providers thereby licensed have sufficient training and experience with the exercise of legal judgment.

The relevant judgment should be exercised with respect to the common good or the public interest but not as discerned directly by a practitioner. Rather, guidance is provided by a conception of the common good as embodied in the positive law of the political community and then applied by practitioners skilled in the craft of legal interpretation.[3] This is what I refer to as the public side of lawyers' duties. The lawyer's role is not defined exclusively by private-law duties; it also has a significant public-law component.[4] By this I do not mean the cliché that the legal profession should be regulated in the public interest, or that lawyers should practice in the public interest. Rather, I mean that lawyers contribute in a vital way to the rule of law by aligning the conduct of clients with public values as embodied in positive law, and not merely considerations of the common good or the public interest.[5]

What lawyers do for clients has significance for democratic self-government and the rule of law. It follows that there is a serious risk that nonlawyers will not be capable of performing this function. If the concern of defenders of UPL regulation is only with the competence and loyalty of paraprofessionals or other nonlawyer service providers, tort and fiduciary law remedies should be sufficient to address them. It is more difficult to address the public side of the duties that nonlawyer providers of legal services will owe. It may be direct regulation by the judiciary, through the promulgation of rules of professional conduct and enforcement through grievance proceedings.[6] It also may occur through unwritten customs and norms acquired as part of a process of professional socialization. In any case, if nonlawyers are permitted to provide legal services, some attention must be paid to the public side, beyond the interest in protecting consumers from careless or inattentive service providers.

By making this argument sympathetically, I do not intend to object to UPL reform. The point, instead, is that proponents of reform should be prepared to counter the objection in its own terms. The hope is to move beyond the endless

3 One of the major themes of the scholarship I have done for most of my career. For a recent (and mercifully brief) summary, see W. Bradley Wendel, *Pluralism, Polarization, and the Common Good: The Possibility of Modus Vivendi Legal Ethics*, 131 Yale L.J. Forum 89 (2021).

4 The two principal intellectual foundations of the ideas to be explored in what follows are Alice Woolley, *The Lawyer as Fiduciary: Defining Private Law Duties in Public Law Relations*, 65 U. Toronto L.J. 285 (2015); and Deborah A. DeMott, *The Lawyer as Agent*, 67 Fordham L. Rev. 301 (1998).

5 I have been exploring this idea recently using fiduciary law and theory. *See* W. Bradley Wendel, *How Can You Have Law without Lawyers? Legal Formalism, Legality, and the Law Governing Lawyers*, *in* Methodology in Private Law Theory: Between New Private Law and *Rechtsdogmatik* (Thilo Kuntz & Paul B. Miller eds., 2023); W. Bradley Wendel, *Should Lawyers Be Loyal to Clients, the Law, or Both?*, 65 Am. J. Juris. 19 (2020).

6 *See* Charles W. Wolfram, Modern Legal Ethics § 2.2.2 (1986) (noting that American courts "have asserted the affirmative power to regulate the legal profession").

cycle of a promising reform idea being met by the usual argument, leading to stasis. The upshot of the argument is not that consumers in need of legal services should have only one option available, in the form of an expensively trained, fully licensed lawyer. It may be possible to meet the needs of consumers for legal services with a human or technologically enabled provider, as long as it is capable of understanding and complying with obligations related to maintaining the rule of law.

Section 4.1 presents three hypotheticals in which nonlawyers engage in what, under most states' definitions, would constitute the UPL. The hypos show that the private duties owed by a provider of services to a consumer of those services do not exhaust the normative space. In addition, there are public duties having to do with the integrity of the legal system. The Reporter of the Third Restatement of Agency, Deborah DeMott, observes that "the law of agency does not by itself capture all of the legal consequences of relationships between lawyers and clients and between lawyers and others to whom the lawyer owes duties."[7] The significance of that proposition is that private-law doctrines such as agency, negligence, and fiduciary duties cannot constitute the whole of regulation of nonlawyer providers of what have traditionally been considered legal services.

The more theoretical part of the chapter, Section 4.2, considers how the duties of lawyers must be understood as including this public-facing aspect. Some regulatory responses seem obvious, like promulgating codes of conduct for nonlawyer service providers. It may be the case, however, that the professional education and socialization of lawyers is more important than it seems at first for the preservation of the public aspect of the role of lawyer. The connection between the practice of law, legal judgment, the rule of law, and democratic self-government is available as an ethical ideal that should inform what lawyers do, even if reality departs from ethical ideals in many cases. This is a problem that UPL reformers need to take seriously, particularly if they hope to overcome the opposition of the organized bar to reform.

Section 4.3 concludes by briefly considering some of the options that are available for preserving the public-facing functions of providers of legal services when those services are provided by nonlawyers. Private-law doctrines from tort, contract, and agency law do not have any readily available "hook" to ensure that nonlawyer service providers interpret and apply the law in a way that is consistent with the interpretive norms of the professional community of lawyers. I do not have firm views about the best way to regulate nonlawyer service providers except to insist that the regulatory approach must be responsive to duties owed on both the private and public sides of the normative ledger.

4.1 CASE STUDIES IN LAWYERS' PRIVATE AND PUBLIC DUTIES

This section presents three hypotheticals. Each of these cases involves legal services that could plausibly be provided by nonlawyers – either humans or some form of

7 DeMott, *supra* note 4, at 301.

artificial intelligence (AI)-enabled technological means. The cases considered here, set in a hypothetical jurisdiction permitting the activities, involve services one could imagine an entrepreneurial group of nonlawyers offering to provide.

4.1.1 *The Startup Company*

Entrepreneurs R Us (ERU), an entity owned and operated by nonlawyers, has been approved through a regulatory sandbox established in State X to provide legal, accounting, and strategic consulting services to small businesses.[8] Among the services it provides is the preparation of documents to form an entity and to document relationships between the entity and its employees, suppliers, and customers. Employees of ERU do not identify themselves as lawyers, accountants, or consultants but refer to themselves as "business service specialists" (BSS). Two principals of a small software business, who had been acting as common law partners, sign a contract with ERU for the purpose of constituting the business as a corporation and drafting contracts with two engineers who had been providing services to the business. The principals tell the BSS that they would prefer to treat the engineers as independent contractors to avoid having to pay workers' compensation and unemployment insurance and to withhold a portion of their Federal Insurance Contributions Act (FICA) taxes. The principals explain that the company is extremely cash-poor at the moment and that the engineers are delighted to work as independent contractors because they anticipate that at some later time they will be in a position to share in the bounty if the company is acquired by a larger technology firm, as is common in the industry. The principals therefore ask the ERU representative to draft independent-contractor agreements for the signatures of the two engineers.

Assume for a moment an omniscient perspective on the case and stipulate to a couple of facts: A reasonable lawyer would recognize that, in the totality of the circumstances, including the number of hours worked and the extent of control exercised by the principals of the business, the engineers should be treated as employees, not independent contractors, under federal and state law. There are no criminal penalties associated with treating the engineers as independent

[8] I have been fascinated by this example ever since it was introduced by clinician and professional responsibility scholar Paul Tremblay, reporting on a matter handled by students in Boston College's entrepreneurship clinic. *See* Paul R. Tremblay, *At Your Service: Lawyer Discretion to Assist Clients in Unlawful Conduct*, 70 Fla. L. Rev. 251 (2018). I initially wrote a brief response to the article in which Tremblay discussed the case, and then returned to the case in a longer theoretical piece. W. Bradley Wendel, *Lawyers' Constrained Fiduciary Duties: A Comment on Paul R. Tremblay,* At Your Service: Lawyer Discretion to Assist Clients in Unlawful Conduct, 70 Fla. L. Rev. F. 7 (2018); W. Bradley Wendel, *Understanding the Complex Loyalty of Lawyers: Dual-Commission, Governance Mandate, and Intrinsic-Limit Analyses, in* Oxford Studies in Private Law Theory: Volume II 159 (Paul B. Miller & John Oberdiek eds., 2023).

contractors – the business is not making any kind of affirmative representation that could be treated as a false statement of fact to a government regulator – but the business is obtaining an economic windfall by not paying for workers' compensation, unemployment, and a share of the engineers' FICA taxes.

4.1.1.1 What Should the ERU Representative Do?

The usual lawyer response is to first consider the prohibition on counseling or assisting a client in conduct the lawyer knows is criminal or fraudulent.[9] The situation is a bit more complicated in the real world, but the hypo stipulates that treating the engineers as independent contractors would not subject them or the drafter of an independent-contractor agreement to criminal penalties, nor would it constitute criminal or civil fraud to treat them as independent contractors. Can a lawyer go ahead and draft the agreement? My answer – which I know many, if not most, lawyers disagree with – is no.

The negative response is based on the complex relationship between a lawyer and client, which is constituted in part by the law of agency but also includes a requirement that the lawyer act only within the limits of the client/principal's legal authorization. As summarized in the Restatement of the Law Governing Lawyers, the most basic obligation of a lawyer is to "proceed in a manner reasonably calculated to advance a client's *lawful* objectives, as defined by the client after consultation."[10] The italicized word indicates that the lawyer can do no more on behalf of a client than the client is authorized to do by the applicable law. It is inconsistent with agency and fiduciary law to believe that the lawyer, as an agent of the company, has the power to create a juridical relationship involving the company and the engineers that is greater than the power actually held by the company. The company does not have the legal authorization to treat the engineers as independent contractors when they should be deemed employees. Lawyers interpret and apply the law that confers power on individuals and entities, but they do not themselves create lawful power. They act only "on the footing of authority" derived from the law.[11]

I do not believe the ERU representative should prepare the independent-contractor agreements. Even though the BSS is not a lawyer, I see no reason why they would not owe the same fiduciary duties of loyalty, competence, and diligence as a lawyer would, as a matter of the common law of agency. The interesting question is whether DeMott's point holds for nonlawyer representatives as well. Recall that she characterized the law-governing lawyers as going beyond the common law of agency and imposing duties that are not neatly captured by the

[9] Model Rules of Pro. Conduct r. 1.2(d) (Am. Bar Ass'n 1983).

[10] Restatement (Third) of the Law Governing Lawyers § 16(1) (Am. L. Inst. 2000).

[11] Wendel, *Understanding the Complex Loyalty of Lawyers*, *supra* note 9, at 168.

agency law duty to follow the instructions of the principal. This is not only because lawyers are subject to supervision by the judiciary but also because control in the attorney–client relationship is not as straightforward as it is in other agency relationships.[12] The client does not have a right to control all aspects of the lawyer's provision of services. Rather, lawyers retain the right, and indeed the duty, to refuse to comply with the client's instructions if it goes beyond the boundaries of what is legally permitted. This does not mean only refraining from counseling or assisting a client to commit a crime or fraud but, as in the startup company case, not purporting to do things for the client that are not adequately supported by the law authorizing the client's conduct.

4.1.2 *The Asylum Seeker*

Affordable Immigration Services (AIS) is a for-profit corporation, owned and staffed by nonlawyers, providing assistance in connection with immigration matters, including applications for work authorization, adjustment of status, naturalization, and asylum.[13] Because it is not affiliated with a nonprofit organization, AIS has not sought approval as an accredited representative by the Department of Justice's (DOJ) Office of Legal Access Programs.[14] Rather, AIS has obtained approval within the sandbox of State X to provide a wide range of legal services. It charges fees for its services and is organized under state law as a for-profit corporation.

A man from an impoverished nation in Central Africa has asked AIS for assistance with an asylum application. His basis for the asylum claim is having suffered persecution in his home country on the grounds of his sexual orientation.[15] Based on the man's statements, made through a friend acting as an interpreter, a representative of AIS completed an application for asylum stating that the man is single, has no children, and was active in his home country in a social group for gay men. The application further claimed that the man was attacked by a religiously conservative, antigay group, which beat him up and threatened to kill him.

An immigration judge found the man's application to be not credible. The man returned to the offices of AIS, this time with a different friend acting as an interpreter, seeking advice about the possibility of appealing the decision. After listening to an explanation of the appellate process, the man asked whether he could bring his wife and three children into the country after he obtained asylum.

[12] DeMott, *supra* note 4, at 304.

[13] This hypo is based on a case handled by the Cornell Law School Asylum and Convention Against Torture Appellate Clinic. Thanks to Estelle McKee and Steve Yale-Loehr for involving me in this case and giving permission to talk about a hypothetical version of it here.

[14] *See* 8 C.F.R. § 1292.1(a)(4).

[15] Federal courts have found that sexual orientation is a "social group" for the purposes of seeking asylum in the United States. *See, for example*, Doe v. Att'y Gen. of U.S., 956 F.3d 135 (3d Cir. 2020); Xochihua-Jaimes v. Barr, 962 F.3d 1175 (9th Cir. 2020); Ayala v. U.S. Att'y Gen., 605 F.3d 941 (11th Cir. 2010).

Taken aback, the AIS representative said the man's application for asylum had stated that he was gay. The man replied that the friend he brought along the first time must have made a mistake. The man was *supporting* gay friends in his home country but was not himself gay. He said the first friend/interpreter must have also been mistaken in stating that the man was single and had no children, but the mistake was understandable since the friend only knew him in the United States, while his family was still in his home country.

4.1.2.1 What Should the AIS Representative Do?

If the representative were a lawyer, he or she would immediately turn to Rule 3.3(a) in the lawyer's state of admission.[16] That rule prohibits knowingly offering false evidence to a tribunal and also requires lawyers to take reasonable remedial measures if they subsequently come to learn that material evidence they have offered was false.[17] The key *mens rea* term of knowledge is defined in the rules as denoting actual (subjective) knowledge of the fact in question.[18] A similar rule exists in the regulations governing the Executive Office for Immigration Review within the DOJ. The regulations loosen the mental state requirement slightly to prohibit either knowingly false statements or statements made with reckless disregard of their falsity.[19] The lawyer's concerns would be twofold: First, is there a requirement to take remedial measures with respect to the application filed with the immigration court? Second, may the lawyer file an appeal of the immigration judge's decision and argue that it was erroneous because the man had been persecuted, or had a well-founded fear of future persecution, on the basis of his sexual orientation?

Answering both of these questions requires engaging with the knowledge element of the rule. The applicant's story has changed, and in a way that suggests he may have been lying on his initial application. However, the language barrier makes it difficult to know whether the reason for the variation is (i) an actual inconsistency in the testimony or (ii) a glitch in the translation. It is possible that the applicant is a gay man who is also married and has children (not an unknown possibility in a conservative society), but in the second interview he stated that he is not gay. The balance of probabilities certainly tips in the direction of a reasonable belief that the testimony on the initial asylum application was false, but this is not yet *knowledge* of falsity. In the criminal defense context, where the constitutional rights of the defendant significantly constrain the professional responsibilities of defense counsel,[20] some courts have interpreted the knowledge standard very strictly.

[16] Model Rules of Pro. Conduct r. 3.3(a) (Am. Bar Ass'n 1983).

[17] "Tribunal" is defined in the rules as including "an administrative agency or other body acting in an adjudicative capacity." *Id.* r. 1.0(m).

[18] *Id.* r 1.0(f).

[19] 8 C.F.R. § 1003.102(c).

[20] *See* Nix v. Whiteside, 475 U.S. 157 (1986).

The Wisconsin Supreme Court, for example, has stated that a lawyer's knowledge, for the purpose of Rule 3.3

> must be based on the client's expressed admission of intent to testify untruthfully. While we recognize that the defendant's admission need not be phrased in "magic words," it must be unambiguous and directly made to the attorney.[21]

The applicant in this case did not come right out and say that he had lied on the application and would continue to lie on the appeal. Because this is not representation of a criminal defendant, it may not be appropriate to apply a heightened knowledge standard. Still, knowledge means actual, subjective knowledge, and in my judgment the attorney does not have it.

Unlike the case of the startup company (Section 4.1.1), the duty not to present false evidence, and the duty to take reasonable remedial measures upon learning that evidence previously presented was false, are imposed by rules of professional conduct applicable to lawyers or "practitioners" appearing before an administrative tribunal. Because immigration matters, by definition, are heard by a tribunal constituted within the DOJ, there will likely be a regulation in place regarding the introduction of false evidence. However, the problem here is not so much regulation, or its absence, but with the substantial training and experience that may be required to exercise judgment in a case like this. The knowledge requirement is not a straightforward matter that can be read off the text of the applicable regulations. The regulation does not expressly reference the rules of professional conduct for lawyers, but a fair inference would be that the term should be given an equivalent meaning. A lawyer researching the application of the knowledge standard would then have to contend with whether the substantial body of case law applying Rule 3.3 in the context of ineffective assistance of counsel claims arising out of the representation of defendants in criminal cases should be applied to civil or administrative proceedings. Finally, one must exercise judgment to determine whether the standard was satisfied in this case.

4.1.3 *Custody Blackmail*

E-Z Divorce markets itself as an online platform assisting consumers with their divorce and other family law matters.[22] It provides a range of services, from document preparation only (comparable to LegalZoom) through an array of interactive help provided by a chatbot or a nonlawyer human customer service specialist (called a "divorce coach"). Customers who select one of the more expensive pricing options

[21] State v. McDowell, 681 N.W.2d 500, 513 (Wis. 2004).

[22] This problem has been discussed in the legal ethics literature for some time. *See, for example*, Katherine R. Kruse, *Beyond Cardboard Clients in Legal Ethics*, 23 GEO. J. LEGAL ETHICS 103, 126 (2010); David Luban, *Partisanship, Betrayal, and Autonomy in the Lawyer-Client Relationship: A Reply to Stephen Ellmann*, 90 COLUM. L. REV. 1004, 1015–16 (1990).

can have their forms reviewed, filed, and served by a divorce coach and can ask questions of the divorce coach in the process of preparing their forms with the assistance of the company's software. E-Z Divorce has been approved by state regulators to provide legal services to consumers.

A father of two young children is considering filing for divorce. He recently got a new job and is concerned that a court order to make substantial maintenance (alimony) payments to his soon-to-be ex-wife would interfere with his hedonistic lifestyle. He is an indifferent father, content to leave most of the responsibilities for caring for his children to their mother. The father signed up for one of the fully featured plans offered by E-Z Divorce and explained his situation to the divorce coach. The coach replied,

> I have seen many people in your situation. Here's something to consider: You can file a petition that seeks joint custody of your children. I know that's the last thing you actually want, but your wife may not know that. She may be willing to give up a big chunk of money in exchange for your "agreement" to permit her to have sole custody of the children.

The father thought this was a brilliant idea and instructed the divorce coach to proceed by preparing a divorce petition seeking joint custody of the couple's children.

Two questions: (1) What do you think of the advice offered by the divorce coach? (2) Would it make a difference to your thinking about this problem if the father had come up with the plan himself and merely directed the divorce coach to fill out the paperwork to seek joint custody?

Although this problem is commonly referred to as "custody blackmail," it does not fall within the prohibition, contained in the rules of professional conduct of some states, on threatening to file criminal charges against an opposing party to gain an advantage in a civil dispute.[23] Nor does it constitute the crime of blackmail, at least under the federal statute.[24] If the divorce coach had been a lawyer, he would have been subject to the State X Rules of Professional Conduct, which state that "a lawyer shall not use means that have no substantial purpose other than to embarrass, delay, or burden a third person."[25] In this case, of course, there is a substantial purpose for the tactic other than embarrassing, delaying, or burdening the wife: It is to decrease the maintenance obligation the husband will eventually incur. Might the tactic

[23] *See, for example*, N.Y. Rules of Pro. Conduct r. 3.4(e), N.Y. State Unified Ct. Sys. (Jan. 1, 2017), https://www.nycourts.gov/legacypdfs/rules/jointappellate/NY-Rules-Prof-Conduct-1200.pdf (last accessed Feb. 24, 2025). A similar prohibition is contained in the rules of professional conduct in Alabama, Connecticut, Georgia, Hawai'i, Idaho, Louisiana, New Jersey, South Carolina, Tennessee, and Vermont.

[24] *See* 18 U.S.C. § 873. For a recent application to a blackmail attempt by a high-profile lawyer, see United States v. Avenatti, 81 F.4th 171 (2nd Cir. 2023).

[25] *See* Model Rules of Pro. Conduct r. 4.4(a) (Am. Bar Ass'n 1983).

constitute "conduct prejudicial to the administration of justice?"[26] Opinions from the American Bar Association (ABA) and other regulators have generally said no, as long as the threat is related to the subject matter of the proceeding – in this case, the divorce.[27] The tactic does not appear to be the type of conduct that subjects lawyers to discipline for "conduct that is prejudicial to the administration of justice,"[28] perhaps owing to the difficulty of proving that the client did not in fact desire custody of the children, as opposed to merely using the custody demand as a bargaining chip.

If there is something wrong with this tactic, it must be wrong with reference to criteria other than the rules of professional conduct, combined with the background criminal law of extortion and blackmail – a portion of the law governing lawyers. Rather than offending against the *law* of lawyering, however, custody blackmail may offend against the *norms* respected by good lawyers. Deborah DeMott argues that "lawyers are distinctive as agents as a consequence of the robust professional culture and standards that define a lawyer's professional identity."[29] These standards "create duties that are not necessarily enforceable by the lawyer's client."[30] She has in mind duties under positive law that are enforceable by courts or judicial branch agencies.

But I would go back before the part about duties to emphasize her appeal to the robust professional culture and professional identity of lawyers. Professional culture and identity can serve as a resource for thinking in normative terms about the practice of law. In exchange for a valuable monopoly on the provision of legal services, lawyers traditionally are believed to practice law in the public interest. This may mean, among other things, saying no to clients who want to do nasty things to others.

I regard custody blackmail as almost certainly permitted by the law governing lawyers but a distasteful thing to do. Others may disagree, but the important thing for present purposes is to see that the debate is internal to what DeMott refers to as the robust professional culture of lawyers. If that culture is capable of supporting norms that can be used to evaluate the conduct of lawyers as permissible or nasty, apart from the lawfulness of the conduct, then it is potentially very useful in curbing the worst excesses of both lawyers and their clients. To the extent the maintenance of this culture depends on professional training and socialization, however, it risks being eroded through loosening of UPL restrictions.[31]

[26] *See id.* r. 8.4(d).

[27] *See* Ass'n of Bar of City of N.Y., Formal Op. 2017-3 (2017); ABA Comm. on Ethics & Pro. Resp., Formal Op. 92-363 (1992).

[28] *See* Annotated Model Rules of Pro. Conduct 727–35 (Ellen J. Bennett & Helen W. Gunnarsson eds., 9th ed. 2019).

[29] DeMott, *supra* note 4, at 306.

[30] *Id.*

[31] *See* Roger C. Cramton & Susan P. Koniak, *Rule, Story, and Commitment in the Teaching of Legal Ethics*, 38 Wm. & Mary L. Rev. 145 (1996); David Luban & Michael Millemann, *Good Judgment: Ethics Teaching in Dark Times*, 9 Geo. J. Legal Ethics 31 (1995).

A different response would be that the rules need to be modified to prohibit this conduct. Those rules could be made applicable to lawyers and nonlawyers, like "divorce coaches," alike. For any given case it may be possible to imagine a rule change that would prohibit nasty conduct like custody blackmail. However, one of legal philosopher H. L. A. Hart's fundamental insights is that rules must be embodied in language and language will always be open-textured.[32] Rules do not determine the scope of their own application and judgment will be required to interpret and apply them. (Consider the previous example, the Asylum Seeker, and the necessity of determining whether the representative has actual, subjective knowledge that the client testified falsely.) Something like DeMott's reliance on the background professional culture of lawyers to inform their conduct is inevitable and cannot be short-circuited by tightening up specific rules here and there. Nonlawyers could certainly be educated and socialized in a professional culture that informs their interpretation of any applicable rules of conduct, but there is no way to avoid difficult interpretive problems altogether.

4.2 THE PUBLIC SIDE: PROFESSIONAL JUDGMENT

The opening paragraph of the Preamble to the ABA's Model Rules of Professional Conduct states that "a lawyer, as a member of the legal profession, is a representative of clients, an officer of the legal system and a public citizen having special responsibility for the quality of justice."[33] This language has launched a thousand platitudinous speeches by bar leaders to law students and newly admitted lawyers, but what does it really mean to say that a lawyer has "special responsibility for the quality of justice"? The key, I believe, is suggested by DeMott's observation that "as members of a profession, lawyers are subject to duties not neatly captured by the consequences of agency."[34] To avoid begging the question, so that the invocation of professionalism becomes simply another version of the usual defense of UPL restrictions, it is helpful to contrast the idea of professionalism here with the law of agency. The agency relationship is characterized by the principal's right to control the agent.[35] As an officer of the court, however, a lawyer is also subject to direct supervision by judicial institutions and, as DeMott contends, "[t]his dimension of the lawyer's position is beyond the explanatory framework of agency law."[36] Alice Woolley similarly notes that the law of fiduciary duties fits uneasily with the foundation of the lawyer–client relationship in "the public law relationship between citizen and state."[37]

[32] H. L. A. Hart, The Concept of Law 120–32 (1961).
[33] Model Rules of Pro. Conduct, Preamble [1] (Am. Bar Ass'n 1983).
[34] DeMott, *supra* note 4, at 301.
[35] *Id.* at 303.
[36] *Id.* at 306.
[37] Woolley, *supra* note 4, at 289.

In this section, I contend that the problem raised by DeMott and Woolley is correctly identified. However, it is misleading to think that their point depends on the direct supervision of lawyers by judicial institutions, often shorthanded as lawyers having the status of officers of the court. Public duties are not a contingent feature of how lawyers are regulated but a conceptual truth about the function lawyers perform for clients in a society committed to the rule of law. That's a mouthful, so more explanation is in order.

Lawyers tend to think about public law as that body of law having to do with relationships between citizens and the state. However, Woolley is not talking about public law but about the public aspect of the role of lawyers, which is related to the function of law and the legal profession in establishing rights and duties among members of a political community. Philip Pettit's description of a social order maps onto what lawyers would think of as the domain of private law, yet it has a public, or social, or communal dimension:

> In speaking of a social order, I have in mind the legally implemented arrangements that determine people's rights and obligations in relation to one another and the limits that these may imply for the privileges and powers that people can individually command.[38]

The second half of this passage should call to mind my treatment of the Startup Company case. People have limits on "the privileges and powers [they] can individually command." The limits are specified by the law that constitutes the juridical relationships that can be created by contracts, different forms of business entities, and other devices of private ordering. As Woolley rightly points out, someone without specialized training cannot access the rights and privileges provided by law – for example, to create a business entity or a contractual relationship with an employee.[39] Thus, lawyers are required to provide this access, but notably it is to the framework of the social order and is therefore not strictly private. The public side of lawyers' duties has to do with access to, and the proper functioning of, the framework of social order established by the positive law of a political community, its lawmaking and law-applying institutions, and those occupational groups (lawyers, judges, and possibly nonlawyer service providers) that keep the system running.

On the private side, the fundamental duty of any agent – which DeMott calls the "fiduciary benchmark" – is that "the agent must interpret the principal's instructions reasonably in light of the principal's wishes as the agent understands them when the agent must decide what action to take."[40] This is a duty owed by lawyers to clients,

[38] Philip Pettit, *Legitimacy and Justice in Republican Perspective*, 65 Current Legal Probs. 59, 60 (2012).

[39] Woolley, *supra* note 4, at 291; *see also* Alice Woolley, *The Lawyer as Advisor and the Practice of the Rule of Law*, 47 U.B.C. L. Rev. 743, 767 (2014).

[40] *See* Deborah D. DeMott, *The Fiduciary Character of Agency and the Interpretation of Instructions*, *in* Philosophical Foundations of Fiduciary Law 321 (Andrew S. Gold & Paul B. Miller eds., 2014).

and serves to ensure that the client is calling the shots in the relationship and the lawyer is not acting paternalistically with respect to the client. As Woolley puts it, "the central function of the lawyer in advising a client is to discern the client's wishes, not to substitute her own."[41] That is fine as far as it goes, but in the Startup Company example, the client's wishes are not the last word. The client wishes to establish a juridical relationship between the corporation and the engineers. It is "juridical" in that various rights, duties, and privileges are supposed to follow from it, applicable to both the parties to the transaction and third parties.[42] The lawyer's work in preparing the independent contract agreements brings into existence a set of relationships constituted by law. Thus, in addition to ensuring that she is clear on the client's instructions, a lawyer in this case must also ensure that she has got the law right insofar as it bears on how the relationship between the company and the engineers can be structured.

Doing this requires judgment. Not since the sustained attack of the American legal realists on "mechanical jurisprudence" has any sensible lawyer believed that it is possible to apply the law deductively in adjudication or when advising clients, that the form of legal norms always has priority over their substance, that law can be applied without consideration of the circumstance of its enactment.[43] Legal rules do not determine the scope of their application, there is quite a bit of creativity involved in figuring out which are the relevant facts, and formal norms are frequently intelligible only against a background of understanding of what their point or purpose must be. In the Startup Company example, the status of the engineers as employees or independent contractors depends on the application of various multi-factor tests that have been used in agency, tort, labor and employment, tax, and other legal contexts.[44] This is not reasoning from first principles about whether it would be in the public interest or the interests of justice to recognize the legal status of independent contractors on these facts. Rather, those judgment calls have been made already, by legislatures, administrative agencies, and judges, and embodied in the form of positive law that is interpreted and applied by lawyers.

My point here is not that nonlawyers or a sophisticated AI system cannot exercise this type of judgment. Rather, the point simply is that the exercise of judgment is necessary to determine whether the engineers should be treated as independent contractors or employees under the applicable law. A similar observation may be made in connection with the judgment required by the providers of legal services in the other hypotheticals. The Asylum Seeker case requires both an interpretation of the applicable law, particularly an understanding of how the knowledge element has been applied in analogous cases, and also a difficult assessment of whether the client

41 Woolley, *supra* note 4, at 295, 306.

42 *See* Wesley Newcomb Hohfeld, *Fundamental Legal Conceptions as Applied in Judicial Reasoning*, 26 Yale L.J. 710 (1917).

43 *See, for example*, Paul B. Miller, *The New Formalism in Private Law*, 66 Am. J. Juris. 175 (2021).

44 *See, for example*, the lengthy list of factors in Restatement (Second) of Agency § 220 (1958).

lied on his application. Granted, immigration and asylum are public law subjects, so it may be easier to see the source of public duties here. But the same sorts of duties of candor to tribunals and third parties would be required if this were a dispute or transaction among private citizens. Any system that allocates rights, duties, and liberties that can be asserted among citizens dealing with each other in potentially contentious circumstances has to do something to ensure that the juridical relationships thereby established have some connection to what is, in fact, the case in the world. Judgment in this case does not pertain to the law establishing the client's rights, duties, and privileges, as in the Startup Company case. Rather, it pertains to the constraints that apply to participants in the process of establishing juridical relationships. These constraints are necessary to the orderly functioning of the entire system, however, and in that sense can be said to be part of the public side of the duties of lawyers or nonlawyer service providers.

The Asylum Seeker case may seem too easy because, no matter how it is regulated at the state level, employees of our hypothetical Affordable Immigration Service are appearing before administrative tribunals, which impose, by regulation, duties comparable to those that would apply to fully licensed lawyers. I stuck close to the facts of the real case when writing up this hypothetical, but it would be possible to take the regulations out of the problem, at least directly, by imagining a client coming to AIS for advice about what to do in order to obtain a work visa, permanent residence, or some other legal right. Now imagine that the AIS representative knows or suspects the client is lying or, even worse, counsels the client to lie. In that case the Justice Department regulations would not apply directly but the untruthfulness of the customer would still be a problem for regulators.

The Custody Blackmail case calls for judgment of a different kind altogether. On the assumption that there is no legal prohibition on making an insincere demand for shared custody as a way of exerting leverage in negotiations over the property settlement in the divorce, the issue is whether we want providers of legal services doing this sort of thing. DeMott refers to professional culture and a lawyer's professional identity.[45] Others may see the matter simply as the application of moral considerations to the representation.[46] In any event, the standards bearing on the exercise of judgment are unwritten, not expressed "officially" in positive law, and applicable by virtue of commitment to the ideals and values of an occupational group. Judgment in this case pertains to what a decent, ethical [lawyer, nonlegal service provider] ought to do. The bracketed terms suggest we can substitute any social or institutional role, but then we have to work out what actions are permissible or impermissible based on the ends and values for which the role is constituted.[47]

[45] DeMott, *supra* note 4, at 306.

[46] *See, for example*, David Luban, Lawyers and Justice (1988).

[47] *See, for example*, Tim Dare, The Counsel of Rogues? A Defence of the Standard Conception of the Lawyer's Role (2009); Arthur Isak Applbaum, Ethics for Adversaries: The Morality of Roles in Public and Professional Life (1999).

In any event, if one believes that the representation should involve counseling the father about the appropriateness (as opposed to lawfulness) of the custody tactic, some account is required to explain how the provider of legal services will acquire the capacity to provide that type of counseling.

As a theoretical matter this is a task for scholars, but as a practical matter it may be understood as an important part of legal education. The Carnegie Report emphasized the notion of professional identity as pertaining to "the skills and inclinations, along with the ethical standards, social roles, and responsibilities, that mark the professional," and "the purposes and attitudes that are guided by the values for which the professional community is responsible."[48] Social roles, responsibilities, and values can be understood in terms of the broader society's expectations for how its system for allocating rights and duties should be administered. Some assertions of rights may be unfair or abusive – a perversion of the process. Determining when this is the case requires . . . you guessed it, judgment. And in this instance that judgment will be developed over time, through experience, as part of membership in a professional community.

4.3 THE REGULATORY QUESTION

This concluding section is quite tentative, not only because the precise form of regulation varies according to the scope of practice allowed to nonlawyer service providers, but also because many of these regulatory responses have proven imperfect when applied to the existing legal profession. Any approach to regulation that is intended to mitigate the access-to-justice problem must be capable of addressing the public side of the duties owed by lawyers or nonlawyer service providers. One pressing issue for the regulation of nonlegal service providers is the relationship between the judgment that is essential to the provision of legal services and the value of independence.[49] Lawyers see themselves as having a fiduciary obligation of loyalty to represent and advise clients solely with reference to the best interests of clients, without regard to competing interests such as financial returns for equity owners of law firms. At the risk of falling back into the traditional defense of UPL restrictions, there may be something worth holding onto in the value of professional independence as it relates to the judgment that must be exercised in situations like those considered in Section 4.1. I worry a bit, however, that the judgment that is essential to the provision of legal services is best (if not only) acquired through a long process of professional education and socialization. It may be possible to replicate this process in the formation of nonlawyer service professionals, but so far that does not appear to be part of the thinking about these regulatory reforms.

48 William M. Sullivan et al., Carnegie Found. for the Advancement of Teaching, Educating Lawyers: Preparation for the Profession of Law (2007).

49 *See* Tom Baker & Rick Swedloff, *Mutually Assured Protection Among Large U.S. Law Firms*, 24 Conn. Ins. L.J. 1, 7–8 (2017).

The Washington State Limited License Legal Technician (LLLT) experiment sought to create a class of legal paraprofessionals, comparable to nurse practitioners or physicians' assistance in medicine, that could deliver legal services at a lower price than the fees charged by lawyers. In addition to an extensive education and licensing process, LLLTs were subject to their own code of professional responsibility, which largely tracked the rules applicable to lawyers.[50] A recent Colorado program goes down the same road: Paraprofessionals who will be licensed to provide legal services in matrimonial matters must have 1,500 hours of substantive legal experience, including 500 hours in Colorado family law; pass a licensing exam and an ethics exam; and satisfy continuing professional education requirements.[51] Those requirements appear to be onerous enough to deter many new entrants from seeking to become licensed paraprofessionals. As Keith Swisher argues, to my mind persuasively, saddling nonlegal service providers with the same educational, licensing, and regulatory regime as lawyers is inconsistent with the goal of increasing access to legal services and not necessary to further regulatory goals of accuracy and accountability.[52]

The Utah reform scheme tries to hold onto some form of traditional regulation by the judiciary of the provision of legal services, while better tailoring the substance of the regulations to the relevant values and objectives. The Utah Supreme Court established an Innovation Office, subject to the direction and control of the court, but charged with fashioning regulations "using an objectives-based and risk-based approach."[53] Importantly, the regulatory objectives encompass both consumer protection and access to justice.[54] These regulatory goals differ from the usual recitation of interests in UPL decisions by courts, which tend to emphasize only the consumer-protection side of the interest balancing.[55] The court also emphasized that regulation should be empirically informed, based on an assessment of the risk to the consumer, and aware of the alternatives available in the market for obtaining similar services.[56]

A comprehensive approach to regulating nonlawyer providers of legal services could attempt to address many of the issues considered in the hypos in Section 4.1. For example, legislation could provide that the attorney–client privilege applies to

[50] Amanda Claxton, *Liberty and Justice for Y'All: Allowing Legal Paraprofessionals to Practice Law to Reduce the Effects of Legal Deserts in Rural Georgia*, 74 Mercer L. Rev. 339, 371 (2022).

[51] *See* Andrea Keckley, *Colo. Supreme Court OKs Legal Paraprofessional Licenses*, Law360 (Mar. 29, 2020), https://www.law360.com/articles/1591238/colo-supreme-court-oks-legal-paraprofessional-licenses (last accessed Feb. 24, 2025).

[52] *See* Keith Swisher, *Death and Ethics: Suffocating or Saving Nonlawyer Practitioners with Lawyer Ethics*, 70 UCLA L. Rev. Discourse 52 (2023).

[53] Utah Sup. Ct. Standing Order No. 15 (as amended Sept. 21, 2022), ¶ 2.3.

[54] *Id.* ¶ 3.1.

[55] *See, for example*, *In re Jackman*, 761 A.2d at 1104; Birbrower v. Superior Ct., *supra* note 2, 949 P.2d at 8; *In re* Eimers, 358 So. 2d 7, 9 (Fla. 1978).

[56] Utah Sup. Ct. Standing Order No. 15 (as amended Sept. 21, 2022), ¶ 3.2.

confidential communications between customers and nonlawyer service providers, in the same way and subject to the same limitations (the crime-fraud exception, etc.) as communications between lawyers and clients. Nonlawyer providers could be subject to enforceable duties of candor to tribunals, to the same extent as lawyers, with respect to their own statements and evidence they submit. The hard part of this approach is not imposing enforceable regulations but training nonlawyer service providers on their application. Something like the knowledge standard in the Asylum Seeker example calls upon fairly sophisticated legal reasoning to determine the appropriateness and limits of analogies with other legal tests to determine an actor's mental state with respect to facts. A first-year criminal law class would be very helpful to someone trying to puzzle out what to do in that case. The Custody Blackmail hypo is different, because in that case the judgment required is not exercised with respect to other areas of positive law but with respect to the values that inform the legal system and the legal profession. Law schools may not do a great job at inspiring students to engage in critical reflection about the values informing the lawyer's role – in fact, the normative curriculum is largely tacit[57] – but at least in theory there is an available site for the consideration of these questions. The values inherent in the provision of legal services are likely to go largely unaddressed if the services are provided by software or humans with limited legal training.

[57] *See* Roger C. Cramton, *Beyond the Ordinary Religion*, 37 J. Legal Educ. 509 (1987); Cramton & Koniak, *supra* note 31, at 154.

PART II

Lessons from the Field

On-the-Ground Efforts to Effect Positive Change

5

What Can Legal Services Reformers Learn from Court Efforts to Assist Self-Represented Litigants?

Judge Carolyn B. Kuhl[*]

When I was appointed to the Superior Court of the State of California for the County of Los Angeles (LASC) in 1995, my first assignment was a felony calendar court, a huge challenge for a lawyer whose legal practice had been "big firm" civil litigation. My reassignment to a courtroom hearing general jurisdiction civil cases a few years later was more familiar terrain. But it also put me in daily contact with colleagues in the same courthouse whose dockets confronted them with a new set of challenges gripping state courts nationwide: a rising tide of self-represented litigants (SRLs) with a profound need for the justice and protection only a court can provide but with few tools with which to navigate a complex system built by and for lawyers.

Soon after my reassignment to our main civil courthouse, I met a judicial colleague who, before his appointment to the bench, had served on the city council of a small city within the jurisdiction of the LASC. Over lunch in the judges' lunchroom one day, the former council member began describing his vision for the future of justice in Los Angeles. He imagined a court system in which every community in Los Angeles would have a court-staffed kiosk where people could go to get advice about how to interact with the court in order to file, prosecute, or defend a civil lawsuit.

My judicial colleague's vision was striking for someone still relatively new to the judicial role. In my mind at that time, courts could only be purely neutral institutions deciding cases brought forward by adversaries. How could the advantages of the adversary system of justice be maintained if the court was providing guidance to one side in litigation?

[*] The author would like to acknowledge the invaluable information provided by Kathleen Dixon, the Managing Self-Help Attorney for Los Angeles Superior Court since 2002, and Snorri Ogata, Chief Information Officer for Los Angeles Superior Court from 2014 to 2023. The fruits of their excellent work are reflected in this chapter. Graham Ambrose, a third-year student at Stanford Law School and a Civil Justice Fellow at the Deborah L. Rhode Center on the Legal Profession, contributed significantly to the research reflected in Section 5.1 of this chapter. And my colleague, Judge William F. Highberger of the Los Angeles Superior Court, generously offered valuable ideas and editorial assistance at all stages of the project.

It turns out that my colleague who envisioned accessible advice for litigants was well ahead of his time. Many judges in the late 1990s took the view that, when pro per litigants (as they were then called) appeared before a judge or sought assistance from court staff, the only proper response was "I am not allowed to give you legal advice; I must treat both sides in a case the same way."[1] But fast forward two decades, a window that includes my term as Presiding Judge of the LASC, and it is clear that American courts have undergone a tectonic shift, even a transformation, in their approach to court-provided guidance and assistance to unrepresented parties. What historically was a pat statement that "the court cannot provide legal advice" has, by necessity, morphed into a more useful but still limited set of resources for unrepresented parties often drowning in legal complexity.

This chapter offers both a history and an assessment of court-annexed assistance for litigants who try to access the court system without counsel and a perspective on whether these efforts, enhanced by a growing menu of digital tools, might plausibly narrow the justice gap by providing these litigants with necessary assistance. At once a history lesson and an in-the-trenches look at a couple of decades of court reforms, my aim is to show how anxieties about judicial and court neutrality have given way to an array of reform options that are producing concrete lessons as the American legal system considers alternatives to conventional, lawyer-centered forms of legal help in a legal system with massive amounts of unmet civil legal need.

Section 5.1 begins with a short, high-level review of efforts by courts around the nation to help SRLs adrift in an ocean of procedure and legalese, gradually abandoning the preexisting view that it was improper to assist SRLs. Section 5.2 offers a more detailed account of LASC's efforts, providing a more focused case

[1] Based on peer group conversations at a national conference on Self-Represented Litigants (SRLs), an American Judicature Society Report recounted that judges recognize "individual and conflicting judicial philosophies [as barriers for SRLs], i.e., 'hands-off' versus activism, and ethical concerns..." AM. JUDICATURE SOC'Y ET AL., A NATIONAL CONFERENCE ON PRO SE LITIGATION: A REPORT AND UPDATE 9 (2001). The "most serious concern of trial judges," according to one late-1990s study of family and probate court judges in Massachusetts, "is their perceived inability to assist a pro se litigant due to their duty to maintain impartiality." Russell Engler, *And Justice for All-Including the Unrepresented Poor: Revisiting the Roles of the Judges, Mediators, and Clerks*, 67 FORDHAM L. REV. 1987, 2070 n.204 (1999) (citing MASS. BAR ASS'N, CHANGING THE CULTURE OF THE PROBATE AND FAMILY COURT 34–47 (1997)). Similarly, the authors of a national report from 1998 concluded "the most serious concern of trial judges" was that the duty of impartiality hampers their ability to help SRLs. *See* JONA GOLDSCHMIDT ET AL., STATE JUST. INST., MEETING THE CHALLENGE OF PRO SE LITIGATION: A REPORT AND GUIDEBOOK FOR JUDGES AND COURT MANAGERS 29 (1998). And a 2000 report from Wisconsin noted that "judges feel like they are in a no-win situation." WISC. PRO SE WORKING GRP., MEETING THE CHALLENGE OF SELF-REPRESENTED LITIGANTS IN WISCONSIN 36 (2000).

The New Hampshire Superior Court noted in the early 1990s, even as SRL numbers grew, that court staff "must remain neutral in all cases and cannot give anyone legal advice." Robert M. Daniszewski, *Coping with the Pro Se Litigant*, 36 N.H. BAR J. 46, 49 (1995); *see also* Ariz. Jud. Ethics Advisory Comm., Op. 88-5 (May 11, 1988) (warning clerks of the court "not to advise the public as to its legal rights and responsibilities").

study of the institutional and ideological challenges of SRL-focused reforms. Some of LASC's efforts to leverage human and technological resources to provide guidance and assistance to SRLs worked well, and others were surprisingly ineffective. Section 5.3, the final section, proposes some "lessons learned" from court efforts to design and oversee self-help services. Those services necessarily fall short of full legal representation. Nevertheless, courts' experiences using supervised nonlawyer resources and technology interfaces to assist SRLs may suggest paths to more cost-effective, high-volume legal services and provide ideas for reformers considering how to enhance access to justice.

5.1 NAVIGATING THE ADVERSARY SYSTEM WITHOUT COUNSEL AND THE RISE OF COURT SELF-HELP SERVICES

As early as the 1990s, judges and court administrators across the nation could see a collision coming. On the one hand, the American legal system was as committed as any in the world to adversarialism, the idea that legal systems work best when the parties – and, more specifically, their lawyers – proofs in a structured, forensic setting to a neutral and passive decision maker who resolves the dispute.[2]

On the other hand, a rising tide of high-stakes but small-scale cases was beginning to flood court dockets: debt collections, evictions, home foreclosures, and child support enforcement actions, among others. These cases were posing particular challenges for judges and court administrators because they tended to pit an institutional plaintiff (a bank, debt buyer, corporate or municipal landlord, the government), nearly always represented by a lawyer, against an individual defendant, nearly always self-represented. In addition, in cases where family members turned to the courts to settle disputes, establish legal relationships, or provide protection (divorce proceedings, guardianship and conservatorship petitions, name change petitions, applications for domestic violence restraining orders), litigants increasingly attempted to navigate the legal system without counsel.

When litigants bring their disputes to court without legal representation, it substantially burdens court operations. Think of a family law proceeding. An SRL who has no idea what to do to solve a custody dispute comes to the courtroom to ask the courtroom clerk for guidance. This interrupts the clerk's efforts to try to organize the court's calendar for the next day. Or a litigant may not understand how to serve her papers, a concept that is not intuitive for most litigants. When the motion is called for hearing, the judge has to explain service of process and continue the motion, further clogging future calendars. As the number of SRLs increases, these delays multiply.

By the late 1990s, it had become clear that complacency was not a sustainable approach to this challenge. Until then, the phenomenon of "pro se litigation" had

[2] *See* Stephan Landsman, The Adversary System 2 (1984).

mostly been the subject of isolated inquiry by individual jurisdictions. Then, in 1998, an important conference – a joint effort of the American Judicature Society, the State Justice Institute, the Open Society Institute, and the American Bar Association – brought together judges and court administrators from across the nation to think through the details and dimensions of the dilemma.[3] SRLs were growing fast: Even in the 1990s SRLs were filing a high proportion of family law cases in California.[4] By 2015 crowded court calendars with substantial SRLs were the norm in family law and some civil courtrooms. A 2015 national survey concluded that lawyers represented both sides in only 24 percent of civil cases and that even in general jurisdiction civil cases only 46 percent of defendants were represented.[5] As the Judicial Council of California observed in its 2019 Benchguide for Handling Cases Involving Self-Represented Litigants, "[t]he traditional passive role for judges works well when well-prepared attorneys represent both parties to a dispute. It doesn't work as well when there is a full calendar of self-represented litigants who are unfamiliar with court rules, processes and evidence while trying to present their cases."[6]

Self-help resources for SRLs initially were thought of as a coping mechanism for courts with crowded civil and family law calendars struggling to move cases forward.[7] As court self-help efforts matured, and as the number of SRLs coming to

3 *See generally* AM. JUDICATURE SOC'Y ET AL., *supra* note 1. The conference was catalyzed by a report issued in 1998 that was the first of its kind to compile nationwide data and research on pro se litigation. *See* GOLDSCHMIDT ET AL., *supra* note 1.

4 One study reported that as early as 1995, pro se litigants in California were filing roughly two-thirds of all divorces and 40 percent of all child custody cases. *See* Frances L. Harrison et al., *California's Family Law Facilitator Program: A New Paradigm for the Courts*, 2 J. CTR. FAMS. CHILD. & CTS. 61, 61 (2000).

5 CIV. JUST. INITIATIVE, NAT'L CTR. STATE CTS., THE LANDSCAPE OF CIVIL LITIGATION IN STATE COURTS 31–32 (2015).

6 JUD. COUNCIL CAL., HANDLING CASES INVOLVING SELF-REPRESENTED LITIGANTS: A BENCHGUIDE FOR JUDICIAL OFFICERS 2-1 (2019) [hereinafter CALIFORNIA BENCHGUIDE RE SRLs]. In 2002, in light of the rising number of SRLs in California courts and growing calls for reform, then-Chief Justice of California Ronald M. George suggested that "the traditional judicial model may not always be the most appropriate, and there may well be better ways to resolve certain disputes." RICHARD ZORZA, THE SELF-HELP FRIENDLY COURT: DESIGNED FROM THE GROUP UP TO WORK FOR PEOPLE WITHOUT LAWYERS 7 (2002). In 2007, the ABA promulgated Rule 2.2 of the Model Code of Judicial Conduct, acknowledging that judges may make "reasonable accommodations" for SRLs. *See* NAT'L CTR. STATE CTS., SELF-REPRESENTED LITIGANTS AND THE CODE OF JUDICIAL CONDUCT 1 (2019), https://www.ncsc.org/__data/assets/pdf_file/0030/15798/proselitigantsjan2016.pdf (last accessed Feb. 14, 2025).

7 *See, for example*, Editorial, *Courts and the Self-Represented*, 82 JUDICATURE 4 (1998) (recognizing that overburdened court staff face "increasing numbers of pro se litigants who ask for explanations of the legal process as it pertains to their cases" and that judges "who expect to play the traditional role of passive arbiter in the litigation process ... may be unable to devote the necessary time to explain the litigation process" and recommending that courts adopt "pro se assistance programs [that are] underway or under consideration in a number of jurisdictions"); *In re Report of the Family Court Steering Committee*, 12 So. 2d 518, 527 (2001) (in light of the fact that "an overwhelmingly large percentage of litigants in family law matters are

court grew, courts came to realize the tragedy starkly articulated in the 2016 Civil Justice Initiative report to the Conference of Chief Justices: "The idealized picture of an adversarial system in which both parties are represented by competent attorneys who can assert all legitimate claims and defenses is, more often than not, an illusion."[8]

Slowly but surely, courts began to experiment, within the limits required for courts to maintain their role as a neutral adjudicator of disputes. Initially, that meant courts providing books, brochures, and forms and online educational tools.[9] Subsequently, it became clear that pamphlets and forms alone could not adequately communicate the complexity of court proceedings and substantive legal requirements. Courts began putting substantial resources into self-help centers where SRLs could meet face-to-face with court personnel to seek help.[10] In the ten years between the mid-90s and mid-00s, some 150 self-help centers were established nationwide.[11] While this required substantial investment of budget resources, scarce space in court facilities,[12] and considerable management oversight, self-help centers became an

unrepresented," and "[i]n response to the pressing need to provide access to the courts in a meaningful manner, self-help programs were developed in all [Florida] circuits"); *Challenge to Justice: A Report on Self-Represented Litigants in NH Courts*, 45 N.H. BAR J. 16, 17 (2005) (noting a "dramatic increase" in the number of SRLs and that both "judges and court staff are often put in the difficult position of assisting a self-represented litigant without impermissibly giving legal advice").

8 NAT'L CTR. STATE CTS., CALL TO ACTION: ACHIEVING CIVIL JUSTICE FOR ALL, RECOMMENDATIONS TO THE CONFERENCE OF CHIEF JUSTICES BY THE CIVIL JUSTICE IMPROVEMENTS COMMITTEE 10 (2016).

9 One example was Florida's Access Initiative, which among other things, democratized legal information by revamping the Florida Supreme Court website with forms, educational tools, and live broadcasting of oral arguments. Robert Craig Waters, *Future of the Florida Judiciary: Chief Justice Gerald Kogan's Access Initiative*, 71 FLA. BAR J. 28 (1997).

10 According to the nonprofit Self-Represented Litigation Network, the first and most famous service center was established in 1994 in the Superior Court of Maricopa County, Arizona. *See* SELF-REPRESENTED LITIG. NETWORK, A DIRECTORY OF COURT-BASED SELF HELP PROGRAMS (2006). Eight full-time court staff at two locations in Phoenix and Mesa helped with court forms and offered generic information to litigants navigating domestic relations or probate issues. *See* GOLDSCHMIDT ET AL., *supra* note 1. Arizona and Utah also pioneered self-help kiosks, in which pro se litigants could receive forms, instructions, and general court information via touch-screen technology. *See id.* at 76–77. Hennepin County, the most populous county in Minnesota, launched a self-help service center in 1996. The center provided a court clerk trained to help SRLs and information about court procedures and legal forms. John M. Stanoch, *Working with Pro Se Litigants: The Minnesota Experience*, 24 WM. MITCHELL L. REV. 297, 309 (1998).

11 Richard Zorza, *Self-Represented Litigants and the Access to Justice Revolution in the State Courts: Cross-Pollinating Perspectives toward a Dialogue for Innovation in the Courts and the Administrative System*, 29 J. NAT'L ASS'N ADMIN. L. JUD. 63, 69 (2009).

12 *See, for example*, Susan M. Palmer, *The State of Pro Se Litigant Education in Vermont*, 27 VT. BAR J. 43, 45 (2001) (quoting the director of family court operations, who noted that the main barrier to democratizing information was the fact that "many courts are limited currently by space and other logistical restrictions"). In West Virginia, a surge in SRLs prompted the state supreme court to establish legal research centers in public libraries where the public could

integral part of many courts' operations.[13] By 2019, California's self-help centers were servicing more than one million court users each year.[14]

In some quarters, these court efforts were controversial. Representatives of the establishment bar even argued that the existence of court-annexed self-help services discouraged use of attorneys.[15] Self-help services provided by courts ordinarily include notifying litigants of pro bono or low-cost options for representation.[16] But some courts apparently thought the primary goal of court-provided self-help resources should be urging litigants to seek attorney representation.[17] Today, however, it is undeniable that existing resources in the legal community have not been able to meet the needs of the litigants who do appear in court – to say nothing of those who have legal needs but do not even attempt to access the courts, or those who are sued but fail to appear.[18]

access LexisNexis, legal research materials, and informational videos. Elliott E. Maynard, *Legal Help Comes to a Library Near You*, 2004 W.V. LAW. 8, 8 (2004). Ventura County, California hired a lawyer to help SRLs out of a custom-ordered 35-foot RV, modeled after a bookmobile library. Terry Carter, *Self-Help Speeds Up*, 87 AM. BAR ASS'N J. 34, 35 (2001). This mobile center visited two locations each day. *Id.* at 37.

13 Of thirty-two states responding to an NCSCs survey in 2022, only eight states did not have some form of self-help center. Of those responding, 84 percent reported that their programs had operated more than five years, and 60 percent reported their programs had operated more than ten years. NAT'L CTR. STATE CTS., COURT-BASED SELF-HELP CENTERS: NATIONAL SURVEY, FINDINGS, RECOMMENDATIONS AND BEST PRACTICES 7 (2022), https://www.ncsc.org/__data/assets/pdf_file/0016/92023/Court-Based-Self-Help-Centers-National-Survey-Findings-Reccomendations-and-Best-Practices23.pdf (last accessed Feb. 14, 2025).

14 *Court Self-Help Centers Offer In-Person, Remote Assistance to Californians Amid Pandemic*, CAL. CTS. NEWSROOM (Apr. 6, 2021), https://newsroom.courts.ca.gov/news/court-self-help-centers-offer-person-remote-assistance-californians-amid-pandemic (last accessed Feb. 14, 2025).

15 *See, for example*, *Law Librarians Heard*, L. LIBR. NEWS (Summer 1997), at 6–7 (citing a co-chair of an ABA committee who attributed the then-emerging "pro se movement" to the advent of self-help centers, legal libraries, kiosks, self-help books, videos, and tapes, the public's inability to afford full-service lawyers, and a "lawyer-bashing mentality").

16 *See, for example*, CAL. ADMIN. OFF. CTS., GUIDELINES FOR THE OPERATION OF SELF-HELP CENTERS IN CALIFORNIA TRIAL COURTS 7–8 (2008) [hereinafter CALIFORNIA SELF-HELP GUIDELINES].

17 Idaho is one example: "The Access Committee recognized that the most effective way to assist litigants is usually to get them legal representation. The thrust of the project, therefore, will be to educate pro se litigants as to the advantages of legal representation, and the manner in which an attorney can assist them with their case." Patrick D. Costello, *Courthouse Assistance Offices*, 42 ADVOC. 13, 13 (1999). *See also*, MO. SUP. CT. JOINT COMM'N TO REV. PRO SE LITIG., REPORT TO THE SUPREME COURT OF MISSOURI & THE MISSOURI BAR (2003) ("Pro se litigants in specific types of cases should be required to participate in an education program that describes the risks and responsibilities of proceeding without representation."); IOWA SUP. CT., GUIDELINES AND INSTRUCTIONS FOR CLERKS WHO ASSIST PRO SE LITIGANTS IN IOWA'S COURTS (2000) ("[I]n many or most situations" the best customer service might be "to advise the litigant to seek the assistance of an attorney").

18 *See, for example*, LEGAL SERVS. CORP., THE JUSTICE GAP: THE UNMET CIVIL LEGAL NEEDS OF LOW-INCOME AMERICANS 19 (2022), justicegap.lsc.gov/the-report/ (reporting that low-income Americans do not get any or enough legal help for 92 percent of their substantial civil legal problems).

Concededly, self-help services can never be the equivalent of legal representation. The necessity that courts maintain neutrality ultimately means that courts cannot recommend a strategy, draft and propound discovery or, challenge the opposing party's factual representations.[19] To state the obvious, a court cannot become an adversary to the party opposing an SRL. However, even careful adherence to that maxim leaves ample room for court-provided and court-hosted services. Courts can provide education about law and procedure, assist in filling out forms with information provided by SRLs, access court records of a litigant's case, and provide options based on the state of the litigated matter. The next section of this chapter offers a closer-in look at how one court – the court where I have had the privilege of serving for nearly thirty years – has attempted to serve the needs of SRLs while hewing to the adversarial fundamentals of the American legal system.

5.2 EFFORTS TO ASSIST SELF-REPRESENTED LITIGANTS AT LASC

LASC is the largest trial court in the country, serving one of the country's most diverse populations. Its prominence and its long experience in providing self-help services to SRLs make it an ideal case study in what has worked well and what has fallen short despite careful design. As reformers in the public and private sectors search for cost-effective, high-volume legal services models or alternative representation models, they should be aware of what courts have learned from their efforts to provide self-help services. The discussion that follows describes and appraises some of the self-help services LASC has implemented or attempted in an effort to leverage human and electronic resources to assist litigants, including efforts to ensure that SRLs have access regardless of the language they speak or their language literacy.

5.2.1 *Leveraging Human Resources*

5.2.1.1 Using an Educational Model to Enhance Service Delivery

In 2002 the Judicial Council of California gave grants to several local courts, including LASC, to encourage development of self-help models. Initially, self-help services were modeled on traditional one-on-one legal representation. A person would come to a courthouse for help and be served by court staff or legal services staff who spoke with the individual, discussed the person's case or legal problem, and provided court forms. Court forms in California are complex, even though (or perhaps because) the forms organized legal topics and required factual responses in an iterative flow. Forms also

[19] A Benchguide produced by the California Judicial Council in 2019 includes an excellent discussion of the legal principles informing what a neutral judicial officer must do and cannot do to assist SRLs. CALIFORNIA BENCHGUIDE RE SRLS, *supra* note 6, at 3-1 to 3-22.

change frequently, often in response to legislative changes. Because of the complexity of court forms, litigants served by the individualized self-help model typically needed to be guided through the process of filling out the forms.

Given the volume of civil and family law cases filed in Los Angeles County,[20] demand for self-help services could not be met using an individual-service delivery model. In subject areas where self-help demand was greatest, particularly in family law, LASC evolved into an educational service delivery model. In 2003, using a model self-help pilot grant, LASC self-help staff observed the types of SRL assistance being provided by several legal aid agencies, and then began experimenting with an SRL workshop model used by the Buhai Center for Family Law. LASC then worked to find ways to reduce the time required for workshops so as to fit into a morning or afternoon session the information needed to fully educate family law litigants about how to make informed decisions in representing themselves.[21]

In family law cases, self-help services provided through an educational delivery model begin at an intake desk at which court staff greets the SRL and asks what they want to accomplish, whether they have a pending case, and what stage their case is at. Importantly, the intake staff person has access to the electronic court docket and can check the status of a litigant's case, if a case already has been filed. Usually, it can be determined rather quickly what type of help the person needs. If there is an immediate need for action (e.g., need for a restraining order or emergency custody order), the SRL is referred to a staff person who can provide prompt individualized assistance.

If there is not an immediate need for action, the SRL is directed to an online or in-person introductory workshop. The introductory workshop for divorce covers topics including service of process, income and expense organization, community and separate property, spousal support, custody and visitation and child support.[22] The goal is to familiarize the SRL with the terminology and basic concepts involved in a divorce or dissolution matter. When conducted in person, the introductory workshop may take about three hours. After the introductory workshop, the family law litigant is required to complete a "homework packet" that tells the litigant what documents must be gathered (e.g., "your paystubs from the past two months") and asks for information such as income for both spouses, monthly expenses, debts, information about children, and schedule of parenting time requested.

[20] In fiscal year 2001–02, 516,251 civil cases and 40,468 family law divorce and separation cases were filed in Los Angeles County. CAL. JUD. COUNCIL, 2003 COURT STATISTICS REPORT 50.1–50.2 (2003).

[21] Details of the workings of LASC's self-help center described in this chapter were provided by Kathleen Dixon, Managing Self-Help Attorney for LASC, in a series of interviews. Notes reflecting the facts she provided are on file with the author.

[22] *Divorce/Dissolution of Marriage Orientation: Workshop 1 of 3*, CAL. SUPERIOR CT., L.A. CNTY., https://www.lacourt.org/selfhelpcourses/dissolution_orientation_menu/story.html (last accessed Feb. 14, 2025).

The "homework packet" is not a form to be filed with the court; it is a guide to gathering factual information relevant to a divorce proceeding.[23]

The SRL is told that family law self-help staff will require the "homework" to be turned in as a "ticket" to attending the next workshop. The divorce process is broken down into a total of three workshops. The second workshop provides step-by-step assistance with filling out court forms to begin or respond to a divorce. The third workshop assists litigants with filling out default judgment forms to complete their divorce if the respondent has not filed a response. Prior to the pandemic, all workshops were in-person. Now the first workshop is online in a format by which the SRL selects topics and moves through slides with written and oral explanations that are accessed at the litigant's own pace. Subsequent workshops are scheduled Webex sessions that require a reservation. The participating SRL can use the share-screen function to ask individual questions about court forms, but the process is less efficient than an in-person workshop.

The educational service model for self-help allows far more litigants to be assisted. Individual assistance continues to be provided to help an SRL who needs specific direction or help with a particular answer on the "homework" or on a court form. But the goal is to communicate information online or in a group setting to the extent litigants are able to comprehend and assist themselves. Notably, the educational model allows both sides in litigation to be assisted: Occasionally court staff even instruct both parties to a divorce proceeding in the same workshop. In other subject areas, such as evictions, self-help assistance is provided by the court to both self-represented landlords and tenants, but different types of assistance are provided.[24]

LASC links family law self-help services to the needs of the litigant in the courtroom. When an SRL appears in court in a family law proceeding and the judge concludes that the litigant has not met a legal requirement (such as service of a motion or filing a required document), the judge can check a box on a standard form, give the form to the litigant, and send the litigant to the self-help center (or to the court website) for assistance with the issue the court has identified.[25] Linking

[23] *Worksheet: Divorce/Dissolution of Marriage Orientation Homework Packet (Workshop 1 of 3)*, Cal. Superior Ct., L.A. Cnty. (July 2021), https://lascpubstorage.blob.core.windows.net/forms/Forms%20Comprehensive%20List/1610-LASC%20SHC%20003.pdf (last accessed Feb. 14, 2025).

[24] Tenants who walk into the self-help center are assisted one-on-one in person or in Webex workshops. Same-day Webex workshops are provided but have limited capacity. Tenants are provided with guidance directed toward completing and filing Answers to unlawful detainer complaints. Self-represented landlords can attend a scheduled series of workshops provided via Webex to educate them about what is required to seek an eviction judgment.

[25] During the COVID-19 pandemic when most or all hearings were by remote video, court staff had to figure out how to use the in-courtroom form indicating the specific need for self-help services. The form obviously could not be handed to a litigant over remote video. The solution was to hold up a QR code to the video camera. The judge told the litigant orally which number or numbers on the form indicated the item(s) needed, and the QR code took the litigant to a

court proceedings to specific self-help services in this way is of great assistance to family law judges in handling their heavy calendars.

LASC has had great success with the educational model. SRLs can move relatively seamlessly between group education and individualized assistance when needed. The court offered a total of 2,126 workshops on eviction, probate, and family law topics from June 2020 through July 2021. Follow-up workshops are well-attended. Over a period in which 680 initial divorce workshops were offered, there were 333 second workshops (assistance with court documents in the divorce process) and 116 third workshops (obtaining a default judgment).[26]

5.2.1.2 Using Student Interns to Assist with Self-Help Services

In 2004 LASC created a JusticeCorps program to bolster self-help resources. The JusticeCorps program is affiliated with the federal AmeriCorps program, which provides benefits to people who agree to participate in approved community programs, such as disaster services and education.[27] JusticeCorps recruits college students and recent college graduates to help provide individualized assistance to SRLs in self-help centers. JusticeCorps college students work part-time during the school year or full-time during the summer. Graduates who had a JusticeCorps internship or other volunteer service experience while in college can apply for a one-year full-time fellowship.

JusticeCorps students and graduate fellows are carefully trained by court staff and legal aid partner staff for the subject area in which they will be working, and they work under the supervision and direction of court staff and legal aid staff.[28] "JusticeCorps members answer questions, help litigants complete court paperwork, and assist in workshops that address the requirements of the various stages of family law, evictions, probate and some civil cases – providing in-depth and individualized services to the litigants."[29]

The JusticeCorps program at LASC has been extraordinarily successful and has significantly extended the resources of the court's self-help services. JusticeCorps also creates opportunities for young people to learn about the law and the judicial

landing page with live links to resources for each item, numbered in the same order as on the form. Interview with Kathleen Dixon, Managing Self-Help Att'y, Cal. Superior Ct., L.A. Cnty. (Mar. 9, 2023) (on file with author).

26 Cal. Superior Ct., L.A. Cnty., Self-Help Report 25 (2022) [hereinafter LASC 2022 Self-Help Report].

27 Staff of the Judicial Council of California assisted LASC in obtaining the AmeriCorps grant. Because of the success of the JusticeCorps program in LASC, Judicial Council staff helped five Bay Area Superior Courts and San Diego Superior Court launch JusticeCorps programs following the model created in LASC. Interview with Kathleen Dixon, Managing Self-Help Att'y, Cal. Superior Ct., L.A. Cnty. (Aug. 12, 2023) (on file with author).

28 Details of the training for JusticeCorps interns and fellows are described at *infra* Section 5.2.1.1.

29 LASC 2022 Self-Help Report, *supra* note 26, at 41.

system and prepares them for careers in the legal field. JusticeCorps at LASC has more than 2,000 alumni.

An important part of the success of the JusticeCorps program is the high standard of service and professionalism to which participants are held. JusticeCorps members wear uniforms and badges. After their training, students officially become part of JusticeCorps by taking an oath administered by a judge of the court during a ceremony to which their families and friends are invited. They promise to "bring Americans together to strengthen our communities," to take action in the face of apathy, to persevere in the face of adversity, and to "get things done" in commitment to "the ideal of equal access to justice for all."[30]

5.2.1.3 Addressing Language Access

LASC provides interpreter services to litigants in over 255 languages.[31] Providing interpreters during court proceedings is not enough. Language access is important for users of the court website, for SRLs using self-help services, and for litigants seeking assistance from the clerk's office or other court staff.

The JusticeCorps program, described above, recruits students who speak another language in their homes. These young people provide a language lifeline for SRLs in the court's self-help program. The court also provides a supplementary salary stipend for court staff with language skills sufficient to allow them to answer the questions of litigants who speak a language other than English. More recently, the court put in place remote telephonic interpreter assistance. Court users identify their spoken language on "I Speak" cards, and they are connected to an interpreter from an outside organization who interprets live through the telephone. This service is provided in self-help center intake counters and clerks' walk-up counters and over the phone through call centers.[32]

[30] The full text of the JusticeCorps oath reads:

> I will get things done for America to make our people safer, smarter, and healthier.
> I will bring Americans together to strengthen our communities.
> Faced with apathy, I will take action.
> Faced with conflict, I will seek common ground.
> Faced with adversity, I will persevere.
> I will carry this commitment with me this year and beyond.
> I am an AmeriCorps member. . . .
> And I am going to get things done.
> As a member of JusticeCorps, I pledge myself to the ideal of equal access to justice for all.

I found the oath so inspiring that I framed a large copy in the reception area of the office of the Presiding Judge. I thought judges and court staff would be reenergized by recalling these ideals.

[31] CAL. SUPERIOR CT., L.A. CNTY., BIENNIAL REPORT 2021–2022, at 22 (2022) [hereinafter LASC BIENNIAL REPORT 2021–2022].

[32] *Id.*

5.2.2 *Leveraging Electronic Resources*

5.2.2.1 Electronic Resources Adjacent to Self-Help Services

Prior to 2020, most self-help services were provided in person. Over time, the information and assistance provided on the LASC website grew, but the court primarily focused on in-person services for SRLs. Although court forms were available online, and the court's self-help centers had computers available for litigants to use to fill out forms while in the self-help facility, most SRLs chose to fill out paper forms. Court staff and legal aid partners who assisted with self-help services generally did not encourage SRLs to use the computers provided (even when completed forms could be filed electronically). As stated by the LASC Managing Self-Help Attorney, who has served in that position since 2002, most staff and legal aid professionals "would not accept that poor people could use computers."[33]

COVID-19 changed this complacency. During the pandemic, most services had to be delivered by remote video or by telephone. If SRLs could use a computer, they were able to have their work checked or ask a question about a specific form by sharing their document electronically with the person assisting them. Staff learned that many SRLs had or could develop computer literacy. Now staff and legal aid professionals working to assist SRLs in person are trained to try to encourage use of the computers provided in the self-help center. Their experience is that most people can use them.

Use of computers by SRLs streamlines the self-help process. If SRLs can use a computer, they can use the court's online resources, either instructional material on the court website or live educational training modules delivered remotely. These resources do not require a trip to a courthouse. Moreover, computer use by SRLs attending in-person training allows for easier review of forms by court staff, correction of forms by the SRL based on the comments of the reviewer, and ultimately filing with the court.

Of course, an SRL may not have access to a computer outside of a courthouse self-help center. The City and LASC public library systems have stepped up to meet that need, and directions for access to library services are featured on the court website. The City of Los Angeles' Public Library Tech2go program allows an adult with a library card to borrow a Google Chromebook and internet hotspot from the library for up to six months. All Los Angeles County public libraries have computer workstations for public use and allow adults with a library card in good standing to borrow a Laptop and Hotspot Kit for three weeks with an option to renew.

[33] Interview with Dixon, *supra* note 27.

5.2.2.2 Website Innovation: "Gina" the Traffic Avatar

In 2016 LASC pioneered providing online services for traffic court litigants using an avatar we named Gina. Gina is an animated cartoon of a woman who serves as a virtual clerk. She greets users and offers assistance in five languages.

First, she helps users locate information printed on their traffic citation. Her instructions are both verbal and transcribed. Once the litigant inputs the unique number of their traffic citation, the court's computer system locates the ticket. Then Gina offers specific options for the litigant. Persons who are eligible for traffic school are told about this option and how to comply with and document the traffic school requirements. An opportunity to set up a payment plan is offered to those who have not previously defaulted on a payment plan. Litigants are told they have an option to continue their hearing date and that they can respond by filing a statement in opposition to the citation in lieu of appearing in court. In each instance, options are clearly explained verbally and in writing simultaneously, and users type the letter or number of the option to indicate their choice. Further instructions follow based on a user's choices.

Gina has been successful, providing assistance that SRLs can and do use and consequently reducing the burdens of in-person appearances, both for SRLs and for the court. She has helped as many as 4,000 people per week. By allowing online payment plans to be established without judicial involvement and by creating the traffic avatar function on the court website, wait times for traffic litigants seeking in-person advice were reduced from hours to an average of twelve minutes. This was hugely significant for litigants. Previously, traffic court litigants had to miss work on one or more days to accomplish a fairly simple traffic court transaction.

5.2.2.3 Online Dispute Resolution

LASC, together with Los Angeles County, has built a seemingly well-designed online dispute resolution (ODR) resource for low-dollar amount cases.[34] The ODR architecture allows parties to begin a negotiation by chat between or among themselves, provides helpful prompts to assist parties in thinking about what to say in making an offer or demand and allows documents to be uploaded and displayed to the opposing party. Importantly, parties are given an option to request that a live mediator, appearing remotely, assist in the negotiation. The participation of a neutral, when requested, helps ensure an even playing field in the negotiation even when one party is more sophisticated than the other.

[34] In California, "institutional filers" are precluded from using the small claims courts because of a restriction providing that a person or entity cannot file more than two small claims cases per year that seek more than $2,500. Cal. Civ. Code § 116.231. In addition, small claims litigants are not allowed to be represented by counsel.

Use of ODR is not mandatory for LASC small claims cases.[35] The ODR platform was used by litigants in 1,400 small claims cases in the period February 2021 through July 2022.[36] To those outside the LASC system, this may seem like a large number. But in fiscal year 2021–22 there were over 22,000 small claims cases filed in Los Angeles County.[37] Thus, only 5 percent of small claims litigants even tried to use the ODR platform. And only 2 percent of small claims cases were settled using the ODR platform.[38]

One problem for use of ODR in the context of small claims cases is the difficulty of notifying parties of the availability of ODR. The court is able to email small claims plaintiffs and encourage them to reach out to the defendant to obtain an agreement to use ODR. But the court does not have access to the Defendant's email. Therefore, it is up to the plaintiff to decide to participate in ODR and then to contact the defendant to explain the ODR resource and encourage the defendant to use it.

Another likely difficulty is the inability of the court to design ODR prompts that address the facts relevant to a particular small claims case. Small claims can involve almost any area of civil law, from real estate to construction defect to the Uniform Commercial Code to tort to contract.[39] Unless a mediator becomes involved, it is likely to be difficult for the parties to evaluate what damages are recoverable and what facts are needed to prove a claim.

The problem of low usage of ODR for small claims cases may have a more fundamental explanation. LASC also developed an ODR platform specifically designed to allow parents in divorce proceedings to negotiate the terms of their parenting plan without having to meet face-to-face. No mediator services are annexed to this ODR tool, but if the parents agree to a plan, the program generates a parenting plan agreement that can be filed for approval by the court. Even where both sides agreed to participate in the negotiation through ODR, a settlement was achieved in only 15 percent of cases.[40]

5.2.2.4 Electronic Guidance for Completion of Court Forms

"Guide and File" was created by Tyler Technologies to help SRLs complete court forms. The user answers specific questions and the answers are used by the

35 By contrast, a Utah pilot project has made use of ODR a mandatory prerequisite in small claims cases. Utah Sup. Ct. Standing Order No. 13 (2018) (revised Jan. 27, 2021).

36 LASC Biennial Report 2021–2022, *supra* note 31, at 39.

37 *Id.* at 47.

38 *Id.* at 39.

39 Debt collection cases ordinarily are not litigated in small claims court in California because of the limit on the number of cases one litigant can file in a year. *See supra* note 38.

40 LASC Biennial Report 2021–2022, *supra* note 31, at 39.

computer program to populate a form that can be electronically filed with the court. The great advantage of the design is that the end product is a document that complies with all court filing requirements.

In fiscal year 2020–21, 980 Guide and File interviews for filing an initial request for divorce were completed by Los Angeles County litigants.[41] But in that fiscal year there were over 29,000 filings for marital dissolution in Los Angeles.[42] In 2020–21, litigants completed 860 requests for domestic violence restraining orders using Guide and File,[43] but over 14,000 such requests were filed.[44]

Customer satisfaction surveys show that most users who complete a Guide and File interview process have a high degree of satisfaction.[45] However, only about one-third of Guide and File interviews that are started by LASC litigants are actually completed.[46] Guide and File interviews can take an hour or two to complete.

5.2.2.5 Addressing Language Access in the Electronic Environment

The court obtained grants to be able to translate portions of the court website into the top five non-English languages used in Los Angeles County – Spanish, Mandarin, Armenian, Korean, and Vietnamese. But information the court provides to SRLs in written form, whether in English or in another language spoken in Los Angeles County, may not be understandable to many people who need court assistance if they have a low level of written language literacy in their native language.

As described above, Gina, the traffic avatar, provides both written and verbal guidance for traffic matters. The court believes that one of the reasons for Gina's success is that she addresses both language and language literacy. The court's self-help educational modules delivered online now also provide information simultaneously in writing and verbally. In addition, the court incorporates icons as nonverbal communication signals, an innovation supported by the research of the National Center for State Courts (NCSCs).[47]

41 LASC 2022 Self-Help Report, *supra* note 26, at 32.

42 Cal. Jud. Council, 2023 Court Statistics Report: Statewide Caseload Trends 138 (2023) [hereinafter 2023 CA Court Statistics Report].

43 LASC 2022 Self-Help Report, *supra* note 26, at 32.

44 2023 CA Court Statistics Report, *supra* note 42, at 138.

45 Cal. Superior Ct., L.A. Cnty., Guide & File Report 15–16 (2022).

46 *Id.* at 22.

47 IAALS has published a guide for effective communication with SRLs, which recommends including advice on very basic issues (such as finding a quiet place to complete forms) and using line drawings to provide a visual roadmap to step-by-step instructions. Lois R. Lupica, Inst. Advancement Am. Legal Sys., Guidelines for Creating Effective Self-Help Information (2019), https://iaals.du.edu/sites/default/files/documents/publications/guidelines_for_creating_effective_self-help_information.pdf (last accessed Feb. 14, 2025).

5.3 LESSONS LEARNED FROM LASC'S SELF-HELP EXPERIENCE THAT MAY BE TRANSFERABLE TO LOW-COST LEGAL REPRESENTATION

This section elaborates on what LASC has learned about leveraging resources to assist SRLs, how to address language access and language literacy, the central importance of early fact-gathering to legal assistance, and the possibility that procedural and substantive law reform can help to close the access-to-justice gap. These insights may be useful to reformers seeking to improve delivery of cost-effective representation to low-income litigants.

5.3.1 *Leveraging Human Resources by Involving Nonlawyers*

Legal representation might achieve economies by incorporating an educational service model similar to that used by LASC early in representation (after initial intake) or at later stages of the representation process, particularly if the educational service model is supplemented with supervised resources similar to JusticeCorps. The parameters governing the assistance nonlawyers are allowed to provide in a court-annexed self-help setting may or may not be appropriate when legal representation is provided, and the author expresses no view on that issue. However, it may be useful to explain the accepted boundaries for provision of court self-help services.

Guidelines for court employees or contract workers providing court-annexed self-help services are derivative of the ethical restrictions that guide how a judicial officer may advise litigants. Neutrality is critical. A judge may not provide assistance to one side in litigation that the judge would withhold from the other side. Judicial ethics rules in California provide: "To ensure impartiality and fairness to all parties, a judge must be objective and open-minded. ... It is not a violation of this Rule, however, for a judge to make reasonable accommodations to ensure pro se litigants the opportunity to have their matters fairly heard."[48]

Translated into the self-help context, the neutrality requirement necessitates that, if LASC provides self-help services in a particular subject area, it must provide assistance to both plaintiffs and defendants. For example, LASC provides self-help services for both self-represented landlords and self-represented tenants in eviction cases. Further, individual guidance should be provided in a manner that maintains the appearance of court neutrality. As stated in the California Administrative Office of the Courts' Guidelines for the Operation of Self-Help Centers in California Trial Courts:

> Services are standardized in that self-help center staff should give the same answer to a question regardless of who asks the question. For example, they can tell a litigant that a declaration needs to be completed and may provide guidance on what

[48] Model Code of Jud. Conduct r. 2.2 cmt. 1, 4 (Am. Bar Ass'n, 2020).

> kinds of facts a court would need in order to decide the issues. The staff may ask appropriate questions to assist in clarifying the facts, and otherwise promote a focus on facts relevant to the court. But the declaration is in the litigant's own words.[49]

In addition to neutrality, competence is essential. A court must provide accurate information when it provides guidance to litigants. If self-help staff advises a litigant that they do not need to complete a particular section on a court-approved form, other court staff should not reject the form as incomplete and the judge should not withhold the relief requested by the litigant on the ground that the form was incomplete. Of course, the point is not that self-help staff can bind a judicial officer. Rather, self-help staff must be adequately trained so that they only provide assistance that is supported by law, court rules, and any local judicial practice.

California guidelines for self-help services require that a self-help attorney oversee the work of nonattorney staff and that a "managing attorney should be responsible for the oversight of all the legal assistance and education provided to the public."[50] The guidelines encourage the use of experienced nonattorney staff so long as they are trained and have access to an attorney:

> Deployment of experienced nonattorney staff to multiple court locations to provide direct services to the public is an excellent way to leverage personnel as long as they are properly qualified and can communicate with at least one attorney working concurrently at one of the court's other self-help center locations who is available for timely consultation.[51]

Training and experience requirements specified in the California guidelines include, *inter alia*: five years' relevant experience for the self-help managing attorney;[52] two years' relevant experience for staff attorneys;[53] for nonattorneys, a high school diploma and two years' experience working with a licensed attorney or three years working for a California court plus a minimum of twenty hours additional training in the relevant area of the law where assistance is provided.[54] Courts are allowed to substitute equivalent experience and training in "appropriate situations."[55]

JusticeCorps volunteers in LASC self-help centers are supervised by LASC staff attorneys or by self-help attorneys provided by legal aid partners. Full-time JusticeCorps Graduate Fellows, who will serve a minimum of 1,700 hours over the course of a year, initially receive two full weeks of training. Then new fellows shadow returning fellows and receive on-the-job training while continuing

49 California Self-Help Guidelines, *supra* note 16, at 7.
50 *Id.* at 11–12.
51 *Id.* at 13.
52 *Id.* at 14.
53 *Id.* at 15.
54 *Id.* at 16.
55 *Id.*

additional training on five Friday afternoons. Additional trainings are added as needed or for enrichment throughout the year. Undergraduate student JusticeCorps members receive most of their training on weekends because they are all full-time college students. They are trained over weekends in September and October with additional weekend follow-up training in January. After at least three full days of training, they begin shadowing staff and being coached onsite while weekend training sessions continue.[56]

LASC has seventy-six full-time court employees who provide self-help services. Of these, twenty-four are attorneys. In addition, self-help services are provided by forty legal aid partner employees working in nine courthouses. In addition, thirty-two full-time JusticeCorps fellows and about seventy part-time JusticeCorps students work under the supervision of LASC employees and legal aid partner employees.[57]

California self-help guidelines provide that "when a litigant cannot be effectively assisted in the court self-help center, prompt referral to appropriate legal assistance should be made whenever possible."[58]

LASC would gladly refer self-help clients to lawyers, publicly funded or otherwise, if those resources were available. Court self-help services are a stop-gap measure, and courts would gratefully redeploy self-help resources to court adjudicatory functions if no-cost or low-cost attorney representation made SRLs vanish. But as circumstances now present themselves, LASC has experimented to make self-help assistance efficient and accessible. Perhaps our innovations can be adapted to make attorney representation more economical.

5.3.2 *Recognizing that Electronic Resources Can Assist Socioeconomically Disadvantaged Individuals*

Experience during the pandemic taught LASC that traditional assumptions about the computer literacy of low-income clients and the availability of computer resources may no longer pose as significant a barrier to reliance on electronic resources as once thought. For attorneys, review of documents or forms shared by a client electronically is likely to be less time-consuming than one-on-one in-person review sessions (both for the legal adviser and for the client).

However, electronic tools must be developed to accommodate individuals with limited language literacy. The principal motivating factor for LASC's creation of Gina, the traffic avatar, was to attempt to assist persons with limited language literacy. Depending on the community served, those seeking to provide low-cost legal assistance may have to address providing service in multiple languages. But all

[56] Interview with Kathleen Dixon, Managing Self-Help Att'y (Aug. 21, 2023) (on file with author).

[57] Interview with Kathleen Dixon, Managing Self-Help Att'y (Aug. 12, 15, 2023) (on file with author).

[58] California Self-Help Guidelines, *supra* note 16, at 16.

low-cost legal services providers are likely to encounter persons with limited language literacy. Use of interactive avatars, verbal as well as written communication, and guidance through nonverbal cues such as icons are tools that legal services providers should consider in their client communications.

What can be learned from LASC's efforts to help SRLs that resulted in tools that are underutilized, such as LASC's ODR and the Guide and File programs? On the front-end, it is important to involve the intended audience in the development and testing of tools for SRLs.[59] On the back-end, empirical research can provide insights into what does and does not work and why. Unfortunately, courts' priorities are and must be managing their daily operations. There is not a great deal of bandwidth for conducting focus groups or empirical studies.

The NCSC and the Institute for the Advancement of the American Legal System (IAALS) have wonderful advice for courts seeking to improve access to justice.[60] But the substantive and procedural laws of each state are different. Each state is required to translate the factual and legal requirements expressed in laws written for (and mostly by) lawyers into tools that are understandable to a nonlawyer. The questions posed by Guide and File in California were written by lawyers. So were the standard California Judicial Council forms. Even with the good advice of NCSC and IAALS, this translation process does not always succeed in its mission.

5.3.3 *The Importance of Early Identification and Assembly of Relevant Facts*

A large part of the success of Gina, the traffic avatar, is that she can provide options specific to the factual and legal circumstances of a particular person and a specific traffic citation. The first thing Gina does after determining which language the user needs is to prompt the traffic litigant to enter the unique identifying number of the citation they received. With this information and the name of the person to whom the ticket was issued, the court's computer can access data concerning the nature of the citation. This central, basic fact allows the court to advise a litigant of the specific options available to them. Is the person who received the citation eligible for traffic school? Can they be offered a payment plan (or have they previously defaulted)? Are they eligible to ask for an automatic deferred payment (or have they previously deferred)? Can they be offered a continued hearing date (how many times have they previously asked for continuance)? What future hearing dates are available? The decision tree is not complicated, but when the computer has access to the

59 *See, for example*, Katherine Alteneder & Eduardo Gonzalez, *Voices in the Civil Justice System: Learning from Self-Represented Litigants and Their Trusted Intermediaries*, Fla. Comm'n on Access to Civ. Just. (2020), https://www.srln.org/system/files/attachments/Voices%20in%20Civil%20Justice%20System_Florida%20JFA_AltenederGonzalez.pdf (last accessed Feb. 14, 2025).

60 *See, for example*, Lupica, *supra* note 47; *Tiny Chat 33: Illustrated Instructions*, Nat'l Ctr. State Cts. (2020), cdm16501.contentdm.oclc.org/digital/collection/p16501coll2/id/121.

underlying facts that determine the legal options for a particular individual, that person can be given clear-cut choices, not just general information.

The court's first version of the traffic avatar provided only general information about possible options for addressing a traffic ticket – not information specific to the particular individual's available options for resolving *their* traffic ticket. This first version of Gina did not ask for the unique identifying number of the citation or access stored data about the nature of the traffic citation and the individual cited. In order for LASC to have information about a particular traffic citation, it had to invest in technology that created an electronic record of each traffic ticket entered by the police department that issued the citation. To achieve this technology improvement, the court had to coordinate with each of the more than forty-five police departments and other law enforcement entities (such as the California Highway Patrol) that operate within Los Angeles County.

The early, more general approach to assisting traffic litigants was much less successful, even though online options for continuing a hearing date, seeking a payment plan, or resolving the ticket through traffic school were available. When LASC was able to move from an educational model (what do I do *if* I get a ticket) to a transactional model (I *got* a ticket, what do I do), utilization of Gina more than tripled.[61] Without the basic facts that shaped the litigant's legal options, online self-help assistance, even when provided by an avatar, fell short of serving the needs of SRLs.

An important component of the success of the education model of self-help used in family law cases is assigning "homework" to the SRL. The "homework" requires the self-represented family law litigant to organize and compile the core documents and information relevant to the legal issues in a particular person's divorce proceeding. The process helps focus the litigant on the issues that will be important to the divorce proceeding rather than points of animosity about the causes of the divorce. As a matter of policy, court staff requires that the "homework" be completed before allowing an SRL to attend the second-level divorce education module. Self-help staff's guidance to a particular SRL (e.g., what forms are essential) is shaped by knowing the issues that will need to be addressed in the divorce proceeding.

Conversely, lack of information about an SRL's particular circumstance has undermined other efforts to provide effective self-help services. Court administrators for family law services very much wanted to create a "chatbot" to assist litigants. The goal was for the chatbot to be able to answer open-text questions typed in by the user. However, without some level of organized information about a particular SRL's circumstances, the inputs were just too complicated for a chatbot to handle. Despite repeated efforts, court administrators only achieved 60 percent accuracy – meaning the chatbot was wrong about 40 percent of the

[61] Interview with Snorri Ogata, former Chief Info. Off., Cal. Superior Ct., L.A. Cnty. (Aug. 15, 2023) (on file with author).

time.[62] The chances of providing erroneous advice simply were too great to allow implementation of a chatbot in this context.[63]

It should not be surprising that gathering the facts relevant to a legal dispute is a critical element of providing appropriate options to a litigant. After all, in most substantial civil litigation, discovery is the most expensive part of the pretrial litigation process.[64] The author of this chapter has argued elsewhere that in categories of simple, repetitive litigation, mandatory, automatic disclosure of specified documents and information should be required at the outset of litigation.[65] Especially in simple, repetitive litigation in which the plaintiff ordinarily controls all information necessary to prove the claim presented (e.g., collections, eviction, and judicial foreclosure cases), there is no reason to require a self-represented defendant to use the adversarial processes of discovery to obtain relevant information about the case.[66]

LASC's experience in assisting SRLs demonstrates that effective guidance is optimized when the core facts on which the outcome of the case will turn are available to the person or technology tool providing assistance early in the litigation. It seems logical that the costs of providing effective legal representation to a low-income individual likewise will be lower if counsel (or any person providing legal guidance) can develop means to obtain core facts at the front-end of the representation.

Applying this principle to simple, repetitive litigation in which the plaintiff ordinarily controls all information necessary to prove the claim, it makes sense to explore policies that would require plaintiffs to make disclosures when they file a complaint or, perhaps, to attach relevant documents to the complaint. California and Oregon have moved in that direction.[67]

5.3.4 *Reducing Legal Complexity*

As discussed above, ODR and Guide and File have had limited utilization in LASC's experience. Courts have made efforts to assist SRLs by providing plain

[62] Interview with Snorri Ogata, former Chief Info. Off., Cal. Superior Ct., L.A. Cnty. (Feb. 16, 2023) (on file with author).

[63] The court does employ chatbots to answer basic questions such as service hours, appointments, case status, and how to obtain particular types of assistance. LASC 2022 Self-Help Report, *supra* note 26, at 38.

[64] Nicholas M. Pace & Laura Zakaras, RAND Inst. Civ. Just., Where the Money Goes: Understanding Litigant Expenditures for Producing Electronic Discovery 1 (2012).

[65] Carolyn B. Kuhl & William F. Highberger, A *Unified Theory of Civil Case Management*, 107 Judicature 35, 40 (2023).

[66] *Id.*

[67] *See* Cal. Civ. Code § 1788.58 (requiring the complaint in a collection action brought by a "debt buyer" to allege specific facts concerning the debt and the non-payment default and requiring that a copy of the contract be attached to the complaint); Or. Unif. Trial Ct. r. 5.180(b) (requiring the complaint in an action by a debt buyer or a debt collector to attach a completed Consumer Debt Collection Disclosure Statement).

language forms but have found that there is an irreducible complexity in substantive and procedural law that makes straightforward forms difficult to achieve.

Consider that the first issue faced by a person in California seeking a court's protection from violent acts of another is which of four different types of restraining orders can provide the legal protection the person needs. The four types of restraining orders – (1) elder or dependent adult abuse protective order, (2) domestic violence restraining order, (3) civil harassment restraining order, and (4) workplace violence restraining order – fall under the jurisdiction of the probate courts, the family law courts and the civil courts, respectively (with workplace violence restraining orders considered a civil court matter). Each type of restraining order has procedures that allow a temporary restraining order to be issued ex parte – a necessary but complex process in and of itself. Some of the distinctions between the types of available relief are so fine that SRLs in LASC sometimes have been sent from the civil filing window to the family law filing window and back again.[68] On the California Judicial Council website, the forms for these types of relief are organized separately: fifty-seven forms for "Domestic Violence Protection," thirty-three forms for "Elder or Dependent Adult Abuse," and thirty-five forms for "Civil Harassment Protection."[69]

Of course, there are relevant distinctions in the circumstances that may give rise to the need for legal protections provided by a restraining order. But are all the fine legal distinctions that have evolved by looking at these remedies separately worth the cost of making the remedies less accessible? I do not pretend to know the answer, but it seems to be a question worthy of study.

Perhaps instead of struggling to simplify complex laws by translating them for use by nonlawyers, we should consider simplifying the law to make remedies and defenses more accessible to SRLs and to reduce costs of providing representation. As suggested above, procedural reform specific to some remedies such as debt collection and eviction (e.g., requiring plaintiffs to provide evidence to prove specific elements of the case at the time the case is filed), may be a path to less complex and costly access to justice. Substantive law in these high-volume cases should be examined as well.

5.4 CONCLUSION

Court-provided self-help resources are by no means a panacea. But those interested in regulatory reform of the legal profession and those interested in cost-effective

[68] To address this untenable situation, LASC shifted the filing and processing of all *ex parte* requests for restraining orders into a single restraining order center, which provided intake, self-help advice, and immediate access to Commissioners who ruled on the *ex parte* submissions regardless of type.

[69] Some of the "forms" are information sheets relevant to a particular issue or form.

representation of litigants in areas of high-volume litigation may find the courts' self-help experiences instructive.

Courts have learned to leverage resources to assist SRLs in a variety of ways. Rather than assigning one staff person to work with one SRL, LASC utilizes an effective education model. With this model, groups of litigants on both sides of certain case types can be helped simultaneously. The court also utilized AmeriCorps funding to create a JusticeCorps cadre of undergraduates and recent college graduates who supplement court self-help services. The pandemic provided a push to leverage the use of computers to assist SRLs who formerly were assumed to be unwilling or unable to use such technology.

Courts also recognize that language access requires more than just relying on Google Translate. LASC invested in a language line to serve court users at self-help and public counter locations. Nevertheless, written language translations may fail to provide for the needs of those who have limited literacy in their native language. Verbal guidance by an avatar or a voice-over provides for greater comprehension than written instructions alone, especially when unfamiliar concepts need to be explained. Use of visual symbols such as icons also provides more effective wayfinding through multilayered material.

LASC has had greater success interacting with SRLs when it can provide answers based on facts specific to the particular litigant's circumstances rather than advice about a general area of law. Early assembly of facts relevant to a litigant's legal problem is critical to more effective guidance and early case evaluation.

Not all seemingly well-designed self-help tools have worked. When courts or others develop tools to interact with individuals seeking help with a legal problem, it is important to involve prospective users in the design. Empirical evaluation of what works and what doesn't is key to determining how to make a better tool to assist litigants.

Finally, it may be time to think differently about the interface between the law and the human experience of individuals. Instead of struggling to translate complex legal principles into concepts that nonlawyers can understand, and instead of acquiescing in the current expense of litigation, perhaps efforts should be directed to simplifying substantive law and tailoring procedure to the fair presentation and adjudication of less complex cases.

6

Civil [Justice] Engineering

Leveraging the Tools of Community, Research, and Fiscal Impact to Build Bridges to Justice

Neil Steinkamp and Samantha DiDomenico

Civil access-to-justice reform pursued through a financially focused, stakeholder-informed approach can drive transformational change. We present a framework and set of techniques, which together we dub "civil justice engineering," for developing effective, scalable policy and procedure for the expansion of civil access to justice informed by qualitative and quantitative data, financial analysis, program evaluation, and stakeholder engagement.

Our framework has been shaped by our work at Stout Risius Ross, LLC (Stout), a global, advisory firm specializing in corporate finance, accounting and transaction advisory, valuation, financial disputes, claims, and investigations. We serve a range of clients, from public corporations to privately held companies in numerous industries. Stout's Transformative Change Consulting practice is a recognized leader in the civil legal aid community and has completed projects involving:

- Strategy consulting for issues relating to access to justice;
- Organizing/facilitating stakeholder listening sessions and focus groups;
- Managing transformative change projects and workflows;
- Operational consulting related to data systems and processes, organizational culture, and employee relations;
- Economic impact assessments and research for civil legal services initiatives;
- Nonprofit budget development, review, and recommendations;
- Cost–benefit and impact analyses for nonprofit initiatives and activities;
- Data-driven program evaluation and implementation; and
- Dispute consulting and damages analyses for low-income individuals and nonprofit organizations.

Stout has provided consulting services to more than forty jurisdictions across the country related to programs assisting people experiencing civil legal issues. In each of these jurisdictions, Stout seeks to understand the local civil justice system, how residents interact with it, and the spectrum of information, assistance, and civil legal resources available for residents – ranging from online legal information, guided interviews and forms, supervised nonlawyers, mediation, community dispute resolution centers, advice and counsel, extensive legal services, and other forms of assistance.

Stout is currently retained as the Independent Evaluator for eviction right to counsel (or access to counsel) programs in Cleveland, Connecticut, Maryland, and Milwaukee. It has conducted eviction right to counsel fiscal return on investment or cost analyses and independent expert reports for advocates, coalitions, bar associations, or government agencies in Baltimore, Broward County, Chattanooga, Delaware, Detroit, Los Angeles County and City, Miami-Dade County, Newark, New York City, New York (outside of New York City), Pennsylvania, Philadelphia, and South Carolina. Many of these engagements have contributed to landmark legislation being passed.

Following the release of Stout's reports in Baltimore, New York City, Philadelphia, Delaware, and Detroit, eviction right to counsel legislation was enacted. In these engagements, Stout worked closely with funders/potential funders, legal services organizations, rental property owners, academics studying housing and eviction, government agencies and the continuum of care, nonprofits serving low-income residents, community organizers, and impacted residents.

Core to our approach is the idea that creating opportunity for change is as much about the analyses and engagement method as it is about the quantitative evaluation of a particular result. By engaging a broad range of local stakeholders, collecting and integrating quantitative and qualitative information, and seeking regular feedback as analyses are developed, civil justice engineering can be used to develop cost–benefit analyses and evaluation techniques that form the basis for collaboration and consensus, both prerequisites for meaningful and durable reforms that expand access to civil justice.

This chapter introduces the civil justice engineering framework and shows how it can further a wide range of access to civil justice initiatives, such as civil right to counsel, court efforts to assist self-represented litigants, an expanded role for nonlawyers or limited-license legal practitioners, effective utilization of brief services and advice programs, and justice initiatives to address racial inequity.

6.1 SITUATING CIVIL JUSTICE ENGINEERING

6.1.1 *Policy-Based Access-to-Justice Reform in the United States: A Brief Overview*

The United States has faced significant challenges in enacting broad, policy-based access to civil justice reform. These challenges arise from a confluence of institutional, political, fiscal, and cultural factors that can impede the development of comprehensive, sustainable reforms. In our experience, obstacles to scalable, sustainable, transformative policy reform have included but are not limited to:

- A propensity for the development of reactive interventions intended to respond to crises rather than a systemic assessment of causes;
- A failure to appreciate the costs of responding to crises when individuals attempt to navigate civil justice issues unassisted;
- An overemphasis on doctrinaire approaches to systemic challenges that require complex solutions;
- A lack of appreciation for the diverse demographic and socioeconomic backgrounds of those seeking assistance in civil justice matters;
- Political divisiveness and entrenched advocacy that impede achieving consensus on broad, scalable, sustainable policy reform;
- Prioritizing short-term results in lieu of investing in long-term, preventative policy change;
- Paralysis arising from the perceived daunting scale of systemic challenges;
- Anxiety and fear arising from the uncertainties of reform; and
- Failure to implement incremental, iterative policy change, instead searching for an immediate, universal solution.

In our experience, the judicial branch specifically can also experience unique obstacles to developing broad reform designed to sustainably improve civil access to justice, such as:

- Concern and frustration stemming from previous attempts to share data with various stakeholders, often related to misuse and misinterpretation of court data;
- Concerns surrounding data quality and data integrity that may reflect poorly on the court or its staff and may compromise any analysis of the data; and
- Apprehension that access-to-justice reforms might slow down case processing and disrupt court operations.

These barriers to change can be overcome. We have observed transformative change when there is an emphasis on incremental progress, acknowledging that no singular policy can comprehensively address all aspects of complex social and justice issues.

6.1.2 *An Introductory Example: The Eviction Right to Counsel Movement in the United States*

One recent example of sustained, scaled, transformative change in civil access to justice in the United States has come from the eviction right to counsel movement, particularly over the last ten years.

In 2015, eviction defendants across America lacked the right to legal representation even after decades of advocacy by tenant organizers, advocates, and other stakeholders. In 2017, New York City passed historic eviction right to counsel legislation.[1] This legislation offered full, extended representation for *all* eligible tenants (individuals with an annual gross household income not over 200 percent of the federal poverty level).[2]

The reform's impact was profound, made evident through New York City's Office of Civil Justice report in 2021, which found that 84 percent of represented tenants were able to stay in their homes.[3] Additionally, during implementation, areas with an eviction-focused right to counsel experienced a reduction in eviction filings of over 30 percent.[4]

The New York City eviction right to counsel legislation sparked a movement that has resulted in legislation being passed in seventeen cities, four states, and one county, where tenants now have a right to counsel or are guaranteed access to counsel for eviction proceedings.[5] The initial results in those jurisdictions demonstrate the impact of this significant expansion of access to civil justice. Based on available data from several jurisdictions, when clients are seeking to avoid an eviction judgment, 76 percent to 79 percent of clients receiving extensive services[6] have been successful in that aim.[7] Of those clients seeking to stay in their homes, 70 percent to 79 percent of clients receiving extensive services have been successful.[8] Of those clients seeking to secure time to find other housing, 42 percent to 88 percent of clients receiving extensive services have been successful.[9]

This expansion in access to civil justice has emerged in jurisdictions with strong tenant organizing movements as well as those with little or no organizing around tenant rights. Change has occurred in the largest of cities as well as smaller cities across various regions (East Coast, West Coast, Midwest, and Mountain Regions). So too has it occurred in places with significant social safety net responses to housing instability and homelessness, as well as in places with a lack of such supportive services.[10]

1 Kriston Kapps, *New York City Guarantees a Lawyer to Every Resident Facing Eviction*, Bloomberg (Aug. 14, 2017, 7:00 AM), https://www.bloomberg.com/news/articles/2017-08-14/new-york-ensures-right-to-counsel-for-all-eviction-cases?embedded-checkout=true (last accessed Feb. 14, 2025).

2 N.Y.C. Admin. Code tit. 26, §§ 26-1301–26-1306.

3 Andrew Scherer, *The Case against Summary Eviction Proceedings: Progress as Racism and Oppression*, 53 Seton Hall L. Rev. 1 (2022).

4 *Id.*

5 Nat'l Coal. for a Civil Right to Coun., *The Right to Counsel for Tenants Facing Eviction: Enacted Legislation*, NCCRC (Nov. 2023), http://civilrighttocounsel.org/uploaded_files/283/RTC_Enacted_Legislation_in_Eviction_Proceedings_FINAL.pdf (last accessed Feb. 14, 2025).

6 "Extensive services" typically means that the lawyer assisting the client works with the client through the final resolution of the dispute.

7 The data underlying these findings are on file with the authors.

8 The data underlying these findings are on file with the authors.

9 The data underlying these findings are on file with the authors.

10 Nat'l Coal. for a Civil Right to Couns., *supra* note 5.

As in New York City, the eviction right to counsel movement and reforms in other areas of civil access to justice have been a decades-long endeavor. Organizers, community-based organizations, civil legal services organizations, bar associations, courts, and countless local stakeholders continue to be the backbone of transformative change and local eviction reform in many communities.

Evaluative reports in these jurisdictions, several completed by the authors, have demonstrated the importance and impact of tenants having representation,[11] but they have also demonstrated the need for iterative implementation techniques, data collection, stakeholder engagement, and the development of a spectrum of resources to assist tenants and rental property owners navigating rental housing disputes.

In this chapter, we discuss how our work has contributed to the efforts of local stakeholders. This should not take away from the extraordinary work of so many local stakeholders who work together to pursue ecosystem change in their communities. To the contrary, as we describe, it is only from the participation, leadership, and engagement of these stakeholders that such change becomes possible. Nor should the pages that follow be taken to suggest that the only means of achieving change is through the methods we describe, or that cost or benefit analyses should be emphasized to the exclusion of equity considerations. Rather, there are many ways in which reform has been, and will be, achieved. We simply and humbly offer our experience as a contribution to, and consideration for, further efforts surrounding local reforms related to access to civil justice.

6.2 AN OVERVIEW OF THE CIVIL JUSTICE ENGINEERING FRAMEWORK: COMPLEMENTING ADVOCACY AND STAKEHOLDER ENGAGEMENT WITH FINANCIAL ANALYSIS

For many jurisdictions, the development of a comprehensive, independent cost–benefit study has informed policymakers and other stakeholders about the potential costs and savings of providing the eviction right to counsel. The development of such studies utilized an innovative combination of academic scholarship and community and stakeholder feedback with the application of quantitative and financial analysis with qualitative context.

6.2.1 *Social Return on Investment and Cost–Benefit Analysis*

A core concept in our civil justice engineering framework is social return on investment (SROI). SROI is a framework used to measure the social and economic value that may be created by an organization or initiative. It aims to assess and

[11] Stout's eviction right to counsel evaluation reports can be found at *Eviction Right to Counsel*, STOUT, https://www.stout.com/en/services/transformative-change-consulting/eviction-right-to-counsel-resources (last accessed Mar. 18, 2024).

quantify the positive impact that an activity generates in relation to the resources invested, going beyond traditional financial measures by incorporating social outcomes into the evaluation.[12]

Closely related to but distinct from SROI is cost–benefit analysis (CBA). CBA is a method employed to assess the potential economic impact and benefits of policy reforms or programs. It involves evaluating the costs associated with implementing the policy and comparing them to the expected benefits for the entities funding the program.[13]

CBA is typically only one aspect of a larger strategy for policy reform regarding access to civil justice. In our experience, reform is not typically based solely on whether it is fiscally prudent, but fiscal impacts (both costs and potential benefits) are relevant considerations and can serve as a critical foundation for further dialogue and collaboration.

CBA is not uncontroversial in policymaking and law. Frank Ackerman and Lisa Heinzerling provide an important critique of CBA, particularly when used as the sole justification for policy reform, arguing that "human life, health, and nature cannot be described meaningfully in monetary terms; they are priceless."[14] In keeping with that critique, Richard L. Revesz and Michael L. Livermore suggest an approach to policy reform that blends the use of CBAs with a compassionate, ethical view of the issues being addressed. They write, "[b]ecause of the complex nature of governmental decisions, we have no choice but to deploy complex analytic tools in order to make the best choices possible … [but we] must exercise statistical compassion by recognizing what numbers of lives saved represent: living and breathing human beings, unique, with rich inner lives and an interlocking web of emotional relationships."[15]

In our civil justice work, we use CBA differently. We do not intend to justify reforms with a CBA but rather to inform the dialogue surrounding reform with quantifiable insight and feedback from local stakeholders. A CBA can allow for informed decision-making, efficient resource allocation, transparency in the decision-making process, advocacy potential, and the ability to iteratively evaluate policy impact and foster accountability. But in isolation, a CBA does not account for

[12] Laura Arrillaga-Andreessen & David Hoyt, *Case Study: An Introduction to Social Return on Investment*, Case SI-65, Stan. Grad. Sch. of Bus. (May 28, 2004), https://www.gsb.stanford.edu/faculty-research/case-studies/introduction-social-return-investment (last accessed Feb. 14, 2025).

[13] Tim Stobierski, *How to Do a Cost–Benefit Analysis & Why It's Important*, Harv. Bus. Sch. Online (Sept. 5. 2019), https://online.hbs.edu/blog/post/cost-benefit-analysis (last accessed Feb. 14, 2025).

[14] Frank Ackerman & Lisa Heinzerling, Priceless: On Knowing the Price of Everything and the Value of Nothing 8 (2004).

[15] Richard L. Revesz & Michael A. Livermore, Retaking Rationality: How Cost–Benefit Analysis Can Better Protect the Environment and Our Health 3 (2008).

the ethical arguments for access to justice. For this reason, discussed below, we recommend that a CBA be utilized within a comprehensive and integrated local approach to access to civil justice reform.

CBAs prior to the passage of such reforms (or the evaluation of the implementation of such reforms after passage, and related potential fiscal impact) have been effective, in part, because of both the comprehensive nature of the related reports and analyses as well as the breadth of contribution from local stakeholders. It is as much about *how* such work is conducted as it is about the quantitative result. By engaging a range of local stakeholders, listening to their perspectives, leveraging and reconciling academic scholarship, collecting and integrating quantitative and qualitative information, and seeking regular feedback as analyses and observations are developed, CBAs form the basis for collaboration that can lead to issue convergence in support of expansion of access to civil justice.

6.2.2 *Leveraging Cost–Benefit Analysis Using an Integrated Approach to Access-to-Justice Reform*

Using this framework, we have assisted jurisdictions across the United States in developing estimates of the fiscal impact of reform related to access to civil justice. This approach incorporates quantitative and qualitative components and often begins well before a reform related to access to civil justice is designed or implemented. Key elements of this approach include, but are not limited to:

- Leveraging the importance of localization by learning from local stakeholders regarding their interest in a particular civil justice reform and developing an understanding of the local civil justice ecosystem;
- Assessing the circumstances parties face through engagement with stakeholders, examining their needs and the role a particular reform has in meeting certain needs and addressing certain circumstances;
- Appreciating that person-centered data is imperfect, thus centering the inquiry on the development of reasonable estimates and transparency regarding preliminary measurement techniques and the need for ongoing assessment;
- Identifying and evaluating quantitative elements for analysis of program costs and potential fiscal impact as well as other impacts;
- Integrating supplemental research and observations;
- Developing estimates of program costs;
- Using prior academic scholarship and stakeholder data, developing estimates of reasonably quantifiable fiscal impacts, and identifying qualitative assessments of other impacts that cannot currently be quantified;
- Assessing opportunities for issue convergence; and
- Identifying opportunities for continued, iterative assessment, evaluation, and refinement, as well as identification of complementary reforms.

The remainder of this chapter will demonstrate how applying this framework can amplify and inform the work of pursuing sustainable, scaled access to civil justice initiatives. We do so by identifying and explaining nine core elements of the approach.

6.3 THE ELEMENTS OF CIVIL JUSTICE ENGINEERING

Element #1: Leveraging the importance of localization by learning from local stakeholders regarding their interest in a particular civil justice reform and developing an understanding of the local civil justice ecosystem.

In our experience, local community stakeholders are typically highly aware of injustices and systemic barriers in their community. Instead of developing recommendations based on our impressions of what should be important to the community, we are guided by feedback from local stakeholders.

For example, in Oklahoma City, Legal Aid knew there were transportation barriers to access to justice, particularly for tenants in eviction proceedings. Public transit could be unreliable, and the bus schedules did not always align with the docket calls at court. Tenants would default in eviction cases because of transportation challenges. Legal aid developed data evaluation elements to measure the frequency of transportation issues shared by clients and are planning to use that data to advocate for changes to docket call times and bus schedules.[16]

Consequently, the work of understanding program costs and potential fiscal impacts often starts at early stages of advocacy. At such stages, the comprehensive, inclusive, and intentional approach described below can inform many elements of advocacy beyond the cost of the proposed reform. It can serve to inform program design based on feedback from multiple stakeholders and can assist in developing coalition, collaboration, and opportunities for issue convergence.

Localization has been critical to propel policy reforms involving civil access to justice. While national trends or generalizable findings furnish insights, a variety of local perceptions, practices, procedures, and stakeholders often require that we uniquely consider the circumstances of each jurisdiction.

Localization also can increase local advocacy and prioritization, fostering accountability and investment within the community. With knowledge of their jurisdiction's peculiarities, local policymakers and stakeholders are better equipped to advocate for and invest in policies that effectively cater to the needs of their constituents.

Detractors may posit that localization leads to excessive temporal and resource burdens; however, in our experience the opposite has been the case. National

[16] Relevant data from intake interviews conducted by legal services organizations and related data collection are on file with the authors.

studies often fail to resonate with local communities and policymakers, leading to tepid support, dialogue, and development. Conversely, localized efforts serve as formidable catalysts for broader movements, effectively inspiring other communities to consider similar reforms.

This work needs to be informed by the views and perspectives of many stakeholders and will be inherently imperfect in measurement techniques – measurement techniques that will be centered on the development of reasonable, reliable, credible metrics but that will necessarily rely on a constellation of imperfect data, research, and qualitative feedback. Independence is an important factor, as findings and observations of this work are not motivated by a particular advocacy position. This can be an important consideration for policymakers interested in understanding the civil justice ecosystem and potential costs and fiscal impact of certain reforms.

Our efforts are to *inform* local efforts to pursue reform in an *independent*[17] manner. We rely on local communities to identify priorities for reform, and we seek to independently advise regarding the costs of implementation and the potential fiscal impacts of those reforms.

As we begin our work, we first, and continually, seek to understand the civil justice ecosystem impacted by the proposed reform. Civil legal issues, whether perceived by the individuals involved as "legal" or not, arise locally. They arise for an individual, a household, and a business owner. They arise in a local neighborhood, local community, city, and county, and with local stakeholders, local courts, and local support services. We are mindful that while our unique experience and expertise working with stakeholders in jurisdictions around the country may inform our work and our dialogue, we must begin our work listening to local stakeholders to understand the local ecosystem – both its history and its present.

Residents, business owners (such as rental property owners or lenders), legal services organizations, community organizers and advocates, attorneys, academic institutions, the courts, policymakers, and other community stakeholders are operating in an intricate, intertwined, and interdependent ecosystem.

We observe this interdependence and interconnectedness throughout our work and uniquely in each jurisdiction. For example, if we consider the eviction ecosystem, we must learn how rental property owners (and their counsel), tenants, courts, civil legal aid organizations, emergency rental assistance administrators, community-based organizations, and other public systems (e.g., emergency shelter, foster care, public schools, healthcare, transportation, police) interact with and upon one another, at what cost (financial and otherwise) and to which party.

We appreciate that we will never fully understand each local ecosystem we work in and certainly not to the extent of the local stakeholders we work with. For this

[17] Throughout our work, our independence is meant to convey that we do not have a vested interest in the outcome nor are we motivated by a particular advocacy position.

reason, throughout our work, we remain open to continually learning about the ecosystem and ensuring, to the extent possible, that those insights and observations are intentionally incorporated in our quantitative and qualitative work. To achieve this, we utilize an immersive stakeholder engagement technique.

Element #2: Assessing the circumstances parties face through engagement with stakeholders, examining their needs and the role a particular reform has in meeting certain needs and addressing certain circumstances.

This approach does not necessarily require us to be subject matter experts in eviction, consumer debt, immigration, guardianship, family law, or other matters of civil access to justice. Instead, we approach our work with curiosity and genuine intrigue about the local justice ecosystem and stakeholders – their history, roles, responsibilities, perceptions, experiences, challenges, current resource constraints; the fiscal impacts and constraints that change can have on them; and the overall capacity for change within a resource-constrained environment.

Intentional, inclusive stakeholder engagement creates the opportunity to continually learn about the ecosystem and to create a collaborative environment that establishes or renews connections among stakeholders. As our work progresses, the stakeholders with whom relationships have been built are continuously re-engaged to discuss emerging issues, review progress, and assess new opportunities and challenges.

Our engagement with stakeholders has included but is not limited to:

- Courts;
- Legal services providers;
- Rental property owners;
- Public housing authorities;
- Rental assistance providers;
- 2-1-1 and other community action call centers;
- Coordinated intake service organizations;
- Legal technology hosts and providers;
- Public libraries;
- Community organizers;
- Continuums of Care (CoC);
- Social benefit administrators;
- Employers;
- City, county, and state government agencies;
- Public education and higher education providers;
- Faith communities;
- Community-based organizations;
- Transportation providers;
- Hospitals and healthcare providers; and
- Homelessness service providers.

In focus groups or interviews, participants share their perspectives and lived experiences regarding the subject matter (e.g., clients or constituents facing eviction or housing instability), potential fiscal and personal impacts, identifying common themes across lived experiences, and considering how we may be able to quantify the costs and benefits of regulatory reform.

When considering with whom to engage, inclusivity and diversity is critical. Engaging with stakeholder groups that have varying experiences, roles, power, perspectives, and perceptions informs the understanding of potential fiscal impacts.

For example, civil legal aid organizations are able to share data and experiences regarding the experiences of their clients, their interactions with the courts and counterparties; and the personnel costs of delivering services (e.g., salaries and benefits). Government and social services agencies are often able to share how they are spending public dollars to respond to certain crises experienced by community members that could be reduced if certain reforms related to access to civil justice were implemented. For example, we have engaged with emergency shelter providers and Continuums of Care[18] throughout the country. In every jurisdiction with which we have engaged, these housing social safety net providers share that a portion of people experiencing homelessness and living in shelters have likely experienced eviction in the past and that the eviction contributed to their need for emergency shelter or other services. This draws a connection between eviction and expensive publicly funded social services, and the link is reinforced by research conducted across the country.[19]

Stakeholders who may not support certain reforms should also be engaged to ensure a comprehensive understanding of potential fiscal impacts. We hear from rental property owners about the challenges they face in providing safe and stable housing, the difficulties accessing rental assistance programs as well as the courts, frustrations with the legal process, and the costs they incur from delays arising from disputes with tenants. We also hear about challenging relationships with their tenants and the rental property owner's efforts to assist in reaching resolutions prior to eviction.

The breadth of this stakeholder engagement helps to prevent bias and demonstrates a commitment to an independent assessment of both opportunities and challenges. In addition, it often uncovers and illuminates new findings that can lead to more informed policy decisions and continued stakeholder collaboration.

[18] A continuum of care is "a concept involving an integrated system of care that guides and tracks patient over time through a comprehensive array of health services spanning all levels of intensity of care." C. Evashwick, *Creating the Continuum of Care* 7 Health Matrix 30 (1989). Stout engages with organizations that are part of the local continuum of care to learn about their perspective on the consequences of the eviction process for local residents based on their interaction with people facing housing instability and homelessness.

[19] *See, for example,* Robert Collinson et al., *Eviction and Poverty in American Cities*, 139 Q.J. of Econ. 57 (Feb. 2024) (finding that eviction orders cause increased homelessness in New York and Chicago).

For instance, it is not uncommon for there to be concerns among rental property owners and their lawyers regarding the impact that expanded access to lawyers for tenants may have. However, lawyers representing rental property owners also consistently indicate that they always prefer to work with a represented tenant rather than an unrepresented tenant and that when lawyers are involved on both sides it is more likely that effective outcomes for both parties can be reached, and often more expeditiously than with an unrepresented tenant, particularly in more complex cases. In some jurisdictions, rental property owners have been vocal supporters of eviction right to counsel programs, particularly when appreciating the complexity of the circumstances tenants are encountering, the ways in which lawyers for tenants are able to effectively resolve these matters, and openness to feedback and recommendations from the rental property owner community – but also seek complementary resources such as sustainable, efficient, and effective emergency rental assistance.

Further, the degree to which tenants facing eviction are experiencing substandard housing conditions is often underappreciated by policymakers but well-understood by courts, legal aid attorneys, and property owners/managers. This information asymmetry typically arises because of a previous lack of structured data collection regarding the presence of these substandard housing conditions. The importance of addressing this information asymmetry arose from initial stakeholder engagement, and its prevalence was understood after implementing revised data collection based on that feedback. As a result, we have found that 60 percent to 80 percent of eviction right to counsel clients in jurisdictions around the country report that they are experiencing at least one (and often many) defective conditions in their home.[20] Figure 6.1's data visualizations are examples of how structured data collection and analysis can inform policymakers and other stakeholders regarding complex circumstances clients can be experiencing and the impact legal representation can have when substantive legal issues are present.[21]

Moreover, in many jurisdictions with an eviction right to counsel, a minority of tenants facing eviction seek legal assistance – however, of those that do, 85 percent to 90 percent are involved in complex disputes with the rental property owner, face severe consequences, are at the lowest income levels,[22] and are likely to need social services if they are not able to achieve their housing goals.[23] This finding has

[20] Relevant data are on file with the authors.

[21] It should be noted that this is not reflective of the conditions of all rental housing but rather is a reflection of the complications that may be contributing to why people are seeking legal assistance. This serves to inform policymakers regarding the complications of the cases and vulnerabilities faced by those these programs seek to serve.

[22] The data underlying these findings are on file with the authors.

[23] The potential need for social services arising from harm, trauma, and disruption from the eviction process is well established by a wide range of studies, intake surveys, and reports conducted by those providing such services, and data collected by legal services organizations from those who are facing such circumstances.

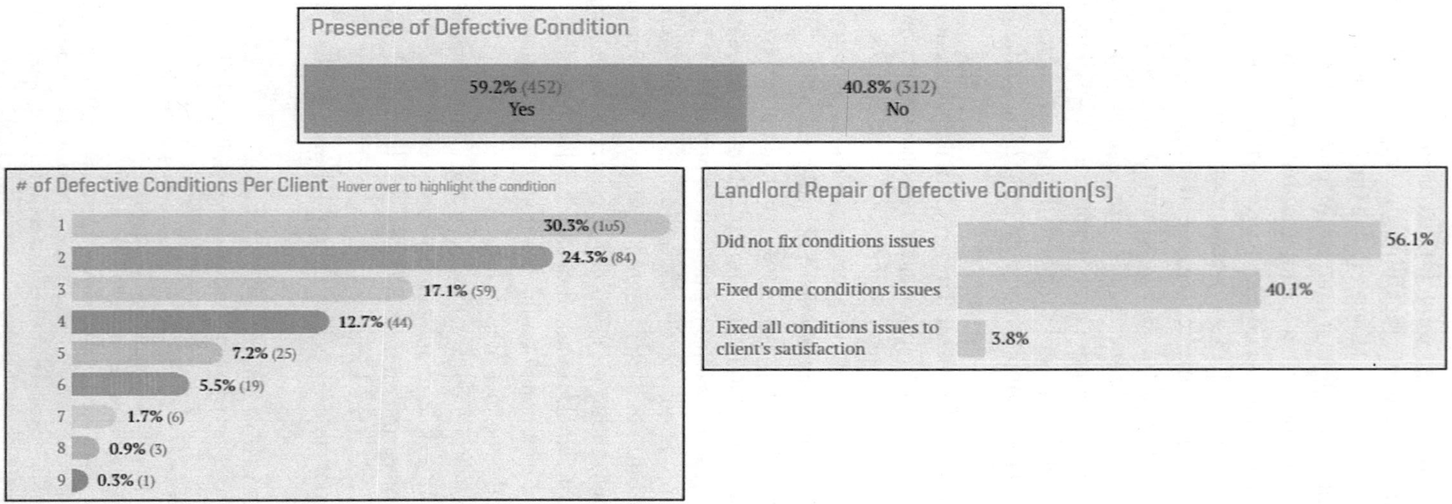

FIGURE 6.1 Exemplar visualization of defective housing conditions.

emphasized the importance of eviction right to counsel legislation to serve the most vulnerable but also has emphasized the need for additional forms of assistance and intervention to serve both rental property owners and tenants in other circumstances.

Policymakers and others often believe that the purpose of legal representation for tenants is to keep people in their homes. However, property owners, legal aid organizations, and community-based organizations often indicated that their tenants did not always want to stay in their homes. Rather, tenants sought legal assistance because their relationship with the rental property owner had often deteriorated beyond repair and the conditions of the homes were often unsafe. Based on this feedback, supplemental data was collected for clients of legal aid organizations to understand what the client's goals were. This data revealed that 30 percent to 45 percent of clients (those facing eviction who sought legal assistance) did not want to stay in their homes.[24] Figure 6.2 provides examples of visualizations showing whether the client wants to stay in their home, and the intersection of whether they want to stay and the presence of defective conditions.

Eviction right to counsel programs and legislation can be critical elements of an ecosystem ensuring justice in rental housing disputes resulting in eviction filings. As we engage stakeholders, we consistently receive feedback about how eviction right to counsel programs provide an essential foundation for housing justice but that they should also be supplemented with other interventions. Many of those interventions are preventative in nature and could decrease the need for more costly interventions downstream. These should be considered complements to or integrated components of an eviction right to counsel. Interventions include sustained emergency rental assistance, mediation, prefiling connection to other social services, relocation assistance, improvements in the substantive landlord/tenant law (such as longer notice periods and just cause eviction protections), transportation assistance, and childcare assistance for in-person court appearances.

Understanding who is likely to access the services and for whom the services may be particularly impactful is important. People with civil legal needs are often experiencing a variety of circumstances and may need a range of services. In eviction right to counsel jurisdictions, we observe common characteristics of eviction right to counsel clients. Our evaluations of the eviction right to counsel programs in three jurisdictions found that tenants seeking representation often do so because they need assistance with the substantive legal issues of their case or potential defenses, or there are challenges within the household exacerbating the trauma of the eviction process. Tenants seeking legal representation in eviction right to counsel jurisdictions are also likely to disproportionately identify as female and African American or black compared to the jurisdiction's overall population.[25]

[24] The data underlying these findings are on file with the authors.

[25] The data underlying these findings are on file with the authors.

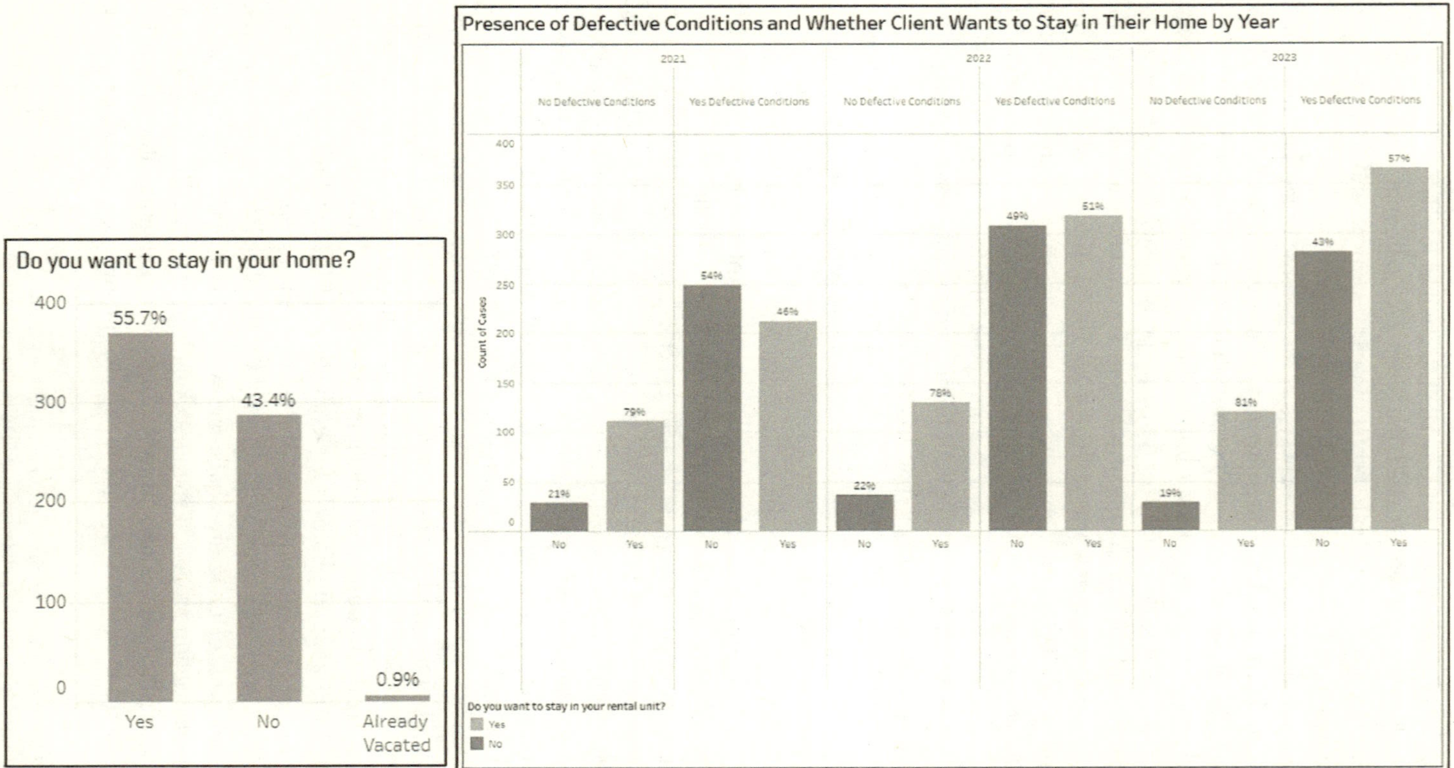

FIGURE 6.2 Exemplar visualization of client preferences regarding housing options.

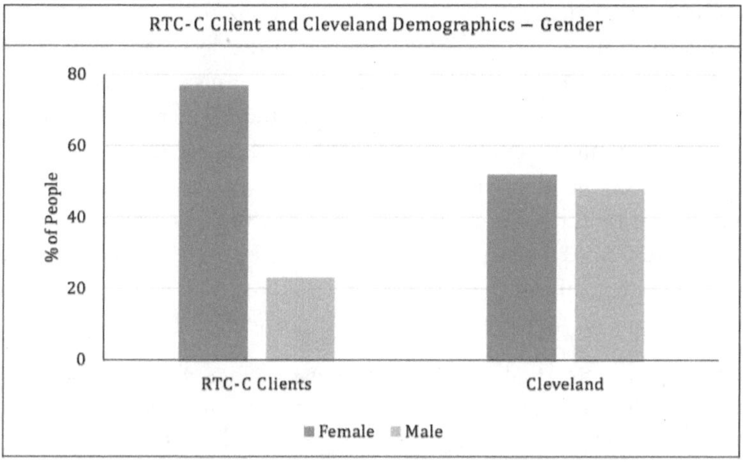

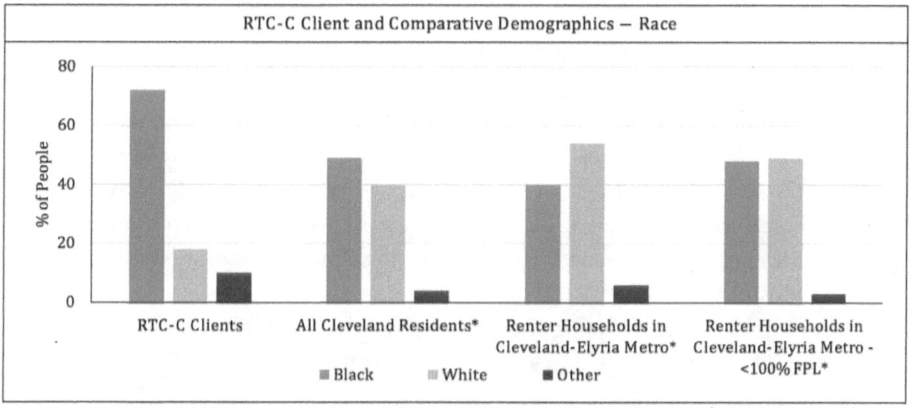

FIGURE 6.3 Comparative demographic metrics for Cleveland right to counsel clients versus Cleveland's overall population.

* All Cleveland Residents includes renters and homeowners. Renter household data is currently only available at the metro level (Cleveland-Elyria Metro), which includes five counties across northeast Ohio.

Figure 6.3 shows comparative metrics for the gender and race of eviction right to counsel clients in Cleveland relative to Cleveland's overall population.

In several right to counsel jurisdictions where we have worked, attorneys representing tenants in eviction matters told us of instances in which they were assisting a tenant where the only issue (a relatively simple one) was the nonpayment of rent. In those attorneys' opinions, the tenant would have been able to navigate the process with other forms of assistance. This does not take away from the impact and importance of an eviction right to counsel in these places but rather reinforces the importance of continued study and evaluation centered on the experiences of the parties involved and the circumstances they face.

Segmenting potential client populations based on circumstances and case characteristics provides insights into the effectiveness and fiscal sustainability of programs, interventions, and service levels. An impactful and informative finding from case and client segmentation analysis would be, for example, that 80 percent of clients who had case or personal circumstances indicating that brief legal services (legal information, advice, assistance connecting with another social service, or assistance negotiating a settlement) would be the form of effective assistance necessary for clients to achieve the goals for their case. This is significantly more meaningful than a broader, less nuanced, and contextualized finding than, for example, that 30 percent of all clients achieved their goals through the receipt of brief services.

Element #3: Appreciating that person-centered data is imperfect, this should center us on the development of reasonable estimates, transparency regarding preliminary measurement techniques, and the need for ongoing assessment.

The variety of unique circumstances people face results in uncertainties regarding the potential impact of service delivery – uncertainties regarding necessary services for a given situation, the cost and longevity of those services, and the short- and long-term fiscal impact. Precise calculations and quantifications for these situations may not always be feasible. Person-centered data is often inherently imperfect, but reasonable estimates can often be developed, particularly when accompanied with transparency regarding the sources of information, limitations of such estimates, and the methods of calculation.

For example, when analyzing the potential fiscal impact of housing instability, we often attempt to estimate the cost savings or redirection of public dollars that could be recognized if fewer people were to experience homelessness (sheltered or unsheltered) because of access to legal representation. There is a significant body of academic research indicating that a portion of people who are evicted will likely experience homelessness and that a subset of the people who experience homelessness will likely enter emergency shelter or require a different housing social safety net response (e.g., rapid rehousing, transitional housing, permanent supportive housing).[26] In addition, local homelessness response providers may also publish reports or provide data

[26] *See, for example*, Howard Rolston et al., *Evaluation of the Homebase Community Prevention Program*, Abt Associates Inc. (June 6, 2013), https://static1.squarespace.com/static/572e5b621d07c088bf6663d9/t/573bd62df85082862032f27b/1463539246596/homebase+report.pdf (last accessed Feb. 14, 2025); NYC Indep. Budget Off., *The Rising Number of Homeless Families in NYC, 2002–2012: A Look at Why Families Were Granted Shelter, the Housing They Had Lived in and Where They Came From* (Nov. 2014), https://www.ibo.nyc.ny.us/iboreports/2014dhs_families_entering_NYC_homeless_shelters.html (last accessed Feb. 14, 2025); Coal. for the Homeless Hous./Harris Cnty., *Capacity and Gaps in the Homeless Residential and Service System, Harris and Fort Bend Counties* (2011), https://irp-cdn.multiscreensite.com/2d521d2c/files/uploaded/Capacity-and-Gaps-in-the-Homeless-Residential-and-Service-System-Harris-and-Fort-Bend-Counties.pdf (last accessed Feb. 14, 2025).

demonstrating the intersection between eviction and shelter entry or other social service responses. We collect, review, and synthesize the data presented in academic studies, as well as local information, and compare it to data civil legal aid providers are collecting regarding where clients would go if they were evicted.

In our experience, the findings from academic studies are often consistent with the civil legal aid provider data and feedback from local social service providers. We leverage these sources of information to develop a quantitative estimate as to the percentage of people who would experience homelessness and likely require a housing social safety net response. We then seek feedback from local stakeholders to ensure the estimates we develop are consistent with their experiences. Once we have an estimate as to the percentage of people who would have likely experienced homelessness but-for legal representation, we review academic studies and local data regarding the annual cost of providing housing social safety net responses. When combined, the incremental number of people who likely avoided needing a housing social safety net response and the annual cost of the housing social safety net response can be used to develop a reasonable, quantitative estimate (informed by qualitative stakeholder feedback) of potential cost savings or opportunities for the redirection of public dollars.

Element #4: Identifying and evaluating quantitative elements for analysis of program costs and potential fiscal impact as well as other impacts.

Through stakeholder engagement, we learn about the availability of quantitative data and prior research that can contribute to analysis of implementation costs, as well as potential fiscal and other impacts.

Stakeholders can often share data they collect through the course of serving their constituents, can identify prior research or publications to inform further analysis, and can identify other stakeholders that may be able to assist in providing quantitative data elements. These same stakeholders then become essential in ensuring a reasonable interpretation and analysis of the data.

In our experience, data collected by local stakeholders often requires significant guidance to appropriately interpret. Examples of data we have received and reviewed include but are not limited to:

- Civil case filing and disposition data;
- Legal services provider de-identified case information;
- Homeless Management Information System (HMIS) data;
- 2-1-1 data;
- US Census data;
- Homelessness response data;
- Foster care entry and exit data;
- Student homelessness and enrollment data; and
- Legal services provider budget and financial data.

This engagement and review of data can also assist in identifying opportunities for expanded data collection and analysis. For example, Figure 6.4 presents data findings that assisted policymakers in understanding the volume of annual eviction filings in Cleveland, the defendant representation rate trend, and defendant representation rates by zip code.[27] This type of visualized data assists in understanding how policy change can impact the total number of filings a jurisdiction is experiencing and identifying whether more residents are being represented through the eviction right to counsel program over time.

Element #5: Integrating supplemental research and observations.

Complex ecosystems simply cannot be defined or fully understood by quantitative data and analysis alone. Further, many stakeholders will not have or will not be able to share quantitative data or data that could be used in robust quantitative analysis. However, many stakeholders can provide a wide range of qualitative feedback, insight, or materials that can be used to provide important history, context, and support for quantitative analysis. This information is essential to demonstrate a more fulsome appreciation for the local civil justice ecosystem. In addition, it provides the ability for stakeholders to contribute to the work, further enabling the development of coalition and the potential for issue convergence. Examples of information used in qualitative assessment and observation include but are not limited to:

- Social program budgets;
- Academic or other research previously conducted about the relevant civil justice ecosystem or matter type;
- Prior program evaluations relevant to the local civil justice ecosystem;
- Articles and investigative reporting about the relevant civil justice ecosystem; and
- Feedback provided in interviews and stakeholder focus groups or listening sessions.

Locally prepared research and the feedback from local stakeholders are complemented by relevant research from other jurisdictions to provide further support for local feedback and create pathways for further engagement.

Element #6: Developing estimates of program costs.

The most prominent question we hear when working on projects related to civil access to justice reform is "What will it cost?"

As such, developing a reasonable, credible, and independent assessment of the expected costs of implementation is an essential element of our work. It is important to ensure such estimates reflect a sustainable model of service delivery consistent with the capacity necessary to provide the services, and the quality necessary to

[27] Relevant data are on file with the authors.

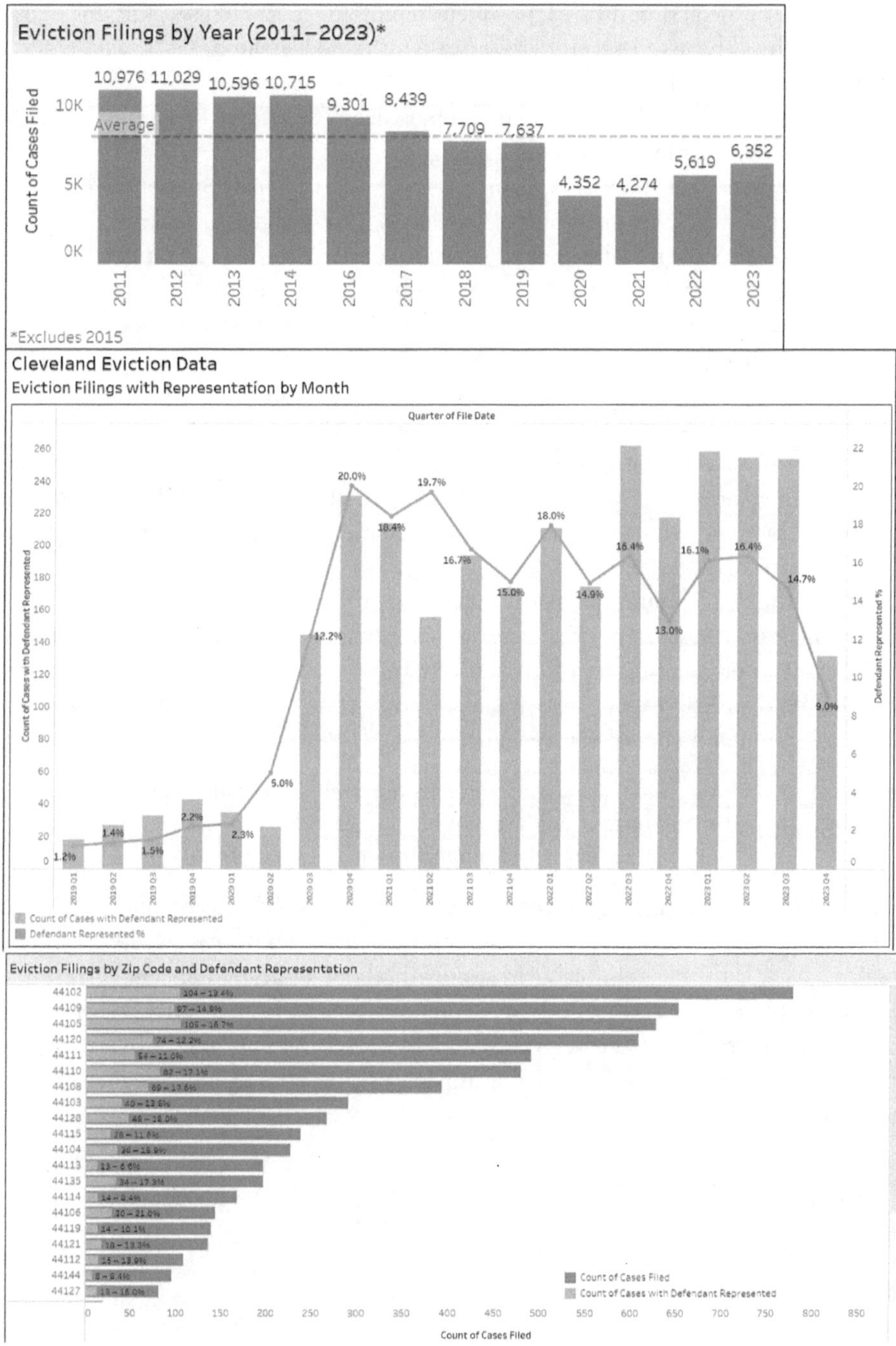

FIGURE 6.4 Eviction data visualizations.

achieve the expected results. This often represents a paradigm shift for those providing the services in severely resource-constrained environments, where such services are necessarily extremely limited.

We have assisted jurisdictions with developing detailed program budgets for a variety of service delivery models. The budgeting exercise includes calculations for the expected number of clients served, estimated caseloads, sustainable personnel expenses (e.g., salaries and benefits for attorneys, paralegals, case managers, intake staff, navigators, and social workers), and program infrastructure (e.g., rent and utilities, office expenses, technology, furniture and equipment, licenses, and dues). The estimated implementation cost of the reform not only informs program and service delivery design but also how the reform may be implemented. Depending on the scale and scope of the reform, it may be appropriate to consider a phased-implementation timeline.

The cost of sustainable implementation provides an important foundation for the assessment of total funding needed but also provides the ability to assess how the potential fiscal and other impacts compare to the costs and availability of sustainable funding. Such measures are not fixed and static. Rather, the costs (and fiscal impacts) can vary if the program design changes. In some instances, program design can be optimized to minimize costs, maximize impact, and maintain the quality of service necessary to achieve programmatic expectations. In other instances, particularly when implementing transformative measures not previously implemented, it may be reasonable to expect cost efficiencies over time as the ecosystem adapts to a new or expanded model of service delivery.

Element #7: Using prior academic scholarship and stakeholder data, developing estimates of reasonably quantifiable fiscal impacts, and identifying qualitative assessment of other impacts not quantified.

The stakeholder engagement process will often reveal significant potential fiscal benefits to states, cities, counties, and municipalities from civil access to justice reform. This is further reinforced by a growing body of academic scholarship that has demonstrated the connections between housing instability or eviction, as well as other forms of trauma, that can give rise to social services responses.[28] Civil access-to-justice reform can have wide-ranging impacts on the lives of individuals, families, neighborhoods, and communities. In our work, we will recognize, research, and

[28] Matthew Desmond & Rachel Tolbert Kimbro, *Eviction's Fallout: Housing, Hardship, and Health*, Social Forces (Feb. 24, 2015), https://scholar.harvard.edu/files/mdesmond/files/desmondkimbro.evictions.fallout.sf2015_2.pdf (last accessed Feb. 14, 2025); Seattle Women's Comm'n. & Hous. Just. Project of the King Cnty. Bar Ass'n., *Losing Home: The Human Cost of Eviction in Seattle* (Sept. 2018), https://www.seattle.gov/documents/Departments/SeattleWomensCommission/LosingHome_9-18-18.pdf (last accessed Feb. 14, 2025); Ctr. on Urb. Poverty and Cmty. Dev., Case W. U., *The Cleveland Eviction Study: Observations in Eviction Court and the Stories of People Facing Eviction* (Oct. 2019), https://case.edu/socialwork/povertycenter/sites/default/files/2019-11/The%20Cleveland%20Eviction%20Study-10242019-fully%20accessible%28r%29.pdf (last accessed Feb. 14, 2025).

discuss these potential impacts, but our quantitative analysis will primarily focus on the potential fiscal impacts that would accrue to the jurisdiction providing the funding for the program. In certain instances, we are mindful that fiscal benefits may accrue to the county or state (e.g., when we are analyzing the fiscal impact to a city) based on the nature of funding for certain social services.

For example, in several jurisdictions, such as Cleveland, we have observed that emergency response to homelessness (including the emergency shelter system), child welfare response, and the primary education system were all funded through the county. While policymakers in the city were interested in allocating funding for an eviction right to counsel and appreciated the holistic benefits that its residents would receive as well as importance of access to the justice system, the financial justification for it was more challenging because it was not providing the funding for social responses that would likely be most impacted.

These fiscal impacts can be considered on a continuum of confidence based on the availability of data, research, feedback, and system characteristics. In our experience, certain fiscal impacts can be reasonably and credibly calculated based on academic scholarship, publicly available data and metrics, and data that is often (or could be) collected by civil legal services organizations or other local stakeholders. Other fiscal impacts cannot be reliably or credibly measured with the data and research available, although feedback from stakeholders and individuals with lived experiences indicates the impacts clearly exist.

As an example, the fiscal impacts associated with residents who experience homelessness and the direct costs of homelessness response and emergency shelter are often more easily quantified using local data and information. However, the impact to property values for neighborhoods experiencing high rates of eviction, or the long-term impacts to health and education for children who experience eviction and persistent housing instability, can be very difficult to measure due to the lack of research and information currently available (both locally and generally on such topics).

The unquantifiable impacts stakeholders describe should also be considered and recognized. The reality of fiscal impacts that cannot be credibly converted to a monetary scale should not be viewed as a limitation. Rather, they are a pathway for continued research and data collection. We have observed firsthand the value of robust, structured data collection in jurisdictions throughout the country that are endeavoring to demonstrate the costs and benefits of regulatory reform related to access to civil justice.

Element #8: Assessing opportunities for issue convergence.

We often observe comprehensive cost–benefit analyses and potential fiscal impact quantifications contributing to the development of local issue convergence.[29]

[29] We use the term "issue convergence" to mean circumstances where stakeholders align on the need for reform and initial steps that can be taken together in pursuit of reform.

Assessing issue convergence requires authentic engagement with a range of local community stakeholders. This engagement should also consider information requests, research, criticism, and questioning. An effective dialogue will require assessments of bias that may arise from the unique perspective and experience of stakeholders and a willingness to respectfully explore the potential for bias and how to interpret, understand, and apply the insights from stakeholder engagement. Through the course of developing this dialogue, we seek to identify common and aligned interests, experiences, and aspirations for change or innovation. We also identify areas of disagreement and concern. These are also valuable contributors to the dialogue and present opportunities to share such concerns from an independent perspective, creating a shared appreciation for the views of other stakeholders, including those who have traditionally been considered adversaries.

In certain instances, we have experienced providers of social services or legal assistance who are informed by their daily experiences but may not appreciate that those daily experiences are largely limited to serving those experiencing the most traumatic and destructive versions of certain civil legal issues or circumstances. In such circumstances, it can often be helpful to broaden the conversation and learn about the experience of system-impacted persons who experience the system differently and do not interact with certain social service or legal service programs. The engagement can then broaden the stakeholders involved and more widely inform the dialogue – with both, the opportunities for issue convergence can increase.

In other instances, for instance, rental property owners may initially oppose contemplated legislation that would expand access to legal representation for tenants. We have talked to dozens of rental property owners and their counsel across the country, and they often express concern that expanded access to legal representation may lead to expected delays in the eviction process due to the presence of a tenant's attorney. They frequently describe these expected delays as potentially contributing to increases in rental arrears and lost rental income.

Rental property owners and their counsel are often accustomed to fast-moving eviction proceedings where tenants fail to appear at the eviction hearing. If they do appear, they are unlikely to be represented, and unlikely to have the necessary specialized knowledge of landlord–tenant law to represent themselves effectively.[30] There are often similar concerns from the courts, which are also accustomed to expeditious eviction proceedings that do not require significant human or financial

[30] Kan. City Eviction Project, *Evictions in the Courts: An Analysis of 106,000 Cases from 2006–2016 in Jackson County* (Jan. 24, 2018), https://static1.squarespace.com/static/59ba0bd359cc68f015b7ff8a/t/5a68e811e4966bee3fb5d6cd/1516824594549/KC+Eviction+Project+-+Courts+Analysis.pdf (last accessed Feb. 14, 2025); Scherer, *supra* note 3, at 51; Nat'l Coal. for a Civil Right to Couns., *Eviction Representation Statistics for Landlords and Tenants Absent Special Intervention* (last modified Nov. 2024), http://civilrighttocounsel.org/uploaded_files/280/Landlord_and_tenant_eviction_rep_stats__NCCRC_.pdf (last accessed Feb. 14, 2025).

resources to adjudicate. Rental property owners also often expect that every tenant will seek legal assistance – regardless of the circumstances the client may be facing, the quality of housing, and the efforts by the landlord to try to provide time or assistance for the tenant.

However, our experience indicates an increased likelihood that cases can be resolved out of court and before the first hearing when both parties are represented, resulting in more efficient and effective case resolutions that has financial benefits for both parties (and the courts). Rental property owners' counsel have shared that they prefer to negotiate and interact with another attorney rather than an unrepresented tenant because it serves their interest: securing an efficient and effective case resolution that often includes emergency rental assistance to pay the rental property owner the back rent owed or creating repayment plans that tenants can reasonably adhere to, thereby increasing the likelihood of a rental property owner being paid the amount of back rent owed.

Rental property owners have also shared with us that the financial cost of identifying, screening, and securing a new tenant is significant, as is the financial cost of preparing a property for re-rental, and vacancies before a new tenant is secured. Because of those costs, their preference is generally to keep a current tenant.

In addition, the ways that tenants respond to delinquency and the receipt of an eviction notice can vary significantly. Not every tenant seeks legal representation. Data collected from eviction right to counsel jurisdictions indicates that those who do seek legal representation are often experiencing a variety of complex issues – such as substandard housing conditions, substantive disputes with the rental property owner, verbal lease agreements, and may be facing severe consequences that could arise from an involuntary displacement.[31] It is possible that many of those who are not seeking legal representation or assistance perceive their circumstances to be largely economic (not legal) and may seek nonlegal forms of assistance. This can inform both communication strategies (to assist tenants in understanding the legal issues associated with eviction cases) as well as complementary services (such as mediation and rental assistance) that may assist with effectively resolving eviction cases when tenants do not seek legal assistance.

Policymakers are also a stakeholder group with financial interest in regulatory reform related to access to civil justice and therefore can be a party to issue convergence. In certain instances, a primary factor for some policymakers when considering a reform is the economics of the reform: what are the costs and benefits, what is the expected return on investment, and is this a fiscally responsible use of taxpayer dollars? We have developed robust cost–benefit analyses of enacted and

[31] STOUT, *Cleveland Eviction Right to Counsel Annual Independent Evaluation January 1, 2022 to December 31, 2022* (Jan. 31, 2023), https://www.stout.com/en/services/transformative-change-consulting/eviction-right-to-counsel-resources (last accessed Feb. 14, 2025).

contemplated eviction right to counsel legislation across the country to inform policymaker decision-making.

Even as issue convergence emerges as a possibility, we continue to embrace an iterative approach to the development of cost–benefit concepts, program design, and implementation considerations. Issue convergence requires continual efforts of genuine and authentic listening and engagement, and there are also often a significant number of unknowns in complex social ecosystems that require ongoing evaluation, assessment, and investigation. Iterative processes of engagement, design, development, implementation, and assessment (repeating) can ensure that an active dialogue is maintained, new insights and challenges are brought forward, and collaboration can continue to foster innovation.

Element #9: Identifying opportunities for continued, iterative assessment, evaluation, and refinement as well as identification of complementary reforms.

Reform will often involve the development and implementation of programs and services not previously provided in a jurisdiction, and certainly not recently. As such, predicting how the civil justice ecosystem will respond and adapt will not be done with perfect precision.

While reasonable estimates can be developed, it is important to acknowledge the limitations of this work and identify the additional data collection, research, and collaboration that will enable the ecosystem to continually evaluate the impact of the reform and identify the complementary services that can further enhance the ecosystem in a financially viable and sustainable manner.

Elements of iterative assessment that can be particularly valuable and impactful include but are not limited to:

- Expanded data collection, analysis, and visualization;
- Integration of data sets from additional data sources;
- Advisory councils to continue to be informed by people with lived experiences;
- Stakeholder engagement and stakeholder working groups;
- Data-informed outreach using local, trusted messengers;
- Focus groups and surveys of people with lived experiences; and
- Consideration of the development of complementary or adjacent resources, programs, policies, or legislation.

A commitment to such iterative assessment, development, and implementation techniques can foster ecosystem collaboration and enhance the likelihood of sustained commitment to innovation by local stakeholders.

6.4 CONCLUSION

The development of a comprehensive, independent cost–benefit study intended to inform policymakers and other stakeholders about the potential costs of providing services intended to expand civil access to justice, as well as the fiscal impact and potential costs savings that could accrue through the passage and effective implementation of such reform, can be a transformative contribution to the dialogue and support necessary to enact and sustain such reform.

However, this work is as much about *how* such analyses are conducted as it is about the quantitative result. By leveraging academic scholarship, engaging a broad range of local stakeholders, genuinely and authentically listening to their perspectives, collecting and integrating both quantitative and qualitative information, and seeking regular feedback as analyses and observations are developed, such cost–benefit analyses form the basis for collaboration and consensus that can lead to issue convergence in support of expansion of access to civil justice.

This approach can inform the work of pursuing sustainable, scaled reform related to many efforts to improve access to civil justice, such as civil right to counsel initiatives, court efforts to assist self-represented litigants, expanding the role of nonlawyers or limited-license legal practitioners, effectively utilizing brief services and advice programs, or developing justice initiatives to address racial inequity. It is also important to acknowledge that other theories of change that are more narrowly constructed may also be successful at achieving discrete change and an improvement in access to civil justice.

In our experience, reform related to access to civil justice that is pursued through a financially focused, stakeholder-informed, research-supported approach can result in significant, transformational, and groundbreaking change in civil access to justice.

7

Beyond Access to Justice

Power, Organizing, and Civil Legal Inequality

Jamila Michener

In the United States, access to legal representation in civil courts is constrained and inequitable. Most people who have justiciable civil legal problems cannot or do not obtain legal assistance.[1] Americans living in and near poverty are disproportionately in need of civil legal protections. In 2022, 74 percent of low-income households experienced at least one civil legal problem, and 39 percent experienced five or more problems – including challenges with health care, housing, disability access, public benefits, domestic violence, and more.[2] Despite grappling with such an extensive range of legal problems, low-income Americans lacked adequate help for 92 percent of them.[3]

The "justice gap" – this rift between legal needs and legal assistance – is driven by both supply and demand. Concerns about the former have understandably dominated approaches to addressing civil legal inequality. Underfunding at the federal, state, and local levels restricts the supply of lawyers available to meet the needs of people facing civil legal problems. For example, legal organizations funded by the Legal Services Corporation – a core institution undergirding the US civil legal infrastructure – are unable to provide enough legal help for 71 percent of the legal problems brought to their doors.[4] Notwithstanding this underfunding, delivering access to legal advice or representation for low-income Americans has long been upheld as a crucial imperative. In 1970, Senator Walter Mondale dubbed legal services, "the most effective poverty program, dollar for dollar."[5] Contemporary evidence supports Mondale's contention. Access to civil legal representation can

1 Rebecca L. Sandefur, *Bridging the Gap: Rethinking Outreach for Greater Access to Justice*, 37 U. Ark. Little Rock L. Rev. 721, 724 (2015); Deborah L. Rhode, Access to Justice (2004).

2 Legal Serv. Corp., The Justice Gap: The Unmet Civil Legal Needs of Low-income Americans 8 (2022).

3 *Id.* at 7.

4 *Id.* at 9.

5 *Legal Services Program of the Office of Economic Opportunity, Hearings before the Subcommittee on Employment, Manpower, and Poverty of the Committee on Labor and Public Welfare, United States Senate*, 91st Cong. 110 (1970) (statement of Sen. Mondale, Member, S. Comm. On Labor and Public Welfare).

narrow health disparities, improve communication between public institutions and impoverished communities, and increase property values and wealth in black communities.[6]

Recognizing these and other benefits, governments have invested in broadening access to legal services. Though the methods for achieving this end have been varied, most have emphasized the supply side of the justice gap: providing lawyers, legal information, and legal help.[7] This chapter begins with a discussion of such supply-side interventions, including (1) right to counsel, (2) legal technologies, and (3) the use of nonlawyers. Each of these has shown promise and attracted public resources. Each also confronts limitations that underscore the imperative of attending to the demand side of the justice gap.

After outlining the limits of supply-side approaches, this chapter turns to the drivers of demand. Most fundamentally, civil legal needs are a product of political processes. Demand for legal help is propelled by a politics of scarcity, inequality, and welfare state retrenchment.[8] Addressing the demand side of the "justice gap" therefore requires the redistribution and reconfiguration of power in American political life. Supply-side approaches to civil legal inequality do not sufficiently account for power. Bringing power to the foreground complements and usefully balances the prevailing preoccupation with increasing the supply of legal resources.

Moving beyond a supply-side emphasis on civil legal systems and toward a demand-side attentiveness to power dynamics within political systems opens a broader horizon of possibilities for change. A demand-side approach posits that when legal interventions lay the groundwork for collective action and facilitate the exercise of power, they can mitigate the demands that necessitate access to justice in the first place. By drawing on in-depth interviews with organized tenants and key examples of legal interventions that catalyze political action, this chapter makes the case that power should be a core concern for anyone seeking to redress civil legal inequality.

7.1 SUPPLY-SIDE APPROACHES: RIGHT TO COUNSEL

To motivate the case for a demand-side focus on power, it's worth considering some of the most salient supply-side approaches. Right to counsel (RTC) is foremost among them. In cities as wide ranging as New York, San Francisco, Boulder,

[6] Jamien P. Cunningham, *An Evaluation of the Federal Legal Services Program: Evidence from Crime Rates and Property Values*, 92 J. URBAN ECON., 76 (2016); Jamien P. Cunningham & Rob Gillezeau, *The Effects of the Neighborhood Legal Services Program on Riots and the Wealth of African Americans*, 4 RSF: THE RUSSELL SAGE FOUND. J. SOC. SCI. 6, 144–57 (2018); James Teufel et al., *Legal Aid Inequities Predict Health Disparities*, 38 HAMLINE L. REV. 329 (2015).

[7] Alissa Rubin Gomez, *Demand Side Justice*, 28 GEO. J. ON POVERTY L. & POL'Y 411, 412–13 (2021).

[8] Jamila Michener, *Legal Aid and Social Policy: Managing a Political Economy of Scarcity*, 706 ANNALS AM. ACAD. POL. & SOC. SCI. 137, 138 (2023).

Minneapolis, Kansas City, and Philadelphia, legislators, judges, community organizations, and denizens have fought for, and won, increased funds for free or low-cost legal counsel in civil proceedings.[9]

These RTC policies take numerous forms. Some are means-tested, and others universal. Some pertain specifically to legal representation in eviction proceedings; a few are broader.[10] Some RTC policies come to fruition through legislative action, others via judicial decisions, still others by executive action.[11] The common thread that runs through all RTC efforts is a mandate to increase the supply of lawyers available to represent or advise people with civil legal needs.

RTC policies can be very effective. In 2017, New York City enacted "Intro 214-B," a pathbreaking expansion of civil legal access.[12] Intro 214-B was intended to provide legal counsel for low-income tenants facing eviction. Prior to the passage of this legislation, roughly 1 percent of New York City tenants were represented by an attorney in eviction cases.[13] Within five years (by the fourth quarter of 2022), 63 percent of tenants in eviction court received legal assistance.[14] Among that group, 78 percent were able to remain in their homes.[15]

9 *See* Nat'l Coal. for a Civil Right to Counsel, *State Status Map*, https://civilrighttocounsel.org/map/ (last accessed Feb. 14, 2025), http://civilrighttocounsel.org/legislative_developments/20232024_civil_right_to_counsel_bills (last accessed Feb. 2, 2024).

10 For example, in 2018, San Francisco voters passed a proposition creating a universal RTC for tenants in eviction cases. *See* S.F. Mayor's Off. of Housing & Cmty. Dev., *Eviction Prevention & Housing Stabilization, Tenant Right to Counsel, Strategy Description*, https://sfmohcd.org/sites/default/files/5.%20Tenant%20Right%20to%20Counsel.pdf (last accessed Mar. 29, 2024). Denver provides free legal representation for "low to moderate income individuals experiencing eviction." Den. Code of Ordinances, § 27-211 et seq. (2024), https://library.municode.com/co/denver/codes/code_of_ordinances?nodeId=TITIIREMUCO_CH27HO_ARTIXTELESE_S27-211LEIN (last accessed Feb. 14, 2025). Other legal areas in which a RTC has been created include parental rights, children's rights, and asset forfeiture. *See* Nat'l Coal. for a Civil Right to Counsel, *supra* note 9.

11 *See* Wash. Rev. Code § 59.18.640 (2021) (RTC for indigent tenants); In the matter of the adoption of A.W.S. and K.R.S., Minor Children, 339 P.3d 413 (2014) (finding a RTC for parent facing involuntary termination of parental rights); Press Release, Phila. Health and Hum. Servs. Managing Director's Off., *City Launches Right to Counsel for Eligible Philadelphia Tenants* (Jan. 21, 2022), https://www.phila.gov/2022-01-31-city-launches-right-to-counsel-for-eligible-philadelphia-tenants/ (last accessed Feb. 14, 2025).

12 Int. 0214-2014, N.Y.C. Council, Comm. on Cts. & L. Servs. (codified at N.Y.C. Admin. Code §§ 26-1301-06), https://legistar.council.nyc.gov/LegislationDetail.aspx?ID=1687978&GUID=29A4594B-9E8A-4C5E-A797-96BDC4F64F80 (last accessed Feb. 14, 2025). *See also* Jamila Michener, *Power from the Margins: Grassroots Mobilization and Urban Expansions of Civil Legal Rights*, 56 Urb. Aff. Rev. 1390, (2020).

13 Task Force to Expand Access to Civ. Legal Servs. in N.Y., *Report to the Chief Judge of the State of New York* 1 (Nov. 2010), https://ww2.nycourts.gov/sites/default/files/document/files/2018-04/CLS-TaskForceREPORT.pdf (last accessed Feb. 24, 2025) (finding that 99 percent of tenants are unrepresented in eviction cases in New York City).

14 N.Y. City Dept. of Soc. Servs., Off. of Civil Just., *Universal Access to Legal Services: A Report on Year Five Implementation in New York City* 5 (Winter 2022), https://a860-gpp.nyc.gov/concern/nyc_government_publications/3t945t63b?locale=en (last accessed Feb. 14 2025).

15 *Id.*

Intro 214-B is just one example of the profound benefits of legal representation for low-income Americans. Nevertheless, even this pivotal RTC legislation has proven insufficient to meet the demand for legal services.[16] Sharp increases in eviction filings in the aftermath of the pandemic were met with a floundering civil legal infrastructure that could not meet the bar set by Intro 214-B. Legal services providers in New York City estimate that they would need roughly $461 million dollars per year to fairly execute current contracts for legal services as well as cover anticipated cases.[17] At present, New York City provides $110 million in funding, falling far short of the target.[18] Despite having a historic RTC law on the books, New York City Mayor Eric Adams has hesitated to bridge this gap.[19]

Funding deficits are only one challenge facing RTC. As widely touted as Intro 2014-B has been, beneficiaries of the law sometimes do not know that they have access to free legal representation, do not understand how to obtain such representation, or are alienated from the legal system altogether. Even proponents and implementers of RTC acknowledge its complexity, difficulty, and cost. Adriene Holder, chief attorney for civil practice at the New York Legal Aid Society, aptly admitted to a NYC reporter that "Right to Counsel is in its infancy stages. . . . [E]veryone wants us to run and twirl but we're barely out of the crawling stage. So, people need to understand that we're going to need to continue to refine how this work is done, but we need resources to do it."[20]

As an attorney, Holder articulates the problem as one of resources, accentuating the supply side of the justice gap. However, it's clear that many people at the racial and economic margins of society face problems that are technically "legal" but cannot ultimately be resolved through legal processes. For example, there were 69,440 residential eviction petitions filed in NYC between July 1, 2021, and June 30, 2022.[21] Among those eviction filings, 54,806 (about 79 percent) were for nonpayment of rent.[22] Though there are legitimate legal issues that prompt nonpayment of rent (e.g., withholding rent due to substandard conditions), a common reason for doing so is not having the money to pay. This holds true for a broad spectrum of civil legal problems that are fundamentally rooted in economic and political systems that do not provide denizens with sufficient material resources to meet basic needs.[23] Legal services providers are inundated by cases because they deal

[16] *Attorney Access*, NAT'L CTR. FOR ACCESS TO JUST., https://ncaj.org/state-rankings/justice-index/attorney-access (last accessed Feb. 3, 2024).

[17] Emma Whitford, *What Would It Take To Fully Fund Right to Counsel for NYC Tenants?*, CITY LIMITS (Apr. 10, 2023), https://citylimits.org/2023/04/10/what-would-it-take-to-fully-fund-right-to-counsel-for-nyc-tenants/ (last accessed Feb. 14, 2025).

[18] *Id.*

[19] *Id.*

[20] *Id.*

[21] *See* N.Y. CITY DEPT. OF SOC. SERVS., *supra* note 14, at 10.

[22] *Id.*

[23] *See* Michener, *supra* note 8, at 139.

with the fallout from such structural deficits. Colleen Shanahan and colleagues make this point as follows.

> The litigants in housing court do not end up behind that door by coincidence. Rather, this is a foreseeable consequence of the absence of affordable and adequate housing, health care, childcare, and education, the absence of fair and equal wages, and the presence of mass incarceration in our society. State civil cases involving debt, family relationships, and children have different names on the courtroom door but similar stories behind those doors.[24]

Economic and political structures engender, maintain, and deepen the deluge of inequalities that are flooding civil legal institutions.[25] Public policies enable housing insecurity, low and stagnating wages, predatory consumer practices, constrained access to public benefits, wage theft, and many other processes that induce precarity.[26] The civil legal system shoulders the resulting burdens, despite not being designed to do so. Colleen Shanahan and her coauthors trenchantly capture this dilemma:

> The work of state civil courts is a daily manifestation of the failure of the executive and legislative branches to disrupt structural inequality or invest in systems of care to mitigate it. These courts operate in the breach to address social needs because they cannot decline the cases presented to them. Thus, the social needs people bring to court are framed as disputes in order to access social provision. ... This leaves state civil courts attempting to address – within the constraints of their dispute resolution design – the social needs of litigants.[27]

In such a context, demand for legal services soars. Right to counsel expansions are meant to mitigate this, and they are an indispensable tool for doing so. However, when deployed solely as a supply-side instrument, RTC has little bearing on larger political-economic conditions. It helps people to (perhaps) survive the "brutal

[24] Colleen F. Shanahan et al., *The Institutional Mismatch of State Civil Courts*, 122 Columbia L. Rev. 1471, 1473 (2022).

[25] *See* Michener, *supra* note 8, at 139; John Whitlow, *Gentrification and Countermovement: The Right to Counsel and New York City's Affordable Housing Crisis*, 46 Fordham Urb. L.J. 1081, 1085 (2019); Kathryn A. Sabbeth, *(Under)Enforcement of Poor Tenants' Rights*, 27 Geo. J. on Poverty L. & Pol'y 97, 120 (2019); Tonya L. Brito et al., *Racial Capitalism in the Civil Courts*, 122 Colum. L. Rev. 1243, 1244–45 (2022).

[26] Daniel J. Galvin, *Deterring Wage Theft: Alt-labor, State Politics, and the Policy Determinants of Minimum Wage Compliance*, 14 Persps. on Pol. 324 (2016); Jamila Michener, Fragmented Democracy: Medicaid, Federalism, and Unequal Politics (2018); Keeanga-Yamahtta Taylor, Race for Profit: How Banks and the Real Estate Industry Undermined Black Homeownership (2019); Mallory E. SoRelle, Democracy Declined: The Failed Politics of Consumer Financial Protection (2020); William W. Franko & Christopher Witko, The New Economic Populism: How States Respond to Economic Inequality (2018).

[27] Shanahan et al., *supra* note 24, at 1474–75.

needs" that emerge from structural inequality but does not disrupt or transform that inequality.[28] This is a basic limitation of supply-side solutions.

7.2 SUPPLY-SIDE LIMITS: LEGAL TECHNOLOGIES

RTC is only one of numerous supply-side approaches. Legal technologies have also been hailed as a route to democratizing access to legal resources.[29] Rapid developments in machine learning and web-based capacities have engendered optimism around the hope that the justice gap can be bridged via low-cost, highly accessible technology-assisted legal service delivery.[30] More than a decade ago, the Legal Services Corporation declared technology "a powerful tool in narrowing the justice gap" and offered recommendations for technological pathways to facilitating access to justice.[31] Some legal scholars have viewed the "great disruption" sparked by swiftly emerging artificial or machine intelligence as a process that will undermine the monopoly of lawyers and "provide benefit to society and clients as legal services become more transparent and affordable to consumers, and access to justice thereby becomes more widely available."[32]

Notwithstanding such confident predictions, there are reasons to be skeptical about the equalizing effects of technological innovations.[33] Successfully leveraging technology to bridge civil legal gaps will be contingent on whether people with legal needs can access the internet, have adequate digital literacy, or have the capacity to adequately articulate their needs when required.[34]

Even further, legal technology cannot circumvent economic and social inequalities. Under some conditions, technology even has the potential to exacerbate disparities, for example, by creating a "two-tiered system" where low-income communities are "stuck with inferior AI-driven assistance."[35] All things considered, technology holds both promise and peril for civil legal inequality. This makes

[28] Martha F. Davis, Brutal Need: Lawyers and the Welfare Rights Movement, 1960–1973 (1995).

[29] Albert H. Yoon, *The Post-Modern Lawyer: Technology and the Democratization of Legal Representation*, 66 U. Toronto L.J. 456 (2016).

[30] Raymond H. Brescia et al., *Embracing Disruption: How Technological Change in the Delivery of Legal Services Can Improve Access to Justice*, 78 Albany L. Rev. 553 (2014).

[31] Legal Services Corp., *Report of the Summit on the Use of Technology to Expand Access to Justice* (Dec. 2013), https://www.lsc.gov/our-impact/publications/other-publications-and-reports/report-summit-use-technology-expand-access (last accessed Feb. 18, 2025).

[32] John O. McGinnis & Russell G. Pearce, *The Great Disruption: How Machine Intelligence Will Transform the Role of Lawyers in the Delivery of Legal Services*, 82 Fordham L. Rev. 3041, 3065–66 (2014).

[33] Emily S. Taylor Poppe, *The Future Is Complicated: AI, Apps & Access to Justice*, 72 Okla. L. Rev. 185 (2019).

[34] *Id.*

[35] Drew Simshaw, *Access to A.I. Justice: Avoiding an Inequitable Two-Tiered System of Legal Services*, 24 Yale J.L. & Tech. 150 (2022).

overreliance on expanding access via supply-side technological innovation an insufficient response to the justice gap.

7.3 SUPPLY-SIDE LIMITS: THE USE OF NONLAWYERS

The use of nonlawyers is another supply-side approach to addressing unmet legal need. Historically, the legal profession in the United States has had relatively high barriers to entry and widespread modes of "self-regulation" that limit who can legally practice law and under what conditions.[36] Lawyers must graduate from an accredited law school, pass the bar exam (in most states), obtain a (state specific) license to practice law, and more.[37] These and other regulations are meant to ensure the integrity of legal practice. But they also limit the supply of lawyers and increase their cost. In the context of high demand, this system creates a challenging context for those seeking access to civil legal resources.[38]

One solution is to increase the supply of practitioners who can address civil legal problems by allowing nonlawyers to practice law in some capacity.[39] For example, in 2014 New York City piloted several programs aimed at leveraging nonlawyer legal expertise to meet civil legal needs. One such program deployed legal navigators to assist self-represented litigants in housing court.[40] These navigators were permitted to perform a wide range of tasks, including substantive responsibilities like answering judges' questions regarding the facts of the case.[41]

Similar efforts have gone even further. In 2012, the Washington Supreme Court passed a rule paving the way for a new category of legal practitioner: Limited License Legal Technicians (LLLTs). Washington thus ushered in "the profession's first paraprofessional licensing scheme that allows nonlawyers to provide legal advice without the supervision of a lawyer."[42] These and other models for expanding the scope of who can provide legal services are encouraging but difficult to sustain. The Washington state program, for example, was sunset in 2023, with no new LLLT licenses being issued thereafter.[43] Though that program gained national recognition

[36] Stanley S. Arkin, *Self-Regulation and Approaches to Maintaining Standards of Professional Integrity*, 30 U. Miami L. Rev. 803 (1976).

[37] Clifford Winston & Quentin Karpilow, *Should the US Eliminate Entry Barriers to the Practice of Law? Perspectives Shaped by Industry Deregulation*, 106 Am. Econ. Rev. Papers & Proc. 171 (2016).

[38] Gillian K. Hadfield, *Higher Demand, Lower Supply – A Comparative Assessment of the Legal Resource Landscape for Ordinary Americans*, 37 Fordham Urban L.J. 129 (2010).

[39] Richard Zorza & David Udell, *New Roles for Non-Lawyers to Increase Access to Justice*, 41 Fordham Urban L. J. 1259 (2014).

[40] *Id.* at 1263.

[41] *Id.*

[42] Rebecca M. Donaldson, *Law by Non-Lawyers: The Limit to Limited License Legal Technicians Increasing Access to Justice*, 42 Seattle U. L. Rev. 1 (2018).

[43] *Sunset of LLT Program*, Wash. State Bar Ass'n (updated Mar. 31, 2023), https://www.wsba.org/for-legal-professionals/join-the-legal-profession-in-wa/limited-license-legal-technicians/decision-to-sunset-lllt-program (last accessed Apr. 2, 2024).

and the (fleeting) endorsement of the Washington State Bar Association, it floundered when the composition of bar's board and the state court changed.[44] Even more broadly, unauthorized practice of law (UPL) regulations across the country prohibit nonlawyers in varied and substantial ways.[45]

Though RTC, legal technologies, and nonlawyer assistance are innovative and important means of tackling civil legal inequality, an exclusive focus on supply-side solutions places a ceiling on the possibilities for transforming the justice landscape. A turn to the demand side – through an emphasis on political power – opens a different horizon of prospects.

7.4 WHY POWER IS PIVOTAL

Power is a complex notion that has been widely theorized in terms of its various faces, forms, and dimensions. For the purposes of this chapter, I define power broadly as the capacity to influence the conditions that shape one's life and community.[46] *Political* power is specifically the capacity to wield influence through the state and other critical political actors (e.g., employers, landlords) as a means of changing the conditions that shape one's life and community.[47] The people and communities with the most inadequate access to civil legal resources – those who are economically and racially marginalized, struggling to survive onslaughts of deprivation and predation in their daily lives – are the very people who often lack political power. Such a dearth of power enables the circumstances that create civil legal problems. So long as power imbalances facilitate material inequities (as is the norm), legal needs (demand) will likely outpace the ability to meet them (supply).

To make concrete the relationships between power and legal need, consider Quiana, a young mother interviewed as a part of a larger research project.[48] After a local code enforcement officer found lead paint in Quiana's home, she tested her four children for lead exposure. Quiana then found out that three of her children had borderline high levels of lead, while her fourth and youngest child – a three-year-old boy – had severely high levels. Despite urging from public health officials,

[44] Lyle Moran, *How Washington Supreme Court's LLLT Program Met Its Demise*, ABA J. (July 9, 2020), https://www.abajournal.com/web/article/how-washingtons-limited-license-legal-technician-program-met-its-demise#:~:text=Meanwhile%2C%20in%20May%2C%20the%20state%20bar's%20treasurer,7%2D2%20in%20June%20to%20sunset%20the%20program (last accessed Feb. 14, 2025).

[45] Derek A. Denckla, *Nonlawyers and the Unauthorized Practice of Law: An Overview of the Legal and Ethical Parameters*, 67 Fordham L. Rev. 2581 (1999).

[46] Jamila Michener, *Racism, Power, and Health Equity: The Case of Tenant Organizing*, 42 Health Affs. 1318 (2023).

[47] Michael L. Rosino, *Boundaries and Barriers: Racialized Dynamics of Political Power*, 10 Socio. Compass 939 (2016).

[48] This project involved systematic in-depth qualitative interviews with tenants. Quiana was interviewed in New York in April 2023. The identities of research participants are protected by using pseudonyms.

Quiana could not afford to relocate. She was unemployed and far down a long waiting list of people eligible to receive section 8 vouchers. Moreover, there was a dearth of affordable rental units in her city. The local department of health fined Quiana's landlord and ordered him to abate the lead, but he did not. When Quiana sought a lawyer to help her address the lead issue, she could not find one. Her local legal services organization focused mostly on eviction cases. They did not have the capacity to take on lead cases.

With her fear and frustration over the situation growing, Quiana stopped paying rent. Her landlord then promptly initiated eviction proceedings. She returned to legal services and only then was able to get an attorney to represent her in housing court. As a result, she was able to temporarily fend off eviction.

Despite receiving civil legal assistance for (some of) her legal problems, Quiana remains in a precarious, unsafe housing situation with an unaccountable landlord looking for a reason to kick her out. Given these circumstances, it would be unsurprising if additional legal problems emerged in her life. Quiana's most fundamental problems, however, are not legal. The primary reasons for her predicament are political-economic: inadequate regulation of predatory landlords, insufficient availability of affordable housing, and an underfunded and ill-equipped housing voucher program. All these issues are the result of political choices that reflect (among other things) the inability of Quiana and people in communities like hers to influence policy to their benefit.

Quiana recognized the problem of power at the core of her dilemma. Facing the double dangers of poisoning and displacement she confessed,

> When it comes to the judges and even code enforcement, I feel like they should be doing more. Because I'm quite sure this is not the only house that's going through situations. So, for [the landlord] to still be out here collecting his rent and half-ass doing his job, I feel like that's where the higher ups should come in ... but it doesn't seem like they're doing anything about it really, and *what can we do*? Like me, for example, I'm trying. I been trying to contact these people and that people, and it's like, *I'm not getting nowhere ... tenants like me, we need a voice, because we're not being heard.*

Though Quiana lived in a city experiencing an enduringly severe crisis of lead poisoning within impoverished communities of color, she was not part of any concerted effort to pressure public officials to address the lead issue or to build safe, affordable housing. By her own account, Quiana lacked the power to change the circumstances that produced her legal problems. Though she did not live in a city with a "right to counsel" in eviction court, it's unlikely that the outcome of her situation would have been different if she had (given that she did have representation in her eviction case). It's similarly implausible to suppose that having access to current advanced legal technology or a nonlawyer legal practitioner would have fundamentally altered Quiana's circumstances. And even if one of these supply-side interventions would have proved effective in Quiana's case, they would do little to change the (similar) conditions faced by many of her neighbors.

On the other hand, when tenants like Quiana organize collectively to exercise power in the face of the inequities that structure their lives, possibilities for more fundamental change emerge.[49] When lawyers and legal institutions go beyond providing access to legal services and toward facilitating collective organizing, people like Quiana are enabled to build power that can alter the conditions that profoundly constrain their life chances.

7.5 HOW POWER CAN MITIGATE LEGAL NEED

To make the case for critically assessing supply-side legal interventions through the lens of power, we must clarify precisely why power is so vital for mitigating legal need. This chapter describes three ways that political organizing to build power can change the conditions that lead to legal problems:

(1) Organizing can help to avoid problems that could have generated legal needs.
(2) Organizing can address problems (through nonlegal means) that generate legal needs.
(3) Organizing can affect policy change to alter conditions underlying legal problems.

Below, I give examples from in-depth qualitative interviews with sixty-seven tenants who organized collectively, each of which illustrates how these mechanisms work to mitigate legal needs.

7.5.1 *Preemptive Organizing to Avoid Problems that Generate Legal Needs*

Some tenant organizations pursued preemptive strategies to help avoid practices that might lead to heightened legal needs. Take, for instance, collective bargaining with landlords: Using the threat of rent strikes or other direct action as leverage, tenant organizations engaged in collective bargaining bring property owners to the table to establish terms that ensure enduringly livable, healthy housing conditions. Tom, an organizer from a large tenant organization in Massachusetts, described the model as follows:

> [W]e were really emphasizing this idea of collective bargaining. . . . You organize a tenant association, and you ask for negotiations with the landlord to secure a long-term contract that ha[s] limited rent increases and addresse[s] conditions. Just like a labor contract, you would try to sign a three-year contract that addresse[s] wages and

[49] Michener, *supra* note 46; Jamila Michener & Mallory SoRelle, *Politics, Power, and Precarity: How Tenant Organizations Transform Local Political Life*, 11 INT. GRP. & ADVOC. 209 (2022).

> working conditions. And we were successful in doing that. We were getting a lot of buildings under contract. … [A] number of landlords decided that it was in their interest financially to work with us, or negotiate with us, rather than trying to evict us, because we could mobilize some pretty serious resources to block evictions. So, we've got a lot of buildings under contract and that really was a qualitative step forward in terms of collective bargaining.

While Tom's union was especially successful, it was not peculiar. Collective bargaining of this sort happens around the country and can act as a mechanism to proactively tackle the conditions that otherwise generate legal needs.

7.5.2 *Responsive Organizing to Address Problems that Generate Legal Needs*

When tenants operate as individuals, they do not have much leverage to hold landlords accountable. Alternatively, when they work collectively, they can use direct pressure tactics like protests and rent strikes to push landlords to meet the very material needs that transform into legal needs when unaddressed. Carlos, a member of a tenant union in Texas, detailed his organizations' "tactics to pressure landlords or management companies to do the right thing":

> We helped organize tenants. … [T]hey'd already had one negotiation with this management company that didn't go so well. … They had no water in the building. … They've been going without water for quite a while, and they finally got it turned back on after the protest and the rent strike. They finally got the water turned back on. [Now] there are still all kinds of other issues – mold in the apartments, other apartments have leaks … [The property management company] don't seem concerned about it. So, that's why rent strikes can continue at least for the foreseeable future … a good number [of tenants] are determined to [keep going].

Carlos and fellow members of his tenant union target specific actors to address harmful housing conditions that might otherwise lead to legal action. If only one or two tenants acted individually by withholding rent (as Quiana did when her landlord would not abate the lead), they could easily end up in housing court facing eviction, and they would likely need a lawyer to prevent displacement. But in the context of collective action, tenants create opportunities to negotiate. And the outcome of those negotiations can circumvent the processes that would have generated legal need.

7.5.3 *Organizing to Affect Policy Change*

A third way that organizing can mitigate legal need is via policy change. From good cause eviction to rent control to affordable housing – tenants around the country build power to address the structural conditions at the root of many legal problems.

Successful policy campaigns can have far-reaching reverberations in the lives of tenants. Consider Joe and Jocelyn, who started a tenant union in a Midwestern city. Soon after launching the union, Joe and Jocelyn discovered the main policy priority of the tenants in their organization: expelling a notorious property management company with a large footprint in the city. As Joe elaborated:

> They wanted them gone, and for good reason, there was a lot of illegal really, really brutal [stuff] going on. So that's the campaign we launched, to get that contract canceled. ... Nobody gave us any chance in hell of winning that campaign ... we had [city] council people saying this will never happen ... we were getting our asses kicked in this campaign. We were not winning. They hired maintenance staff to intimidate us. ... I got regular death threats against my daughter. Throughout this campaign every leader that spoke out was retaliated against from breaking windshields to evictions. But we just kept base building. We just kept knocking on doors. We just kept building relationships and we had meetings with the housing authority director.

Having identified an important cause of the problems facing tenants in their city, Joe and Jocelyn's union focused on weakening the "power structure" represented by people like the city housing director to achieve their policy goal of driving out a major property management company. To this end, they engaged in strategic institutional negotiation.[50] Though they identified the housing director as a primary roadblock, she was highly respected and behaved differently in closed-door conversations with tenant union members than she did publicly. So, their strategy was to push her "to treat our residents in public the way she treats them in private meetings." Joe believed that "what grows in the dark dies in the light of exposure" and anticipated that making a public spectacle of the housing director would create productive political pressure. This is precisely what happened. Joe describes it this way:

> We were able to get a committee hearing with [city] council and a resolution saying that the council supported cancelling this contract. We showed up really powerful that day. We filled up half the room. Our members told really powerful stories about the most egregious shit happening, and then [the housing director] literally got up there and did everything short of calling them liars. And [the city contract with the management company] was canceled four days later.

Jocelyn and Joe worked with hundreds of tenants in their city, most of whom were black women, to achieve a policy change that directly addressed the very housing conditions that often landed tenants in court. Indeed, they initially wanted a RTC campaign to be their first policy effort. But most members of the union preferred that they begin the union's work with ousting the management company that had long plagued the city. Following the lead of the tenants by letting their needs

[50] Jamila Michener, *Health Justice through the Lens of Power*, 50 J.L. Med. & Ethics 656 (2022).

determine the policy agenda of the union, Joe and Jocelyn developed a winning strategy and overcame the odds that seemed stacked against them at first. By building political power instead of legal capacity, they met the very needs that might have morphed into legal problems if left unaddressed. By doing so, they built their power further, creating a positive feedback cycle:

> [T]hat was our first campaign, and we built a really solid base out of that ... If you're in [this city] and you lived in public housing in the last ten years, chances are you've experienced this management group. Chances are your family experienced abuse by them. So, we built a lot of credibility on that. It's like, okay, this isn't just another nonprofit. ... These folks can actually deliver material demands, can actually make promises to working class people and deliver on them.

Joe, Jocelyn, and the tenants they organized took direct political action to drive policy change in their city. Their efforts centered on changes that would be meaningful in the lives of race-class marginalized tenants, altering the processes that create legal needs in the first place.

7.6 DEMAND-SIDE LEGAL INTERVENTIONS

Given the limits of the supply-side provision of legal services and the promise of building power through political organizing, it is tempting to underestimate the continued importance of civil legal infrastructure and resources. However, eschewing legal interventions in the current political economy risks doing great harm because many people would suffer more acute deprivation in the absence of legal protections. Further still, spurning legal tactics misses a potentially imperative opportunity to use the law as a means of forging countervailing power.[51] In this view, a strategic and complementary mix of supply and demand approaches is optimal.

What do demand-side legal interventions look like? All the attention given to supply has obscured the prospects for moving beyond accessing justice and toward wielding power.[52] Though an exhaustive accounting of those prospects is beyond the scope of this chapter, the remaining sections surface two examples that point in the direction of this fundamentally important shift: (1) using supply-side policies like RTC and use of nonlawyers as a path to power and (2) leveraging legal protections to support political organizing.

7.6.1 *From Supply to Demand: RTC as a Springboard*

Supply-side policies can complement and enhance efforts to build power in the marginalized communities that face the most debilitating legal problems. In some

[51] Kate Andrias & Benjamin I. Sachs, *Constructing Countervailing Power: Law and Organizing in an Era of Political Inequality*, 130 Yale L.J. 546 (2021).

[52] Sameer M. Ashar & Annie Lai, *Access to Power*, 148 Daedalus 82 (2019).

ways, this can happen inadvertently through policy feedback processes. For example, my coauthor Mallory SoRelle and I have found that people with civil legal problems who have legal representation have higher levels of political efficacy and are more likely to participate in politics.[53] In this way, policies that expand access to civil legal representation can "feedback" into the political system and boost the participation of people within racially and economically marginalized communities.[54]

There are also strategic and intentional ways of translating supply-side policies into demand-side gains. One example is Intro 1529 – a recently enacted law in NYC known as "The Power to Organize" bill. Intro 1529 amends the administrative code of the city of New York to require the Office of the Civil Justice (OCJ) coordinator to collaborate with community groups in engaging tenants around their civil legal rights and creating community infrastructure to enable tenants to protect those rights.[55] Such infrastructure can include holding tenant workshops and trainings, supporting the formation of tenant associations, and referring tenants to community organizations.

Like Intro 2014-B, Intro 1529 was developed and advanced by community organizers in collaboration with city council members and lawyers.[56] Media reports referred to the bill as promoting "tenants' right to organize."[57] In local meetings, tenant organizers explicitly talked about the limits of RTC/Intro 214-B and the necessity to both reinforce RTC through organizing efforts and use RTC as a springboard for funding organizing to build more power.[58] In this way, Intro 214-B together with Intro 1529 offer a model for addressing both the supply and the demand side of civil justice by pushing for both access to legal resources and increased organizing power. The complementary logic of these bills exemplifies how providing people with civil legal representation can be an entry point into cultivating political power.

7.6.2 *Abating Demand: Using Law to Sustain Organizing*

Leveraging civil law as a tool to buttress community organizing against the actors that provoke demand for legal services is also an important and direct means of

53 Jamila Michener & Mallory SoRelle, Uncivil Democracy: Power, Politics, and Civil Justice (forthcoming).

54 Jamila Michener, *Policy Feedback in a Racialized Polity*, 47 Pol'y Stud. J. 423 (2019).

55 Int. 1529-2019, N.Y.C. Council, Comm. Gen. Welfare (codified at N.Y.C. Admin. Code, §§ 26-1304(c); 26-1306), https://legistar.council.nyc.gov/LegislationDetail.aspx?ID=3923900&GUID=93564381-0704-43F3-9599-244BA2545155 (last accessed Feb. 14, 2025).

56 Michener, *supra* note 12.

57 Jonathan Sperling, *Coalition Urges City to Promote Tenants' Right to Organize*, Queens Daily Eagle (Dec. 13, 2019), https://queenseagle.com/all/2019/12/13/coalition-urges-city-to-promote-tenants-right-to-organize (last accessed Feb. 14, 2025).

58 Author's ethnographic observation of tenant organizations (2020 and 2021).

abating such demand.[59] For example, landlords that rent unsafe properties or perpetrate unethical practices are one driver of legal need.[60] As discussed in the previous section, providing legal support for organized groups of tenants that fight against such landlords – as opposed to only providing legal representation to each individual tenant – is an example of a demand-side, power-centered approach. This is not a new idea. Community lawyering and movement lawyering are longstanding and continued forms of resistance to structural inequalities.[61] Nevertheless, there is a disconnect between legal practitioners who prioritize increasing access to justice and those who seek to build power within the communities that are most bereft of such justice. John Whitlow, director of CUNY School of Law Community and Economic Development Clinic, incisively articulates the contours of this disconnect:

> [R]ight to counsel should be viewed as a limited intervention that operates when eviction is imminent, i.e. after the structural sources of displacement have done their work. Failure to recognize the limits of the RTC – and of access to justice paradigms more generally – naturalizes those structural sources and legitimates as normal the widening inequalities produced by our current political-economic and social order. Challenging inequality and displacement in a deep and lasting way requires moving beyond access to justice.[62]

One means of "challenging inequality and displacement in a deep and lasting way" is by offering legal support to tenant organizations as they marshal such challenges. For instance, consider the circumstances of tenants in Crest Hill Apartments, a privately owned recently renovated eighty-unit building.[63] Because Crest Hill has rent-stabilized apartments, it is one of the only affordable options for low-income tenants in the Northeastern community where the building is located. For this reason, many Crest Hill tenants welcomed the opportunity to rent in an affordably priced recently renovated building.

However, when a small child in the complex fell ill and a local pediatrician identified lead poisoning as the underlying problem, Crest Hill tenants discovered

[59] John Whitlow, *Community Law Clinics in the Neoliberal City: Assessing CUNY's Tenant Law and Organizing Project*, 20 CUNY L. Rev. 351 (2017).

[60] Philip M. E. Garboden & Eva Rosen, *Serial Filing: How Landlords Use the Threat of Eviction*, 18 City & Cmty. 638 (2019).

[61] Karen Gargamelli & Jay Kim, *Common Law's Lawyering Model: Transforming Individual Crises into Opportunities for Community Organizing*, 16 CUNY L. Rev. 201 (2012); Nicholas Hartigan, *No One Leaves: Community Mobilization as a Response to the Foreclosure Crisis in Massachusetts*, 45 Harv. C.R.-C.L. L. Rev. 181 (2010).

[62] John Whitlow, *Beyond Access to Justice: Challenging the Neoliberal Roots of Hypergentrification*, L. & Pol. Eco. Blog (Apr. 9, 2018), https://lpeproject.org/blog/beyond-access-to-justice-challenging-the-neoliberal-roots-of-hyper-gentrification/ (last accessed Feb. 14, 2025). Whitlow is not alone in advancing a vision that looks beyond access to justice to more fundamental structural transformation that contributes to "social reconstruction rather than social reproduction." *See, for example*, Sameer M. Ashar, *Law Clinics and Collective Mobilization*, 14 Clinical L. Rev. 359 (2008).

[63] Based on author's interview with tenant organizer in state in the Northeast (October 2022).

that they were living in conditions that were perilous for their health. Per state law, the lead poisoning diagnosis triggered automatic reporting to the local Department of Health, which then involved the Environmental Protection Agency (EPA). The EPA was legally mandated to test every unit in the building where children younger than six years old lived. Testing revealed that some units had nearly 50,000 micrograms of lead dust per square foot, relative to the EPA limit of 10 micrograms.

Tenants were infuriated. Many of the children in the building had been experiencing respiratory and other health issues. Melissa, a young mother in the building with some experience in political organizing, learned about the threat of lead toxicity and jumped right into action:

> [I]t was such an egregious revelation that . . . I was like, we have to have a meeting – a tenants meeting. There's just no option. We have to deal with this. And if we do it individually, there's just too many units for it to get mishandled by management . . . it was obvious . . . I literally have to do this. So I put up fliers around the building.

Melissa spread the word and Crest Hill tenants quickly had an initial meeting. Soon, the tenants in the building formed a tenant union to collectively confront the lead hazard that was sickening their families:

> So that first meeting, we had thirty people or so. It was a really good first meeting. And we just talked about the lead issue and how we were going to address it. And it was mostly giving people information on how to schedule their inspections, things like that . . . [T]he second meeting I broached the subject of a tenant union . . . it's so egregious that . . . we just have to proceed as quickly as possible . . . to move swiftly in order to protect kids in this building, let alone everyone else. And so, we got a majority support verbally at that meeting. And then me and a handful of other people brought the union petition around the buildings.

Within a month, three-quarters of the units in the building signed the petition. But the building owner was completely indifferent to tenant demands. Crest Hill was one of many buildings they owned, and paltry state fines did not outweigh the significant cost of lead abatement.

Crest Hill tenants pursued multiple strategies for holding the owner accountable. One strategy involved seeking legal help:

> [I]t came to light that not only is there a chronic, a systematic lead issue. There's also severe water damage and leaking . . . [and] fuzzy mold growth . . . our spore counts in here are very high . . . [so] it escalated pretty quickly in terms of our actions . . . [we] had to hire a civil attorney. With children involved, obviously, affecting their health . . . [I]t's for our own protection . . . [So]there's a housing court case. The first family filed with the housing court in January. Five more families, including us, joined for February. So now, we're paying rent into an escrow account. Ten more people are joining the rent strike for March.

Though the housing court case was a means of redress in its own right, it was also a mechanism to support organizing. The most obvious leverage that Crest Hill tenants had against their delinquent owner was the money they paid for rent. But tenants feared that withholding rent would risk eviction. Even though the building was hazardous, it was the only option for many tenants, especially short of any settlement or support to facilitate their move. So, if Crest Hill tenants wanted to organize a rent strike against the building owner, they needed protection from eviction while doing so. The civil proceeding afforded such protection by allowing tenants to pay their rent into an escrow that could be withheld from the landlord while the case was pending. This cleared the way for tenants to pursue more risky strategies, including direct action (protests, rallies, press conferences) in combination with a coordinated rent strike. In the absence of assurances from a civil attorney, many tenants would not have participated in these activities.

Crest Hill tenants navigated the boundaries between legal strategies and building grassroots power with a keen understanding of the relationship between the two, which Melissa articulated this way:

> [I]t can be really important to separate out the legal from the power building because Americans especially will go straight to the legal system as their only avenue. So, initially, everyone was going straight to that: "We got to hire the lawyer and sue [the owner]..." But even at the first meeting, I was saying, "if we are only going through the legal system, we will quickly become extremely frustrated and stop any kind of actual struggle against ownership and management because there are so many gaps."
>
> And a good lesson for the tenants was the Department of Health finished their legal mandate to only inspect units with kids under six, and tenants were like, "how can that be possible? How can they not be in charge of inspecting the rest of the units?" People were saying, "that can't be what the law is because that's not sufficient." And it's like, I hear you that it's not how it should be, but that is the reality ... the law is not made for tenants. It is not directed at tenants. It is to protect landlords and property ownership, to encourage property ownership. And what you're hearing is true, but we can't just get frustrated. We have to just take that information, find out what the gap is between where regulation stops and where we want it to be, and that gap is where we have to organize until we get the living conditions that we want to get.

At the core of these observations is an acknowledgment of the distinct but symbiotic relationship between legal and organizing approaches. The explicit use of lawyers in support of community organizing efforts goes beyond the case-based approach implicit in many access-to-justice efforts, and toward collective action that can help larger groups of people face more fundamental problems. In this view, policies seeking to advance access to justice through supply-side approaches like RTC, legal technology, and the use of nonlawyers are necessary, but not sufficient. It is pivotal to complement such policies with demand-side statutes that protect people from retaliation for organizing, strengthen collective bargaining rights, provide funding for lawyers to support community organizations, and more.

8

The Puzzle of Anemic "Legal Tech" and the Future of Legal Services

David Freeman Engstrom and Jess X. Lu

A puzzle hangs over legal tech: Why isn't there more of it, particularly the sort that helps ordinary people?

Conditions have long seemed ripe for a legal tech renaissance. While there remains debate about where to assign blame for the justice gap, its magnitude is undeniable. A parade of "legal needs" surveys in recent decades shows that a hundred million or more Americans experience one or more civil justice problems each year yet receive no help in resolving them.[1] Take this decades-long crisis of immense, unmet civil legal need and add in rapid advances in technology, especially artificial intelligence (AI), and one would expect a robust "direct-to-consumer" (DTC) legal tech sector that provides affordable, tech-enabled solutions to fill the justice gap.

And yet, investment in DTC legal tech – just one measure of an industry's health and potential – has languished compared to lawyer-driven software applications, such as Harvey or Casetext. Beyond LegalZoom and RocketLawyer, DTC legal tech is a footnote in a market dominated by law firms and corporate buyers.[2] And investment in DTC legal tech is a pittance compared to "fintech." Think here of Robinhood, a commission-free stock trading tool that has received a hefty $6 billion in funding,[3] more than ten times even LegalZoom.[4] Becky Sandefur, the dean of access-to-justice

1 *See* L. Servs. Corp., 2022 *Justice Gap Study* (2022), https://justicegap.lsc.gov/resource/2022-justice-gap-report/ (last accessed Feb. 14, 2025); Rebecca L. Sandefur & James Teufel, *Assessing America's Access to Civil Justice Crisis*, 11 U.C. Irvine L. Rev. 753, 757, 769–70 (2021); Deborah L. Rhode, *Access to Justice*, 69 Fordham L. Rev. 1785 (2001); Deborah L. Rhode, *Access to Justice: Again, Still*, 73 Fordham L. Rev. 1013 (2004).

2 Direct-to-consumer legal services have received only an estimated 0.6 percent of total investment in legal tech, broadly defined, from 1984 to 2020. Bob Ambrogi, *Exclusive Analysis: The True Story of Legal Tech Funding, 1984–2020*, LawSites (Sept. 12, 2022), https://www.lawnext.com/2022/09/exclusive-analysis-the-true-story-of-legal-tech-funding-1984-2020.html (last accessed Feb. 14, 2025).

3 *Robinhood Company Financials*, CrunchBase, https://www.crunchbase.com/organization/robinhood/company_financials (last accessed Feb. 14, 2025).

4 *LegalZoom Company Financials*, CrunchBase, https://www.crunchbase.com/organization/legalzoom-com/company_financials (last accessed Feb. 14, 2025).

scholars,[5] concluded in a 2019 report that legal tech tools serving "non-lawyers" are "restricted and limited" in functionality and "only partly match the types of justice problems most commonly reported by Americans."[6] A more recent report from Duke University reached the same conclusion: "justice tech"[7] has struggled to overcome "system barriers."[8] As one "justice tech" founder recounted, "I had a big dream and I knew it would be hard, but I had no idea."[9]

So why hasn't a robust DTC legal tech market emerged? At least three explanations have so far dominated the debate. The first (and most common) blames restrictive rules that say that only lawyers can practice law (i.e., prohibitions on "unauthorized practice of law," or UPL) or own law firms (i.e., Rule 5.4's bar on fee-sharing).[10] The former limits functionality, consigning DTC legal tech tools to form-filling and "document assembly," thus providing only limited help to those in need. The latter bar DTC providers that are not fully lawyer-owned – like LegalZoom – from employing lawyers to supplement their tech-based services. A second prominent theory is insufficiently potent technology: Automated tools, even sophisticated AI-based ones, cannot perform the all-important translational work – cutting through legalese and explaining options and outcomes in plain language – that is necessary when serving unsophisticated lay clients.[11] While not a problem for legal tech directed at lawyers, it's a major hurdle for tools that aim to serve people who need actionable advice in clear, understandable, and bite-sized forms. A third explanation focuses on courts' technology systems: Looking across some 14,000 court jurisdictions in the United States, one sees a checkerboard of technology and data infrastructures. The resulting technological Babel makes impossible the scale necessary to induce tech providers to invest time and capital in developing and

5 Professor Sandefur also coauthored the first chapter in this volume.

6 Rebecca Sandefur, *Legal Tech for Non-Lawyers: Report of the Survey of US Legal Technologies*, Am. Bar Found. (2019), https://www.americanbarfoundation.org/resources/legal-tech-for-non-lawyers-report-of-the-survey-of-us-legal-technologies/ (last accessed Feb. 14, 2025).

7 Using a much more expansive definition than that of Suffolk University, and including many legal tech models outside of DTC legal services, the Duke study defined "justice tech" as "companies and programs that create technology solutions to help people navigate legal matters with tech solutions that foster hope, independence, and self-empowerment and contribute to a fairer legal system." Duke at 08.

8 Kelli M. Raker, *From Founded to Funded: Challenges and Visions for Justice Tech*, Duke Ctr. on L. & Tech. 3 (2023), https://law.duke.edu/sites/default/files/images/embed/from_founded_to_funded_challenges_visions_for_justice_tech_oct2023.pdf [hereinafter "Duke Report"] (last accessed Feb. 14, 2025).

9 *Id.*

10 Gillian K. Hadfield, *The Cost of Law: Promoting Access to Justice through the (Un)corporate Practice of Law*, 38 Int'l Rev. L. & Econ. 44, 53 (2014). *See also* Gillian K. Hadfield & Deborah L. Rhode, *How to Regulate Legal Services to Promote Access, Innovation, and the Quality of Lawyering*, 67 Hastings L.J. 1191, 1193–94 (2016); Gillian K. Hadfield, *Legal Barriers to Innovation*, 31 Regulation 14 (2008).

11 John Armour & Mari Sako, *Lawtech: Leveling the Playing Field in Legal Services?*, *in* Legal Tech and the Future of Civil Justice 53–55 (David Freeman Engstrom ed., 2023).

then maintaining robust, user-friendly systems that serve customers with very limited ability to pay.

This chapter argues that undergirding each of these explanations is a deeper and potentially intractable problem. Though barriers such as restrictive rules, weak tech, or the court technology checkerboard are commonly invoked, they fail to account for the limited scale and longevity of most DTC legal tech. The better explanation for anemic legal tech – or at least a core component of a complete one – is the uniquely challenging market economics of providing low- and medium-income Americans with legal services. Facing already narrow margins, DTC legal tech is locked in an unwinnable race to attract and retain customers who only need their services once – and, worse, may not realize they need them at all. Lowering other barriers – say, by lifting the lawyer's monopoly, or leveraging newly potent forms of generative AI – might give DTC legal tech room to breathe, but doing so cannot alone solve the underlying problem: To build sustainable models, DTC legal tech needs passive income streams and enterprise-level customers.

That conclusion, withering as it is, is crucial to thinking about the future of legal services and access to justice. For instance, it is possible that "regulatory reform" advocates have it wrong, at least as to technology-based legal services. If liberalized legal services rules are unlikely to yield a flowering of DTC legal tech anytime soon, then perhaps the access-to-justice movement should be investing its limited capital, both political and real, in efforts to build out human-centered models of legal services delivery, such as the community justice worker movement.[12] By extension, perhaps legal tech entrepreneurs should focus on devising tools that extend the reach of the human providers, beleaguered and overwhelmed, that already dot the civil justice landscape. Even more bracing, perhaps legal tech developers should be creating tools that serve courts, not self-represented litigants.

As we note below, courts in the coming years will face a "make or buy" choice. "Make" means court-connected, court-hosted systems, including court portals, remote hearings, online dispute resolution (ODR), digital self-help, or e-filing, whereas "buy" means courts structuring themselves, particularly their technology and data systems, to be more accessible to intermediaries, especially DTC legal tech providers, who serve self-represented litigants. Make and buy require very different infrastructures, and it's not at all obvious that courts, perennially underfunded, have the money to do even one, let alone both. But if DTC legal tech is doomed, and budget-constrained courts must choose, then "make" – taxpayer-financed, "public option" legal tech – may be the wiser investment.

We develop these ideas using a mix of theory and evidence. The first section below reviews the "usual suspects" – three common explanations for anemic DTC legal tech. The next section sets forth our market- and business-centered theory, thus building a fuller account of the challenges facing DTC legal tech. A third section

[12] *See* Chapter 1 of this volume.

reports our research, including interviews, with six DTC legal tech providers, chosen to reflect a cross-section of the current market landscape, and then maps them to the full set of "barrier" theories. A final section considers the implications of a DTC legal tech sector that may never get fully off the ground.

A few orienting notes on scope: First, our inquiry focuses on DTC legal tech providers: client-facing providers that use technology to deliver legal services. We thus bracket legal tech tools that instead automate law practice via a "technology assist"[13] to lawyers and legal workers.[14] Moreover, we focus on legal tech providers that offer *actual* legal services, defined broadly as "help with a justiciable issue."[15] As such, we exclude story-telling tools, reminder tools, and digital signature tools which, while client-facing, do not provide a legal service; we also exclude "legal marketplaces," which merely connect consumers to an (often traditional) legal services provider.[16] Finally, we include DTC legal tech providers whose end users are individuals and/or small businesses, but not lawyers or large corporations. In so doing, we employ a broader definition of "consumer" than previous studies.[17] By defining consumers to include small businesses in addition to individuals, we focus on tools within the so-called PeopleLaw segment of the legal services industry, as distinct from corporate-facing BigLaw or legal aid.[18] In serving ordinary

[13] R. Grossman & Gordon V. Cormack, *Technology-Assisted Review in E-Discovery Can Be More Effective and More Efficient Than Exhaustive Manual Review*, 17 RICH. J.L. & TECH. (2011).

[14] *See* David Freeman Engstrom & Jonah B. Gelbach, *Legal Tech, Civil Procedure, and the Future of Adversarialism*, 169 U. PA. L. REV. 1001, 1017–18 (2021) (offering a taxonomy of legal tech applications). Suffolk University's Legal IT Lab has also created a useful taxonomy of legal tech, segmenting the space by use case: technology used by legal workers, technology built for legal workers, technology for clients, technology that performs a traditional lawyer role, marketplace tools, and technology used by courts. *What Legal Technology Is*, SUFFOLK L. TECH CLASS (Aug. 2020), https://suffolklitlab.org/legal-tech-class/docs/legal-tech-overview/legal-tech-overview (last accessed May 13, 2024).

[15] Our definition of legal services is inclusive of things like document assembly, which is not technically considered a legal service under laws governing the unlicensed practice of law (UPL). This concept was codified in LegalZoom's consent agreement with the North Carolina Bar Association. *See* LegalZoom.com, Inc. v. N.C. State Bar, No. 11 CVS 15111, 2015 WL 6441853, at *1 (N.C. Super. Ct. Oct. 22, 2015). In August 2019, the American Bar Association adopted best practices for online legal document providers that included similar constraints. *See generally Resolution 10A: ABA Best Practice Guidelines for Online Legal Document Providers*, AM. BAR ASS'N HOUSE OF DELEGATES (Aug. 12–13, 2019), https://www.americanbar.org/content/dam/aba/directories/policy/annual-2019/10a-annual-2019.pdf (last accessed Feb. 14, 2025).

[16] Attorney-client matching service Atticus is an example of a legal marketplace, and thus outside of the express scope of this study. We nonetheless include Atticus because it is illustrative of how regulatory constraints shape business models.

[17] An example is the 2019 Sandefur study, which studied only "digital legal tools for nonlawyer users" who were "individual members of the public working on their own problems or nonlawyers such as social workers or community organizers working directly with the public." *See* SANDEFUR, *supra* note 6, at 3.

[18] For more information on this terminology, *see* David Freeman Engstrom, *Introduction*, in LEGAL TECH AND THE FUTURE OF CIVIL JUSTICE 6 (David Freeman Engstrom ed., 2023).

individuals and not organizational clients, PeopleLaw sits at the cusp of the justice gap: individuals and businesses who do not qualify for legal aid but who also cannot afford traditional legal services.

8.1 THE USUAL SUSPECTS: "BARRIER" THEORIES

Three explanations have dominated the debate about anemic "justice tech." Each, however, raises hard questions about where the real problem lies. This section reviews each explanation to set the stage for our own market- and business-focused account of why DTC legal tech has languished.

8.1.1 *Restrictive Rules and Regulatory Reform*

The most common explanation for anemic legal tech is regulatory constraints on law practice. In the US context, two types of restrictions are most salient. The first is the prohibition on UPL. The second is Rule 5.4's bar on fee-sharing, which limits investment in law firms to lawyers and prevents investors who are not lawyers and organizations that are not law firms to own, invest in, and profit from the sale of legal services. Notably, numerous states have relaxed, or are considering relaxing, these regulations.[19] But as it stands, these rules continue to constrain the services that legal tech providers can offer.[20]

However, whether liberalizing reforms can unleash new entity- and technology-based modes of legal services delivery remains unproven. In the United Kingdom, where UPL was already more relaxed, loosening fee-sharing rules to permit non-lawyer investment in legal services providers has had an underwhelming impact on innovation. While the majority of such providers in the United Kingdom serve individual consumers or small businesses,[21] a comparative study of nonlawyer ownership in Canada, Australia, England, and Wales concluded that outside investment's impacts on access to justice remain limited outside of certain practice areas, such as personal injury.[22] Moreover, it's unclear whether the benefits of these

[19] For more on those reforms, see, for example, the Introduction of this volume; Marco Poggio, *The Issues Access to Justice Leaders Are Watching in 2024*, LAW360 (Jan. 5, 2024), https://www.law360.com/articles/1779365/the-issues-access-to-justice-leaders-are-watching-in-2024 (last accessed Feb. 14, 2025) (describing status of regulatory reform efforts in a number of states).

[20] At the same time, Rule 5.4 cuts off fully compliant legal services providers, particularly law firms, from the financing sources, including venture capital and other equity stake, that have revolutionized the rest of the economy. *See* Hadfield, *Legal Barriers*, *supra* note 10.

[21] Mari Sako & Richard Parnham, *Technology and Innovation in Legal Services: Final Report for the Solicitors Regulation Authority* 7, SRA (2021), https://www.sra.org.uk/globalassets/documents/sra/research/full-report-technology-and-innovation-in-legal-services.pdf (last accessed Feb. 14, 2025).

[22] Memorandum from Jasminka Kalajdzic on alternative business structure research to the Ont. Trial Lawyers Ass'n. (Dec. 1, 2014), https://otlablog.com/wp-content/uploads/2015/01/Dr-Kalajdzic-Study-on-NLO.pdf (last accessed Feb. 14, 2025).

economies of scale are consistently passed on to consumers. While greater nonlawyer investment generally *has* promoted technological innovation and the development of new legal services,[23] evidence is mixed on whether reforms have moved the needle on price.[24]

8.1.2 *Weak AI*

A second common explanation for anemic DTC legal tech is that AI is simply not potent enough to productize PeopleLaw. One theory is that, unlike legal tech for BigLaw, legal tech for PeopleLaw must interface directly with individuals and small business owners who require lay translation of legal concepts,[25] something natural language processing (NLP) technology, powerful as it is, has struggled to do.[26]

The "weak AI" explanation for languishing legal tech is an important one, but it is hardly decisive. After an "AI winter" of relative stasis, AI is once more undergoing staggering leaps in potency with the arrival of powerful "large language models," or LLMs – a branch of "generative AI" that is capable of producing clear, plain language text. Champions see a two-fold promise. First, new AI systems are plainly better than earlier generations of NLP at translating plain language into legalese and vice versa.[27] As already noted, lay-to-legal translation is essential if you want to build usable tools. Second, increased translational capacities might mean that new generative AI systems can take lay narratives – an individual's plain language explanation of a problem – and then map them to legal ontologies, pathways, and even

[23] Stephen Roper et al., *Innovation in Legal Services: A Report for the Solicitors Regulation Authority and the Legal Services Board* 22, SRA (2015), https://www.sra.org.uk/globalassets/documents/sra/research/innovation-report.pdf?ver-sion = 4a1aba (last accessed Feb. 18, 2025).

[24] For instance, a 2018 survey suggests that technological innovation unlocked by ABS status reduced costs for one-third of surveyed providers, though it is unclear if they then passed those cost savings on to consumers. L. Servs. Bd., 2018 *Technology and Innovation in Legal Services Main Report* 5 (Nov. 2018), https://legalservicesboard.org.uk/wp-content/media/Innovation-survey-2018-report-FINAL-2.pdf (last accessed Feb. 24, 2025). By contrast, a 2020 report asserts that ABSs are more likely to offer fixed-fee and low-cost services as compared to non-ABS legal entities. L. Servs. Bd., 2020 *Evidence Compendium* 64 (2020), https://legalservicesboard.org.uk/wp-content/uploads/2020/11/The-State-of-Legal-Services-Evidence-Compendium-FINAL.pdf (last accessed Feb. 24, 2025). However, there is no evidence that overall affordability has improved: Indeed, a 2020 study of the quoted prices of legal services in England and Wales found more indications of price increases rather than decreases. L. Servs. Bd., *Prices of Individual Consumer Legal Services* 7 (Sept. 2020), https://www.legalservicesboard.org.uk/wp-content/uploads/2020/09/Prices-of-Individual-Consumer-Legal-Services-Sept-2020-1.pdf (last accessed Feb. 24, 2025).

[25] Armour & Sako, *supra* note 11, at 54–56.

[26] *Id.* at 58–60.

[27] *See* Neel Guha et al., *LegalBench: A Collaboratively Built Benchmark for Measuring Legal Reasoning in Large Language Models*, *in* Advances in Neural Information Processing Systems 36 (S. Koyejo et al. eds., 2024).

likely outcomes.[28] For the first time, AI might be potent enough to plausibly offer actionable advice to self-represented litigants on options and outcomes.

Current prognostications, however, may miss some important points. For starters, generative AI may not move the needle as much as some think. Much of existing DTC legal tech does not rely on cutting-edge technologies: Document assembly, for instance, is relatively low-tech, using simple automation engines to help self-represented litigants answer complaints and avoid default judgments.[29] The value-add of sophisticated generative AI systems may not be as robust as some assume.

Moreover, to be both reliable and cost-effective, AI must adapt to an ever-shifting constellation of substantive and procedural rules across jurisdictions. Direct-to-consumer legal tech providers have to this point relied solely on human lawyers to manually update their tools as laws change or new rules and regulations are issued. Here, too, questions remain about how soon, or even whether, newly potent forms of AI can handle subtly and ever-changing laws and regulations without human intervention.

Time will tell whether continuing AI advances can make meaningful progress on these problems. But, for the moment, weak AI does not offer anything approaching a fully satisfactory theory for the current state of DTC legal tech. For some applications, current tech capabilities seem more than ample. For others, continued AI advances may hold the key.

8.1.3 *The Court Technology Checkerboard*

A third common explanation for anemic DTC legal tech extends from American federalism. In a nutshell, most PeopleLaw clients have a limited ability to pay. So for providers, scale is king. However, in addition to the variations in substantive and procedural law just noted, a checkerboard of technology systems, particularly e-filing systems, and data infrastructures across thousands of local court jurisdictions make scaling services nearly impossible.

More specifically, DTC legal tech is limited by two types of jurisdictional complexity.[30] First, patchwork systems create jurisdictional differences in what forms litigants need to e-file, what requirements they need to meet, and what system – both front-end and back-end – litigants e-file through. Filing requirements are a key pain point that increases the complexity of delivering clients filing-ready documents;

28 *See* Margaret D. Hagan, *Good AI Legal Help, Bad AI Legal Help: Establishing Quality Standards for Responses to People's Legal Problem Stories*, JURIX AI AND ACCESS TO JUST. WORKSHOP (2023), https://drive.google.com/file/d/14CitzBksHiu_2x8W2eT-vBe_JNYOcOhM/view?usp=drive_link (last accessed Apr. 2, 2024).

29 Interview with Kimball Parker, CEO of SixFifty (Feb. 3, 2023) [hereinafter "Parker Interview"].

30 Filing complexity not only focuses on the complexity of the laws themselves but also encompasses procedural complexity around filing requirements.

DTC legal tech often requires full-time lawyers to manually track and update requirements across the jurisdictions they serve.[31] Second, even if technologists find a way to track and code around jurisdictional differences, self-represented litigants cannot e-file at all in many states[32] and, even where they can, they can only do so in limited case types. Filing fees – and e-filing can often introduce additional fees – pose an additional burden; there are no consistent digital payment systems, so some jurisdictions require litigants to pay in person.[33]

As with the other commonly invoked barriers to robust DTC legal tech, the state and local checkerboard of technology systems and data infrastructures might improve, and efforts are underway to develop common, jurisdiction-spanning data standards.[34] Unless automated approaches can replace brute-force monitoring and updating, the checkerboard problem – complex, incongruous, and confusing requirements that vary state to state and even courthouse to courthouse – will remain a threat to low-cost delivery models. At the same time, the technology checkerboard plainly has less to say about federal-level innovation, not to mention large states with relatively unified court systems. As with the other explanations, the checkerboard is, at best, a partial explanation for anemic legal tech.

* * *

In short, even if rules were liberalized, AI continued to vault ahead, and the checkerboard made more uniform, DTC legal tech still faces substantial barriers. The next section begins to sketch them.

8.2 A NEW TAKE: MARKET BARRIERS TO ROBUST DTC LEGAL TECH

What else might explain anemic legal tech? This section develops an alternative, market-based theory focused on legal tech providers as businesses – and, very often, startups – and the shape of the markets they seek to serve. To flesh out its particulars, it draws on theory and industry analogues to propose a three-step, market-based explanation: Legal tech lacks a sustainable customer base because (i) limited customer demand and (ii) high customer-acquisition costs produce (iii) an acute "lifetime value trap." The rest of this section elaborates on each of these challenges.

[31] Interview with Erin Levine, Founder of Hello Divorce (Jan. 31, 2023) [hereinafter "Levine Interview"].

[32] Nat'l Ctr. for State Cts., Self-represented Efiling: Surveying the Accessible Implementations 3 (2022).

[33] *See* George Simons, *Civil Court Fees Block Justice Even in Well-Intentioned States*, Bloomberg Law (Feb. 23, 2022), https://news.bloomberglaw.com/us-law-week/civil-court-fees-block-justice-even-in-well-intentioned-states (last accessed Feb. 18, 2025).

[34] *See Filing Fairness Project*, Stan. L. Sch., https://filingfairnessproject.law.stanford.edu/ (last accessed May 1, 2024).

PeopleLaw – the market that DTC legal tech is best positioned to serve – has been flooded with lawyers for decades,[35] yet it remains notorious for its lack of profitability.[36] The vast majority of PeopleLaw is bespoke and labor-intensive, and there isn't much room to lower prices when the average solo practitioner already earns less than $60,000 (and may be facing significant law school debt).[37] And while legal tech has often served those priced out of traditional PeopleLaw, that market likely cannot sustain the scale necessary for a tech startup to grow, particularly where legal tech providers typically face stiff competition to attract individual customers.[38]

With the ever-increasing cost of digital marketing, including the rising ticket price of search engine optimization (SEO), legal tech must dramatically increase the dollar value of each client to break even, let alone turn a profit. While this problem may be addressed by building a steady base of loyal, returning customers, demand in PeopleLaw is hardly consistent: Customers are less likely to need another divorce than they are a replacement pair of their favorite brand-named sneakers. To solve this problem, other consumer services segments – health tech and platform tech – have redefined the customer: Instead of individual users, they serve enterprises that come with big-ticket contracts and reliable revenue. But there is no clear enterprise customer, at least not yet, for legal tech to tap into.

8.2.1 *Limited Customer Demand*

In general, legal markets are hindered by informational asymmetries that artificially curb demand: People do not understand their true legal needs, and do not seek appropriate representation. One way to combat low demand is to target services to specific markets: Think here of personal injury lawyers' billboards, which make the nature of their services crystal clear. But when providers tailor their offerings to a legal services niche particularized enough to passively attract customers – such as sole business proprietors or divorcees – that niche often has too few clients to justify the expense of serving it.

8.2.2 *High Customer-Acquisition Costs*

Even if a legal tech provider can crack the demand problem and generate interest in their services within their target demographic, founders note that "it still [takes] a lot

[35] Benjamin H. Barton, *Regulation, Culture, Markets: The Future of Legal Tech, in* LEGAL TECH AND THE FUTURE OF CIVIL JUSTICE 30–32 (David Freeman Engstrom ed., 2023).

[36] WILLIAM D. HENDERSON, LEGAL MARKET LANDSCAPE REPORT 13–15 (2018).

[37] Barton, *supra* note 35, at 30–32.

[38] *See, for example*, LegalZoom's marketing spend. LegalZoom, *United States Securities and Exchange Commission form* S-1 69 (2021), https://www.sec.gov/Archives/edgar/data/1286139/000119312521182939/d146270ds1.htm (last accessed Feb. 18, 2025).

of work to convert that interest into a paying customer."[39] This is because customer-acquisition costs (CAC) are incredibly high. Traditional, low-tech methods don't seem to work in the legal tech space: Finding consumers by word of mouth can be "challenging" and take "more time than they originally planned."[40] In general, overcrowding in DTC markets has driven up the price of digital advertising,[41] eliminated any arbitrage, and made the customer-acquisition math much more challenging.[42] For legal tech, even in markets where users understand their specific legal need, intense competition between providers can render legal services financially inaccessible. Take immigration, for example: Provider overcrowding has made SEO on immigration-related terms so expensive that many for-profit providers charge fees in the thousands to recoup advertising costs.[43]

8.2.3 *The Lifetime Value Trap*

A DTC brand's success hinges on how much headroom there is between customer lifetime value (LTV) and CAC.[44] Now that CAC has skyrocketed, it is "widely accepted" that firms should direct more effort into retaining existing customers than attracting new ones.[45] Yet there are only two ways to boost LTV: repeat customers, or customer cross-sell. DTC legal tech is set up for failure on both.

Where consumer demand is steady – for example, in consumer goods – the key to repeat customers is loyalty: getting your customer to stick with you over your competitors. Customer-centric, interaction-based marketing models are the current gold standard for increasing customer loyalty and, thus, LTV.[46] Consistent touch-points allow companies to gather nuanced customer data that can predict and even generate demand. Allbirds, a DTC shoe brand, can use the data of existing customers to estimate how often a particular customer will need to replace their shoes, and to build customer profiles that allow it to maximize each dollar spent on CAC. The same relatively straightforward calculation is possible for razors, laundry detergent,

[39] Duke Report, *supra* note 8, at 17.

[40] *Id.*

[41] V. Kumar, Customer Lifetime Value – The Path to Profitability, 2 Foundations and Trends in Marketing 1 (2008); V. Kasturi Rangan et al., *How Direct-to-Consumer Brands Can Continue to Grow*, 99 Harv. Bus. Rev. 101 (2021), https://hbr.org/2021/11/how-direct-to-consumer-brands-can-continue-to-grow.

[42] Leonard A. Schlesinger et al., *Reinventing the Direct-to-Consumer Business Model*, Harv. Bus. Rev. Online (2020), https://hbr.org/2020/03/reinventing-the-direct-to-consumer-business-model (last accessed Feb. 18, 2025).

[43] Interview with Jonathan Petts, Co-Founder & CEO of Upsolve (Mar. 1, 2023) [hereinafter "Petts Interview"]; *The Green Card Explained*, Boundless, https://www.boundless.com/immigration-resources/the-green-card-explained/ (last accessed May 13, 2024).

[44] Kumar, *supra* note 41; Rangan et al., *supra* note 41.

[45] Ali T. Jahrom et al., *Managing B2B Customer Churn, Retention and Profitability*, 43 Indus. Mktg. Mgmt. 1258 (2014).

[46] Kumar, *supra* note 41, at 85–89.

and all manner of consumer goods that are used up and regularly repurchased. And in consumer goods, cross-sell opportunities are often obvious: A company can easily expand into selling shaving cream alongside razors.

A common strategy among DTC companies is to build customer loyalty by expanding beyond their initial product offerings to create a complementary ecosystem of products and services. Peloton, for instance, initially offered big-ticket exercise bikes but quickly expanded to offer digital exercise class subscriptions, exercise apparel, and wellness programming.[47] It thus transformed from a bike retailer to a holistic exercise company with the ability to collect and use customer data to drive growth.

Direct-to-consumer companies that provide services, not goods, also leverage consumer data to drive LTV.[48] By interfacing directly with consumers, DTC brands can generate huge troves of data about usage preferences. TurboTax, for example, sells customer data to generate advertisements[49] and targets users with "offers"[50] – that is, upsells them.[51] And perhaps most important of all, the relentlessness of annual taxes means that TurboTax enjoys repeat customers – and, even better, customers with increasingly complex needs over a lifetime – with little investment required on their part.

Where building loyalty among individual customers is impracticable, DTC service providers often turn to enterprise-level customers: companies, not individuals, who purchase big-ticket and renewable contracts. Subscriptions sold to enterprises, not individuals, are also generally more profitable: While Amazon's marketplace generates more revenue, its cloud solutions – sold only to enterprises – account for the lion's share of Amazon's profits.[52] Similarly, many health tech players have made insurers and employers their core customers.[53] More complex healthcare services use a B2B subscription model: Livongo, a diabetes management platform, is free to the individual user but paid for by employers, health plans, or health providers.[54]

[47] *See* Kumar, *supra* note 41; Rangan et al., *supra* note 41.

[48] *Id.*

[49] Courteney Brown, *What Intuit Knows about You*, Axios (May 29, 2019), https://www.axios.com/2019/05/29/what-intuit-knows-about-you (last accessed Feb. 18, 2025).

[50] Geoffrey A. Fowler, *You Agreed to What? Tax Sites Want Your Data for More than Boarding*, Wash. Post (Apr. 12, 2020), https://www.washingtonpost.com/technology/2022/04/12/tax-prep-privacy/ (last accessed Feb. 18, 2025).

[51] Paul Kiel & Justin Elliott, *TurboTax and Others Charged at least 14 Million Americans for Tax Prep*, ProPublica (Feb. 5, 2020), https://www.propublica.org/article/turbotax-and-others-charged-at-least-14-million-americans-for-tax-prep-that-should-have-been-free-audit-finds (last accessed Feb. 18, 2025).

[52] Alexander Gleiss et al., *An Apple a Day – How the Platform Economy Impacts Value Creation in the Healthcare Market*, 31 Elec. Mkts. 849, 853 (2021).

[53] *Id.* at 865.

[54] *Livongo FAQs* 2020, Univ. of Tex. (2021), https://www.utsystem.edu/sites/default/files/documents/publication/2021/ut-select-livongo-overview-faqs/livongo-faq-2020.pdf (last accessed May 13, 2024).

Most importantly, enterprise-level contracts serve as vital cash infusions that give startups with limited equity – like most legal tech – the capital they need to scale and grow.[55] Biotechnology startups often get early "revenues" from contracts with large pharmaceutical companies, providing both cash flow and visibility into on-hand capital for longer-term investments.[56] This ability to forecast is particularly important in maturing startups looking to scale.[57] Major cash infusions are especially vital for legal services startups that, because of Rule 5.4, cannot raise outside investment using asset-backed guarantees and do not have outside equity to pad their cash flows.

Structural forces prevent legal tech from implementing each of these traditional strategies. First and foremost, legal tech cannot rely on predictable demand to increase LTV. Unlike shoes, people do not always need legal services. And the more specialized the legal service is, the rarer the potential repeat customers or cross-sell opportunities become. This creates a tension between increasing specialization of legal tech – the very unbundling of legal services that some view as a necessary precursor to lower-cost legal services[58] – and a DTC legal tech provider's ability to generate sustainable LTV.

Second, traditional enterprise customers do not exist for legal services, likely due in part to the lack of legal insurance. In the United States, there is little legal insurance outside of medical malpractice for doctors.[59] Employers, reliable enterprise customers, are unlikely to offer legal insurance on a large scale: Unlike healthcare, where both employer and employee have a vested interest in the employee's health, employees often have legal needs that are actually *adverse* to their employers – for instance, issues around benefits or even claims against the employer itself.

Third, enterprises unique to legal services are poorly positioned to support and scale DTC legal tech. BigLaw seems the obvious choice: Because firms can invest in DTC legal tech without running afoul of UPL or Rule 5.4, they can give small startups the credibility needed to win customer trust. But the economics of BigLaw are not designed to withstand the major up-front investment required to stand up a legal tech startup. A new DTC legal tech provider must spend at least six months to a year fine-tuning SEO to hit the right searches and convert leads to revenue[60] – an

[55] *See* Antonio Davila et al., *Building Sustainable High-Growth Startup Companies: Management Systems as an Accelerator*, 52 Cal. Mgmt. Rev. 79 (2010); Gunter Festel et al., *Valuation of Early Stage High-tech Start-up Companies*, 18 Int'l J. of Bus. 217 (2013).

[56] Davila et al., *supra* note 55, at 97; Paull Dunn & Leo Cheatham, *Fundamentals of Small Business Financial Management for Startup, Survival, Growth, and Changing Economic Circumstances*, 19 Managerial Fin. 1 (1993).

[57] Festel et al., *supra* note 55, at 217.

[58] Hadfield, *Cost of Law*, *supra* note 10, at 52–53; *see also* Hadfield, *Legal Barriers*, *supra* note 10.

[59] Tom Baker, The Medical Malpractice Myth (2005). By contrast, legal insurance in Europe is relatively ubiquitous. Anthony Heyes et al., *Legal Expenses Insurance, Risk Aversion and Litigation*, 24 Int'l Rev. L. & Econ. 107 (2004).

[60] Parker Interview, *supra* note 29.

expensive process even without the years required to create the document assembly tool in the first place.[61] Cash-strapped courts could, in theory, be a promising enterprise customer for established providers, supplying them with a steady stream of litigant-clients, but they face high hurdles in supporting startups.

Finally, the nature of legal services creates barriers to legal tech companies building holistic product suites for which customers have ongoing needs. For instance, Hello Divorce – a DTC legal tech company described in more detail below – followed the "Peleton-model" and introduced nonlegal services that extend the lifetime of its divorce clients. But the introduction of those services required careful, resource-intensive navigation around strict UPL and Rule 5.4 prohibitions. Even then, the lack of perpetual demand for legal services creates issues. While Peloton customers will likely only buy one bike – just as Hello Divorce customers will likely only get one divorce – exercise and wellness are ongoing needs; divorce counseling is not. Direct-to-consumer legal tech must not only stave off competition; it must also contend with a more existential question: If I solve my client's legal problem, will they ever need me again?

8.3 THE BARRIERS IN OPERATION: CASE STUDIES IN LEGAL TECH

This section puts data on what, to this point, has been mostly open-ended theorizing about the workings of the legal tech marketplace. We do so by running the various theories – both the "usual suspects" and our new, market-based way of thinking – through a select set of legal tech providers, as summarized in Table 8.1.[62] These legal tech offerings represent a rough cross-section of the nascent DTC industry in terms of each entity's services type (from online software wizards that generate ready-to-file legal documents to legal advice from humans), the subject-matter area of those services, the entity's organizational structure, its fee structure (including its for-profit or nonprofit status and its sources of revenue), and its geographic scope. Taken together, these companies offer an ideal workbench to explore how the different possible explanations for the industry's anemic status operate and intersect across different segments of the market. They also make plain our central thesis, as summarized in Figure 8.1. While conventional explanations for anemic DTC legal

[61] Anett Erdmann et al., *Search Engine Optimization: The Long-Term Strategy of Keyword Choice*, 144 J. Bus. Rsch. 650 (2022). Interviews with founders showed that document assembly tools require months to years of time and investment to set up. *See* Petts Interview, *supra* note 43; Parker Interview, *supra* note 29; Levine Interview, *supra* note 31.

[62] We have chosen six providers of various sizes at different levels of maturity that offer different services at different scopes. Note that, while Atticus does not fall within our definition of DTC legal, we nonetheless include it as an interesting analogue to Hello Divorce. Both case studies illustrate how regulation impacts business model design, which then impacts service delivery and scalability.

TABLE 8.1 *Six case studies of legal tech providers*

	Scope	Structure	Services			Fees			
			Document assembly	Legal advice	Attorney-client matching	One-time customer transaction fees	Ongoing customer subscription fees	Attorney referral fees	Grants or individual donations
Hello Divorce: generates and files divorce documents; connects clients with lawyers at its sister firm, Levine Law	Multi-State	Dual-Entity	✓	✓	✓		✓	✓	
Atticus: legal marketplace that performs client intake and connects users with vetted outside lawyers; focused on social security and disability	National	Dual-Entity			✓			✓	
Tenant Power Toolkit: generates and files documents for tenants facing eviction in California with a focus on the L.A. courts	CA	Stand-Alone	✓						✓
LegalZoom: offers document production, filing, and legal advice for small business owners and solo proprietors	National	Stand-Alone	✓	✓		✓	✓	✓	
Upsolve: generates but does not file, chapter 7 bankruptcy documents	National	Stand-Alone	✓					✓	✓
SixFifty: SaaS company offering employers platform-level employment and privacy solutions with one-off document assembly available on their website	National	Wholly Owned Subsidiary of Wilson Sonsini	✓	✓		✓	✓		

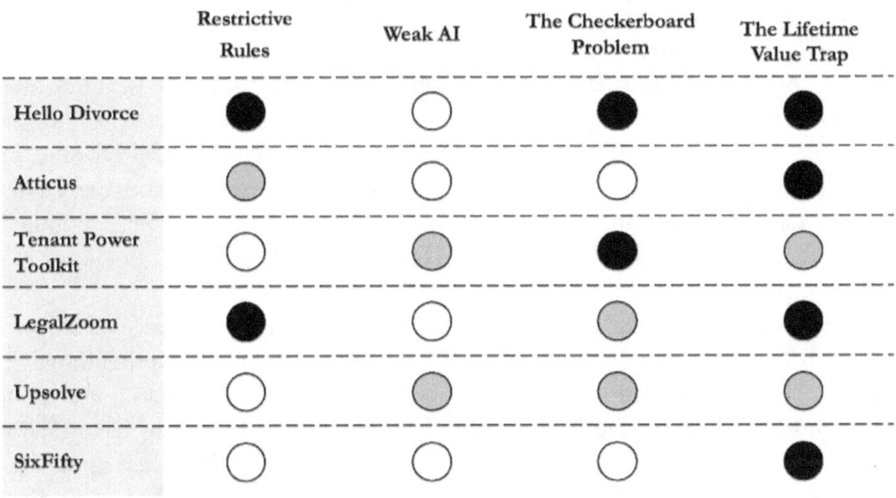

FIGURE 8.1 Impact: degree to which a barrier restricts scale.
A black circle indicates that the barrier has a significant and negative effect on the provider such that lifting the barrier would enable the provider to scale, grow, or otherwise offer better services to their clients; a gray circle indicates that the barrier limits scalability or profitability in minor ways; a white circle indicates that the barrier has no or minimal impact.

tech – restrictive lawyer rules, weak AI, and the jurisdiction-by-jurisdiction technology checkerboard – might explain languishing legal tech as to some subset of DTC providers, only our market-based theory can fully explain lagging legal tech across the board.

8.3.1 *Restrictive Rules: Why Hello Divorce Struggles When Atticus Does Not*

Restrictive rules have shaped what services American legal tech can offer and how their businesses are structured. But just how much explanatory power do they carry, and how, exactly, do rule restrictions limit available business models when trained on particular providers?

Key to answering those questions is to see the *combined* effects of UPL and Rule 5.4, not one or the other operating alone. For instance, LegalZoom's core business focuses on document assembly, which is not affected by UPL rules or changes to them. Rule 5.4's constraint on nonlawyer ownership, however, adds a further layer of complexity by limiting provision of legal advice *even by full-fledged lawyers*. In the United States, LegalZoom's nonlawyer ownership means it cannot hire attorneys to provide direct legal advice to its customers – a major disadvantage when competing against traditional law firms. But in the UK and Arizona, which permit nonlawyer ownership in some circumstances, LegalZoom employs licensed attorneys to provide permitted legal services. And it makes a mint in doing so – those legal services are a major profit driver, increasing transaction volume and allowing LegalZoom to charge a premium over its tech-only services.[63]

But workarounds of Rule 5.4 in the United States are few. New ventures must either forego outside funding or adopt convoluted dual-entity structures to allow the tech side to receive funding while the law firm itself does not. Hello Divorce, for instance, operates both Hello Divorce, a technology company, and the Levine Family Law Group, a full-service law firm, as separate entities through a complicated "dual-entity" model in order to skirt both UPL and Rule 5.4 restrictions. And doing so is costly.

To see why, consider first that Hello Divorce provides digital DIY divorce products across document assembly, e-filing, credit repair, and other financial services.[64] Its online platform also offers access to expert help from in-house mediators and lawyers at Levine Law.[65] Users pay a monthly subscription fee of $99 to access the DIY web-based tool and additional fees for financial coaching or legal services.[66] The Levine Family Law Group, a long-standing family law practice, provides those legal services,[67] which are used by approximately 50 percent of Hello Divorce's clients.[68] Those clients sign a fee agreement with Levine Law, not Hello Divorce.[69] But in order to provide legal services through the Hello Divorce app – which hosts all scheduling, correspondence, and documents – Levine Law pays Hello Divorce a monthly administrative fee of $4,750.[70]

These crisscrossing contracts are a direct product of restrictive regulation. Lest it violate UPL, Hello Divorce the tech company cannot hire lawyers to provide legal services; its technology cannot provide legal services, nor can its paralegals offer legal advice.[71] But under Rule 5.4, Levine Law cannot split legal fees with Hello Divorce. And since Rule 5.4 bans nonlawyer investment, Hello Divorce cannot collect legal fees directly from customers or own an in-house law firm. Nor can Levine Law support Hello Divorce as a wholly owned subsidiary: It is unlikely any law firm

63 LegalZoom S-1, *supra* note 38, at 170.

64 E-Mail from Erin Levine, Founder of Hello Divorce (Sept. 19, 2022) (on file with author) [hereinafter "Levine E-Mail"].

65 Levine Interview, *supra* note 31.

66 *How an Attorney-turned-Entrepreneur Is Using Legal Technology to Reshape Divorce Law*, Clio Customer Stories, https://www.clio.com/customers/how-an-attorney-turned-entrepreneur-is-using-legal-technology-to-reshape-divorce-law/ (last accessed Jan. 7, 2024).

67 *Id.*

68 *Id.*

69 Erin Levine, *Legal Fee Revenue Model*, Canva, Slide 4-6, https://www.canva.com/design/DAEv10ZG1Js/9TxWJDrhBSAkdyTH07i6cQ/view?utm_content=DAEv10ZG1Js&utm_campaign=designshare&utm_medium=link2&utm_source=sharebutton (last accessed Jan. 7, 2024) (hereinafter "Hello Divorce Investor Materials").

70 Clio, *supra* note 66; Hello Divorce Investor Materials, *supra* note 69, at 6.

71 California is one of many jurisdictions that requires paralegals to be supervised by a lawyer in a firm to give legal advice. Hello Divorce Investor Materials, Slide 3, *supra* note 69.

outside of resource-rich BigLaw can afford to shoulder the costs of scaling a startup, especially since Rule 5.4 cuts off access to loans and outside capital.

This convoluted structure, while end-running UPL and Rule 5.4, brings substantial operational complexity, making the business more expensive, harder to run, and less attractive to investors. For starters, Hello Divorce cannot enjoy basic economies of scale such as shared software subscriptions, malpractice insurance, workers comp, and cybersecurity.[72]

The dual-entity workaround also restricts the flow of capital between Levine Law and Hello Divorce. Venture capital and private equity can only be directed to Hello Divorce,[73] while legal services revenue must flow into Levine Law. Thus, venture funding cannot be used to pay attorney salaries – Levine Law's biggest cost bucket.[74] The dual-entity structure's mismatched cash flows also split value between the two companies, making Hello Divorce appear less profitable – and less attractive to investors – on paper.[75]

In stark contrast to Hello Divorce, Atticus[76] – an "attorney-client matching" service – has set up a dual-entity model that works simply because there is no UPL risk to mitigate. Atticus does not provide direct legal services, or anything approaching legal services, and no money exchanges hands between Atticus and individual users. Atticus' "front-facing" entity, a law firm licensed in California, acquires clients, screens them, and matches them 1:1 with a vetted attorney in the Atticus network.[77] Those network providers then pay Atticus a referral fee in compliance with Rule 1.5e and applicable state-level regulations. While Hello Divorce's "front facing" entity is its technology platform,[78] Atticus' "tech" entity serves as its back-office: a venture capital-backed Delaware C corporation that owns the tech platform and manages spending across both entities.[79] Thus, Atticus is subject to far less regulatory scrutiny,[80] especially because its services do not compete directly with attorneys.[81] Atticus actually makes the existing legal monopoly

72 Levine Interview, *supra* note 31.

73 *Id.*

74 *Id.*.

75 *Id.*; *see supra* Table 8.1.

76 Interview with Sam Byker, Founder of Atticus (Feb. 7, 2023) (hereinafter "Byker Interview"). Atticus styles itself as a legal primary care doctor: It diagnoses legal need and direct users to the proper specialist.

77 *Id.*

78 This is in part out of necessity; if Levine Law ran Hello Divorce, it would be more difficult to argue that Hello Divorce does not provide legal services.

79 *Id.* The arms-length relationship between these two entities is governed by a complex, twenty-page Master of Services agreement.

80 Barton, *supra* note 35, at 29.

81 Unauthorized practice of law complaints are almost always generated by lawyers, no aggrieved members of the public. *See* Deborah L. Rhode & Lucy Buford Ricca, *Protecting the Profession or the Public? Rethinking Unauthorized-Practice Enforcement*, 82 FORDHAM L. REV. 2587 (2014). This is especially true in PeopleLaw, where competition between lawyers is fierce. *See* Barton, *supra* note 35, at 30; *see also* Benjamin H. Barton & Deborah L. Rhode, *Access to*

work better by solving a mismatch between demand and supply. Rather than competing over the same client pool, Atticus helps existing PeopleLaw attorneys scale their services by finding them clients – including clients who may not otherwise pursue legal help at all.

In short, restrictive rules have plenty of explanatory value when it comes to key segments of the legal tech industry. Just ask Levine Law and Hello Divorce. But, as Atticus' success shows, they hardly explain anemic legal tech across the board.

8.3.2 *Weak AI: The Upside of Generative AI for the Tenant Power Toolkit*

Consider another "usual suspect:" that underpowered AI has prevented DTC legal tech from building the tools necessary to scale PeopleLaw solutions. But even "full-powered" AI is not positioned to address DTC legal tech's – and particularly, DTC document assembly tools', most pressing issues. As noted previously, much document assembly is technologically simple: Providers plug complicated legal expertise into a technologically basic software wizard. Instead, the most labor- and capital-intensive phase is hiring lawyers to (1) create a plain language logic tree and (2) track ever-changing procedural and substantive requirements.[82]

While these pain points constrain scale, generative AI is hardly a panacea. AI may never be capable of replacing lawyer translations, especially in more complex areas of the law. Plain language translations require precision and difficult judgment calls: Translating law into plain language is uniquely challenging because it carries inherent risks of over- or under-specification, creating a trade-off between making legal language understandable and retaining its original meaning.[83] Given this complexity, it may be some time before NLP can take the reins. And as discussed in Section 8.3.3, so long as technology cannot itself brute-force through the court technology checkerboard, scaling across jurisdiction remains prohibitively costly. In short, while some blame "weak" AI for "weak" DTC legal tech, "stronger" AI is unlikely to have the capabilities necessary to meaningfully jumpstart more effective DTC document assembly tools.

Still, as highlighted by the Tenant Power Toolkit, some providers may nonetheless benefit from next-generation AI. Currently, the toolkit asks a series of plain

Justice and Routine Legal Services: New Technologies Meet Bar Regulators, 70 Hastings L.J. 955, 985–86 (2019).

82 *See, for example*, SixFifty's document assembly tool. Parker Interview, *supra* note 29.

83 *See, for example*, Hanjo Hamann & Friedemann Vogel, *Evidence-Based Jurisprudence Meets Legal Linguistics – Unlikely Blends Made in Germany*, 1 BYU L. Rev. 1474 (2017); Michael Curtotti & Erin McCreath, A *Right to Access Implies a Right to Know: An Open Online Platform on Research on the Readability of Law*, 1 J. of Open Access to L. 1 (2013); Robert O. Charrow & Veda R. Charrow, *Making Legal Language Understandable: A Psycholinguistic Study of Jury Instructions*, 79 Colum. L. Rev. 1306 (1979); Zsolt Ződi, *The Limits of Plain Legal Language: Understanding the Comprehensible Style in Law*, 15 Int'l J.L. Context 246 (2019); Michael Blaise, *The Rise of Plain Language Laws*, 76 U. Miami. L. Rev. 447 (2022).

language questions to gauge eligibility and generate legal documents – such as fee waivers, proof of service, or even answers – for California tenants who have been served eviction papers.[84] While the toolkit can e-serve and e-file documents via One Legal, it can do so only in California.[85] Its scale and scope is limited by the pace at which human lawyers can design new plain language logic trees or translate existing ones, and the number of jurisdictions it can actually file in. Could generative AI enable the toolkit to reach more users by translating and simplifying its existing services?

Perhaps. First, generative AI can help providers like the Tenant Power Toolkit serve non-English speaking clients by instantly translating existing document assembly tools into languages beyond English. Often, the people Tenant Power Toolkit seeks to serve require a tool in their native language.[86] This time-consuming translation work is currently done by humans. As AI improves, even if it cannot create the logic trees themselves, it may offer a reliable and lower-cost solution to extending the reach of human-created tools.[87]

Second, generative AI can make existing tools more accessible by reducing the number of questions users must answer. Branching logic trees are time-consuming. The Tenant Power Toolkit finds that users often do not complete the process, having underestimated how long and complex the tool is.[88] Upsolve, another tool catered toward low-income folks, has cited similar issues.[89] Here too, generative AI may present a novel solution: Users could type in a plain language problem that AI would then map onto legal questions and outcomes with no need for elaborate Q&A-like branching.

Even so, while AI could simplify logic trees – asking fewer questions and instead using technology trained on lawyer-made datasets to sift through the information the client provides – for most DTC legal tech providers, this is a nice-to-have and not a need-to-have: Document assembly tools have worked effectively as they are.

8.3.3 *The Court Technology Checkerboard: A Problem LegalZoom Monetizes and Upsolve Avoids*

Turning to the last of the conventional explanations, to what extent does the state- and local-level checkerboard of laws and court technology systems affect Table 8.1's menu of legal tech providers? For many, the combined complexity of state laws and

84 *About Us*, The Tenant Power Toolkit, https://tenantpowertoolkit.org/about (last accessed Apr. 19, 2024); Interview with The Debt Collective (Dec. 4, 2023) (hereinafter "Debt Collective Interview").

85 Debt Collective Interview, *supra* note 84

86 *Id.*

87 *Id.*

88 *Id.*

89 Petts Interview, *supra* note 43.

filing requirements makes expanding to new geographies expensive and labor-intensive. Return, briefly, to Hello Divorce. Each day, several of its clients' forms are rejected not because they are incorrect but because the filing requirements have changed since the online tool prepared their documents.[90] Hello Divorce must employ a full-time lawyer to track and update filing requirements down to the county level, as courthouses often change their requirements with little or no notice.[91] Because the cost of filing alone makes serving additional states highly expensive,[92] the court technology checkerboard directly limits geographic scalability: Solutions built for one jurisdiction often cannot solve the same problem for clients in a different location.[93]

Two strategies have been successful in overcoming the checkerboard problem: (1) finding an area where the law is uniform, but filing is not, as LegalZoom has or (2) limiting services to document preparation only, like Upsolve.

LegalZoom operates across 50 states and more than 3,000 counties in the United States; its core business is generating and then filing documents for small businesses.[94] LegalZoom has achieved such scale by monetizing the checkerboard problem. While LLC formation implicates different laws and regulations at the local, state, and even federal levels,[95] the basic steps for setting up an LLC are consistent across all states.[96] By choosing a relatively uniform area of the law, LegalZoom was instead able to focus its resources on tracking and coding the different filing requirements of each jurisdiction.

Perhaps counter-intuitively, because its solution actually *solves* filing complexity, simplification of state-by-state systems poses a major risk: LegalZoom's investor materials highlight that "if U.S. state agencies increase their offerings for free and easy-to-use business formation services such as ... filing portals to the public, it could have a significant adverse effect on our business."[97]

But for Upsolve – which, as a reminder, assembles but does not file chapter 7 bankruptcy forms – such filing portals would make its services more accessible and effective. An estimated 40 percent of Upsolve users drop off at filing because courts are inconsistent in their treatment of self-represented litigants.[98] Generally, e-filing remains too complex for Upsolve's online tool to integrate, especially as

90 Levine Interview, *supra* note 31.
91 *Id.*
92 *Id.*
93 Duke Report, *supra* note 8, at 25.
94 LegalZoom S-1, *supra* note 38, at 1.
95 *Id.* at 4, 23.
96 These include choosing a name and filing articles with the secretary of state. *LLC Regulations: Everything You Need to Know*, UpCounsel (updated Feb. 1, 2023), https://www.upcounsel.com/llc-regulations (last accessed Feb. 18, 2025).
97 LegalZoom S-1, *supra* note 38, at 25.
98 Petts Interview, *supra* note 43; *see also* NCSC, *supra* note 32.

requirements continue to change.[99] Despite expanding its scope in other ways – offering information and referrals to help customers with other types of bankruptcy, piloting consumer debt relief advocates in New York City, and building a new online tool for immigration – Upsolve's technology-enabled services remain narrow: They assemble, but do not file, legal forms.

Here again, the checkerboard argument is complicated. Refraction through a more market-based model suggests that inter-jurisdictional variation is at once a threat and an important source of value.

8.3.4 *The Lifetime Value Trap: A Challenge for All For-Profit Providers*

Turn, now, to our market-based theory of anemic legal tech, which proceeds from the premise that low demand and high advertising costs have made customer acquisition expensive, so DTC legal tech providers must find a way to make each customer, once acquired, more profitable. As reflected in Figure 8.1, for-profit providers universally struggle to escape the LTV trap. Only for nonprofit providers – Upsolve and the Tenant Power Toolkit – do the economics of customer acquisition and retention have only minor impacts.

8.3.4.1 Customer Acquisition

At first blush, one obvious solution to the LTV trap is for legal tech to partner with law firms, allowing them to tap into an established client base. Our case studies, however, demonstrate that referral rates are low. SixFifty is a wholly owned subsidiary of Silicon Valley law firm Wilson Sonsini that provides platform solutions that customers, usually small businesses, use as part of their daily operations.[100] These solutions focus on streamlining common document assembly processes, not just fulfilling one-off document needs, and are marketed as legal automation software.[101] One of the very few legal tech players with direct ties to a BigLaw law firm, SixFifty nonetheless maintains a careful distance from Wilson Sonsini, using standard UPL disclaimers despite relaxed regulations in its home state of Utah.

While SixFifty and Wilson Sonsini do cross-refer customers – SixFifty even offers Wilson Sonsini clients a "friends and family" discount – those referrals almost never result in new business for either entity.[102] Poor referral rates are largely attributable to low customer overlap: Customers go to SixFifty and Wilson Sonsini for entirely

[99] *Electronic Self-Representation (eSR) Bankruptcy Petition Preparation System for* Chapter 7 *and* Chapter 13, U.S. Bankr Ct., https://www.cacb.uscourts.gov/esr.

[100] ALM Media, *Wilson Sonsini Launches New Software Developer*, Yahoo News (Feb. 4, 2019), https://news.yahoo.com/wilson-sonsini-launches-software-developer-053019611.html (last accessed Feb. 18, 2025).

[101] *Id.*

[102] Parker Interview, *supra* note 29.

different needs.[103] We see similar mismatch between customers of Hello Divorce and Levine Law.[104] Law firms make "chandeliers" – they handle multimillion-dollar deals and disputes – while document assembly tools standardize "lightbulb" solutions for simpler problems.

Instead of relying on referrals, most DTC legal tech providers turn to digital advertising to attract new clients. For some, it's an easier task. People in need of a divorce, for instance, know they have a legal need and often make predictable searches, making it easy for Hello Divorce to target potential clients.[105] In other areas – particularly in large and diffuse markets – SEO is expensive and imprecise. LegalZoom, for example, generally targets small business owners; sales and marketing is their largest operating expense, amounting to nearly one-third of total revenue.[106] But even if a company has resources to spend on SEO, it may not be an effective distribution channel. In immigration, for instance, the high volume of both general and specific searches (e.g., "immigration help" or Violence Against Women Act (VAWA) application") and providers' need to target outreach based on their subspecialty (e.g., Deferred Action for Childhood Arrivals (DACA) work permits) makes the SEO strategy impracticable.[107]

8.3.4.2 Customer Retention

To increase LTV, many providers prioritize cross-sell. As previously noted, because no one *plans* to get divorced more than once, Hello Divorce has shifted its focus to more holistic lawyer-alternatives such as financial counseling and marriage mediators to extend the lifetime of each client.[108] LegalZoom also focuses on driving additional purchases and cross-sell for its customers,[109] including by upselling its customers to higher margin solutions.[110] For example, LegalZoom plans to expand credentialled-professional-assisted offerings[111] similar to those offered by HelloDivorce.

Another way to boost customer retention is through subscriptions.[112] Despite being a key component of LegalZoom's strategy to enhance LTV – in fact, its

[103] *Id.*
[104] Levine Interview, *supra* note 31.
[105] *Id.*
[106] *Id.* From 2019 to 2021, increases in both net income and net revenue were essentially offset by increased marketing spend. *Id.* at 69.
[107] Petts Interview, *supra* note 43.
[108] Levine Interview, *supra* note 31.
[109] LegalZoom S-1, *supra* note 38, at 72.
[110] *Id.* at 9.
[111] *Id.*
[112] *See* Frank v. Cespedes & Jacco van der Kooij, *The Rebirth of Software as a Service*, HARV. BUS. REV. ONLINE (2023), https://hbr.org/2023/04/the-rebirth-of-software-as-a-service (last accessed Feb. 18, 2025). *See also* LegalZoom S-1, *supra* note 38, at 75 ("the number of subscription units [is] an important metric since subscriptions enable us to increase lifetime value through deeper, longer-term relationships with customers").

"business depends substantially on [] subscribers renewing their subscriptions"[113] – growth in one-time transactions continues to outpace growth in subscriptions.[114] And an all-in subscription strategy comes with a major pitfall: Deferred revenue as a result of subscription units can make cash flows dependent on the size, timing, and terms of subscription agreements.[115]

SixFifty, for its part, has successfully combined cross-sell *and* subscriptions by building a suite of complementary products that allows it to naturally sell existing customers additional products (e.g., selling an employee handbook customer a subscription to its severance paperwork tool). This is partially attributable to the substantive legal areas it serves: Every business enterprise that interfaces with consumers must remain compliant with ever-changing privacy and employment regulations. Bundling multiple types of compliance under one vendor simplifies the process for small HR and legal departments; for example, they only need to be trained on and use one platform solution. SixFifty also occupies a niche where legal need is ongoing: Year after year, employers will need to hire, onboard, and let go of employees.

8.3.4.3 Escaping the Lifetime Value Trap

The LTV-to-CAC ratio, which compares the value of a customer over their lifetime to the cost of acquiring them, is the primary measure of DTC profitability.[116] For ecommerce, a ratio greater than 3:1 is considered "good."[117] In SaaS,[118] industry benchmarks place the average LTV-to-CAC ratio at 3:1 for business services and 6:1 for financial services.[119] DTC legal tech, which straddles ecommerce and SaaS, likely sees much lower – and thus unsustainable – LTV-to-CAC ratios.

LegalZoom, for its part, "aims to achieve" a ratio of 3:1 within twenty-five months.[120] Because LegalZoom does not publish (and in fact claims not to know)[121] its customer churn rate, it's difficult to calculate its exact LTV-to-CAC ratio based on publicly available data. That its *goal* is a ratio of 3:1 suggests that LegalZoom's actual ratio is lower, and thus, below industry benchmarks.

[113] LegalZoom S-1, *supra* note 38, at 24.

[114] *Id.* at 74–76, 84 (measuring growth in both volume and revenue).

[115] *Id.* at 21.

[116] *CAC to LTV Ratio*, Corp. Fin. Inst., https://corporatefinanceinstitute.com/resources/valuation/cac-ltv-ratio/ (last accessed Apr. 19, 2024).

[117] *Id.* DTC brands are notorious for disguising customer acquisition costs on their balance sheets, tucking them into the general selling, general, and administrative (SG&A) expense bucket. *See* Rangan et al., *supra* note 41.

[118] SaaS, or "Software as a Service," companies license centrally hosted software platforms to their clients on a subscription basis. Think Salesforce, Shopify, or even Zoom.

[119] Evan Bailyn, *The SaaS LTV to CAC Ratio*, First Page Sage (updated Apr. 10, 2024), https://firstpagesage.com/seo-blog/the-saas-ltv-to-cac-ratio-fc/ (last accessed Feb. 18, 2025).

[120] LegalZoom S-1, *supra* note 38, at 72.

[121] *Id.* at 24.

By contrast, SixFifty achieves a 3:1 LTV-to-CAC ratio,[122] putting it on par with other business services but below analogous financial services. But SixFifty is likely unique among its legal tech peers; its primary customers are businesses with large annual contracts and thus higher average LTV.[123] By contrast, LegalZoom must retain a subscription customer for ninety days to recoup acquisition costs.[124] Despite enjoying higher LTV, SixFifty's CAC is likely to remain high because it uses a traditional sales motion reliant on SEO. Even this legal tech success story is doomed to chase LTV through cross-selling or by retaining subscription customers for as long as possible.

* * *

More so than the "usual suspects," market-based barriers to growth explain anemic legal tech. Through these case studies, we can trace the universal profitability struggle to a single, relatively simple culprit: the customer. Scholars envision DTC legal tech serving individuals in need of unbundled, specialized legal services.[125] But demand for such services is uniquely fickle: Customers rarely understand their own legal need and, unlike annual check-ups or taxes, specialized legal need is rarely ongoing. By serving their clients, providers often render themselves moot. And given high CAC costs, one-off clients cannot sustain DTC legal tech. If we want to move the needle on access to justice, we need to accept the reality that leaving legal tech growth up to the "market" might mean that effective, scalable legal tech for ordinary people remains out of reach.

8.4 IMPLICATIONS

To this point, we have identified and tested an alternative, market-based theory for lagging DTC legal tech that provides a fuller, industry-spanning explanation than the standard arguments around restrictive rules, weak AI, or the court technology checkerboard. This section builds out some of the implications of our findings for the future of legal services and access to justice. Two loom largest. First, the structural challenges facing DTC legal tech hold important lessons for current "regulatory reform" efforts, and they may even tip the scales away from liberalization strategies that aim to foster a robust, competitive legal tech marketplace. Second, market-based barriers to a robust DTC legal tech ecosystem may have fundamental implications for how courts should see their role, and build out their own technology and data infrastuctures, as the civil justice system enters its next chapter.

[122] Parker Interview, *supra* note 29.
[123] *Id.*
[124] LegalZoom S-1, *supra* note 38, at 2.
[125] *See* Hadfield, *Legal Barriers*, *supra* note 10.

8.4.1 *Is Regulatory Reform a Wrong Turn?*

Our market-based theory offers a cautionary note, perhaps even waves bright red flags, for theories of regulatory reform that aim to foster, or otherwise depend upon, a robust DTC legal tech market as a way to serve the millions who currently face civil justice problems without meaningful legal help.

Regulatory reform, while a complex amalgam of reform impulses, can be distilled into three basic flavors. *Entity-level* reform efforts aim to relax UPL, Rule 5.4, or both in order to permit entities – from already-existing ones, such as law firms or LegalZoom, to new tech startups – to devise new, entity-level legal services delivery models. Direct-to-consumer legal tech finds its footing in this entity-level flavor. *Role-based* reforms call for new, top-down licensure schemes to mint new classes of legal professionals – think physician assistants or nurse practitioners for law – with entry requirements, ongoing educational and reporting requirements, and regulatory oversight patterned after current regulation of the legal profession.[126] But a third flavor, "community justice workers," is gaining steam.[127] Drawing from both entity – and role-based approaches, this new reform model calls for deputizing certain trusted legal services providers – for instance, legal aid groups – to hire, train, and oversee new types of nonlawyer service providers, rather than top-down licensure, in order to extend their reach. This trio of reform flavors is currently jockeying for position across dozens of states as access-to-justice concerns move more squarely onto legal and political radars.

The deep, market-based challenges facing DTC legal tech plainly present a significant challenge to the first, entity-level approach – and may even tip the scales in favor of the other models. Indeed, if one-to-many legal services are unlikely to flourish, and if sandbox reforms, as in Utah, or ABS systems, as in Arizona, cannot yield a robust, competitive marketplace of DTC legal tech providers, then perhaps reformers should put their eggs in other baskets. Seeking political change is not costless. Reformers must be careful to spend their limited real and political capital wisely, and in ways that will achieve movement ends, rather than seeking change for change's sake.

To be sure, this chapter's anatomy of the market-based challenges facing DTC legal tech does not perform a full-dress analysis of the relative economic viability of all three reform models. Role-based reforms suffer from economic challenges of their own: The quality of services and the fees charged by newly minted paraprofessionals will almost certainly be directly proportional to entry and training costs and the stringency of regulatory oversight. And even a significant discount off the fees charged by lawyers – currently averaging $300 per hour – will still price most

[126] *See* David Freeman Engstrom et al., Legal Innovation after Reform: Evidence from Regulatory Change 10 (2022) (discussing entity and role reforms).

[127] *See* Chapter 1 of this volume.

Americans out of the market. The community justice worker approach has problems of its own, as it depends on legal aid and other providers who are perennially funding-strapped and may not be inclined to take on significant new oversight duties in support of a model that, in effect, cannibalizes their own service provision.

Here, then, lies a more bracing possibility: Perhaps regulatory reform is itself a wrong turn – a market-based move that cannot solve the core market failure that is fueling reform calls in the first place. Perhaps, in other words, we should be seeking other ways to narrow the justice gap and serve the millions who must navigate a complex civil justice system with little or no help. That leads directly to a second implication: the role of courts, and the technology choices they make, as they prepare for the next chapter of the civil justice system.

8.4.2 *Courts' Make-or-Buy Choice*

A second, and related, implication of our findings goes to how courts can best leverage potent new legal technologies, particularly with the advent of generative AI, for self-represented court users.

In the current court tech landscape, we see the challenge facing courts as a version of "make or buy." Courts can "make" new legal services by creating virtual self-help centers, from simple chatbots to a full-scale, end-to-end digital courthouse front door where court users can come, input a plain language description of a problem, and get back actionable information and advice, be routed to other appropriate forms of legal help, or access needed form-filing and e-filing tools. Courts can also offer court-hosted online dispute resolution (ODR) platforms. The first ODR platforms at eBay and PayPal were simple gathering places where disputants could gather, usually asynchronously, and bargain their way to a settlement.[128] But with generative AI, we can glimpse more advanced versions – call it ODR 2.0 – that primes the disputants with information, including, perhaps, a prediction as to how the case would come out if litigated to a judgment in court.[129]

Alternatively, courts can "buy" assistance for self-represented litigants by improving accessibility and inter-connectivity – for instance, through application programming interfaces (APIs), or by adopting common data standards – and by taking other measures, such as lowering e-filing barriers, to make it easier for legal tech providers to provide fully integrated services to self-represented litigants.[130]

Neither "make" nor "buy" is without deep challenges. As already noted at length, "buy" depends on a robust legal tech marketplace that may not materialize even with substantial relaxation of regulatory constraints on legal services and more

[128] *See* David Freeman Engstrom, *Digital Civil Procedure*, 169 U. Pa. L. Rev. 2243, 2273 (2021).

[129] *Id.*

[130] Such is the theory behind Stanford's Filing Fairness Project, a multi-jurisdictional effort to modernize court filing systems and related technology and data infrastructures. *See Filing Fairness Project*, *supra* note 34.

standardized, less checkerboard-like court technology and data infrastructures. The uniquely challenging market economics of serving moderate and low-income Americans may simply be too much to support a truly robust marketplace of legal services providers.

"Make" can seem no less daunting. Above all, it requires significant technical capacity that few courts currently have. Indeed, courts are woefully lacking in IT expertise, never mind AI. And, even if they partner with one of the purveyors of foundational, open-source LLMs in order to harness the newest and most potent forms of generative AI, significant in-house work will need to be done to customize and improve the accuracy of the models. As a result, partnering may be necessary in the age of generative AI, but partnering only partially solves the problem of limited court technical capacity.

Still, a reasonable conclusion is that "make" may be the better course, particularly if budget-strapped courts can only choose one. More bracingly, it's possible that "make" is the *only* plausible path forward, particularly in the parts of the civil justice system where access concerns are most acute – the parade of debt collection actions, evictions, and family law matters that now dominate state court dockets. In that part of the civil justice system, as the average litigant's ability to pay moves toward zero and profit margins thin, the market-based critique advanced in this chapter, and the uniquely challenging market economics of serving low- and even medium-income Americans, gains even greater purchase, leaving courts and policymakers with few other levers. Indeed, if a truly robust DTC legal tech marketplace is doomed from the start, then court-hosted, taxpayer-financed, "public option" legal tech – not selective, privately offered services serving the relatively better off – may be the wiser and fairer use of limited public funds.

8.5 CONCLUSION

This chapter has squarely asked the question that has long hung over legal tech: Why has DTC legal tech that serves individuals and small businesses directly not risen up amidst massive unmet civil legal needs? Our answer is a disheartening one: Inclusive legal tech may never materialize, at least not at a scale that can more than dent the problem of access to justice, because of the uniquely challenging market economics of serving ordinary people. But there is power in that recognition, for it can push us to consider what other measures might be necessary to make the civil justice system more open and fairer for all.

PART III

The Comparative Lens

What Can Be Learned from Others?

9

How Power Undermined the Medical Profession

Allison K. Hoffman

Mere decades ago, ambitious college students who wanted a lucrative career dreamed of being doctors. Today, they imagine a future as venture capitalists. Over the course of the twentieth century, the medical profession in the United States aggrandized power and profit and is now watching it begin to slip away.[1] Although there is no single explanation for this meteoric rise and gradual decline, this chapter argues that one factor has been the profession's own success. As medical science advanced, it afforded doctors increasing authority and, acting through professional associations, they used this authority to shape the law to protect their turf and their profits. And it also, I argue, had a terrible side effect. Because buried within the rise of professional autonomy and power was also the profession's sharp decline – a decline that may hold important lessons for reformists focused on building a new era of the legal profession.

In medicine, the twentieth century ushered in scientific advances and the beginning of modern medicine and, with it, the growth of a powerful profession.[2] As Paul Starr described in his classic 1982 tome, "the profession has been able to turn its authority into social privilege, economic power, and political power. In the distribution of rewards from medicine, the medical profession, as the highest-paid occupation in our society, receives a radically disproportionate share."[3]

Led by associations, most prominently the American Medical Association (AMA), doctors worked assiduously throughout the twentieth century to concentrate their power and to maximize professional sovereignty. And it worked. Doctors wrested control over both state and federal laws and policies regulating the delivery of medicine.[4] They suppressed efforts to impose market competition in health care,

[1] Mind you, medicine remains a lucrative profession for the meantime, certainly more so on average than law.

[2] Paul Starr, The Social Transformation of Medicine (1982).

[3] *Id.* at 5.

[4] Timothy S. Jost, *Introduction*, *in* Regulation of the Healthcare Professions 2–3 (Timothy S. Jost ed., 1997).

which threatened to displace physician authority with consumer authority.[5] And they used their power to bend payment policies in their favor.

This aggregation of power enabled doctors to control supply, influence prices, and limit their exposure to critique and liability. And it built enduring structures that served to reproduce authority through legislative and market pressure.[6] It came, at times, at the expense of patients and taxpayers, as health care costs skyrocketed. It also produced less than ideal patient and physician experiences, including the seven-minute doctor's office visit that we've all experienced, a period too short to diagnose or to manage any complex health situation.

Physicians have commanded high prices and profits. The startling irony is that the profits that physicians worked so hard to generate, accumulate, and protect have now lured in outside investors – corporate health systems, insurers, and, most recently, private equity companies – looking to extract these profits.

Early evidence suggests that this corporatization has not markedly increased access to medical care, maybe diminishing quality, and has undoubtedly changed the patient experience and the nature of the medical profession. Doctors are beginning to look like one small input into a larger medical economy, and patient care has become often impersonal. Medical doctors now operate in ways unrecognizable to doctors of a generation prior. After a century of resisting external control, they rarely run their own shops, or, increasingly, even group practices. They are more often beholden to large corporate entities. Medicine still enjoys some benefits of professionalism: high pay, respect, and job security. Yet, the practice of medicine is undoubtedly in decline, measured not only by decreasing autonomy but also by decreasing satisfaction and respect.[7]

Focused on efficiency more than professionalism, the new health care economy will come to value workers who can perform tasks at lower labor costs, thereby eroding the turf and earnings that doctors worked so assiduously to defend. Advanced practice nurses, pharmacists, and others are no longer mere "physician extenders." They are increasingly central players. Yet, all these providers have become corporatized and commodified, as the most astute observers like Paul Starr and Tim Jost predicted four decades ago at the nascence of the decline of the profession.[8]

This chapter engages in a thought experiment. It asks: If doctors had pursued a different strategy, could they have retained the profits they worked so hard to earn – and would this alternative system have been better, both for physicians and their

5 See, for example, id. at 3; CLARK C. HAVIGHURST, DEREGULATING THE HEALTH CARE INDUSTRY: PLANNING FOR COMPETITION 89 (1982) (discussing how self-regulation by the medical profession contributed to anticompetitive conditions in health care).

6 STARR, *supra* note 2, at 19.

7 For the beginnings of this decline, *see id.* at 391. *See also* Eyal Press, *Standard of Care*, N.Y. TIMES MAG. (June 18, 2023).

8 STARR, *supra* note 2, at 428, 444–49; Jost, *supra* note 4, at 4–5.

patients? This question is important in its own right and also because this inquiry holds crucial lessons for medicine's sister profession: law. In some ways, law and medicine (or access to justice and access to care), although often analogized, may not be similar enough to compare. But some larger themes and questions might transcend these differences. This chapter considers why law has not gone the way of medicine and whether medicine's trajectory might offer law a cautionary tale. Does gatekeeping help or hinder a profession? How might resistance of government funding and of corporate ownership be a preservation strategy and what does that mean for nascent efforts to allow corporate investors in law firms? And what does the nature of the profession mean, at the end of the day, for the people it serves?

This chapter couldn't possibly answer all these questions. By asking them, however, it probes the importance of the link between the character of the profession and access to quality services, and it illuminates how understanding medicine might deepen, enrich, and complicate conversations about law reform.

9.1 THE PROFESSION'S CONTROL OVER THE REGULATION AND BOUNDARIES OF THE PROFESSION

9.1.1 *The Rise of Associations and the Self-Regulation of Medicine*

The very idea of what the medical profession is and who it includes was largely constructed by professional associations through efforts to shape regulation of the practice of medicine. The AMA, chief among medical professional associations for many decades, was founded in the 1840s when the profession was wholly unregulated.[9] The next decades brought increased reliance on doctors, who became more capable at helping patients.[10] A profession formed that, using legal tools, defined its own boundaries, sought self-protection, and set its own obligations and standards.

Physicians, represented by the AMA starting in the mid-nineteenth century and joined over the course of the twentieth century by specialty associations, led efforts to shape the face of medical regulation. Framed as necessary to protect patients and ensure good care, these efforts served also to insulate the profession from competition.[11] Four primary efforts ultimately sought to bolster and protect physicians and their earnings. The first three – licensure laws, scope-of-practice restrictions, and medical education pipeline control – suppressed the size of the profession and reserved certain domains of practice only for physicians. The final one,

9 STARR, *supra* note 2, at 18.

10 *Id.* at 18, 145.

11 *But see* Gabriel Scheffler & Ryan Nunn, *Occupational Licensing and the Limits of Public Choice Theory*, 4 ADMIN. L. REV. ACCORD 25, 33–34 (2019) (arguing that the public choice account of licensure may be overstated, that early licensure laws were at least in part motivated by driving out unqualified practitioners, and that they improved quality).

corporate practice of medicine laws, attempted to limit nonphysician interference with medical practice. They all have close corollaries in law.

9.1.1.1 Licensure and the Unlicensed Practice of Medicine

First, physicians sought to limit who could practice medicine with strict licensure requirements. Modern licensure laws, which emerged in the nineteenth century, are codified in state practice acts and require graduation from accredited schools and passage of examination to practice.[12] Practitioners argued that these laws would protect the public from quackery, and they did to some degree,[13] but licensure laws also became a tool to police the bounds of the profession, tamping down supply.[14]

Licensure laws were developed state-by-state, based on state police powers, and their broad wording meant that many activities might constitute "medical practice," which was reserved for physicians. In these laws' current form, the term "medical practice" continues to encompass wide swaths of activities: One author describes these laws as constructing a "practically limitless range of activity within the exclusive power of medicine," possibly even reaching mundane activities like ear piercing or blogging.[15] Bill Sage and Linda Aiken describe medicine as "noteworthy among modern professions for having staked out far more territory than physicians themselves can service, and for managing that territory by delegating duties to other professions who remain subject to physician control and supervision."[16] This delegation structure later began to crumble, as discussed below.

Despite being passed in the name of high-quality care, licensure laws are rarely invoked to police poor-quality care.[17] They have, however, been used to discipline complementary or alternative medical practitioners as engaged in the illegal practice of medicine, a violation that is punishable criminally.[18] New private and public structures developed in the 1980s–90s to attempt to regulate quality more directly. Some identified this moment in time as the beginning of bureaucratic control over, or the proletarianization, of practice.[19]

[12] Timothy Stoltzfus Jost, *Oversight of the Quality of Medical Care: Regulation, Management, or the Market?*, 37 ARIZ. L. REV. 825, 828 (1995).

[13] Scheffler & Nunn, *supra* note 11, at 34.

[14] Jost, *supra* note 12, at 829.

[15] Sandra Johnson, *Structure of Governmental Oversight of Quality in Healthcare*, *in* THE OXFORD HANDBOOK OF U.S. HEALTH LAW 503 (I. Glenn Cohen et al. eds., 2016).

[16] William M. Sage & Linda H. Aiken, *Regulating Interdisciplinary Practice*, *in* REGULATION OF THE HEALTHCARE PROFESSIONS 74 (Timothy S. Jost ed., 1997).

[17] Nadia Sawicki, *Character Competence, and the Principles of Medical Discipline*, 13 J. HEALTH CARE L. & POL'Y 285 (2010).

[18] Johnson, *supra* note 15, at 500, 504. Some states allow complementary or alternative practices in "Health Freedom Acts," or by licensing them separately. *Id.* at 504.

[19] Jost, *supra* note 12, at 829, n.73.

9.1.1.2 Depressing Supply through Medical Education

The medical profession also constrained the supply of physicians by limiting its own pipeline.[20] Toward the end of the nineteenth century, medicine was a growth industry; the number of medical schools was on the rise and women were entering medicine in increasing numbers, including through training in elite institutions where they were welcomed because they brought much-needed financial contributions.[21] In 1904, however, the AMA halted this expansion with the creation of a Council on Medical Education that began grading institutions and, in 1906, fully approved only half of the 160 medical schools in existence.[22] State licensure boards adopted the heightened requirements espoused by the AMA, including moving from a two- to a four-year course of study, pushing many medical schools out of business.[23]

This standardization already underway was hastened by the 1910 Flexner Report, written for the Carnegie Foundation by Abraham Flexner, a doctor trained at Johns Hopkins University in what he characterized as the ideal of experimental science-based education.[24] He criticized the overproduction of medical schools as "private ventures, money making in sprit and object" and "wholly didactic," instead of institutions focused on training doctors clinically.[25] He made the case that a prior college degree in fundamental sciences and language should be a prerequisite for medical education, which, itself, should be based on doing, not watching.[26]

In the following decades, more than half of medical schools merged or closed, including five of seven historically Black medical schools (Howard University College of Medicine and Meharry Medical College remained).[27] Medical schools limited admissions for women, and alternative medicine was sidelined or extinguished.[28] This decline in medical training depressed medical care, exacerbating shortages in rural areas and poor areas.[29]

Following this initial narrowing of admission came a second one with the creation of specialties, starting with ophthalmology in 1916.[30] A system of self-

[20] *Id.* at 830.
[21] STARR, *supra* note 2, at 117.
[22] *Id.* at 118.
[23] *Id.*
[24] Abraham Flexner, MEDICAL EDUCATION IN THE UNITED STATES AND CANADA: A REPORT TO THE CARNEGIE FOUNDATION FOR THE ADVANCEMENT OF TEACHING (1910); *see* STARR, *supra* note 2, at 188.
[25] Flexner, *supra* note 24, at 3–6.
[26] *Id.* at 53, 90, 125.
[27] Louis W. Sullivan & Ilana Suez Mittman, *The State of Diversity in the Health Professions a Century after Flexner*, 85 ACAD. MED. 246 (2010).
[28] STARR, *supra* note 2, at 124; Frank W. Stahnisch & Marja Verhoef, *The Flexner Report of 1910 and its Impact on Complementary and Alternative Medicine and Psychiatry in North America in the 20th Century*, EVID.-BASED COMPLEMENTARY & ALT. MED. (2012).
[29] STARR, *supra* note 2, at 125.
[30] Jost, *supra* note 12, at 830.

regulatory specialty boards was developed to exercise control over various specialties, and the Advisory Board for Medical Specialties was formed in 1933.[31] The division of the profession into specialties created more particularized claims to expertise and, in turn, enhanced payment. Today, and traceable to efforts by the AMA, doctor shortages persist at critical levels, especially in primary care where compensation lags behind most specialties.

9.1.1.3 Scope of Practice

After shrinking the pool of doctors, physicians preserved maximal authority by limiting the care nonphysician health care professionals could provide. Scope-of-practice laws, which both license and constrain practice, dictated who could do what among nurses, nurse practitioners, naturopathic doctors, acupuncturists, nurse midwives, and others. For example, when nurse practitioner training began, these laws determined whether nurse practitioners could diagnose conditions, prescribe medication (including controlled substances), and treat chronic conditions independent of physician supervision[32] and also set the structure of physician supervision required.[33] The providers regulated by scope-of-practice laws were even called "physician extenders," a term that emphasized their role, as secondary to physicians.[34] These laws have become controversial as evidence mounts that lifting these restrictions increases access to care without compromising quality,[35] but the AMA continues to resist their liberalization.[36]

9.1.1.4 Corporate Practice of Medicine Restrictions

A fourth and final way that physicians tried, but ultimately failed, to retain maximal control was through state prohibitions against the "corporate practice" of medicine.

[31] *Id.*

[32] *State Practice Environment*, AM. ASS'N NURSE PRACTITIONERS (updated Oct. 2024), https://www.aanp.org/advocacy/state/state-practice-environment (last accessed Mar. 12, 2023).

[33] *Id. See also* Chapter 8 in this volume.

[34] These laws are criticized as anticompetitive. FED. TRADE COMM'N, POLICY PERSPECTIVES: COMPETITION AND THE REGULATION OF ADVANCED PRACTICE NURSES 20 (2014); E. Kathleen Adams & Sara Markowitz, *Improving Efficiency in the Health-Care System: Removing Anticompetitive Barriers for Advanced Practice Registered Nurses and Physician Assistants*, THE HAMILTON PROJECT (June 2018).

[35] *See, for example,* Mary O. Mundinger et al., *Primary Care Outcomes in Patients Treated by Nurse Practitioners or Physicians: A Randomized Trial*, 283 JAMA 59 (Jan. 5, 2000) (showing that random assignment to a primary care nurse practitioner or doctor produced similar outcomes); Sara Markowitz et al., *Competitive Effects of Scope of Practice Restrictions: Public Health or Public Harm?*, 55 J. HEALTH ECON. 201 (2017) (showing that practice restrictions on nurse midwives increase rates of induced labor and Cesarean section birth with no effect on health outcomes).

[36] *AMA Successfully Fights Scope of Practice Expansions that Threaten Patient Safety*, AM. MED. ASS'N (May 15, 2023), https://www.ama-assn.org/practice-management/scope-practice/ama-successfully-fights-scope-practice-expansions-threaten (last accessed Feb. 18, 2025).

Some feared that when those acting in the service of patients were controlled externally, it could infuse profitmaking into their consciousness and tarnish the profession. Common laws and statutes in most states thus restricted business and managerial control over medical practice. But as medicine began to look more like a business than a calling over the latter half of the twentieth century, corporate practice of medicine laws were circumvented, repealed, overturned, limited, or unenforced.

9.2 THE MEDICAL PROFESSION'S CONTROL OVER PRICES

The emergence of modern health care financing, including the 1965 passage of Medicare and Medicaid and the growth of managed care beginning in the 1970s, threatened the imposition of external controls over medical practice. In the 1970s–80s, health care prices soared, and questions over health care quality provoked a movement toward quality management and improvement.

Having public and private insurers as powerful intermediaries could, in theory, have swiftly tempered professional influence. To the contrary, the introduction of external financing brought an infusion of spending that increased the stakes of payment policy, and the profession's use of its political capital to shape this policy intensified. This section traces how the profession used its influence to shape insurance into a tool for profitmaking.

9.2.1 *Medicare Fuels the Profession*

The early to mid-twentieth century brought debates over the government's role in financing health care, and the AMA resisted government-financed health care because of the fear that it would bring regulation along with the financing. Although the AMA contributed to the defeat of national health insurance, Medicare passed in 1965 over AMA resistance.[37]

Yet, instead of Medicare bringing professional regulation, the profession has since shaped the program for its benefit. Medicare has created a steady and reliable funding stream for inpatient and outpatient care. The Medicare Act provided that outpatient care would be compensated at rates that were "reasonable" or "customary," terms that became defined based on the amounts that doctors billed for care.[38] This squishy statutory language fanned the flames of medical inflation through the 1970s, and as doctors' billed amounts increased, Medicare's price tag ballooned.[39]

[37] Theodore R. Marmor, The Politics of Medicare 77 (2nd ed. 2000).

[38] *Medicare Coverage Determination Process*, Ctrs. for Medicare & Medicaid Servs. (last modified Sept. 10, 2024), https://www.cms.gov/Medicare/Coverage/DeterminationProcess (last accessed Apr. 25, 2023).

[39] Marmor, *supra* note 37, at 89.

The Medicare Act also delivered an explicit promise not to interfere with the profession. In its very first section, the statute provides:

> Nothing in this subchapter shall be construed to authorize any Federal officer or employee to exercise any supervision or control over the practice of medicine or the manner in which medical services are provided, or over the selection, tenure, or compensation of any officer or employee of any institution, agency, or person providing health services; or to exercise any supervision or control over the administration or operation of any such institution, agency, or person.[40]

Although Medicare has undoubtedly deeply shaped health care delivery, this provision has cabined payment and quality reform. As just one example, the Affordable Care Act (ACA) created a body to study comparative cost effectiveness to pay more for higher-value care.[41] Although this Patient-Centered Outcomes Research Institute (PCORI) was formed, it was prohibited from considering the relative cost of treatments; rather it was only allowed to consider the effectiveness of treatments.[42] This means that if two treatments are both effective but they vary wildly in price, their relative prices are not allowed to factor into PCORI-funded analysis.[43]

Physicians also directly influence reimbursement rates in various ways. For example, in 1992 Medicare transitioned to paying doctors based on a relative scale of how much effort goes into different categories of care.[44] Medicare sets the amount paid for a base unit, and a committee of the AMA called the RVS Update Committee (RUC) determines the multiplier for each type of encounter. The AMA Board of Trustees selects the RUC chair, and specialty societies nominate individual members. Of thirty-two current members, over two-thirds represent specialties, and in 2023 only four were women (practicing in pediatrics, geriatrics, osteopathy, and primary care).[45] This means that regulators defer to doctors – and a skewed sample of doctors, at that – to determine how much Medicare pays for a therapy session versus a surgeon's fee for a knee replacement versus a pediatric well visit.

Primary care doctors, whose work is relatively undervalued through this process, have also accreted power through policies including so-called value-based models of care. The ACA created a Center for Medicare & Medicaid Innovation

[40] Pub. L. No. 89–97, tit. I, §102(a), 79 Stat. 291 (1965).

[41] Alan M. Garber & Harold C. Sox, *The Role of Costs in Comparative Effectiveness Research*, 29 Health Affs. 1805, 1806 (2010).

[42] *Id.* at 1806.

[43] *Id.* at 1806–07; *What Is PCORI's Official Policy on Cost and Cost-Effectiveness Analysis?*, PCORI (last updated Sept. 1, 2023), https://www.pcori.org/funding-opportunities/applicant-and-awardee-resources/frequently-asked-questions/collecting-data-costs-and-economic-burdens-faqs (last accessed Feb. 24, 2025) (last accessed Apr. 25, 2023).

[44] Marmor, *supra* note 37, at 113.

[45] *Composition of the RVS Update Committee (RUC)*, Am. Med. Ass'n, https://www.ama-assn.org/about/rvs-update-committee-ruc/composition-rvs-update-committee-ruc (last accessed Mar. 9, 2023).

(CMMI, now called the CMS Innovation Center) within CMS to test new payment models,[46] which pay bonuses when patients achieve health outcomes within spending parameters. Primary care doctors are the lynchpin to success and profit in these models. This fact has drawn the attention of corporate investors in primary care. Over the past decade, corporate investors have begun to aggregate primary care doctors into formal or informal networks. These typically private-equity-backed entities (e.g., Oak Street Health, ChenMed, and One Medical) have, in turn, begun to change the nature of primary care practice, as discussed below.

9.2.2 *Consolidation and Power over Private Insurers*

The story of private insurance was much the same (until recently): Despite insurer efforts to manage cost inflation, the profession gained the upper hand by consolidating to preserve and enhance their rates. Initially, private fee-for-service insurance did not restrict the providers or medical care someone could use.[47] During the 1980s–90s, managed care gained steam as an attempt at cost control. Insurance companies created limited networks and began to push back on prices with credible threats that they would exclude providers from their networks if their prices were too high.[48]

That period was short lived. Patients protested overly restrictive networks. Hospitals and doctors consolidated in ways that aggrandized their own power vis-à-vis insurers. Even when the Federal Trade Commission (FTC) attempted to slow provider consolidation, courts backed doctors and hospitals in their resistance of managed care.[49] The end result has been high prices and insurers and employers who are price takers, unable to negotiate down rates. Even large employers increasingly express frustration at their inability to control prices in employee health plans.[50]

That said, the tides may be turning, as insurers like UnitedHealth Group have over the past decade sought to regain the upper hand by acquiring physician practices and steering patients toward doctors who are under their control.[51]

[46] *About the CMS Innovation Center*, CTRS. FOR MEDICARE & MEDICAID SERVS. (updated Aug. 14, 2023), https://innovation.cms.gov/about (last accessed Apr. 25, 2023).

[47] Jon Gabel et al., *Withering on the Vine: The Decline of Indemnity Health Insurance*, 19 HEALTH AFFS. 152 (2000).

[48] *Id.*

[49] *See, for example*, FTC v. Tenet, 186 F.3d 1045 (8th Cir. 1999) (rejecting the FTC's antitrust challenge to a merger between two hospitals).

[50] Kaiser Family Found. & Purchaser Bus. Grp. on Health, *How Corporate Executives View Rising Health Care Costs and the Role of Government* 5–6 (2021), https://www.pbgh.org/wp-content/uploads/2021/04/9704-How-Corporate-Executives-View-Rising-Health-Care-Costs-and-the-Role-of-Government-v2.pdf (last accessed Feb. 18, 2025).

[51] Reed Abelson, *UnitedHealth Buys Large Doctors Group as Lines Blur in Health Care*, N.Y. TIMES (Dec. 6, 2017); John Tozzi, *UnitedHealth Chases 10,000 More Doctors for Biggest U.S. Network*, BLOOMBERG (Mar. 5, 2021), https://www.bloomberg.com/news/articles/2021-03-05/uni

This trend is beginning to shift the power dynamic between insurers and doctors, as discussed below.

9.3 WHAT A CENTURY OF AGGREGATION OF REGULATORY AND MARKET POWER PRODUCES

For a century, doctors worked on turf building and defending until they became one of the most valuable pawns in the game of health care, second perhaps only to patented drugs and medical devices in an industry that constitutes nearly one-fifth of the economy. Yet, what these efforts have produced for practicing physicians is far from what was initially envisioned. Even worse, at the macro level, it may be contributing to the erosion of high-quality and humanely delivered medical care.

9.3.1 *Modern Professional Threats: Employment and Investment*

9.3.1.1 Physician Employment

Physician employment has accelerated dramatically, and the form and nature of employment have become complex. Initially, doctors were either in private practice or employed by hospital systems, but practices are now owned in various forms by physicians, hospitals, and/or corporations, and corporate ownership includes insurers, private equity firms, and others.[52] By one conservative count, over half of doctors are now employees, rather than owners of their own practice, including 66 percent of doctors under age forty and nearly 60 percent in fields including family medicine and pediatrics that used to be the hallmarks of independent physician practice.[53] Another study estimated that three-quarters of physicians were employed in 2022, up from just over 60 percent three years prior.[54] Even in surgical subspecialties, which have long resisted this trend, over one-third of doctors are now employees.[55] The COVID-19 pandemic accelerated this trend.[56]

tedhealth-s-deal-machine-scoops-up-covid-hit-doctor-groups#xj4y7vzkg (last accessed Feb. 18, 2025).

[52] Eliza Daily, *Physician Employment Is Changing. What Does that Mean for the Industry?*, ADVISORY BOARD (Apr. 26, 2022), https://www.advisory.com/daily-briefing/2022/04/27/physician-employment (last accessed Feb. 18, 2025).

[53] Carol K. Kane, *Policy Research Perspectives, Recent Changes in Physician Practice Arrangements: Private Practice Dropped to Less than 50 Percent of Physicians in 2020* 12–13, AM. MED. ASS'N (2021), https://www.ama-assn.org/system/files/2021-05/2020-prp-physician-practice-arrangements.pdf (last accessed Feb. 18, 2025).

[54] Avalere Health, *COVID-19's Impact on Acquisitions of Physician Practices and Physician Employment 2019–2021* 11–13 (2022), http://www.physiciansadvocacyinstitute.org/Portals/0/assets/docs/PAI-Research/PAI%20Avalere%20Physician%20Employment%20Trends%20Study%202019-21%20Final.pdf (last accessed Feb. 18, 2025).

[55] Kane, *supra* note 53, at 13.

[56] Avalere Health, *supra* note 54, at 14–16.

One early factor that led to increasing physician employment, at first mostly by hospitals and health systems, was the promise of data – especially big data – to drive better or more efficient care in institutional settings.[57] Some arguments for employment are still based on the hope that patient care can be better managed in more integrated settings.

A more skeptical take, though, is that doctors are now subject to an extremely complicated system of reimbursement, and lay managers can better navigate it.[58] When for-profit corporations take over nonprofit hospitals, for example, billing goes up even if there are no changes in the actual care provided.[59]

9.3.1.2 United Is No Longer Just an Insurer

Meanwhile, it's not just the share of physicians who are employed that is changing; it's also who employs them. Although most physician employment is still by hospitals, the fastest-growing segment is by corporate groups, including insurers and private equity firms.[60] In 2021, UnitedHealth Group, under its OptumHealth Unit, employed or controlled (in whole or part) over 53,000 doctors, about 5 percent of US physicians, more than the largest US health systems (Ascension, HCA Healthcare, and Kaiser Permanente).[61] This piece of United's overall business is expanding quickly, tripling its revenue from 2015 to 2020.[62] Other insurers including Humana Corp. and CVS Health Corp., which owns Aetna, are also expanding into health care delivery.

These insurers often pay doctors through value-based arrangements, and recent acquisitions focus on primary care doctors who are gatekeepers to the health care system. This strategy is especially important for Medicare Advantage business, which is the private health plan option for Medicare enrollees. In Medicare Advantage, health plans are paid a fixed amount per month per enrollee who selects their plans, but this amount can be adjusted upward through a risk-adjustment payment if the enrollee is identified by a provider as higher risk.[63] Corporations game

[57] Jost, *supra* note 12, at 838.

[58] Independent practices must employ an increasing number of administrative staff to navigate this complexity. Robert Kocher, *The Downside of Health Care Job Growth*, Harv. Bus. Rev. Online (Sept. 23, 2013), https://hbr.org/2013/09/the-downside-of-health-care-job-growth (last accessed Feb. 18, 2025).

[59] Elaine M. Silverman et al., *The Association between For-Profit Hospital Ownership and Medicare Spending*, 341 New Eng. J. Med. 420 (Aug. 5, 1999), https://www.nejm.org/doi/full/10.1056/NEJM199908053410606 (last accessed Feb. 18, 2025).

[60] Kane, *supra* note 53, at 16; Avalere Health, *supra* note 54, at 13.

[61] Tozzi, *supra* note 51.

[62] *Id.*

[63] Martha Hostetter & Sarah Klein, *Taking Stock of Medicare Advantage: Risk Adjustment*, Commonw. Fund Blog (Feb. 17, 2022), https://www.commonwealthfund.org/blog/2022/taking-stock-medicare-advantage-risk-adjustment (last accessed Feb. 18, 2025).

risk-adjustment payments and increase reimbursement, in part by encouraging doctors to indicate that patients are sicker.[64]

Now, over half of Medicare's sixty-five million enrollees select a private plan and, eventually, it is likely all will.[65] The top players in Medicare Advantage, measured by share of enrollees,[66] are among the most active physician practice acquirers, focusing on those physicians who are in a position to influence risk-adjustment payments.

9.3.1.3 The Entrance of Private Equity

Other outside investors, including private equity firms, have been the most recent and aggressive entrants. Private equity firms will extract at least some of the wealth the medical profession labored to create as they seek profit. Regulators are taking notice, slowly.[67]

In some sectors, the influx of private equity capital might be beneficial, but in health care (and other fields like law where labor intensity produces value), it is harder to see the promise. As one report put it, private equity is "focused on short-term revenue generation and consolidation and not on the long-term wellbeing of patients. This in turn leads to pressure to prioritize revenue over quality of care, to overburden health care companies with debt, strip their assets, and put them at risk of long-term failure."[68]

A major problem is that corporate investors can profit without improving patient care.[69] Private equity firms have a short investment lifespan of generally ten or fewer years, during which the best way to achieve a higher sales price is through consolidation, which produces two benefits. First, larger networks of providers have more bargaining power to demand higher prices. Second, larger companies earn a higher multiplier when sold, just on account of being larger.[70]

Private equity investment in health care has accelerated dramatically over the past decade. Although it can be difficult to estimate because not all deals are reported,

64 *Id.*

65 Nancy Ochieng et al., *Medicare Advantage in 2024: Enrollment Update and Key Trends*, Kaiser Fam. Found. (Aug. 8, 2024), https://www.kff.org/medicare/issue-brief/medicare-advantage-in-2024-enrollment-update-and-key-trends/ (last accessed Feb. 24, 2025).

66 *Id.* (UnitedHealth [29 percent share]; Humana [18 percent share]; and CVS Health [11 percent share]).

67 Annie Railton et al., *PE Investment in Healthcare Attracting Greater Federal Scrutiny*, N.Y. L.J. (June 30, 2021), https://www.goodwinlaw.com/-/media/files/news-and-events/press-posts/07_02-nylj-pe-healthcare-fca.pdf (last accessed Feb. 18, 2025); *see also* Erin Fuse Brown & Mark Hall, *Private Equity and the Corporatization of Health Care*, 76 Stan. L. Rev. 527 (Mar. 2024).

68 Richard M. Scheffler et al., *Soaring Private Equity Investment in the Healthcare Sector: Consolidation Accelerated, Competition Undermined, and Patients at Risk* 2, AAI (2021), https://publichealth.berkeley.edu/wp-content/uploads/2021/05/Private-Equity-I-Healthcare-Report-FINAL.pdf (last accessed Feb. 20, 2025).

69 *Id.* at 6.

70 *Id.* at 7.

one source estimates that annual deals increased from $45 billion in 2010 to nearly $120 billion in 2019.[71] Health care accounted for nearly 20 percent of reported private equity deals in 2020, making it the second-largest sector for investment.[72] A large majority of private equity buyouts are of clinics and outpatient care, followed by elder and disabled care.[73]

Private equity is driving consolidation in outpatient care, rolling smaller physician groups into large national companies.[74] One target has been physician staffing services that themselves aggregate physicians and contract with hospitals that need hospitalists, emergency medicine doctors, and anesthesiologists.[75]

Consider one example featured in a recent report.[76] Advanced Dermatology and Cosmetic Surgery (ADCS), founded in Florida in 1989, is a physician practice management firm that began to buy up physician practices in 2009. Private equity firm Audax acquired ADCS and added dozens of additional physician practices.[77] ADCS is now the largest dermatology practice across 12 states with 145 physician partners and 1.5 million patient visits a year.[78] Audax sold to another private equity firm, and likely made money simply by growing ADCS' revenue, even with no improvements in care.[79] For patients, this type of consolidation often makes health care less personal and more expensive.

Private-equity-driven consolidation is pervading primary care too. In Medicare Advantage, the private equity-funded aggregators described above gather physicians into networks. They are then acquired, often by Medicare Advantage organizations. For example, Oak Street's was acquired in February 2023 by CVS Health for $10.6 billion and One Medical by Amazon for $3.9 billion as part of a possible strategy of entering Medicare Advantage.[80] The companies can use these relationships to steer patients from public Medicare to their private Medicare

[71] *Id.* at 2; *see also* Eileen Appelbaum & Rosemary Batt, Inst. for New Econ. Thinking, Private Equity Buyouts in Healthcare: Who Wins, Who Loses? (2020).

[72] Scheffler et al., *supra* note 68, at 8 (using data from PitchBook).

[73] *Id.* at 11.

[74] *See, for example,* Jane M. Zhu et al., *Private Equity Acquisitions of Physician Medical Groups across Specialties, 2013–2016*, 323 JAMA Rsch. Letter 663 (Feb. 18, 2020).

[75] Appelbaum & Batt, *supra* note 71, at 56–66.

[76] Scheffler et al., *supra* note 68, at 26.

[77] *Id.* at 26–27.

[78] Harvest Partners, *Advanced Dermatology & Cosmetic Surgery*, https://www.harvestpartners.com/advanced-dermatology-cosmetic-surgery (last accessed Sept. 13, 2023). Note that these large firms evade antitrust scrutiny because they grow through small deals, none of which is large enough to trigger Hart Scott Rodino's review.

[79] Scheffler et al., *supra* note 68, at 30, 33.

[80] Michelle F. Davis et al., *CVS Pays $10.6B for Oak Street Health Primary Care Centers*, ALM Benefits Pro (Feb. 8, 2023), https://www.benefitspro.com/2023/02/08/cvs-pays-10-6b-for-oak-street-health-primary-care-centers/ (last accessed Feb. 20, 2025); Heather Landi, *Amazon Closes $3.9B One Medical Deal as It Builds out Healthcare Strategy*, Fierce Healthcare (Feb. 22, 2023), https://www.fiercehealthcare.com/providers/amazon-closes-39b-one-medical-deal-build-its-ambitions-healthcare-player (last accessed Feb. 20, 2025).

Advantage plans where doctors become a key to profitmaking through risk adjustment, as discussed above.[81]

9.3.2 *Change Emerges: Possibly Too Little Too Late*

In recent years, physicians and their priorities have noticeably shifted. Physicians are trying to regroup and regain control over their professional lives through labor efforts including unionization. And laws aimed at turf protection have begun to recede, hastened by the COVID-19 pandemic. These efforts may be too late, however, to redirect the trajectory of the profession.

So far, this chapter has portrayed doctors and the profession as monolithic, which was untrue even in the days when most doctors were male, white, politically conservative members of the AMA, and the AMA spoke on their behalf on policy. In recent decades, doctors have become much more heterogeneous.[82] Doctors are seeking more varied ends out of medical practice. They are more than ever prioritizing work-life balance more than or co-equal to other career goals.[83] The AMA's power and membership has declined, evident during ACA debates when new groups like Doctors for America spoke on behalf of an emerging progressive and public health-oriented wing of the profession.[84] And even the AMA seeks to evolve. In June 2019, the AMA nearly passed a proposal to eschew opposition to single-payer health care reform.[85]

The COVID-19 pandemic hastened health policy reforms, undoing many of the overly restrictive laws that produced a glaring shortage of primary care doctors in many communities. For example, all fifty states temporarily waived in-state licensure requirements, which allowed providers to cross state boundaries to practice, and all but one applied this waiver to telehealth too.[86] Most states with restrictive scope-of-practice laws allowed nonphysician providers to do increasingly more, practicing to the top of their training and ability, rather than to an artificially set boundary.[87]

[81] Richard Kronick, *Projected Coding Intensity in Medicare Advantage Could Increase Medicare Spending by $20 Billion Over Ten Years*, 36 Health Affs. 320 (2017).

[82] *Doctor Demographics and Statistics in the US*, Zippia, https://www.zippia.com/doctor-jobs/demographics/ (last accessed Aug. 29, 2023).

[83] NEJM Career Center, *Understanding Millennial Physician Job Seekers: An Updated Look* 8 (2022), http://resources.nejmcareercenter.org/wp-content/uploads/MillennialStudyUpdate2022.pdf (last accessed Feb. 20, 2025).

[84] Doctors for America, *What We Do, Doctors for America*, https://doctorsforamerica.org/what-we-do/ (last accessed Mar. 13, 2023).

[85] Abigail Abrams, *A New Generation of Activist Doctors Is Fighting for Medicare for All*, Time (Oct. 24, 2019).

[86] Allison K. Hoffman & Simone Hussussian, *Covid-19 and Access to Medical Care in the United States*, Reg. Rev. (May 26, 2020), https://www.theregreview.org/2020/05/26/hoffman-hussussian-covid-19-access-medical-care-united-states/ (last accessed Feb. 20, 2025).

[87] Am. Ass'n of Nurse Practitioners, *COVID-19 State Emergency Response: Temporarily Suspended and Waived Practice Agreement Requirements*, https://www.aanp.org/advocacy/state/covid-19-state-emergency-response-temporarily-suspended-and-waived-practice-agreement-requirements (last accessed Mar. 12, 2023).

Some, although a small minority of, states made these expansions to scope-of-practice permanent.[88]

The boundaries of medical practice continue to shift after the pandemic. In the first months of 2023, state lawmakers introduced 200 bills that would, for example, allow pharmacists to administer vaccines or prescribe hormonal contraceptives and that would allow optometrists to inject local anesthesia for minor procedures.[89] Likewise, both the federal and the state governments relaxed laws on telemedicine.[90] And some states, and Medicare, created parity rules for reimbursing telehealth and in-person visits the same amounts.[91]

But rebuilding the profession with a more capacious vision of who is part of it may prove impossible after the effects of over a century of protectionism. Nurses are leaving the profession, and nursing shortages are increasingly acute.[92] In turn, private equity is buying up travel nursing agencies that place nurses in high-need areas across the country at a premium.[93] It seems that current efforts to increase access to care and redefine the bounds of the profession may be limited by a path set in motion a century prior.

9.3.3 *The Impact of the Fall of the Medical Profession on Patients*

This chapter focuses on the medical profession and its regulation, but anyone who has been a patient knows who loses in the end when regulation is motivated by factors other than access to high-quality care. It has been evident for some time that the profession depressed supply and access to care in harmful ways, especially in low-income and rural areas, and efforts to turn the tide are likely insufficient to make up for a century of contraction.

What is more recently surfacing is that the increasing corporatization of health care delivery is also bad for our health. Physicians report pressure to provide more care by reducing the time with each patient, detracting from the quality of care in some cases.[94] The rise of the corporatization of health care has led to providers

88 *Id.* (reporting that Massachusetts, Maine, New York, Nebraska, and Kansas made permanent or are considering making permanent waivers of practice agreement requirements).

89 Daniel Payne, *The ______ Will See You Now: How the Pandemic Could Change Who Treats You*, POLTICOPRO (Apr. 11, 2023), https://subscriber.politicopro.com/article/2023/04/the-will-see-you-now-how-the-pandemic-could-change-who-treats-you-00091256 (last accessed Feb. 20, 2025).

90 Hoffman & Hussussian, *supra* note 86.

91 *Id.*

92 *Id.*

93 Mary Bugbee, *Profiting in Crisis: Exploring Private Equity's Investments in Travel Nursing Amidst a Critical Nursing Shortage and a Pandemic*, PRIVATE EQUITY STAKEHOLDER PROJECT (2022), https://pestakeholder.org/wp-content/uploads/2022/10/PE_travelnursing_FINAL-1.pdf (last accessed Feb. 20, 2025).

94 Mark W. Friedberg et al., *Factors Affecting Physician Professional Satisfaction and Their Implications for Patient Care, Health Systems, and Health Policy*, 3 RAND HEALTH Q. 1

feeling they must fit more "billable" patients into shorter increments of time, resulting in care that they feel is insufficient or even unethical and increasing cynicism among providers.[95]

Subjective patient experience suffers. Data from the Harris Poll indicates that more than 70 percent of adults feel the health care system is failing to meet their needs in at least one way.[96] Examples of this failure include the length of waiting time to schedule an appointment, coordinating across several providers, and not understanding recommendations from health care providers.[97]

Meanwhile, the United States has fallen farther behind peers in common health metrics such as life expectancy at birth and infant mortality.[98] Disease burden, which takes into account both premature death and years of living with disability, is higher in the United States than elsewhere.[99] The United States also ranks last among its peer countries in measures of health access and quality, negatively impacting population health.[100] The United States has among the lowest rates of physician visits and lowest number of hospital beds in the world, yet its health care spending is the world's highest.[101]

Specific evidence on corporate ownership is not encouraging either. Medicare Advantage plans are driving up the cost of Medicare without adding concomitant value. These private plans profited early on by enrolling healthier populations.[102] Most have been accused of fraud by whistleblowers and/or the government.[103] They fail to serve patients with complex health needs,[104] and their enrollees are more

(2014), https://www.rand.org/pubs/periodicals/health-quarterly/issues/v3/n4/01.html (last accessed Feb. 20, 2025).

95 Marie G. Rudden, "A *Weird Culture of Coercion*": *The Impact of Health Care Corporatization on Clinicians*, 19 INT'L J. APPLIED PSYCHOANALYTIC STUD. 270 (2022).

96 Am. Acad. of Physician Assistants, *The Harris Poll*, https://www.aapa.org/research/patient-experience/ (last accessed Sept. 13, 2023); Jamie Ducharme, *More than 70% of Americans Feel Failed by the Health Care System*, TIME (May 16, 2023).

97 *Id.*

98 Nisha Kurani & Emma Wager, *How Does the Quality of the U.S. Health System Compare to Other Countries?*, PETERSON-KFF HEALTH SYS. TRACKER (Sept. 30, 2021), https://www.healthsystemtracker.org/chart-collection/quality-u-s-healthcare-system-compare-countries/ (last accessed Feb. 20, 2025).

99 *Id.*

100 *Id.*

101 Munira Z. Gunja et al., *U.S. Health Care from a Global Perspective, 2022: Accelerating Spending, Worsening Outcomes*, COMMONWEALTH FUND (Jan. 31, 2023), https://www.commonwealthfund.org/publications/issue-briefs/2023/jan/us-health-care-global-perspective-2022 (last accessed Feb. 20, 2025).

102 RANDALL S. BROWN ET AL., MATHEMATICA POL'Y RSCH INC., THE MEDICARE RISK PROGRAM FOR HMOS: FINAL SUMMARY REPORT ON FINDINGS FROM THE EVALUATION xvii–xx (Feb. 18, 1993).

103 Reed Abelson & Margot Sanger-Katz, *The Cash Monster Was Insatiable': How Insurers Exploited Medicare for Billions*, N.Y. TIMES UPSHOT (Oct. 8, 2022), https://www.nytimes.com/2022/10/08/upshot/medicare-advantage-fraud-allegations.html (last accessed Feb. 20, 2025).

104 David J. Meyers et al., *Analysis of Drivers of Disenrollment and Plan Switching among Medicare Advantage Beneficiaries*, 179 JAMA INTERNAL MED. 525 (2019).

likely to enter lower-quality nursing home facilities.[105] Evidence suggests that Medicare Advantage plans are wrongly denying care in as much as one-fifth of cases, threatening the viability of rural hospitals.[106]

As another example, early evidence on private equity investment in physician practices suggests that patients may end up paying more or getting unnecessary care. A Kaiser Health News investigation of private-equity-owned outpatient care reported $500 million in False Claims Act settlements for overbilling, and a series of articles uncovered stories of unnecessary and poor-quality care, including of a two-year-old who died after a private-equity-owned dental clinic performed unnecessary root canals and placed crowns on baby teeth.[107] A study in JAMA of 578 private equity-acquired physician practices in dermatology, gastroenterology, and ophthalmology showed increases in health care spending and use.[108] In the case of dermatology and ADCS, noted above, after private equity investment, dermatology practices refocused on the sale of retail skincare products and self-pay elective procedures, and employees reported that the company cut back on essential supplies and provided care with questionable value and safety.[109] Research suggests that nursing homes with private equity ownership produce lower quality of care – including increased emergency department visits and hospitalizations for patients – at higher prices.[110] And a shocking recent study revealed a 25 percent increase in preventable hospital-acquired injuries – like falls and central line or surgical site infections – after private equity hospital acquisitions.[111]

105 David J. Meyers et al., *Medicare Advantage Enrollees More Likely to Enter Lower-Quality Nursing Homes Compared to Fee-For-Service Enrollees*, 37 HEALTH AFFS. 78 (2018).

106 Gretchen Morgenson & Lisa Cavazuti, *By Denying Claims, Medicare Advantage Plans Hurt Rural Hospitals, Say CEOs*, NBC NEWS (Dec. 15, 2023), https://finance.yahoo.com/news/denying-claims-medicare-advantage-plans-123041741.html (last accessed Feb. 20, 2025).

107 Fred Schulte, *Sick Profit: Investigating Private Equity's Stealthy Takeover of Health Care across Cities and Specialties*, KFF HEALTH NEWS (Nov. 14, 2022), https://kffhealthnews.org/news/article/private-equity-takeover-health-care-cities-specialties/ (last accessed Feb. 20, 2025).

108 Yashaswini Singh et al., *Association of Private Equity Acquisition of Physician Practices with Changes in Health Care Spending and Utilization*, 3 JAMA HEALTH F. e222886 (2022), https://jamanetwork.com/journals/jama-health-forum/fullarticle/2795946 (last accessed Feb. 20, 2025) (reporting an average 20 percent increase in charges per claim and a 16.3 percent increase in number of encounters).

109 Scheffler et al., *supra* note 68, at 34; Katie Hafner & Griffin Palmer, *Skin Cancers Rise, Along with Questionable Treatments*, N.Y. TIMES (Nov. 20, 2017), https://www.nytimes.com/2017/11/20/health/dermatology-skin-cancer.html (last accessed Feb. 20, 2025).

110 *See, for example*, ATUL GUPTA ET AL., NAT'L BUREAU OF ECON. RSCH., OWNER INCENTIVES AND PERFORMANCE IN HEALTHCARE: PRIVATE EQUITY INVESTMENT IN NURSING HOMES (2021), https://ssrn.com/abstract=3790212 (last accessed Feb. 20, 2025) (showing 10 percent increases in short-term mortality of Medicare patients with private equity ownership of nursing homes, or 20,150 lives lost due to private equity ownership over twelve years, declines in other measures of well-being including mobility, and a 11 percent increase in taxpayer spending per patient); Robert Tyler Braun et al., *Association of Private Equity Investment in US Nursing Homes with the Quality and Cost of Care for Long-Stay Residents*, 2 JAMA HEALTH F. e213817 (2021).

111 Sneha Kannan et al., *Changes in Hospital Adverse Events and Patient Outcomes Associated with Private Equity Acquisition*, 330 JAMA 2365 (2023).

In the end, patients suffer as medicine overly focuses on profits. When profit seeking is imposed through external controls and management, it becomes increasingly difficult for doctors and others to provide any counterbalance, regardless of their own intentions or motivations.

9.4 THOUGHTS FOR THE LEGAL PROFESSION

How does the legal profession avoid the fate of the medical profession? Initially, law and medicine progressed in step. Over the past century, law has used many of the same tools as medicine to protect profits and bolster professional standing: restrictive supply requirements with accreditation limiting the pool of lawyers, which, like the supply restrictions in medicine, had a disproportionate effect on women and underrepresented minorities; licensure laws for turf protection; bans on corporate ownership; and strict supervision requirements for lawyer extenders such as legal assistants and paralegals. The American Bar Association (ABA) sought control in the same way the AMA did, with only one letter's difference.

Yet, today's legal profession looks very different from medicine. Lawyers are still the only ones who can practice law. Law has largely resisted entry of outside investors like private equity, and, although insurance also plays a key role in modern legal practice, it is as a client to firms, not as an owner of them. Many lawyers are not employees, and those who are employed tend to be employed by their fellow lawyers, organized under a partnership model or by cities, states, or the federal government.

Still, in law, many are advocating for the abolition of Rules 5.4(b) and (d), which prevent fee-sharing and nonlawyer ownership. The forward-looking question is this: How does the legal profession improve access to legal services without opening the portals that devoured the medical profession? Since I come to this volume as an interloper in the access-to-justice conversation, I end with loosely formed thoughts on how the arc of the medical profession might frame some hard questions for the legal one about practice authority and capital. These are intended as beginning questions, not as answers.

9.4.1 *Who Can Practice? Questioning the Boundaries of the Profession*

One hypothesis running through this chapter is that the medical profession was too restrictive when shaping the bounds of practice authority. Contraction of medical education and narrow practice rules might have rooted out some bad practices of medicine, but when people can't see a doctor, it can quickly become a crisis.[112]

To address shortages, the profession allowed "physician extenders," assuming that they would never be a good substitute for a doctor and that physicians could control

[112] STARR, *supra* note 2, at 382.

them. Yet, as evidence emerged that an advanced practice nurse can provide good care, independent of a doctor, justifications for control dissipated.

Maybe law has not yet found the tipping point of an access crisis, but if it hasn't, it may be nearing one. The number of people who have unmet need for legal assistance has surged.[113] At this pivotal moment, the legal profession and the ABA can still help to shape a solution that thoughtfully considers the role of paraprofessionals, nonlawyer professionals, and technology including artificial intelligence, rather than being an impediment to it.

Medicine suggests that holding on too tight to the boundaries of practice might lead to a short-term boon but a long-term unraveling. So, a first reflection is: If the legal profession embraces a more capacious model of legal services, can broader practice authority be part of the solution, rather than an impediment to be overcome?

9.4.2 *How to Fund Access to Legal Services*

Even if more people could offer legal services in various forms, the harder challenge is an external one of how to fund legal services for people who cannot afford them (which is most people). And perhaps the lesson of medicine in this space is that there is no easy answer.

Legal aid societies have existed since the mid-nineteenth century, shifting through various models and funding sources over time.[114] By 1965, most major cities in the United States had some formal, local legal aid program.[115] Most adopted a traditional model of charitable, individualized, case-by-case assistance.[116]

The Economic Opportunity Act of 1964 (EOA) marked the first time Congress provided federal funding for legal aid.[117] The Act created the Office of Economic Opportunity (OEO) to administer EOA funds,[118] which relied on local community

[113] L. Servs. Corp., *The Justice Gap Report* (2022), https://www.lsc.gov/our-impact/publications/other-publications-and-reports/2017-justice-gap-report (last accessed Feb. 20, 2025).

[114] Scott Cummings & Jeffrey Selbin, *Poverty Law: United States, in* International Encyclopedia of the Social & Behavioral Sciences 3 (James D. Wright ed., 2015); William P. Quigley, *The Demise of Law Reform and the Triumph of Legal Aid: Congress and the Legal Services Corporation from the 1960's to the 1990's*, 17 St. Louis U. Pub. L. Rev. 241, 244 (1998).

[115] Alan Houseman & Linda E. Perle, Securing Equal Justice for All: A Brief History of Civil Legal Assistance in the United States 8 (2018); Shaun Ossei-Owusu, *Civil vs. Criminal Legal Aid*, 94 S. Cal. L. Rev. 1573 (2021) (describing the first cities to establish legal aid organizations outside of New York, Boston, and Chicago).

[116] Houseman & Perle, *supra* note 115, at 8. A minority at times sought systemic changes in the law.

[117] Cummings & Selbin, *supra* note 114, at 3–4.

[118] Note, *The Legal Services Corporation: Curtailing Political Influence*, 81 Yale L.J. 231, 236 (1972); Cummings & Selbin, *supra* note 114, at 3; Clinton Bamberger, *Legal Services Program of the Office of Economic Opportunity*, 41 Notre Dame L. Rev. 847, 852 (1966); Quigley, *supra* note 114, at 245.

action agencies to disburse these funds. Private attorneys opposed OEO models on several grounds, including that with federal funding might come the specter of greater regulation of the legal profession.[119]

In 1971, an ABA committee recommended the creation of a private, nonprofit corporation that would replace OEO.[120] And a 1974 law succeeded with the creation of the Legal Services Corporation (LSC), a nonprofit corporation headed by an independent, bipartisan board.[121] After a brief rise, however, Congress began to limit the use of LSC funding, culminating in the election of Ronald Reagan in 1980 who proposed its complete elimination.[122] President Reagan failed to achieve this vision, but LSC has been on a funding roller coaster since.[123]

Some bar associations endorsed an alternative, middle-ground proposal for federally funded legal aid: Judicare.[124] Judicare would have used federal funds to pay for poor clients to seek private services, like Medicare and Medicaid.[125] But John Robb, the then-Chairman of the Standing Committee on Legal Aid and Indigent Defendants of the American Bar Association, rejected following the path of medicine, arguing presciently in 1967 that doctors may "have paid too high a price for what may well prove to be a short lived prosperity."[126] Despite some testing of Judicare models, it never took hold in more than very limited ways.[127]

Instead of one, central funding model, various decentralized ones have emerged. On the criminal side, states and cities help to fund defense attorneys. On the civil side, for example, programs funded through interest on lawyers' trust accounts (IOLTA), the second-largest source of legal aid funding after LSC, pay for legal services using interest accrued from trust accounts in which lawyers hold client funds.[128] These programs were created by state rules of professional conduct, state legislatures, or state supreme courts, and have existed in every state and the District of Columbia since 1997.[129]

[119] *See* Bamberger, *supra* note 118, at 849; John D. Robb, *Alternate Legal Assistance Plans*, 14 CATH. LAW. 127, 138 (1968).

[120] Houseman & Perle, *supra* note 115, at 21.

[121] *See* Legal Services Corporation Act of 1974, Pub. L. No. 93-355, 88 Stat. 378 (1974).

[122] Cummings & Selbin, *supra* note 114, at 8.

[123] Quigley, *supra* note 114, at 261; Cummings & Selbin, *supra* note 114, at 8; Carl Rauscher, *LSC Requests $1.5 Billion to Confront Widening Justice Gap amid Pandemic Hardships*, LEGAL SERVS. CORP. (Mar. 9, 2023), https://www.lsc.gov/press-release/lsc-requests-15-billion-confront-widening-justice-gap-amid-pandemic-hardships (last accessed Feb. 20, 2025).

[124] *See* Joseph F. Preloznik, *Wisconsin Judicare: An Experiment in Legal Services*, 57 A.B.A. J. 1179, 1179–80 (1971).

[125] Robb, *supra* note 119, at 128.

[126] *Id.* at 140.

[127] Houseman & Perle, *supra* note 115, at 27.

[128] *Id.* at 43.

[129] Andrew Arthur, Comment, *A Good Rule, Poorly Written: How the Financial Crisis Highlighted the Inadequacy of IOLTA Rate Rules*, 64 CATH. U. L. REV. 729, 732–33, 745 (2015); Hillary A. Webber, *Note, Equal Justice under the Law: Why IOLTA Programs Do Not Violate the First Amendment*, 53 AM. U. L. REV. 491, 496 (2003).

The United States spent over $4.5 trillion on health care in 2022, including over $1 trillion on professional services, such as physician and clinical services.[130] In contrast, the entire legal services market is not even $400 billion. And total legal aid funding including LSC and IOLTA was just $2.8 billion in 2021, barely a drop in the bucket.[131]

Although the lack of federal funding impedes access to justice, lessons from medicine suggest it also avoids traps. Medicare and Medicaid brought an infusion of federal money into health care and, with it, a host of problems including steep health care cost inflation, which regulators have lacked the reach and the will to curb. Instead, they turn to market competition with hopes that it will do so, handing over program administration to corporate participants in those markets. With some exceptions, these efforts have failed to save money or improve care quality; in fact, they've done the opposite.[132]

Maybe uniform federal funding would have avoided these traps. If, in 1965, Congress had passed a national health insurance system, we might see more coherent price regulation where the greatest friction occurs between regulators, on one hand, and doctors and hospitals, on the other, over reimbursement rates. The medical profession (ironically, considering the AMA's deep resistance to such an approach) might have fared better in that alternative world. But a partial solution in health care has accelerated the undermining of the profession.

This lesson from medicine suggests that the challenge for the law is how to get to funding levels that approach the need for legal services while resisting the problems that powerful, yet fragmented federal programs can create. This challenge is obviously formidable.

9.4.3 *Whether to Resist Corporatization*

A related question is whether to allow corporate money to fill shortfalls. Here, medicine's trajectory suggests the legal profession "proceed with caution." Had corporate practice of medicine prohibitions stayed in place and been enforced, corporate interests likely wouldn't have been excluded wholly, as evinced by the many workarounds of these laws. But at the same time, there likely would have been stronger legal teeth to resist dramatic corporatization.[133]

[130] Micah Hartman et al., *National Health Care Spending in 2022: Growth Similar to Prepandemic Rates*, 43 Health Affs. 6 (2024).

[131] ABArray National Data, *U.S. Funding for Legal Aid* (Nov. 30, 2022), https://public.tableau.com/app/profile/abarray/viz/ABArrayNationalData/NationalLegalAidFunding (last accessed Feb. 20, 2025).

[132] Allison K. Hoffman, *Health Care's Market Bureaucracy*, 66 UCLA L. Rev. 1926 (2019).

[133] *See* Brown & Hall, *supra* note 67, at 54 (considering whether corporate practice of medicine doctrine could be invoked to push back on private equity investment in health care).

Prohibitions on corporate ownership in the law, in contrast, have been in place and effective for nearly a century. Every state bar association, except the District of Columbia, adopted ABA Rule 5.4, which prohibits nonlawyer ownership of law firms, despite having faced resistance among firms.[134]

Yet, recently, a few states have adopted reforms permitting nonlawyers to own law firms. Arizona eliminated Rule 5.4 on a permanent basis, whereas Utah began a two-year pilot period to experiment with allowing law firm ownership by nonlawyers.[135] In their wake, California and North Carolina established committees to investigate similar reforms.[136]

Law firms see eliminating Rule 5.4 as enabling new ways for them to access capital, which under the rule is only possible if equity partners invest more in the firm or through a bank loan.[137] Without Rule 5.4, external investors can buy equity in the firm, producing capital without debt.[138] Eliminating Rule 5.4 could also institutionalize adjacent legal competencies outside of law firms,[139] or allow marketing, tax planning, or wealth management entities to obtain ownership interest in legal services.[140]

Some thoughtful scholars and other stakeholders suggest that the elimination of Rule 5.4 could benefit lawyers and promote access to justice.[141] They highlight potential increases in consumer access to services and innovation in the legal market, and some early experimentation affirms this possibility.[142]

Yet, medicine offers a cautionary tale about lifting such barriers whole cloth, especially without monitoring which corporate interests can enter and how. Corporate investment in health care illustrates the unintended consequences that could follow if states are not careful about keeping a close eye on the precise form

[134] Conrad J. Jacoby, *Practice Innovations: Non-Lawyer Ownership of Law Firms – Are Winds of Change Coming for Rule 5.4?*, Reuters (Mar. 31, 2022), https://www.reuters.com/legal/legalindustry/practice-innovations-non-lawyer-ownership-law-firms-are-winds-change-coming-rule-2022-03-31/ (last accessed Feb. 20, 2025).

[135] Lyle Moran, *Arizona Approves Nonlawyer Ownership, Nonlawyer Licensees in Access-to-Justice Reforms*, A.B.A. J. (Aug. 28, 2020).

[136] Conn Kavanaugh, *Lawyer Ownership of Law Firms: Coming to a Jurisdiction Near You?*, JD Supra (June 3, 2021).

[137] Tyler Cobb, *Have Your Cake and Eat It Too! Appropriately Harnessing the Advantages of Nonlawyer Ownership*, 54 Ariz. L. Rev. 765, 776 (2012).

[138] *See, for example*, Brett Cole, *Slater and Gordon, Australian Law Firm, to Acquire Arm of Quindell of Britain*, N.Y. Times (Mar. 29, 2015); Brandon Kochkodin, *Why Law Firms Could Be Private Equity's Next Conquest*, Forbes (Feb. 26, 2024).

[139] Sara Merken, *Arizona Approves Five More Entities for New Legal Business Structure*, Reuters (Aug. 27, 2021).

[140] *Id.*

[141] *See, for example*, Jason Solomon et al., *How Reforming Rule 5.4 Would Benefit Lawyers and Consumers, Promote Innovation, and Increase Access to Justice*, Stan. Ctr. Legal Pro. (Apr. 2020); Ralph Baxter, *Dereliction of Duty: State-Bar Inaction in Response to America's Access-to-Justice Crisis*, 132 Yale L.J. F. 228, 235 (2022).

[142] David Freeman Engstrom et al., Legal Innovation after Reform: Evidence from Regulatory Change (2022).

diversification takes. It might be that such reforms open the floodgates but, without sufficient consumer protections and regulations, do not meaningfully expand access to justice.

9.5 CONCLUSION

We may never know exactly what factor or factors caused the medical profession's decline. Maybe what lawyers should learn most is that working to preserve one's own turf and earnings, rather than focusing on what is best for clients, harms the core values that make something a profession. It matters less whether it was the medical profession's aggressive self-regulation or its defeat of national health insurance or its exertion of control over reimbursement. When a profession works to aggrandize power and wealth and, in the process, loses sight of why it was accorded professional respect in the first place, it has become less a profession and more a business. There is certainly a lesson there for lawyers.

10

Lessons from Medicine's Experiment with Nurse Practitioners and Physician Assistants

Philip G. Peters, Jr.

The idea of independent legal paraprofessionals offering legal services in currently underserved areas at more affordable price points is gaining traction across the country. Over the past several years, an increasing number of states have been studying and moving forward with licensing paraprofessionals, including Arizona, Utah, Oregon, Minnesota, Colorado, and New Hampshire.[1] When arguing in favor of the licensure of nonlawyer legal advocates, reform proponents almost inevitably draw analogies to nurse practitioners (NPs) and physician assistants (PAs).[2] But many law reformers know relatively little about these mid-level health care providers or whether it is *actually* true that these providers furnish accessible and affordable high-quality care. This chapter addresses this knowledge gap and, in so doing, looks for lessons that the experience of mid-level health care providers offers for access-to-justice reforms.

In both law and medicine, the most important question raised by the creation of middle tiers of providers is whether mid-level providers can provide high-quality services despite their shorter training periods. An important subsidiary question is whether, by virtue of their less expensive training, they increase the access of underserved populations to care. This chapter looks for clues in the significant body of empirical evidence about their work.

This chapter also identifies important differences between the medical and legal marketplaces that may determine whether nonlawyer advocates can duplicate the successes of NPs. The most important differences are the widespread presence of insurance in medicine and the chronic shortage of primary care physicians.

[1] Nora Freeman Engstrom & James Stone, *Auto Clubs and the Lost Origins of the Access-to-Justice Crisis*, 134 Yale L.J. 123 (Oct. 2024) (compiling citations).

[2] *See, for example*, Nora Freeman Engstrom, *Effective Deregulation: A Look under the Hood of State Civil Courts*, Jotwell (Oct. 31, 2022), https://legalpro.jotwell.com/effective-deregulation-a-look-under-the-hood-of-state-civil-courts/ (last accessed Feb. 3, 2025); Stephen Daniels & James Bowers, *Alternative Legal Professionals and Access to Justice: Failure, Success, and the Evolving Influence of the Washington State LLLT Program (The Genie Is Out of the Bottle)*, 71 DePaul L. Rev. 227, 240–41 (2022).

In addition, medicine has a long history of accommodating a wide variety of medical professions of varying scope and stature, ranging from ophthalmologists to audiologists, and from nurses to X-ray techs. In the field of law, by contrast, attorneys have largely reserved the entire field to themselves. As a result, the arrival of nonlawyer advocates has the potential to be much more disruptive and existentially disquieting than the emergence of NPs was to physicians.

The remainder of this chapter unfolds as follows. Section 10.1 begins by exploring how modern medicine has accommodated multiple categories of nonphysician health care providers for over a century. It then traces the origins of the NP and PA professions and the reactions of physicians. Section 10.2 describes the impact that NPs and PAs have had on patient care, focusing on the quality of services they provide and their impact on access to care for both rural and uninsured patients. Section 10.3 then explores the lessons that this medical story offers for improving access to legal services.

10.1 THE RISE OF NURSE PRACTITIONERS AND PHYSICIAN ASSISTANTS

At their inception in the 1960s, NPs were a novel hybrid of nurse and physician. Unlike nurses, they had the authority to order tests, diagnose conditions, and select treatments, albeit under the supervision of a physician. That authority crossed a boundary that physicians had previously reserved for themselves. This sharing of core physician powers made NPs a naturally attractive analogy for law reformers seeking to create a new category of mid-level legal professionals with some of the powers previously held exclusively by attorneys, such as negotiating a settlement or appearing before a tribunal. These reformers could equally well have relied on an analogy to PAs, whose scope of practice largely mirrors that of NPs.

In the field of law, however, proposals to delegate this kind of authority to mid-level practitioners have generated far more opposition from the organized bar than medical reformers faced when creating the NP and PA professions in the mid-1960s. Several aspects of the health care environment in the twentieth century may help explain medicine's warmer reception.

10.1.1 *The Long History of Multiple Health Care Professions*

In medicine, limited license medical specialists have long shared the health care field with physicians. These limited license professionals range from doctorate-level nonphysicians who have full authority to treat a limited range of maladies free from the supervision of a physician, like dentists and optometrists, to mid-level providers who can care for virtually all patients but can only provide a limited set of services, like registered and practical nurses. To handle even more discrete tasks, medicine has also created dozens of more limited allied health professions, like radiology techs and phlebotomists. This division of labor is a fundamental aspect of the delivery of modern medicine. Without it, health care would be much more expensive and much less accessible.

Medicine's division of labor began over a century ago. At that time, the parameters of acceptable "medical" practice were not well defined. In the late nineteenth and early twentieth centuries, allopathic physicians (MDs) were fighting and defeating homeopaths, naturopaths, and, for a time, osteopaths for control over the practice of medicine.[3] All three forms of alternative medicine arose as a reaction against traditional medicine, which at that time was often harsh and sometimes harmful. The first, homeopathy, was created in the late eighteenth century around two key precepts: First, the Law of Similars dictated that patients be treated with remedies that would generate symptoms similar to those being experienced by the patient ("like cures like") and, second, the Law of Infinitesimals called for prescriptions to be very, very highly diluted.[4] Naturopathy also arose in the 1890s. It sought to prevent and cure disease by stimulating the body's natural healing abilities. One of the founders defined it as a broad discipline that included practices like hydrotherapy, herbal medicine, homeopathy, and a healthy diet.[5] To a large extent, naturopaths opposed surgery and prescription drugs.[6] Early osteopathy, for its part, was created in the 1890s around the belief that diagnosing and treating the musculoskeletal system could successfully treat most illnesses, including those involving internal organs and the brain.[7]

Allopathic physicians argued that all three approaches were unproven, in some cases scientifically implausible, and likely to keep patients away from conventional care that could help them.[8] As a result, physicians successfully pushed homeopathy and naturopathy to the margins of the field. In the second half of the twentieth century, they abandoned their objections to osteopathy after it embraced evidence-based medicine.

While this fight was taking place in hospitals and state legislatures, other medical professions were cementing their own place in the health care marketplace. For example, nursing, optometry, and pharmacy all had their first state practice acts in place by 1903.[9] Podiatrists (foot doctors) began organizing as a profession in the early

3 Ruth Horowitz, In the Public Interest: Medical Licensing and the Disciplinary Process (2012).

4 *See* Viola Maria Schulz et al., *Systematic Review of Conceptual Criticisms of Homeopathy*, 9(11) Heliyon E21287, 1-2 (2023).

5 *See Unsolved: Naturopathy*, HandWiki (Jan. 24, 2024), https://handwiki.org/wiki/Unsolved:Naturopathy (last accessed Feb. 3, 2025).

6 *See id.*

7 *See* Abigail Zuger, *Scorned No More, Osteopathy Is on the Rise*, N.Y. Times (Feb. 7, 1998), at F1 (reviewing the changes in training and the increased receptiveness of physicians).

8 *See, for example, Id.*

9 *See* Harold L. Wilensky, *The Professionalism of Everyone?* 70 Am. J. Socio. 137, 1423 tbl. 1 (1964). All states had optometry practice acts by 1921. *The History of the American Optometric Assn.*, Am. Optometric Ass'n, https://www.aoa.org/archives/ (last accessed Aug. 4, 2023);

1900s, and by 1923 at least twenty-three states had enacted practice acts that granted them the right to diagnose and treat diseases of the foot without physician supervision, thus eliminating the risk of prosecution for the unauthorized practice of medicine.[10]

Physical therapists (PTs) and occupational therapists gained credibility during World War I when they were given status as "reconstruction aides" for badly injured soldiers.[11] The arrival of polio cemented their roles. All these professions had limited licenses that overlapped with the general, unrestricted health care license of physicians.

Physicians did not campaign against nurses and PTs as they had against naturopaths and homeopaths, perhaps because nurses and PTs worked under the direction of a physician. Optometrists were not so lucky. They dueled with physicians in state courts and legislatures for decades over their right to exist as a separate profession (was refraction "the practice of medicine"?) and then over the scope of their practice.[12] Those battles continued to rage throughout the twentieth century as the two professions battled over optometrists' freedom to use new innovations such as diagnostic eye drops and therapeutic lasers.[13]

Following World War II, new technologies quickly expanded the use of laboratory tests and diagnostic imaging. For each of these tasks, new staff were needed. Each staffing specialty eventually coalesced into a new limited license profession. Many fell into the category that universities now call the "allied health professions." They include laboratory techs and techs for every major kind of imaging device, including diagnostic radiography, computed tomography (CT), magnetic resonance imaging (MRI), nuclear medicine, and ultrasound.[14] These licenses can be quite

Diane Benefiel, *The Story of Nurse Licensure*, 36 NURSE EDUC. 16, 16 (2011) ("By 1923, all 48 states had passed some form of nursing licensure legislation. ... In 1938, New York passed the first mandatory nurse licensure legislation.")

10 *See* Louis T. Bogy, *Podiatry*, TEX. HIST. SOC'Y (1995), https://www.tshaonline.org/handbook/entries/podiatry (last accessed Feb. 3, 2025) (number of practice acts); *Historical Highlights of APMA*, APMA, https://www.apma.org/about-apma/governance/who-we-are/historical-highlights-of-apma/ (last accessed Feb. 3, 2025). Podiatry is "the medical care and treatment of the human foot." *Podiatry*, MERRIAM-WEBSTER DICTIONARY, https://www.merriam-webster.com/dictionary/podiatry#:~:text=Kids%20Definition-,podiatry,treatment%20of%20the%20human%20foot (last accessed Aug. 4, 2023).

11 *See A Brief History of Occupational Therapy*, MY OT SPOT (Sept. 6, 2019, last updated May 13, 2023), https://www.myotspot.com/tag/ot-history/ (last accessed Aug. 2, 2023); *History of the Occupational Therapy Profession*, PRINCE EDWARD I. C. OF OCCUPATIONAL THERAPISTS, https://www.peiot.org/pei-ot-history (last accessed Feb. 3, 2025).

12 *See* Bill Kekevian, *Legalizing Optometry: A Behind-The-Scenes Look at the People, the Moments and the Legislation That Made the Profession What It Is Today*, REV. OF OPTOMETRY (2016), https://www.reviewofoptometry.com/article/legalizing-optometry#:~:text=Optometry's%20first%20licensure%20law%2C%20passed,and%20as%20recently%20as%202008 (last accessed Feb. 3, 2025).

13 *See id.*

14 *See* Christine Harris, *Evolution of a Profession: A Rad-Tech's Reflections*, 50 APPLIED RADIOLOGY 28 (2021), https://appliedradiology.com/articles/evolution-of-a-profession-a-rad-

specialized; Arizona, for instance, licenses nine different kinds of radiologic technologists.[15]

Emergency Medical Technicians (EMTs) and paramedics have a different origin story. Their professions arose in response to a 1966 national report on auto accident injuries. The report revealed that vehicle accidents in 1965 killed more Americans than were lost in the entire Korean War.[16] A seriously injured accident victim had a better chance of survival in a combat zone than on the side of the road. The report called for the standardization of training for emergency response personnel. Soon after, Congress passed the National Highway Traffic Safety Act of 1966, which standardized emergency medical service training and promoted state involvement.[17]

Today, the number of limited license health care professions is vast. California now licenses acupuncturists, audiologists, chiropractors, clinical social workers, contact lens dispensers/spectacle lens dispensers, dental assistants, dental hygienists, dentists, educational psychologists, hearing aid dispensers, marriage and family therapists, midwives, naturopathic doctors, NPs, occupational therapists, opticians, optometrists, osteopathic physicians, pharmacists, pharmacy technicians, PTs, PAs, physicians, podiatric medical doctors, professional clinical counselors, psychiatric technicians, psychiatrists, psychologists, registered nurses, respiratory therapists, speech-language pathologists, and vocational nurses.[18] At any given time, one or more will be wrestling with physicians over the boundaries of their permitted scope of practice. But on the whole, the many health care professions have learned to accommodate one another.

In short, physicians have shared the field of medicine with other limited license professionals from the very earliest days of modern allopathic dominance. This sharing and specialization allow the delivery of higher-quality services in a more efficient manner. It delegates less complex and less remunerative tasks to less expensively trained providers, saving time for physicians to provide more

tech-s-reflections (last accessed Feb. 3, 2025). In 1970, four states had legislation and by 1995, thirty-three states did. *History of the American Society of Radiologic Technologists*, AM. SOC'Y RADIOLOGIC TECHNOLOGISTS, https://www.asrt.org/main/about-asrt/museum-and-archives/asrt-history (last accessed Aug. 4, 2023).

[15] *See Special Licensing*, ARIZ. DEP'T HEALTH SERV., https://www.azdhs.gov/licensing/special/index.php#mrt-provider-info (last accessed Aug. 23, 2023).

[16] *See* Dennis Edgerly, *Birth of EMS: The History of the Paramedic*, 38(12) J. EMERGENCY MED. SERV. 10 (2013), https://www.jems.com/administration-and-leadership/birth-ems-history-paramedic/ (last accessed Feb. 3, 2025); Joshua Bucher and Hashim Q. Zaidi, *A Brief History of Emergency Medical Services in the United States*, EMRA, https://www.emra.org/about-emra/history/ems-history (last accessed Aug. 4, 2023).

[17] *See* Bucher and Zaidi, *supra* note 16.

[18] *See Consumer's Guide to Healthcare Providers*, CAL. DEP'T HUMAN AFFS. (Jan. 2014), https://www.dca.ca.gov/publications/healthcare_providers.shtml (last accessed Aug. 1, 2023).

complicated (and more highly remunerated) services. In medicine, the widespread sharing of duties from the top to the bottom has normalized it.

The story in law is markedly different. According to scholars Rebecca L. Sandefur and Matthew Burnett, "[b]y the middle of the 20th century, American lawyers had successfully captured most of the tasks of the practice of law, including negotiation and legal advice."[19] Since then lawyers have kept the territory securely to themselves. While several formal and informal exceptions exist,[20] they are only now emerging from the margins of the profession. In law, unlike medicine, their arrival constitutes an assault on normalcy.

10.1.2 *The Spread of Health Insurance, the Emergence of Physician Scarcity, and the Growth of NPs and PAs*

Two other historical factors were crucially important to the early acceptance of NPs and PAs. One was the emergence of widespread health insurance after World War II. The second was the shortage of primary care physicians that followed in its wake. NPs and PAs were viewed as part of the solution.

Both professions arose in the aftermath of World War II and the War on Poverty, the occurrence of both the events having changed medicine. During World War II, employers used health insurance coverage as a way to sidestep four years of wartime wage controls.[21] As a consequence, the percentage of the population with health insurance skyrocketed from 9 percent before World War II to nearly 70 percent by 1960.[22] Enrollment grew from 20,662,000 in 1940 to nearly 142,334,000 in 1950.[23] The pool of insured Americans grew again in 1965 when President Lydon Johnson signed legislation creating Medicare and Medicaid. Nineteen million Americans signed up for Medicare in the first year alone.[24]

Yet, just as the ranks of the insured were swelling, the number of new primary care physicians was dropping; physicians were moving away from primary care

[19] *See* Chapter 17 in this volume.

[20] *Id.* at 7 (noting that nonlawyers are permitted to serve clients before several federal administrative agencies); Engstrom, *supra* note 2 (describing lay advocates who assist clients in cities across the country in matters ranging from domestic violence to child welfare).

[21] Justin Barr & Scott H. Podolsky, A *National Medical Response to Crisis – The Legacy of World War II*, 383 N. Engl. J. Med. 613 (2020); George B. Moseley III, *The U.S. Health Care Non-System, 1908–2008*, 10 AMA J. Ethics 324, 325–26 (2008).

[22] Alex Blumberg & Adam Davidson, *Accidents of History Created U.S. Health System*, All Things Considered (Oct. 22, 2009), https://www.npr.org/2009/10/22/114045132/accidents-of-history-created-u-s-health-system (last accessed Aug. 23, 2023).

[23] Melissa Thomasson, *Health Insurance in the United States*, EH.Net Encyclopedia (Apr. 18, 2003), www.eh.net/encyclopedia/article/thomasson.insurance.health.us (last accessed Aug. 23, 2023).

[24] *See A Brief History of Medicare in America*, Medicare Res., https://www.medicareresources.org/basic-medicare-information/brief-history-of-medicare/ (last accessed Aug. 4, 2023).

toward specialties.[25] As a result, America had far too few primary care providers to serve this growing pool of insurance-card-carrying patients.[26]

Facing this crisis in capacity, some individual physicians began training staff to provide routine care and office procedures.[27] Delegation of routine care to nurses was also expanding. To finesse the unauthorized practice of medicine issues, nursing, physician, and hospital associations periodically published joint statements supporting this practice.[28] But the arrangement was unstable. Then, the NP and PA professions were born.

The history of NPs begins in 1965 with the efforts of Loretta Ford, a former public health nurse and a professor of nursing. She teamed up with Henry Silver, a pediatrician, to create a post-registered nurse (RN) curriculum at the University of Colorado for advanced training in pediatric care. Motivating Ford was her awareness that rural public health nurses often visited new mothers and newborns who needed services that were outside the scope of their nursing licensure, such as the diagnosis and treatment of an infection. Yet, no rural physicians were available to legally provide these services.[29] Ford believed that nurses could fill that need if provided with specialized training. In hindsight, her quest strongly resembles the desire of today's law reformers to expand and legalize the help that nonlawyer community advocates can provide to clients who would otherwise have no legal assistance at all.

To some extent, Ford was building on past precedent. In 1925, Congress created the Frontier Nursing Service, which allowed trained nurses to serve as midwives.[30] Then in 1930, the Federal Bureau of Prisons deployed former military corpsmen to provide health care in prisons.[31] California did the same in 1949.[32] And in the 1940s, Alaska started training community health workers to serve in remote areas.[33] We see a similar phenomenon in law today as nonlawyer advocates are both formally and informally expanding their roles in several niches like domestic violence proceedings.[34]

From the outset, NPs had a substantially wider scope of practice than that of registered nurses. The licensing laws allowed NPs, unlike nurses, *to diagnose and*

[25] *See* Barr & Podolsky, *supra* note 21 ("World War II also fundamentally transformed health care provision nationwide. By rewarding physicians' board certification with rank and pay, the military catalyzed medical specialization in post-war America.").

[26] *See* Reginald D. Carter, *Exploring Opportunities and Challenges*, 7, 11, *in* Physician Assistants as Social Innovators in Healthcare (2022).

[27] *Id.* at 12.

[28] *See* Carter, *supra* note 26, at 14.

[29] She felt that the medical profession should solve the shortage of primary care physicians itself. *See Loretta Ford on the Evolution of the NP Role*, YouTube (uploaded May 2, 2016), https://www.youtube.com/watch?v=2pHbCw_HS-8 (last accessed Apr. 11, 2023).

[30] *See* Carter, *supra* note 26, at 12.

[31] *Id.*

[32] *Id.*

[33] *Id.*

[34] *See* Engstrom, *supra* note 2.

treat medical conditions in their area of training under the supervision of a physician. With physician oversight, they could admit patients, order imaging or lab tests, and later, write prescriptions.

At the same time, NPs were intended to complement and collaborate with physicians, not replace them.[35] Ford was careful to use wording that would not anger physicians.[36] Nearly all NPs were female, like the RN pool from which they were drawn, and nearly all MDs were male. Although many nursing schools did not welcome the new hybrid, they did not stand in the way of NP practice acts.[37]

The first PA program also started in 1965. Its student body consisted of four medics returning from the Vietnam War. Eugene A. Stead, an MD and the program's creator, felt that the rapid training programs taken by these medics during the war could be adapted to train a cadre of quickly, but highly, trained medical assistants to help remedy the shortage of physicians. He used funding from the National Heart Institute to establish the first program at Duke in 1965.[38]

Although both professions require two years of additional coursework, their entry path and training are different. NP programs require that the applicant be an RN with some practice experience.[39] Students take two years of classwork and clinical training in a specialty area, like pediatrics. By contrast, most PA programs accept any bachelor's degree.[40] Like medical schools, however, they have substantial science course prerequisites and require the taking of a competitive examination.[41] Some programs also require prior experience in health care such as being a paramedic or medical assistant.[42] PAs then take a two-year course of classes and clinical work that is essentially a condensed version of medical school.[43] They do not specialize during this basic training. And because there is no medical residency, they can go directly to work after the two-year program, cutting six years off the training of an MD.

[35] *See* A. Keeling, *Historical Perspectives on an Expanded Role for Nursing*, 20 OJIN: ONLINE J. OF ISSUES IN NURSING 2 (2015) (recalling that Ford wanted NPs to work collaboratively with MDs initially to address common childhood health problems during well baby checks).

[36] *See Loretta Ford Documentary*, YOUTUBE (uploaded Nov. 5, 2019), https://www.youtube.com/watch?v=-Shw9wFswOI (last accessed Jan. 7, 2023).

[37] *See* Elizabeth Landau, *Nurse Practitioners Were "Lone Rangers," Founder Says*, CNN (Oct. 1, 2011), https://www.cnn.com/2011/09/30/health/living-well/loretta-ford-nurse-practitioner/index.html (last accessed Feb. 3, 2025).

[38] *See* Roderick S. Hooker & Reginald D. Carter, *From Concept to Reality* 19, 23–24, *in* PHYSICIAN ASSISTANTS AS SOCIAL INNOVATORS IN HEALTHCARE (2022).

[39] *See Nurse Practitioner Career Overview*, NURSEJOURNAL.ORG (updated Mar. 3, 2023), https://nursejournal.org/nurse-practitioner/ (last accessed Aug. 24, 2023) (stating that most programs require two years of RN experience).

[40] *See Become a PA*, AM. ASS'N OF PHYSICIANS' ASSISTANTS, https://www.aapa.org/career-central/become-a-pa/ (listing common classes) (last accessed Aug. 24, 2023).

[41] *Id.*

[42] *See* Bureau of Lab. Stat., U.S. Dep't of Labor, *Physician Assistants*, OCCUPATIONAL OUTLOOK HANDBOOK (last modified Aug. 29, 2024), https://www.bls.gov/ooh/healthcare/physician-assistants.htm (last accessed Apr. 12, 2023).

[43] *See* Hooker & Carter, *supra* note 38, at 23.

After graduation, PAs, like NPs, practice under the direction of a supervising physician. But unlike NPs, the supervising physician determines the PA's legal scope of practice.[44] If their supervising physician permits, they too can order tests, diagnose illnesses, and select treatments. In most cases, their practice is essentially identical to that of NPs, and, in clinical practice, PAs commonly work side-by-side with NPs doing identical work.[45]

Both fields are growing more rapidly than physicians. According to the Bureau of Labor Statistics, the growth rate between 2021 and 2031 is expected to be 3% for physicians,[46] 28% for PAs,[47] and 40% for NPs.[48] Both NPs and PAs are regularly ranked at or near the top of the *U.S. News and World Report* rankings of the best jobs in health care and the best jobs overall.[49] In 2021, NPs averaged $120,680 annually,[50] and PAs averaged $121,530.[51]

In the early years, neither NPs nor PAs faced opposition from organized medicine. Several factors may explain this acquiescence. First, as noted above, health care had a long tradition of utilizing trained and licensed mid-level providers to assist physicians. Second, physicians benefitted from the arrival of the new mid-level professionals (unlike the professionalization of optometry). They got better-trained assistants to whom they could delegate more complex tasks while still billing all the services in their own name. The new staff also freed them to undertake more lucrative procedures with their own time. Third, the new professionals were clearly subordinate to the physicians who supervised and directed their work. Physician primacy was not challenged. No patients were lost. Fourth, the health care marketplace had too few physicians, especially in primary care. Help was needed. Fifth, the

44 *See id.* at 36.

45 *See* Erin Sarzynski & Henry Barry, *Current Evidence and Controversies: Advanced Practice Providers in Healthcare*, 25 Am. J. Managed Care 366, 366 (2019) ("Despite differences in training and licensure, APPs have considerable overlap in their scope of practice."; there were "few differences in their roles and perception of care by administrators."); Karen Donelan et al., *Perspectives of Physicians and Nurse Practitioners on Primary Care Practice*, 368 N. Engl. J. Med. 1898, 1903 (2013) ("Both physicians and NPs agree that they perform largely the same services.").

46 *See* Bureau of Lab. Stat., U.S. Dep't of Labor, *Physicians and Surgeons*, Occupational Outlook Handbook (last modified Aug. 29, 2024), https://www.bls.gov/ooh/healthcare/physicians-and-surgeons.htm (last accessed Aug. 23, 2023).

47 Bureau of Lab. Stat., U.S. Dep't of Labor, *supra* note 42.

48 Bureau of Lab. Stat., U.S. Dep't of Labor, *Nurse Anesthetists, Nurse Midwives, and Nurse Practitioners*, Occupational Outlook Handbook (last modified Aug. 29, 2024), https://www.bls.gov/ooh/healthcare/nurse-anesthetists-nurse-midwives-and-nurse-practitioners.htm (last accessed Apr. 12, 2023).

49 *See, for example*, *Nurse Practitioner Role Named "Best Job That Helps People,"* Am. Ass'n of Nurse Prac. (Mar. 13, 2023), https://www.aanp.org/news-feed/nurse-practitioner-role-named-best-job-that-helps-people (last accessed Feb. 3, 2025); *Physician Assistant*, USNews, https://money.usnews.com/careers/best-jobs/physician-assistant (last accessed Aug. 23, 2023) ("#2 in Best Health Care Jobs; #4 in 100 Best Jobs.").

50 Bureau of Lab. Stat., U.S. Dep't of Labor, *supra* note 48.

51 Bureau of Lab. Stat., U.S. Dep't of Labor, *supra* note 48.

field had an ample pool of insurance funds from which to pay the new mid-level providers.

10.1.3 *The Political Winds Changed When NPs and PAs Sought Independence from Physician Direction*

The honeymoon with physicians did not last. Today, NPs and PAs want full independence from physician oversight.[52] Faced with the prospect of NP and PA independence and the accompanying threat to physician income, organized medicine is fiercely fighting these state legislative proposals.

Of course, the objections expressed publicly by physicians do not focus on the protection of their turf. Instead, three other arguments are commonly voiced. The first is that quality will be impaired if NPs and PAs are given too much independence. Physicians don't believe that mid-level providers deliver the same quality of care that physicians do, especially in complex cases.[53] Second, physicians insist that mid-level providers are no more likely than physicians to serve low-income and underserved patients.[54] These two contentions will be familiar to reformers who are trying to authorize mid-level legal practitioners. Third, physicians contend that NPs will overuse medical procedures like imaging and lab tests to protect against mistakes caused by their weaker education and training, driving up health care costs.[55]

The issue of quality is the most important of these objections. Here, NPs have benefited from a large and growing body of favorable outcomes data refuting physicians' claims. The strong evidence that NPs and PAs provide high-quality care has enabled NPs to enlist the help of important allies like the American Enterprise

[52] *Utah's New Law Will Improve Patients' Health Care Access*, AM. ASS'N OF NURSE PRAC. (Mar. 16, 2023), https://www.prnewswire.com/news-releases/utahs-new-law-will-improve-patients-health-care-access-301774618.html#:~:text=Spencer%20Cox%20and%20the%20Utah, from%20nurse%20practitioners%20(NPs).&text=Utah%20is%20now%20the%2027th,to%20 adopt%20Full%20Practice%20Authority (last accessed Aug. 23, 2023).

[53] *See, for example*, Donelan et al., *supra* note 45, at 1902. In a survey, two-thirds of physicians believed that doctors provide higher-quality examinations and consultations. *Id.* Only 18 percent of physicians felt NPs should lead medical homes, compared to 82 percent of NPs. Only 4 percent of physicians felt NPs should be paid equally for providing the same service, while 64 percent of NPs disagreed. *Id.*

[54] *See Scope of Practice: Key Tools & Resources*, AM. MED. ASS'N (Jan. 7, 2025), https://www.ama-assn.org/practice-management/scope-practice/scope-practice-key-tools-resources (last accessed Feb. 3, 2025) (stating that "[t]he AMA created over 4,500 geomaps to demonstrate that expanding scope does not equal expanding access to care").

[55] *See, for example*, *AMA Issue Brief: Expanding Nurse Practitioner Scope of Practice Leads to Increased Utilization of Health Care Resources*, AM. MED. ASS'N (2022), https://amascopeofpractice.org/wp-content/uploads/2023/01/Issue-Brief-2023-NP-Increased-Utilization-of-Health-Care-Resources-FINAL.pdf; *AAFP Warns of Dangers in Bill to Expand NPPs' Practice Scope*, AM. ASS'N OF FAMILY PHYSICIANS, https://www.aafp.org/news/government-medicine/npp-scope-letter.html (last accessed Jan. 30, 2024).

Institute,[56] the Brookings Institute,[57] the Institute of Medicine,[58] the Robert Wood Johnson Foundation,[59] the American Association of Retired Persons (AARP),[60] the Federal Trade Commission (FTC),[61] and the National Governors Association.[62] NPs have even enlisted some of the physician lobby's usual allies, like health insurers, hospital associations, and chambers of commerce. Their supporters see the removal of NP scope-of-practice restrictions as a way to bring down costs and make access to health care more equitable.[63] To this end, the Robert Wood Johnson Foundation allied with the AARP to launch *The Future of Nursing: Campaign for Action*, a nationwide initiative for state law reform.[64]

State by state, the fundraising and the recruitment of consumer groups by the National Association of Nurse Practitioners has been very sophisticated.[65] The NP coalition in New Jersey, for example, included AARP New Jersey, the Chamber of Commerce, the Horizon Foundation of New Jersey (Blue Cross Blue Shield's corporate foundation in New Jersey), and the New Jersey Hospital Association.[66] In Texas, NPs enlisted individual nursing organizations, hospitals, health care systems, businesses, and educational institutions, along with the Texas Association of Business and the Texas Hospital Association.[67]

This combination of favorable outcomes, important allies, and polished campaigning convinced lawmakers in twenty-seven states to enact Full Practice Authority legislation for NPs.[68] These laws empower NPs to diagnose conditions

[56] Peter Buerhaus, Nurse Practitioners: A Solution to America's Primary Care Crisis (2018).

[57] E. Kathleen Adams & Sara Markowitz, Improving Efficiency in the Health-Care System: Removing Anticompetitive Barriers for Advanced Practice Registered Nurses and Physician Assistants (2010).

[58] Inst. Medicine, The Future of Nursing (2010) [hereinafter, Future of Nursing 2010].

[59] *Future of Nursing: Campaign for Action*, Robert Wood Johnson Found., https://beta.rwjf.org/en/grants/grantee-stories/programs/future-of-nursing–campaign-for-action.html (last accessed Aug. 23, 2023).

[60] *Campaign for Action*, AARP, https://campaignforaction.org/ (last accessed Aug. 25, 2023).

[61] *See* Daniel J. Gilman & Tara Isa Koslov, *Policy Perspectives: Competition and the Regulation of Advanced Practice Nurses*, FTC (Mar. 2014), https://www.ftc.gov/system/files/documents/reports/policy-perspectives-competition-regulation-advanced-practice-nurses/140307aprnpolicypaper.pdf (last accessed Feb. 24, 2025).

[62] Nat'l Governors Ass'n, The Role of Nurse Practitioners in Meeting Increasing Demand for Primary Care (2012).

[63] *See* Inst. of Medicine, The Future of Nursing 2020–2030: Charting a Path to Achieve Health Equity 7, 86 (2021) [hereinafter, Future of Nursing 2020–2030].

[64] *See supra* notes 51 and 52.

[65] *See* Stephen Isaacs & Paul Jellinek, Accept No Substitute: A Report on Scope of Practice 21–22 (2012).

[66] *Id.* at 23.

[67] *Id.*

[68] *Utah's New Law*, *supra* note 52.

and to order and implement treatments *without the need for a collaborative relationship with a physician.*[69] PAs are now working to enact similar legislation.

But physician groups have raised their game considerably since the first NP full-practice laws were passed. In the past few years, they have reached out more vigorously to physicians, residents, and medical students in each state where NP or PA scope-of-practice bills have been introduced. The American Medical Association (AMA) has prepared members-only talking points and posted them on its web page.[70] State by state, the AMA is helping local medical societies fashion a strong response when scope-of-practice reform bills are introduced.[71] Going forward, both NPs and PAs will face stiffer opposition.[72]

10.1.4 *Reviewing the Story*

In the 1960s, NPs and PAs were accepted into medicine without organized resistance. In hindsight, this is surprising. Each profession was permitted, under supervision, to diagnose and treat patients. Physicians could easily have perceived the delegation of their core medical powers to be an unacceptable intrusion into the central work of physicians. But they did not. The explanations for this peaceful entry may provide useful clues for law reformers. So, too, will the very different reaction that physicians had when NPs later sought freedom from physician oversight.

When the first NP and PA programs were created, the appearance of new mid-level health care providers was a routine occurrence. No existential norms were threatened. More importantly, physicians benefited financially from the arrival of these highly trained assistants. At the same time, the new professionals did not challenge physician primacy. Crucially, the new mid-level professionals would not be taking patients away from physicians. With a chronic shortage of primary care providers, there were patients enough to go around. Lastly, the practice of medicine was blessed with an ample pool of insurance funds from which to pay the new mid-level providers without taking a slice of the pie from physicians.

Law reformers can duplicate some of these favorable conditions with careful crafting of boundaries, as discussed further in Section 10.3. But the absence of

[69] *See, for example*, N.H. Stat. 326-B:11 (2024); N.D. Admin. Code 54-05-03.1-03.2 (2023); *Issues at a Glance: Full Practice Authority*, Am. Ass'n of Nurse Prac. (revised Aug. 2024), https://www.aanp.org/advocacy/advocacy-resource/policy-briefs/issues-full-practice-brief (last accessed Jan. 28, 2024); Nat. Council of St. Bds of Nursing, Model Act (2021). NPs are supervised by the state board of nursing rather than the board of medicine. *Id.* The AANP now strongly disfavors the term "midlevel provider." Am. Assn. Nurse Prac., *Id.*

[70] *See Scope of Practice*, *supra* note 54.

[71] *Id.*

[72] The AMA says it has recently defeated both NPs and PAs in half a dozen states. *See Advocacy in Action: Fighting Scope Creep*, Am. Med. Ass'n (updated Aug. 14, 2023), https://www.ama-assn.org/practice-management/scope-practice/advocacy-action-fighting-scope-creep (last accessed Aug. 24, 2023).

insurance, the lack of a tradition of sharing the legal ecosystem, and the oversupply of JDs are three environmental differences that pose unique challenges for law reformers. They, too, are discussed in Section 10.3.

NPs lost the support of physicians when they sought independence from physician oversight. Freed from physician oversight, NPs could set up their own practices, compete for patients, potentially lower prices, and acquire a status akin to a physician, at the top of the medical hierarchy. As NPs sought this greater independence and prestige, physicians began to view NPs as a financial threat, rather than a financial windfall. This new perspective caused a shift in physicians' attitudes toward NPs – a shift that also offers lessons for law reform.

10.2 THE OUTCOMES RESEARCH: NPS AND PAS DELIVER HIGH-QUALITY CARE

As noted above, NPs offer a naturally attractive analogy for law reformers working to create a category of licensed, mid-level legal professionals. This section examines the impact that NPs have had on patient care, focusing especially on the quality of services rendered and the impact on access to care for both insured and uninsured patients.

In the six decades since Loretta Ford created the first NP program, dozens of studies have investigated the care provided by NPs and, to a lesser extent, PAs. Although the studies all have limitations, they consistently find that both professions deliver high-quality care. Recent research also suggests that NPs modestly increase access to care. The positive findings about quality of care in particular have helped NPs and PAs recruit a wide variety of important allies in their current quest for full independence.

10.2.1 *Quality of Care*

The quality of care provided by NPs has been studied much more than care provided by PAs. The studies of NP quality of care use data from a variety of practice settings and contexts, including primary care, nursing homes, Veterans hospitals, Medicare recipients, and emergency departments, and they employ many methodological and statistical approaches. Yet, the findings have been surprisingly consistent and positive: The number of studies finding that NP care is equal to or better than the care provided by physicians vastly outnumber the unfavorable ones. As a result, the major literature reviews have consistently concluded that, on balance, NPs provide care that is equal to or better than care provided by physicians, though reservations are sometimes expressed about the most complex cases.[73]

[73] *See, for example,* Melanie Swan et al., *Quality of Primary Care by Advanced Practice Nurses: A Systematic Review,* 27 INT. J. QUAL. H. CARE 396, 396, 400 (2015) (RCTs find equal or better

These findings have been relied upon in several important public policy reports encouraging the growth of the NP supply and the expansion of their scope of practice, including reports from the Office of Technology Assessment,[74] the Institute of Medicine,[75] and the province of British Columbia.[76]

The only regular reservation is the desire for more research on complex cases.[77] However, the research on tough cases is growing. For example, an important 2019 review of the studies on acute and critical care by Ruth Kleinpell and her colleagues found evidence of improved patient outcomes when supervised NPs and PAs deliver care. The positive metrics included:[78]

1. Fewer complications
2. Less time on ventilation
3. More use of clinical practice guidelines
4. Improved laboratory test use
5. Increased palliative care consultations
6. Reduced length of hospital stay
7. Reduced readmissions
8. Improved discharge time
9. Longer ICU survival rates
10. Better patient care management

outcomes for physiologic measures, such as blood pressure and glucose outcomes, cholesterol); Brigitte Fong Yeong Woo et al., *The Impact of the Advanced Practice Nursing Role on Quality of Care, Clinical Outcomes, Patient Satisfaction, and Cost in the Emergency and Critical Care Settings: A Systematic Review*, 15 HUM. RES. HEALTH 63, 63 (2017) (reporting that "the involvement of nurses in advanced practice in emergency and critical care improves the length of stay, time to consultation/treatment, mortality, patient satisfaction, and cost savings"); Ruth Kleinpell et al., *Nurse Practitioners and Physician Assistants in Acute and Critical Care: A Concise Review of the Literature and Data 2008–18*, 47 CRIT. CARE MED. 1441, 1446 (2019) (reviewing studies of acute and critical care and finding equal or better outcomes).

74 U.S. Congress, Off. Tech. Assessment, NURSE PRACTITIONERS, PHYSICIAN ASSISTANTS, AND CERTIFIED NURSE-MIDWIVES: A POLICY ANALYSIS 5 (1986) ("The weight of the evidence indicates that, within their areas of competence, NPs, PAs, and CNMs provide care whose quality is equivalent to that of care provided by physicians.").

75 *See* FUTURE OF NURSING 2020–2030, *supra* note 63.

76 *See* SABRINA T. WONG & VICKI FARRALLY, THE UTILIZATION OF NURSE PRACTITIONERS AND PHYSICIAN ASSISTANTS: A RESEARCH SYNTHESIS (2014). This comprehensive report was prepared on behalf of the Nursing Research Advisory Council to provide decisionmakers in British Columbia, Canada, with a comprehensive international review and synthesis of the research literature pertaining to nurse practitioners and physician assistants.

Examining fourteen systematic reviews between 1981 and 2011, it found consistent evidence that NPs and PAs "within their scope of practice," provide "equivalent quality of care compared to their physician counterparts and they are well-accepted by patients."

77 *See, for example*, Sarzynski & Barry, *supra* note 45, at 367 (calling for more research on acute care and complex patients).

78 *See* Kleinpell et al., *supra* note 73, at 1446.

The literature also has positive findings on many other metrics, including blood pressure, glucose outcomes, cholesterol,[79] C-sections,[80] mental-health-related mortality,[81] and mortality more generally.[82] A much smaller set of studies have yielded negative findings, often around drug prescribing.[83] In addition, patients often prefer the care provided by NPs, feeling that NPs offer a more holistic approach than physicians.[84] NPs score consistently higher on patient satisfaction.[85]

The least favorable review of NP care was published in 2019 by Erin Sarzynski and John Barry, both MDs. They concluded that the studies offer "mixed results."[86] On the one hand, NPs had positive findings on studies such as the retrospective study of twenty million community health center patients that found equal or better results for NPs on quality metrics like smoking cessation, depression treatment, statin therapy, physical exams, patient education, imaging, medication use, return visits, and referrals.[87] On the other hand, other studies found that MDs ordered fewer unnecessary antibiotics for acute infections[88] and made fewer specialist referrals for patients with diabetes.[89] In the end, the authors conceded that "[p]hysicians' arguments about quality are largely unfounded, at least for common health concerns."[90]

79 *See* Swan et al., *supra* note 73, at 400.

80 *See* Future of Nursing 2020–2030, *supra* note 63, at 81.

81 *See id.* at 150.

82 *See* Woo et al., *supra* note 73, at 63.

83 *See, for example*, Michael I. Ellenbogen & Jodi B. Segal, *Differences in Opioid Prescribing among Generalist Physicians, Nurse Practitioners, and Physician Assistants*, 21 Pain Med. 76 (2020) (relatively high rates of opioid prescribing among NPs and PAs, especially at the upper margins); Evan L. Dvorin et al., *High Frequency of Systemic Corticosteroid Use for Acute Respiratory Tract Illnesses in Ambulatory Settings*, 178 JAMA Internal Med. 852 (2018) (more inappropriate obsolete steroid use for acute respiratory tract infections).

84 *Id.*

85 *See, for example*, Elena Kraus & James M. DuBois, *Knowing Your Limits: A Qualitative Study of Physician and Nurse Practitioner Perspectives on NP Independence in Primary Care*, 32 J. Gen. Internal Med. 284 (2017).

86 *See* Sarzynski & Barry, *supra* note 45, at 367.

87 That study is E. T. Kurtzman & B. S. Barnow, *A Comparison of Nurse Practitioners, Physician Assistants, and Primary Care Physicians' Patterns of Practice and Quality of Care in Health Centers*, 55 Med. Care 615 (2017).

88 *See* Johanna E. Bellon et al., *Comparing Advanced Practice Providers and Physicians as Providers of E-Visits*, 21 Telemed. J. eHealth 1019 (2015).

89 *See* Yong-Fang Kuo et al., *Diabetes Mellitus Care Provided by Nurse Practitioners vs Primary Care Physicians*, 63 J. Am. Geriatric Soc'y 1980 (2015); Danny R. Hughes et al., *A Comparison of Diagnostic Imaging Ordering Patterns between Advanced Practice Clinicians and Primary Care Physicians Following Office-Based Evaluation and Management Visits*, 175 JAMA Internal Med. 101 (2015).

90 *See* Sarzynski & Barry, *supra* note 45, at 367. A more recent prepublication manuscript claims to have found that patients who saw NPs in VA emergency departments had more "preventable hospitalizations" within thirty days of their visit, but it used criteria from the Agency for Healthcare Research and Quality that may also be measuring the intervening care provided in the VA hospitals after admission and any outpatient care that the patients received in the thirty days after being seen in the VA ED. *See* David C. Chan Jr. & Yiqun Chen, *The*

Researchers have done much less research on PA outcomes. Most studies that include PAs have combined the outcomes of PAs and NPs and reached favorable results.[91] When analyzed separately, PA outcomes seem to be very similar to those of NPs.[92]

Two pairs of recent studies with large databases deserve individual mention. In the first set, Peter Buerhaus and his coauthors used a Medicare primary care database that they adjusted for patient severity and found that patients receiving primary care from NPs were less likely to have preventable hospital admissions, hospital readmissions within thirty days of being discharged, inappropriate emergency department visits, and low-value MRIs associated with low back pain.[93] Physicians, however, had more positive findings for the number of cancer screenings (such as mammography screenings for breast cancer and colonoscopies for colorectal cancer).[94] In a second study using the same data, the authors narrowed their inquiry to Medicare beneficiaries with a disability or a very low income and had virtually the same findings.[95]

The other set of studies looked at complex diabetes patients in the Veterans Affairs (VA) system and found that NP and PA team leaders achieved control equivalent to that of physicians for blood glucose, blood pressure, and cholesterol.[96] The second study examining the same data set determined that patients of the NPs and PA team leaders were less likely to be hospitalized or to have an emergency room (ER) visit due to an ambulatory care-sensitive condition, even after adjusting for differences in

Productivity of Professions: Evidence from the Emergency Department, NAT'L BUR. OF ECON. RSCH. 9, 15 (June 2023), https://www.nber.org/system/files/working_papers/w30608/w30608.pdf (last accessed Feb. 24, 2025); *Prevention Quality Indicator Methods*, AGENCY FOR HEALTHCARE RSCH. & QUALITY INDICATORS, https://qualityindicators.ahrq.gov/measures/pqi_resources (last accessed May 2, 2023).

91 *See* Wong & Farrally, *supra* note 76 at 30, 34 (very favorable overall).

92 *See, for example*, Sarzynski & Barry, *supra* note 45, at 367 ("Quality of care is similar among NPs, PAs, and physicians for routine patient presentations, but evidence is less robust for complex patients."); George L. Jackson et al., *Intermediate Diabetes Outcomes in Patients Managed by Physicians, Nurse Practitioners, or Physician Assistants: A Cohort Study*, 169 ANN. INTERN. MED. 825, 825 (2018) (no difference); George Goldberg et al., *Physician's Extenders; Performance in Air Force Clinics*, 19 MED. CARE 951, 951(1981) ("Physician's assistants performed at least as well as physicians on 25 out of 28 nonredundant process–of–care criteria; ... In a comparison of physician's assistants with nurse practitioners, the two groups' performance was not significantly different.").

93 *See* BUERHAUS, *supra* note 56, at 484, 487.

94 *Id.* The authors concluded that each profession had "different strengths." *Id.* at 484.

95 *See* Catherine M. DesRoches et al., *The Quality of Primary Care Provided by Nurse Practitioners to Vulnerable Medicare Beneficiaries*, 65 NURSING OUTLOOK 679, 686–87 (2017) (finding that NP patients had a lower risk of preventable hospitalizations and emergency department use, less low-value imaging for low back pain and, unlike the larger study, equal chronic disease management but were less likely to have eye screenings or cancer screenings).

96 *See* Jackson et al., *supra* note 92, at 825.

patients' medical and social complexity.[97] In a third study, the authors extended their inquiry to less complex diabetes patients, finding that, here too, patients of NPs and PAs had fewer inpatient admissions and less emergency department use than patients of physicians.

The VA studies are especially useful because they minimize two of the most significant potential biases in this research. First, physician consultation is minimal in the VA system.[98] Second, "incident to" billing is not applicable to VA patients. And because the authors investigated both routine and very complex patient care, the authors concluded that their studies provide "further evidence that NPs and PAs may be appropriately used as primary care providers, as opposed to being limited to supplement the care of physicians within primary care settings."[99]

Recent studies have also found favorable NP outcomes in states where collaboration is no longer required. A study by Jennifer Perloff and her colleagues in 2017 found that NP independence had no effect on patient outcomes, including ambulatory care-sensitive hospital admissions.[100] Another study by Jeffrey Traczynski and Victoria Udalova found that "allowing NPs to practice and prescribe drugs without physician oversight increases medical care for underserved populations and reduces ER use for conditions responsive to primary care."[101] In a study using VA data, Chuan Fen Liu and associates found "comparable or better outcomes achieved at similar costs for patients [with chronic diseases, including diabetes, IHD, and hypertension] across differing levels of comorbidity, suggesting NPs as PCPs need not be limited to less complex patients."[102] The only contrary findings deal with prescription practices,[103] especially the overprescribing of controlled substances.[104] More definitive studies on that issue are needed.

Concerns about quality of care have also led some critics to suggest that the use of mid-level providers will generate excessive medical malpractice claims.[105] But the

[97] *See* Perri A. Morgan et al., *Impact of Physicians, Nurse Practitioners, and Physician Assistants on Utilization and Costs for Complex Patients*, 38 HEALTH AFFS. 1028, 1031–32 (2019).

[98] *See Id.* at 1031.

[99] *Id.* at 1035.

[100] *See* Jennifer Perloff et al., *Association of State-Level Restrictions in Nurse Practitioner Scope of Practice with the Quality of Primary Care Provided to Medicare Beneficiaries*, 76 MED. CARE RES. REV. 597 (2019) (no effect); *see also* Morris M. Kleiner et al., *Relaxing Occupational Licensing Requirements: Analyzing Wages and Prices for a Medical Service*, 59 J. L. & ECON. 261, 283–84 (2016) (no effect on mortality).

[101] *See* Jeffrey Traczynski & Victoria Udalova, *Nurse Practitioner Independence, Health Care Utilization, and Health Outcomes*, 58 J. HEALTH ECON. 90, 104 (2018).

[102] Chuan Fen Liu et al., *Outcomes of Primary Care Delivery by Nurse Practitioners: Utilization, Cost, and Quality of Care*, 55 HEALTH SERV. RES. 178, 187 (2020).

[103] *See* KIHWAN BAE ET AL., MARYLAND'S HEALTH CARE LESSON FOR PENNSYLVANIA: HOW FULL PRACTICE AUTHORITY CAN INCREASE ACCESS AND IMPROVE OUTCOME 15 (2022) (reviewing the research).

[104] *See id.* at 16–17 (collecting the studies).

[105] Bavneet Walia et al., *Increased Reliance on Physician Assistants: An Access-Quality Trade-Off?*, 10 J. MARK. ACCESS & HEALTH POL'Y 2030559 (2022).

data show the opposite – NPs and PAs are far less likely to have a paid malpractice claim than physicians.[106]

Critics sometimes note that many studies, until quite recently, had any of three potential limitations.[107] None of the potential shortcomings, however, warrant a different conclusion about NP or PA quality of care. The first limitation is that most of the studies used data that lacked information about the extent of physician consultation with the NPs.[108] Thus, they did not provide information about the outcomes that would occur if NPs were acting independently. However, these studies firmly established that NPs provide equivalent quality of care when in a collaborative relationship with a physician. That finding alone was a major reaffirmation of the NP model. In addition, more recent studies have looked at the care provided by NPs and PAs when they are not working under physician supervision and their findings are equally favorable, as noted above in the discussion of the VA studies and studies from states where NPs can practice independently.

Second, some researchers worry about the potentially distorting effects of a current Medicare billing practice that permits the attribution of care provided primarily by NPs and PAs to MDs. In particular, "incident to" billing allows physicians who have participated in the care of a patient to submit claims in their own name even though a mid-level practitioner provided most of the services. Because services billed in the name of an NP or PA receive only 85 percent of the physician's fee from Medicare, Medicaid, and private insurers, hospitals and

[106] Using data from the National Practitioner's Data Bank, two studies looking at the years from 1991 to 2007 and from 2005 to 2014 found that the average physician is many times more likely than an NP or PA to make a medical malpractice payment. *See* Douglas Brock et al., *Physician Assistant and Nurse Practitioner Malpractice Trends*, 74 MED. CARE RES. & REV. 613 (2016); Roderick S. Hooker et al., *Does the Employment of Physician Assistants and Nurse Practitioners Increase Liability?* 95 J. MED. LICENSURE & DISCIPLINE 6 (2009). Despite these statistics, a 2022 article concluded that PAs are more prone to diagnostic error than physicians are. *See* Walia et al., *supra* note 105. That conclusion is incorrect. Because PAs much less often perform surgery, their paid claims for diagnostic error form a larger fraction of their total paid claims than for physicians. On this basis, the authors concluded that "the healthcare system currently invites upon itself some level of unnecessary medical diagnostic error" by relying on providers with less training, many of whom may not have been admitted to medical school. But they misinterpret the data. Physicians have so many more paid claims per capita, that the average NP or PA's odds of a paid claim for diagnostic error are still much lower than those of the average physician.

[107] In addition to the concerns raised in the text, critics have worried about lack of generalizability from one medical setting to another. That concern should disappear as the number of studies across multiple settings grows. Another weakness is the rarity of randomized controlled studies, but the consistency of the findings using a variety of other credible research designs reduces the significance of this weakness. *See also* ISAACS & JELLINEK, *supra* note 65 (concluding that physicians will not emphasize the studies on quality).

[108] *See, for example*, Kleinpell et al., *supra* note 73, at 1446 (noting that the studies "omitted information on degree of physician oversight and consultation"); ELLEN MCCLEERY ET AL., EVIDENCE BRIEF: THE QUALITY OF CARE PROVIDED BY ADVANCED PRACTICE NURSES 3–6 (2014).

practice groups have a financial incentive to bill in the physician's name.[109] And because the extent of this practice is unknown, researchers who use insurance claims databases will inevitably assign some patient care to MDs that was primarily provided by NPs or PAs. Fortunately, the policy will be tightened in 2024. Furthermore, the VA studies described above did not have this risk and still found that NPs and PAs provided equivalent quality of care.

Third, several studies have found that NPs see patients who, on average, are less complex and less acute than the patients seen by physicians.[110] As a result, some of the reviews expressing confidence in the care provided by NPs have also expressed caution about the body of research looking at NP care of complex or critical illnesses.[111] But the recent series of VA studies and the two Buerhaus Medicare studies provide preliminary reassurance on this issue; both accounted for patient severity and had positive findings.[112]

Overall, the existing research justifies the conclusion that NPs and PAs, in their areas of specialization, provide care that is the same or better than care provided by physicians. While individual studies often have weaknesses, they collectively present a strong case for NP and PA quality of care.

The positive patient outcomes generated by NPs and PAs strongly support the claim by law reformers that mid-level professionals can provide high-quality services in their area of specialization if given suitable education and experience.

10.2.2 *Impact on Affordability and Access*

A primary goal of mid-level legal licensure is to make legal representation for simple matters more affordable. As it stands now, many Americans cannot afford to hire a lawyer. Legal access reform seeks to create categories of mid-level legal providers who are trained more economically than lawyers and, as a result, can charge lower fees and work for lower salaries. But, some wonder, will it work? Will opening up a new breed of practitioner really promote access and reduce costs?

[109] *See, for example*, Peter Buerhaus et al., *Quality of Primary Care Provided to Medicare Beneficiaries by Nurse Practitioners and Physicians*, 56 Med. Care, 484, 488 (2018); Phyllis Maguire, *Split Visit Billing Rules for Physicians and NPs/PAs*, Today's Hospitalist (Jan. 2022).

[110] *See, for example*, Perri A. Morgan et al., *Factors Associated with Having a Physician, Nurse Practitioner, or Physician Assistant as Primary Care Provider for Veterans with Diabetes Mellitus*, 54 Inquiry 46958017712762 (2017) (noting that "patients with physician PCPs are modestly more medically complex than those with NP or PA PCPs"); McCleery, *supra* note 108, at 4–5.

[111] *See, for example*, Sarzynski & Barry, *supra* note 45, at 367 (noting that questions remain about complex patients); Future of Nursing 2020–2030, *supra* note 63 (finding outcome of equivalent limited to services "within scope").

[112] A related question that has not yet been studied is whether NPs and PA are appropriately referring patients whose complexity tests the limits of their training. Some state practice acts require this. *See infra* text at notes 148–149.

Here again, the story in medicine, and particularly the experience of NPs and PAs, is instructive. NPs and PAs earn roughly half the wages of primary care physicians. In May 2021, according to the Bureau of Labor Statistics, the median income for NPs was $123,780 annually,[113] and the median income for PAs was $121,530.[114] The median for family medicine physicians was $235,930[115] and for internal medicine doctors $242,190.[116] Thus, NPs generate substantially lower salaries per full-time-equivalent.

However, the savings in labor cost *per patient* are reduced because NPs and PAs have historically generated less revenue than physicians. In mixed provider groups, NPs commonly see fewer patients,[117] see patients with less complex ailments,[118] work fewer hours,[119] have longer visits,[120] and generate costs for physician oversight.[121] These factors make it difficult to calculate the precise degree to which hiring NPs saves an employer money. The calculation is further complicated by the possibility that the longer visits associated with NPs save health care costs later by generating fewer hospitalizations and less unnecessary imaging down the road.[122]

Regardless, private practice physicians regularly employ NPs and PAs (rather than more physicians) to help keep their practices profitable.[123] According to a 2009 survey for the National Center for Health Statistics, half of all office-based physicians employed advanced practice nurses or PAs.[124] A report for the Physicians Foundation explains that physicians had been "[f]aced with declining reimbursement rates and the need to increase patient volume in order to keep their practices afloat."[125] Hiring NPs and PAs allows physician practices to increase their volume at lower cost.[126] Hiring

[113] *See* Bureau of Lab. Stat., U.S. Dep't of Labor, *supra* note 48.

[114] *See* Bureau of Lab. Stat., U.S. Dep't of Labor, *supra* note 42.

[115] *See* Bureau of Lab. Stat., U.S. Dep't of Labor, *supra* note 46.

[116] *Id.*

[117] *See, for example*, Sarzynski & Barry, *supra* note 45, at 368 (reporting that MDs see 30 percent more patients than NPs and are often paid to supervise NPs); Buerhaus et al., *supra* note 109, at 14 (reporting that NPs see fewer patients per week); Liu et al., *supra* note 102, at 186 ("An NP's panel size at VA is expected to be 75 percent of an MDs in order to give NPs sufficient time to manage their patients.").

[118] *See supra* note 110.

[119] *See, for example*, Buerhaus et al., *supra* note 109, at 14 ("On average, PCNPs work fewer hours per week than PCMDs (37 hours versus 46 hours)."); Donelan et al., *supra* note 45, at 1898 (reporting that, in survey of MDs and NPs, physicians reported working longer hours).

[120] *See* Swan et al., *supra* note 73, at 396.

[121] *See* Sarzynski & Barry, *supra* note 45, at 368 (noting that MDs are often paid to supervise NPs).

[122] *See* Liu et al., *supra* note 102, at 186 ("Reduced panel size may translate to greater access and time spent with individual patients, which in turn may translate into fewer hospitalizations."); Morgan et al., *supra* note 110, at 1031 (reduced size could help explain favorable findings).

[123] *See* Isaac & Jellinek, *supra* note 65, at 10–11.

[124] *Id.* (49.1 percent).

[125] *Id.*

[126] *Id.*

NPs and PAs also allows hospital-contracted groups, like hospitalists and ER groups, to offer the hospital lower terms.[127]

To the extent that these interpretations of recent events are correct, then NPs and PAs have helped hospitals and physician groups remain viable despite the price concessions demanded by insurance companies. Those concessions may, in turn, have tempered the rise in prices paid for health care services and the premiums paid for health insurance. If so, a marginal improvement in access to health insurance and, thus, health care may have resulted.

At present, the only concrete evidence of cost reduction is found in a 2016 study that found that prices for child well-care visits were lower by 3 to 16 percent in states with independent NPs,[128] and another 2016 study finding that clinics with more nonphysicians had "lower prices for office visits."[129] The impact of NPs on prices is likely to grow as NPs begin setting up independent practices. This tempering of medical price increases improves access to medical care for uninsured middle-class patients, but it helps account for the strong political opposition of the AMA to NP independence.

NPs also increase access by providing crucial staffing for community health centers (CHCs). Community health centers' reliance on NPs and PAs has increased in recent years,[130] as these clinics have had difficulty recruiting and retaining physicians.[131] Today, over half of the primary care positions in CHCs are filled by NPs and PAs.[132] As a result, the rise of NPs and PAs has helped the clinics continue providing care to their uninsured and underinsured patients.

Urgent care clinics and retail clinics also rely heavily on mid-level health care providers. Urgent care clinics offer self-paying patients a lower-cost alternative to an ER visit.[133] Average ER visits are four to ten times more expensive than urgent care clinics depending on the patient's condition.[134] Retail clinics also reduce ER visits and

[127] *See* Maguire, *supra* note 109.

[128] *See* Kleiner et al., *supra note* 100, 261.

[129] Michael R. Richards & Daniel Polsky, *Influence of Provider Mix and Regulation on Primary Care Services Supplied to US Patients*, 11 Health Econ. Pol'y L. 193, 193 (2016).

[130] *See* Kurtzman & Barnow, *supra* note 87, at 1.

[131] *See id.* at 6 (citing R. A. Rosenblatt et al., *Shortages of Medical Personnel in Community Health Centers: Implications for Planned Expansion*, 295 JAMA 1042 (2006)).

[132] *See* Karen Eseta Mulitalo et al., *How PAs Have Brought Innovation to Primary Care, in* Physicians Assistants as Social Innovators in Healthcare 65, 72–73 (2022); Kurtzman & Barnow, *supra* note 87, at 1–2.

[133] *See* Lindsay Allen et al., *The Impact of Urgent Care Centers on Nonemergent Emergency Department Visits*, 56 Health Serv. Rsch. 721, 722 (2021).

> We found that having an open urgent care center in a ZIP code reduced the total number of ED visits by residents in that ZIP code by 17.2% ($P < 0.05$), due largely to decreases in visits for less emergent conditions. … We found that urgent care centers reduced the total number of uninsured and Medicaid visits to the ED by 21% ($P < 0.05$) and 29.1% ($P < 0.05$), respectively."

[134] *See id.* (reporting that clinic care is on average ten times less expensive); *id.* at 727 (reporting that nonemergent visits are about four times less expensive, a cost of $156 as against $570).

are primarily staffed by NPs.[135] By staffing these two kinds of storefront clinics at lower salaries than those of physicians, mid-level medical providers may be keeping retail prices for routine medical care lower than they otherwise would be. To that extent, they are improving access to care for people who are uninsured or have extremely high deductibles. Unfortunately, the magnitude of that impact remains unmeasured.

In the field of law, mid-level legal practitioners have the same potential to generate lower prices for basic services, making those services more accessible to middle-class clients. As with NPs, this beneficial pricing effect can occur regardless of whether the nonlawyer advocates work within a law firm, set up their own practices, or work for a nonprofit.

NPs and PAs have also had a positive impact on the availability of medical care in rural areas. Many studies have found that NPs and PAs are more likely than all physicians except family medicine physicians to practice in rural areas and Health Professional Shortage Areas (HPSAs).[136] Of course, the AMA vigorously denies that NPs are more likely than physicians to work in underserved areas. To prove its case, the AMA has created a geomapping computer program to demonstrate that NPs cluster in "the same geographic locations as physicians."[137] But the public cannot access this tool.

Finally, NPs are more likely to treat Medicaid beneficiaries.[138] They even improve the willingness of physicians to accept new Medicaid patients.[139]

To summarize, NPs and PAs have had a positive impact on access to care for uninsured patients. They do this most dramatically by providing essential staffing for free clinics. They also staff the relatively low-cost urgent care and retail clinics visited by many uninsured and underinsured patients. Furthermore, there are signs that the availability of NPs and PAs is tempering price increases for primary care in general. NPs and PAs have also had a positive impact on the availability of medical care in

[135] *Id.* at 722. Retail clinics lack some of the services of urgent care clinics, like repair of lacerations, but their out-of-pocket costs tend to be lower. *Id.* at 722–23.

[136] *See, for example, The Distribution of the U.S. Primary Care Workforce*, AGENCY FOR HEALTHCARE RSCH. & QUALITY, https://www.ahrq.gov/research/findings/factsheets/primary/pcwork3/index.html (last accessed Mar. 26, 2024) (table 2); Keith B. Naylor et al., *Geographic Variation in Spatial Accessibility of U.S. Healthcare Providers*, 14 PLOS ONE 1 (2019) (NPs and family practice physicians more rural than other physicians as assessed by driving distance). PA distribution is also more rural than physicians. *See* Mulitalo et al., *supra* note 132, at 71–72 (collecting studies).

[137] *Health Workforce Mapper*, AM. MED. ASS'N, https://www.ama-assn.org/about/research/health-workforce-mapper (last accessed Jan. 31, 2024).

[138] *See, for example*, Peter Buerhaus et al., *Practice Characteristics of Primary Care Nurse Practitioners and Physicians*, 63 NURSING OUTLOOK 144, 144 (2015); Jennifer Perloff et al., *Comparing the Cost of Care Provided to Medicare Beneficiaries Assigned to Primary Care Nurse Practitioners and Physicians*, 51 HEALTH SERV. RSCH. 1407, 1414 (2016) (beneficiaries assigned to NPs were more likely to be on Medicaid).

[139] *See* Richards & Polsky, *supra* note 129, at 193 ("We find clinics with more non-physician clinicians are associated with better access for Medicaid patients and lower prices for office visits.").

rural areas. Licensed nonlawyer legal practitioners could have a similar tempering effect on prices for basic legal services. They could also provide a pool of lower-priced practitioners to staff new, innovative clinics in areas like eviction and debt collection where clients lack the funds to hire attorneys.

10.3 TYING THE PIECES TOGETHER: LESSONS FOR LAW

For law reformers looking at the experience in medicine, two positive findings stand out. First, high-quality services can, indeed, be delivered by mid-level practitioners who are trained at a lower cost than that required to train the top tier of the profession. Second, professions can exist with many kinds of limited license professions. Medicine has dozens of them. And their proliferation has not shaken the foundation of the profession. Medicine uses limited license specialists to deliver high-quality health care in a more efficient manner.

However, the field of law differs from that of medicine in at least three important ways that impose barriers to the licensing of mid-level legal practitioners. One crucial difference is the absence of a legal equivalent to health insurance. A second is the long-standing shortage of physicians. A third is the long custom of using mid-level licensed providers in medicine. As a result, physicians did not view the creation of new categories of mid-level health care providers as a zero-sum game, at least when the new tiers were under the direction of physicians. The health care marketplace provided enough patients with insurance to support both physicians and nonphysicians. As a result, physicians did not collectively oppose the creation of the NP and PA professions, nor did they oppose emergence of the professions of EMT and paramedic or the numerous categories of mental health counselors. They made no organized efforts to temper the very rapid growth in the number of NP and PA programs. Only when these mid-level providers began to ask for powers that would make them nearly equivalent to physicians did opposition intensify.

These important differences between the legal and medical markets mean that law reformers face more practical and political barriers than Loretta Ford did. This section looks first at the objections raised to limited license legal professionals and how those objections have been addressed in medicine. It then looks for strategic lessons in the successful efforts by NPs and, to a lesser extent PAs, to enact state-enabling laws.

10.3.1 *Practical and Political Barriers*

The primary objections are summarized in the committee reports of three states that rejected or tabled proposals for limited license legal professionals – Montana,[140]

[140] Minutes, *Mont. Supreme Court Access to Justice Comm'n* (Dec. 8, 2017) https://courts.mt.gov/external/supreme/boards/a2j/minutes/12-8-17min.pdf (last accessed Feb. 24, 2025) (reporting that

Illinois,[141] and Virginia.[142] My review of these reports shows that critics of nonlawyer licensure offer a few recurrent refrains:

1. Legal representation by nonlawyers will be sloppy. A two-tier system of justice will result.
2. For-profit nonlawyer advocates will not serve underserved or low-income people.
3. Limited license legal practitioners will not be able to earn a living, even if they serve primarily middle-class clients.
4. We already have an oversupply of lawyers. Mid-level licensees will threaten their livelihoods.

In this final section, I examine these concerns, against the factual template that medicine supplies.

The first and most important concern raised by opponents of limited license legal professions is the fear that nonlawyers will provide inferior representation.[143] According to this view, even matters that appear simple can be complex. While the evidence about mid-level medical professionals is reassuring, we know much less about the effectiveness of nonlawyers.[144] More research is badly needed.

The research proving that NPs and PAs had outcomes comparable to physicians literally opened doors across the country. It led directly to influential national reports from the Office of Technology Assessment in 1986 and the Institute of Medicine twice in the twentieth century. It even prompted the FTC to question the legality of limitations on medical practice. And it generated an unexpected array of allies across the health care sector.

If law reformers can produce similar proof of the quality of representation provided by nonlawyer advocates, the odds of legislative success will grow dramatically. But doing so will be difficult. Obtaining high-quality outcomes data in the

"the LLLT committee decided to recommend that Montana not pursue the LLLT model") [hereinafter Montana Minutes].

141 2016 Report and Recommendations of the Illinois State Bar Association's Task Force on the Future of Legal Services (Oct. 4, 2016) [hereinafter, Illinois Report].

142 The Study Committee on the Future of Law Practice, *Report: The Study Committee on the Future of Law Practice* (Sept. 14, 2016), https://iaals.du.edu/sites/default/files/documents/publications/va_report_of_the_study_committee.pdf (last accessed Feb. 24, 2025) (appearing to take a "wait and see" approach) [hereinafter, Virginia Report].

143 *See, for example*, Illinois Report, *supra* note 141, at 19 (explaining that the goal is to protect clients from mistakes of the ignorant and schemes of the unscrupulous).

144 *See, for example*, Anna E. Carpenter et al., *Trial and Error: Lawyers and Nonlawyer Advocates*, 42 L. & Soc. Inquiry 1023, 1024 (2017) ("Scholars know very little about the effectiveness of nonlawyers."); Elizabeth Chambliss, *Law School Training for Licensed Legal Technicians – Implications for the Consumer Market*, 65 S.C. L. Rev. 579, 601 (2014) (explaining that "we know very little about the relative quality of different types of legal services providers").

context of small, state-specific nonlawyer programs is challenging.[145] One obstacle is the absence of large data sets like the medical records kept by Medicare and the Veterans Administration. Another is the lack of standardization across state reform proposals.[146] Innovative ideas will be needed, such as a multistate collaboration using a shared reform model.[147] Or collaboration with a large state or federal agency like the Veterans Administration using, for example, specially trained nonlawyers to assist veterans with their claims for benefits. (My law school currently uses supervised student interns to do this work.)

While we wait, the preliminary clues are reassuring. Nonlawyers do nearly as well as lawyers on simple matters.[148] Specialized training is crucially important – more even than generalized experience.[149] These findings point toward narrowly focused training on routine matters accompanied by clear boundaries on the scope of practice that mirror the training.

Limited licensure advocates can also draft their proposals in ways designed to maximize the odds of good outcomes. At the front end, simplification of judicial forms and procedures would be a wonderful start. And at the tail end, nonlawyers could be required to have in place a preexisting relationship with a practicing lawyer for swift consultations when matters become unexpectedly complex. In medicine, NPs routinely turn to MDs in the most complex cases and internists who are stumped call-in other specialists like cardiologists or urologists. In fact, the NP licensing laws in some states expressly require as much. North Dakota, for example, requires that an NP "recognize individual limits of knowledge, skills, and abilities and plan for situations beyond the licensee's expertise."[150] And New Hampshire's statute governing advanced practice registered nurses (APRNs), including NPs, states:

Each APRN shall be accountable to clients and the board:

(b) For *recognizing limits* of knowledge and experience and planning for the management of situations beyond the APRN's expertise; and
(c) For *consulting with or referring* clients to other health care providers as appropriate.[151]

[145] *See* Chambliss, *supra* note 144, at 602 ("Quality assessment is also impeded by the decentralized, fragmented nature of civil legal services delivery, which relies on a wide variety of delivery models in addition to private practice.").
[146] *Id.*
[147] *See* Chapter 13 in this volume.
[148] *See* Rebecca L. Sandefur, *Legal Advice from Nonlawyers: Consumer Demand, Provider Quality, and Public Harms*, 16 STAN. J. C.R. & C.L. 283, 304–05 (2020) ("Findings from a systematic review of forty years of U.S. research comparing lawyer and nonlawyer performance bear out the importance of complexity. ... [W]hile nonlawyer advocates can be very good at some things, they may be not always be appropriate when clients face complex legal issues.").
[149] *Id.* at 305.
[150] N.D. Admin. Code, 54-05-03.1-03.2 (2023).
[151] N.H. Stat. 326-B:11.II (2023) (emphasis added).

Lawyers do this, too, but new nonlawyer practitioners may not know the tradition or have the relationships needed to accomplish it. To cure this, establishment of a relationship with a lawyer could be built into clinical training. Adding protective features like these may influence the votes of open-minded judges and legislators.

Finally, law reformers can improve quality control and reassure critics by borrowing from medicine and giving lawyers an oversight role. To keep costs down, one lawyer could be permitted to supervise multiple mid-level providers. This oversight need not be too costly or intrusive; it could occur at the end of each day, much like attending physicians review the charts of residents, or each week just as some supervising physicians meet with collaborating NPs.

The second important objection to the licensure of nonlawyer advocates is the belief that for-profit, mid-level legal professionals will not serve low-income people.[152] Here, the absence of an analog to health insurance is crucially important. Fees will have to be paid, and critics fear that they will be too high for low-income clients. According to a dissenting judge on the Washington Supreme Court, Washington's pilot program was "incompatible with meeting the needs of low-income individuals," and had "shifted to becoming a moderate means effort."[153] For many law reformers, this is a major shortcoming.

The problem of retail cost has led some advocates to recommend that the length and cost of training for limited licenses be reduced. This shifts the best medical analogy away from the training of NPs and PAs and toward the training of EMTs and paramedics. Their education and training are much cheaper than that of MDs, NPs, and even RNs. And their entry prerequisites are less demanding. As a result, their pay is lower and their scope of practice more limited. This may align well with some nonlawyer niches being considered by reformers.

But this option faces a couple of obstacles. One is its tension with the goal of high-quality representation. To thread the needle, the training will have to be tightly aligned with the scope of practice, as is true for many mid-level medical professionals. A second problem is that these trained and licensed "legal paramedics" may make less money than an untrained and unlicensed paralegal. If their income drops to that of paralegals, as happened for some mid-level practitioners in Washington,[154]

[152] *See* ILLINOIS REPORT, *supra* note 141, at 26 ("The needs of the underserved who cannot afford to pay for legal services are likely not going to benefit from the implementation of a for-profit LLLT program."). Virginia noted the absence of data. Virginia Report, *supra* note 142, at 17 ("There is little data to measure the programs' impact on access to legal services.").

[153] *See generally In re* Proposed Amendments to APR 28–Limited License Legal Technician Rules, Order No. 25700-A-1258 (Wash. 2019) (Gonzalez, J., dissenting). His remarks are discussed in Daniels & Bowers, *supra* note 2, at 259.

[154] *See also* THOMAS M. CLARKE & REBECCA L. SANDEFUR, PRELIMINARY EVALUATION OF THE WASHINGTON STATE LIMITED LICENSE LEGAL TECHNICIAN PROGRAM 13 (2017) ("A hypothetical business model that charges fees between those of a paralegal and a lawyer seems viable, but current actual fees [in Washington] are mostly the same as a traditional paralegal. Where the LLLTs are operating a pure LLLT practice, their fees tend to be moderately higher than that of paralegals.").

then potential license applicants will have no financial incentive to pay the training costs associated with the limited license.[155] But if their incomes settle higher, then low-income clients will not be able to afford their services. To serve low-income clients, subsidies will be needed.

Another strategy for surmounting the problem of retail cost is to recruit existing community advocates to become licensed mid-level legal professionals, and then to subsidize their training. This may already be happening informally in the federal agencies that allow nonlawyer representatives to assist claimants. And, in Chapter 1 of this volume, Sandefur and Burnett describe several similar state programs.[156] In Delaware and Texas, for example, nonlawyers can represent tenants and landlords. Alaska allows nonlawyer Community Justice Workers to be trained and supervised by Alaska Legal Services Corporation. Most work in remote Alaska Native communities that have no lawyers. Arizona has a Licensed Legal Advocate program for domestic violence cases. In addition, Utah has a legal safe space that it calls a "sandbox." Programs in the sandbox receive waivers from the unauthorized practice of law prohibitions. One potential advantage of these grassroots programs is their potential, not only to help underserved clients solve their legal problems but also to change their trust in, understanding of, and engagement with the law.[157]

A third objection raised by critics of limited licenses is that the holders will not be able to earn a living even if they serve primarily middle-class clients.[158] This issue did not surface in medicine because that system largely serves patients who have insurance, including Medicaid and Medicare. Consequently, salaries for mid-level medical professionals are good, jobs are plentiful, and there are more applicants for mid-level career programs than there are slots, even though the educational costs are substantial.

Because legal practice lacks any equivalent to health insurance, the financial viability of mid-level practitioners is still an open question. The experience in Washington was an inauspicious start. One review concluded that "[m]ost LLLTs struggle to attract enough clients to sustain a viable business."[159] One barrier is that consumers may be confused about the services that limited license providers are

[155] EMTs, paramedics and imaging technologists just need a high school diploma or associate degree. Would that suffice for some highly targeted nonlawyer niches as long as they first received a year of specific legal training? That idea requires considerably more thought.

[156] *See* Chapter 1 in this volume.

[157] *See id.* at 9 (recommending that objective).

[158] *See* Clarke & Sandefur, *supra* note 154, at 13; Daniels & Bowers, *supra* note 2, at 262 (observing that "sustainability has become a major concern not only in Washington State but also in other states as well"); Illinois Report, *supra* note 141, at 26–27 ("In addition, given the rise of internet based alternative legal services that provide forms and do-it-yourself services (both for-profit and non-profit), the economic viability of LLLT's may be in doubt.").

[159] *See* Clarke & Sandefur, *supra* note 154, at 13. The committee in Montana assigned to consider the issue noted that "the level of training required for the license would be a significant barrier to participation." Montana Minutes, *supra* note 140, at 3.

authorized and qualified to perform.[160] In addition, many people do not want to involve the formal legal system.[161] Others "do not understand their issues to be legal, and so do not see them as proper objects of legal action."[162] In many instances, the amounts in dispute don't warrant hiring a representative.[163]

Nevertheless, the universe of underserved middle-class Americans is so vast that the effort to serve them makes sense, even though some trial and error will be necessary to find models that work. The Institute for Advancement of the American Legal System at the University of Denver clearly thinks so.[164] It released a report in June 2023 called "Allied Legal Professionals: A National Framework," containing national recommendations to guide states considering programs to train and license a new tier of "allied legal professionals."[165] The Institute is working with three national paralegal organizations to create this national template. Its summary of the new profession closely resembles that of NPs, and they expressly make that analogy. The proposal contemplates a tier of licensed legal practitioners whose lower training costs (lower than Washington's) will make their services affordable for middle-class Americans. They recommend independence from attorney oversight, even in court. Their plan targets clients with enough purchasing power to buy lower-cost legal services.[166] Because it contemplates the recruitment of paying clients, this proposal will face intense opposition from the bar.

This prospect of competition for clients fuels the last and most incendiary objection to authorizing mid-level legal practitioners. Many members of the bar view the legalization of mid-level legal professionals as a threat to their livelihoods. For them, it is a zero-sum game.

[160] *See* Illinois Report, *supra* note 141, at 27 ("[T]he Task Force believes there is a real possibility for consumers to be misled by unsupervised LLLT's attempting to perform services they are neither qualified nor authorized to perform."); Clarke & Sandefur, *supra* note 154, at 9 ("Clients [in Washington] were sometimes confused about exactly what LLLTs could and could not do.").

[161] *See* Rebecca L. Sandefur & Matthew Burnett, *All Together Now: Building a Shared Access to Justice Research Framework for Theoretical Insight and Actionable Intelligence*, Oñati Socio-L. Ser. 1330, 1342 (July 28, 2024) https://opo.iisj.net/index.php/osls/article/view/1437, at 3 ("For many issues, people simply attempt to handle problems on their own."); Chambliss, *supra* note 144, at 587 (observing that "simply lowering rates does not address problems of consumer engagement").

[162] *See* Sandefur & Burnett, *supra* note 159, at 3.

[163] *See* Aebra Coe, *Like It or Not, Law May Open Its Doors to Nonlawyers*, Law360 (Sept. 22, 2019) (noting that a 2015 study by the National Center for State Courts "found that in many civil cases the cost of hiring a lawyer is often more expensive than the value of the amount in dispute, as three-quarters of all judgments in the state courts during the year were less than $5,100").

[164] *See Allied Legal Professionals*, Inst. for Advancement of the Am. L. Sys., https://iaals.du.edu/projects/allied-legal-professionals (last accessed Aug. 28, 2023); Michael Houlberg & Natalie Anne Knowlton, Allied Legal Professionals: A National Framework for Program Growth (2023).

[165] *See* Houlberg & Knowlton, *supra* note 164.

[166] *See id.* at 18, 28.

In medicine, the reaction of physicians to the creation of mid-level professions has been dramatically different. In that field, the various tiers of licensed health care professions facilitate the work of physicians. Their presence frees physicians to devote time to services that are more remunerative. For example, PAs can handle post-op clinic visits while the supervising physicians perform more procedures. Hospital nurses can provide the continuous patient care that the admitting physicians require. And insurance pays for it all. In short, the widespread presence of health insurance and the shortage of physicians combine to produce a dramatically different climate for the deployment of mid-level professionals.[167] That fabric of cooperation has only recently frayed as NPs and then PAs have begun to seek full independence from physicians and, thus, the ability to threaten the business of physicians.

In the debate over law reform, many members of the bar already see a threat to their business. And they are responding as many physicians have done to the call for full NP independence.

10.3.2 *Lessons from the Successful Law Reform Efforts in Medicine*

Justice reformers could potentially reduce the pushback from practicing lawyers by borrowing from the initial NP and PA profiles and designing plans that provide some benefit to practicing lawyers. This will be a controversial tactic. But the potential tactical value makes it worth consideration. For example, the practice act could mandate one supervising lawyer for every five community law workers. As noted above, this supervision need not be very expensive or intrusive.[168]

A second way to borrow from the successful experience in medicine is to create boundaries on the new profession's scope of practice that reduce the perceived threat to practicing lawyers. Practicing lawyers can help identify the niches that they cannot afford to serve, and their acquiescence will materially improve the odds of legislative success.

Unfortunately, none of this is likely to soften the plight of most unemployed or underemployed lawyers. Indeed, some critics of limited licenses seem to be asking that we put young lawyers to work before adding to the supply of legal practitioners. But these lawyers could already be serving the needs of these clients if they felt they could make a living doing so. Legal services are simply too expensive for a self-pay

[167] Law reformers do not seek a status equivalent to lawyers (with the possible exception of the Institute's proposal for Legal Practitioners). In that respect, their proposals are more like the original plans to create the NP and PA fields or the EMT and paramedic professions.

[168] At the same time, this arrangement will have the very beneficial effect of requiring the *ex ante* establishment of a relationship between each mid-level provider and a practicing attorney. That will ensure that each community advocate knows a lawyer to whom unexpectedly complex cases can be referred.

market. There are no lessons in medicine for solving this dilemma. Some kind of financial assistance will be necessary.

Practicing lawyers and reformers will have their fiercest fights over those clients whose incomes place them near the border between those who can afford to hire a lawyer and those who can't. The closer that a proposal for nonlawyer licensure comes to that border, the fiercer the opposition will be. And the less critical the new license will be. It would be very helpful to have more information about the characteristics of this boundary territory.

The legislative success of NPs over the past sixty years also suggests one additional tactic that has nothing to do with the merits of the proposal. That tactic is to nationalize the campaign for mid-level lawyer services. That means establishing one or more national organizations whose job it is to doggedly recruit allies, develop and promulgate a consistent narrative, and develop leaders. It can also draft model legislation. The Institute for Advancement of the American Legal System at the University of Denver may be angling for this role.

One of the organization's jobs should be recruitment of allies in the federal agencies. This "federalizing" strategy proved very beneficial for NPs and PAs. In 1977, the American Nurses Association had its first success in Washington, D.C. Congress passed the Rural Health Clinic Act of 1977 providing funding to increase the use of NPs and PAs working in rural health centers. It required that 50 percent of services in these clinics come from NPs and PAs.[169] Next, Elliott Richardson, the Secretary of Health, Education and Welfare, established the Committee to Study Extended Roles for Nurses to consider the feasibility of expanding nursing practice. In 1971, the committee recommended expanding the use of NPs.[170] One result was increased federal funding for the training of NPs in areas such as family, adult, and emergency practice.[171] In 1986, the Office of Technology Assessment published a comprehensive literature review concluding that NPs and PAs in primary and ambulatory care provided care as good as the care provided by physicians "within their areas of competence."[172]

In 1989, President George H. W. Bush signed the Omnibus Reconciliation Act authorizing federal reimbursement for NPs in rural areas outside of health clinics.[173]

[169] *See* Hooker & Carter, *supra* note 38, at 30; Nira Al-Agba & Rebekah Bernard, Patients at Risk: The Rise of the Nurse Practitioner and Physician Assistant in Healthcare 4 (2020).

[170] *See* U.S. Dep't of Health, Educ. & Welfare, Extending the Scope of Nursing Practice: A Report of the Secretary's Committee to Study Extended Roles for Nurses 4, 12 (1971) (declaring that "we believe that extending the scope of nursing practice is essential").

[171] Arlene W. Keeling, *Historical Perspectives on an Expanded Role for Nursing*, 20 OJIN: Online J. of Issues in Nursing (May 31, 2015), https://ojin.nursingworld.org/table-of-contents/volume-20-2015/number-2-may-2015/historical-perspectives-expanded-role-nursing/ (last accessed Feb. 24, 2025).

[172] *See* Office of Technology Assessment, *supra* note 74, at 5.

[173] *See* Al-Agba & Bernard, *supra* note 169, at 4.

A decade later, President Clinton signed the Budget Reconciliation Act of 1997, allowing Medicare to pay for NP services regardless of geographic location. In that same year, the Robert Wood Johnson Foundation began to fund Executive Nurse Health Policy Fellowships to place nurses in positions of policy leadership at the state and national levels.[174]

In 2010 the Institute of Medicine published an influential report called *The Future of Nursing* in which it recommended expanded NP scope of authority.[175] In 2012, the National Governors Association concluded that NP care was comparable to physician care and called for loosening of restrictions on the practice.[176] Two years later, the FTC concluded that restrictions on practice were no longer needed and could be anticompetitive.[177]

Following enactment of the Affordable Care Act of 2010 and the *Future of Nursing*, the Robert Wood Johnson Foundation allied with the AARP to launch *The Future of Nursing: Campaign for Action*, a nationwide initiative for state law reform.[178] As noted above, NPs now have full practice authority in the majority of states.

In a similar vein, today's law reformers can build on the federalizing efforts that others have already begun. Several federal agencies have welcomed nonlawyer representatives who assist beneficiaries who are very often overwhelmed by the bureaucratic process. Much more of that is possible.

Once the effort has allies, a narrative, and great outcomes, the prospects for further reform legislation will be much improved. So too will the odds of funding to subsidize low-income clients.

10.4 CONCLUSION

High-quality services can be delivered by mid-level practitioners who are trained at a lower cost than that required to train the top tier of the profession. Medicine has dozens of these professions – and has had them for over a century. The two examined in this chapter – NPs and PAs – have patient outcomes that equal those of physicians. Moreover, researchers have repeated these positive findings in a wide variety of settings using many different methods and metrics. In addition, NPs and

[174] *See id.* at 5.

[175] *See* The Future of Nursing 2010, *supra* note 58.

[176] *See* Nat'l Governors Ass'n, *supra* note 62, at 11 (concluding that NP care is comparable to that of physician care and that "states might consider changing scope of practice restrictions and assuring adequate reimbursement for their services as a way of incentivizing greater NP involvement in the provision of primary care").

[177] *See* Gilman & Koslov, *supra* note 61.

[178] *State Implementation Program*, Robert Wood Johnson Found., https://ccna7.vermilion.com/our-network/grantee-and-award-programs/state-implementation-program/ (last accessed Apr. 30, 2023).

PAs provide this care at lower cost than physicians and in underserved areas where it is difficult to recruit physicians.

Now law reformers are creating and evaluating new mid-level licenses in the field of law. If the early outcomes are good, then ensuing proposals can be drafted with provisions designed to convince doubters that quality will be high.

Because the law has no analog to health insurance, however, the programs will also have to bring fees down. To do so, training programs will need to be lean and focused. Trial and error will eventually reveal some good ones. Once models that offer excellent outcomes at substantially reduced cost are developed, the search for sustainable funding will be much easier.

11

The Statutory Influence of Tribal Lay Advocates*

Lauren van Schilfgaarde

There is a lawyer shortage in Indian country.[1] Comparable to Indigenous people across the globe, Native Americans lack access to justice in strikingly disproportionate numbers compared to non-Natives.[2] This is in part because typical access to justice initiatives tend to fail rural communities, and particularly Native communities.[3] First, there are not enough Native attorneys. While Native Americans are approximately 1.6 percent of the US population, they represent only 0.3 percent of the legal profession, a disproportionality that has been observed as "stark beyond measure."[4] In addition to education-access barriers, this disproportionality is rooted in historical efforts to bar Natives from participating in the American legal system, including from serving on juries,[5] as

* The author's sincere gratitude to the research assistance from Felix Murphet, commentary from Mica Llerandi, and the insight engagement of the Stanford Law School's New Voices in Access to Justice Convening.

1 Lisa R. Pruitt et al., *Legal Deserts: A Multi-State Perspective on Rural Access to Justice*, 13 Harv. L. & Pol'y Rev. 15, 119 (2018) (noting "South Dakota's Native American population suffers from a particularly dire shortage of lawyers"). "Indian country" is both a legal term of art to describe the Tribal lands on which Tribes exercise their sovereign authority (18 U.S.C. § 1551) and a euphemism to describe Tribes, Tribal communities, and the contexts in which they live.

2 *See generally* U.N. Expert Mechanism on the Rights of Indigenous Peoples, *Access to Justice in the Promotion and Protection of the Rights of Indigenous Peoples*, A/HRC/24/50 (2013); Inst. for the Study of Human Rights, Colum. Univ., Indigenous Peoples' Access to Justice, Including Truth and Reconciliation (Wilton Littlechild & Elsa Stamatopoulou eds., 2014).

3 Michele Statz et al., *"They Had Access, But They Didn't Get Justice": Why Prevailing Access to Justice Initiatives Fail Rural Americans*, 28 Geo. J. on Poverty L. & Pol'y 321 (2021) (using empirical data from the "Northland," including intentional examinations of Native communities in Wisconsin and Minnesota, to unveil the failure of typical access to justice initiatives like technology, pro se self-help forms, and finding a dearth of private pro bono attorneys).

4 Nat'l Native American Bar Ass'n, The Pursuit of Inclusion: An In-Depth Exploration of the Experiences and Perspectives of Native American Attorneys in the Legal Profession 10 (2015).

5 Elk v. Wilkins, 112 U.S. 94, 102 (1884) (exempting Native Americans born on Tribal lands from birthright citizenship, and thereby excluding them from federal jury service); Equal Just.

witnesses,[6] and even from U.S. citizenship.[7] Second, non-Native attorneys are not filling the gap. There are not enough resources to attract attorney representatives, including woefully underfunded court systems[8] coupled with insufficient compensation and housing for attorneys.[9] Yet, the legal needs in Indian country are extensive. The vestiges of historical oppression against Natives manifest in devastating metrics, including the country's highest rates of poverty and unemployment.[10]

Intriguingly, however, access to justice initiatives within Indian country do not exclusively focus on expanding access to attorneys,[11] largely because Tribal legal traditions are not wholly dependent on lawyers. For example, the practice of Tribal law, an intellectual tradition dating back millennia, does not center the lawyer but instead centers community customs and expectations. Further, Native Americans' practices in Tribal court, which reflect their long-established legal traditions and

INITIATIVE, RACE AND THE JURY: ILLEGAL RACIAL DISCRIMINATION IN JURY SELECTION 35–36 (2021) (noting federal courts continue to disproportionately exclude Native Americans from jury service).

6 *See, for example,* People v. Hall, 4 Cal. 399 (Cal. 1854) (upholding the Act Concerning Civil Cases of April 16, 1850, which provided that "No Black or Mulatto person, or Indian, shall be allowed to give evidence in favor of, or against a white man").

7 Indian Citizenship Act, Pub. L. 68-175, 43 Stat. 253 (1924) (conferring birthright citizenship on all noncitizen Indians); United States v. Nice, 241 U.S. 598 (1916) (holding that U.S. citizenship is compatible with Tribal citizenship).

8 U.S. COMM'N ON C.R., BROKEN PROMISES: CONTINUING FEDERAL FUNDING SHORTFALL FOR NATIVE AMERICANS 8 (Dec. 2018), https://www.usccr.gov/files/pubs/2018/12-20-Broken-Promises.pdf (last accessed Feb. 4, 2025) (finding that funding for Tribal courts is inadequate); Lindsay Cutler, *Tribal Sovereignty, Tribal Court Legitimacy and Public Defense*, 63 UCLA L. REV. 1752, 1756 (2016) ("[T]he decision not to extend a statutory right to appointed counsel in tribal courts was driven by a recognition of tribal sovereignty, but perhaps more so by a concern about federal funding."); Comm. on the Elimination of Discrimination Against Women (CEDAW), *General Recommendation No. 39 on the Rights of Indigenous Women and Girls*, CEDAW/C/GC/39, at ¶ 28 (2022) (noting the international propensity for Indigenous justice systems to be underfunded and/or unsupported, and that nation-states have an obligation to ensure their support).

9 *See, for example,* Dominque Alan Fenton, *Poor on a Native American Reservation? Good Luck Getting a Lawyer*, THE MARSHALL PROJECT (June 13, 2016), https://www.themarshallproject.org/2016/06/13/poor-on-a-native-american-reservation-good-luck-getting-a-lawyer (last accessed Feb. 4, 2025) (describing the lack of public defense counsel at the Oglala Sioux Tribal Court); Pruitt et al., *supra* note 1, at 116–17 (noting despite disproportionately high rural poverty rates, rural areas tend to receive disproportionately less legal aid funding); Joseph Kunkel & Aspen Global Leadership Network, *Indian Country's Housing Crisis Is a Public Health Crisis*, ASPEN INSTITUTE (June 26, 2020), https://www.aspeninstitute.org/blog-posts/indian-countrys-housing-crisis-is-a-public-health-crisis/ (last accessed Feb. 4, 2025) (noting while "the Department of Housing and Urban Development (HUD) has found that Indian Country faces a deficit of 68,000 housing units per year, the real need is likely triple that").

10 U.S. COMM'N ON C.R., *supra* note 8, at 8.

11 Compare with the American Bar Association's (ABA) preferred strategy for increasing access to justice by focusing on increasing access to lawyers. Deborah L. Rhode & Scott Cummings, *Access to Justice: Looking Back, Thinking Ahead*, 30 GEO. J. LEGAL ETHICS 485, 489 (2017).

continue as recognized expressions of their Tribal sovereignty,[12] were established without the formal equivalent of the lawyer.[13] The hundreds of Tribal courts across Indian country operate around and with lawyers,[14] but also with experts in Tribal customary law, like elders, and with traditional processes and remedies, like peacemaking and restorative reparations. Lawyers tend to have a crippling lack of familiarity with Tribal courts and a false sense that Tribal law is an inferior practice area.[15] Thus, even assuming attorneys came flocking to the Tribal court, *and* the Tribe had sufficient funds and political will to hire them on behalf of the Tribe, a law school-trained, state-barred attorney may nevertheless still lack the necessary legal and cultural competence to meet the needs of the Tribal court.[16]

Outside of Indian country, the broader access to justice movement is increasingly calling for options apart from lawyers.[17] Given the historical evolution of Tribal courts and their creative innovations to accommodate nonlawyer practitioners, Tribal courts may offer some useful insight for broader access to justice initiatives. As just one type of response, numerous Tribal codes expressly provide for lay advocates as authorized representatives to appear before the court despite not being a member of a state bar, and/or not having attended an American Bar Association (ABA)-accredited law school. Lay advocates offer unique access to justice opportunities, including filling a gap between prohibitively expensive attorneys and pro se representation. But we should resist framing lay advocates as simply attorney replacements. Attorneys are presently mired in their own legitimacy crisis, experiencing a professional fissuring that is undermining the special monopoly traditionally claimed by attorneys as defenders of the rule of law and democracy itself.[18] There may be an appetite for a model of lay advocacy that expands beyond just a

[12] *See, for example,* United States v. Wheeler, 435 U.S. 313, 322–23 (1978) (describing Tribes as "self-governing sovereign political communities" with "the inherent power to prescribe laws for their members and to punish infractions of those laws").

[13] Wanda D. McCaslin, *Introduction: Reweaving the Fabrics of Life, in* Justice as Healing: Indigenous Ways 88 (Wanda D. McCaslin ed., 2005). ("For indigenous Peoples, law is far more than rules to be obeyed. Law is found within our language, customs, and practices. … These are not passed on through lectures or written codes.")

[14] Steven W. Perry et al., *Tribal Courts in the United States, 2014 – Statistical Tables,* Bureau of Just. Stat., Off. of Just. Programs, U.S. Dep't of Just. 11 (July 2021), https://bjs.ojp.gov/sites/g/files/xyckuh236/files/media/document/tcus14st_o.pdf.

[15] Gloria Valencia-Weber, *Indian Law on State Bar Exams: A Situational Report,* Fed. Law. (Mar./Apr. 2007), https://www.fedbar.org/wp-content/uploads/2007/03/focuson-valenciaweber-0307-pdf-1.pdf (last accessed Feb. 4, 2025) (arguing for the inclusion of Indian law on state bar exams, in part, to recognize and legitimate Indian law, challenge disrespect of Tribal governments, and serve the general interests of the state).

[16] CEDAW, *supra* note 8, ¶ 30 (finding internationally, non-Indigenous justice systems have a higher likelihood of subjecting Indigenous people to racism, structural and systemic racial discrimination, and procedures that are not culturally appropriate).

[17] Rhode & Cummings, *supra* note 11, at 490 ("The public wants more access to justice, not necessarily more access to lawyers."). *See also, for example,* Chapter 1 in this volume.

[18] Scott Cummings, *Lawyers in Backsliding Democracy,* 112 Calif. L. Rev. 513 at 518–19 (Apr. 2024).

second-best solution or resource of last resort, and toward a more capacious conception. Can lay advocates offer meaningful representation? Are they sufficiently competent? Are they accountable? Do they satisfy the clients – and communities – they serve?[19] Tribal court lay advocates have practiced for decades and offer some answers to these timely and critically important questions.

In particular, the Tribal experience can help to answer these burning questions because Tribes have the sovereign autonomy to design and operate their Tribal courts, including the authority to deviate from well-established federal and state constitutional norms, though with notable constraints detailed below. Tribes are integrating social services into case plans, experimenting with restorative justice, weaving in cultural concepts, language, and teachings, and building out Tribal law jurisprudence.[20] Notably, Tribal lay advocates have disrupted the notion that their efforts are a compromise on competency. For some Tribes, the fact that lay advocates are more likely to be from the community and more likely to stay within the community makes them *more competent advocates* than outside lawyers.

This chapter examines Tribal codes to determine the extent to which Tribes have codified the eligibility of lay advocates to appear in Tribal courts, and how, if at all, Tribes have contended with ethical concerns surrounding lay advocates, including their competence and accountability. It reveals how Tribal codes expressly incorporate cultural elements into the lay advocate's role. By examining Tribal codes, this chapter provides insight into Tribal views on lay advocates' ability to enhance Tribal members' access to justice and also sheds light on potential guardrails to ensure that lay advocates provide ethical and effective representation.

The chapter proceeds in two sections. Section 11.1 examines the legal structure and history of Tribal courts, including why these courts embrace lay advocates. Section 11.2 then turns to Tribal codes and canvasses what these codes say about the ethical requirements of, and qualifications for, lay advocates. This inquiry reveals that Tribes are using lay advocates to expand the pool of eligible representatives before the court. But they are also prioritizing customary law and community such that lay advocates may have the potential to enhance the level of representation within the Tribal court.

11.1 EXCEPTIONAL TRIBAL COURTS

Tribal courts are the judicial arms of sovereign Indian nations, which are distinct both from the United States and from each other. Tribal powers neither arise from

[19] Rhode & Cummings, *supra* note 11, at 490.

[20] *See generally* Matthew L. M. Fletcher, American Indian Tribal Law (2nd ed. 2020); Lauren van Schilfgaarde, *Restorative Justice as Regenerative Tribal Jurisdiction*, 112 Calif. L. Rev. 101 (2024).

nor are created by the Constitution of the United States.[21] Tribal courts are instead extra-constitutional – that is, the U.S. Constitution and its attendant due process protections simply do not apply.[22] Nor does the Fourteenth Amendment of the U.S. Constitution incorporate federal due process protections to Tribes.[23] The lack of incorporation extends to prominent U.S. Supreme Court decisions, such as the right to legal counsel[24] and the right for that counsel to be effective.[25] Instead, Tribes make their own Tribal laws and determine how those laws are to be interpreted.

The Tribal court remains an oft-neglected and misunderstood juridical structure within the American legal system.[26] There is no central depository of Tribal law, nor has there been any meaningful comparative study of lay advocates within Tribal systems. In fact, the first study of the mere existence of Tribal courts was published only in 2021, and excluded all of Alaska.[27] Federal courts have frequently relied upon the perceived foreignness of Tribal courts to justify undermining Tribal sovereign authority.[28]

While Tribes are distinct, Tribes exist within the United States under the plenary authority of Congress.[29] Congress can unilaterally recognize, restrict, and/or encroach upon Tribal authority. Congress has done just that, statutorily recognizing Tribal courts[30] but also restricting that authority in numerous instances and

[21] Talton v. Mayes, 163 U.S. 376, 384 (1896) (holding the Fifth Amendment's grand jury requirement does not apply to the Cherokee Nation).

[22] *Id.* at 383–84.

[23] *Id.* at 383–84. *See also* United States v. Doherty, 126 F.3d 769, 777 (6th Cir. 1997) ("*Talton* has come to stand for the proposition that neither the Bill of Rights nor the Fourteenth Amendment operates to constrain the governmental actions of Indian tribes.") (citations omitted) (quoting Santa Clara Pueblo v. Martinez, 436 U.S. 49, 56 (1978)).

[24] Gideon v. Wainwright, 372 U.S. 335 (1963) (holding the Sixth Amendment guarantees counsel in criminal proceedings and extends that guarantee to states through the Due Process Clause of the Fourteenth Amendment).

[25] Strickland v. Washington, 466 U.S. 668 (1984).

[26] Elizabeth Reese, *The Other American Law*, 73 Stan. L. Rev. 555, 578 (2021) (noting the "current omission of tribal law from the mainstream is not because tribal law is inherently unworthy of our attention," but because of a history of marginalization).

[27] Perry et al., *supra* note 14. Of the 574 federally recognized Tribes, 229 are located within the state of Alaska. However, given jurisdictional and infrastructure limitations, there are likely far fewer operational Tribal courts within Alaska.

[28] *See, for example*, Nevada v. Hicks, 533 U.S. 353, 384 (2001) ("The resulting law applicable in tribal courts is a complex 'mix of tribal codes and federal, state, and traditional law,' . . . which would be unusually difficult for an outsider to sort out.").

[29] United States v. Kagama, 118 U.S. 375, 377 (1886) (holding Congress has a duty of protection to Tribes and a corresponding plenary power). Hon. Orville M. Olney & David H. Getches, *Indian Courts and the Future: Report of the NAICJA Long Range Planning Project*, Nat'l Am. Indian Ct. Judges Ass'n 2 (1978), https://www.ojp.gov/ncjrs/virtual-library/abstracts/indian-courts-and-future-report-naicja-national-american-indian (last accessed Feb. 4, 2025) (noting that the development and implementation of robust Tribal court systems have not stymied incursions on Tribal authority to self-govern).

[30] *See, for example*, Indian Reorganization Act of June 18, 1934, Pub. L. No. 73-383, 48 Stat. 984 (1934) (codified as amended at 25 U.S.C. §§ 461–66, 470–76, 478–79); Violence Against

contexts.[31] As Tribal judicial actions came to impact white settlers, federal policy increasingly became concerned with the substance of Tribal judicial systems.[32] The Indian Civil Rights Act (ICRA) of 1968 is one of the most consequential legislative influences on Tribal courts.[33] Broadly, anti-subordination efforts have focused on the promotion of individual civil rights, including through national oversight, rights-based frameworks, and judicial solicitude.[34] Under this theory, rights-based individual freedoms are most relevant when contrasted against an oppressive government from which the people require protection. The protection of those rights – such as the right to due process, including through representation by counsel – is presumed to take place in the context of judiciaries overseeing parties facing off as adversaries. The ICRA endorses this constitutional framework by statutorily extending due process requirements comparable to the U.S. Constitution's Bill of Rights onto Tribes.[35] But in doing so, it also cements the adversarial system, overseen by a powerful centralized government, as the statutorily mandated judicial system of Tribes.

While the ICRA statutorily requires Tribal courts to ensure litigants receive "due process" and "equal protection,"[36] the ICRA does not incorporate the body of federal case law that informs the substance of those terms in American law.[37] Consequently, the reasonings of constitutional bulwarks like *Strickland*,[38] *Gideon*,[39] and *Miranda*[40] do not automatically extend to Tribal governments, and

Women Reauthorization Act of 2005, Pub. L. No. 109-62, tit. IV, 119 Stat. 2960 (2005) (requiring state and federal courts to extend full faith and credit to Tribally issued protection orders).

31 *See, for example*, General Crimes Act, ch. 92, 3 Stat. 383 (1817) (codified as amended at 18 U.S.C. § 1152) (extending federal concurrent criminal jurisdiction onto Tribal lands); Major Crimes Act, ch. 341, 23 Stat. 385 (1885) (codified as amended at 18 U.S. § 1153) (further extending federal concurrent criminal jurisdiction onto Tribal lands), and Act of Aug. 15, 1953, Pub. L. No. 67, Stat. 588 (1953) (codified as amended at 18 U.S.C. § 1162) (extending state concurrent criminal and civil adjudicatory jurisdiction onto some Tribal lands).

32 *See generally* van Schilfgaarde, *supra* note 20 (tracing the history of CFR Courts as the introduction of the adversarial, rights-based judicial system to Tribes, coupled with federal restrictions on how Tribes can operate those systems).

33 Pub. L. 90-284, 82 Stat. 77 (Apr. 11, 1968) (codified as amended at 25 U.S.C. §§ 1301–05); *see also generally* The Indian Civil Rights Act at Forty (Kristen Carpenter et al. eds., 2012) (examining the impacts of the Indian Civil Rights Act forty years after its enactment).

34 Maggie Blackhawk, *Federal Indian Law as Paradigm within Public Law*, 132 Harv. L. Rev. 1787, 1797 (2019).

35 25 U.S.C. § 1302(a).

36 *Id.* § 1302(a)(8).

37 Santa Clara Pueblo v. Martinez, *supra* note 23, at 62 (holding the ICRA has no federal cause of action beyond habeas corpus, and upholding Tribal sovereign immunity).

38 Strickland v. Washington, *supra* note 25.

39 Gideon v. Wainwright, *supra* note 24 (holding the Sixth Amendment's guarantee of a right to assistance of counsel applies to states by way of the Fourteenth Amendment).

40 Miranda v. Arizona, 384 U.S. 346 (1966) (holding the Fifth Amendment requires law enforcement officials to advise suspects of their right to remain silent and to obtain an attorney during interrogations while in police custody).

Tribes must determine the substance of due process and equal protection rights. Many Tribes have nevertheless elected to incorporate comparable protections, including due to pressures to adopt Western legal norms.[41] But there are also instances in which Tribes diverge.[42]

In addition to federal case law exceptionalism, the ICRA differs substantively from the US Constitution. For example, the ICRA imposes a sentencing limitation on Tribal courts, effectively demoting Tribal legal systems to misdemeanor courts.[43] In regard to attorney representation, the ICRA is most notably contrary to constitutional protections in its acknowledgment, and then workaround, of *Gideon*, providing that no Tribe may "deny to any person in a criminal proceeding" the right "*at his own expense* to have the assistance of counsel for his defense."[44] Tribes cannot prevent someone from hiring a defense attorney, but they do not have to fund it. The lack of federally mandated, Tribal government-funded criminal legal defense has been cited as a significant barrier for the future of Tribal courts.[45] Some Tribes have guaranteed the right to counsel for indigent defendants in their own Tribal law.[46] But broadly, most Tribes either cannot afford or have failed to prioritize building a robust public defender and/or legal services office. As a result, the adversarial model of two equally positioned adversaries remains largely theoretical in Tribal courts.

Congress could have required that Tribes provide state-barred attorneys to criminal defendants in Tribal court. So too could Congress have funded that public defense. Instead, the ICRA is an example of federal attempts to encourage the adoption of the Anglo-adversarial model, while also recognizing some Tribal self-

[41] Carrie E. Garrow & Sarah Deer, Tribal Criminal Law and Procedure 202 (2004) ("[T]he introduction of Anglo-American models of police, jails, and more coercive governmental power has required tribal governments to protect individuals from overbearing governments and intrusions upon their liberty").

[42] *See, for example*, Navajo Nation v. Rodriguez, 2004 WL 5658107 (Navajo Dec. 16, 2004) (interpreting the ICRA not to include a requirement for a *Miranda*-type warning from law enforcement but relying on the Navajo principle of *hazhǫ́'ógo*, meaning loosely that patience and respect are required when dealing with another human being).

[43] 25 U.S.C. § 1302(b)-(c) (limiting Tribal imprisonment authority to one year and a fine of $5,000). In 2010, Congress raised the sentencing limitation to three years but attached conditional due process requirements. Tribal Law and Order Act of 2010, Pub. L. 111-211, 124 Stat. 2258.

[44] 25 U.S.C. § 1302(a)(6).

[45] Samuel Macomber, Note, *Disparate Defense in Tribal Courts: The Unequal Rights to Counsel as a Barrier to Expansion of Tribal Court Criminal Jurisdiction*, 106 Cornell L. Rev. 275 (2020).

[46] *See, for example*, Osage Nation Code tit. 5, § 1-111 (providing the right to counsel for criminal defendants, but only in cases of extreme financial hardship, and only where imprisonment is being sought); United Keetoowah Band of Cherokee Indians in Oklahoma Tribal Code, 2022 Courts Act, ch. 11, Rule 1106(a) (providing that the Court will pay for indigent defense, but only if there are sufficient funds); Salt River Pima-Maricopa Indian Community Code of Ordinances, ch. 5, art. iv, Rule 6.1 (providing for indigent defense, but only if the defendant is charged with an offense that carries a potential sentence of imprisonment exceeding one year).

government. In doing so, Congress reserved some, albeit small, space for Tribal innovation.

Section 11.2 explains that Tribes are seemingly using that space to do something remarkable through Tribal lay advocate programs. In so doing, they are not only addressing the access-to-justice gap but also bridging their traditional customs with the Western court model. Within a historical context of pressures to abandon traditional dispute resolution in exchange for adopting the Anglo-adversarial model, Tribes have created a space for lay advocates – and these lay advocates are serving as a liaison between the traditional and Western justice models.

11.2 TRIBAL LAY ADVOCATES IN TRIBAL CODE

Tribal lay advocates are representatives authorized to appear in the Tribal court without some or all of the credentials required of an attorney. Tribal codes reveal the instances in which Tribes have statutorily recognized, and even prioritized, the role of the lay advocate within the Tribal judiciary. There is no current scholarship as to when Tribal lay advocates began to proliferate in Tribal courts, how their roles within the Tribal judiciary have materialized in reflection of and beyond the Tribal code, how they have influenced other Tribal legal bodies, or how they impact litigants within Tribal courts. However, we can look to a snapshot of Tribal codes as a current statutory expression of Tribal court praxis – praxis that has trickled up to legislative recognition.[47]

Not all Tribal codes are publicly available. Of those that are, only a few are available on typical legal search engines.[48] While there have been attempts to centralize Tribal codes, it is nevertheless still best practice to verify codes with individual Tribes.[49] For this project, we visited publicly available Tribal websites with publicly posted Tribal codes and searched for provisions regarding attorney or legal practitioner regulation, and specific terms such as "attorney," "lawyer," "lay advocate," or "spokesperson(man)(woman)." In total, we visited 129 Tribal websites representing 24 states. Because Tribal courts tend to be underdeveloped within Public Law 280 jurisdictions, Tribes located in Public Law 280 states, including Alaska and California, tend to be underrepresented. Our research was not exhaustively comprehensive of all Tribal codes. Rather, we sought a diversity of content – that is, variations among the codes in order to showcase a panoply of potential

[47] Tribal code is but one lens to examine Tribal law approaches to lay advocates. The advantage of examining Tribal code is both its increasing availability, but also its bluntness in revealing the degrees of Tribal endorsements of lay advocates. Note the snapshots below do not represent all Tribal codes, in part because not all Tribal codes are publicly available.

[48] Reese, *supra* note 26, at 622 ("Even for experts working in tribal law, there is a lot we do not know and – because we have yet to build a reliable and consistent infrastructure – cannot find out easily.")

[49] *Id.* at 623.

approaches to lay advocates. Of the Tribal websites visited, twenty-three did not make their codes publicly available, and twenty-four codes did not include a relevant provision regarding lay advocates. Eighty-two codes did include such a provision. Numerous provisions were substantively similar to each other. Drawing on these codes, this chapter offers a rough mapping of the role of lay advocates in various Tribal courts.

11.2.1 *Right to Representation*

As noted above, the ICRA extends to a criminal defendant in Tribal court only the right of counsel "at his own expense."[50] A Tribe may expand this guarantee in Tribal law to provide defendants with a right to an attorney in certain circumstances.[51] But some Tribes have used lay advocates to provide more representation to defendants. For example, the Nooksack Indian Tribe guarantees representation for criminal defendants at the expense of the Tribe, and this guarantee applies to non-attorney-appointed advocates.[52]

11.2.2 *Qualifications for Lay Advocates*

Tribal definitions for lay advocates vary. But generally, Tribal codes define a lay advocate as someone authorized to practice before the Tribal court but who did not graduate from an ABA-accredited law school.[53] Many Tribal courts, however, require both attorneys and lay advocates to obtain a license to practice.[54] For instance, the Hoopa Valley Tribal Court of Appeals confirmed that both attorneys and non-attorneys fall under the regulation of spokespersons, another term for lay advocate, who may appear before the Hoopa Valley Tribal Court.[55]

[50] 25 U.S.C. § 1302(6).

[51] *See, for example,* Boos v. Yazzie, 6 Nav. R. 211, 214 (Nav. Sup. Ct. 1990) (recognizing a right to counsel for indigent criminal defendants in section 7 of the Navajo Nation Bill of Rights); Osage Nation Code tit. 5, § 1-111 (providing counsel for criminal defendants, but only in cases of extreme financial hardship and where imprisonment is sought); Salt River Pima-Maricopa Indian Community Code of Ordinances, ch. 5, art. iv, Rule 6.1 providing for indigent defense, but only if the defendant is charged with an offense that carries a potential sentence of imprisonment exceeding one year).

[52] Nooksack Indian Tribal Code § 10.02.010 (noting if the defendant is found guilty, they must pay a $50 fee for their representation, subject to waiver if the defendant is unable to pay or was a minor at the time of the offense).

[53] *See, for example,* White Mountain Apache Judicial Code § 2.27; Yurok Tribal Code § 2.05.010 (though section 2.10.810 of the Yurok Tribal Code also allows for spokespeople to be admitted at the discretion of the hearing judge).

[54] *See, for example,* White Mountain Apache Judicial Code § 2.26; Mohegan Tribe of Indians of Connecticut Code of Ordinances, pt. II, ch. 1, art. I., § 1-36 (requiring spokespeople to be admitted to the Mohegan Tribal Court Bar).

[55] In the Matter of Robertson, 4 NICS App. 11, 116 (Hoopa Valley Tribal Ct. App. 1996).

Some Tribal codes reference a Tribal bar, referencing the existence of a Tribal bar established outside of the code, while some specifically establish a Tribal bar and make membership in such bar its own criteria for lay advocates to appear before the Tribal court.[56] The Citizen Potawatomi Nation clarifies that lay advocates are "[e]ntitled to the same rights, privileges, obligations, and duties, and [ ] accorded all the honors to the same extent as any attorney admitted to practice before the Courts of the Tribe within [the] reservation."[57]

Crucially, Tribal codes tend to frame lay advocates as more than nonlawyers or attorney replacements. As explained further below, Tribal codes incorporate additional qualifications, such as tiered priorities for Tribal members and Native Americans who are close to the community and have familiarity with Tribal law. These added qualification criteria suggest that Tribes expect their lay advocates to possess expertise distinct from that of a lawyer.

11.2.3 *Priority for Tribal Members*

Many Tribal codes that provide for lay advocates have cabined and/or tiered their eligibility pool to give priority to Tribal members when authorizing individuals to appear before the Court as lay advocates.[58] The Blue Lake Rancheria Code provides for appearances by "counsel" who must be admitted to the bar of any state,[59] and for "spokesperson[s]," defined as "any person not admitted to a bar of any state who is a tribal member or a relative of a party and speaks for any party in a case filed in the Tribal Court."[60] The Fort McDowell Yavapai Nation extends lay advocate eligibility

[56] *See, for example*, Burns Paiute Tribal Code § 1.1.180; Confederated Tribes of the Umatilla Indian Reservation Rules of Court, Rule 11(e); Klamath Tribal Codes tit. 2, § 11.35(b)(2); Kalispel Tribe Law & Order Code, § 1-12.01; Lummi Nation Code, § 1.05.010. Note that not only has Tribal bar membership garnered implicit recognition from Congress, but organizations like the ABA now recognize Tribal bar membership as an eligible entry point into the broader American legal profession. American Bar Association Res. 11-4 (2014) (amending constitutional amendment § 3.1 to include individuals in good standing with federally recognized Tribal courts).

[57] Citizen Potawatomi Nation Tribal Code, Rule 8-1-101(C).

[58] *See, for example*, White Mountain Apache Judicial Code § 2.27(B)(1); Leech Lake Band of Ojibwe Judicial Code tit. 1, pt. v, § 3 (extending lay advocate eligibility to a member of the Band or a member of another Band affiliated with the Minnesota Chippewa Tribe); Lower Sioux Indian Community Judicial Code § 1.22; Prairie Island Indian Community Tribal Code, Courts Ordinance § 9(a); White Earth Nation Judicial Code, ch. v, § 1; Mississippi Band of Choctaw Indians Tribal Code tit. 1, § 1-4-3 (limiting lay advocate eligibility to either a member of the Tribe or of another federally recognized American Indian Tribe); Citizen Potawatomi Nation Tribal Code, Rule 8-1-101(C) (limiting lay advocate eligibility to members of a federally recognized Tribe); Miami Tribe of Oklahoma Judicial Code §§ 2.25, 2.26(D) (limiting lay advocate eligibility to Tribal members, or to members of a federally recognized Tribe who are also licensed to practice in any other Indian Tribal Court in Oklahoma on a case-by-case basis).

[59] Blue Lake Rancheria Tribal Code, Ordinance No. 07-01, § 11.1.1.010(A).

[60] *Id.* § 11.1.1.010(E).

to any Indian person.[61] The White Mountain Apache Tribe permits non-Tribal members to be licensed as an advocate, but they must either be employed by the Tribe or a public defender organization approved by the Tribe and also must be licensed and in good standing with at least one other Tribal jurisdiction.[62] Among their enumerated methods for demonstrating competency, the Ho-Chunk Nation lists admission to practice before another Tribal court, or being a Ho-Chunk Tribal member representing another Tribal member.[63]

These Tribes appear to be actively engaged in negotiating the tradeoffs between attorneys and non-attorneys, as well as Tribal members or Natives and non-Natives, in the provision of legal representation. A Tribal member attorney offers the maximum potential for competence: legal training, accreditation, and professional accountability, coupled with a likelihood for community, cultural, custom, and linguistic familiarity. A Native non-Tribal member attorney offers at least a familiarity with Tribal communities broadly and an appreciation for Tribal law and how to navigate it. A non-Native attorney may lack cultural credibility but brings their legal training. Conversely, Tribal member lay advocates may lack formal legal training, but they are more likely to bring a familiarity with Tribal law, including customary law, as well as community norms and practices. Similarly, Native non-Tribal members, non-attorneys may lack specific familiarity with this Tribal community but offer a familiarity with Tribal law generally. By requiring lay advocates to be Tribal members, Tribes validate the notion that legal representatives are most effective when equipped with intimate knowledge of the community and culture in which the litigation takes place. Proximity to the Tribe is but one competency metric. The provisions below evince a different method for measuring Tribal law competence.

11.2.4 *Tribal Law Training*

Lay advocates may definitionally be distinguished from attorneys by their lack of law school training, but many Tribal codes require that lay advocates have some legal training, experience, and/or that they demonstrate legal skills. Those requirements suggest that Tribal law advocates are not "less-than-attorneys" but rather are customary law experts.

[61] Fort McDowell Yavapai Nation Law & Order Code § 1-25.

[62] White Mountain Apache Judicial Code § 2.27(B)(2). *See also* Mohegan Tribe of Indians of Connecticut Code of Ordinances, pt. II, ch. 1, art. I., § 1-37(c) (permitting spokespersons to represent litigants only in minor civil actions, unless they are also admitted and in good standing in a foreign jurisdiction); Mashpee Wampanoag Tribe, Administrative Order #20 (extending lay advocate eligibility only to those who have been admitted as attorneys to the Bar of "any Tribe, State, or Federal Court"). However, law students are exempted from this requirement and may appear before the Tribal Court for any case. White Mountain Apache Judicial Code § 2.27(D).

[63] Ho-Chunk Nation Code, Rules for Admission to Practice, Rule II(1)-(5).

Consider Tribal codes that require a specific familiarity with the Tribe's laws and federal Indian law generally, a requirement that is woefully lacking for state-barred attorneys.[64] For example, the Cherokee Nation defines lay advocates as "[a]ny lay person demonstrating experience or education in Indian law and the laws of Cherokee Nation."[65] The Leech Lake Band of Ojibwe requires that lay advocates be familiar with "the Constitution of the Minnesota Chippewa Tribe, the by-laws of the Band, and the codes, statutes and ordinances of the Band."[66] The Bois Forte Band of Chippewa requires that lay persons attest that they will abide by the rules and principles of the Tribal court and code, and that they have an understanding of the law, but only as it pertains to their client's case.[67]

Some Tribes require that lay advocates pass a Tribal law exam.[68] Tribal law exams vary in scope and difficulty but tend to be administered by the Tribal court or the Tribal bar and test familiarity with Tribal law and court procedure. They can range from brief personal attestations to arduous multiday examinations.[69]

Other Tribes do not require that lay advocates pass a Tribal bar exam but impose other requirements to ensure that the advocate is familiar with Tribal law. The White Earth Nation, for instance, requires that lay advocates file an affidavit that they have studied and are familiar with Tribal law.[70] The Pascua Yaqui Tribe requires that each attorney and lay advocate attend a four-hour class on Pascua Yaqui law and court procedure and complete a certification class every two years.[71] Similarly, the Iowa Tribe of Oklahoma has a Tribal practice program designed to familiarize

64 Valencia-Weber, *supra* note 15 (arguing for the inclusion of Indian law on state bar exams); Seminole Tribe of Florida Tribal Code § 3-117; Sovereign Nation of the Chitimacha Code of Justice tit. I, § 501(b); Sault Ste. Marie Tribe of Chippewa Indians Tribal Code § 87.110.

65 Cherokee Nation Tribal Code appendix I to tit. 20, Rule 140. *See also* Fond du Lac Band of Lake Superior Chippewa Tribal Civil Code § 113; Burns Paiute Tribal Code § 1.1.81 (requiring spokesmen to swear they have read and are familiar with the Tribal law and order code).

66 Leech Lake Band of Ojibwe Judicial Code tit. 1, pt. v, § 3.

67 Bois Forte Band of Chippewa Tribal Code § 114(b).

68 *See, for example,* Kickapoo Tribe in Kansas Tribal Code, Rule 106; The Laws of the Gros Ventre & Assiniboine Tribes tit. 1, § X(B); Crow Tribe of Montana Tribal Code § 3-7-702; Winnebago Tribal Code § 1-400(5); Citizen Potawatomi Nation Tribal Code, Rule 8-1-101(C); Iowa Tribe of Oklahoma Tribal Code, Rule 101(C); Keweenaw Bay Indian Community Code of Ordinances § 1.208(C)(1); Klamath Tribal Codes tit. 2, § 11.35(b)(3).

69 *See, for example,* Navajo Nation Bar Association Bylaws, section V (detailing the format and scope of the Navajo Nation Bar Examination to include being offered twice a year, and to cover Navajo Common Law, the Navajo Nation Code, Navajo Nation Supreme Court decisions, as well as federal Indian law, contracts, criminal law, Navajo Fundamental law, Navajo civil and criminal procedure, Navajo peacemaking, Navajo property law, Navajo rules of evidence, Navajo rules of professional conduct, torts, and the Treaty of 1868). *Also see, for example,* Reno-Sparks Indian Colony Tribal Code, § 1-80-020(a) (requiring representatives to state an oath that they are "familiar with the Tribal Law and Order Code").

70 White Earth Nation Judicial Code, ch. v, § 2.

71 Pascua Yaqui Tribal Code tit. 3, ch. 1-4, § 20.

applicants with practice before the Tribal court.[72] In contrast, the Hoh Tribe requires that lay advocates demonstrate "knowledge of the culture and traditions of the Hoh people,"[73] potentially gesturing to the unique potential for lay advocates to use their cultural knowledge to supplement the building of customary law.[74]

To capture some of the basic legal skills that law school is credited with imparting, some lay advocate competency provisions require advocates to demonstrate certain skills. The Fort McDowell Yavapai Nation holds non-attorney advocates to the same standards of knowledge and ability as are expected of attorneys.[75] The Seminole Tribe and the Sault Ste. Marie Tribe of Chippewa Indians require that lay advocates possess good communication skills, have legal work experience, and the ability to perform legal research.[76] By contrast, the Mississippi Band of Choctaw Indians Tribal Code requires the Chief Justice to assess the competence of lay advocates prior to their admission to practice before the Choctaw courts.[77]

11.2.5 *Ethical Advocacy*

Once lay advocates are qualified, Tribal codes are primarily concerned with the substance of lay advocates' work. Like competence, the Tribal codes seek to narrow the professional responsibility gap between attorneys and advocates by extending comparable expectations to attorneys and Tribal lay advocates. In doing so, Tribes are generating a novel body of ethical rules particular to lay advocates.

11.2.5.1 Acceptance of Risk

Some Tribes require litigants to acknowledge their lay advocate is not an attorney and accept the risk.[78] Taking this tack, the Hopi Tribe and the Pascua Yaqui Tribe

72 Iowa Tribe of Oklahoma Tribal Code tit. I, Rule 101(B). The Rules presently describe the Tribal practice program as an aspirational program they desire for the Committee on Iowa Tribe of Oklahoma Committee on Admissions and Grievances to establish.

73 Hoh Law & Order Code § 1.8.16. *See also* Seminole Tribe of Florida Tribal Code § 3-117(H) (requiring lay advocates to have legal experience in Tribal court, and know and understand Tribal traditions and customs).

74 *See, for example,* van Schilfgaarde, *supra* note 20, at 103, 139 (noting the work of Tribes to increasingly incorporate "custom and tradition within Tribal justice systems to help transform such systems back into truly Indigenous systems").

75 Fort McDowell Yavapai Nation Law & Order Code § 1-25.

76 Seminole Tribe of Florida Tribal Code § 3-117; Sault Ste. Marie Tribe of Chippewa Indians Tribal Code § 87.110.

77 Mississippi Band of Choctaw Indians Tribal Code tit. I, § 1-4-1. The code does not specify how the Chief Justice makes this assessment, giving them total discretion.

78 *See, for example,* Kiowa Indian Tribe of Oklahoma Code of Law tit. 1, § 1.6.5 (limiting lay advocates to civil matters, traffic violations, and misdemeanor criminal matters, but only if the defendant knowingly waives their right to an attorney); Klamath Tribal Codes tit. 2, § 11.35(c) (permitting lay advocates for any criminal matters, but only if the defendant has knowingly waived their right to counsel).

permit lay advocates for criminal cases but only when the defendant has knowingly waived their rights to counsel.[79] Some codes reflect higher expectations of lay advocates. For example, the Fort McDowell Yavapai Nation statutorily holds non-attorney advocates to the same standards of knowledge and ability as are expected of attorneys,[80] clarifying that persons who retain the services of non-attorney advocates do so at their own risk.[81] In contrast, the Cherokee Nation requires that litigants make a verified statement they understand the lay advocate is not a trained lawyer, but also permits malpractice claims against lay advocates who fail to uphold the same standards of expertise as a trained, licensed lawyer.[82] The Colorado River Indian Tribes explicitly shift the burden to the Tribal court to advise parties who are not represented by an attorney of their right to request a jury.[83] These provisions help to put the litigant on notice that lay advocates are not barred as attorneys, while preserving some protections for the litigant, including an expectation of performance by the lay advocate.

11.2.5.2 Ethical Requirements and Expectations

Some Tribal codes impose significant ethical expectations for lay advocate performance and accountability. For example, some codes define lay advocates as officers of the court[84] and/or extend the Tribal rules of professional ethics to both attorneys and lay advocates.[85] The Pascua Yaqui Tribe incorporates the ABA Model Rules of Professional Conduct to lay advocates.[86] The Fort McDowell Yavapai Nation adopts the ABA Model Rules for both attorneys and lay advocates, alongside "such standards as may be established by tribal law or court rule in performances of their duties as legal counsel,"[87] while the Keweenaw Bay Indian Community provides seven ethical rules applicable to all "practitioners" before the Court.[88]

[79] Hopi Code § 1.6.5; Pascua Yaqui Tribal Code tit. 3, ch. 1-4, § 40.

[80] Fort McDowell Yavapai Nation Law & Order Code § 1-25.

[81] *Id.*

[82] *Id.*

[83] Colorado River Indian Tribes Law & Order Code, art. II, § 203(h).

[84] *See, for example*, White Mountain Apache Judicial Code § 2.22(C).

[85] *See, for example, Id.* § 2.27; Sovereign Nation of the Chitimacha Code of Justice tit. I, §§ 504, 505(a); Sault Ste. Marie Tribe of Chippewa Indians Tribal Code § 87.106; Crow Tribal Code § 3-7-702; Winnebago Tribe of Nebraska Tribal Code tit. 1, art. 4, § 1-400(3); Pueblo of Zuni Tribal Code § 1-5-1; Cheyenne River Sioux Tribal Code § 1-5-6; Flandreau Santee Sioux Law & Order Code tit. 1, § 1-5-1.

[86] Pascua Yaqui Tribal Code tit. 3, ch. 1-4, § 10. *See also* Mohegan Tribe of Indians of Connecticut Code of Ordinances, pt. II, ch. 1, art. I., § 1-7 (extending the Connecticut Rules of Professional Conduct to non-attorneys). *See also* Mashpee Wampanoag Tribe, Administrative Order #7 (adopting the Massachusetts Rules of Professional Conduct); In re Adoption of Revised Rules of Professional Conduct for Attorneys, Ho-Chunk Nation Supreme Court SCR 20:1.1.5 (Feb. 22, 2016) (adopting the Wisconsin Rules of Professional Conduct).

[87] Fort McDowell Yavapai Nation Law & Order Code § 1-25(D).

[88] Keweenaw Bay Indian Community Tribal Code tit. § 2-47.

Some codes have adopted ethical rules that are particular to lay advocates. Numerous Tribal code provisions require that the lay advocate be of good moral character and/or not have criminal convictions.[89] The Citizen Potawatomi Nation requires that lay advocates pass a moral fitness assessment.[90] The Seminole Tribe requires lay advocates to only follow the portion of the ABA Model Rules relating to the attorney-client relationship, candor, and integrity,[91] and the Nooksack Indian Tribe has a distinct Advocate's Code of Conduct and imposes additional responsibilities on professional attorneys.[92] The Mohegan Tribe of Connecticut permits the Chief Judge to waive certain Rules of Professional Conduct "for the purpose of application to non-attorney spokespersons, but shall enforce them to the maximum extent possible," that is – the court will enforce the remaining applicable rules as applied to non-attorney spokespersons to the maximum extent applicable.[93] Nevertheless, under the Mohegan Tribal Code, spokespeople may be held in contempt of court for misbehavior, other willful neglect, a violation of duty in their rule,[94] and in a section specifically directed at spokespersons, for "failing to maintain the respect due the Mohegan Tribal Court or engaging in offensive conduct in the courtroom."[95]

Other Tribal codes stop short of applying broad ethical codes of conduct to lay advocacy and instead adopt specific, discrete ethical provisions that apply to lay advocates. The Seminole Tribe, for instance, will remove lay advocates if they "knowingly disrespect[] the customs and traditions of the Tribe."[96] The Bois Forte Band of Chippewa requires that lay persons attest that they will advocate for their client's position.[97] The Burns Paiute requires lay advocates to swear they will maintain the respect due the Tribal court, will not represent a suit that appears to them to be unjust, and employ such means only as are consistent with truth and honor.[98]

The Yurok Tribe's governing principles for their rules of court seemingly go one step further, reflecting not only on lay advocate expectations but also on how the law generally should be applied in consideration of lay advocate participation.

89 *See, for example*, Mississippi Band of Choctaw Indians Tribal Code tit. 1, § 1-4-3 (requiring "good moral character"); Turtle Mountain Band of Chippewa Indians Tribal Codes tit. 2, § 2.1401; Burns Paiute Tribal Code § 1.1.81(a); Sovereign Nation of the Chitimacha Code of Justice tit. I, § 501(b) (in addition, the Code requires that lay counselors must not have been convicted of a felony in any jurisdiction and must not have been convicted of child abuse or neglect in any jurisdiction).

90 Citizen Potawatomi Nation Tribal Code tit. 8, Rule 8-1-101(C).

91 Seminole Tribe of Florida Tribal Code § 3-119.

92 Nooksack Indian Tribal Code § 10.02.010.

93 Mohegan Tribe of Indians of Connecticut Code of Ordinances, pt. II, ch. 1, art. I., § 1-8(a).

94 *Id.* § 1-60(a)(3).

95 *Id.* at pt. II, ch. 1, art. I., § 1-42.

96 Seminole Tribe of Florida Tribal Code § 3-120.

97 Ho Chunk Nation Tribal Code, Rules for Admission to Practice, Rule 1(A).

98 Burns Paiute Tribal Code § 1.1.81(d)–(f).

The Tribe requires lay advocates to "conduct themselves in a fashion that respects the individuals involved in the Court process and is consistent with the sovereign rights and responsibilities set out in the preamble of the Yurok Constitution and inherent in Yurok cultural practices."[99] At the same time, the Tribal code recognizes that its courts should account for lay advocate participation when resolving disputes, noting the following.

> In establishing these rules, the Yurok Tribal Council and the Yurok Court are aware that many times people will come before the Court without formal representation or with spokespersons who may not be law-trained. These rules are not meant to create an environment that favors law-trained represented persons and will not be enforced in such a manner as to create such an outcome. Rather, the rules are meant to guide the parties to a fair and just resolution by providing a framework for the resolution of issues.[100]

The Yurok Tribe has centered its values on guiding "parties to a fair and just resolution." While the Tribe does not relieve lay advocates of accountability, these governing principles explicitly signal a more flexible statutory interpretation rubric to be employed in light of lay advocate participation.

11.2.5.3 Effective Advocacy

Some Tribes have adopted ineffective assistance of counsel standards. In U.S. constitutional law the standard for effective assistance of counsel in criminal trials is established in *Strickland v. Washington*, which provides that counsel is ineffective where "counsel's conduct so undermined the proper functioning of the adversarial process that the trial cannot be relied on as having produced a just result."[101] Because the ICRA does not provide a right to counsel, and because Tribes are not compelled to follow *Strickland*, Tribes are not required to guarantee effective assistance of counsel unless they do so through Tribal law.[102] The Hopi Tribe has done just that, adopting the *Strickland* standard as applied to attorneys (but not lay advocates).[103]

In 2005, the Hualapai Court of Appeals followed suit in *Bender v. Hualapai Tribe*, including the requirement that the attorney's actions be reasonable under the circumstances in light of prevailing professional norms.[104] Notably, *Bender* extends the *Strickland* test to non-attorney lay advocates. In compliance with the Hualapai

99 *Id.* § 2.20.050.

100 Yurok Tribal Code § 2.10.010.

101 466 U.S. at 692–93.

102 Kimmelman v. Morrison, 477 U.S. 365, 377 (1985) (explaining that "the right to counsel is the right to effective assistance of counsel").

103 Navasie v. Hopi Tribe, No. 98AC000015 (Nov. 16, 1999), 1999.NAHT.0000010.

104 Bender v. Hualapai Tribe, 2005-AP-001, 5 (Hualapai Court of Appeals, 2005).

Constitution,[105] the Tribe provided the appellant with an advocate at trial, not a licensed attorney. The Hualapai Court noted that the professional norms used to determine the standard of professional conduct must take into account the difference between licensed attorneys and non-attorney advocates,[106] and that the standard must take into account the different contexts of Tribal and non-Native legal systems.[107] However, the court held that even a lay advocate should have been expected to request a continuance to adequately prepare, to protest the absence of a preliminary hearing, or both.[108] The lay advocate was consequently found to have provided ineffective assistance.[109]

11.3 CONCLUSION

The Tribal code offers just one small window into the role of the lay advocate within Tribal courts. But the code reveals promising insights. Tribal courts, particularly within the criminal realm, are severely limited in the authority they can exercise, while also pressured to assert that surviving authority in a specifically Anglo-adversarial way. Yet, despite operating Anglo-adversarial-type courts, and despite suffering a lack of lawyers, the Tribal code makes clear that the lay advocate is serving more than just a gap-filler for lawyers.

Lay advocate eligibility criteria often prioritize Tribal members and familiarity with Tribal law. The lay advocate is not just offering some legal training; they are offering a wholly new form of competence to the Tribal court – enhancing the Tribal court's legitimacy and the building of Tribal law. Ethical protocols, meanwhile, are being applied to the lay advocate in ways that suggest lay advocates can operate within their own realm of accountability, transparency, and community norms.

Outside of Tribal courts, lay advocate critics have raised concerns over the quality and performance of nonlawyers, including those who are licensed and regulated.[110] The fact that some Tribes specifically exclude lay advocates from practice suggests they may harbor similar concerns.[111] But for at least some Tribes, Tribal lay advocates are "welcome in the courtroom."[112] The codification of lay advocacy reveals a

[105] Hualapai Constitution, art. VI, § 13(c) (providing that a criminal defendant is entitled to "the assistance of an advocate for his defense admitted to practice before the Tribal Courts").

[106] Bender v. Hualapai Tribe, 2005-AP-001, *supra* note 104, at 6.

[107] *Id.*

[108] *Id.*

[109] *Id.*

[110] Statz et al., *supra* note 3, at 356 (citing Deborah L. Rhode & Lucy Buford Ricca, *Protecting the Profession or the Public: Rethinking Unauthorized-Practice Enforcement*, 82 Fordham L. Rev. 2587, 2593–94 (2014).

[111] *See, for example*, Osage Nation Code tit. 5, § 1-111(c) ("Lay counselors not admitted to any state bar association . . . are prohibited from appearing before the Courts to represent any party".).

[112] Statz et al., *supra* note 3, at 359.

concerted effort to provide enhanced access to advocacy that is likely more familiar with the Tribal court process. And given their ties to Tribal communities, cultures, and traditions, Tribal lay advocates may assist in enhancing dignity within the Anglo-adversarial process.[113] Access to justice requires access not just to legal information but additional human resources. To the extent the attorney serves as a bridge between "access" and "justice,"[114] the lay advocate too can be a bridge – for the advancement of Tribal law, for the preservation of Tribal custom, and for the substantive access of Tribal communities to Tribal justice.

[113] *Id.* at 373 (noting procedural due process, at its most basic, is notice and an opportunity to be heard, which requires a connection to human dignity).
[114] *Id.* at 374.

12

Necessary but Insufficient?

Reforms to Legal Services Regulation, Technology, and the Role of the Courts in Increasing Access to Justice in England and Wales

Natalie Byrom

The introduction of the Legal Services Act 2007[1] (LSA 2007) was heralded as a "comprehensive and profound" shift in legal services regulation,[2] whose stated intention was to "put consumers first."[3] The LSA 2007 emerged in response to recommendations of successive reviews[4] confirming that the legal services market was not working for individual consumers – complaints were high, redress mechanisms were inadequate, and gaps in provision left people unable to access justice. The LSA 2007 aimed to remedy these issues through clarifying routes to redress, weakening the lawyers' monopoly on the delivery of legal services and thereby increasing access to justice. Taken together, these reforms resulted in the creation of a regulatory framework that has been described as among the least restrictive in the world.[5] However, the decision to retain as part of the LSA 2007 a regulatory regime structured around professional titles and the affirmation of six "reserved activities"[6] – which are arguably unrelated to "any conception of relative public,

[1] Legal Services Act 2007, https://www.legislation.gov.uk/ukpga/2007/29/part/1 (last accessed Feb. 4, 2025).

[2] Myles V. Lynk, *Implications of the UK Legal Services Act 2007 for US Law Practice and Legal Ethics*, 23 PRO LAW. 26, 27 (2015).

[3] Dep't Const. Affs., *The Future of Legal Services: Putting Consumers First*, CM 6679 (2005), https://assets.publishing.service.gov.uk/media/5a7c000740f0b63f7572ab8b/6679.pdf (last accessed Feb. 4, 2025).

[4] John Flood, *Will There Be Fallout from Clementi? The Repercussions for the Legal Profession after the Legal Services Act 2007*, 2012 MICH. ST. L. REV. 537 (2012).

[5] Stephen Mayson, *Independent Review of Legal Services Regulation: Assessment of the Current Regulatory Framework* 4 (UCL Ctr. Ethics & L., Working Paper LSR-0, 2020), https://www.ucl.ac.uk/ethics-law/sites/ethics_law/files/irlsr_wp_lsr-0_assessment_final_0.pdf (last accessed Feb. 4, 2025).

[6] These activities are "exercising rights of audience and rights to conduct litigation; preparing documents that relate principally to the transfer or registration of land and applications for probate; carrying out notarial functions; and administering oaths." The provision of legal advice is not a reserved activity under the Legal Services Act 2007.

market or consumer risks in the twenty-first century"[7] – has created complexity and uncertainty that have undermined innovation in the interests of access to justice. Crucially, the reforms have failed to reorient the market toward the delivery of legal services to individuals on low incomes, a position exacerbated by the subsequent withdrawal of public funding for civil, family, and criminal legal aid in 2013. This combination of factors has led to a dramatic increase in the number of people representing themselves in legal proceedings, which in turn, has placed significant pressure on the courts and tribunals.

In the face of growing delays and a government unwilling to invest in the court system in the absence of extensive reform, in 2014, the Ministry of Justice and Senior Judiciary set in motion plans to harness technology to improve the efficiency of the courts by introducing new digital ways of working. By 2016, the scale and scope of these plans had been significantly expanded to include the adoption of in-court digital technology, online dispute resolution (ODR), online hearings, an expanded role for Case Officers,[8] and reductions in the workforce and physical court estate[9] – creating a £1.3 billion public sector technology program "unmatched anywhere in the world" in terms of breadth and aspiration. The reform program intended to produce a "single online system for starting and managing cases" that would "help people to understand their rights and what options are open to them"[10] and encourage earlier settlement of cases and uptake of alternative dispute resolution. Original proposals for this single online system included the intention to create automated processes to help litigants understand their rights and provide them with basic legal advice – making the justice system more navigable for self-represented litigants. Crucially, these new systems would not primarily be purchased "off the shelf" from the private sector but designed and built by HM Courts and Tribunals Service (HMCTS)[11] with input from the judiciary and other key stakeholders.[12]

7 Stephen Mayson, *Independent Review of Legal Services Regulation: The Scope of Legal Services Regulation* 5 (Working Paper LSR-2, 2020), https://www.ucl.ac.uk/ethics-law/sites/ethics_law/files/irlsr_wp_lsr-2_scope_final.pdf (last accessed Feb. 4, 2025).

8 These are administrative staff with delegated judicial powers to facilitate earlier settlement between parties.

9 Bos. Consulting Grp., *HM Courts and Tribunals Service Reform Programme: Independent Review* 3 (2016), https://www.transformjustice.org.uk/wp-content/uploads/2023/11/BCG-Report-for-Release.pdf (last accessed Feb. 5, 2025).

10 Ministry of Just. et al., *Transforming Our Justice System* 6 (2016), https://assets.publishing.service.gov.uk/media/5a803d9ae5274a2e8ab4f019/joint-vision-statement.pdf [hereinafter Ministry of Justice Report] (last accessed Feb. 4, 2025).

11 An executive agency of the Ministry of Justice, jointly accountable to the Lord Chancellor and the Senior Judiciary for the administration of the courts. For a detailed examination of the adequacy of arrangements for the governance of HMCTS and their impact on the effective administration of the courts, please see Natalie Byrom, *Where Has My Justice Gone? Current Issues in Access to Justice in England and Wales*, Nuffield Found. (2024), https://www.nuffieldfoundation.org/wp-content/uploads/2024/Where-has-my-justice-gone.pdf (last accessed Feb. 4, 2025).

12 Bos. Consulting Grp., *supra* note 9, at 4.

The stated aim of these reforms was to produce a courts and tribunals system that is "just, and proportionate and accessible to everyone."[13]

Almost from its inception, the reform program was beset by delays and challenges.[14] Between 2017 and 2020 the program was repeatedly scaled back and the timetable for delivery extended.[15] By 2019, official communications from HMCTS seemed to indicate that they were quietly retreating from proposals for a publicly funded and designed pre-court automated process to help parties understand their rights – arguably the flagship initiative of the program in terms of improving access to justice.[16] The COVID-19 pandemic served to exacerbate existing issues, diverting key staff to focus on recovery plans and delaying the roll-out of existing projects,[17] while also intensifying significant case backlogs. By February 2023, the UK National Audit Office reported that even though HMCTS had only £120 million left of its total £1.3 billion budget, only twenty-four out of forty-four reform projects had been completed.[18]

In the face of a reform program that has failed to deliver on its original ambition and scope, and the absence of further public funding, the government and senior judiciary are now, once again, looking to the market to deliver solutions that will reduce pressure on the courts and increase access to justice. In November 2023, the Lord Chancellor[19] and senior judiciary announced a new vision for the future of civil and family courts and tribunals,[20] one that will harness technology and data standards to join up information, support, and dispute resolution services provided by the private sector. This future digital justice system has been described by the

[13] Ministry of Justice Report, *supra* note 10, at 4.

[14] Nat'l Audit Off., *Early Progress in Transforming Courts and Tribunals Session* 24 (2018), https://www.nao.org.uk/wp-content/uploads/2018/05/Early-progess-in-transforming-courts-and-tribunals.pdf (last accessed Feb. 4, 2025).

[15] Nat'l Audit Off., *Progress on the Courts and Tribunals Reform Programme Session* 17 (2023), https://www.nao.org.uk/wp-content/uploads/2023/02/progress-on-courts-and-tribunals-reform-programme-1.pdf [hereinafter Nat'l Audit 2023] (last accessed Feb. 4, 2025).

[16] Susan Acland-Hood, *How Do We Work out When to Stick, and When to Twist?*, Inside HMCTS (Feb. 28, 2019), https://insidehmcts.blog.gov.uk/2019/02/28/how-do-we-work-out-when-to-stick-and-when-to-twist/ (last accessed Feb. 4, 2025).

[17] Nat'l Audit 2023, *supra* note 15, at 15.

[18] *Id.* at 48.

[19] The Lord Chancellor and Secretary of State for Justice is appointed by the Monarch on the advice of the Prime Minister and is a senior member of cabinet. By law, the Lord Chancellor is the minister of the Crown responsible for the administration of the courts and legal aid in England and Wales. In their capacity as Secretary of State for Justice, the Lord Chancellor also administers the prison system and probation services in England and Wales. Prior to 2005, the Lord Chancellor was also head of the judiciary and a senior judge of the House of Lords in its judicial capacity. However, under the Constitutional Reform Act 2005, the Lord Chancellor was replaced as head of the judiciary by the Lord Chief Justice, and the Lord Chancellor may no longer sit as a judge.

[20] Ministry of Just. et al., *Vision for the Future of Civil and Family Courts and Tribunals*, U.K. Gov't (Nov. 20, 2023), https://www.gov.uk/government/news/vision-for-the-future-of-civil-and-family-courts-and-tribunals (last accessed Feb. 4, 2025).

Senior Judiciary as a "public private partnership"[21] that moves "away from state controlled centralised systems"[22] – signaling a clear departure from the approach underpinning the court reform program.

As part of this vision, data standards specified and governed by a newly created committee – the Online Procedure Rule Committee (OPRC) – will be used to support the seamless transfer of client data between private sector digital information, advice, and dispute resolution providers, and eventually onto the courts, where necessary.[23] This new vision raises several fundamental questions relating to:

- the willingness of the market to deliver digital information, advice, and dispute resolution services aimed at individual consumers on low incomes – particularly those with legal problems in the areas of law formerly funded by legal aid;
- the incentives for private providers to transfer cases to the public justice system;
- the willingness of private companies to participate in a court-centric set of technical and data standards and the impact on fairness and access to justice should they choose to demur; and
- the capacity of the OPRC to oversee the delivery of proposals that appear, on the basis of existing information, to surpass in aspiration, scope, and difficulty of previous initiatives in financial services, specifically the UK Open Banking initiative[24] – which has itself been described as "ambitious, complex and world leading."[25]

Finally, the proposals, which rely on the existence and widespread public adoption of private sector digital information, advice, and dispute resolution services, call into question the adequacy of the scope of regulation established by LSA 2007.

[21] Lord Just. Colin Birss, *The 24th Competition Law Association Burrell Lecture: Is a Focus on Data the Way to Improve Access to Justice in Multifaceted World?*, U.K. JUDICIARY (Dec. 6, 2023), https://www.judiciary.uk/speech-by-lord-justice-colin-birss-is-a-focus-on-data-the-way-to-improve-access-to-justice-in-a-multifaceted-world/ (last accessed Feb. 4, 2025).

[22] *Id.*

[23] *Id.*

[24] The UK Open Banking initiative was developed to implement European-level legislation – the second Payment Services Directive – which was introduced with the aim of increasing competition in the payments sector through improving transparency, innovation, and supporting customer choice, while also improving consumer protection. Open banking allows customers to securely share data with trusted third parties so that a broad range of businesses can compete to provide bank customers with better financial services, more choice, and lower prices. This sharing has been made possible through mandating data standards and the creation of Application Programme Interfaces built to an open standard developed in partnership with industry.

[25] *See* KIRSTEN BAKER, COMPETITION & MKTS. AUTH., OPEN BANKING LESSONS LEARNED REVIEW 3 (2022).

Research[26] increasingly suggests that the focus of the LSA 2007 on reserved activities and titles has created uncertainty, which has hindered the growth of new technology-based models of legal advice and support. Further, the structure of the LSA 2007 has placed many providers of technology-assisted legal information and advice services outside of the scope of legal services regulation. Successive research has highlighted the "credibility gap"[27] affecting unregulated businesses, particularly those that operate in the tech and data space, and the impact of this gap on public trust and adoption.[28] The imperative to successfully implement this latest set of reforms may therefore finally force a wholesale reconsideration of the regime established by the LSA 2007, specifically, the replacement of existing reserved activities and title-based regulation with a principled, risk-based approach capable of encompassing currently unregulated digital information, advice, and dispute resolution services.

This chapter is structured as follows. Section 12.1 briefly outlines the measures introduced as part of the LSA 2007, specifically focusing on those elements of the regulatory framework that were intended to increase access to justice. Section 12.2 presents a critical appraisal of these reforms and their impact. Section 12.3 describes the attempts made by government and the senior judiciary between 2015 and 2023 to harness public sector technology to address access-to-justice challenges in England and Wales, focusing principally on the digital court reform program. Section 12.4 describes some of the issues with delivery that have plagued the reform program, with a particular focus on one of the flagship initiatives intended to improve access to justice for individual consumers – the Online Solutions Court. Section 12.5 outlines what is currently known about new plans to leverage services designed and operated by the private sector to deliver digital pathways to and through the justice system, while Section 12.6 concludes the chapter by presenting some of the key questions that these nascent plans pose – questions with significant implications for the future of legal service regulation in England and Wales.

12.1 THE LEGAL SERVICES ACT 2007: REFORMING REGULATION TO INCREASE ACCESS TO JUSTICE?

The LSA 2007 was introduced to tackle systemic issues with the operation of the legal services market – particularly the parts of the sector that serve individual, rather than corporate clients. By 2004, complaints against legal service providers for

[26] Legal Servs. Bd., *Technology and Innovation in Legal Services: An Analysis of a 2022 Survey of Legal Service Providers* 10 (2023), https://legalservicesboard.org.uk/wp-content/uploads/2023/06/20230425-Tech-and-Innov-survey-2022-Designed.pdf (last accessed Feb. 4, 2025).

[27] Legal Servs. Bd., *The State of Legal Services 2020: Narrative Volume* 47–48 (2020), https://legalservicesboard.org.uk/wp-content/uploads/2020/11/The-State-of-Legal-Services-Narrative-Volume_Final.pdf (last accessed Feb. 4, 2025).

[28] Ctr. for Data, Ethics & Innovation, AI Barometer Report 4 (2020).

issues including inadequate professional service, misconduct, and negligence[29] were high. In 2005, the Law Society, a consumer rights organization, reported that one-third of people considered that they had received poor service from the lawyer they had instructed.[30] Mechanisms for resolution and redress in relation to complaints, then operated by the bodies representing the profession, were "inefficient and inept,"[31] leading to extensive delays and rising backlogs. In parallel, successive independent reviews highlighted the complexity and incoherence of the regulatory regime for the legal services market, which was then overseen by twenty-two separate regulators whose remits were poorly aligned and who often failed to communicate with each other,[32] creating confusion and gaps in protection for consumers. Finally, an investigation by the Office of Fair Trading[33] raised concerns that the "lawyers monopoly" on the provision of legal services was distorting competition, negatively affecting quality and price,[34] and could no longer be justified as serving the public interest.[35]

A seminal review of the regulation of legal services, commissioned by government and led by Sir David Clementi, found that the framework that existed in 2004 had no clear objectives or principles and was inflexible, overly complex, and lacking in transparency and accountability.[36] Existing complaints mechanisms run by lawyers themselves were, at a level of principle, inadequate to secure consumer confidence.[37] In relation to competition, Clementi found that there was real and growing pressure from consumers and others as to whether the restrictive practices of the main professional bodies could still be justified. Overall, Clementi concluded, existing arrangements had "insufficient regard for the interests of consumers"[38] and should therefore be urgently reformed.

The measures introduced by the LSA 2007 were intended to address these issues by putting "the consumer first" and delivering a "simpler, more consistent regulatory framework."[39] Objectives for regulation, including the duty to improve access to justice and increase citizens understanding of their rights and duties, were introduced.[40] A new overarching regulator, the Legal Services Board, was created to

[29] Flood, *supra* note 4, at 540.
[30] *Id.* at 541.
[31] *Id.*
[32] *Id.* at 543.
[33] This is a non-ministerial government department responsible for protecting consumer interests across the UK between 1973 and April 1, 2014. *See Office of Fair Trading*, U.K. Gov'T, https://www.gov.uk/government/organisations/office-of-fair-trading (last accessed Apr. 25, 2024).
[34] Dep't Const. Affs., *supra* note 3, at 15.
[35] Flood, *supra* note 4, at 539.
[36] Dep't Const. Affs., *supra* note 34, at 17.
[37] *Id.*
[38] *Id.*
[39] *Id.* at 8.
[40] Mayson, *supra* note 5, at 3.

oversee ten frontline regulators[41] and the principle that the regulation of professionals should be independent from the representation of them was enshrined in statute[42] – addressing concerns about regulatory capture. New, clearer routes for dealing with complaint resolution and redress were introduced through the creation of the Office for Legal Complaints and the Legal Ombudsman, and a Legal Services Consumer Panel was created to ensure that the perspectives of consumers of legal services were heard and considered by regulators.

The LSA 2007 also instituted reforms to existing rules that stated that law firms had to be wholly owned by qualified lawyers through the introduction of Alternative Business Structures (ABSs). The ABSs permitted the participation in law firms of those who are not legally qualified – whether are owners, managers, or investors. In doing so, the LSA 2007 supported the ownership of legal practices by a supermarket or investment bank.[43] The creation of ABSs aimed to reduce the fragmentation[44] of the part of the profession that served individual consumers through supporting the creation of larger, multidisciplinary organizations offering both legal and nonlegal services, for example, car insurance and legal services for accident claims.[45] Through improving access to both capital and economies of scale, it was hoped that ABSs would improve access to justice – making services cheaper and closing gaps in coverage that impacted negatively on those in rural areas and less mobile consumers.[46] Improved access to capital would also, it was hoped, support innovative service delivery models through enabling firms to invest in technology, tools, and infrastructure – supporting organizations to meet legal need at scale.[47]

While the introduction of the LSA 2007 was heralded as a "comprehensive and profound shift" in legal services regulation,[48] it left one aspect of the former regime largely untouched: the set of "reserved activities"[49] that can only be undertaken by those who are appropriately qualified and expressly authorized to do so – whether

[41] These were the Solicitors Regulation Authority, the Bar Standards Board, CILEx Regulation, the Master of the Faculties, the Council for Licensed Conveyancers, the Intellectual Property Regulation Board, the Costs Lawyers Standards Board, the Institute of Chartered Accountants in England & Wales, the Institute of Chartered Accountants in Scotland, and the Association of Chartered Certified Accountants.

[42] This led to the creation of new, separate regulatory arms for the Law Society and the Bar Council – the Solicitors Regulation Authority and the Bar Standards Board.

[43] One of the first licensed ABSs was Cooperative Legal Services, owned and run by the supermarket chain, Cooperative. Flood, *supra* note 4, at 549.

[44] At the time the LSA 2007 was introduced, the English legal profession consisted of 169,002 lawyers comprising 150,128 solicitors and 15,387 barristers. There were approximately 10,400 solicitors firms, most of which (84.8 percent) had four partners or fewer – to serve a population of 62 million people. Flood, *supra* note 4, at 539.

[45] *Id.* at 548.

[46] *Id.*

[47] Dep't Const. Affs., *supra* note 34, at 21.

[48] Lynk, *supra* note 2, at 27.

[49] These activities are "exercising rights of audience and rights to conduct litigation; preparing documents that relate principally to the transfer or registration of land and applications for

individuals or entities.[50] The legal profession's monopoly is created and sustained through these six reserved legal activities, which vary significantly in content and scope.

The rationale for the decision to affirm rather than review these activities is unclear, especially since, it has been argued, the reserved activities are "not derived from any systematic or principled approach to regulation" but rather stem from "a collection of historical practices, political expediencies and anachronisms."[51] Legal activities outside the scope of the reserved activities, including the provision of legal advice, are not regulated under the LSA 2007 unless they are delivered by a legally qualified professional. This creates a curious disparity whereby legal professionals providing legal advice[52] are regulated for the delivery of that advice by the regulator for their profession, while those who are not legally qualified are not regulated for providing the same service.[53] Where non-reserved activities, for example, the provision of legal information and advice, are provided by those who are *not* legally qualified, these activities cannot be regulated by a legal services regulator, leaving consumers who rely on these services unable to access redress, other than that provided by general consumer law or under voluntary codes of practice.[54] The idiosyncratic nature of these arrangements has led to a framework that is still confusing, disproportionate, and inadequate to protect consumers from risk,[55] particularly in the context of the rise of legal technology designed to substitute for, rather than augment, services provided by legal professionals.

12.2 THE IMPACT OF THE LEGAL SERVICES ACT 2007 ON ACCESS TO JUSTICE IN ENGLAND AND WALES

Despite the stated objectives of the LSA 2007, including explicit commitments to protect consumers and improve access to justice, a growing body of evidence suggests that the revised regulatory requirements have failed to adequately address either the transactional or systemic harms that undermine access to justice in England and Wales. The following section explores what is known about the nature and impact of these harms in greater detail.

probate; carrying out notarial functions; and administering oaths." The provision of legal advice is not a reserved activity under the LSA 2007.

50 Inst. of Chartered Accts. in Eng. & Wales, *An Overview of the Legal Services Act 2007* (2017), https://www.icaew.com/-/media/corporate/files/regulations/probate-and-abs/an-overview-of-the-legal-services-act-2007.ashx (last accessed Feb. 4, 2025).

51 Mayson, *supra* note 7, at 5.

52 For example, a solicitor, barrister, or licenced conveyancer.

53 Mayson, *supra* note 7, at 5.

54 *Id.*

55 Stephen Mayson, *Independent Review of Legal Services Regulation: The Focus of Legal Services Regulation* 30 (Working Paper LSR-3, 2020), https://www.ucl.ac.uk/ethics-law/sites/ethics_law/files/irlsr_wp_lsr-3_focus_final.pdf (last accessed Feb. 4, 2025).

12.2.1 *Transactional Harms*

Transactional harms are harms that accrue from the "unsatisfactory engagement of legal services,"[56] such as receiving inaccurate or inappropriate legal results, failing to exercise legal rights, or purchasing unnecessary or inappropriate legal services,[57] which can lead to both economic and wider forms of detriment. The scope of the LSA 2007 resulted in the creation of a large unregulated sector of legal service providers. Research published by the Legal Services Board in 2022 suggests that unregulated businesses have up to a 9 percent share of the overall legal services market serving individual consumers.[58] The same research found that while most people were satisfied with the service provided by all types of providers, those using unregulated providers were most likely to report dissatisfaction with the service they received. Limited data gathered from consumer rights charities and ombudsmen schemes suggests that issues with unregulated providers (such as receiving poor advice) have negative impacts on consumers including lost time, lost money, and worse health or well-being.[59] The true scale of transactional harms experienced by users of the unregulated legal sector is arguably obscured by the fact that the limited data that does exist is derived from consumer complaints. The exclusion of consumers of unregulated legal services from access to the accessible, centralized redress schemes created by the LSA 2007 has created significant barriers to reporting harms in the very parts of the legal services market that are subject to the least *ex ante* quality assurance and regulatory oversight. In the absence of access to bodies like the Office for Legal Complaints and Legal Ombudsmen, individuals who purchase services from unregulated legal service providers must rely on remedies under consumer law or voluntary codes of practice, which are difficult to access. Excluding consumers of unregulated legal services from centralized complaint and redress mechanisms also undermines the ability of regulators and policymakers to gather data on the prevalence of harm. While the Office for Legal Complaints and the Legal Ombudsman are required to collect and publish data on the scale and nature of the complaints they receive, no such requirements exist in relation to consumer law or codes of practice.

The decision to affirm rather than review or replace the preexisting reserved activities has created gaps in oversight and redress that expose individual consumers to transactional harms. In particular, the failure to bring the provision of initial legal

56 Stephen Mayson, UCL Ctr. for Ethics & L., *Consumer Harm and Legal Services: From Fig Leaf to Legal Well-being*, Supplementary Report of the Independent Review of Legal Services Regulation, at v (2022), https://www.ucl.ac.uk/ethics-law/sites/ethics_law/files/irlsr_supplementary_report_2022_final_220413.pdf (last accessed Feb. 4, 2025).

57 *Id.*

58 Legal Servs. Bd., *Mapping Unregulated Legal Services: Research Report* 5 (2022), https://legalservicesboard.org.uk/wp-content/uploads/2022/06/20220616-Mapping-unregulated-legal-services-FINAL-1.pdf (last accessed Feb. 4, 2025).

59 *Id.* at 6.

information and advice within the scope of the LSA 2007 exposes consumers to the risk that they may fail to exercise their legal rights or receive inappropriate legal services. Successive research studies have found that legal problem-resolution strategy is strongly correlated with accurate understanding of rights, awareness of legal services, and correct problem characterization.[60] As such, access to accurate and appropriate initial information and advice is a fundamental prerequisite for securing effective legal services and outcomes. The fact that the provision of initial legal information and advice currently falls outside the scope of legal services regulation (unless provided by a legal professional) exposes consumers to risk particularly in the context of the shift to technology-assisted and online models of legal information and advice, which has been led by organizations and individuals not regulated under the LSA 2007. Research published by the Legal Services Board in 2022 found that unregulated firms are more likely than firms overall to use technology (e.g., apps, chatbots, and interactive websites) to deliver services to consumers.[61] As researchers have observed, the kinds of "one-to-many" models of legal information and advice facilitated by technology have the potential to damage more people, more quickly, than a single rogue human can.[62] This risk has been recognized by both the Legal Services Board and the Competition and Markets Authority (CMA), with the latter advocating for a wholesale review of the LSA 2007 as early as 2016.

12.2.2 *Systemic Harms*

In addition to exposing consumers to transactional harms, the LSA 2007 has failed to address the systemic harm created by the fact that the market is unable to supply: "[A]ny or enough providers of legal services who are competent, local, accessible, and affordable for the legal needs in question."[63] The LSA 2007 was introduced one year prior to the global financial crisis and three years before a change of government that ushered in a series of policies aimed at significantly reducing public spending on legal services for those on low incomes. In 2010 the incoming center-right government required the Ministry of Justice to find "budget cuts of around £2 billion from an overall budget of £9.8 billion."[64] In response, the then Lord

[60] This is true in addition to other factors, including legal confidence and social norms. *See, for example*, Pascoe Pleasence et al., How People Understand and Interact with the Law ii (2015); OECD & Open Soc'y Founds., Legal Needs Surveys and Access to Justice (2019).

[61] Legal Servs. Bd., *supra* note 26, at 9.

[62] Alison Hook, *The Use and Regulation of Technology in the Legal Sector beyond England and Wales*, Rsch. Paper for the Legal Servs. Bd. 52 (2019), https://www.legalservicesboard.org.uk/wp-content/uploads/2019/07/International-AH-Report-VfP-4-Jul-2019.pdf (last accessed Feb. 4, 2025).

[63] Mayson, *supra* note 56, at 4.

[64] House of Commons Just. Comm., *Impact of Changes to Civil Legal Aid under Part 1 of the Legal Aid, Sentencing and Punishment of Offenders Act 2012*, at 5 (2015), https://publications.parliament.uk/pa/cm201415/cmselect/cmjust/311/311.pdf (last accessed Feb. 4, 2025).

Chancellor introduced legislation – the Legal Aid, Sentencing and Punishment of Offenders Act 2012 (LASPO) – with the intention of drastically reducing the amount of public funding available to support the provision of legal information, advice, and representation in relation to both civil and criminal law matters. Official figures demonstrate that following the enactment of LASPO, central government funding for civil legal advice and representation has fallen by one-third.[65]

In the face of this new funding landscape, measures introduced as part of the LSA 2007 intended to increase the number of consumer-focused legal service providers have proved inadequate. In the absence of public funding, the market has failed to respond effectively to the growing numbers of people experiencing unmet legal need. Research published by the Legal Services Board in 2020 demonstrates that every year, 3.6 million people across England and Wales have an unmet legal need involving a dispute.[66] Far from encouraging more provision in areas of consumer law, "the 'centre of gravity' in private practice has shifted further toward the generally more lucrative areas of business, commercial and institutional law and away from the needs of individual consumers and their everyday legal problems."[67] The lack of accessible legal advice and representation has also increased pressure on the courts as more people attempt to represent themselves in legal proceedings.[68] As one expert remarked, the reforms to regulation do "not appear to have revolutionized access to justice in the U.K."[69]

12.3 COMPENSATING FOR MARKET FAILURE: DIGITAL COURT REFORM TO THE RESCUE?

As early as 2014, it was becoming clear that the courts and tribunals in England and Wales were unable to cope with the substantial increase in self-represented litigants, many of which experienced difficulties in effectively presenting their case.[70] A cross-party committee of parliamentarians concluded that the court system would require "more funding to cope."[71] However, an increase in funding, without significant reform attached, was not to prove forthcoming. Speeches published by members of the Senior Judiciary confirmed that they too were confronted with "the need to

[65] In 2010–11 the civil legal aid budget was £1.346 billion, compared with £873 million in 2022–23. The criminal legal aid budget was £1.542 billion in 2010–11, declining to £926 million in 2022–23. *See* D. Clark, *Resource Department Expenditure Limit (RDEL) of Criminal and Civil Legal Aid in England and Wales from 2005/06 to 2021/22*, STATISTA (Dec. 6, 2023), https://www.statista.com/statistics/1098628/legal-aid-spending-in-england-and-wales/ (last accessed Feb. 4, 2025).

[66] Legal Servs. Bd., *supra* note 27, at 21.

[67] Mayson, *supra* note 56, at 5.

[68] House of Commons Just. Comm., *supra* note 64 at 4.

[69] David Freeman Engstrom & R. J. Vogt, *The New Judicial Governance: Courts, Data, and the Future of Civil Justice*, 72 DEPAUL L. REV. 171, 225 (2022).

[70] House of Commons Just. Comm., *supra* note 64 at 4.

[71] *Id.*

reform which is necessitated by the retrenchment of the State."[72] In this context, it was argued that the courts would have to think boldly and consider a combination of reforms in parallel, including shifting to more inquisitorial processes, simplifying court procedures, modernizing court technology, and adopting new "virtual" approaches for preliminary hearings.[73] The then-master of the rolls (the head of civil justice) went further still, stating that without radical change England and Wales would face nothing less than the "managed decline" of its justice system.[74]

In March 2014, a memo to judges and court staff announced the approval of a reform program with a budget of £375 million over five years, to commence in 2015–16. The aim of the program was to create a "sustainable and affordable system" that would also "enable the legal profession and other justice agencies to adopt more efficient and cost saving working practices by using digital technology in their dealings with the courts and tribunals."[75] From 2015 onward, several reviews exploring options for reform took place. One group, led by Professor Richard Susskind, drew inspiration from projects in the Netherlands and Canada and recommended the creation of "a new online court utilising online dispute resolution (ODR) techniques to secure efficient and effective access to justice for individuals who did not have access to a lawyer."[76] A subsequent review of the structure of the civil courts, led by Lord Justice Briggs, broadly adopted the recommendations of Professor Susskind's working group as part of plans to create a "wholly new, standalone Online Court – the Online Solutions Court."[77]

The Online Solutions Court designed by Lord Justice Briggs was structured around a three-stage process, designed to support self-represented litigants to resolve low-value claims. Stage 1 of the Online Court used decision trees to help litigants understand the nature of their legal problem and assist them in finding appropriate sources of advice, help, and support.[78] If having progressed through Stage 1, litigants were unable to resolve their issue via alternative means, they would then be supported through an automated online process to complete an application form and submit relevant documents, before progressing to Stage 2. The second stage of the Online

[72] Roger John Laugharne Thomas, Baron Thomas of Cwmgiedd, Lord C.J. of Eng. & Wales, *Reshaping Justice*, Address to Justice 3 (2014); *see also* Letter from Chris Graylin, Lord Chancellor & Sec'y St. Just. et al. (n.d.), https://www.judiciary.uk/wp-content/uploads/JCO/Documents/News+Release/REFORMING-HM-COURTS-AND-TRIBUNALS_2_.pdf (last accessed Feb. 4, 2025).

[73] Roger John Laugharne Thomas, *supra* note 72, at 4.

[74] Terence Etherton, Master of the Rolls, *The Civil Court of the Future*, Lord Slynn Memorial Lecture (June 14, 2017), https://www.judiciary.uk/wp-content/uploads/2017/06/slynn-lecture-mr-civil-court-of-the-future-20170615.pdf (last accessed Feb. 4, 2025).

[75] Letter from Lord Thomas of Cwmgiedd, Lord C.J. of Eng. & Wales et al. 1 (Mar. 28, 2014), https://www.judiciary.uk/wp-content/uploads/2014/03/joint-letter-to-judges-and-staff-hmcts-reform.pdf (last accessed Feb. 4, 2025).

[76] Etherton, *supra* note 74, at 6.

[77] *Id.* at 6.

[78] *Id.* at 9.

Court would enlist case officers – court administrators supervised by judges – to manage claims and facilitate settlement via a range of methods including mediation, online alternative dispute resolution, and early neutral evaluation.[79] If resolution was not reached via Stage 2, litigants would then proceed to Stage 3, where their claim would be adjudicated by a judge, either online, via telephone, or on the papers. Of the three stages articulated as part of his vision for the Online Solutions Court, Lord Justice Briggs considered Stage 1 to be the most important. He even went so far as to describe "interactive triage" as the "main feature of his reforms" stating that without it the court would be "as unnavigable as before."[80]

Initially, prospects for the full implementation of the Online Solutions Court looked promising. In December 2015 Lord Justice Briggs reported that his proposals were being "actively developed by the HM Courts and Tribunals Service" and that "funding is now in place for design, testing and implementation."[81] Since then, the ambition, scope, and budget, if not the timeframe for completion, had been repeatedly increased. By the autumn of 2016, the overall budget for court reform had nearly doubled.[82] Consultants brought in to advise HMCTS on their plans described the overall breadth and aspiration of the reform program as "unmatched anywhere in the world,"[83] stating that "no other system has attempted a reform programme that is so broad in terms of widespread adoption of digitalization, introduction of structural changes in court personnel and rationalisation of estate and workforce."[84] What is more, the new digital services contemplated as part of the reform program would not primarily be purchased "off the shelf" but designed and built by HMCTS with input from the judiciary and other key stakeholders, albeit with extensive support from teams of external consultants and staff on fixed term and temporary contracts.[85] Beyond improving the efficiency of the courts, successful delivery of the reform program was positioned as critical to the delivery of a range of wider access-to-justice policies: specifically, those intended to pump-prime the nascent LawTech sector[86] by encouraging innovation and improving access to court data.

79 *Id.*

80 Frederick Wilmot-Smith, *Justice eBay Style*, London Rev. Books (Sept. 26, 2019), https://www.lrb.co.uk/the-paper/v41/n18/frederick-wilmot-smith/justice-ebay-style (last accessed Feb. 4, 2025).

81 Lord Justice Briggs, Judiciary of Eng. & Wales, *Civil Courts Structure Review: Interim Report* 75–76 (2015), https://www.judiciary.uk/wp-content/uploads/2016/01/CCSR-interim-report-dec-15-final-31.pdf (last accessed Feb. 4, 2025).

82 Joshua Rozenberg, *The Online Court: Will IT Work?*, Legal Educ. Found. (July 2020), https://long-reads.thelegaleducationfoundation.org/hmcts-reform/ (last accessed Feb. 4, 2025).

83 Bos. Consulting Grp., *supra* note 9, at 4.

84 *Id.*

85 *Id.*

86 Ministry of Just., *Legal Support: The Way Ahead*, OGL (2019), https://assets.publishing.service.gov.uk/media/5c5b3a0840f0b676e6ddc6dc/legal-support-the-way-ahead.pdf (last accessed Feb. 4, 2025).

12.4 FAILURE TO DELIVER: THE CURIOUS CASE OF THE ONLINE SOLUTIONS COURT

The recommendations made by Lord Justice Briggs, including the proposal for the creation of an Online Solutions Court, were accepted and formally endorsed by the Senior Judiciary in a joint statement published in January 2017.[87] A speech published in June 2017 by the newly appointed Master of the Rolls seemed to confirm that plans to introduce an Online Solutions Court – including the Stage 1 "interactive triage" that Lord Justice Briggs considered to be the "main feature" of his proposals – were still a crucial element of the overall program.

However, by January 2019, any mention of Stage 1 with its "automated, interactive triage" had been dropped altogether from official communications published by HMCTS. At this point, HMCTS published a document articulating their revised vision for the reform program.[88] All mention of Stage 1 was omitted. Instead, and as had been the case prior to reform, the document stated that the journey for users would begin at the point at which they completed a claim form, which they could at that point already do online.

At the time of writing, new systems matching Lord Justice Brigg's vision have still not been launched, but neither has their abandonment been formally announced by government. In total and as described in the introduction above, only twenty-four of the planned forty-four reform projects have been marked as complete by HMCTS, and less than £120 million of the £1.3 billion budget allocated remains. The National Audit Office, reviewing the progress of the court reform program for the third time in 2023, found that:

> it remains difficult to understand whether HMCTS has delivered the full intended scope for projects that it classes as complete. This is because HMCTS classes a project as complete when it considers that the service provides sufficient functionality, even if HMCTS has not developed all the service's intended scope.[89]

Damningly, the National Audit Office reported that HMCTS may itself not know whether projects have delivered on their original promise – due to a failure to either

[87] Press Release, Cts. & Tribunals Judiciary, *Civil Courts Structure Review: Joint Statement from the Lord Chief Justice and the Master of the Rolls* (Jan. 6, 2017), https://www.judiciary.uk/guidance-and-resources/civil-courts-structure-review-joint-statement-from-the-lord-chief-justice-and-the-master-of-the-rolls/ (last accessed Feb. 4, 2025).

[88] H.M. Cts. & Tribunals Serv., *Putting People at the Heart of Reform: Response to PAC Recommendation* 2 JUST. MATTERS (Jan. 2019), https://assets.publishing.service.gov.uk/media/5c5405a0e5274a49487aef54/Public_Accounts_Committee_Recommendation_2_31_Jan_2019.pdf (last accessed Feb. 4, 2025).

[89] H.M. Cts. & Tribunals Serv., *Progress on the Courts and Tribunals Reform Programme* 21 (Feb. 2022–23), https://www.nao.org.uk/reports/progress-on-the-courts-and-tribunals-reform-programme/ (last accessed Feb. 4, 2025).

adequately define and document the initial scope of projects or routinely monitor the outstanding work needed to deliver them.[90]

12.5 A NEW VISION FOR THE FUTURE? BACK TO THE MARKET TO DELIVER A DIGITAL JUSTICE SYSTEM

In the face of growing awareness that the digital reform program had failed to deliver its original ambition and scope, despite HMCTS having spent 90 percent of the agreed £1.3 billion budget, a different approach was urgently needed. The imperative to reform the courts and tribunals to reduce their ongoing cost had not disappeared – in fact, the context of significant case backlogs across the civil and family courts and tribunals,[91] exacerbated by the COVID-19 pandemic, strengthened the imperative to improve efficiency. However, a challenging fiscal environment precipitated by a range of global and domestic factors[92] rendered the prospect of further significant government investment in the courts and tribunals system unlikely.

In response to this environment, in November 2023, the Lord Chancellor and senior judiciary announced a new vision for the future of civil and family courts and tribunals.[93] Their short published statement sets out a bold ambition to harness AI and technology to create a joined-up process for people attempting to navigate third- and private-sector providers of information, advice, and dispute resolution, and facilitate seamless transfer to the courts where necessary.[94] The OPRC, established by the Judicial Review and Courts Act 2022, is intended to play a key role in delivering this vision, by using its powers to set rules and standards, including data standards, for both online court-based dispute resolution services and "digital pre-action portals and other processes."[95] The Master of the Rolls, Sir Geoffrey Vos, inaugural Chair of the OPRC, had previously stated that the creation of the OPRC signaled an end to the fixation on court-based systems, and the beginning of a process of creating a "truly holistic Digital Justice System."[96] The focus of the OPRC's rulemaking will be on "providing architectural coherence and integration"[97] between private and non-court providers of dispute resolution services and

[90] Nat'l Audit 2023, *supra* note 15, at 48.

[91] Byrom, *supra* note 11.

[92] Daniel Harari et al., *Rising Cost of Living in the UK* 20, House of Commons Libr. (2024), https://researchbriefings.files.parliament.uk/documents/CBP-9428/CBP-9428.pdf (last accessed Feb. 4, 2025).

[93] Ministry of Just. et al., *supra* note 20.

[94] *Id.*

[95] Sir Geoffrey Vos, Master of the Rolls, Keynote Address to the Ombudsman Ass'n, *Driving System Change and Addressing Injustice* (June 21, 2023), https://www.judiciary.uk/speech-by-the-master-of-the-rolls-driving-system-change-and-addressing-injustice/ (last accessed Feb. 4, 2025).

[96] *Id.*

[97] *Id.*

the formal justice system. This would be achieved, Vos argued, through the process of both (1) dictating high-level standards for the dispute resolution processes within the OPRC's remit and (2) setting common technical standards for digital dispute resolution platforms, including specifying the design of application programming interfaces (APIs) to support the seamless transfer of data from dispute resolution services to the courts.[98]

Lord Justice Birss, the Deputy Head of Civil Justice, elaborated on this vision in late 2023[99] and early 2024.[100] He explained that a "holistic Digital Justice System" would have four key elements. First, the aim is no longer to create a single digital "front door" to the courts, supported by a state-run "interactive triage" system for the different legal issues.[101] Instead of the public sector taking responsibility for building a "single … monolithic IT programme at huge cost and with huge complexity,"[102] routes into the court system will be designed by the private and not-for-profit sectors.[103] Providing these dispute resolution providers adhere to the data standard specified by the OPRC, they will be able to access APIs to support them in transferring cases seamlessly from their platforms to the courts. Second, the cost of building and updating digital information, advice, and dispute resolution services will be borne by the private and not-for-profit providers who develop them.[104] Accordingly, both the cost of developing digital pre-action entry-routes and the "prohibitive burden of maintenance"[105] will not be borne by government, cementing the delivery of the digital justice system as a "public private partnership."[106] Third, the data standards specified by the OPRC will be based on fields in the common database created to manage cases across the civil and family courts and tribunals.[107] This will facilitate the easy transfer of cases from private dispute resolution providers to the courts, reducing the need for users to re-enter

98 *Id.*

99 Birss, *supra* note 21.

100 Colin Birss, Lord J., Deputy Head of Just., Speech to King's College London L. Sch., *Future Visions of Justice* (Mar. 18, 2024), https://www.judiciary.uk/speech-by-the-deputy-head-of-civil-justice-future-visions-of-justice/ (last accessed Feb. 4, 2025).

101 See Birss, supra note 21. Now you might think that part of the solution to many of these problems is what has been called in the past 'a single point of entry'. If only there was a single place – a single website let's say – maybe run by the Government – to which everyone could go and it would ask them what their problem was and tell them authoritatively where they needed to go and what to do. And at one stage our thinking was centred around a set up like this. And something like that looks like that may still have a role to play. However, it does raise some difficulties and the point of this address is to explain why a data standards approach offers advantages. (Birss, *supra* note 21.)

102 *Id.*

103 *Id.*

104 *Id.*

105 *Id.*

106 *Id.*

107 *Id.*

information or upload the same documents to multiple systems.[108] Fourth, over time this data standard could be adopted by a wider range of providers, including early legal advice and assistance services, enabling seamless transfer of data from the start of individuals' advice-seeking journey and helping an individual litigant "navigate through the whole of the digital justice system before they ever get to court."[109]

12.6 DELIVERING THE NEW VISION: QUESTIONS AND CONSIDERATIONS

The goals of the new vision for the digital justice system, especially those that relate to simplifying the experience of navigating both legal services and the courts for individual consumers, are laudable. However, for the proposals as currently expressed to be implemented successfully, a series of issues and questions must be addressed. These are outlined in the concluding section of the chapter (Section 12.7).

12.6.1 *Is the Market Capable of Delivering Digital Legal Information, Advice, and Dispute Resolution Services in the Areas of Law Where There Is the Most Significant Unmet Legal Need?*

As noted above, reforms to the regulation of legal services introduced by the LSA 2007 have failed to encourage the development of new business models[110] that deliver effective services to low-income, high-need clients. As a consequence, the state has been forced to step in to fund the creation of high-quality, free, or low-cost online legal information – either by designing services themselves or by providing grants to charities to deliver and maintain these services. The fragility of existing providers was highlighted last year when the cessation of a government grant to a charitable provider of legal information threatened the continuing existence of the service.[111] There are multiple recent examples of government being forced to step in to design, commission, or fund online legal information and signposting services

[108] Lord Justice Birss provides the following explanation:

> The vision is that the provider's system will – because it rests on the same building blocks – then be able to refer them on, this next stage may then involve further advice and/or bringing a civil, family or tribunal claim into the courts and tribunals system. The person selects the option to start a court action. The system has the information to do this for them, and they can then immediately see their claim on the court's system. . . . The data flows to where it is needed when it needs to do so. The data standards will in time mean that all this happens smoothly, without the person having to repeatedly tell their story or repeatedly upload documents. (*Id.*)

[109] *Id.*

[110] Legal Servs. Bd., *supra* note 27, at 12.

[111] Mondipa Fouzder, *Legal Help Website Faces Uncertain Future after Funding Ends*, L. Soc'y Gazette (July 3, 2023), https://www.lawgazette.co.uk/news/legal-help-website-faces-uncertain-future-after-funding-ends/5116516.article (last accessed Feb. 4, 2025).

where the market has failed to provide them, including the housing disrepair tool,[112] the recently issued tender for an Online Support and Advice Grant to deliver a digital service capable of providing litigants in person with legal support and advice in relation to civil, family, and tribunal problems,[113] and the announcement in the spring budget of funding for a digital "one-stop shop" for people experiencing family law issues, described as "a new online information and guidance tool to support earlier resolution of family disputes and divert cases away from the family courts, where appropriate."[114]

Issues also exist with the willingness and capacity of the market to deliver online and digital dispute resolution services in the areas of law where unmet legal need is most persistent. While several ombudsmen schemes and providers of alternative dispute resolution do exist,[115] the extent to which their services are currently delivered online is unclear. Only 3 companies out of 365 listed on the government-funded LawTech UK ecosystem tracker are described as providing digital dispute resolution services to consumers.[116] These challenges are reflected in global studies exploring the development of private, as opposed to court-based ODR schemes. As researchers noted in 2021, "ODR has not been able to find a suitable business model to motivate ODR service providers to provide sustainable services."[117] Further work is needed to understand why there has been such limited activity to date, and what support from regulators and government may be needed to develop the market further.

12.6.2 *Are There Sufficient Incentives for Private Dispute Resolution Providers to Transfer Cases to the Courts?*

The OPRC has the power to make rules that provide "for the transfer by electronic means of information held for the purposes of an online dispute resolution service to a court or tribunal."[118] Widespread adoption of the data and technical standards set by the OPRC is critical to delivering a joined-up digital justice system and reducing barriers to access for individuals and businesses. However, under the existing

[112] Richa Sharma & Michael Hay, *Housing Disrepair Online Signposting Tool: Summary of Monitoring Data and Stakeholder Interviews*, Ministry of Just. (2023), https://assets.publishing.service.gov.uk/media/6555e142046ed4000d8b99ce/MOJ_HousingDisrepairOST.pdf (last accessed Feb. 4, 2025).

[113] Ministry of Just., *Online Support and Advice Grant (OSAG Legal Support)*, Bidstats (Jan. 16, 2024), https://bidstats.uk/tenders/2024/W03/814809135 (last accessed Feb. 4, 2025).

[114] HM Treas., Spring Budget 2024, at 69 (2024).

[115] *See infra* Section 6.3.

[116] *LawtechUK Ecosystem Tracker*, LawTech UK, https://lawtechuk.io/ecosystem/ (last accessed Apr. 25, 2024).

[117] Online Dispute Resolution: Theory and Practice – A Treatise on Technology and Dispute Resolution 591 (Mohamed S. Abdel Wahab et al. eds., 2d ed. 2021).

[118] Judicial Review and Courts Act 2022, c. 35 § (1)(a) (UK), https://www.legislation.gov.uk/ukpga/2022/35/section/24 (last accessed Feb. 4, 2025).

framework, only those ODR services that wish to transfer cases to the courts will be required to abide by the data and technical standards specified by the OPRC. This may pose a challenge for the delivery of the new vision as it is unclear whether the existing business models adopted by private ODR and alternative dispute resolution (ADR) providers incentivize them to facilitate the "seamless transfer"[119] of cases to the courts.

To explain further, private ODR systems are "created by contract and rely on the agreement of the participants for their legitimacy."[120] Private ODR systems, particularly in the consumer or commercial space, are often funded by one of the parties, or one category party to a dispute (e.g., the Official Injury Claim portal, which is funded by the Motor Insurance Bureau). In many cases, businesses are able to choose which ADR or ODR provider they use; as a consequence, the marketing material produced by private ODR and ADR providers tends to emphasize their flexibility – in the sense that procedures need not always apply "strict rules of law" and their confidentiality – which enables firms to avoid the risk of "adverse publicity and reputational damage that could arise from a court case."[121] Accordingly, the business model adopted by private ODR and ADR providers creates an incentive *not* to make the transfer of cases to the courts easier, threatening the viability of new proposals.

12.6.3 *Will the Market Agree to Meet the Needs of the Public Justice System in Relation to Collecting Data to Monitor Fairness and Address Inequality of Access?*

Even where ODR providers wish to support seamless transfer of cases to the courts, it is unclear whether they will be willing to adapt their data collection practices to meet the needs of the public justice system. As noted by researchers:

> Private ODR systems are created by contract and rely on the agreement of the participants for their legitimacy. Public systems, on the other hand, are created by law and rely on the ability to protect the broad range of interests law serves – distributive justice, substantive equality, political freedom, and democratic participation – for their legitimacy. A private system is free to take the interests of only the parties to a dispute into account, but a public system must consider the interests of third parties, the legal system as a whole, and the background set of moral, social, political, and legal norms that make contract-based relationships possible. A public dispute resolution system must produce outcomes that are fair and just, not just convenient, efficient, and cheap.[122]

[119] Birss, *supra* note 21.
[120] Robert J. Condlin, *Online Dispute Resolution: Stinky, Repugnant, or Drab*, 18 Cardozo J. Conflict Res. 717, 733 (2017).
[121] *Alternative Dispute Resolution*, BusinessCompanion (last updated May 2024), https://www.businesscompanion.info/en/quick-guides/consumer-contracts/alternative-dispute-resolution (last accessed Feb. 4, 2025).
[122] Condlin, *supra* note 120, at 733–34 (citations omitted).

One way in which the courts in England and Wales have sought to demonstrate that reformed digital processes produce outcomes that are fair and just is by introducing new data collection practices to monitor the impact of digitized services on the experience of users with particular demographic and protected characteristics under the Equality Act 2010.[123] Users of digitized services are asked to complete a short questionnaire about their demographic and protected characteristics at the point at which they make an application to the courts or respond to an existing case.[124] This data is being used to undertake "access to justice impact assessments"[125] designed to identify, fix, and monitor barriers to access to justice for users from different demographic groups. To date, access-to-justice impact assessments have been completed for digital services dealing with divorce, probate, social security and child support, and online civil money claims. These impact assessments have revealed that in relation to probate and divorce service cases filed by users from ethnic minority groups were more likely to experience delays or be stopped than those filed by white applicants.[126] The findings of these impact assessments are now being used to improve services, demonstrating the importance and utility of the new data collection practices HMCTS have introduced. Private ODR providers are not required to collect or publish data on the fairness of their processes or monitor data on the demographic and protected characteristics of users. It is unclear whether they would be willing to amend their practices to support this data collection – particularly if doing so incurs additional costs. However, if they do not collect this data and are still permitted to "seamlessly transfer" cases to the courts, the opportunity to monitor fairness may be lost, undoing the significant recent progress that has been made to harness digital systems to improve the transparency, accountability, and fairness of the courts.

12.6.4 *Does the OPRC Have the Mandate and Resources Needed to Deliver the New Holistic Digital Justice System? Lessons from UK Financial Services*

Proposals to harness data and technical standards to deliver joined-up legal services and systems are unprecedented in the context of the justice system in England and

[123] Edafe Onerhime, *Monitoring Equality in Digital Public Services*, Open Data Inst. (2020), https://research.thelegaleducationfoundation.org/research-learning/funded-research/monitoring-equality-in-digital-public-services (last accessed Feb. 4, 2025).

[124] *HMCTS Protected Characteristics Questionnaire – Data on Users of Reformed Services*, U.K. Gov't (Nov. 16, 2023), https://www.gov.uk/government/publications/hmcts-protected-characteristics-questionnaire-2023/hmcts-protected-characteristics-questionnaire-data-on-users-of-reformed-services (last accessed Feb. 4, 2025).

[125] H.M. Cts. & Tribunals Serv., *Assessing Access to Justice in HMCTS Services – Summary Report*, U.K. Gov't (2023), https://www.gov.uk/government/publications/assessing-access-to-justice-in-hmcts-services/assessing-access-to-justice-in-hmcts-services-summary-report (last accessed Feb. 4, 2025).

[126] *Id.*

Wales. However, initiatives of the kind described by the Master of the Rolls and Lord Justice Birss do exist and have been implemented in the context of the UK financial services industry as part of the UK Open Banking Initiative, which was created to make it easier for customers to compare and switch banks by supporting the secure sharing and transfer of personal data.

The UK Open Banking initiative was developed in response to concerns that there was too little competition in the banking sector and that this absence of competition was undermining innovation and harming consumers. An investigation led by the CMA found that across the United Kingdom, the "four largest banks account for over 70 percent of main Personal Current Accounts and collectively have lost less than 5% market share since 2005 – despite the fact that 90 percent of consumers would benefit from switching to a cheaper product."[127] To remedy this situation, in 2017 the CMA issued an order, the Retail Banking Market Investigation Order[128] (2017 Order) which compelled the UK's nine biggest banks to open their data to third parties. The proposals contemplated the sharing of two different kinds of data in two different standardized formats. First, under the new UK Open Banking regime, the nine largest UK banks would be required to release as open data reference information about the location of their branches and ATMs, the details of their different products, and data on service quality, to an agreed data standard.[129] Second, the UK Open Banking framework made it possible for customers to securely share limited transaction data with other banks and third parties through the use of APIs.

The aim of the CMA in passing the 2017 Order was to create the infrastructure to support the publication and sharing of a limited set of clearly defined data between organizations in a concentrated market.[130] To achieve this aim, the CMA mandated the creation of an independent organization (the Open Banking Implementation Entity ("OBIE")),[131] funded by industry, with an average FTE headcount of over 100

[127] Comp. & Mkts. Auth., *Retail Banking Market Investigation: Final Report*, at x–xi (2016), https://assets.publishing.service.gov.uk/media/57ac9667e5274a0f6c00007a/retail-banking-market-investigation-full-final-report.pdf (last accessed Feb. 4, 2025).

[128] Comp. & Mkts. Auth., *The Retail Banking Market Investigation Order 2017* (2017), https://assets.publishing.service.gov.uk/media/5a759cc7ed915d506ee80283/retail-banking-market-investigation-order-2017.pdf (last accessed Feb. 4, 2025).

[129] Rowland Manthorpe, *To Change How You Use Money, Open Banking Must Break Banks*, WIRED (Oct. 16, 2017), https://www.wired.com/story/psd2-future-of-banking/ (last accessed Feb. 4, 2025).

[130] By 2022 it was reported that there were over 300 service providers enrolled in the OBIE service directory. *See* BAKER, *supra* note 25, at 3.

[131] The (OBIE) was created to "agree, consult upon, implement, maintain and make widely available without charge open and common banking standards" for the reference and transaction data specified in the 2017 Order. *The Future Oversight of the CMA's Open Banking Remedies: Response to Consultation*, COMP. & MKTS. AUTH. 2 (2022). The OBIE was established as an independent company, Open Banking Limited, funded by the nine largest UK banks and was originally overseen by the CMA. *Id.*

staff, and annual operating costs ranging between £32.7 million and £47 million.[132] The Open Banking Implementation Entity was given the power to mandate adoption of the data and technical standards developed by the nine largest UK banks with a combined market share of over 90 percent of the UK's consumer and small business accounts.[133] Additional regulatory oversight of the use of application program interfaces to guard against fraud and misuse was provided by the Financial Conduct Authority, an extremely well-resourced regulator, with support from the Information Commissioners Office. Even so, by the end of the implementation period in 2023, only six out of nine of the UK's largest banks had adopted the standards required to implement Open Banking.

In contrast, the proposals outlined for the delivery of the new holistic digital justice system contemplate creating standards and Application Programme Interfaces to support the sharing of what could amount to a considerable volume of personal and case-level data, much of which is currently unstructured. The detail of the data to be shared has not been defined. Unlike the retail banking sector, the legal services sector is highly fragmented – with nearly 9,600 firms providing services for consumers and small corporates.[134] This figure does not include not-for-profit providers and charities, or the eighty existing approved Alternative Dispute Resolution Providers and twenty Ombudsmen schemes. The body tasked with developing and specifying data and technical standards across this diffuse range of stakeholders is the Online Procedure Rule Committee, a committee comprising six members (three judicial members appointed by the Lord Chief Justice and three expert members appointed by the Lord Chancellor) supported by two sub-committees[135] staffed by volunteer members. The Ministry of Justice has allocated just £10,000 per year to pay for travel, subsistence, and publications. The impact statement published by the Ministry of Justice states that any additional costs associated with digitizing services or providing additional digital support will be funded by the HMCTS Court Reform Programme – it is not clear whether the creation and implementation of data and technical standards is included in this,[136] or who will fund this work if resource is not made available by government.

[132] OBIE, *Annual Report* 2020, at 29 (2020), https://assets.foleon.com/eu-central-1/de-uploads-7e3kk3/48197/obie-ra-artwork-10096a5716bf30-2.5853a6c2c203.pdf (last accessed Feb. 4, 2025).

[133] Press Release, Comp. & Mkts. Auth., *Millions of Customers Benefit as Open Banking Reaches Milestone* (Jan. 12, 2023), https://www.gov.uk/government/news/millions-of-customers-benefit-as-open-banking-reaches-milestone (last accessed Feb. 4, 2025).

[134] PricewaterhouseCoopers LLP, *UK Legal Services Market Report* 2022, at 6 (2022), https://www.pwc.co.uk/industries/assets/uk-legal-services-market-report-2022.pdf (last accessed Feb. 4, 2025).

[135] *Online Procedure Rule Sub-committee Member*, U.K. Gov't (Nov. 2023), https://web.archive.org/web/20240419152736/https://apply-for-public-appointment.service.gov.uk/roles/7909 (archived page) (last accessed Feb. 4, 2025).

[136] Ministry of Just., *Judicial Review and Courts Bill: Overarching Impact Assessment* 3 (2021), https://publications.parliament.uk/pa/bills/cbill/58-02/0152/JudicialReviewandCourtsBilloverarchingIAfinal.pdf (last accessed Feb. 4, 2025).

A timetable for implementation, or agreed definition of either the vision or goal, has not yet been published, and an explanation of how access to the APIs will be regulated and by whom has not yet been provided. These details may yet be forthcoming.

It is still early days, but the experience of Open Banking, an initiative that has been described as "ambitious, complex and world leading"[137] despite its comparatively limited scope, when contrasted with the new vision articulated for the digital justice system of the future, demonstrates the importance of moving swiftly to provide.

12.6.5 *What Changes to Regulation May Be Needed to Support the Adoption of Online Information, Advice, and Dispute Resolution Services?*

The delivery of the new vision for the digital justice system relies on consumers adopting and using private online information, advice, and dispute resolution services. However, as described above in Section 12.2, many of these services fall outside of the scope of existing legal services regulation, exposing consumers to the risks of transactional harms for which there is little accessible or meaningful redress. Research published by the Legal Services Board shows both that consumers are "more dissatisfied with the service they receive from unregulated providers"[138] and further that the absence of regulation and effective redress leaves unregulated businesses facing a "credibility gap" that may inhibit their growth.[139] The UK government-funded Centre for Data, Ethics and Innovation has highlighted both that an absence of clear regulatory standards and quality assurance is a key driver of public distrust,[140] and further that "in the absence of trust, consumers are unlikely to use new technologies or share the data needed to build them."[141] The imperative to deliver the new vision for a digital justice system may therefore strengthen calls to review and extend the regulatory framework established by the LSA 2007.

12.7 CONCLUSION

This chapter has attempted to demonstrate, by reference to the experience of England and Wales, that deregulation of legal service provision, while superficially attractive, is not a panacea to the access-to-justice crisis. Deregulation alone is unlikely to be sufficient to prevent market failure in the provision of effective legal services to high-need individuals on low incomes. In relation to the prospect of harnessing technology to advance access to justice, deregulation may in fact prove

[137] *See* BAKER, *supra* note 25, at 3.
[138] Legal Servs. Bd., *supra* note 27, at 34.
[139] *Id.* at 47–48.
[140] AI BAROMETER REPORT, *supra* note 28, at 4.
[141] *Id.* at 6.

counterproductive. Evidence suggests that lack of regulation may increase uncertainty for providers and foster mistrust that reduces, rather than increases the prospect of consumer adoption. As such, rather than deregulation, reregulation of legal service provision may be required – with new, evidence-based frameworks structured to respond flexibly and effectively to sources of systemic and transactional harm, including those posed by advancements in technology.

In relation to the role that courts themselves might play in encouraging new services that address legal need, judges and policymakers in England and Wales have offered two approaches. The first focused on investing in improvements in court technology to make it easier for self-represented litigants to understand their rights and navigate court processes, thereby reducing the need for legal services. This approach was exemplified by the proposal to create a new Online Solutions Court. Lack of publicly available information about why exactly the Online Solutions Court has failed to materialize makes it difficult to draw firm conclusions about the viability of this approach, although successful experience in other jurisdictions offers encouragement.

The second and most recent suggestion for the role that courts might play in improving pre-court legal services is both more novel and more speculative. It relies on the courts using their new powers to set data standards to encourage a shift in the way legal services are designed and delivered. Proponents argue that the desire of private providers to support the seamless transfer of cases to the courts will encourage the adoption of court-defined approaches to collecting and sharing data. These common standards will make it easier for individuals to transfer between providers, reducing referral fatigue and improving the navigability of legal services in the pre-court space. While successful implementation could prove transformative, at present, these proposals pose significant questions, and their complexity suggests that reaching answers may take some time. In the context of a growing access-to-justice crisis, the most pressing question is arguably whether consumers, and indeed the courts, can afford to wait.

13

Legal Tech Companies and Access to Justice in Germany*

Giesela Rühl

German civil courts enjoy a sterling reputation worldwide. According to the 2022 World Justice Project Rule of Law Index, for example, the German civil justice system ranks 4th out of 140 countries.[1] However, beneath the surface is growing cause for concern: For more than two decades, the number of cases newly submitted to German civil courts has been decreasing. This holds particularly true for the first instance local courts (*Amtsgerichte*)[2] that hear civil cases with a disputed value up to €5,000 (approx. 5,300 USD).[3] In these yeoman courts of the German system, annual filings have declined by almost 1 million cases over the past twenty-five years, from roughly 1.7 million in 1995 to some 700,000 in 2021,[4]

* The author wishes to thank the participants of the New Voices in Access to Justice Workshop at Stanford Law School, the fellows of the Rhode Center for the Legal Profession of Stanford Law School, and the participants of the CodeX Lunch Discussion Group for their helpful comments. Thanks are also due to Jakob Horn and Lino Binggeli from Humboldt University for their valuable assistance in the preparation of this chapter.

1 See *Germany: Civil Justice*, WORLD JUST. PROJECT (2022), https://worldjusticeproject.org/rule-of-law-index/country/2022/Germany/Civil%20Justice/ (last accessed Feb. 5, 2025).

2 The German civil justice system knows two different courts that may hear cases in first instance: local courts *(Amtsgerichte)* and regional courts *(Landgerichte)*. Local courts hear cases up to a value of €5,000, whereas regional courts are competent for cases exceeding a value of €5,000. *See* Gerichtsverfassungsgesetz (GVG) [Germany's Ct. Const. Act]; 1950 Bundesgesetzblatt I (BGBl. I). [Federal Law Gazette] at 455 (Ger.), §§ 23 no. 1, 71(1). There are a total of 638 local courts and 115 regional courts. For a more detailed description of the German civil justice system, including recent law reforms, see PETER MURRAY & ROLF STÜRNER, GERMAN CIVIL JUSTICE (2004); Giesela Rühl, *Preparing Germany for the 21st Century: The Reform of the Code of Civil Procedure*, 6.6 GERMAN L. J. 909 (2005).

3 Note that a loss of cases can also be observed for the regional courts (*Landgerichte*). However, that loss is not as intense. With 422,995 newly submitted cases in 1996, the intake decreased by approximately 32 percent to 289,714 in 2018. It must be noted, though, that for the regional courts, numbers have gone up since 2019 to a total of 362,890 newly submitted cases in 2021. See STATISTISCHES BUNDESAMT [FEDERAL STATISTICAL OFFICE], FACHSERIE 10 REIHE 2.1-2008 36 (Oct. 21, 2009); STATISTISCHES BUNDESAMT [FEDERAL STATISTICAL OFFICE], FACHSERIE 10 REIHE 2.1-2021 43 (Aug. 5, 2022).

4 In 1995 local courts received a total of 1,751,448 civil cases, whereas they only received a total of 753,926 civil cases in 2021. See STATISTISCHES BUNDESAMT [FEDERAL STATISTICAL OFFICE],

most of them contract claims (notably construction, insurance, sales, and lease contracts).[5]

Is this a problem? At first glance, one might be inclined to say no. Arguing that fewer cases mean less work for courts, one could think that declining case numbers are a good thing. A closer look, however, reveals that the story is more complicated: Fewer court cases probably mean that fewer claims are being enforced. To be sure, it could be that the number of cases before German courts has fallen because people have fewer legal problems and, therefore, do not need to seek assistance from the court. Or it could be that more cases are being settled through alternative dispute resolution mechanisms such as arbitration or mediation. But these reasons, even if they are true, cannot explain the staggering loss of one million cases per year.[6] Instead, chances are that a significant number of lower-value claims simply go unenforced, suggesting that Germany – like the United States – has an access-to-justice problem, albeit one with different contours: In the United States, financially distressed, self-represented individual *defendants* do not know how to navigate the court system when sued by highly professional institutional plaintiffs.[7] In Germany, by contrast, individual *plaintiffs* (very often, consumers) are refraining from pursuing their claims in court.

On closer inspection, however, things might not be as bad as they appear. In fact, like in the United States, a growing cast of nonlawyer, technology-fueled service providers have entered the German legal services market in the past ten or so years. Commonly referred to as "legal tech companies," they use digital technologies to automate, simplify, and thus improve the enforcement of lower-value, especially consumer claims. More specifically, they take easily standardizable, well-structured claims, check their legitimacy (largely) automatically with the help of algorithms and, in close cases, enforce them in return for a contingency fee.

Probably the best-known German legal tech company of this sort is the company Flightright.[8] It enforces passengers' rights under the European Air Passenger Rights Regulation[9] – a European Regulation that requires airlines to pay passengers

FACHSERIE 10 REIHE 2.1-2008 12 (Oct. 21, 2009); STATISTISCHES BUNDESAMT [FEDERAL STATISTICAL OFFICE], FACHSERIE 10 REIHE 2.1-2021 13 (Aug. 5, 2022).

5 See GERHARD WAGNER, RECHTSSTANDORT DEUTSCHLAND IM WETTBEWERB 93-9, 120 f. (2017); Caroline Meller-Hannich et al., *Abschlussbericht zum Forschungsvorhaben "Erforschung der Ursachen des Rückgangs der Eingangszahlen bei Zivilgerichten"* 40–56 (2023), https://bmj.de/SharedDocs/Downloads/DE/Fachinformationen/Abschlussbericht_Eingangszahlen_Zivilgerichte.html (last accessed Feb. 4, 2025).

6 *See* Hanns Prütting, *Rückgang der Klageeingangszahlen bei Gericht,* DEUTSCHE RICHTERZEITUNG (DRIZ) 62 (2018) (with further references).

7 For a detailed discussion, see Daniel Wilf-Townsend, Assembly-line Plaintiffs, 135 HARV. L. REV. 1704 (2022).

8 FLIGHTRIGHT, https://www.flightright.com (last accessed Feb. 5, 2025).

9 Regulation (EC) No. 261/2004 of the European Parliament and of the Council of February 11, 2004, establishing common rules on compensation and assistance to passengers in the event of denied boarding and of cancellation or long delay of flights, 2004 O.J. (L 47) 1.

compensation in case of cancellation, denied boarding, or long delays. According to Flightright, it has helped more than six million air passengers (Europe-wide) receive compensation, amounting to €430 million over the past ten years.[10] The secret of Flightright's success includes the following:

- a database with over eighty million records, fed daily with flight data from all over Europe as well as information on strikes and weather conditions;
- an algorithm that can (allegedly) determine within seconds, by means of data matching, whether a specific passenger is entitled to compensation;
- and, finally, an attractively designed website that allows passengers to check the legitimacy of a claim within a few seconds with the help of a structured questionnaire.

Flightright, however, has not only developed a very profitable business model and helped air passengers to enforce their rights. It has also revolutionized the out-of-court enforcement of lower-value claims, notably consumer rights, and offers a showcase for how consumers can benefit from digitization to enforce their legal rights. In fact, following in Flightright's footsteps, a large number of legal tech companies are now active in Germany. According to a recent tally on the website "future-law.eu"[11] there are now more than twenty companies actively contributing to the enforcement of consumer rights. These include companies dealing with the enforcement of tenants' rights against landlords, and companies dealing with policyholders' rights against insurance companies. All these companies are now well-known to large parts of the population and have become extremely popular: They are easily accessible via the internet, offer fast and unbureaucratic processes, and – most importantly – exempt consumers from any cost risk.

Legal tech companies, however, have not been uniformly met with joy and excitement. To the contrary, the legal profession has, over the past years, turned out to be skeptical – and at times even hostile – to the growing presence of legal tech companies. Some lawyers and lawyers' organizations (including bar associations) have identified legal tech companies as rivals in the legal services market and initiated a discussion about whether legal tech companies should be allowed to do what they do – and whether they are illegally providing legal services. These discussions have since led to various rulings of the German Federal Court of Justice (*Bundesgerichtshof – BGH*) as well as the adoption of a new federal law that specifically targets legal tech companies, the so-called Legal Tech Act 2021.[12]

[10] Fun fact: six million is also the number of cases that all 638 German lower courts (*Amtsgerichte*) have dealt with in the same period.

[11] Legal Tech Map Germany 2024, https://future-law.eu/wp-content/uploads/2024/10/Legal-Tech-Map-Germany-10-2024-1.pdf (last accessed Feb. 5, 2025).

[12] Gesetz zur Förderung verbrauchergerechter Angebote im Rechtsdienstleistungsmarkt of 10 August 2021 [Legal Tech Gesetz] [Legal Tech Act], 2021 Bundesgesetzblatt I [BGBl. I] [Federal Law Gazette] at 3415 (Ger.).

In the following chapter, I critically engage with these developments and their implications for access to justice in Germany. I start in Section 13.1 by outlining the regulatory environment for the provision of legal, and legal tech, services in Germany. In Section 13.2, I turn to the case law of the Federal Court of Justice, followed by a discussion in Section 13.3 of the Legal Tech Act of 2021. In the final Section, I offer some conclusions and an outlook on the future of legal tech. Overall, I hypothesize that access to justice in Germany has benefitted from legal tech companies but that important issues remain to be addressed.

13.1 PROVISION OF LEGAL TECH SERVICES: THE REGULATORY ENVIRONMENT

As in many other countries, including the United States, Germany's legal services marketplace is heavily regulated. At the heart of the regulatory landscape are two statutes: the Federal Code for Lawyers (*Bundesrechtsanwaltsordnung – BRAO*)[13] and the Act on Out-of-Court Legal Services (*Rechtsdienstleistungsgesetz – RDG*).[14] As in the United States and elsewhere, these laws essentially reserve the right to provide legal services to formally admitted attorneys[15] – that is, to professionals who are subject to strict rules on education and professional conduct. However, unlike in the United States, attorneys do not enjoy a complete monopoly.[16] Instead, the Act on

[13] Bundesrechtsanwaltsordung of 1 August 1959 [BRAO] [hereinafter Federal Code for Lawyers], 1959 Bundesgesetzblatt I [BGBl. I] [Federal Law Gazette] at 565 (Ger.), (official) English translation available at https://www.gesetze-im-internet.de/englisch_brao/index.html (last accessed Feb. 4, 2025). The Federal Code for Lawyers contains the basic regulations on admission to the bar and on the rights and duties of practicing as a lawyer. It is supplemented by the Berufsordnung der Rechtsanwältinnen und Rechtsanwälte [BORA] [Professional Code of Conduct for Lawyers] [hereinafter Professional Code of Conduct for Lawyers] and the Fachanwaltsordnung [FAO] [Specialist Lawyer Code]. For foreign (European) lawyers working in Germany, the Gesetz über die Tätigkeit europäischer Rechtsanwälte in Deutschland of 9 March 2000 [EuRAG] [Law Regulating the Activities of European Lawyers in Germany] 2000 Bundesgesetzblatt I [BGBl. I] [Federal Law Gazette] at 182, 1349 (Ger.), applies. It implements a number of EU directives.

[14] Gesetz über außergerichtliche Rechtsdienstleistungen of 12 December 2007 [RDG] [Act on Out-of-Court Legal Services] [hereinafter Act on Out-of-Court Legal Services], 2007 Bundesgesetzblatt I (BGBl. I) [Federal Law Gazette] 2840 (Ger.), (official) English translation available at https://www.gesetze-im-internet.de/englisch_rdg/index.html (last accessed Feb. 4, 2025). The Act on Out-of-Court Legal Services defines the notion of "legal services" and regulates, in the interest of consumer protection, which nonlawyer services may offer legal services out of court (as opposed to in court). With regard to in-court proceedings, additional provisions are to be found in the applicable rules of procedure, notably the Zivilprozessordnung of 30 January 1877 [ZPO] [Code of Civil Procedure] 1877 Reichsgerichtsblatt [RGBl.] [Imperial Law Gazette] at 83 (Ger.).

[15] Section 3(1) of the Federal Code for Lawyers describes the attorney as the "designated and independent counsel in all legal matters" (in and out of court).

[16] Note that recently multiple US states have introduced reforms relaxing the long-standing restrictions on who can practice law and offer legal services. See for a more detailed discussion and empirical analysis David Engstrom et al., *Legal Innovation after Reform: Evidence from*

Out-of-Court Legal Services allows certain groups of nonlawyers to provide legal services out of court under certain conditions.[17] According to section 10(1) of the Act, for example, registered debt collection services (*Inkassodienstleister*) may collect outstanding payments out of court and may offer associated legal services without an attorney's license (so-called debt collection license, or *Inkassolizenz*).[18] The provision has long been part of the German regulation of the legal services market. And for the better part of its existence, it did not receive a lot of attention: It was broadly accepted that debts can be collected with the help of nonlawyer, specialist debt collection agencies that are subject to much less regulation than attorneys.[19] Nobody argued that debt collection was something that needed to be accomplished by attorneys.

In recent years, however, section 10(1) no. 1 of the Act on Out-of-Court Legal Services has become the focal point of a heated debate. That is because legal tech companies like Flightright resort to the debt collection license under the Act on Out-of-Court Legal Services to offer their services, even though these companies are run by persons who qualify as attorneys.[20] More specifically, some lawyers have initiated a debate about whether section 10(1) no. 1 of the Act allows legal tech companies to do what they do – or whether these companies are illegally providing legal services.[21]

The opponents of a liberalized approach to the provision of legal services make two points. First, they claim that the offerings of legal tech companies take on work that exceeds the scope of classic debt collection services because they do not only focus on the collection of undisputed claims but also take on cases that are difficult and unclear (and, hence, would otherwise be prone to end up in court). In addition, they argue that legal tech companies offer services that are only loosely associated with the collection of debt.

Regulatory Change, Deborah L. Rhode Ctr. on the Legal Prof. (Sept. 2022), https://law.stanford.edu/wp-content/uploads/2022/09/SLS-CLP-Regulatory-Reform-REPORTExecSum-9.26.pdf (last accessed Feb. 4, 2025).

[17] The exceptions are limited to the provision of legal services out of court. For in-court proceedings, lawyers essentially enjoy a full monopoly with very few exceptions being enshrined in § 79(2) of the Code of Civil Procedure.

[18] Section 10(1) of the Act on Out-of-Court Legal Services reads (in official English translation): "Natural and legal persons and companies without legal personality registered with the competent authority (registered persons) may provide legal services in the following fields on the basis of special expertise: 1. collection services."

[19] See *infra* Section 13.1.

[20] It should be noted, however, that the day-to-day service, notably the handling of individual cases, is done by nonlawyers like law students or law graduates who are not admitted to the German bar.

[21] *See, for example*, Bundesrechtsanwaltskammer [BRAK] [German Federal Bar Association], *Stellungnahme Nr. 10 zum Regierungsentwurf zur Förderung verbrauchergerechter Angebote im Rechtsdienstleistungsmarkt* 4 (Feb. 2021), https://www.bundestag.de/resource/blob/837104/5f4e0c397786967cf32050caeab689db/stellungnahme-brak_wessels-data.pdf (last accessed Feb. 4, 2025).

A prominent example that illustrates the first point is Lexfox (now active under the name CONNY), a legal tech company that helps tenants navigate the German federal rent control scheme adopted in 2015 (the so-called rent brake – *Mietpreisbremse*).[22] Under the rent control scheme, the rent that landlords can charge when renting out apartments must not exceed a certain threshold. However, the rent control scheme only kicks in under certain (substantive and formal) conditions. In addition, it can be rather difficult to assess the permissible rent in an individual case because various factors have to be taken into account. Lexfox, therefore, must check the availability of the "rent brake" by collecting information from the landlord, and then it must calculate the permissible rent before it can actually ask for payment. Accordingly, Lexfox offers services much closer to those of an attorney than to those of a classic debt collection service. Indeed, Lexfox's website frames its services as "reduction of rent" and not as "collection of outstanding payments."[23]

The second point raised by opponents of a liberalized approach is closely related to the first: While legal tech companies offer services that resemble the services offered by attorneys, they are subject to much less regulation. Under the Federal Code for Lawyers (*Bundesrechtsanwaltsordnung – BRAO*)[24] and the Act on the Remuneration of Lawyers (*Rechtsanwaltsvergütungsgesetz – RVG*)[25], for example, attorneys are subject to a number of restrictions: They must not take on financial investors;[26] they must not take over legal costs, especially litigation costs for clients;[27] and they may only agree on contingency fees or other forms of payment based on success under very strict conditions.[28]

Debt collection services, in contrast, are not subject to any of these rules. Just as any other company, they can take on investors, finance legal costs (including

[22] Bürgerliches Gesetzbuch of 18 August 1896 [BGB] [Civil Code] Rechtsgesetzblatt [RGBl] [Imperial Law Gazette] (Ger.) §§ 556d to 556g at 195.

[23] Conny, https://conny.de/en/rent/rent-control-b (last accessed Feb. 4, 2025).

[24] Federal Code for Lawyers 565, *supra* note 13.

[25] Gesetz über die Vergütung der Rechtsanwältinnen und Rechtsanwälte of 15 March 2022 [RVG] [Act on the Remuneration of Lawyers] [hereinafter Act on the Remuneration of Lawyers], 2004 Bundesgesetzblatt I [BGBl. I] [Federal Law Gazette] at 718 (Ger.), (official) English translation available at https://www.gesetze-im-internet.de/englisch_rvg/index.html (last accessed Feb. 4, 2025).

[26] Federal Code for Lawyers §§ 59c(1), 59i(3).

[27] Federal Code for Lawyers § 49b(2) (sentence 2).

[28] According to § 49b(2) (sentence 2) of the Federal Code for Lawyers and § 4a(1) of the Act on the Remuneration of Lawyers (as in force before adoption of the Legal Tech Act 2021), attorneys are only allowed to charge a contingency fee in a particular case if the client in question, in light of his or her economic abilities, would otherwise be deterred from pursuing legal action. Further discrepancies are described by Matthias Kilian, *Verbrauchergerechte Angebote im Rechtsdienstleistungsmarkt – Warum der Gesetzentwurf nicht das erreicht, was er vorgibt, erreichen zu wollen*, AnwaltsBlatt online [AnwBl. online] 102, 106 (2021); Hans-Jürgen Hellwig, *BGH zu Lexfox: BRAO, RDG und das unionsrechtliche Kohärenzerfordernis: Neue Freiheiten für Anwältinnen und Anwälte bei der Berufsausübung*, AnwaltsBlatt online [AnwBl. online] 260, 263 (2020).

litigation costs) for their clients, and offer their services on a contingency fee basis.[29] In addition, debt collection services are subject to much more lenient rules with regard to regulation of conduct: While attorneys have to follow strict rules relating to, among others, the handling of conflicts of interest,[30] client information,[31] and third-party funds,[32] debt collection services are under no comparable regulation.[33] Finally, the requirements for admission are much different. While becoming an attorney in Germany takes two state exams and at least six years of training (four years of law school; two years of practical training),[34] debt collection service providers must only provide proof of expertise (*Sachkundenachweise*),[35] which can be obtained through participation in a 120-hour training course (*Sachkundelehrgang*), including a written test.[36] Other than that, they are not subject to any regulation.[37]

Thus, opponents of a liberalized approach protest that legal tech companies, in practice, offer services that are similar to (or identical to) the services traditionally offered by lawyers but that they are not able to ensure the same kind of quality as lawyers. As a consequence, they conclude that, in the interest of consumer protection, legal tech companies should not be allowed to offer services under the debt collection license of the Act on Out-of-Court Legal Services.

13.2 LEGALITY OF LEGAL TECH SERVICES: CASE LAW

The above discussion shows that legal tech companies in Germany face similar opposition from lawyers and lawyers' organizations as they do in the United States. And, as in the United States, the legality of legal tech companies and their business models has been challenged in the courts.[38] However, so far, all attempts to strike down the business models of legal tech companies in Germany have been unsuccessful. Notably, the German Federal Court of Justice has turned out to be very legal tech-friendly and has held, starting with the pioneering *Lexfox I* judgment, that the Act on Out-of-Court Legal Services allows legal tech companies to do what they do.

29 This is the very reason why legal tech companies do not even wish to register as attorneys (even though most of them could because they are run by lawyers who have the necessary qualifications).

30 Federal Code for Lawyers § 43a(4).

31 Federal Code for Lawyers § 43a(2); Strafgesetzbuch [StGB] [Penal Code] 1998 Bundesgesetzblatt I [BGBl. I] [Imperial Law Gazette] at 3322, § 203(1) no. 3 (Ger.).

32 Federal Code for Lawyers § 43a(7); Professional Code of Conduct for Lawyers § 4.

33 See, however, the changes that the Legal Tech Act has brought about. See *infra* Section 13.3.

34 For a more detailed description, see *Study Law in Germany 2024*, Keystone Law Studies (2024), https://www.lawstudies.com/countries/germany# (last accessed Feb. 4, 2025).

35 Act on Out-of-Court Legal Services § 11(1).

36 Verordnung zum Rechtsdienstleistungsgesetz of 19 June 2008 [RDV] [Regulation relating to the Act on Out-of-Court Legal Services], 2008 Bundesgesetzblatt I [BGBl. I] [Federal Law Gazette] at 1069, § 4 (Ger.).

37 See, however, the changes that the Legal Tech Act has brought about. See *infra* Section 13.3.

38 For litigation in the United States, see, for example, Upsolve, Inc. v. James, 604 F. Supp. 3d 97 (S.D.N.Y. 2022).

13.2.1 *The* Lexfox I *Judgment of the Federal Court of Justice*

The *Lexfox I* judgment, rendered in 2019, revolved around a Berlin tenant who had used Lexfox's online services to check whether his rent was in line with the German federal rent control scheme (the so-called rent brake).[39] When Lexfox's online rent calculator indicated that his rent was too high, he assigned all his rights and claims under his tenancy agreement (including any right to repayment of overpaid rent) to Lexfox, which promised to enforce the tenant's rights and claims for a contingency fee. Lexfox reached out to the landlord, made a formal complaint about the rent brake violation, and asked for additional information in order to determine the permissible rent, to demand repayment of the overpaid rent, and to request that the landlord agree to charge only the permissible rent in the future. The landlord, however, refused to cooperate, and Lexfox took the case to court (along with the help of an attorney).[40] Lexfox was successful before the local court (*Amtsgericht – AG*) of Berlin.[41] On appeal, however, the regional court (*Landgericht – LG*) of Berlin rejected Lexfox's claim, holding that the assignment of rights and claims under the tenancy agreement had been invalid because the enforcement of the "rent brake" required the provision of fully fledged legal services – not those covered by the debt collection license under section 10(1) no. 1 of the Act on Out-of-Court Legal Services.[42] Lexfox appealed to the highest German civil court, the Federal Court of Justice (*Bundesgerichtshof – BGH*), teeing up a ruling on the appropriate reach of the debt collection license and, incidentally, on the permissibility of Lexfox's business model.[43]

In its eighty-page judgment, the Federal Court of Justice reversed the regional court's decision.[44] It held that the services offered by Lexfox were covered by the debt collection license, and thus lawful, and also that the tenant's assignment of rights and claims had been fully valid. According to the court, section 10(1) no. 1 of the Act on Out-of-Court Legal Services not only allowed for the classic collection of (undisputed) outstanding payments but also included more complex tasks, such as the collection of information about a claim and taking steps to meet the requirements to bring a formal claim, including through letters of complaint.[45] Pointing

39 Bundesgerichtshof [BGH] [Federal Court of Justice], Nov. 27, 2019, Neue Juristische Wochenschrift [NJW] 208 (2020) (Ger.) – *Lexfox I.*

40 Legal tech companies that are registered as debt collection services may not represent their customers in court. Rather, section 79(1) of the German Civil Code requires debt collection services to hire an external attorney to go to court.

41 Amtsgericht Berlin-Lichtenberg [AG Berlin-Lichtenberg] [Local Court Berlin-Lichtenberg], Dec. 12, 2017-6 C 194/17, Beck-Rechtsprechung [BeckRS] 151479 (2017) (Ger.).

42 Landgericht Berlin [LG Berlin] [Regional Court Berlin], Aug. 28, 2018, Beck-Rechtsprechung [BeckRS] 2018, 19885 (Ger.).

43 Bundesgerichtshof [BGH] [Federal Court of Justice], Nov. 17, 2019, Neue Juristische Wochenschrift [NJW] 208 (2020) (Ger.) – *Lexfox I.*

44 *Id.* ¶¶ 38, 97.

45 *Id.*¶ 100.

out that the Act on Out-of-Court Legal Services was meant to liberalize and hence, to open, the market for out-of-court legal services to nonlawyers, the court held that the Act allowed nonlawyers with sufficient expertise in a certain area to offer legal services. For this reason – and in light of the basic right to freely choose a profession enshrined in Article 12 of the German Constitution[46] – the Act's exceptions, including the provisions encompassing debt collection in section 10(1) no. 1 had to be interpreted broadly, not narrowly, and with reference to the legislature's intention to protect consumers from unqualified legal service providers.[47] Since Lexfox possessed the required expertise, there was no reason to assume that it should not be allowed to offer its services. There was, in other words, no need to protect consumers from Lexfox.

13.2.2 *Further Judgments of the Federal Court of Justice*

With its *Lexfox I* judgment, the Federal Court of Justice established a very broad scope of debt collection under section 10(1) no. 1 and allowed substantial overlap between the services of legal tech companies and the services traditionally offered by attorneys. At the same time, the court interpreted the Act on Out-of-Court Legal Services in a very liberal way prohibiting the provision of legal services by nonlawyers only where such a prohibition is necessary to protect consumers.

In subsequent judgments, the court confirmed and applied an equally liberal approach to other legal tech companies.[48] In July 2021, for example, the court held that the business model of Airdeal was covered by the debt collection license of

[46] Grundgesetz für die Bundesrepublik Deutschland of 23 May 1949 [GG] [Basic Law for the Federal Republic of Germany], 1949 Bundesgesetzblatt I [BGBl. I] [Federal Law Gazette] at 1 (Ger.).

[47] Section 1(1) of the Act on Out-of-Court Legal Services expressly provides that the purpose of the Act is to protect citizens from unqualified legal services.

[48] *Cf.* Bundesgerichtshof [BGH] [Federal Court of Justice], Apr. 8, 2020, Neue Juristische Wochenschrift – Rechtsprechungsreport [NJW-RR] 779, para. 30 (2020) (Ger.) – *Lexfox II*; Bundesgerichtshof [BGH] [Federal Court of Justice] May 6, 2020, Beck-Rechtsprechung [BeckRS] 11460 (2020) (Ger.) – *Lexfox III*; Bundesgerichtshof [BGH] [Federal Court of Justice] May 27, 2020, Beck-Rechtsprechung [BeckRS] 16800 (2020) (Ger.) – *Lexfox IV*; Bundesgerichtshof [BGH] [Federal Court of Justice] May 27, 2020, Beck-Rechtsprechung [BeckRS] 15829 (2020) (Ger.) – *Lexfox V*; Bundesgerichtshof [BGH] Federal Court of Justice] May 27, 2020, Neue Zeitschrift für Mietrecht [NZM] 551, para. 43 (2020) (Ger.) – *Lexfox VI*; Bundesgerichtshof [BGH] [Federal Court of Justice] May 27, 2020, Beck-Rechtsprechung [BeckRS] 16799 (2020) (Ger.) – *Lexfox VII*; Bundesgerichtshof [BGH] [Federal Court of Justice] May 27, 2020, Beck-Rechtsprechung [BeckRS] 15802 (2020) (Ger.) – *Lexfox VIII*; Bundesgerichtshof [BGH] [Federal Court of Justice] Jan. 19, 2022 – VIII ZR 220/21, para. 28 (juris) (Ger.) – *Lexfox IX*; Bundesgerichtshof [BGH] [Federal Court of Justice] Jan. 19, 2022 – VIII ZR 122/21, para. 28 (juris) (Ger.) – *Lexfox X*; Bundesgerichtshof [BGH] Federal Court of Justice] Jan. 19, 2022 – VIII ZR 123/21, para. 27 (Ger.) – *Lexfox XI*; Bundesgerichtshof [BGH] [Federal Court of Justice] Jan. 19, 2022 – VIII ZR 196/21, para. 26 (juris) (Ger.) – *Lexfox XII*.

section 10(1) no. 1 of the Act.[49] Airdeal had collected claims by way of assignment from Air Berlin customers whose flights had been canceled as a result of the company's insolvency.[50] Airdeal's detractors argued that this service exceeded Airdeal's rights as a debt collection service, pointing out that Airdeal did not even attempt to collect the claims out of court, but instead sought court enforcement right away (with the help of an attorney).[51] The Federal Court of Justice, however, held that the debt collection license did not require debt collection services to enforce claims out of court first before seeking enforcement in court. Rather, the license also covered business models that primarily (or exclusively) envisioned court enforcement of claims (with the help of an attorney).[52] In a similar vein, the court decided, in June and October, 2022, that a debt collection license gives legal tech companies the right to collect damages claims from a large number of consumers (including claims that were subject to foreign law) in order to enforce them in court.[53] It is, therefore, fair to conclude that legal tech companies enjoy great freedom to offer their services under the debt collection license of the Act on Out-of-Court Legal Services.[54] In fact, as of today, every business model premised

[49] Bundesgerichtshof [BGH] [Federal Court of Justice] July 13, 2021, Neue Juristische Wochenschrift [NJW] 3046 (2021) (Ger.).

[50] Air Berlin was a German airline and at its peak Germany's second-biggest air passenger carrier. It filed for insolvency on August 15, 2017, and ceased to operate on October 27, 2017. *See* Richard Weiss, *Air Berlin Riles for Insolvency as Etihad Pulls Funding Plug*, BLOOMBERG (Aug. 15, 2017), https://www.bloomberg.com/news/articles/2017-08-15/air-berlin-files-for-insolvency-after-etihad-withdraws-support (last accessed Feb. 4, 2025); *Air Berlin leitet den Sinkflug ein*, AERO.DE (Oct. 9, 2017, 1:58 PM), https://www.aero.de/news-27642/Air-Berlin-leitet-den-Sinkflug-ein.html (last accessed Feb. 4, 2025).

[51] For an overview, see Martin Henssler, *Vom Anwaltsmarkt zum Markt für Rechtsdienstleistungen*, ANWALTSBLATT ONLINE [ANWBL. ONLINE] 168, at 169–73 (2020). In addition, it was argued that the collection (and enforcement) of a large number of claims would violate (former) section 606(1) of the Code of Civil Procedure. According to this provision, a model declaratory action (Musterfeststellungsklage) may only be filed by certain institutions and organizations and without intention to make a profit. *Id.* at 169. The Federal Court of Justice, however, rejected this argument pointing to the fact that (former) section 606 (1) only applies to model declaratory action within the meaning of the Code of Civil Procedure – and not to other ways of collecting and enforcing larger numbers of claims.

[52] Bundesgerichtshof [BGH] [Federal Court of Justice] July 13, 2021, Neue Juristische Wochenschrift [NJW] 3046, para. 16-44 (2021) (Ger.). Note that section 79(1) of the German Civil Code requires debt collection services to hire an external attorney to go to court.

[53] Bundesgerichtshof [BGH] [Federal Court of Justice] June 13, 2022, Neue Juristische Wochenschrift [NJW] 3350 (2022); Bundesgerichtshof [BGH] [Federal Court of Justice] Oct. 10, 2022, Verbraucher und Recht [VuR] 25 (2022).

[54] It should be noted, though, that even after the *Lexfox I* judgment, various lower instance courts held that the business model of some legal tech companies violated the Act on Out-of-Court Legal Services. However, all these judgments were later overturned. *See, for example*, Landgericht München I [LG München I] [Regional Court Munich I] Feb. 7, 2020, Beck-Rechtsprechung [BeckRS] 841 (2020) (Ger) – *financialright*; Landgericht Braunschweig [LG Braunschweig] [Regional Court Braunschweig] Apr. 30, 2020, Beck-Rechtsprechung [BeckRS] 7267 (Ger.), Beck-Rechtsprechung [BeckRS] 7267 (2020) (Ger.); Landgericht Ingolstadt [LG Ingoldstadt] [Regional Court Ingolstadt] Aug. 7, 2020, Beck-Rechtsprechung [BeckRS] 18773

on a debt collection license and considered by the court has been upheld and considered to be in line with the Act.[55]

13.3 NEW RULES AND REGULATIONS: THE LEGAL TECH ACT 2021

The above-described judgments of the Federal Court of Justice have answered a number of pressing questions revolving around the legality of legal tech companies. However, they did not end the discussion about the regulation of legal tech companies. In fact, the very liberal approach of the Federal Court of Justice – and the ongoing criticism by lawyers and lawyers' organizations – sparked a discussion about an adjustment of the applicable legal framework. This discussion eventually led to the adoption in 2021 of the Act for the Promotion of Consumer-oriented Offers in the Legal Services Market *(Gesetz zur Förderung verbrauchergerechter Angebote im Rechtsdienstleistungsmarkt)*, commonly known and referred to as the Legal Tech Act.[56]

13.3.1 *Main Thrusts and Noteworthy Changes*

The Legal Tech Act has two main thrusts:[57] First, it is meant to mitigate the earlier described imbalance between the regulation of attorneys, on the one hand, and the regulation of debt collection services, on the other, thus leveling the playing field

(2022) (Ger.); Landgericht Augsburg [LG Augsburg] [Regional Court Augsburg] Oct. 27, 2020, Beck-Rechtsprechung [BeckRS] 30625 (2020) (Ger.).

55 In addition to legal tech companies that operate as debt collection services, the Federal Court of Justice has also upheld other legal tech business models. In September 2021, for example, the court decided that the business model of Smartlaw (https://www.smartlaw.de) was in line with the Act on Out-of-Court Legal Services. Smartlaw does not engage in the enforcement of consumer claims but helps consumers (and companies) to (automatically) create legal documents that the Local Bar Association of Hamburg *(Rechtsanwaltskammer Hamburg)* considered to be illegal under the provisions of the Act on Out-of-Court Legal Services. The Federal Court of Justice, however, rejected this view and held that Smartlaw was allowed to offer its services, arguing that the digital creation of legal documents does not amount to the provision of legal services in the meaning of section 2(1) of the Act. According to section 2(1) of the Act legal service is any activity in concrete third-party matters as soon as it requires a legal examination of the individual case. *See* Bundesgerichtshof [BGH] [Federal Court of Justice] Sept. 9, 2021, Neue Juristische Wochenschrift [NJW] 3125 (2021) (Ger.).

56 Gesetz zur Förderung verbrauchergerechter Angebote im Rechtsdienstleistungsmarkt of 10 August 2021 [Legal Tech Gesetz] [Legal Tech Act], 2021 Bundesgesetzblatt I [BGBl. I] [Federal Law Gazette] at 3415 (Ger.).

57 Entwurf eines Gesetzes zur Förderung verbrauchergerechter Angebote im Rechtsdienstleistungsmarkt [Draft Legal Tech Act], Deutscher Bundestag: Drucksachen [BT-Drs.] [Printed Matter of the German Federal Parliament] 19/27673, at 1 (Ger.), available at https://dserver.bundestag.de/btd/19/276/1927673.pdf (last accessed Feb. 4, 2025). For a detailed presentation of the Act, including its purposes, see Martin Fries, *De minimis curat mercator: Legal Tech wird Gesetz*, NEUE JURISTISCHE WOCHENSCHRIFT [NJW] 2537 (2021); Tim Günther, *Das neue Legal Tech Gesetz. Zwischenlösung für den Rechtsdienstleistungsmarkt*, ZEITSCHRIFT FÜR MULTIMEDIA UND RECHT [MMR] 764 (2021).

between the two. Second, it is intended to provide consumers with better protection when they make use of debt collection services.

To reach these goals, the Legal Tech Act first loosens some of the traditional legal restrictions for attorneys. Most importantly, it allows lawyers to charge a contingency fee where three conditions are met: (1) where a plaintiff asserts a monetary claim up to a limit of €2,000;[58] (2) where the attorney provides out-of-court debt collection services, typically in payment order or enforcement proceedings;[59] and (3) where the client would otherwise be deterred from pursuing legal action.[60] In addition, the Act allows attorneys to take over the costs associated with enforcing the client's rights, notably the costs of litigation, where the attorney provides out-of-court debt collection services, provided that the attorney charges a contingency fee at the same time.[61] It follows that attorneys engaged in debt collection are largely put on par with legal tech companies.

True to its name, however, the Legal Tech Act does not just regulate attorneys. It also takes on the regulation relating to legal tech companies. To begin with, the Act tightens the requirements for admission as a debt collection service under section 10(1) no. 1 of the Act on Out-of-Court Legal Services. According to section 13(2) of the Legal Tech Act, applicants must now describe in their application for registration what they plan to do and in which legal areas they will operate. This requirement allows the competent registration agency to check the admissibility of the respective business model at the time of registration, thus avoiding the uncertainty that results if admissibility can only be checked later during civil proceedings (as in the Lexfox case).[62] The registration agency may also, at the time of registration, ask for proof of expertise in addition to participation in the previously mentioned 120-hour training course (*Sachkundelehrgang*).[63] Finally, the Act establishes new disclosure obligations that debt collection services must fulfill toward consumer-clients. In particular, it requires debt collection services to inform consumers about (1) alternative options to ensure the consumer's rights if the company wishes to charge a contingency fee; (2) the details of any agreement with a third-party litigation funder; and (3) the details of the legal tech company's right to enter into settlement agreements.[64] Additional disclosure obligations relate to situations where a debt collection service declines to enforce a particular claim, and require the debt collection service to inform the consumer why it declined to pursue their claim.[65]

[58] Act on the Remuneration of Lawyers § 4a(1) (sentence 1, no. 1).

[59] Act on the Remuneration of Lawyers § 4a(1) (sentence 1, no. 2).

[60] Act on the Remuneration of Lawyers § 4a(1) (sentence 1, no. 3).

[61] Federal Code for Lawyers § 49b(2) (sentence 2).

[62] Up until 2021, admissibility of a business model was not checked by the authorities at the time of registration. Rather, it was checked during civil proceedings when discussing the right of action (standing) of the legal tech company in question (just as in the *Lexfox I* judgment).

[63] Regulation Relating to the Act on Out-of-Court Legal Services § 2(1) (sentence 4).

[64] Act on Out-of-Court Legal Services § 13b(1) (nos. 1–3).

[65] Act on Out-of-Court Legal Services § 13b(2).

The company must indicate whether it inquired into the legal legitimacy of their claim, and if so whether this has been done automatically, such as with algorithms. Consumers must be further informed that the decision not to enforce the claim does not affect other forms of enforcement, whether in-court or via alternative dispute resolution mechanisms.

13.3.2 *Consequences for the Legal Services Market*

As evident above, the Legal Tech Act has brought about some key changes to the regulatory landscape relating both to attorneys and to legal tech companies that offer their service under section 10(1) no. 1 of the Act on Out-of-Court Legal Services. Overall, however, the changes are rather limited.[66] In the literature, they have rightly been described as a "small step"[67] and mere "cosmetic correction."[68]

To begin with, the Act loosens restrictions for attorneys only with regard to debt collection services – that is, with regard to the area where there is immediate competition from nonlawyers like Lexfox and Airdeal. It does not, however, loosen the restrictions for any other kinds of services attorneys offer – areas where competition from legal tech companies may emerge. In particular, the Legal Tech Act does not touch upon the "big" issues of lawyer regulation, notably the general ban on attorneys working on a contingency fee basis, the general bans regarding litigation funding, and, most importantly, the general ban on seeking outside financial investment from nonlawyers (fee-splitting). As a consequence, the Act essentially sidelines attorneys from any substantial use of legal technology beyond debt collection, and it prevents them from providing the same kind of consumer-friendly and efficient services that legal tech companies offer. Thus, it fails to actually create the intended level-playing field.[69]

The Legal Tech Act applies an equally cautious approach to the regulation of legal tech companies. In particular, it does not specifically say that legal tech companies may offer their services under the Act on Out-of-Court Legal Services. It leaves courts to decide the permissibility of other legal tech business models under the Act on a case-by-case basis.[70] Thus, it fails to provide prospective legal tech

66 See Gerhard Wagner & Till Weskamm, *Anspruchsbündelung durch Legal Tech: Im Dschungel des RDG*, in Festschrift für Martin Henssler 1605, 1609–10 (2023).

67 Volker Römermann, *Legal Tech-Gesetz: Ein (allzu) kleiner Schritt in die richtige Richtung*, Recht Digital [RDi] 217 (2021).

68 Fries, *supra* note 57, at 2540.

69 It should be noted, though, that there is nothing that prevents lawyers from offering debt collection services in addition to their legal services. In this case, however, the debt collection offering must be independent of the legal services offering to avoid the restrictions that apply to attorneys.

70 The registration under the Act on Out-of-Court Legal Services does not have any binding effect. This means that civil courts can declare business models of legal tech companies illegal despite their valid registration (and admission) by the competent registration authority.

companies with much-needed legal certainty.[71] In addition, the Act only requires debt collection services to make certain disclosures to consumers. While this may theoretically increase transparency it is more than likely that most consumers will fail to read or take note of the information provided.[72]

Against this background, the debate about the regulation of legal (and tech) services will have to go on. Among the issues to be considered is whether the above-mentioned restrictions that continue to apply to attorneys should be abandoned.[73] In particular, the debate will consider whether attorneys should generally be allowed to work on a contingency fee basis, to fund litigation, and to take financial investors on board.[74] In addition, the evolving legal tech scene will have to be monitored to determine whether further legislative action is needed, and in particular whether legal tech companies should be required to prove their legal competence beyond current requirements. To be sure, legal tech companies have – thus far – only improved the enforcement of consumer claims. However, since there is virtually no regulation in place that could ensure quality – for example in the form of regulation relating to legal expertise – there is a potential risk that the situation may change in the future.[75] In the best interest of consumers, it is therefore necessary to remain careful and to react should regulation become necessary.

13.4 CONCLUSION

Legal tech companies have thus far enriched the German legal services market and have helped to mitigate the access-to-justice problem that Germany

[71] It should be noted, though, that the legislature has – slightly – amended the definition of "debt collection services" to be found in section 2(2), sentence 1 of the Act on Out-of-Court Legal Services. It now emphasizes that debt collection services also include the legal examination and provision of advice relating to the collection of debts. However, this amendment is generally understood as a mere codification of the case law of the Federal Court of Justice in re *Lexfox*. See Fries, *supra* note 57, at 2538; Wagner & Weskamm, *supra* note 66, at 1610.

[72] *See* Fries, *supra* note 57, at 2540 (accord).

[73] The coalition agreement of the current German government promises to modify the ban of contingency fees and to analyze whether the ban of nonlawyer ownership of law firms is still necessary. *See Koalitionsvertrag 2021–2025 zwischen der Sozialdemokratischen Partei Deutschlands (SPD), Bündnis 90/Den Grünen und den Freien Demokraten (FDP), Mehr Fortschritt wagen.* Bündnis für Freiheit, Gerechtigkeit und Nachhaltigkeit 89 (2021), https://www.spd.de/fileadmin/Dokumente/Koalitionsvertrag/Koalitionsvertrag_2021-2025.pdf (last accessed Feb. 4, 2025).

[74] Note that there is a chance that at least some of the restrictions, notably the ban on nonlawyer ownership of law firms will have to be abandoned: the Bayerischer Anwaltsgerichtshof [Bavarian Lawyers' Court] has recently submitted a preliminary question to the Court of Justice of the European Union [CJEU] inquiring whether the strict ban on nonlawyer ownership of law firms is in line with European Union law, notably the European freedoms of capital movement, services, and establishment. See Bayerischer Anwaltsgerichtshof [BayAGH] [Bavarian Lawyers' Court], Apr. 20, 2023, Anwaltsblatt online [AnwBl. Online] 283 (2023).

[75] *See* Fries, *supra* note 57, at 2538 (accord).

faces.[76] They have also, so far at least, survived attempts from the organized bar to narrow or even terminate their business models. Thanks to both the German courts, in particular the Federal Court of Justice, as well as the German legislature, legal tech companies are allowed to offer their services under the debt collection service exception of the Act on Out-of-Court Legal Services. Without openly admitting it, the courts and the federal legislature have recognized that legal tech companies make a positive difference for consumers who wish to enforce lower-value claims.[77] In addition, these actors have made clear that they are not willing to let legal tech companies – particularly those devoted to enforcing lower-value, mostly consumer, claims – fall prey to the kind of "lawyer protectionism" that underlies much of the criticism voiced against digital legal service providers. For champions of liberalization, these are welcome developments.

It is regrettable, however, that the German federal legislature has – so far – refrained from taking a closer look at the overall regulatory landscape for the provision of legal services and notably the strict regulation of the legal profession. With the Legal Tech Act, it has only loosened, and not eliminated, some of the restrictions that attorneys currently face. And it has done so in a very limited fashion, namely with regard to the collection of debt. In contrast, it has not analyzed whether the remaining restrictions – especially those relating to the admission of financial investors, the funding of litigation, and the use of contingency fees – are actually necessary in order to protect consumers. Since the German legislature has also refrained from subjecting legal tech companies to stricter regulation (beyond the minimal regulations in the Legal Tech Act), the German legal services market will remain bifurcated, with heavily regulated attorneys and lightly regulated legal tech companies. In the years to come, we will, therefore, need to better understand the benefits and costs of that bifurcation – whether it resulted from a clear-eyed assessment by legislators and courts, or

[76] Römermann, *supra* note 67, at 221–24; Gerhard Wagner, *Algorithmisierte Rechtsdurchsetzung*, 222 ARCHIV FÜR DIE CIVILISTISCHE PRAXIS [AcP] 56, 59–60 (2022); Wagner & Weskamm, *supra* note 66, at 1624.

[77] Despite all this it should be noted that legal tech companies are also creating problems. The most important one relates to the German civil justice system: Legal tech companies are increasingly enforcing claims in court (with the support of attorneys). Using technology that allows them to file a large number of (similar) cases quickly and efficiently in an assembly-line way. As a consequence, some German civil courts have been flooded with (a large number of) very similar cases. There is currently a discussion going on how to make sure that German civil courts can adequately deal with these kinds of "mass claims." For an overview, see Deutscher Richterbund (German Judges Association), *Arbeitsgemeinschaft Massenverfahren* (May 13, 2022), https://www.drb.de/fileadmin/DRB/pdf/Stellungnahmen/2022/Loesungsvorschlaege_AG_Massenverfahren.pdf (last accessed Feb. 4, 2025), as well as CDU/CSU-Fraktion des Deutschen Bundestags, *Kollaps der Ziviljustiz verhindern – Wirksame Regelungen zur Bewältigung von Massenverfahren schaffen*, DEUTSCHER BUNDESTAG: DRUCKSACHEN [BT-DRS.] [Printed Matter of the German Federal Parliament] 20/5560, at 2 (Ger.), https://dserver.bundestag.de/btd/20/055/2005560.pdf (last accessed Feb. 4, 2025).

whether it is instead just the result of path dependency and muddling through. If the latter proves to be the case, which seems more than likely, Germany will have to completely overhaul its legal services market in order to regulate attorneys and other legal services providers, including legal tech companies in essentially the same – and most likely, a more liberal – way. In particular, it will have to introduce rules that allow legal service providers across the board to resort to outside funding, to finance litigation via equity or other sources, and to work on a contingency fee basis, at least under certain conditions.

However, even if the German legal services market is ultimately liberalized along these lines – which is, in the end, a political and thus unpredictable process – the access-to-justice problems that Germany is facing will most likely remain. In fact, a recent study, commissioned by the Federal Ministry of Justice (*Bundesjustizministerium – BMJ*) concluded that the dramatic loss of cases that German courts have experienced during the past twenty-five years can be attributed in significant part to features of the German civil justice system.[78] In particular, the report found that the relatively high costs of pursuing a claim, the complexity and the length of civil proceedings,[79] and uncertainty regarding case outcomes lead many people not to seek justice in the courts.[80] It is, therefore, to be welcomed that efforts are currently being made to improve the German court system. In fact, a Working Group commissioned by the German judiciary submitted a number of proposals for the modernization of the German civil justice system in 2020.[81] Since then, the German Federal Ministry of Justice has been intensively gathering and discussing ideas for how to make the German court system more appealing and more accessible for consumers and nonlawyers in general.[82] And while nothing has been decided or implemented yet, it has become clear that any reform package will set out to improve not only access to courts but also the conduct of court proceedings through the use of digital technology, notably self-help systems that use guided interviews or chatbots inspired by legal tech companies. In addition, it is noteworthy that some German Federal States are currently experimenting with the use of artificial intelligence to deal with assembly-line claims that have reached German

[78] Meller-Hannich et al., *supra* note 5, at 317–21 and 340–41.

[79] It should be noted, however, that civil proceedings take less time in Germany than in most other countries. See, for example, EUROPEAN COMM'N, THE 2022 EU JUSTICE SCOREBOARD 11, figs. 7, 8 (2022), https://commission.europa.eu/system/files/2022-05/eu_justice_scoreboard_2022.pdf (last accessed Feb. 4, 2025).

[80] Meller-Hannich et al., *supra* note 5, at 340.

[81] Arbeitsgruppe, *"Modernisierung des Zivilprozesses" im Auftrag der Pra sidentinnen und Präsidenten der Oberlandesgerichte, des Kammergerichts, des Bayerischen Obersten Landesgerichts und des Bundesgerichthofs, Modernisierung des Zivilprozesses* (Dec. 2021), https://www.justiz.bayern.de/media/images/behoerden-und-gerichte/oberlandesgerichte/nuernberg/diskussionspapier_ag_modernisierung.pdf (last accessed Feb. 4, 2025).

[82] An overview of the ideas and projects that are currently being discussed is available at *Projects, Insights, Strategy*, DIGITAL SERVICE, //digitalservice.bund.de/en/blog (last accessed Feb. 5, 2025).

courts in recent years as a result of legal tech companies' efforts to bring and enforce lower-value claims.[83] While these experiments are still in an early stage and limited to certain types of claims, they show where the path is leading. One may, therefore, hope that – in conjunction with the top-down attempts to modernize and digitalize the German court system – German courts will soon adopt the measures necessary to increase the attractiveness of the German civil justice system, thereby furthering the delivery of justice.

83 Bettina Mielke, *Künstliche Intelligenz in der Justiz. Sechs Einsatzbereiche am Beispiel von aktuellen Pilotprojekten*, LEGAL-TECH.DE (Nov. 28, 2023), https://legal-tech.de/kuenstliche-intelligenz-in-der-justiz-pilotprojekte/ (last accessed Feb. 4, 2025).

PART IV

New Frontiers

Charting the Future of Legal Services

14

Professional Speech, the *Lochnerized* First Amendment, and the Unauthorized Practice of Law

Genevieve Lakier

The First Amendment has not traditionally been a powerful tool in the access-to-justice toolbox, but that may be about to change. Recent shifts in First Amendment doctrine have destabilized the law of professional regulation and called into question the constitutionality of even decades-old professional licensing laws. Access-to-justice advocates have taken advantage of this sea change in First Amendment law to challenge the constitutionality of the state bans on the unauthorized practice of law (UPL) that pose what many advocates believe to be an insuperable barrier to access to justice in many states. These challenges appear in at least one case to be succeeding.

In *Upsolve, Inc. v. James*, a federal district court held that New York state laws that prohibit nonlawyers from engaging in the UPL likely could not be constitutionally enforced against the nonlawyer Justice Advocates whom an access-to-justice nonprofit, Upsolve Inc., wanted to train to help poor New Yorkers defend themselves against debt collection lawsuits.[1] More specifically, the district court found that enforcement of the state's UPL laws likely violated both Upsolve's and the Justice Advocates' First Amendment rights because it imposed a content-based restriction on their speech.[2]

In reaching this conclusion, the district court relied on two recent Supreme Court cases that suggest, in marked contrast to the cases that came before them, that the same First Amendment principles that govern the regulation of speech in the public sphere also apply to regulations of the professional marketplace – at least, some of the time. The *Upsolve* decision is thus significant not only because it represents the first time in U.S. history that a federal court has interpreted the First Amendment to prohibit the enforcement of a ban on the UPL against nonlawyers who wish to give personalized legal advice to individual clients. It is also significant because it suggests how what some scholars have critically described as the "Lochnerian" turn in First

1 Upsolve, Inc. v. James, 604 F. Supp. 3d 97 (S.D.N.Y. 2022). The relevant statutes include N.Y. Judiciary Law §§ 478, 484.

2 Upsolve, Inc. v. James, *supra* note 1, at 104–05.

Amendment law – namely, the increasing scrutiny that courts apply to laws that regulate the expressive practices of market actors – might be used to limit the reach of UPL laws, thereby enabling organizations like Upsolve to experiment with nonlawyer-based solutions to the access-to-justice crisis in the United States.[3] *Upsolve* is currently on appeal, but even if it is ultimately overturned, the decision provides a proof of concept for similar challenges elsewhere.

For access-to-justice advocates, this development is obviously a welcome one. Although recent years have seen some notable successes in the fight against the trade monopoly that lawyers have traditionally claimed over the provision of legal services, resistance by the judiciary and the established bar has frustrated otherwise promising avenues of reform.[4] In this context, the First Amendment may offer a useful alternative to ordinary politics, and one that may be less prone to the pathologies of self-dealing than other mechanisms of legal change.

The intrusion of the First Amendment into what was previously a largely de-constitutionalized area of law also has potential downsides, however. Scholars have criticized the Lochnerian turn in First Amendment jurisprudence for its imperial tendencies – that is to say, for its tendency to constitutionalize ever greater swathes of commercial regulation, thereby making it difficult for the government to protect consumers against fraud and exploitation, or advance other important regulatory goals.[5] This tendency is also evident in the professional speech cases. As I discuss below, in order to craft what it insisted was a narrow ruling in *Upsolve*, the district court relied upon a distinction between speech and conduct that is wholly unconvincing and susceptible to challenge. In practice, then, the logic of the opinion is sweeping; it could very easily be interpreted to mean that UPL laws violate the First Amendment, not only when they prohibit nonlawyers from giving personalized advice to clients but also when they prohibit nonlawyers from filing briefs in court or arguing cases. The opinion also could be extended to protect for-profit entities from state regulation, not just nonprofit advocacy organizations like Upsolve.

It is possible, then, that the Lochnerized First Amendment could help deregulate the entire arena of legal licensing just in time for the arrival of ChatGPT 5 and subsequent advances in generative artificial intelligence. It is not at all obvious that

[3] *See, for example*, Sorrell v. IMS Health Inc., 564 U.S. 552, 602–03 (2011) (criticizing the decision to apply heightened scrutiny to a regulation of commercial speech for "reawaken[ing] *Lochner*'s pre-New Deal threat of substituting judicial for democratic decisionmaking where ordinary economic regulation is at issue"); Robert Post & Amanda Shanor, *Adam Smith's First Amendment*, 128 Harv. L. Rev. F. 165 (2015). For a fuller exploration of this point, see Genevieve Lakier, *The First Amendment's Real Lochner Problem*, 87 U. Chi. L. Rev. 1241 (2020).

[4] Stephen P. Younger, *The Pitfalls and False Promises of Nonlawyer Ownership of Law Firms*, 132 Yale L.J. F. 259, 265–67 (2022).

[5] *See, for example*, Post & Shanor, *supra* note 3, at 166 (warning of the tendency of the recent cases to "*constitutionalize* the unregulated operation of the laissez-faire commercial marketplace" thereby imposing "a straitjacket [on] our institutions of democratic governance").

the ends that access to justice advocates seek would be advanced by this degree of deregulation. Improving access to justice does not mean leaving legal consumers at the mercy of hucksters, the incompetent, or the hallucinations of generative AI. And yet, in principle at least, this is the deregulatory outcome that the constitutionaliza tion of legal licensing could achieve.

In practice, however, this outcome seems quite unlikely. Courts that have applied the new precedents to strike down regulations of professional speech in other contexts have tended to do so narrowly. Older understandings of where and how the First Amendment applies are not so easily altered, and courts continue to insist that much of the existing regulatory framework survives the recent precedents. This is likely to be especially true of cases that call into question the privileges of the professional bar.[6]

The *Upsolve* decision certainly suggests as much. As I explain below, in reaching the conclusion that enforcement of New York's UPL laws against the Justice Advocates program would likely violate the First Amendment, the district court could have relied upon a different, much older but arguably more on-point set of Supreme Court precedents that hold that professional licensing laws and other regulations of professional speech violate the First Amendment when their enforcement threatens important democratic interests, including the democratic interest in ensuring meaningful access to the courts. So far, these precedents have not been interpreted to apply to efforts by nonlawyers to facilitate access to justice, but they absolutely could be. After all, as Rebecca Sandefur and Matthew Burnett point out in their contribution to this volume, the inability of poor Americans to access the courts is "not just a problem of social welfare policy or justice service delivery; it is a failure of democracy" – and one that makes it impossible to ensure the fundamental legal equality that self-government requires.[7]

Despite the obvious relevance of these older cases, the district court decided to rely instead upon the newer precedents because, the opinion suggests, it believed them to have *less* sweeping implications for the regulation of the legal profession. This is because, rather than relying upon a thick concept like democracy, the new cases rely instead upon the much thinner – and more judicially manipulable – distinction between speech and conduct. What the *Upsolve* decision thus suggests, somewhat surprisingly perhaps, is that the new doctrinal framework, with its overriding emphasis on content neutrality as the core commitment of First Amendment law, may be attractive to courts deciding UPL cases precisely because it can be wielded to permit only a very limited alteration to the regulatory status quo. If so, this

[6] *See* Kathleen M. Sullivan, *The Intersection of Free Speech and the Legal Profession: Constraints on Lawyers' First Amendment Rights*, 67 Fordham L. Rev. 569, 580–81 (1998) (noting courts' tendency to extend "greater deference to state interest in regulating lawyer speech than the comparable speech of others").

[7] *See* Chapter 1 in this volume.

means that access-to-justice advocates should not think of constitutional litigation as an *alternative* to regulatory reform but instead as one of the means of spurring it. It also means, however, that it will be up to access-to-justice advocates to explain to courts why certain kinds of legal representation should be treated as speech for First Amendment purposes and why other kinds of legal representation should not be. It will be up to advocates, in other words, to infuse the arid framework of the Lochnerian First Amendment with the democratic values and concerns that have traditionally informed the First Amendment cases – albeit imperfectly – and that continue to inspire the access-to-justice movement.

The chapter proceeds in three sections. Section 14.1 describes the doctrinal shift that underpins recent efforts to challenge UPL laws on First Amendment grounds. Section 14.2 explores the reasoning and the complexities of the district court's decision in the *Upsolve* case. Section 14.3 examines its implications for access to justice and charts a more sensible path forward.

14.1 FIRST AMENDMENT BOUNDARIES AND THE REGULATION OF PROFESSIONAL SPEECH

The First Amendment guarantees that the government shall make "no law abridging the freedom of speech."[8] Despite the seeming absolutism of its language, however, this guarantee has never been understood to mean that the government may never enforce laws that restrict what private persons say, or even that it must always satisfy strict judicial scrutiny when it does so. Instead, the First Amendment's Speech Clause has been interpreted to provide very little constraint – and in some cases no constraint whatsoever – on the government when it regulates certain kinds of speech or regulates speech in certain kinds of ways. There is, as Fred Schauer notes, a "vast expanse of human communication that lies beyond the boundaries of the First Amendment."[9]

What kinds of speech or speech regulations lie beyond the First Amendment's boundaries has shifted over time, however. Where courts locate those boundaries reflects a contestable, and often contested, view of what kinds of speech need to be rendered mostly off-limits to regulation in order to protect the interests that the First Amendment protects. As judicial conceptions of those interests change, so too do the First Amendment's boundaries.

This fact – the mutability of the First Amendment's boundaries – has become starkly evident in recent years. As many commentators have noted, the court's changing understanding of the values that the First Amendment protects, and the means by which it protects them, has produced a noticeable expansion in the kinds

8 U.S. Const. amend. I.

9 Frederick Schauer, *The Boundaries of the First Amendment: A Preliminary Exploration of Constitutional Salience*, 117 HARV. L. REV. 1765, 1784 (2004).

of speech, and speech regulations, that are granted some degree of constitutional protection by the courts.[10]

One of the areas in which this change has been evident, if also highly contested, has been the law of professional regulation. Notwithstanding the fact that much of what lawyers, therapists, accountants, and doctors do when they provide service to clients is to listen and to speak, courts have traditionally interpreted the First Amendment to impose very few constraints on the government when it restricts who can practice these "speaking professions," and what they can say when they do.[11] Some courts have held that – as the Fourth Circuit put it recently – when the government "regulate[s] professionals providing personalized advice in a private setting to a paying client ... [t]he First Amendment does not come into play."[12] Other courts have reviewed licensing laws and other regulations of professional expression under a rather generous intermediate scrutiny standard.[13] The result has been, in both of these lines of cases, to vest states with "broad power to regulate the practice of [the professions]."[14]

In recent years, however, the scope of this broad power to regulate professional speech has come into question, as a result of the Supreme Court's turn away from what we might call "the democratic theory" of the Speech Clause that motivated the earlier, deferential approach, and its embrace instead of a broader, what some have described as Lochnerian, view of the Speech Clause's means and ends.

In this section, I explore the still somewhat tentative shift that has taken place in the past few years in judicial understandings of the constraints the First Amendment imposes on the government when it regulates professional speech, before examining in the next section how that shift impacted the district court's analysis of the constitutionality of New York's UPL laws in *Upsolve*.

14.1.1 *The Democratic Theory of Professional Regulation and the First Amendment*

The reason why courts have traditionally granted government actors broad discretion to regulate professional speech is because they have tended to view these kinds of regulations as efforts to regulate the commercial marketplace, not the political

[10] *See, for example*, Amanda Shanor, *First Amendment Coverage*, 93 N.Y.U. L. REV. 318, 322 (2018) ("The First Amendment's borders are now in a period of great transformation – largely expansion, and rapid, at that").

[11] Lowe v. S.E.C., 472 U.S. 181, 228 (1985) (White, J., concurring).

[12] Nat'l Ass'n for the Advancement of Multijurisdictional Prac. v. Lynch, 826 F.3d 195–96 (4th Cir. 2016).

[13] *See for example*, Mothershed v. Justices of Sup. Ct., 410 F.3d 602 (9th Cir. 2005) (applying intermediate scrutiny to state rule that barred out-of-state attorneys from providing legal representation in the state).

[14] United Mine Workers v. Ill. State Bar Ass'n, 389 U.S. 217, 222 (1967) (noting that this principle is "beyond question").

sphere. For this reason, courts have tended to assume that these kinds of laws pose very little threat to the democratic interests that, until very recently, were assumed to be the primary interests that the Speech Clause protects.[15]

Justice Robert Jackson was perhaps the first, and certainly one of the most influential, jurists to articulate this view of how professional regulations fit into the First Amendment. In his concurring opinion in *Thomas v. Collins* in 1945, Jackson asserted that, while the First Amendment prevents the government from "stop[ping] an unlicensed person from making a speech about the rights of man or the rights of labor" the First Amendment does *not* prevent the government from "forbidding one without its license to practice law as a vocation."[16] The First Amendment applies differently in these two classes of cases, Jackson explained, due to the "different effects [the two kinds of government regulations] had ... on interests which the state [was] empowered to protect." Laws that license who can practice law as a vocation attempt to protect members of the public "against the untrustworthy, the incompetent, or the irresponsible, or against unauthorized representation of agency," and this is obviously a legitimate thing for a democratic government to attempt to do.[17] In contrast, laws that license what Jackson described as public "speech-making" about the law do not protect consumers against this kind of abuse.[18] This is because, in these cases, there is no agency relationship for them to protect. Instead, the only purpose of these laws is to prevent the public from hearing what the government considered to be "false doctrine," and this is not a purpose that the government can legitimately pursue, consistent with the democratic principles that underpin the First Amendment. To the contrary, Jackson insisted, it was "[t]he very purpose of the First Amendment ... to foreclose [the government] from assuming [this kind of] guardianship of the public mind."[19]

In the decades after *Collins*, courts largely agreed that laws that license the professions, or regulate what professionals can say in the course of their professional activities, ordinarily pose little problem from a First Amendment standpoint because what they regulate is not speech addressed to a public audience, on matters of public concern.[20] Instead, they typically restrict speech that emerges out of and relates to

15 *See, for example,* Lillian R. BeVier, *The First Amendment and Political Speech: An Inquiry into the Substance and Limits of Principle*, 30 STAN. L. REV. 299, 309 (1978) ("[T]he constitutional process of self-government provides an indispensable clue to the meaning of the first amendment").

16 323 U.S. 516, 544 (1945) (Jackson, J., concurring).

17 *Id.* at 545.

18 *Id.*

19 *Id.* at 547.

20 *See, for example,* Planned Parenthood of Se. Pa. v. Casey, 505 U.S. 833, 884 (1992); Schware v. Bd. of Bar Exam'rs, 353 U.S. 232, 239 (1957); Lawline v. Am. Bar Ass'n, 956 F.2d 1378, 1386 (7th Cir. 1992); *see generally* Robert Post, *Informed Consent to Abortion: A First Amendment Analysis of Compelled Physician Speech*, 2007 U. ILL. L. REV. 939, 951 (2007).

the private, agency relationship between a professional and a client.[21] This means, courts assumed, that professional licensing laws and other kinds of professional speech regulations do not ordinarily threaten the "uninhibited, robust, and wide-open" public debate about public matters that the First Amendment protects in the name of democracy.[22] Instead, they protect important interests – not only the significant consumer welfare interest that Jackson identified in his concurrence but other public goods, such as the integrity of the justice system in the United States.[23]

Because courts viewed these laws as attempts to regulate the commercial practice of being a lawyer or accountant or doctor, rather than as an effort by the government to patrol the boundaries of public discourse, they tended to treat them as incidental rather than direct regulations of speech, and for that reason apply only very deferential scrutiny – if they applied any constitutional scrutiny at all.[24] This was true even when these laws made obvious speaker and content-based distinctions – as professional licensing laws commonly do.[25]

There were exceptions to this general rule of deference. First, in cases where the government attempted to use professional speech regulations to target speech that did *not* arise out of the relationship between a professional and a client, but instead addressed a public audience and touched on matters of more general public concern, courts did not defer to the government – just as Jackson's concurrence suggested that they should not. Instead, they tended to characterize the government's actions not as an incidental regulation of speech but as a "regulation of speaking or publishing as such" to which the very speech-protective rules that govern the content-based regulation of speech in the public forum apply.[26]

Second, courts strictly scrutinized governmental regulations when they understood enforcement of the regulations to threaten important democratic interests. For example, in a limited set of cases, the court recognized that the enforcement of

[21] Nat'l Ass'n for the Advancement of Multijurisdictional Prac. v. Lynch, *supra* note 12, at 196 ("The government may regulate professionals providing personalized advice in a private setting to a paying client ... [because i]n this context, the professional's speech is incidental to the conduct of the profession") (quotation omitted).

[22] New York Times Co. v. Sullivan, 376 U.S. 254, 270 (1964).

[23] *See* Goldfarb v. Va. State Bar, 421 U.S. 773, 792–93 (1975) (recognizing that the state interest "in regulating lawyers is especially great since lawyers are essential to the primary governmental function of administering justice").

[24] *See, for example,* Lowe v. S.E.C., *supra* note 11, at 232 ("If the government enacts generally applicable licensing provisions limiting the class of persons who may practice the profession, it cannot be said to have enacted a limitation on freedom of speech or the press subject to First Amendment scrutiny"); People v. Shell, 148 P.3d 162, 173–74 (Colo. 2006) (same).

[25] *See* Section 14.2 for discussion of the content-based and speaker-based nature of these kinds of laws.

[26] Lowe v. S.E.C., *supra* note 11, at 232 (White, J., concurring); *see also* Bailey v. Huggins Diagnostic & Rehab. Ctr., Inc., 952 P.2d 768, 773 (Colo. App. 1997); Dacey v. N.Y. Cnty. Laws.' Ass'n, 423 F.2d 188 (2d Cir. 1969).

professional regulations against cause-oriented lawyers could undermine democratically important equality interests, and therefore required stricter constitutional scrutiny than otherwise was required.

Most famously, perhaps, in *NAACP v. Button*, the court held that a Virginia anti-solicitation law could not be used to prevent the racial justice advocacy organization the National Association for the Advancement of Colored People (NAACP) from connecting organization-funded attorneys to potential litigants in school desegregation cases unless the government could demonstrate that, in the circumstances of the case, enforcement of the law furthered a "compelling" state interest.[27] The First Amendment required this showing, the court explained, because of the important democratic interests that would be imperiled by enforcement of the anti-solicitation law, given the fact that, for the NAACP, "litigation [was] not a technique of resolving private differences [bu]t a means for achieving the lawful objectives of equality of treatment . . . for the members of the Negro community in this country."[28] Because the court recognized that the professional activities of the NAACP lawyers constituted "a form of political expression" that, in a country riven by racialized politics, represented "the sole practicable avenue open to a minority to petition for [a] redress of grievances," the court refused to apply the deferential scrutiny that applied in cases in which the government used anti-solicitation laws to prevent "the oppressive, malicious, or avaricious use of the legal process for purely private gain."[29]

In later cases, the court reached the same conclusion about the enforcement of anti-solicitation and UPL laws against other kinds of legal advocacy groups. In *In re Primus*, for example, the court held that South Carolina's anti-solicitation rules could not be applied to the American Civil Liberties Union (ACLU) without satisfying strict scrutiny because the organization "engaged in extensive educational and lobbying activities" and "devoted much of [its] funds and energies to an extensive program of assisting certain kinds of litigation on behalf of [its] declared purposes."[30]

And in a series of cases involving union litigation support programs, the court held that state professional regulations could not be used to prohibit trade unions from connecting their members to union-subsidized lawyers who could represent them in

[27] Nat'l Ass'n for Advancement of Colored People v. Button, 371 U.S. 415, 439 (1963) ("[W]here there is a significant encroachment upon personal liberty, the State may prevail only upon showing a subordinating interest which is compelling").

[28] *Id.* at 429.

[29] *Id.* at 443, at 431 ("The NAACP is not a conventional political party; but the litigation it assists, while serving to vindicate the legal rights of members of the American Negro community, at the same time and perhaps more importantly, makes possible the distinctive contribution of a minority group to the ideas and beliefs of our society.").

[30] *Primus*, 436 U.S. at 427–28 (concluding that "[f]or the ACLU, as for the NAACP, 'litigation is not a technique of resolving private differences'; it is 'a form of political expression' and 'political association'" (quoting Nat'l Ass'n for Advancement of Colored People v. Button, *supra* note 27, at 429, 431)).

workers' compensation lawsuits without satisfying strict scrutiny.[31] Although these litigation programs were less self-consciously political than those at issue in *Button* or *Primus*, the court recognized that they nevertheless vindicated the same "fundamental First Amendment right" to engage in "collective activity ... to obtain meaningful access to the courts" that those cases recognized.[32]

Despite the court's embrace in these cases of a quite expansive view of what kinds of litigation activities vindicate democratic values, the number of cases in which the First Amendment was interpreted by lower courts to meaningfully limit the government's power over the professions turned out to be relatively few. Even when professionals spoke to a public audience, if their speech emerged out of and related to their relationship to a client, the court made clear that something far less that the rigorous standard of strict scrutiny should apply.[33] The court also made clear that the rights recognized by the *Button* line of cases only applied to nonprofit groups and actors. It was only where "political expression or association is at issue," the court explained in *In re Primus*, that the First Amendment does not "tolerate[] the degree of imprecision that often characterizes government regulation of the conduct of commercial affairs."[34]

Lower courts accordingly interpreted these precedents narrowly, to not apply to any group that might have economically self-interested reasons to engage in collective action to facilitate clients' access to the courts.[35] Courts also rejected the idea that these precedents had anything to say about the enforcement of UPL laws, or other professional regulations, against *nonlawyers*.[36] In case after case, they rejected the idea that the trade monopolies created by professional licensing regimes posed any threat to the fundamental First Amendment right that the *Button* and *Primus* and union cases recognized. Courts instead measured infringements against this fundamental right against the baseline of the existing licensing system.

The result of this rather narrow, even we might say conservative, reading of the *Button* line of cases was a body of law that made the First Amendment useful as a mechanism for challenging the efforts by state governments to repress

31 United Transp. Union v. State Bar of Mich., 401 U.S. 576 (1971); United Mine Workers v. Ill. State Bar Ass'n, *supra* note 14, at 217; Bhd. of R.R. Trainmen v. Virginia, 377 U.S. 1 (1964).

32 United Transp. Union v. State Bar of Mich., *supra* note 31, at 585–86 ("The common thread running through our decisions in *Button* [and] *Trainmen* ... is that collective activity undertaken to obtain meaningful access to the courts is a fundamental right within the protection of the First Amendment").

33 *See* Gentile v. State Bar of Nev., 501 U.S. 1030, 1033 (1991).

34 *Id.* at 430–31.

35 *See, for example*, Cap. Associated Indus., Inc. v. Stein, 922 F.3d 198 (4th Cir. 2019).

36 *See, for example*, S. Christian Leadership Conf. v. Sup. Ct., 252 F.3d 781, 790 (5th Cir. 2001) (noting that the "major difference between this case and *Button* and *Primus* is ... that the student practitioners are not licensed members of the bar" and that "[t]he ability of students to represent clients as attorneys in legal matters is entirely the relatively recent creation of the L [egal] S[ervices] C[orporation] and continues to exist entirely at the LSC's complete discretion").

well-established legal advocacy groups like the NAACP, but largely useless as a mechanism for challenging the regulatory status quo when it came to legal licensing. This doctrinal state of affairs made good sense in a world in which the First Amendment was understood primarily as a mechanism for safeguarding the autonomy of public discourse from governmental control. In this world, the First Amendment had very little relevance to the regulation of the commercial market, including its less profit-oriented corners.

This was the world in which the crisis of legitimacy that helped usher in the modern constitutional order was created. By drawing the somewhat blunt distinction that Jackson's concurrence in *Collins* drew between the regulation of the public sphere and the regulation of profit-oriented activity, the court was able to justify vigorous judicial protection of First Amendment rights even in a post-*Lochner* age. Perhaps for this reason, this view of how the First Amendment worked and what it achieved remained largely unquestioned for many decades.

Beginning in the 1970s, however, members of the court began to express growing dissatisfaction with the assumptions that underpinned the New Deal and post-New Deal First Amendment cases. More specifically, members of the court began to question the sharp distinction between the political and the commercial realms when it came to thinking about the First Amendment's means and ends. The result was a shift in the rules that governed many areas of First Amendment law, including, recently, and in still somewhat uncertain ways, professional speech.

14.1.2 *The Lochnerian First Amendment*

The significant change in the composition of the Supreme Court that occurred under President Nixon produced a marked change in the tone and content of the Supreme Court's First Amendment jurisprudence. The Burger Court's First Amendment opinions emphasized, to a much greater than had previously been true, the importance of the Speech Clause as a guarantor of individual expressive autonomy, not just democratic rights and values.[37] At the same time, both liberal and conservative members of the court increasingly began to question the assumption that underpinned Justice Jackson's *Collins* concurrence, and many of the other early and mid-twentieth-century cases: namely, that the commercial marketplace was *not* an important arena for political discussion and debate, and that regulations of commercial relationships did not therefore threaten to create a "guardianship of the public mind." They recognized instead that, just like the speech that appears in newspapers, books, and public ceremonies, the speech that takes place on billboards, in boardrooms, and in doctor's offices can, and in some cases clearly does, shape public attitudes and beliefs, and that regulations of the commercial marketplace can consequently serve political ends, as well as consumer welfarist ones.

[37] *See* Lakier, *supra* note 3, at 1317–25 (describing the shift).

The result of this changing view of the interests that the First Amendment protected was a marked shift in how the court analyzed the constitutionality of laws that regulated speech and expressive conduct in the commercial marketplace. This shift first became evident in the Court's commercial advertising cases.[38] Eventually, however, this shift in the court's view of the First Amendment also made its impact felt in the case law dealing with professional speech and licensing.

Two decisions in particular suggested a very different approach to the constitutional review of professional regulation than courts had taken so far. The first of these decisions was *Holder v. Humanitarian Law Project*, which the court decided in 2010.[39] The law at issue in *Holder* – a provision in the Patriot Act that made it a crime to provide "material support" to designated foreign terrorist organizations – was not what anyone would describe as a regulation of professional speech.[40] It was enacted to combat the distinctive harms associated with international terrorism, not the harms that flowed from untrustworthy or incompetent professional services. Nevertheless, because what the plaintiffs challenged in the case was the part of the law that defined material support to include the provision of "expert advice and assistance" to foreign terrorist organizations, the question it forced the court to confront was essentially the same question that confronted courts all the time in professional licensing cases: namely, what standard of scrutiny should apply to laws that restrict the provision of expert advice and assistance?[41] As the previous section makes clear, when confronted with this question in the professional regulation context, courts prior to 2010 almost invariably applied the deferential standard of scrutiny that First Amendment doctrine required when the government regulated speech only incidentally.

In *Holder*, however, the court insisted that the ban on providing expert advice to foreign terrorist organizations could not be treated as an incidental regulation of speech because application of the law turned on the *content* of the advice being provided and, more specifically, turned on whether that advice was "derived from scientific, technical or other specialized knowledge."[42] In cases where "the conduct triggering coverage under the statute consists of communicating a message," the court wrote, the law cannot be considered an incidental regulation of speech and courts must "[apply] a more demanding standard."[43]

The implications for the professional speech cases were obvious. After all, virtually all professional licensing laws make the distinction between expert and

[38] *See, for example*, Bates v. State Bar of Ariz., 433 U.S. 350 (1977); Va. Pharmacy Bd. v. Va. Consumer Council, 425 U.S. 748 (1976); Post & Shanor, *supra* note 3, at 167–68.

[39] Holder v. Humanitarian Law Project, 561 U.S. 1 (2010).

[40] *Id.* at 8–9.

[41] *Id.* at 21.

[42] *Id.* at 27–28 (quoting 18 U.S.C. § 2339A).

[43] *Id.* at 28 (quoting Texas v. Johnson, 491 U.S. 397, 403–04 (1989)).

non-expert advice-giving that the *Holder* Court insisted was content-based.[44] This is not surprising: The purpose of these laws is, after all, to limit who can claim to be expert in particular ways, and to structure the practice of that expertise. *Holder* thus very strongly suggested that many professional licensing laws should henceforth be treated as content-based regulations of speech, rather than as general regulations of conduct that only incidentally target speech.

This was certainly how some lower courts interpreted the decision. For example, in *King v. New Jersey*, the Third Circuit relied upon *Holder* to conclude that a New Jersey law prohibiting licensed counselors from using therapeutic methods to attempt to change the sexual orientation of their minor clients could not be considered an incidental speech regulation because application of the law turned on the content of the counselors' speech to their clients.[45] "Speech is speech," the Third Circuit insisted, "and it must be analyzed as such for purposes of the First Amendment."[46] The Eleventh Circuit relied upon *Holder* to reach the same conclusion about a Florida law that prohibited physicians from asking patients whether they possessed firearms in their home, or from noting as much in their medical records.[47] Here too, because the law turned on the content of what the physician said, the Eleventh Circuit concluded that, under *Holder*, it could no longer be treated as a regulation of conduct that only incidentally restricted speech.

The significance of this change for the actual regulation of the professions was not immediately apparent, however. This is because even those courts that interpreted *Holder* to change how they performed the incidental regulation of speech analysis quickly devised a new means of justifying a deferential standard of review in professional speech cases. They argued that, even if these regulations could no longer be considered incidental regulations of speech, they nevertheless triggered deferential scrutiny because the speech they directly regulated fell into a newly identified category of low-value speech that was not fully protected by the First Amendment.[48]

44 Post, *supra* note 20, at 949–50 ("[I]n the context of [professional] practice we insist upon competence, not debate, and so we subject professional speech to an entirely different regulatory regime. We closely monitor the messages conveyed by professional speech, and we sanction viewpoints that are false when measured by the 'knowledge ... ordinarily possessed and exercised by [professionals] in good standing.'") (quoting Larsen v. Yelle, 246 N.W.2d 841, 844 (Minn. 1976)).

45 King v. Governor of the State of New Jersey, 767 F.3d 216 (3d Cir. 2014).

46 *Id.* at 228.

47 Wollschlaeger v. Governor of State of Fla., 814 F.3d 1159, 1183–84 (11th Cir. 2015). The decision was incredibly contested. *See* Wollschlaeger v. Governor of Fla., 649 F. App'x 647 (11th Cir. 2016), *aff'd in part and rev'd in part en banc*, 848 F.3d 1293 (11th Cir. 2017).

48 *See, for example*, King v. Governor, *supra* note 45, at 232; *see also* Moore-King v. Cnty of Chesterfield, Va., 708 F.3d 560, 569 (4th Cir. 2013) (identifying a category of "professional speech" that the government could "license and regulate ... without running afoul of the First Amendment").

In 2018, however, the court appeared to decisively reject this new-wine-in-old-bottles approach to the constitutional analysis in professional speech cases when, in its decision in *National Institute for Life v. Becerra,* it insisted that professional speech was not in fact a low-value category of speech under the First Amendment.[49] Instead, the court made explicit what *Holder* had only implicitly suggested: When the government imposes a content-based restriction on what professionals can say to their clients or potential clients, courts should apply the same presumption of unconstitutionality they apply to the content-based regulations of public speech – at least in cases where, Justice Thomas wrote somewhat cryptically in his majority opinion, the government regulates professional "speech as speech."[50]

Courts should treat content-based regulations of professional speech with the same distaste they treated content-based regulations of public speech, Justice Thomas asserted, because in both cases, the content-based regulation of speech threatens important First Amendment values. Content-based regulations of professional speech could, like content-based regulations of other kinds of speech, be motivated by a desire "to suppress unpopular ideas or information" rather than any "legitimate regulatory goal."[51] Even when they aren't, Justice Thomas warned, they nevertheless interfere with the truth-promoting ends of the First Amendment:

> [W]hen the government polices the content of professional speech, it can fail to "preserve an uninhibited marketplace of ideas in which truth will ultimately prevail." Professionals might have a host of good-faith disagreements, both with each other and with the government, on many topics in their respective fields. Doctors and nurses might disagree about the ethics of assisted suicide or the benefits of medical marijuana; lawyers and marriage counselors might disagree about the prudence of prenuptial agreements or the wisdom of divorce; bankers and accountants might disagree about the amount of money that should be devoted to savings or the benefits of tax reform. "[T]he best test of truth is the power of the thought to get itself accepted in the competition of the market," and the people lose when the government is the one deciding which ideas should prevail.[52]

In this remarkable passage, Justice Thomas appeared to not only reject the idea that professional speech was a low-value category of speech for purposes of the First Amendment. He also appeared to reject the core assumption that underpinned Justice Jackson's *Collins* concurrence and the rest of the seventy-odd years of professional speech cases. This assumption was, of course, that the content-based regulation of professional speech did *not* pose the same threat to First Amendment interests and values as the content-based regulation of speech about matters of

49 Nat'l Inst. of Fam. & Life Advocs. v. Becerra, 138 S. Ct. 2361 (2018).

50 *Id.* at 2374.

51 *Id.*

52 *Id.* at 2374–75 (quoting McCullen v. Coakley, 134 S. Ct. 2518, 2529 (2014) and Abrams v. United States, 250 U.S. 616, 630 (1919) (Holmes, J., dissenting)).

public concern because it regulated speech that emerged out of a commercial relationship – and a relationship that was characterized, as many commercial relationships are, by significant inequalities of power and knowledge – and therefore served important and legitimate ends that the content-based regulation of the public sphere did not further. The quote above suggests instead that courts should show the same skepticism to regulations of professional speech as they show to laws that regulate public discourse because the physician's waiting room is just as important a place for what Justice Holmes called "the free trade in ideas" as the Speakers' Corner in Hyde Park.[53]

In fact, notwithstanding the passage above, the *Becerra* opinion implicitly acknowledged that the government possesses greater power to regulate professional speech than to regulate speech in the public sphere. Justice Thomas noted, for example, that "the First Amendment does not prevent restrictions directed at commerce or conduct from imposing incidental burdens on speech" and asserted that "[l]ongstanding torts for professional malpractice" as well as laws that require informed consent before medical procedures should still be characterized as "regulations of professional conduct that incidentally burden speech."[54] Thomas asserted as much even though these laws clearly would not, in many instances at least, qualify as incidental regulations of speech under the rule set out in *Holder*.[55] The obvious implication of this assertion is that, when it comes to the kinds of speech acts to which these laws apply, the First Amendment rule against content-based regulation that governs regulation of the public forum does not apply – just as Jackson's concurrence suggested it should not.

The opinion nevertheless made clear that the category of otherwise content-based speech acts that now could be treated as incidental regulations of professional conduct was considerably narrower than it had traditionally been understood to be. It no longer includes virtually anything the professional speaker says in the course of serving a client. Instead, there has to be some kind of direct "tie[]" between the speech targeted by the regulation and a professional act or procedure.[56] The court did not explain what it means for a regulation of professional speech to be

53 Abrams v. United States, *supra* note 52, at 630.

54 Nat'l Inst. of Fam. & Life Advocs. v. Becerra, *supra* note 49, at 2373.

55 Whether professionals violate informed consent laws, or commit tortious malpractice, often depends on "what they say." Holder v. Humanitarian Law Project, *supra* note 39, at 27. As Robert Post notes, "doctors are routinely held liable for malpractice . . . for failing to inform patients in a timely way of an accurate diagnosis, for failing to give patients proper instructions, for failing to ask patients necessary questions, or for failing to refer a patient to an appropriate specialist." Post, *supra* note 20, at 950–51. This makes it hard to understand how these kinds of laws could be considered incidental under the *Holder* rule.

56 Nat'l Inst. of Fam. & Life Advocs. v. Becerra, *supra* note 49, at 2373–74 (rejecting the claim that the law at issue in the case constituted an incidental regulation of speech because it did not "facilitate informed consent to a medical procedure" and was "not tied to a procedure at all" but "applies to all interactions between a covered facility and its clients, regardless of whether a medical procedure is ever sought, offered, or performed").

sufficiently "tied to a procedure" to warrant deferential scrutiny.[57] But the strong implication of the passage quoted above was that professionals could not be sanctioned for merely communicating their opinion to their clients – that when the government did so, it regulated "speech as such" and therefore had to satisfy the demanding standards of strict scrutiny.

Understood as such, *Becerra* appeared to authorize, even perhaps require, the "expansion [of the First Amendment] into areas long thought impervious to constitutional law" – specifically, areas "of economic regulation . . . courts had abandoned to the legislatures after the *Lochner* disaster."[58] This was certainly how some courts interpreted the decision. Although some courts interpreted *Becerra* narrowly, as merely reinstituting the doctrinal state of affairs that existed prior to *Holder*,[59] others read it in combination with *Holder* to require a markedly different approach to the constitutional analysis in professional speech and licensing cases. One of the courts that did so was the district court that decided the *Upsolve* case. In the next section I discuss the details and reasoning of that case, and what it tells us about the complexities of the Lochnerian turn in First Amendment jurisprudence, before exploring in Section 14.3 the normative implications of the decision for the access-to-justice movement.

14.2 THE *UPSOLVE* LITIGATION

Upsolve involved an as-applied challenge to the UPL laws that have been on the books, in one form or another, in New York since the early twentieth century.[60] The challenge was brought by the nonprofit access-to-justice organization, Upsolve, Inc.

Founded in 2016, Upsolve represents a new breed of legal aid. Started by a Harvard undergraduate, a lawyer, and an engineer, Upsolve received funding not only from traditional supporters of legal aid, like the Legal Services Corporation, but also from tech funders, like Y Combinator and Google CEO Eric Schmidt.[61] And rather than providing individual clients the services of pro bono lawyers, the organization instead employed tech tools to help expand access to justice to poor Americans. Indeed, the organization's signature product was an app that helped individuals file for Chapter 7 bankruptcy.[62]

57 *Id.*

58 Daniel J. H. Greenwood, *First Amendment Imperialism*, 1999 UTAH L. REV. 659, 659–61 (1999).

59 *See infra notes* 107–108 and accompanying text.

60 Laurel Rigertas, *The Birth of the Movement to Prohibit the Unauthorized Practice of Law*, 37 QUINNIPIAC L. REV. 97, 117–21 (2019) (chronicling the emergence of the UPL regime in New York at the behest of the newly created bar associations in the late nineteenth and early twentieth centuries).

61 Danny Crichton, *YC-Backed Upsolve Is Automating Bankruptcy for Everyone*, TECHCRUNCH (Jan. 16, 2019), https://techcrunch.com/2019/01/16/upsolve-bankruptcy/ (last accessed Feb. 20, 2025).

62 For details of how the app operated, see *In re* Peterson, No. 19-24045, 2022 WL 1800949, at *8 (Bankr. D. Md. June 1, 2022).

Upsolve did not rely on technology alone to help its users, however. The organization recognized, as it should, that human advice and assistance represented an important part of any effort to expand access to the courts. It consequently integrated human review and assistance into the operation of its bankruptcy app.[63] And soon after launching the app, Upsolve began to develop plans for a non-technology-based access-to-justice program in New York.

The program, which Upsolve called the "Access to Justice Movement" (AJM), would train nonlawyer "Justice Advocates" to help defendants in debt collection lawsuits fill out the one-page form that the state provided those served with debt collection complaints.[64] Although the form was intended to help unrepresented defendants figure out how to respond to a complaint served against them, it failed to communicate in a manner that was always easy to understand. Its language was too technical, and it assumed a basic knowledge of the institutions and processes of the legal system that many defendants did not possess.[65] The job Upsolve envisaged for the Justice Advocates was to help make the form easier to use for more of the roughly 85 percent of defendants in debt collection lawsuits who either chose not to, or did not have the resources to, procure a lawyer.[66] The Advocates would do so by explaining to individual clients what the various questions on the form meant in ordinary language, and by advising clients how they should answer them.

In its complaint, Upsolve claimed that the only thing stopping it from starting the new program was the threat of prosecution under New York's UPL laws.[67] This threat is not insignificant. Like many other states, New York's UPL laws allow the imposition of criminal as well as civil penalties on anyone who engages in the UPL.[68] And although these laws, like similar statutes in other states, do not define what it means to engage in the UPL, New York courts had for many years interpreted them to prohibit, among other things, "the giving of legal advice and counsel" by all but duly licensed attorneys.[69] This meant that the laws forbade the

[63] Upsolve, *Internal Policy on Not Providing Legal Advice for Employees*, https://upsolve.org/no-legal-advice/ (last accessed Feb. 20, 2025) (describing the human review built into the Upsolve process).

[64] Complaint at 17, Upsolve, Inc. v. James, *supra* note 1, (No. 1:22-cv-00627).

[65] As Upsolve pointed out in its complaint, the form required defendants to know (among other things) whether service of the complaint against them "was not correct as a matter of law," or whether the statute of limitation that applied to the suit against them had run out. *Id.* at 11–12. Neither of these questions are likely to be easy to answer for nonlawyer defendants.

[66] *Id.* at 6–7.

[67] Upsolve, Inc. v. James, *supra* note 1, at 107.

[68] *See* N.Y. Judiciary Law §§ 476-a, 478, 484, 485, 750, 753 (proscribing the unauthorized practice of law and providing for criminal and civil penalties on the practice); Matter of Rowe, 80 N.Y.2d 336, 341–42 (N.Y. 1992) (defining the practice of law in New York as "the rendering of legal advice and opinions directed to particular clients")

[69] Spivak v. Sachs, 16 N.Y.2d 163, 166 (1965) ("It is settled that the practice of law forbidden in this State . . . to all but duly licensed New York attorneys includes legal advice and counsel as well as appearing in the courts and holding oneself out as a lawyer") (citing cases).

one thing that the Justice Advocates would be trained to do: provide their "legal advice and opinions . . . to particular clients."[70]

In an effort to establish the legality of the new program notwithstanding the hostile statutory terrain, Upsolve turned to a higher power: the First Amendment. It filed suit in federal court, seeking a declaratory judgment that enforcement of the UPL laws against the Justice Advocates program would violate its First Amendment rights, and those of the Justice Advocates.

To support this claim, Upsolve made two arguments. Its first argument relied heavily on the *Button* line of cases. Upsolve argued that, just like the lawyers in those cases, the Justice Advocates possessed a fundamental right to engage in "collective activity to obtain meaningful access to the courts" that would be infringed were they prevented by the UPL laws from providing help and assistance to defendants faced with debt collection actions against them.[71]

This argument was a strong one. The parallels between the cases were striking. Like the NAACP and the ACLU, Upsolve was a nonprofit organization that provided legal services to clients, not because it wanted to make a profit but because doing so furthered its vision of a just democratic society. The organization described itself as a "movement to fight for a legal & financial system we can all access."[72] In its legal filings, it described the Justice Advocates program as a project of political advocacy that worked to ensure that all New Yorkers can access their legal rights with the goal of "fight[ing] the cycle of poverty and drawing attention to the shortcomings of the justice system for low-income New Yorkers."[73]

Furthermore, as in *Button* and *Primus*, the risk that commercial considerations would undermine how Upsolve promoted these grand democratic purposes appeared very low. This was because, like the NAACP and ACLU programs, there were no monetary stakes for the AJM program. Neither the Advocates nor Upsolve profited from the unrepresented defendants who participated in the program. Thus, for Upsolve, as in *Button* and *Primus*, there was little reason to worry that application of state law was necessary to prevent "the oppressive, malicious, or avaricious use of the legal process for purely private gain."[74]

Nevertheless, despite the strength of the analogy that Upsolve was able to draw between its aims and activities and those of the organizations that had famously prevailed in earlier access-to-justice cases, the district court rejected the idea that Justice Advocates possessed the same fundamental right to engage in "collective activity . . . to obtain meaningful access to the courts" as the lawyers in *Button* and

[70] Matter of Rowe, *supra* note 68, at 341.

[71] Upsolve, Inc. v. James, *supra* note 1, at 110.

[72] UPSOLVE, https://upsolve.org/ (last accessed Mar. 9, 2024).

[73] Memorandum in Support of Plaintiffs' Motion for a Preliminary Injunction, Upsolve, Inc. v. James, *supra* note 1, at 97 (No. 1:22-cv-00627), 2022 WL 1057475, at *11.

[74] *Id.*

Primus did.[75] Instead, the district court interpreted the principles articulated in *Button* and *Primus* to apply only to the associational and expressive activities of *licensed* attorneys. The court suggested, further, that the fundamental right those cases recognized might apply only to certain kinds of litigation campaigns – those in which licensed attorneys "sought to vindicate constitutional rights, such as equal protection against discriminatory laws," not more basic rights, like the right to access justice.[76]

The district court's opinion strongly suggested that the reason why the court adopted this exceedingly narrow interpretation of the relevant precedents – one that is, it is worth pointing out, very difficult to reconcile with the facts of the union litigation cases – was because the court feared that any other interpretation would have too destabilizing an effect on the regulatory landscape.[77] Were the First Amendment interpreted to grant nonlawyers a fundamental right to "[p]romote access to the courts," the court warned, the result would be to "allow any non-lawyer, so long as they do not charge a fee, to bootstrap a right to practice law."[78] It would mean that "[c]lients in any type of civil lawsuit would . . . enjoy the right to full non-lawyer representation."[79] Clearly alarmed by the specter of this deregulated world, the court adamantly rejected the idea that the democratic interests protected by the First Amendment access-to-justice cases were implicated here.

In marked contrast to the earlier cases, however, the district court's rejection of the relevance of the *Button* line of cases did not doom Upsolve's challenge. Instead, the court picked up the second argument that Upsolve made to challenge the enforcement of the UPL laws against the Justice Advocates program, and concluded that, even if the Justice Advocates lacked a fundamental First Amendment right to promote access to the courts, they nonetheless possessed a different fundamental First Amendment right not to be regulated by a content- or speaker-based law – and a right that was likely to be violated in this case. The court rejected Upsolve's *democracy* argument, in other words, but it accepted its *content neutrality* one.

The court's acceptance of this second argument required it to reject and/or distinguish what it acknowledged to be the significant body of prior case law that

75 Upsolve, Inc. v. James, *supra* note 1, at 111.

76 *Id.*

77 The Court was quite explicit in the union cases that the First Amendment protected the right to associate to facilitate access to justice even when only statutory rights were at stake. *See* United Transp. Union v. State Bar of Mich., *supra* note 31, at 585 (noting that the "basic right to group legal action" protected "a cooperative union of workers seeking to assist its members in effectively asserting claims under the [Federal Employers' Liability Act]"); Bhd. of R.R. Trainmen v. Virginia, *supra* note 31, at 5 ("It cannot be seriously doubted that the First Amendment's guarantees of free speech, petition and assembly give railroad workers the right to gather together for the lawful purpose of helping and advising one another in asserting . . . statutory rights which would be vain and futile if the workers could not talk together freely as to the best course to follow.").

78 Upsolve, Inc. v. James, *supra* note 1, at 111.

79 *Id.*

assumed that lawyers (or, as in this case, nonlawyers) had no right to be regulated by content-neutral laws when they engaged in the practice of law.[80] In order to justify putting aside this very significant body of law, the court turned, as it had to, to more recent and more binding authority – namely, the decisions in *Holder* and *Becerra*.

The district court interpreted *Becerra* to stand for the proposition that, at least when they regulate "pure speech," professional licensing laws are subject to the same neutrality obligations as any other laws. "*Becerra* undermined the notion," the court wrote, that "licensing requirements are somehow *sui generis* under the First Amendment merely because they target professionals."[81] More specifically, the court argued, *Becerra* undermined the idea that the government could use the tool of professional licensing to "transform pure speech" into conduct and "evade First Amendment scrutiny altogether."[82]

This meant, the court concluded, that the crucial question in the case – or at least, the question that determined what level of scrutiny applied to Upsolve's First Amendment challenge – was not, as courts had previously assumed, whether the UPL laws regulated speech directed at a public audience about matters of public concern, or regulated speech that emerged out of the agency relationship between a professional expert and a client. Instead, the crucial question was whether the kind of activities the Justice Advocates wished to engage in constituted speech or something else called "conduct."[83]

The district court invoked *Holder*, in turn, for the proposition that the provision of personalized advice to another was an act of speech, not conduct.[84] This meant, the court asserted, that even if the use of UPL laws to prevent nonlawyers from filing briefs or from arguing cases could continue to be treated as an incidental regulation of speech, the same was not true when it came to the use of UPL laws to prohibit nonlawyers from providing individual clients with out-of-court legal advice.[85] The use of the law in this context had to be considered a direct regulation of speech – and more than that, under the logic of *Holder*, it had to be considered a *content-based* regulation of speech.[86] This was because, the district court explained, like the material support statute in *Holder*, application of New York's UPL ban depended on what the Justice Advocates said. The fact that the ban prohibited the Justice

80 *Id.* at 112 (acknowledging that "[t]here is no doubt [that] lower courts have overwhelmingly concluded that UPL statutes regulate professional 'conduct' and merely burden a non-lawyer's speech incidentally").

81 *Id.* at 116.

82 *Id.*

83 *Id.* at 112 (noting that "plaintiff's claim hinges on whether the act of giving legal advice should be conceptualized as conduct or speech").

84 *Id.* at 114.

85 *Id.* at 112 (noting that, although in the past, nonlawyers "have been excluded from 'drafting' pleadings and 'filing' legal documents" without triggering heightened First Amendment scrutiny, "[t]hese conduct-focused cases are inapposite, as Plaintiffs do not seek to do any of these activities" but instead seek merely to provide "out-of-court verbal advice").

86 *Id.* at 114.

Advocates from providing only advice about matters related to their legal rights and responsibilities, but did not prevent them from advising clients about any other topic, made the law "by definition [a] content-based [regulation of] speech" under *Holder*.[87] The logic of that opinion, it wrote, fit "seamlessly" with this one.[88]

The court accordingly held that enforcement of the UPL law against the Justice Advocates program would be consistent with the First Amendment only if the government could demonstrate that enforcement of the ban, in the specific circumstances in which it applied, furthered a compelling governmental interest by the least speech-restrictive means.[89] And the court ultimately concluded that, in all likelihood, New York could not meet this heavy burden.

Although the district court acknowledged that the interests New York invoked to defend its UPL laws – namely, protecting the welfare of legal consumers and safeguarding the integrity of the courts – are generally compelling interests for a government to pursue, it rejected the claim that these interests were compelling as applied to the Justice Advocates program.[90] According to the court, the fact that Upsolve permitted the Justice Advocates to only advise clients about a limited number of matters, did not allow them to appear in court or file legal documents on behalf of their clients, and required them to alert clients to the need for attorney representation when the problems posed by their cases proved too complex meant that the program posed little threat to the interests of legal consumers.[91] To the contrary: By giving clients who otherwise could not afford a lawyer some amount of legal advice, it promoted the welfare of legal consumers, as well as the integrity of the New York courts.[92]

The court also found that New York's ban on the provision of legal advice by nonlawyers was not narrowly tailored because there were many other ways that the state could protect the interests of legal consumers against incompetent advice-givers. It could – as it in fact did – sanction after the fact those who provided erroneous advice.[93] It could also require Justice Advocates to disclose to clients their (lack of) legal training and the limited scope of their services.[94] It could even require Justice Advocates and other nonlawyers to pass through a certification

[87] *Id.*

[88] *Id.*

[89] *Id.* at 117. The court also found that strict scrutiny was warranted because New York's ban on UPL made a speaker-based discrimination, and one that, as applied to the Justice Advocates, reflected a content preference. *Id.* at 115. Because this argument dovetails with the argument about content-based discrimination, I do not discuss it separately. Nevertheless, technically, the court found the New York laws to engage in two separate kinds of (presumptively unconstitutional) discrimination.

[90] *Id.* at 117.

[91] *Id.* at 118.

[92] *Id.* at 118.

[93] *Id.* at 119.

[94] *Id.*

process similar to, but less rigorous than, the one licensed attorneys had to satisfy.[95] The court held, in other words, that New York could *regulate* the provision of legal advice by nonlawyers. What it could not do was simply ban it.

The district court consequently reached a conclusion that no prior court had reached: Nonlawyers possess a First Amendment right to provide out-of-court legal advice to individual clients, at least when they do so as part of an adequately structured and safeguarded legal aid program. The decision, in this respect, demonstrates quite vividly the expansiveness of the Lochnerian First Amendment. It suggests how the decisions in *Becerra* and *Holder* could be interpreted by lower courts to call into question the constitutionality of licensing regimes – in this case, the UPL laws – that had for decades escaped serious constitutional challenge.

The decision also demonstrates, however, the complexity of this project of First Amendment expansion. Scholars have warned that the Lochnerized First Amendment could be used to effectively "constitutionaliz[e] the unregulated operation of the laissez-faire commercial marketplace," thereby imposing "a strait-jacket [on] our institutions of democratic governance."[96] But this is not the best reading of what the decision in *Upsolve* accomplishes. Rather than simply reading a laissez-faire vision of constitutional liberty into the First Amendment, the decision instead protects what not only access-to-justice advocates but the court itself had in prior decades recognized to be a fundamentally important democratic right. It protects the right of "[l]aymen . . . to associate together . . . to preserve and enforce rights granted them under federal [and state] laws."[97] This is true even if it does so on the basis of a formalist claim about the distinction between speech and conduct, rather than by reasoning more pragmatically about the kinds of rights that individuals need to possess to fully participate in democratic society, as the *Button* line of cases do.

Indeed, it may very well have been *because* of the formality of the content neutrality argument *Upsolve* made – *because* it did not require the court to reach potentially contested conclusions about the democratic deficits of the existing licensing regime – that the district court was willing to accept it. Whatever the case, the result was an opinion that protects democratic interests, not just commercial ones.

Nor does the opinion impose anything like a "straight jacket" on market regulation. To the contrary: The opinion makes clear that legislatures and state courts retain significant power under the court's interpretation of the First Amendment to regulate nonlawyer legal advocacy and advice-giving in all sorts of ways. Indeed, the district court went out of its way to emphasize the "narrowness" of its holding in this respect.[98]

95 *Id.*

96 Post & Shanor, *supra* note 3, at 166.

97 Bhd. of R.R. Trainmen v. Virginia, *supra* note 31, at 7.

98 Upsolve, Inc. v. James, *supra* note 1, at 111–12 ("At the outset, the Court underscores that an abstract 'right to practice law' is not at issue in this narrow challenge. . . . '[T]he issue here is a

The trouble the court took to emphasize this aspect of its ruling suggests another reason why the court may have embraced the plaintiffs' content neutrality argument: It may have believed it imposed *less* of a straightjacket on the regulation of the professions than an argument based on the *Button* line of cases because it would apply only to the provision of out-of-court legal advice, rather than to other kinds of legal practice. It is not at all clear that this perception – if indeed it was what motivated the court to rule as it did – is an accurate one, however. Judicial recognition that Justice Advocates possessed a fundamental right to engage in collective action to facilitate access to the courts would not necessarily mean that future courts would have to grant "clients in any type of civil lawsuit . . . the right to full non-lawyer representation," as the district court warned. It would only mean that courts would have to apply strict scrutiny in all cases in which UPL laws prevent nonprofit groups from providing clients with non-licensed legal assistance. And, although strict scrutiny is a rigorous standard, its application is obviously not always fatal in fact. It is perfectly plausible that, even under such a standard, courts could and would find that a ban on the nonlawyer provision of complex legal tasks such as drafting briefs or arguing in court furthered the state's compelling interests in the welfare of legal consumers and the integrity of the justice system, even if a wholesale ban on the nonlawyer provision of other legal advice wouldn't pass muster.

At the same time, the fact that the decision in *Upsolve* was grounded in the Justice Advocates' right to content neutrality, not their right to engage in collective political expression, meant that the right the court articulated could potentially be invoked by for-profit actors quite unlike Upsolve. After all, most of the alternative mechanisms that the district court cited as support for its conclusion that New York possessed alternative, less speech-restrictive means to achieve its regulatory objectives – legal malpractice liability, disclosure requirements, and the like – could easily be adopted by commercial actors also.

Viewed objectively, it is safe to say as a result that the *Upsolve* decision is in some respects broader than a ruling based on the *Button* line of cases would have been, even if in other respects it may be somewhat narrower. What it reflects, overall, is a doctrinal logic that results in a *different* distribution of First Amendment rights than an approach grounded in an access-to-justice logic would have produced.

Nevertheless, this was no doubt a ruling that was intended to fit within, rather than undermine, New York's existing regulatory framework. Indeed, one way to read the opinion was as a spur to the New York courts and legislatures not to deregulate but to regulate more expansively by creating a two-tier system of regulation and licensing for law, similar to that which exists in medicine. How should access-to-justice advocates feel then about this far-from-radical but also quite significant

narrow one: whether the First Amendment protects the precise legal advice that Plaintiffs seek to provide, in the precise setting in which they intend to provide it. The Court holds that it does.'").

decision? And what are its implications going forward? These are the questions I take up in the final section.

14.3 IMPLICATIONS

The district court's decision in *Upsolve* is clearly good news for access to justice. As advocates have long argued, the serious crisis of legal representation that besets so much of the American legal system is unlikely to be solved without significant reform to the existing regulatory system and to the monopoly that the licensed bar enjoys over the practice of law in the vast majority of states.[99]

The trial court's opinion in *Upsolve* provides an avenue for reform of this kind in states where ordinary regulatory pathways are blocked. It not only gives the green light to Upsolve's experimental project in New York; it lays out the doctrinal argument that advocates in other states can make to demand reform, and it also provides persuasive authority they can rely on when they do so. Indeed, advocates have already taken advantage of the opportunity it offers. In South Carolina, the NAACP recently filed a First Amendment lawsuit, challenging the constitutionality of enforcing the state's UPL laws against the organization's proposed Housing Advocates program, which would train nonlawyers to provide assistance to individuals faced with eviction.[100] In its brief, the organization heavily cited *Upsolve* as support for its claim that the application of the law to the Housing Advocates program triggered strict scrutiny, because it represented a "content-based regulation of ... speech."[101] And while there are signs that the South Carolina district court is attempting to avoid having to deal with the difficult First Amendment question it raises, similar constitutional challenges are very likely to emerge in other states before too long.[102]

If these lawsuits succeed, the result will be, as the previous section makes clear, only a limited alteration to the existing licensing regime, but nevertheless a significant one. This is because even relatively simple legal advice – such as, for example, the advice the Justice Advocates are instructed to provide their clients, to whenever possible "deny the allegations" in complaints filed against them – can help avoid

[99] *See, for example*, Gillian K. Hadfield, *Legal Markets*, 60 J. ECON. LITERATURE 1264 (2022); Deborah L. Rhode, *Access to Justice: A Roadmap for Reform*, 41 FORDHAM URB. L.J. 1227 (2014); Rebecca L. Sandefur, *Legal Advice from Nonlawyers: Consumer Demand, Provider Quality, and Public Harms*, 16 STAN. J. C.R.-C.L. 283 (2020).

[100] *See* S.C. State Conf. of NAACP v. Wilson, No. 2:23-CV-01121-DCN, 2023 WL 5207978, at *1 (D.S.C. Aug. 14, 2023).

[101] Memorandum in Support of Plaintiffs' Motion for a Preliminary Injunction at *16-17, S.C. State Conf. of NAACP v. Wilson (D.S.C. 2023) (No. 2:23-CV-01121-DCN).

[102] In a recent order, the district court invoked the doctrine of Pullman Abstention to stay the case until the South Carolina Supreme Court has an opportunity to determine whether the Housing Advocate program did in fact violate the state's UPL laws. S.C. State Conf. of NAACP v. Wilson, *supra* note 100, at *9. The NAACP is currently appealing this decision.

some of the most serious harms produced by the crisis of legal representation, such as the harm of default judgments. And it is the kind of advice that can be imparted to nonlawyers relatively easily, as the twenty-eight-page Justice Advocates training guide makes clear. A limitation on the monopoly of legal work by lawyers therefore provides an opportunity for access-to-justice organizations like Upsolve to address some of the most egregious and easily addressed problems caused by the crisis of representation in the United States, while still providing the professional bar the power to dictate who can engage in more complex, and less easily trainable, lawyerly tasks.

This is not to say that granting nonlawyers the power to provide this kind of advice poses no risks to the consumer welfare and judicial integrity interests that New York and other states insist are served by UPL laws. Indeed, many of the most established legal aid organizations in the state filed an amicus brief in support of New York state because they believed that granting a First Amendment right to the Justice Advocates to provide individualized legal advice would do more harm than good.[103] More specifically, these organizations argued that extending a First Amendment right to Justice Advocates to provide individualized legal services would create a kind of two-tier system of justice, in which those with sufficient economic resources to pay for a lawyer would receive the kind of nuanced and tailored advice that legal education enables, whereas those without the money to pay for a lawyer would have to rely upon the inevitably simplified – and for that reason, sometimes wrong – advice of those trained by an eighteen-page manual.[104] The aid organizations warned that this two-tier system of justice would not only be stratified along class lines but also racially – the result being to force the "Black and Latinx communities that are … disproportionately impacted by debt collection abuses" to rely upon "lower-quality legal services" than other communities receive, thereby only "further entrench[ing] the harms of a discriminatory, two-tiered financial system."[105]

These organizations are likely correct that what the decision in *Upsolve* enables is not, by any means, a fully egalitarian market in legal services. They are also almost certainly correct that the inequalities will continue to be manifested along racial as well as class lines. And they are also likely correct that, in some cases, the advice a Justice Advocate provides a client may not only be unhelpful but may be wrong in a legally meaningful respect – that it will result in precisely the non-easily remediable kind of harm the licensing system is meant to prevent.

[103] Brief of Consumer Law Experts et al. as Amici Curiae Opposing Plaintiffs' Motion for a Preliminary Injunction, Upsolve, Inc. v. James, *supra* note 1, at 97 (No. 1:22-cv-00627).

[104] *Id.* at 8 (arguing that "the [Justice Advocates] Training Guide adopts a one-size-fits-all model of advice that ignores potential claims and defenses available to the consumer, including advising consumers who may not have been served yet to file an answer, at the risk of waiving jurisdiction defenses, and advis[es] consumers using oversimplified calculations of statutes of limitations, among other problems").

[105] *Id.*

Nevertheless, given the seriousness of the crisis of legal representation in New York, the number of cases in which their advice will result in worse outcomes for defendants is apt to be low. After all, most of the clients that the Justice Advocates serve do not now have a choice to go to a licensed attorney. There are too few legal aid organizations in New York to provide services to the vast majority of unrepresented debtors. Therefore, most clients of the Justice Advocates face a choice not between advice from a licensed attorney or a minimally trained layperson, but between advice from a trained layperson or no advice whatsoever. It is hard to see how providing the option of advice from a Justice Advocate will result in a *more* inequitable system of justice than the system that currently exists in New York. The Justice Advocates may in a few cases give imperfect advice. But it is likely that in many more, they will help litigants navigate a confusing and complex legal terrain – and, at the bare minimum, lower the incredibly high number of default judgments that plague the system.[106]

Nevertheless, the fact that the decision in *Upsolve* blesses what is not only a significant but a controversial, and indeed bitterly contested, revision to the existing licensing system means that its holding will no doubt be challenged. The constitutional argument it relies upon is likely to come under pressure from two directions – both from those seeking to narrow its reach and those seeking to expand it.

First, and most obviously, the decision's rather expansive interpretation of *Holder* and *Becerra* can and likely will be contested, both on appeal and in other cases. Those who want to challenge the decision on these grounds will have plenty of fodder. As I noted in Section 14.1, many other courts have interpreted those decisions much more narrowly than the *Upsolve* court did.

For example, in *Capital Associated Industries, Inc. v. Stein*, the Fourth Circuit held that a ban on the practice of law by corporations "fit[] within NIFLA's exception for professional regulations that incidentally affect speech" because the ban didn't "target the communicative aspects of practicing law, such as the advice lawyers may give to clients" – that is to say, it didn't limit what specific advice lawyers could give clients – but merely "focus[ed] more broadly on the question of who may conduct themselves as a lawyer."[107] Because the ban did not discriminate on the basis of viewpoint, in other words, but merely imposed speaker-based restrictions on who could speak about certain topics, the Fourth Circuit found it to be an incidental regulation of speech, regardless of the holding in *Becerra*.

Similarly, in *Tingley v. Ferguson*, the Ninth Circuit interpreted *Becerra* to hold only that professional speech was not a historically established low-value category of expression, but to otherwise permit professional regulations to be characterized as incidental regulations of speech so long as they allow the professional to

[106] Estimates on default rates in New York consumer bankruptcy court range from 70 to 95 percent. Complaint, *supra* note 64, at 6.

[107] Cap. Associated Indus., Inc. v. Stein, *supra* note 35, at 208.

communicate their personal opinions to clients in other contexts than the regulated one.[108]

These decisions illustrate how some courts can, have, and are domesticating *Becerra* by reading it to do little more than get rid of the newly invented low-value category of professional speech. In their rather unabashed effort to interpret *Becerra* as a decision that did not do much to alter the doctrinal status quo, these decisions are hard to square with the expansive and impassioned language of Justice Thomas's opinion. But they are not obviously inconsistent with its holding; and as the earlier discussion suggests, *Becerra* is by no means the clearest decision or a decision that reflects a court entirely certain about how far the First Amendment does or should extend into the broad terrain of professional regulation. On appeal, the Second Circuit could easily rely upon these decisions to reject the conclusion reached by the district court in *Upsolve* and reaffirm the constitutionality of UPL laws.

The decision could also be challenged from the opposite direction: Litigants could argue that the specific speech/conduct distinction *Upsolve* relies upon makes no sense as a doctrinal matter, and, on that basis, push for a broader constitutional ruling than the self-consciously "narrow" one that the *Upsolve* district court fashioned. Such a challenge would not be hard to mount. The district court did very little to explain, let alone justify, the distinction it drew between laws that regulate who can provide out-of-court-verbal advice (which it determined to be speech) and laws that regulate who can draft pleadings on behalf of clients, or argue cases in court (conduct). And it is not terribly easy to come up with a doctrinal justification for that distinction. As a matter of black letter law, all that is required for conduct to qualify as speech for First Amendment purposes is that it reflects "an intent to convey a particularized message . . . and . . . the likelihood was great that the message would be understood by those who viewed it."[109] These conditions are almost certainly going to be met virtually any time someone writes a brief for a client, or argues a case in court. The logic of *Holder* applies here too, "seamlessly."

Later courts, therefore, could quite easily interpret the content discrimination principle that the district court relied upon in *Upsolve* to reach a much more sweeping ruling. This does not mean that later courts will *have* to apply the content discrimination logic more broadly than the *Upsolve* court did. As Section 14.1 makes clear, the boundaries of the First Amendment have always been shaped by courts' conception of the ends the First Amendment is supposed to further. And the acts of filing a brief or making arguments in court are obviously much more complicated expressive acts than the act of giving a client verbal advice; to be successfully performed, they require much more nonverbal conduct. Their status as speech may therefore not be as intuitively obvious to courts as the simpler act of providing out-of-court legal advice may be.

[108] Tingley v. Ferguson, 47 F.4th 1055, 1073 (9th Cir. 2022).
[109] Texas v. Johnson, *supra* note 43, at 404.

Nevertheless, there is no obvious doctrinal reason why a later court could not make the same argument that the *Upsolve* court did to conclude that the enforcement of UPL laws against nonlawyers who wish to draft pleadings or argue cases in court also triggers strict scrutiny. The result, obviously, would be a reading of the First Amendment that imposes far greater constraints on the power of state legislatures and judiciaries to license the practice of law than the *Upsolve* decision does.

The fact that the decision could be challenged from two different directions highlights the uncertain inflection point at which we stand. It reflects the deep uncertainty evident in the case law about precisely what the Supreme Court's recent cases mean for the regulation of the professions, including the regulation of the legal profession. Given this uncertainty, and the perhaps insoluble indeterminacy built into the speech/conduct distinction itself, it is hard to say what the consequences of the *Upsolve* decision will be. An opinion that was crafted self-consciously to impose a narrow constraint on New York's power to regulate the practice of law could be interpreted to stand for a much broader proposition than it intended to convey, or it could end up reversed by the Second Circuit.

This does not make the decision unimportant. To the contrary, the district court's opinion is a powerful illustration of how the Supreme Court's changing conception of the First Amendment's means and ends can and is being used to disrupt the regulatory status quo when it comes to the regulation of the professions. But the fact that the constitutional reasoning in the case has not yet gained a broader foothold in First Amendment cases, and that it remains vulnerable from multiple directions, means that access-to-justice advocates cannot take the decision, or its holding, for granted.

Instead, the lack of clarity that plagues the professional speech cases means that advocates have now both the opportunity and perhaps also the obligation to explain to courts why one interpretation of the decision is preferable to others – to help courts, in other words, theorize the (currently quite unclear) relationship that does and should exist between the First Amendment and the licensing of legal services. As the discussion in Section 14.2 suggests, this explanation may have to be made in the rather formalist language employed in the *Holder* and *Becerra* decisions, and in *Upsolve* itself. It may have to rely on arguments about what properly counts as speech or conduct for First Amendment purposes, and what counts as a direct or incidental regulation of speech. But it need not be insensitive to the democratic interests and concerns that have long motivated both the access-to-justice movement *and* many of the First Amendment cases.

To put it another way: Given the lack of consensus about precisely what *Holder* and *Becerra* mean, there is an opportunity for advocates and litigants to push the courts to craft a First Amendment jurisprudence that, even if not self-consciously grounded in the democratic interests and values that played such an obvious role in the *Button* line of cases, advance them nonetheless. Yet, engaging with courts about the proper meaning and wider implications of the *Upsolve* decision will require advocates to come up with answers to some difficult questions.

First, it will require advocates to decide whether they want to pursue a constitutional path of legal reform. The generally forbidding nature of the First Amendment terrain, up until very recently, has meant that the access-to-justice movement has not expended a great deal of effort on constitutional argument. Most of the reform efforts have focused on convincing state courts – the institutions that have traditionally been tasked with the responsibility of defining and enforcing UPL rules – to change their rules and regulations. Turning to the First Amendment as a mechanism of regulatory change will require the movement to shift both its language and strategy and to devote far more energy to arguing how ensuring better access to the courts advances other, democratic aims.

Yet, if advocates decide to pick up the arguments relied upon by the district court in the *Upsolve* case, they will have to decide how broadly they want those arguments to apply. Most importantly, perhaps, they will have to decide whether these arguments should be extended to for-profit actors like LegalZoom, which like Upsolve helps legal consumers complete important legal filings.[110] As Section 14.2 suggests, for-profit actors could easily argue that they have the same First Amendment right to content-neutral regulation as nonprofits like Upsolve do. Were they to succeed in convincing courts of this argument, the result would be very likely a significant expansion in the reach of nonlawyer service providers, given the scale of businesses like LegalZoom and the upside potential of the market in general.

Affirmatively making this argument would require, however, dispensing with the assumption that has underpinned the access-to-justice cases for seventy years: namely, that the First Amendment only really protects the associational rights of political, that is, nonprofit, legal advocacy organizations. Advocates, and courts also, will need to decide whether they are willing to move so far away from the traditional understanding of what kinds of collective associations possess significant democratic importance and pose sufficiently little threat to the welfare of legal consumers to be entitled to the assiduous constitutional protections against professional regulations that nonprofits like the NAACP and the ACLU traditionally received. This will require evaluating whether the benefits to access to justice in terms of scale and efficiency outweigh the obvious risk to consumer welfare that the introduction of a profit motive introduces. This chapter is obviously not the place to answer this question. But it is a question that *Upsolve* clearly poses – and that, it strongly suggests, both courts and access-to-justice advocates will have to confront sooner or later.

Similarly, advocates and courts will have to decide whether the logic relied upon by the *Upsolve* court should be extended to other acts of legal representation. Should nonlawyers like the Justice Advocates be able to not only advise clients about how to

110 Hadfield, *supra* note 99, at 1301.

fill out legal forms but make arguments on their behalf, either in pleadings, or in court? In reality this question is twofold: Is activity of this sort the kind of expressive conduct that the First Amendment protects? And if so, do state governments possess a compelling reason to nevertheless limit who can engage in these expressive tasks? The broad but uncertain language employed by the court in both *Holder* and *Becerra* leaves both of these questions open.

As this discussion suggests, rather than revealing anything definitive about the meaning of the Lochnerized First Amendment, what the decision in *Upsolve* instead does is put on the table a number of important questions that it was impossible, or at least unimportant, to ask before. Perhaps the most important takeaway of this chapter, then, is that the meaning of how the First Amendment applies to the regulation of the legal profession is not fixed. Perhaps more than at any time in recent history, it is up for grabs. This is an opportunity for access-to-justice advocates, even if it is one that comes with some amount of peril.

14.4 CONCLUSION

A common criticism of the Lochnerian turn in First Amendment jurisprudence is that it produces a free speech jurisprudence that protects interests – economic efficiency, consumer choice – far removed from the democratic interests that the Speech Clause was enacted to protect. As this chapter suggests, the story is somewhat more complicated. The constitutionalized deregulation that the Supreme Court's recent First Amendment cases authorize and enable has obviously economically liberalizing effects. But it also can and has been wielded to advance democratic interests that were poorly served by a body of law that distinguished categorically between the commercial and the political spheres. How useful the new Lochnerian First Amendment will in the end be to the access-to-justice movement and its democratic aspirations remains to be seen. But the decision in *Upsolve* suggests its potential as a spur to reform.

For academics, as well as access-to-justice advocates, the possibilities opened up by the more "imperial" First Amendment are important to keep in mind when assessing its costs and benefits. Instead of surrendering the Lochnerized First Amendment to those who wish to wield it for purely economically deregulatory ends, they may be able to seize it, in this context at least, to further some of the most fundamental of democratic interests the First Amendment cases recognize. But doing so will require coming up with a theory of what the First Amendment should mean in this context, and to whom it should apply. These are arguments that access-to-justice advocates have little experience or history making. There is good reason to think that that should now change.

15

Rethinking "Our Bar Federalism"

David Freeman Engstrom and Daniel B. Rodriguez[*]

It's hard to look at the current structure of American legal services regulation and not conclude that "Our Bar Federalism," as Justice Black might have put it, has outlived its usefulness.[1] Fifty states maintain their own rules and their own regulatory apparatus in overseeing a legal profession and a legal services industry that are now demonstrably national and even multinational in scope. Worse, the American civil justice system is in the grips of an access-to-justice crisis, and the state-by-state regime of restrictive rules that props up the lawyers' monopoly is plainly a core cause. Worse still, bar federalism's duplicative and inequality-fueling outputs will only grow more outmoded in the years to come as new legal services delivery models proliferate in the age of AI.[2] Indeed, the current balkanized, fifty-state scheme will increasingly look downright provincial and retrograde as new technologies remake the legal services industry and offer robust and scalable ways to serve the millions of Americans who, facing debt collections, evictions, divorce, child custody battles, small business struggles, and end-of-life decisions, navigate a complex legal system alone. Rosy invocation of "laboratories of democracy," among other federalism values that perennially feature in American politics, rings increasingly hollow in an embattled civil justice system that sits on the cusp of some of its most significant change in a century.

In this chapter, we argue that the time has come to rethink "Our Bar Federalism." We do so in three steps. First, we ask how we got here by stepping through the mix of path dependencies, political economy, and competing constitutional doctrines that created bar federalism in the first place and then made it

* The authors thank Bob Gordon for valuable feedback and Ari Berman for outstanding research assistance.

1 Though the term "our federalism" has appeared dozens of times in the US Supreme Court's decisions, the capitalized and more breathless version ("Our Federalism") was first used by Justice Black in Younger v. Harris, 401 U.S. 37, 44 (1971).

2 *See generally* David Freeman Engstrom, Ed., Legal Tech and the Future of Civil Justice (2023).

stick. Second, we examine bar federalism in a changing world and argue that bar federalism *should* and, just as important, *could* change. Third, we ask *how* the system might change. Weighing tradeoffs across four possible futures for bar federalism, we settle on a "hybrid" state and federal approach, with state bars continuing to regulate lawyers but federal regulators overseeing the rest, as the best way to move to a system that better aligns with the present and future realities of the American civil justice system.

15.1 HOW DID WE GET HERE? BAR FEDERALISM'S ORIGINS

The regulation of legal services has always been, from colonial times to postindustrial America, a state and even local endeavor. Why so? Three factors have bequeathed us the current system of bar federalism: (1) simple colonial-to-state path dependencies, (2) a lawyer political economy with a markedly small-firm and solo-practitioner skew, and (3) the constitutional limbo resulting from competing federalism doctrines and norms. The first of these helped set into place the basic state-centered model that exists today. The second and third ensured that it stuck.

15.1.1 *Path Dependencies and Patchworks*

A running start at explaining bar federalism's origins is simple colonial-to-state path dependencies. Each colony had its own governance systems, its own courts, and its own understandings of English and local law. Lawyers were trained in common law (save in Louisiana), but common law was not so common. Instead, colonies featured their own blend of common, customary, local, and statutory law. As the legal profession grew in size and importance alongside the economy, colonies devised similarly kaleidoscopic ways to admit lawyers to practice, and also vested different authorities, from individual courts to royal governors to legislatures, with the power to oversee those admissions.[3] A decentralized approach to regulating legal services made sense where substantive law, procedure, and institutions varied so dramatically. When colonies became states, these differences persisted.

Bar associations emerged within this patchwork in the seventeenth century. Importantly, however, the arc of legal services regulation did not always bend toward the current lawyers' monopoly. After the Revolution, then gaining momentum during the Jacksonian era, many states actively *deregulated* the bar. Fueled by distrust of England-trained specialists, the role of lawyers in postwar debt collection,

[3] Thomas M. Alpert, *The Inherent Power of the Courts to Regulate the Practice of Law: An Historical Analysis*, 32 Buffalo L. Rev. 525, 531–32 (1983) (describing the "hodgepodge" of authorities that regulated the colony-to-state and post-Revolutionary legal profession); Benjamin H. Barton, The Judge-Lawyer Bias in the American Legal System 110 (2011) (same).

and anti-elitist fear of an insurgent class of oligopolists,[4] states stripped bar admission requirements of education or training components,[5] and some entirely eliminated requirements for appearing in court.[6]

The professionalization projects of the latter part of the nineteenth and early part of the twentieth centuries would reverse this deregulatory trend, but the checkerboard of laws, rules, and institutions inherited from two centuries of colony-by-colony and state-by-state evolution helped to establish, then reify, bar federalism in two ways. First, state and local variation fueled arguments – still in circulation today – that state-overseen licensure, testing, and discipline are needed to ensure competency.[7] Particularly in an era before electronic research and modern communications and travel, state control over entry and discipline seemed the best way to assure familiarity with state and local law and practice. Second, the state-by-state checkerboard created vested interests in each state's constellation of rules and approaches – and thus potent political headwinds for any effort to alter them. By the early twentieth century, as newly powerful state bar associations came to dot the American legal landscape, the basic pattern was set – and, with it, a distinctive state-centered bar politics that has proven highly resistant to change.

15.1.2 *Bar Politics and the Political Economy of Legal Services*

As the nation industrialized and emerged from the Civil War, lawyers began to think beyond locality and consider the benefits of professional organization.[8] It was only after 1870 that bar associations – a "definite and permanent organization of lawyers for purposes of the profession" – emerged as organizations that could also

[4] ROSCOE POUND, THE LAWYER FROM ANTIQUITY TO MODERN TIMES: WITH PARTICULAR REFERENCE TO THE DEVELOPMENT OF BAR ASSOCIATIONS IN THE UNITED STATES 179–82, 225–41 (1953) (explaining how fear of oligopoly, among other arguments, fueled bar deregulation); *see also* RICHARD L. ABEL, AMERICAN LAWYERS 40 (1989) (explaining how the egalitarian ideology of the Jacksonian era "was hostile to state-supported monopolies, as it was to all forms of inequality").

[5] POUND, *supra* note 4, at 5, 179–81 (cataloging the lack of entry requirements and noncredentialed status of many bar entrants).

[6] BARTON, *supra* note 3, at 111 (canvassing states and noting that Maine, Wisconsin, and Indiana removed all requirements for appearing in state courts).

[7] *See* ABEL, *supra* note 4, at 117, 124 (noting continuing use of nonreciprocity in some states, justified, at least in part, on competence grounds); Michael J. Thomas, *The American Lawyer's Next Hurdle: The State Based Bar Examination System*, 24 J. LEGAL PROF. 235, 244 (2000) (noting continued opposition to a national bar exam based in "familiarity with local law"). For a recent case law example, see Nat'l Ass'n for the Advancement of Multijurisdiction Prac., (NAAMJP) v. Simandle, 658 F. App'x 127, 137 (3d Cir. 2016) (crediting "familiarity with state law" as a rationale for rule limiting federal court admission to attorneys licensed to practice in state court).

[8] Philip J. Wickser, *Bar Associations*, 15 CORNELL L. REV. 390, 404 (1930).

regulate the legal profession.[9] Within a decade, some 126 localities had bar associations.[10] States also created bar associations, and, though many started as "paper organizations,"[11] they steadily gained support and authority because of their usefulness, from the high-minded promotion of "effective administration of discipline" and jurisprudential excellence[12] to the low-minded aim of keeping out "undesirable" elements, including immigrants and Black Americans.[13] By 1923, every state had an active bar association, with a set of powers that reflected each state's unique path and politics.[14]

But now, it was too late to fathom anything but bar federalism because a distinct political economy of lawyering had emerged around professionalization. Its first feature was a convergence of big- and small-state incentives around restrictions on lawyer mobility. Large states such as New York wanted to control entry and restrict admission and vigorously resisted surrendering that authority.[15] Smaller ones wanted to restrict competition from big-city lawyers, particularly out-of-state ones.[16] As professionalization unfolded, bar protectionism was not so much about managing the threat posed by nonlawyers – though there was plenty of that[17] – but rather managing the threat posed by out-of-state lawyers.

9 POUND, *supra* note 4, at 253–54.

10 *Id.* at 254, 259–69 (cataloging the development of local bar associations).

11 Wickser, *supra* note 8, at 403; *see also* ABEL, *supra* note 4, at 46.

12 Margaret Canary, Note, *The Importance of Lawyers' Control over Regulation of the Legal Profession: A History of Self-Regulation, from the Long Parliament of 1641 to the Alabama State Bar*, 46 J. LEGAL PROF. 309, 319–20 (2022); Frank E. Atwood, *Objectives and Methods of Bar Integration*, 20 ABA L. J. 203 (1934) (advocating an integrated bar because state bars could "expose[] unworthy applicants" to the courts for disbarment, advance jurisprudence through "meetings, periodicals, [and] conferences," and promote the economic welfare of lawyers).

13 Alpert, *supra* note 3, at 544.

14 POUND, *supra* note 4, at 272.

15 *See* Wickser, *supra* note 8, at 10 (describing how the New York City Bar Association was "definitely cold toward any project of federation"); William E. Flowers, *The Practice of Law by Out-of-State Attorneys*, 20 VAND. L. REV. 1276, 1302 n.17 (1967) ("New York first recognized office practice as forbidden to other than admitted attorneys in 1919 by statutory construction.").

16 *See, for example,* John W. Oliver, Kan. City Bar, *Big City or Country – Where to Start to Practice*, 4 J. MO. B. 113, 126 (1948) (expressing concern about competition from "city law schools" and from "Harvard, Michigan and other outstate schools"); *see also* JEROLD S. AUERBACH, UNEQUAL JUSTICE: LAWYERS AND SOCIAL CHANGE IN MODERN AMERICA 42–43, 97 (1977) (describing how early restrictions on attorney advertising and educational requirements were designed to disfavor urban lawyers).

17 In 1870, Bar Associations began to focus on legal work outside the courts, which featured competitors like insurance companies, collection agencies, banks, accountants, and more. ABEL, *supra* note 4, at 112. As a result, between 1905 and 1940, 400 state and local bar associations created committees on the UPL. *Id.* at 113. External competition to the bar began to pose material economic threats as early as 1880, particularly in the fields of real estate transactions, debt collection, and trusts and estates. JAMES WILLARD HURST, THE GROWTH OF AMERICAN LAW: THE LAW MAKERS 319–20 (1950); *see also* Ronen Shamir, *Professionalism and Monopoly of Expertise: Lawyers and Administrative Law, 1933–1937*, 27 LAW & SOC'Y REV. 361, 371–74 (1993) (providing examples of legislation against UPL).

The second feature of an emerging political economy of legal services was a pronounced small-firm and solo-practitioner skew. In 1872, only fourteen law firms nationwide boasted more than three lawyers, the largest only six.[18] Even by 1914, a little more than 200 firms claimed 4 or more lawyers in the nation's ten largest cities. And as late as 1948, a stunning 61 percent of American lawyers remained solo practitioners,[19] and fewer than 5 percent of firms had eight or more lawyers.[20]

The small-firm and solo-practitioner skew of the American legal profession first fueled, then sustained, bar federalism. Rules requiring that out-of-state lawyers hire local ones and that those lawyers "meaningfully" participate in representations created a profitable cottage industry of "local counsel."[21] The profession's small-firm skew also translated into substantial power within bar associations. Armed with arguments about the value of state-specific legal knowledge and the extra-legal benefits of a robust local bar,[22] the profession's journeymen – solo and small-firm practitioners – have controlled bar associations and even the ABA's House of Delegates, which has consistently blocked proposals for a more open and mobile profession.[23] Ironically, state bar associations have become the monopoly feared by Jacksonian critics, but more the yeoman than the oligarchical sort.[24]

18 Benjamin H. Barton, Glass Half Full: The Decline and Rebirth of the Legal Profession 23, 25 (2015).

19 Robert L. Nelson, *Futures of American Lawyers: A Demographic Profile of a Changing Profession in a Changing Society*, 44 Case W. Res. L. Rev. 345, 370 (1994).

20 Barton, *supra* note 18, at 26.

21 Eli Wald, *Federalizing Legal Ethics, Nationalizing Law Practice, and the Future of the American Legal Profession in A Global Age*, 48 San Diego L. Rev. 489, 522 (2011) (noting requirement under Rule 5.5(c)(1)).

22 Stephen Gillers, *Lessons from Multijurisdictional Practice Commission*, 44 Ariz. L. Rev. 685 (2002).

23 On the ABA's early domination by smaller firms and solos, see James R. Silkenat & Harvey B. Rubenstein, *Small Firm Lawyers: An ABA Opportunity*, GPSolo (Jan./Feb. 2011), at 7, https://www.americanbar.org/content/dam/aba/publications/gp_solo_magazine/2011/full_issue_2011_january_february_28_1.pdf ("In its early days, the American Bar Association (ABA), like most law-related organizations, was composed primarily of solo and small firm practitioners."); Richard L. Abel, *The Transformation of the American Legal Profession*, 20 Law & Soc'y Rev. 7, 10 (1986) (describing solo practitioners as the dominant kind of lawyer from the 1940s through 1960s). On House of Delegates opposition to reforms promoting openness and mobility, see Thomas D. Morgan, *The Evolving Concept of Professional Responsibility*, 90 Harv. L. Rev. 702, 715–16 (1977) (describing the House of Delegates' amendment to rules on lawyer advertising, whose "effect is to preserve the balkanization of practice characteristically found today and to protect the small town practitioner from attempted inroads from his or her big city cousin"); Abel, *supra* note 4, at 12 ("Solo and small firm practitioners are most deeply affected by competition from new entrants, who engage in advertising and price cutting."); Henry S. Drinker, *Legal Specialists: Specialized Legal Service*, 41 A.B.A. J. 690, 692 (1955) (discussing the House of Delegates' rejection of a rule that would allow a lawyer to advertise his services to other lawyers); Susan Gilbert & Larry Lempert, *The Nonlawyer Partner: Moderate Proposals Deserve a Chance*, 2 Geo. J. Legal Ethics 383, 383 (1988) (describing the House of Delegates' rejection of a rule that would allow nonlawyers to have managerial roles at law firms).

24 *See, for example*, Abel, *supra* note 4, at 114–15 (concluding that efforts to reform UPL rules were a minority view and of limited success); *see also* Robert W. Gordon, *Lawyers, the Legal*

15.1.3 *Federalism's Ambiguities*

If simple path dependencies created a patchwork of approaches with a set of vested interests to match, then a final force ensured that bar federalism stuck: Bar federalism has long sat in a kind of constitutional limbo, held in place by competing dictates of vertical and horizontal federalism.

On one side of this limbo, two constitutional doctrines have, however shakily, bolstered bar federalism. First, regulation of the bar, the Supreme Court has repeatedly said, sits squarely at the center of state police powers, and perhaps even *exclusively* within such powers.[25] State bar regulation aims, according to a representative court formulation, "to protect the public against imposition and incompetence of persons professing to be qualified to practice law,"[26] "maintain[] high professional standards among those who practice law within its borders,"[27] and "preserve respect for the administration of justice."[28]

The further notion that bar regulation might rest *exclusively* with states has come in more tentative packaging. Perhaps the strongest statement is *Leis v. Flynt*, in which the Supreme Court described regulation of the bar as a power "left exclusively to the States."[29] In *Leis*, the court thus stated what was only implied in *Konigsberg v. State Bar of California* two decades earlier, when Justice Harlan cautioned his colleagues to be "reluctant and slow" to intervene in state bar regulation on account of federalism sensitivities.[30] This may explain why, as would be consistent with Tenth Amendment doctrine, federal incursions into state bar regulation have been largely limited to remedying constitutional violations – for instance, the *Bates* Court's invalidation of prohibitions on attorney advertising on

Profession & Access to Justice in the United States: A Brief History, 148 Daedalus 177, 186 (2019) (describing current challenges to UPL rules).

25 *See* United Mine Workers v. Ill. State Bar, 389 U.S. 217, 222 (1967) ("That the States have broad power to regulate the practice of law is, of course, beyond question."); Bradwell v. Illinois, 83 U.S. 142 (1872) (Bradley, J., concurring) (arguing that the regulation of professions, including the legal profession "fairly belongs to the police power of the State"); Bates v. State Bar of Arizona, 433 U.S. 350, 361 (1977) ("[T]he regulation of the activities of the bar is at the core of the State's power to protect the public.").

26 Bd. of Comm'rs Miss. State Bar v. Collins, 214 Miss. 782, 800 (1952).

27 NAACP v. Button, 371 U.S. 415, 456 (1963) (Harlan, J., dissenting); Bates, *supra* note 25, at 361 (recognizing that "the regulation of the activities of the bar is at the core of the State's power to protect the public").

28 United Mine Workers, *supra* note 25, at 223.

29 439 U.S. 438, 442 (1979) ("Since the founding of the Republic, the licensing and regulation of lawyers has been left exclusively to the States and the District of Columbia within their respective jurisdictions. The States prescribe the qualifications for admission to practice and the standards of professional conduct. They also are responsible for the discipline of lawyers.").

30 *See* 353 U.S. 252, 276 (1957) (Harlan, J., dissenting); *see also* Schware v. Bd. of Bar Exam., 353 U.S. 232, 249 (1957) (Frankfurter, J., concurring).

First Amendment grounds,[31] or preemption of state regulation by the Sixth Amendment right to counsel.[32] Dicta though they might be, language in *Leis*, *Konigsberg*, and elsewhere[33] has provided something of a protective shield against federal incursions on state authority.

The second constitutional buttress is the notion, worked out over time by state supreme courts under the banner of "inherent powers," that regulating the legal profession is solely the province of courts. Before 1870, state legislatures and courts "rarely fought over the control of the legal profession."[34] Legislatures could set general requirements for admission, but courts had inherent powers to disbar specific lawyers.[35] That changed in the 1870s when states, concerned with the state of legal practice and the resistance of state legislatures to enact higher standards, began to justify the idea of courts' *exclusive* regulation of the legal profession.[36] In the absence of an "express grant" of regulatory authority by a state constitution, state courts asserted, authority over the bar must "be exercised by the department to which it naturally belongs."[37]

[31] *See* Bates, *supra* note 25, at 350–84; *In re* Summers, 325 U.S. 561, 570–71 (1925) (noting that only a bar decision "which violated a federal right secured by the Fourteenth Amendment would authorize our intervention").

[32] *See* Spanos v. Skouras Theaters, 364 F.2d 161 (2d Cir. 1966); U.S. v. Bergamo, 154 F.2d 31 (3d Cir. 1946).

[33] *See, for example*, Goldfarb v. Va. State Bar, 421 U.S. 773, 792 (1975) ("The interest of the States in regulating lawyers is especially great since lawyers are essential to the primary governmental function of administering justice, and have historically been 'officers of the courts.'"); Supreme Court of New Hampshire v. Piper, 470 U.S. 274, at 292 (1985) (Rehnquist, J., dissenting)

> Certain aspects of legal practice are distinctly and intentionally *nonnational*. ... Put simply, the State has a substantial interest in creating its own set of laws responsive to its own local interests, and it is reasonable for a State to decide that those people who have been trained to analyze law and policy are better equipped to write those state laws and adjudicate cases arising under them

Mason v. Florida Bar, 208 F.3d 952, 956 (11th Cir. 2000) (noting that states have "both a general interest in protecting consumers, as well as a special responsibility to regulate lawyers").

[34] Alpert, *supra* note 3, at 533.

[35] *Id.* at 534.

[36] Benjamin H. Barton, *An Institutional Analysis of Lawyer Regulation: Who Should Control Lawyer Regulation – Courts, Legislatures, or the Market*, 37 Ga. L. Rev. 1167, 1173 (2003); *see also* Barton, *supra* note 3, at 113–19 (explaining that, under the inherent powers doctrine, some state supreme courts invalidated bar integration statutes and instead integrated by judicial order); Charles W. Wolfram, *Inherent Powers in the Crucible of Lawyer Self-Protection: Reflections on the LLP Campaign*, 39 S. Tex. L. Rev. 359, 374–75 (1998) (compiling cases).

[37] *See, for example*, *In re* Integration of Neb. State Bar Ass'n, 133 Neb. 283, 275 N.W. 265, 266 (1937). Because lawyers were "historically ... 'officers of the courts,'" their regulation by the court was proper. Goldfarb v. Va. State Bar, *supra* note 33, at 792; *see also* Schware v. Bd. of Bar Exam., *supra* note 30, at 248 ("In the United States the courts exercise ultimate control."); *In re* Griffiths, 413 U.S. 717, 732 (1973) (Burger, J., dissenting) ("The role of a lawyer as an officer of the court predates the Constitution; it was carried over from the English system and became firmly embedded in our tradition."). *See generally* Alpert, *supra* note 3, at 538–39 (explaining that, to push for greater professionalization, courts "us[ed] the traditional characterization of

Some acrobatics are required to get from "inherent powers" to bar federalism. The first step is that, if regulating legal services is solely a judicial responsibility, Congress can no more do it than state legislatures. Step two excludes federal courts from the menu of possible bar regulators by applying Article III's limiting of federal judicial power to "cases and controversies." Two steps later, only state courts remain standing. The end result is hardly an ironclad shield, and litigants and legislatures have made gradual inroads against a self-claimed judicial monopoly, moving some states toward something more like shared powers.[38] Even so, and as we'll see, the combination of *Leis* and "inherent powers" has been influential as bar federalism has beaten back efforts at nationalization.

On the other side of the constitutional limbo are horizontal federalism constraints, particularly limits on state-on-state discrimination under the Privileges and Immunities Clause and Dormant Commerce Clause. A pivotal moment came in *Supreme Court of New Hampshire v. Piper*, where the Court held that New Hampshire's rule rejecting a bar applicant who lived just beyond state lines violated the Privileges and Immunities clause.[39] *Piper* thus completes the constitutional limbo within which bar federalism sits. When "inherent powers" and the possibility in *Leis* and elsewhere that legal services regulation is an *exclusively* state power are combined with *Piper*'s horizontal federalism limits, bar federalism emerges as at once mandatory and illegal – an exclusive state preserve, and yet constitutionally troubled in many of its particular applications.

Bar federalism's ambiguous legal status, of course, is hardly an ironclad barrier to federalization. It is also worth noting that legal limbo's contours may be shifting. Growing concerns about access to justice – a topic we turn to below – are spurring new legal challenges to lawyer regulation that could further limit state power. As Genevieve Lakier notes in Chapter 14, nonlawyer legal services providers have begun to mount 1st Amendment challenges against state "unauthorized practice of law" (UPL) rules, reviving a legal battle last fought in the 1960s over the provision of "group legal services." The other new legal entrant is antitrust, which was the site of protracted battles between LegalZoom and state attorneys general in the 1990s, but is

lawyers as officers of the court and then claim[ed] that [legislative] interference with these officers in turn interfered with the functioning of the judicial branch") (citing *Ex Parte Burr*, 22 U.S. 529, 531 (1824)).

38 Alpert, *supra* note 3, at 551–52; *see also* BARTON, *supra* note 3, at 139.

39 Supreme Court of New Hampshire v. Piper, *supra* note 33, at 275. On *Piper*'s wider importance, see Linda Greenhouse, *Business and the Law: Competition and Lawyers*, N.Y. TIMES (Dec. 25, 1984), https://www.nytimes.com/1984/12/25/business/business-and-the-law-competition-and-lawyers.html (last accessed Feb. 1, 2025). The Court's post-*Piper* decisions have steadily grown even more skeptical of state bar regulation of law practice. *See, for example*, Supreme Court of Virginia v. Friedman, 487 U.S. 59 (1988) (striking down a Virginia bar rule authorizing admission "on motion" but only for permanent Virginia residents); Barnard v. Thornstenn, 489 U.S. 546 (1989) (rejecting the claims of the Virgin Islands that special circumstances attendant to the geography and context of legal practice in that territory warranted a rule outright prohibiting nonresident attorneys from bar admission).

resurfacing again as a way to exert pressure on state bars to open up an increasingly lawyerless civil justice system to new legal services providers.[40] At least for the moment, however, neither of these developments has yet shifted the core of bar federalism's legal limbo, which continues to enervate federal-level reforms.

15.1.4 *Federalizing Feints*

Each of these forces has been on full display as bar federalism has turned back challenges to the authority of states and state bar associations by consumer advocates, national bar associations, and federal agencies.[41] For instance, the American Bar Association (ABA) has repeatedly fallen short in its efforts to nationalize self-regulation, whether through its efforts, beginning in 1908, to establish a national Canon of Ethics,[42] or its failed attempts to unify membership with state bar associations, which arguably only served to empower states via the creation of the House of Delegates with robust state representation.[43] Only the grueling thirty-year effort by the National Conference of Bar Examiners to create the multistate bar exam achieved its full aim.[44] In countering these attempts at ABA expansionism, state bars have proven adept at proactively adopting self-regulation to assuage concerns or lobbying Congress, leaving the ABA mostly a font of recommended rules.[45] Even the ABA's role as accreditor of law schools relies upon the acquiescence by (most, but not all) state authorities in their decisions to tie bar admission to ABA approval.

Perhaps the most revealing struggle came in the late 1970s when the Federal Trade Commission (FTC) explored a direct regulatory role in legal services as part of wider investigations into how state regulation might be inhibiting competition in the professions. First up were pharmacists, but soon the agency launched a preliminary investigation into legal services, covering licensing requirements, UPL, advertising, restrictions on forms of practice, and "restrictions on the development of

[40] As an example, the Antitrust Division of the U.S. Department of Justice recently sent a "letter of interest" to the North Carolina legislature in aid of its consideration of a proposal to loosen the state's UPL rules to permit qualified nonlawyer representatives to offer limited legal services, reminding legislators of DOJ's work on the "competitive effects of restrictions on the practice of law," including "undue restrictions on competition between lawyers and nonlawyers that are not necessary to address legitimate and substantiated harms to consumers or are not sufficiently narrowly drawn to minimize anticompetitive effects." Letter from Maggie Goodlander, Deputy Assistant Attorney General, to North Carolina General Assembly (Feb. 14, 2023).

[41] Michael J. Powell, *Developments in the Regulation of Lawyers: Competing Segments and Market, Client, and Government Controls*, 64 Soc. Forces 281, 293–94 (1985); Alpert, *supra* note 3, at 548.

[42] Fred C. Zacharias, *Federalizing Legal Ethics*, 73 Tex. L. Rev. 335, 338 (1994).

[43] Powell, *supra* note 41, at 291–92.

[44] John Eckler & Joe E. Covington, *The New Multistate Bar Examination*, 57 ABA J. 1117, 1118 (1971).

[45] *Id.* at 293–94; Alpert, *supra* note 3, at 548.

alternative systems for delivery of legal services."[46] Only the investigation into those restrictions went forward, but even that yielded a violent response, including a resolution from the Southern Conference of Bar Presidents as the General Accounting Office neared clearance of a questionnaire to be sent out to state bars, which called for the FTC to forego any further action until Congress could consider its jurisdiction over the professions.[47] Other bar associations encouraged lawyers to "respond to this intrusion by contacting directly [their] elected representative[s] and expressing [their] personal as well as general indignation at the outrage being perpetrated upon the profession."[48] These fire alarms worked, and Senators introduced amendments that prohibited the FTC's use of funds for investigating the legal profession.[49] That response amounted to a clear shot across the bow, and a clear sign, Stanford Law's Bill Baxter reported, that the FTC had taken on one of the "sacred cows" of American politics and run afoul of powerful bar associations with "real political clout."[50]

The State Bar of Texas was particularly hostile, establishing in 1982 a twenty-one-person standing committee on federal laws and regulations affecting the bar.[51] The committee's chief activity was to appear before congressional committees to oppose FTC's authority to regulate professionals. Texas bar president Orrin Johnson, channeling bar federalism's constitutional limbo, observed that "the instrusion [sic] of the Federal Trade Commission violated the historic relationship between state and federal governments . . . [T]hat members of the bar were regulated by the judicial branch of the government of Texas and were therefore a part of the very fabric of the judicial system of Texas."[52]

[46] Marc A. Comras, *Are We Heading toward Federal Regulation of the Legal Profession?*, Docket Call, ABA (Spring 1979).

[47] *FTC Future Discussed as Lawyer Probe Renews*, LawScope, ABA J. (Sept. 1980).

[48] B. M. Westberry, *FTC Seeks Control of Legal Profession*, 43 Ky. Bench & B. 8 (1979); *see also Hearing on FTC Activities Concerning Professionals before the S. Comm. on Com., Sci., and Transp.* 97th Cong. 51 (1981) (statement of Mark White, Att'y Gen. of Texas) ("[T]he State of Texas requests Congressional legislation which will clearly instruct the FTC that it has no power to investigate or regulate agencies of the State such as the State Bar of Texas"); *see also id.* at 62 (statement of Robert Van Vooren, Board member, Iowa State Bar Association)

> ("[T]he Iowa State Bar Association considers the pending inquiry by the FTC, and any rulemaking activities by the FTC incident to the regulation of the practice of law in Iowa, to be an unnecessary and unconstitutional intrusion by the Federal Trade Commission into the affairs of State government that traditionally have been adequately handled by the supreme court of Iowa under the express mandate of the constitution of the State of Iowa.").

[49] *FTC "Profession-Probes" Under Fire in Senate*, 65 ABA J. 1618, 1618 (1979).

[50] *FTC Future Discussed as Lawyer Probe Renews*, *supra* note 47.

[51] *See Lawyers Seek a Loophole*, Newsweek at 11 (Aug. 1, 1983); *FTC Chairman Vows to Fight on Lawyer Regulation*, Hous. Post at 10A (Aug. 1, 1983).

[52] Philip Wilson, *Federal Laws and Regulations Affecting the Bar*, 46 Tex. B.J. 857, 858 (1983).

In short, a mix of path dependencies, politics, and law explains how we arrived at the current system of bar federalism, and why it has stuck. The next section explains why it may be time to move in another direction, and why it just might be possible.

15.2 WHY COULD AND SHOULD WE CHANGE NOW? BAR FEDERALISM IN THE TWENTY-FIRST CENTURY

If powerful forces created and then sustained bar federalism, any call for reform must answer some obvious questions: Why change now? And supposing we wanted to, is change even possible? This section argues that change is indeed possible because of two tectonic shifts in the American legal landscape: (1) a rapidly evolving legal services industry and (2) a deepening access-to-justice crisis. Together, these shifts have eroded the conditions that have long held bar federalism in place while simultaneously exposing the flaws of a balkanized, fifty-state approach to legal services regulation. Our analysis thus builds upon and supports the larger case for reforming American legal services regulation in order to bring it into line with the twenty-first-century realities of an embattled civil justice system.

15.2.1 *A New Political Economy of Lawyering*

Among the changes making it possible to rethink bar federalism, few are more important than the changing structure of the legal profession and the legal services marketplace. As previously noted, the American bar has been, for most of its history, a small-scale affair. But the bar's localist skew has changed dramatically since the postwar period. In 1948, nine out of ten American lawyers were private practitioners, and two-thirds of them – and a stunning 61 percent of all US lawyers – were solo practitioners.[53] But by 1960, only 46 percent were solo practitioners,[54] and the best recent evidence (from 2000) puts the number at one in three.[55]

Much of this change has come through steady growth in the size and reach of law firms. In the late 1950s, only thirty-eight firms reported more than fifty lawyers, half of those in New York City. By the mid-1980s, more than 500 firms could make that claim.[56] Firm size has only increased from there, spurred on by mergers beginning in the 1990s.[57] In 1980, 17 percent of practitioners were in offices with just 2 lawyers, and only 7 percent were in offices of 100 or more. But fast forward three decades and

53 Nelson, *supra* note 19, at 370.

54 *Id.*

55 Gerard J. Clark, *American Lawyers in the 2000: An Introduction*, 33 SUFFOLK U. L. REV. 293 (2000).

56 Mark Galanter & Thomas M. Palay, *Why the Big Get Bigger: The Promotion-to-Partner Tournament and the Growth of Large Law Firms*, 76 VA. L. REV. 747, 749 (1990).

57 Albert Yoon, *Competition and the Evolution of Large Law Firms*, 63 DEPAUL L. REV. 697, 713 (2014); William D. Henderson & Marc Galanter, *The Elastic Tournament: The Second Transformation of the Big Law Firm*, 60 STAN. L. REV. 1867, 1882–83 (2008).

those numbers flip: In 2006, only 12 percent of practitioners were in offices of 2 lawyers, while fully 33 percent were in firms of more than 100 lawyers.[58]

An important consequence is that law practice has become increasingly multi-jurisdictional.[59] But firm growth is not the only reason. Fissuring, disaggregation, and unbundling of legal services have also widened multi-jurisdictionality by growing the ranks of specialized providers.[60] Technology, from virtual courts to computerized research, has also made it much easier to practice nationally, and continuing advances in AI will no doubt further lower multi-jurisdictional barriers.[61] Once limited to a few superfirms and a finite set of regional ones, law firm operations now regularly spill across state borders. Indeed, by 2004, 57 percent of lawyers worked in "multi-office firms," and more than 10 percent of lawyers worked at firms with at least ten offices.[62]

Another consequence of firm growth is subtler. There was a time when American lawyers were nearly all independent practitioners, answerable only to themselves. Now most lawyers work in entities (for instance, large firms organized as limited liability partnerships), and most are employees of one sort or another. Put differently, the growing entities that increasingly populate the American legal services industry have introduced significant bureaucratic complexity to law practice. Hierarchy has intensified – a predictable result of increases in the size, internal differentiation, stratification, and geographic dispersion of firms.[63] Growing bureaucratic complexity has, in turn, steadily eroded the hegemony of private practice. Unlike days of yore, most American lawyers are buried deep within complex bureaucracies, answerable to higher-ups – rainmaker partners, executive committees, compensation committees – not merely their clients.

Taken together, these changes have eroded two features of the political economy of lawyering that had sustained bar federalism since colonial times. First, as the

58 Clara N. Carson & Jeeyon Park, Am. Bar Ass'n, The Lawyer Statistical Report: The U.S. Legal Profession in 2005 6 (2005).

59 *See* Zacharias, *supra* note 42, at 335 (noting "increasingly national character of the legal profession"); Henderson & Galanter, *supra* note 57, at 1882–83 (noting the emergence of the "national law firm").

60 Milton C. Regan & Palmer T. Heenan, *Supply Chains and Porous Boundaries: The Disaggregation of Legal Services*, 78 Fordham L. Rev. 2137 (2010).

61 *See generally* Andrew Perlman, *The Implications of ChatGPT for Legal Services and Society*, The Practice (Mar./Apr. 2023), https://clp.law.harvard.edu/knowledge-hub/magazine/issues/generative-ai-in-the-legal-profession/the-implications-of-chatgpt-for-legal-services-and-society/ (last accessed Feb. 1, 2023).

62 George P. Baker & Rachel Parkin, *The Changing Structure of the Legal Services Industry and the Careers of Lawyers*, 84 N.C. L. Rev. 1635, 1662–63 (2006). Among the 100 largest US firms, the number of lawyers based in "branch offices" increased some sixfold between 1978 and 1987. Abel, *supra* note 4, at 10. By then, the 100 largest law firms maintained an average of five branch offices. Mary C. Daly, *Resolving Ethical Conflicts in Multijurisdictional Practice – Is Model Rule 8.5 the Answer, an Answer, or No Answer at All?*, 36 S. Tex. L. Rev. 715, 727 (1995).

63 Abel, *supra* note 4, at 10.

localist skew of the American bar has receded, the balance of power within bar associations, including the ABA, has tilted away from its yeoman roots.[64] Second, the decline of solo practitioners and the increasing entity orientation of the American legal profession has worked a subtle but critically important change in lawyers' professional standing. Professional independence – a concept at the core of lawyer self-regulation and the "inherent powers" doctrine – is more shibboleth than reality when most lawyers belong to a large entity. Similarly, law's claim as a public-regarding profession rather than a brute business is wearing thin in a world of rampant firm consolidations, obsessive focus on per-partner profits, and free-agent movement between firms.[65]

A second tectonic force is also changing the political economy of lawyering, and it is a grim one: After decades of neglect, access to justice has roared onto legal and political radars, fueled by a growing realization that the civil justice system is in crisis. In some three-quarters of the twenty million civil cases filed in state courts each year, one side lacks a lawyer.[66] Most of these cases are highly consequential, if low-dollar, matters: debt collections, evictions, mortgage foreclosures, and certain types of family law, such as child support enforcement. And these are only the cases – and the litigants – that are visible on dockets. Beneath them lie tens of millions more Americans who have genuine legal problems but never make it to court at all.[67]

A crisis on this scale has many causes, consequences, and potential cures.[68] But for present purposes, an important effect has been to erode American lawyers' claim as guardians of the public interest. Indeed, many see the access-to-justice crisis as, at

[64] *See, for example*, Silkenat & Rubenstein, *supra* note 23, at 7 (discussing dwindling presence and influence of solo practitioners in the ABA); *ABA Body Approves Contentious Guidelines*, 1 J. OF BUS. at 25, 34 (Mar. 16, 2016) (describing House of Delegates' approval of rules for nontraditional legal services over the protests of smaller firms). Interestingly, now disadvantaged in competition, small firms and solos have begun to *favor* rules that would open the profession. *See, for example*, Russell G. Pearce, *A Cautionary Tale from the Multidisciplinary Practice Debate: How the Traditionalists Lost Professionalism*, 72 TEMP. L. REV. 985, 994 (1999) (discussing small firm and solo practitioner support and endorsement of Multi-Disciplinary Practices [MDPs]).

[65] *See* Tyler J. Replogle, *The Business of Law: Evolution of the Legal Services Market*, 6 MICH. BUS. & ENTREPRENEURIAL REV. 287 (2017) (tracking key changes in the business orientation of law firms); Gillers, *supra* note 22 (noting that weakening local bars reduces lawyers' ability to serve as local leaders, community organizers, and benefactors).

[66] For the 75 percent figure, see NAT'L CTR. FOR STATE CTS., THE LANDSCAPE OF CIVIL LITIGATION IN STATE COURTS iv (2015).

[67] *See generally* Rebecca L. Sandefur, *What We Know and Need to Know about the Legal Needs of the Public*, 67 S.C. L. REV. 443 (2016). The most recent national survey found that only 14 percent of legal problems "involved courts." *Id.* at 448. This fact indicates that, although the pro se crisis is itself a national disgrace, that crisis represents only the visible tip of a much larger iceberg.

[68] *See* David Freeman Engstrom & Nora Freeman Engstrom, *The Making of the A2J Crisis*, 75 STAN. L. REV. ONLINE 145 (2024).

least in part, the result of lawyer protectionism. Nor has the legal profession done itself any favors in this regard by blocking even limited reforms designed to increase access to legal help. Fueled by leading scholars and key idea entrepreneurs, a movement is afoot to relax the usual rules that say that only lawyers can practice law (UPL) or own law firms (Rule 5.4 and state equivalents) in order to welcome new providers into the system, whether human or software.[69] First up in 2020 was Utah, which created a "regulatory sandbox" within which new legal services providers can seek waivers of UPL and Rule 5.4. Soon after, Arizona unfurled reforms of its own, authorizing paraprofessionals (think nurse practitioners for law) and erasing Rule 5.4 by allowing legal services providers to seek status as "alternative business structures" (ABSs) and thus tap nonlawyer capital and talent to drive innovation. A critical mass of other states are considering, or have considered, similar ways to reconfigure regulation of legal services.[70]

The verdict remains out on these reforms, which, at three years old, have only just begun to generate empirical evidence about what types of innovation can result.[71] The important point is that American lawyers are not distinguishing themselves in their reflexive opposition to even the *suggestion* of reform. In 2022, a California State Bar working group tasked only with *studying* reform options was unceremoniously shut down by the state legislature's judiciary chairs when the plaintiffs' bar complained.[72] At the national level, the ABA House of Delegates, a mere two years after specifically calling for experimentation, passed a resolution reaffirming Model Rule 5.4 and insisting that nonlawyer ownership of law firms is dangerous.[73] Reflexive bar opposition to reforms of this sort, even when designed to operate in the civil justice system's lower precincts and so posing little threat to lawyers' bottom lines, has not won lawyers new admirers and is deepening public perception that law has become more guild than profession.

[69] The first of these restrictions takes the form of prohibitions, present in all fifty states, on "unauthorized practice of law," or UPL. The second restriction comes in the form of the prohibition on fee-splitting in Rule 5.4 of the Rules of Professional Responsibility and state-level equivalents.

[70] Sam Skolnik, *By the Numbers: 10 States Allowed Non-Lawyers to Offer Services*, BLOOMBERG (Dec. 28, 2023 5:00AM EST), https://news.bloomberglaw.com/business-and-practice/by-the-numbers-10-states-allowed-non-lawyers-to-offer-services (last accessed Feb. 20, 2025).

[71] DAVID FREEMAN ENGSTROM et al., LEGAL INNOVATION AFTER REFORM: EVIDENCE FROM REGULATORY CHANGE (Sept. 2022).

[72] David Freeman Engstrom & Nora Freeman Engstrom, *Why Do Blue States Keep Prioritizing Lawyers over Low-Income Americans?*, SLATE (Oct. 17, 2022), https://slate.com/news-and-politics/2022/10/blue-states-legal-services-lawyers-fail.html (last accessed Feb. 20, 2025).

[73] In August of 2022, the ABA House of Delegates adopted Resolution 402, reaffirming long-standing policy (dating from 2000) advocating opposition to nonlawyer investment in law firms. See *American Bar Association's House of Delegates Adopts Resolution on Nonlawyer Ownership of Law Firms and Sharing Legal Fees with Nonlawyers, Which Was Sponsored and Proposed by the Illinois State Bar Association*, ILL. STATE BAR ASS'N (Aug. 9, 2022), https://www.isba.org/barnews/2022/08/americanbarassociationshouseofdeleg (last accessed Feb. 20, 2025).

15.2.2 *Regulatory Mismatch, Legal Innovation, and Access to Justice*

Tectonic shifts in the political economy of lawyering are thus powerful reasons why bar federalism *could* change. But a fast-changing legal services industry also provides good reason for why the current system of bar federalism *should* change. Indeed, bar federalism will be increasingly costly in both resource and innovation terms – and it will look outmoded and downright retrograde in an increasingly entity- and tech-based, multi-jurisdictional legal services industry.

A useful starting point for thinking about bar federalism's costs is the so-called values of federalism – a set of principles lurking in the background as the Framers negotiated the Constitution's specific enumerations of power.[74] As summarized by the Supreme Court in *Gregory v. Ashcroft*, federalism:

> assures a decentralized government that will be more sensitive to the diverse needs of a heterogenous society; it increases opportunity for citizen involvement in democratic processes; it allows for more innovation and experimentation in government; and it makes government more responsive by putting the States in competition for a mobile citizenry.[75]

Cutting across these benefits is a kind of covering principle for distributing power among government tiers: subsidiarity. That principle maintains that policymaking authority should be sited at the lowest level of government that can internalize all costs and benefits.[76] The result is something like a rebuttable presumption in favor of decentralization: Push policy authority down whenever possible to maximize preference satisfaction, opportunities for democratic participation, and experimentation, except where sufficiently large inter-jurisdictional spillovers or other defects compel a federal response.[77]

Viewed through the lens of subsidiarity, bar federalism is a costly scheme that is increasingly ill-adapted to the realities of the twenty-first-century legal services industry. Some of the thinking about bar federalism's costs is not

74 Michael W. McConnell, *Federalism: Evaluating the Founders' Design*, 54 U. Chi. L. Rev. 1484, 1493 (1987).

75 Gregory v. Ashcroft, 501 U.S. 452, 458 (1991).

76 *See, for example*, Neil S. Siegel & Robert D. Cooter, *Collective Action Federalism: A General Theory of Article I, Section* 8, 63 Stan. L. Rev. 115 (2010) (summarizing a body of theory built atop assumptions that local residents have better information about the costs and benefits of policies and stronger incentives to hold officials accountable for policy choices); McConnell, *supra* note 74, at 1507 (reviewing Raoul Berger, Federalism: The Founders' Design and offering a classic synthesis).

77 Federalism debates have always been in part functional and utilitarian, steeped in the language of costs, benefits, and externalities and the disciplining effects of mobility, in part democratic, steeped in the language of civic republicanism, and in part de-ontological, built upon rights talk and preservation of individual liberties. *See* Roderick Hills, *Federalism and Public Choice*, *in* Law and Public Choice (D. Farber & A. O'Connell eds., 2009).

new.[78] State-by-state rules have long been thought to impose steep compliance costs on increasingly multi-jurisdictional legal practice. Disparate and "splintered" rules around confidentiality, lawyer obligations to third parties and courts, advertising, and supervision of nonlawyers all bring significant compliance costs for jurisdiction-straddling practitioners – costs that are then passed on to consumers.[79] Because many legal markets span states, conflicting rules may particularly affect advertising costs.[80] This is significant for a legal profession that already spends most of its time, perhaps as much as two-thirds, drumming up business.[81]

Systemic costs are also high. Among them are sovereignty costs, where the state with the most restrictive standard calls the tune.[82] Bar federalism is also costly *itself* to maintain. Funding fifty different regulators to oversee an industry that increasingly spans jurisdictions is a needless drain on the public fisc. Without appropriate coordination, a fifty-state balkanized set of enforcement regimes needlessly duplicates regulatory efforts and squanders valuable social resources while generating "minimal gains."[83]

An even more compelling argument than simple costs may be that the current system of bar federalism is simply not equipped to regulate twenty-first-century legal services. As David Wilkins's field-shaping exposition long ago explained, American legal services regulation primarily takes three forms: (1) "disciplinary controls," via rule enforcement overseen by state supreme courts and bar associations;[84] (2) "liability controls," enforced via private lawsuits asserting legal malpractice claims; and (3) "institutional controls," as vested in institutions where lawyers work, such as court- or SEC-imposed sanctions under Federal Rule of Civil Procedure 11 or SEC Rule 2(e), respectively.[85] None of these approaches, however, fits well with the new wave of tech-fueled, entity-based, and jurisdiction-spanning legal services. Even without regulatory reform relaxing restrictive rules, "legal tech" companies are growing fast and providing "unbundled" services, such as document assembly,

[78] *See generally* Zacharias, *supra* note 42; *see also* Charles Silver, *What We Don't Know Can Hurt Us*, 43 Akron L. Rev. 1009 (2010); Wald, *supra* note 21, at 501.

[79] *See* Zacharias, *supra* note 42, at 346; *see also* Wald, *supra* note 21, at 494–512 (collecting arguments and evidence).

[80] For discussion that advertising is increasingly internet-based (or at least cross-border), see Zacharias, *supra* note 42, at 348.

[81] *See* Gillian K. Hadfield, *Legal Markets*, 60 J. Econ. Literature 1264, 1293 (2022).

[82] *See* Zacharias, *supra* note 42, at 346 (noting "lowest common denominator" effect).

[83] David B. Wilkins, *Who Should Regulate Lawyers?*, 105 Harv. L. Rev. 799, 873 (1992); *see also* Wald, *supra* note 21, at 512.

[84] These take at least two forms, including traditional bar disciplinary systems and California's modified approach, with a formally independent Bar Court. Cal. Bus. & Prof. Code § 6086.5 (creating Bar Court and the State Bar Discipline Monitor).

[85] *See* Wilkins, *supra* note 83, at 835–47. For more on "federalization through contextualization" via court and agency rules, see Daniel R. Coquillette & Judith A. McMorrow, *Zacharias's Prophecy: The Federalization of Legal Ethics through Legislative, Court, and Agency Regulation*, 48 San Diego L. Rev. 123, 126 (2011).

directly to consumers. One need not be a dreamy futurist to think that, going forward, legal services will less and less resemble the one-to-one, encompassing attorney-client relationship that has prevailed to this point.[86] Instead, it seems likely and perhaps even inevitable that a large proportion of legal services will be delivered at scale by entities in a one-to-many model using a mix of lawyers, nonlawyers, and software.

As this new world unfolds, the current duplicative, fifty-state approach is likely to grow even more expensive and outmoded. Regulation of legal services will look different in at least three ways. First, regulation of legal services will increasingly be entity-based, with regulatory oversight and enforcement focused not on "individual lawyer impropriety" within the confines of a particular attorney–client representation but rather on the full set of organizational procedures, routines, and systems new entity-based providers use to deliver legal services.[87] A second difference follows: Regulatory oversight will largely focus not on gross and even spectacular individual-level failures, as in the current attorney disciplinary system, but rather what Wilkins, albeit in a different era, referred to as "low-level negligence."[88] That is, effective oversight will often require unearthing coding problems, bias, or flawed user interfaces that cause individually small but collectively large harms to clients in systems operating at scale, not just gross, individual-level shortfalls in legal knowledge or violations of legal ethical rules. Third, all this means that regulation of legal services will be a highly technical process, because judging the quality of new modes of representation and types of outputs will often require regulators to understand a provider's design, implementation, and oversight of software or other technical systems that produced these outputs. It also likely means deploying data and data analytics, which may be the only way to identify and weigh the significance of system design and implementation choices that generate low-level negligence.

A final difference is that much regulatory oversight will be regular, not episodic, performed through audits or other resource-intensive and technocratic ways of evaluating systems. A fifty-state, balkanized system designed around individual-level, ex-post disciplinary controls – controls that, even in the best of circumstances, can capture only the most egregious conduct[89] – will lack the resources and the technical capacity to do any of this well.[90]

[86] Gillian K. Hadfield, *The Cost of Law: Promoting Access to Justice through the (Un)corporate Practice of Law*, 38 Int'l Rev. L. & Econ. 43, 53 (2014).

[87] *See* William D. Henderson, *Legal Market Landscape Report*, State Bar of Calif. 27 (July 2018), https://board.calbar.ca.gov/docs/agendaItem/Public/agendaitem1000022382.pdf (last accessed Feb. 24, 2025).

[88] Wilkins, *supra* note 83, at 848.

[89] David Wilkins, *Legal Realism for Lawyers*, 104 Harv. L. Rev. 468, 493 (1990).

[90] For development of this argument, see David Freeman Engstrom & R. J. Vogt, *The New Judicial Governance: Courts, Data, and the Future of Civil Justice*, 72 DePaul L. Rev. 171 (2023).

The argument that bar federalism suppresses innovation is trickier. The question that has hung over "legal tech" in recent decades is why there is not more of it. A particular puzzle is why there is so little direct-to-consumer legal tech that serves the millions of self-represented litigants within the system.[91] At least three explanations have risen to the top. The first is insufficiently advanced technology: Automated tools, including sophisticated AI-based ones, cannot perform the all-important translational work – cutting through legalese and explaining options and outcomes in plain language – that is necessary when serving unsophisticated lay clients.[92] A second theory is that, looking across some 14,000 court jurisdictions in the United States, one sees a checkerboard of court technology systems and data infrastructures. The resulting technological Babel defeats the scale necessary to induce tech providers to invest time and capital in developing and then maintaining robust and user-friendly systems that serve individuals with very limited ability to pay.[93]

Neither of these explanations indicts *bar* federalism specifically, but a third one does: The current balkanized, fifty-state approach to legal services regulation stymies innovation because one of its chief products is regulatory uncertainty. Innovation in legal services delivery models requires investment in research and development to create new products and processes. Innovation also requires new organizational forms, developed by private entities in the shadow of extant governmental institutions and current rules of the road. Embarking on new forms and models of legal service delivery is expensive and risky in a system of fifty different rules.[94] Worse, bar federalism is murky even by conventional regulatory standards. For starters, separation-of-powers struggles around "inherent powers" mean that the *location* of regulatory authority is uncertain in many states. Exclusively courts? Shared powers between courts and legislatures? State bar organizations operating under delegated power? Yet even in states where court authority is clear, judicial rulemaking is, as Hadfield has put it, "unsystematic and opaque."[95] Rules that operate on lawyers are often elaborated either via bar disciplinary proceedings or court-promulgated rules that are not subject to public hearings or the notice-and-comment process that are the norm, or even required, in the political branches. The end result is a political

[91] Rebecca Sandefur, *Legal Tech for Non-Lawyers: Report of the Survey of US Legal Technologies*, Am. Bar Found. (2019), https://www.americanbarfoundation.org/resources/legal-tech-for-non-lawyers-report-of-the-survey-of-us-legal-technologies/ (last accessed Feb. 1, 2025); Rebecca L. Sandefur et al., *Seconds to Impact?: Regulatory Reform, New Kinds of Legal Services, and Increased Access to Justice*, 84 Law & Contemp. Probs. 69 (2021).

[92] John Armour & Mari Sako, *Lawtech: Leveling the Playing Field in Legal Services?*, *in* Legal Tech and the Future of Civil Justice (David Freeman Engstrom ed., 2023).

[93] This is the theory of change of the Filing Fairness Project, launched in 2022, at Stanford Law School. *See* Filing Fairness Project, *Deborah L. Rhode Center on the Legal Profession*, https://law.stanford.edu/filing-fairness-project/ (last accessed Mar. 27, 2024).

[94] Hadfield, *supra* note 86 at 55.

[95] *Id.*

and policy catch-22. To gain traction, reforms that aim to relax the rules and open up the system need proof of concept. But in the current system, at least, no demonstration of success is possible.

In sum, we are at a critical point in the access-to-justice struggle because legal services regulation is balkanized in ways that resist change – a resistance that is out of whack with the realities of the civil justice system. Bar federalism will bring steadily increasing regulatory costs in a world of digitally provided, one-to-many legal services provided at scale. And though bar federalism's effect on innovation remains less than fully understood, all signs point away from maintaining "Our Bar Federalism." In the final section, we explore some preliminary ideas about how to move the access-to-justice needle forward.

15.3 A WAY FORWARD FOR REGULATING LEGAL SERVICES

The story told thus far is persistent bar federalism, the result of stakeholders following patterns set long ago by state bar authorities and judges, and a regulatory scheme that is increasingly ill-adapted to the twenty-first-century realities of a changing legal services industry and civil justice system. In short, we see the conditions as ripe for rethinking. In this section, we thus bracket arguments about whether bar federalism could or should change. Instead, we ask: Accepting that some degree of change is needed, what is the best way to achieve it?

Consider, as a start, three possible futures for American legal services regulation. The first continues the current trajectory: A state-by-state muddling through in the hope that reform experiments in Utah, Arizona, and elsewhere might push us to a new and better equilibrium as we learn what works and what doesn't. While we should not be naive in supposing that evidence and analysis will move those who have interests in opposing reform, the past year or two gives at least some reason to believe in the capacity of reform-minded stakeholders to take what we are learning through clear-headed, data-driven scrutiny and build mechanisms of change. A second option is that states might instead forge regional compacts using the process prescribed by Article 1, section 10, of the Constitution.[96] The subject matter of these compacts might include reciprocity in the admission of lawyers and nonlawyers to practice, common standards of training and discipline, and shared mechanisms of enforcement as a way to share benefits and burdens and enable a more frictionless scheme of lawyering and legal services. A third, and very different, possibility is to excavate bar federalism root and branch and move to full-scale federalization.[97] This would likely mean a federal agency, whether already established or a new and purpose-built one, to oversee lawyers and new nonlawyer service providers and enforce new federal standards for admission,

[96] *See generally* CONG. RSCH. SERV., INTERSTATE COMPACTS: AN OVERVIEW (Aug. 15, 2022).

[97] For earlier versions of this proposal, see Zacharias, *supra* note 42; Wald, *supra* note 21.

discipline, and "unauthorized practice of law," whether articulated by Congress or the agency itself.

We favor a fourth option: a federal-state hybrid. There are several ways to hybridize legal services regulation by allocating some authority at the federal level and some at the state level.[98] Our proposal divides labor by maintaining current state authority over traditional "role" regulation, while vesting federal regulators, whether in an existing or new agency, with responsibility for "entity" regulation. Put another way, a hybrid approach would retain the current state-level system of ex-post disciplinary and liability controls for conventional, one-to-one delivery of legal services by lawyers and paraprofessionals. But one-to-many service models, delivered by entities at scale using a mix of lawyers, nonlawyers, and software, would come within the jurisdiction of a new federal regulatory authority.

Hybridizing legal services regulation would, in our view, combine many of the virtues of the other reform possibilities while avoiding some of their vices. By preserving state control over "role" regulation, a hybrid approach would retain some of subsidiarity's virtues, capturing local knowledge while facilitating continued experimentation among states. Leaving regulation of conventional lawyering in the hands of state authorities also acknowledges that one-to-one interactions, however complex as a matter of adjudication as law and legal process become more complex themselves, still involve at their core professional relationships between lawyers and clients. Where, however, legal services are delivered on a one-to-many basis, the professional relationship is less about the lawyer behind the desk and the client opposite and more about service delivery on a wider and commoditized scale. Borders become impediments and the fifty disparate regulatory regimes impose tremendous and unnecessary transaction costs. When software risks eating the world, as the saying goes, it behooves us to think of structural solutions that meet technology and globalization where they are, rather than where parochial visions of a legal profession long past might want them to be.

Many questions, and many details, remain to be worked out. As already noted, a puzzle that hangs over the legal tech world is why, even as AI has galloped ahead, direct-to-consumer legal technologies that might assist millions of self-represented litigants have remained a relatively small part of the legal tech ecosystem. If the answer to that question is restrictive rules, then federalization could pay potentially large dividends: A single set of rules, and rules designed with one-to-many legal service models in mind, could unlock new and innovative ways to provide legal help that are chilled in the current fifty-state system. If the answer instead is that the checkerboard of technology and data infrastructures across 14,000 court jurisdictions

[98] Different from our hybrid approach, Wald proposed an "intermediary approach" in which the federal government relaxes the prohibition on multi-jurisdictional practice in Rule 5.5, allowing lawyers to practice nationally, but states retain control over admission, licensing, and discipline. Wald, *supra* note 21, at 531.

defeats the scale tech providers need to invest in robust, user-friendly platforms, then centralizing and standardizing the rules may not accomplish much.

There are other risks, too. Critics might object that, by reducing regulatory uncertainty, a hybrid model might indeed spur at least some innovation among legal tech providers, but only at the cost of valuable state-level experimentation as to the optimal mix of regulation needed to spur innovation while also placing guardrails around it. This concern is worrying, but it is hardly fatal. For starters, the "laboratories of democracy" idea, while a venerated one, has taken a beating of late, raising questions about the ability of any decentralized system to generate useable information about policy interventions.[99] Innovation in Utah and Arizona, while promising, is surely different from what one might expect in very different legal markets in California or Texas. The larger blind spot in this critique, as hinted at above, is that state courts currently lack much technical capacity – and, perhaps more importantly, they lack the power of the purse to change that fact. These shortcomings raise significant questions about the current fifty-state system's ability to perform the job in the first place, let alone drive a flowering of ideas about how to do it well. Put alternatively, even if states were, in theory, promising sources of innovation, capacity constraints make it highly improbable they could carry out this promise. Finally, recall that legal tech providers need scale to justify investment in services designed to reach consumers who, almost by definition, have limited ability to pay. Unless the regulatory uncertainty that defines the current system can be reduced at scale, across states, there may not be much new legal tech innovation for the current fifty-state system to use as an experimental testbed.

A second concern is that a new federal role could provide defenders of the current lawyer-dominated status quo with a one-stop-shop for exerting influence, yielding federal rules that are as stringent as, or even more stringent than, the current fifty-state approach. A version of this concern comes from Ben Barton, who worries that new regulatory schemes might end up imposing more restrictive rules than at present, particularly in the lower precincts of the system, where lawyers' bottom lines are less threatened, leaving a salutary zone of independence.[100] On this view, a new federal regulatory role might end up spurring less, not more, innovation in legal services relative to the present.

Here, too, the concern is worth considering but hardly fatal. To begin, lawyers may not prove nearly so efficacious in defending their monopoly. As already noted,

[99] *See, for example*, Edward L. Rubin & Malcolm Feeley, *Federalism: Some Notes on a National Neurosis*, 41 UCLA L. Rev. 903, 924 (1994) (questioning whether decentralized experiments will generate useful information); Susan Rose-Ackerman, *Risk Taking and Reelection: Does Federalism Promote Innovation?*, 9 J. Legal Stud. 593, 615–16 (1980) (arguing that policy innovation will be an underproduced public good because risk-averse politicians will free-ride rather than risk failed innovation).

[100] Benjamin H. Barton, *The Future of American Legal Tech: Regulation, Culture, Markets*, in Legal Tech and the Future of Civil Justice (David Freeman Engstrom ed., 2023); *see also* Zacharias, *supra* note 42, at 379.

lawyers are fast losing the moral high ground in a civil justice system in the throes of an access crisis that they have presided over. Moreover, once the regulatory debate is pushed into a data-driven consumer protection framing, lawyers' claims to expertise lose some of their force. Even the argument, just noted, that legal tech enjoys significant latitude in the part of the civil justice system where so few have lawyers may not be quite right. Legal tech entrepreneurs say otherwise, claiming a substantial chilling effect because of the mere possibility of UPL enforcement. And all of this ignores the fact that many innovations, particularly technology-based ones, start in mainstream consumer markets and then work their way down. Like the smartphone, new one-to-many legal services models may start in areas such as divorce, with many middle-class clients in need of low-cost services, and only then work their way to eviction or debt collection, once the myriad components of a winning business model have been refined.

This only scratches the surface of the many challenges and critiques of a new hybrid federal-state role. While we leave such detail for another day, we note, in summary, that a hybrid approach presents a potentially more balanced and also more achievable approach. Reducing the balkanization of legal services provides concrete benefits, and we suggest the hard work of thinking about reforms that move in this direction while preserving what is best, or at least tenable, in intrastate regulation.

15.4 CONCLUSION

We would do well to rethink "Our Bar Federalism." The way in which it is configured has the worst elements of federalism's theory and architecture without the best elements. As a consequence, we cannot confront in a systematic, constructive way the many flaws in our scheme of lawyering and legal services regulation. And we cannot ensure that the settling of certain contentious matters by smart regulation will be implemented across the nation, thereby ensuring a more efficient, efficacious interstate flow of human capital of lawyers and legal service providers.

16

Access to Advice as a Linchpin of Family Justice

Rebecca Aviel

Most Americans simply cannot afford legal representation in the traditional model, and family law is repeatedly invoked as an illustrative context in which this lack of access is stark: By some estimates, 80 to 90 percent of family cases involve at least one unrepresented party.[1] Family court systems around the country have responded to this reality by establishing robust self-help centers and working to simplify court forms and procedures to better meet the needs of self-represented litigants in divorce and child custody matters. As just one example in a rising tide of innovation, self-represented litigants in Colorado can obtain information and assistance – but not representation or legal advice – from Self-Represented Litigant Coordinators, who are judicial employees located in the self-help center of each judicial district.[2] The website for the state court system offers court-approved forms and plain language instructions, including flowcharts and short explanatory videos on electronic filing for non-attorneys.[3] The judges who handle domestic relations matters are assisted by Family Court Facilitators, who work with the parties to move the case to resolution,

[1] Natalie Anne Knowlton et al., *Cases without Counsel: Research on Experiences of Self-representation in U.S. Family Court* 1, Inst. for the Advancement of the Am. L. Sys. (2016), https://iaals.du.edu/sites/default/files/documents/publications/cases_without_counsel_research_report.pdf (last accessed Feb. 3, 2025); Deborah L. Rhode & Lucy Buford Ricca, *Protecting the Profession or the Public? Rethinking Unauthorized-Practice Enforcement*, 82 Fordham L. Rev. 2587, 2607 (2014); *see also* Nat'l Ctr. for State Cts. Family Just. Inst., *The Landscape of Domestic Relations Cases in State Court* ii (2018), https://iaals.du.edu/sites/default/files/documents/publications/fji-landscape-report.pdf (last accessed Feb. 3, 2025) (examining eleven jurisdictions and finding that 72 percent of cases involved at least one self-represented litigant).

[2] S. Ct. of Colo., Off. of the Chief Just., *Chief Justice Directive* 13-01 (2023), https://www.coloradojudicial.gov/sites/default/files/2023-08/13-01.pdf (last accessed Feb. 3, 2025) (specifying what can and cannot be provided to self-represented litigants by self-help staff).

[3] *See, for example, Flowchart – Divorce of Legal Separation NO Minor Children*, Colo. Jud. Branch (undated), https://www.courts.state.co.us/userfiles/file/Court_Probation/04th_Judicial_District/El_Paso/Domestic%20Forms/FCF%20500%20Flowchart%20Dissolution%20or%20Legal%20Separation%20No%20Minor%20Children.pdf (last accessed Feb. 3, 2025); *Efiling for Non-Attorneys*, Colo. Jud. Branch (undated), https://www.coloradojudicial.gov/taxonomy/term/959 (last accessed Feb. 3, 2025).

and family court matters are governed by a special rule of civil procedure that requires courts to actively manage cases in a way that is tailored to the particular needs of each family.[4]

As important as these initiatives are, it is hard to avoid the impression that they are crisis measures – more band-aid than cure. They address the inability of litigants to obtain counsel rather than reflecting an affirmative sense of what civil justice should look like.[5] Litigants moving through family court systems that have been adjusted to be navigable without an attorney will find it much easier to successfully file for and complete a divorce as compared to systems that continue to operate on the fiction of attorney involvement.[6] But even in the jurisdictions that have done the most retrofitting, self-represented litigants must pursue their cases without the benefit of legal strategy, analysis, or advice.[7] A couple that intends to resolve their divorce swiftly and amicably with minimum transaction costs might need to complete the entire process without ever understanding whether the house they have been living in is separate or marital property. As Russell Engler explained so incisively more than twenty years ago, "most assistance needed by unrepresented litigants is likely to involve what would fall within an intellectually honest definition of legal advice."[8]

Against this backdrop, advocates for family law reform have wisely noted that traditional full-fledged representation in the adversarial model, even where available, is not well-suited to many domestic relations litigants in any event.[9] Litigants who come to court because they are divorcing, need an allocation of parental responsibilities, or are otherwise undergoing some kind of family transition have a highly distinctive set of needs and interests that don't appear in other contexts.[10] Family law's particular qualities – the need to protect children and the uniquely intertwined financial relationship between the parties – have led reformers to invest in systems that offer multiple pathways to resolution, depending on the degree of

4 Colo. State Ct. Admin. Off., *Domestic Relations Triage Project Final Report* (Aug. 2018), https://www.ncsc.org/__data/assets/pdf_file/0023/18833/co-scao-report-final-w-app.pdf (last accessed Feb. 3, 2025).

5 Jessica K. Steinberg, *Demand-Side Reform in the Poor People's Court*, 7 Conn. L. Rev. 741, 762 (2015).

6 *See, for example*, D. James Greiner et al., *Using Random Assignment to Measure Court Accessibility for Low-Income Divorce Seekers*, 118 Proc. Nat'l Acad. Scis. e2009086118 (Apr. 6, 2021) (reporting numerous procedural barriers making divorce systems inaccessible to unrepresented litigants).

7 *See supra* note 2 (specifying that court staff cannot provide strategy, analysis, or advice).

8 Russell Engler, *And Justice for All-Including the Unrepresented Poor: Revisiting the Roles of the Judges, Mediators, and Clerks*, 67 Fordham L. Rev. 1987, 2026 (1999).

9 Rebecca Aviel, *Why Civil Gideon Won't Fix Family Law*, 122 Yale L.J. 2106, 2109 (2013) (explaining that most family law litigants "want proceedings that are shorter, simpler, cheaper, more personal, more collaborative, and less adversarial").

10 We are focused here on custody disputes between parents whose relationship is dissolving rather than state-initiated proceedings in which the state is seeking to obtain custody of an abused or neglected child or to terminate parental rights altogether; nor do we address cases where a third party asserts custodial rights to the child in question.

conflict and complexity presented by each family's circumstances.[11] Some divorcing couples who meet eligibility criteria regarding minor children and marital assets may be able to convert the terms of their agreement into a decree without even appearing in court.[12] Others will be able to arrive at an agreement after mediation or assistance from a court-assigned parenting coordinator. Adversarial procedures resulting in a judicial determination of rights and responsibilities are limited to those cases that truly cannot be resolved with a more streamlined, problem-solving approach. These structural reform efforts de-emphasize the role of counsel in resolving family law cases – reflecting both a pragmatic acknowledgement that the army of lawyers that would be needed to serve domestic relations litigants is not about to materialize, and a genuine sense that many families are better served by a system that does not run on the kind of individualized partisan advocacy that is taken to be the lawyer's stock-in-trade.

As much as we should celebrate these efforts, we must also be candid about the role that legal expertise continues to play in achieving justice in family law. As long as we remain committed to the substantive principles that family law regimes seek to advance, and aspire to bring family law matters to resolutions that are aligned with these substantive principles, litigants should have some access to core legal competencies – especially the provision of advice. In this sense family law, for all its exceptionalist qualities, is not so different from other areas of law: Legal advice still matters. To make it accessible in the face of persistent resource constraints, the legal profession must be willing to expand the range of postures in which it is possible for litigants to get legal advice and the categories of professionals who are allowed to provide it.

The challenge, present in other legal areas where access concerns are acute but hitting family law with particular force, is how to leverage family law's mix of exceptionalist and universalist attributes to create an array of avenues for obtaining meaningful and affordable legal advice. The options we might offer in family law

[11] Because claims of exceptionalism are vulnerable to the identification of relevant similarities, it is worth clarifying at the outset that the point is not to make an argument of exceptionalism for its own sake. The argument is simply that several of family law's distinctive qualities are relevant to improving access to justice for divorcing couples. Some of family law's unique attributes offer cost-reduction opportunities that aren't available in other contexts – the fact that some divorcing couples have interests that are more aligned than they are adverse allows for the possibility of joint representation where it would be inappropriate in a landlord–tenant dispute. Conversely, some of family law's distinctive qualities produce constraints – the need to monitor and protect the interests of children limits the extent to which we should feel comfortable converting family law entirely to a private settlement regime. The essential point is that family law litigants should be offered a menu of resolution pathways and services that are uniquely tailored to the specific circumstances of family law, even if we wouldn't accept those arrangements in other contexts. And to be sure, a comprehensive access-to-justice strategy for family law will borrow liberally from other areas where promising.

[12] *See, for example*, *JDF 1018: Affidavit for Decree without Appearance*, Colo. Jud. Branch (Mar. 1, 2024), https://www.courts.state.co.us/Forms/PDF/JDF1018.pdf (last accessed Apr. 18, 2024).

will not translate seamlessly to all other contexts, as we will see. Indeed, what will work for some family law litigants would be inappropriate for others. But the exercise reveals a broader point: The most comprehensive access-to-justice strategies will include both Transubstantive interventions as well as subject-specific ones. The question is how to benefit from this pluralism while managing the added complexity that it brings. Section 16.1 shows how family law differs in key respects from the adversarial paradigm assumed by the American civil justice system. Section 16.2 explains that family law litigants are nonetheless navigating a system of legal rules, meant to effectuate profoundly consequential judgments about family obligations and various forms of dependency, and that in at least some subset of cases legal advice is critical to arriving at outcomes that are tolerably aligned with these substantive principles. Building from these observations, Section 16.3 considers various strategies for making legal advice more affordable and accessible to a wider range of family law litigants.

16.1 FAMILY LAW EXCEPTIONALISM

We might begin by observing that married couples who seek a divorce are required to use the judicial system to dissolve their marriage, no matter how deeply they agree that the marriage should end, and no matter how aligned they are regarding child custody, the distribution of debts and assets, and support obligations. Unlike parties to a contract dispute, or neighbors quarreling over a property line, or indeed any other type of civil matter, a divorcing couple may not negotiate and resolve their affairs without resort to the courts in any American jurisdiction.[13] Family law has undergone a profound transformation away from the fault-based, adversarial systems of yesteryear, in which spouses had to prove specific types of marital fault in order to obtain a divorce.[14] But for all that has changed, this feature of family law remains the same – though notably, in many jurisdictions divorcing spouses may now proceed as joint petitioners rather than opposing parties.[15] We will discuss in more detail the substantive legal principles that are said to justify this mandatory resort to the judicial system, but for now we sidestep such normative questions to instead make a simple but important observation: The presence of divorcing spouses in the judicial system says nothing about their adversity or alignment on the core issues of their dissolution. In other contexts, we might be able to assume that litigants are in court

[13] *See* Margaret Ryznar & Angélique Devaux, *Voilà! Taking the Judge Out of Divorce*, 42 SEATTLE U. L. REV. 161, 162 (2018) ("[A] fundamental premise in American law is that divorce constitutes a civil judicial process."); *see also* Hon. Lynda B. Munro (ret.) et al., *Administrative Divorce Trends and Implications*, 50 FAM. L.Q. 427, 428 (2016).

[14] *See, for example*, Rebecca Aviel, *Family Law and the New Access to Justice*, 86 FORDHAM L. REV. 2279, 2280 (2018) (explaining that until the 1960s and 1970s, divorce was only available to an "innocent" spouse who could prove that his or her partner had committed a specific type of misconduct – such as adultery, cruelty, or abandonment).

[15] Rebecca Aviel, *Counsel for the Divorce*, 55 B.C. L. REV. 1099, 1126 (2014).

because they are adversarial. But that's not necessarily true for divorcing spouses – in fact, a recent study conducted by the Family Justice Initiative found that 64 percent of domestic relations cases were filed as uncontested.[16] Divorcing spouses are in court, no matter how collegial or aligned their interests may be, simply because that is the only way they may dissolve the marriage.[17] This has important implications for designing access-to-justice solutions because it reminds us not to treat divorcing spouses as necessarily adverse to one another in a way that is analogous to other civil litigants. They might be able to benefit from legal service delivery models that would be categorically unethical and inappropriate for other litigants.

Another way in which family law is distinctive is the impact on children whose parents are undergoing dissolution. Family law rests on something of a paradox: The substantive principles that govern family law have as one of their chief objectives the protection of children's interests, but the process by which these principles are adjudicated and applied in individual cases can undermine this core objective.[18] The statutes that govern child custody instruct courts to weigh numerous factors designed to identify the best interests of the child,[19] and child support regimes have been repeatedly reformed to ensure adequate support for children after family dissolution.[20] The principles that govern the distribution of marital property and the award of spousal support also take into account children's interests. In allocating marital property between divorcing spouses, courts are instructed to consider whether to award "the family home or the right to live therein for a reasonable period to the spouse with whom any children reside the majority of the time."[21] Alimony statutes, which typically require a demonstration that the spouse seeking support is economically dependent, allow for the court to arrive at this conclusion either because the spouse is unable to support herself "through appropriate employment or is the custodian of a child whose condition or circumstances make it inappropriate for the spouse to be required to seek employment outside the home."[22] A court applying this provision could conclude that someone is eligible for spousal support – even if she is capable of obtaining adequate employment – because she cares for a child who would be best served by having her continue to stay home.

And yet amidst all of these substantive principles that express concern for the interests of children, a nearly universal consensus has emerged among scholars and advocates that divorce litigation itself is so harmful for children that avoiding it

[16] *See also* Nat'l Ctr. for State Cts., *supra* note 1, at i.

[17] See *supra* note 13 and accompanying text.

[18] *See, for example,* Jon Elster, *Solomonic Judgments: Against the Best Interest of the Child*, 54 U. Chi. L. Rev. 1, 11–12 (1987) (asserting that the best-interests standard is "self-defeating, in that finely tuned consideration of the best interests of each particular child is likely to impose 'process costs' that on balance tend to make children worse off").

[19] *See, for example,* Colo. Rev. Stat. Ann. § 14-10-124 (West).

[20] *See* Laura W. Morgan, *Child Support Fifty Years Later*, 42 Fam. L.Q. 365, 366 (2008).

[21] Colo. Rev. Stat. Ann. § 14-10-113.

[22] Colo. Rev. Stat. Ann. § 14-10-114.

should be one of the central features of family court reform.[23] This consensus has been so well-established that only a brief refresher is necessary here: The essential point is that because litigation puts parents in the position of adversaries, it actively generates hostility rather than simply reflecting some preexisting, static level of conflict that the parents bring with them simply by virtue of the end of the relationship. As the process drags on parties become more entrenched in their positions, and the resulting delay and uncertainty create anxiety and confusion for the children involved.

In addition to this uniquely powerful concern for the interests of third parties, family law matters present a financial relationship between the litigants that is without a convincing analogue in other areas of civil justice. There are surely cases where a spouse might have access to separate funds, gifted by a wealthy parent perhaps, to pay for their own representation. But for the most part, the spouses are both drawing on a single, joint pool of assets to fund litigation costs, and this is precisely the pool of assets whose favorable distribution they would be seeking to achieve. Consider a divorce where one spouse feels that they should receive more than 50 percent of the value of the marital house, perhaps because they contributed substantially more to the property's acquisition and improvement. This could well be a colorable legal claim: Most of the statutes that govern marital property don't require strictly equal division, and instead allow judges to make a distribution that is equitable based on individual circumstances, guided by statutory factors such as contribution.[24] But in a divorce where each spouse is represented by their own attorney in the conventional way, the spouse seeking the larger share will have to consider whether it is worth spending money on two lawyers to achieve this preferential result. This expense can quickly overtake the value of the increased share that the spouse was pursuing.

The need to engage in this calculus is particularly acute, given that dissolution produces various social and financial concerns that might reasonably appear more important to divorcing couples than obtaining the assistance of counsel. If a divorcing couple has limited resources to expend on professional assistance, it isn't obvious that they are better off spending those funds on a lawyer rather than a financial advisor, a tax accountant, or a child psychologist. In a recent study of divorcing spouses who chose to proceed without counsel, researchers repeatedly heard that a key part of the decision was to free up the funds that would have gone to attorney fees for family needs such as education and housing.[25] One study

[23] Michael Saini, *Triage as an Innovative Framework for Domestic Relations Cases*, Presentation at Modern Families, Innovative Courts: The 2015 Domestic Relations Best Practice Court Institute for Judges, Magistrates, Family Court Facilitators and Sherlocks (June 1–3, 2015) (PowerPoint on file with author) ("Everyone who works in family law . . . agrees on two things: family court is not good for families, and litigation is not good for children.").

[24] *See, for example*, Colo. Rev. Stat. Ann. § 14-10-113.

[25] Knowlton et al., *supra* note 1, at 12–15.

participant, "facing a rent and a mortgage, payments on two vehicles, and two insurance policies, concluded the money that would have been spent on an attorney would be better spent split between themselves."[26] Others emphasized the desire to redirect funds toward the children of the marriage:

- "As I was having conversations with the attorneys, it became clear to me that representation was not an efficient use of resources that were very, very limited that I could actually be using toward my children."
- "I'd much rather put that money toward supporting children than trying to fight to get them."
- "We have kids in college, and there just wasn't any reason to spend money on something – we just didn't need it."[27]

Decisions about whether to obtain legal assistance for a marital dissolution are seen as family budgeting assessments:

> My ex-partner and I looked at the expenses involved in each of us having a lawyer. We looked at the expenses of one of us having a lawyer and one not having a lawyer. We looked at the expenses of being represented for paperwork, by a paralegal, just to make the process clear so that we didn't have to return. And that's the method that we chose.[28]

For all these reasons, scholars and advocates have emphasized that models designed for other contexts are inapt for family law. Family law systems must prioritize problem-solving and private agreement over litigation and adjudication, and treat the parties as the best source of insight as to "what processes and services are best suited to a healthy reorganization for that family."[29] And yet, as much as we want to design systems that reduce antagonism and move away from the adversary nature of family dispute resolution, we must keep in mind that family law litigants are navigating a system that is fundamentally a legal one, in several important ways. Our growing appreciation for the value of self-determination in family court, and our need to grapple with the painful resource constraints that characterize the American civil justice system, more generally, ought not to obscure our recognition that even family court is a system in which legal expertise still has a meaningful role to play.

16.2 FAMILY LAW AS A SYSTEM OF LEGAL RULES

The process that governs family dissolution is obviously a legal system in the sense that parties file motions, appear in court, and litigate toward a judgment. But more

[26] *Id.* at 15.
[27] *Id.*
[28] *Id.*
[29] Fam. Just. Initiative, *Principles for Family Justice Reform* 4 (2019), https://iaals.du.edu/sites/default/files/documents/publications/family_justice_initiative_principles.pdf (last accessed Feb. 3, 2025).

importantly, these judgments are meant to bear some relationship to substantive legal principles that express and operationalize critically important norms about family decision-making and the rights and duties that family members owe each other. The space for private ordering has grown substantially over the past decades,[30] but family law is a long way from being a system that seeks only to facilitate private agreements and resolve disputes according to the terms of any such agreements, although those are certainly important functions.[31]

Family law seeks to protect vulnerable individuals and manage the inescapable social phenomenon of intersecting forms of dependency. Children are obviously dependent on the adults who care for them; family law also recognizes that adults may arrive at the end of a marriage with significant economic dependency caused by their caregiving role in the family. The paradigm case is a couple who decides jointly during the marriage, as many still do, that the overall welfare of the family would be maximized if one spouse were to put her own educational and professional pursuits on hold to manage the household and care for the couple's children. Such an arrangement allows the other spouse to devote time and energy to professional advancement, resulting in an enhanced income stream that benefits the entire family during the marriage. But if the marriage dissolves, the economic dependency fostered by this arrangement is solely born by the caregiving spouse, while the other spouse walks away from the marriage with professional and financial prospects that reflect the family's investment in his career.[32] The pattern is so familiar that it is captured with a shorthand reference to the "displaced homemaker."[33]

The substantive legal principles that govern family law reflect a judgment about how the economic risks of such an arrangement should be allocated. As Anne Alstott observes, "family law rules that establish financial relationships and liability between individuals constitute a form of social insurance."[34] To protect against unfairness and to encourage adults to make decisions that are in the best interest of the whole family unit while the marriage is intact, the law treats marriage as an economic partnership. The couple earns and spends as a unit, and both parties have claims to the acquired assets of the marital estate. The fruit of marital labor belongs to the couple, not the individual laboring spouse.[35] Upon dissolution, each spouse is entitled to a share of that fruit because each contributed to its creation.

[30] Brian H. Bix, *Private Ordering and Family Law*, 23 J. AM. ACAD. MATRIM. LAW. 249, 285 (2010).

[31] Carl E. Schneider, *The Channeling Function in Family Law*, 20 HOFSTRA L. REV. 495, 497 (1992).

[32] *See, for example*, Lorenz v. Lorenz, Supreme Court of New York, Appellate Division, 63 A.D.3d 1361 (2009). At the time of divorce, the husband's annual income was roughly $100,000, while the wife's was around $20,000, which the court attributed in part to the effects of marital decision-making.

[33] *See, for example*, *In re* Marriage of Wilson, 201 Cal. App. 3d 913, 918 (Ct. App. 1988).

[34] Anne L. Alstott, *Private Tragedies? Family Law as Social Insurance*, 4 HARV. L. & POL'Y REV. 3, 4 (2010).

[35] *Principles of the Law of Family Dissolution* § 4.03 (AM. L. INST. 2002).

The enforcement of these principles is a big part of why the state still plays quite a robust role at the end of a marriage – not by adjudicating fault as it used to do, but by monitoring and supervising the terms of dissolution, a role that is effectuated through the requirement that those seeking divorce obtain a judicial decree.[36] States require divorces to happen in the courthouse, rather than in an administrative office resembling the county clerk's office where real estate titles are recorded, to effectuate the economic partnership and child welfare norms to which family law is committed.

These norms are considered so important that divorcing spouses are given less autonomy than any other civil litigants to deviate from these principles.[37] Courts no longer categorically reject prenuptial agreements as per se unenforceable or presumptively invalid, but such agreements are subject to heightened scrutiny, including robust disclosure requirements.[38] Divorce settlement agreements likewise are subject to both procedural and substantive fairness review.[39] Family law's economic partnership norms are more than simply default rules around which parties may contract to their own satisfaction.[40]

None of this, of course, is set in stone. Lawmakers must consider whether there are groups of couples whose circumstances are so unlikely to implicate these concerns that they should be allowed to opt out entirely of meaningful dissolution review. That's precisely the idea underlying simplified dissolution procedures, an important innovation offered in a growing number of jurisdictions.[41] Although the details vary, the unifying theme is that couples who meet certain eligibility requirements and agree on the terms of their dissolution can convert their agreement into a formal divorce decree with minimal time and process, sometimes without even appearing in court.[42] In Illinois, for example, couples without children are eligible

[36] There are other reasons as well, including the detection of and appropriate response to domestic violence. Colo. Rev. Stat. Ann. § 14-10-107.8 (requiring parties filing divorce petitions "to disclose to the court the existence of any prior temporary or permanent restraining orders and civil protection orders to prevent domestic abuse").

[37] *In re* Marriage of Manzo, 659 P.2d 669, 674 (Colo. 1983) (noting that "because of the fiduciary relationship between husband and wife, separation agreements generally are closely scrutinized by the courts, and such agreements are more readily set aside in equity under circumstances that would be insufficient to nullify an ordinary contract").

[38] *See, for example,* Edwardson v. Edwardson, 798 S.W.2d 941, 945 (Ky. 1990).

[39] Colo. Rev. Stat. Ann. § 14-10-112 (instructing courts to review separation agreements for unconscionability). Such review is undertaken in light of the statutory criteria governing property distribution. *See In re* Marriage of Lowery, 568 P.2d 103 (Colo. 1977).

[40] Part of the reason for that is the state's own interest in privatizing dependency. The Uniform Premarital Agreement Act specifies that if the modification or elimination of spousal support in a premarital agreement would cause a spouse to be eligible for public assistance at the time of separation, "a court, notwithstanding the terms of the agreement, may require the other party to provide support to the extent necessary to avoid that eligibility." Uniform Premarital Agreement Act § 6(b).

[41] *See* Munro (ret.) et al., *supra* note 13, at 428 (discussing the benefits of summary dissolution).

[42] Aviel, *supra* note 14, at 2283.

for simplified dissolution if the marriage lasted less than eight years; neither spouse owns real estate; the entire marital estate is valued at $50,000 or less; neither spouse is dependent on the other for support; neither makes more than $30,000 per year nor does their combined annual income exceed $60,000; there are no jointly held retirement benefits; and the combined value of any benefits either spouse holds is less than $10,000.[43]

There is ample room for productive debate about whether a larger range of couples should be eligible for this kind of streamlined process, or even administrative rather than judicial divorce. And the debate should take into account a realistic assessment of how many couples will have access to the kind of legal advice that would conceivably allow them to benefit from family law's substantive principles and attendant judicial review. But as it currently stands, family law reflects an ambition, however imperfectly realized, that goes beyond simply effectuating private agreements, and few advocate for a systematic overhaul that would move substantive family law principles in that direction. Simplification is a crucial part of family law reform, but at a certain point it collides with our commitment to the substantive principles that form the foundation of family law.

To see these dynamics in action, consider a couple in their early thirties, without children, who are divorcing after six years of marriage. Each spouse has a college degree and has been working for the duration of the marriage. The wife works at a nonprofit organization that focuses on the resettlement of refugees, earning about $50,000 a year, while the husband works as an investment banker for a national firm, earning anywhere from $250,000 to $350,000 a year, depending on bonuses. Upon marriage the couple decided that they would not merge their finances, a practice that has grown more common in recent decades.[44] Each has their own account into which they deposit their respective paychecks, and they have a joint checking account from which to pay shared expenses. Each moves funds from their own account to the shared account as needed to pay for their half of the couple's bills. Upon deciding to end the marriage, the couple might begin from the premise that they will each walk away with the funds in their own account and half of whatever might be residually remaining in the joint account. After all, the very practice of keeping separate accounts suggests some underlying notion of what belongs to whom – the couple might feel that by keeping their finances separate they have already resolved the question of how the assets will be distributed at the end of the relationship.

A lawyer, on the other hand, would readily identify and apply the fruit-of-marital-labor principle to this couple's situation, and would see that the husband's account

[43] 750 Ill. Comp. Stat. Ann. 5/452.

[44] Joe Pinkser, *Should Couples Merge Their Finances?*, ATLANTIC (Apr. 20, 2022), https://www.theatlantic.com/family/archive/2022/04/how-couples-should-manage-finances-hybrid-model/629607/ (last accessed Feb. 3, 2025).

was in fact marital property.[45] In some jurisdictions it would be subject to an equal distribution, while in others it would be subject to equitable distribution, based on factors such as the parties' respective contributions to the marital estate and the economic circumstances they will face after the marriage ends. To appreciate the importance of having access to this legal advice, we do not need to take a position on what the parties will or should do with this knowledge. The parties might choose to proceed as they would have previously, arriving at an agreement that leaves the husband with more of the proceeds from his salary than a court might award in a judicial determination, subject to the kind of review discussed above.[46] But it is fair to assume that the parties will bargain differently with one another with this knowledge, and that if we believe in the substantive principles that underlie marital property distribution, that this is a good thing. Without it, left only to their intuitions about what is "theirs," their agreement will be at odds with the core principle that the fruit of marital labor belongs to the couple – not because the parties knowingly contracted around it but because the insight wasn't available. And this is a fact pattern that intentionally sidesteps some of the more pressing issues that arise in family law matters: custody of minor children, a displaced homemaker, domestic violence, or a jointly owned business that would require professional expertise to partition fairly.[47]

What reformers must continue to grapple with is the extent to which family courts should be willing to sign off on agreements that smoothly and quickly proceed to a resolution that no court would order when applying the substantive legal principles in an adjudicative posture. On the surface, the agreement does tolerably well on some of the metrics that are commonly used to evaluate civil justice reforms – speed, reduction of transaction costs, and self-determination, at least in some superficial sense. But it does poorly when judged against the substantive principles that family law seeks to advance – marriage as an economic partnership – and without the wife's understanding of this core legal principle, it is hard to say that there has been a knowing and voluntary waiver.[48] Even as we move steadily and laudably toward more autonomy in the dissolution of marriage, offering litigants a bypass around slow and costly judicial procedures that they would prefer to avoid, we should be

45 These principles are sufficiently determinate that a competent lawyer should be able to identify and predictively apply them from a posture of neutral assessment rather than partisan advocacy.

46 While judicial review offers something of a failsafe, a system that makes the advice available early on in the process, so that parties can incorporate it into their agreement, is better than one that operationalizes the substantive principles only by having a judge refuse to accept an excessively lop-sided agreement.

47 In a well-functioning triage system, cases with these features would not be eligible for simplified procedures but would be flagged for additional services and interventions.

48 It could be argued that the wife's participation in keeping separate accounts during the marriage should be treated as a functional waiver of any claims to the husband's earnings and manifests an intention to be governed by the practice of financial separation instead of whatever the default legal principles would offer. Marital property principles could be revised to reflect this view, but that's not how they are currently understood.

candid about what it means for systems to ratify agreements in the absence of legal advice. Agreements may not only deviate significantly from substantive legal principles, which is one thing, but will rest on a lack of knowledge about substantive legal entitlements.

This is the conundrum: We want to facilitate private agreement, both out of an authentic commitment to promoting self-determination and reducing adversarialism in family matters, and as a realistic response to the overwhelming caseloads and resource constraints that characterize family court. And yet, for all that has changed in the law of marriage and divorce over the past sixty years, we continue to think that there is a social benefit to having a law of families that is more than just a set of mechanisms for effectuating private agreements. As long as we think it a worthy social endeavor to regulate families in this way, rather than just facilitating purely private decision-making about the distribution of assets upon dissolution, we'll have difficult decisions to make about when we allow litigants to opt out of the judicial procedures that operationalize family law's social insurance and risk-allocation objectives. Simplified dissolution pathways in their current form are largely designed to allow opt-out only for those couples whose circumstances are less likely to implicate economic partnership and child welfare concerns – shorter marriages with few assets and no children. (The couple depicted above would not even be eligible for simplified dissolution in Illinois, for example, because their incomes are too high.)

If we could imagine more affordable access to legal advice, so that more litigants were choosing dissolution pathways with some basic knowledge about how the law applies to their circumstances, we might feel more comfortable allowing a much wider range of couples to forego judicial review. Enhancing access to advice can thus soften – although surely not eliminate – the tension between speed, simplification, and self-determination, on the one hand, and family law's substantive commitments on the other. Legal expertise was once necessary to navigate the compulsory adversarial nature of adjudicative divorce proceedings; now it might be the key to allowing more and more couples to opt out while maintaining some residual commitment to family law's substantive principles.

We now can see clearly that, for all its exceptional qualities, family law shares something in common with other areas plagued by pervasive unmet legal needs. For at least some subset of participants, meaningful access to justice requires some access to legal advice: the identification of governing legal principles and the application of those principles to an individual's particular circumstances. This is not to diminish the work that has been done to provide various other forms of valuable assistance to self-represented litigants; some of the notable efforts in this vein, in addition to the simplification initiatives mentioned above, include converting court documents and forms into plain language, document preparation software and other technological assistance, and "concierge" or "navigator" models of assistance in which court staff provide "personalized assistance, but not legal advice, for self-represented parties."[49] But it is clear that none of this is intended to function as legal advice. Indeed, discussions of the optimal role for court staff to play in domestic relations matters routinely emphasize the need to steer clear of providing legal advice.[50]

An honest appraisal of access to justice for family law litigants would acknowledge the importance of legal advice, at least for some subset of unrepresented litigants, and would note what a large range of couples there are whose assets are substantial enough to benefit from legal assistance, but whose resources are sufficiently limited that the couple will reasonably hesitate before diverting those funds to lawyer's fees – the family law version of the "missing middle." No matter how well-trained, hard-working, and sensitive to the specialized needs of domestic relations litigants, a bevy of court staff sidling up to the line between legal information and legal advice, or automated, AI-based advice keyed to modal rather than edge situations, falls short of what our aspirations should be. Reforms that work around the margins of the provision of legal advice are important, and we should continue to explore ways to shrink the set of litigants for whom access to advice will make a meaningful difference in the substantive justice of their resolutions – but a comprehensive strategy will attend to the fundamental importance of advice.

16.3 ACCESS TO ADVICE AS A LINCHPIN OF FAMILY JUSTICE

We've seen that in order to develop an appropriate access-to-justice strategy for family law, we must both carefully attend to family law's exceptionalist attributes, and yet also recognize that, for all the transformation family law has already undergone, it continues to be a legal system governed by substantive principles, such that just resolutions will in some instances require legal advice of the sort that is still very hard to come by for most Americans. We have the foundation to understand that among the many innovative solutions being proposed and implemented, family court reform must also offer expanded access to legal advice – meaning, of course, opportunities to obtain advice, and potentially related legal services such as negotiation and document drafting, at a lower price point than what traditional representation at market rates would entail. We can now squarely consider various

[49] Fam. Just. Initiative, *A Model Process for Family Justice Initiative Pathways* 2 (2019), https://nationalcenterforstatecourts.app.box.com/s/620evvuopo8bzvfigt7505cmhx6se2kq (last accessed Feb. 3, 2025).

States using this kind of model include Alaska, California, Maryland, and Oregon. *Family Law Self-Help Center*, ALASKA CT. SYS., https://courts.alaska.gov/shc/index.htm (last accessed Mar. 21, 2024); *Self-Help Guide: Families and Children*, CAL. CTS., https://selfhelp.courts.ca.gov/families-and-children (last accessed Mar. 21, 2024); *Family Court Help Centers*, MD. CTS., https://www.mdcourts.gov/family/familyselfhelp (last accessed Mar. 21, 2024); *Family Law Self-Help*, OR. JUD. BRANCH, https://www.courts.oregon.gov/programs/family/selfhelp/Pages/default.aspx (last accessed Mar. 21, 2024).

[50] *See* Fam. Just. Initiative, *supra* note 49, at 17.

ways this might be achieved. Some of these possibilities, like the acceptance of joint representation as a legitimate form of unbundled legal services, will draw on family law's distinctive attributes to propose a model that would not transfer well to other areas of unmet legal needs. Others, like early neutral evaluation, involve family law borrowing a mechanism from other areas of law and refashioning it to meet access-to-justice objectives for family law litigants. The goal is to convert family law's particular mix of distinctive and generalizable attributes into a wider range of opportunities for obtaining meaningful and affordable legal advice.

16.3.1 *Unbundling Legal Advice from Partisan Advocacy*

The revision of the rules of professional conduct to explicitly allow limited scope representation, whereby "the client is in charge of selecting one or several discrete lawyering tasks contained within the full-service package," was a significant milestone in expanding access to advice.[51] A robust literature now examines the connection between "unbundling" and access to justice, for the straightforward reason that it allows clients with limited financial resources to obtain some legal services even if they cannot afford full representation.[52] Online divorce platforms like Hello Divorce reflect the newest approach to unbundling, offering clients a range of tech-enabled plans and services that can include consultation with an attorney.[53] But for all the innovation that's out there, unbundling has yet to achieve its full potential in enhancing access to advice for family law. One of the reasons for that is the legal profession's continued insistence that advice and related services can only be provided in a posture of individualized partisan advocacy, thus foreclosing the joint representation of amicably divorcing spouses by a single lawyer. This possibility seems shocking if we continue to assume that divorcing spouses are analogous to other civil litigants. But it follows naturally from one of the distinctive qualities of family law considered above: Divorcing spouses are not necessarily adverse to each other in the ways that would foreclose a joint representation.

Lest one be tempted to scoff at the idea that anyone going through a divorce would agree to such a thing, it turns out that many divorcing couples seek precisely that, and reasonably so – they don't want to hire two different attorneys to assist each spouse on an individualized basis, but they believe that they would benefit from some legal expertise in the course of their dissolution. They seek a particular type of

[51] Forrest S. Mosten, Unbundling Legal Services: A Guide to Delivering Legal Services a la Carte 1–2 (2000).

[52] *See, for example*, Molly M. Jennings & D. James Greiner, *The Evolution of Unbundling in Litigation Matters: Three Case Studies and a Literature Review*, 89 Denv. U. L. Rev. 825 (2012). Researchers have raised questions about the effectiveness of limited scope assistance as compared to full representation. *See, for example*, D. James Greiner et al., *The Limits of Unbundled Legal Assistance: A Randomized Study in a Massachusetts District Court and Prospects for the Future*, 126 Harv. L. Rev. 901, 906 (2013).

[53] See hello divorce, https://hellodivorce.com/ (last accessed Mar. 21, 2024).

limited scope representation, "in which a single lawyer provides them with guidance as to the set of interests they share; assists them in arriving at a negotiated resolution of all divorce-related issues; and provides them with the drafting expertise necessary to make their agreement clear, concrete, and comprehensive."[54] Such couples are repeatedly told with the utmost conviction that this would be a categorical violation of the ethical rules, specifically the prohibition on conflicts of interest.[55] As I have previously explained, this conclusion rests on a paternalistic and insufficiently nuanced assessment of adversity in divorce, a misunderstanding of how much can be "usefully explained to a divorcing couple from an impartial stance about the law that governs the dissolution of marriage," and a failure to appreciate the extent to which a couple can benefit from a lawyer's expert advocacy for their potentially substantial shared interests in "minimizing transaction costs, maximizing the total value of the marital estate at the time of the dissolution, and reducing the negative impact of the divorce on any children."[56]

To be sure, joint representation isn't for everyone – on the contrary, it is an arrangement that would work only for a very particular subset of divorcing couples. But it illustrates a broader point that access-to-justice strategies need not be uniform across or even within subject areas, and that attending to the unique needs and interests of sub-groups within sub-groups can reveal opportunities to provide access to advice in new and cheaper formulations. Joint representation should be available as part of a broader menu of options to obtain legal advice without engaging in full-fledged adversarial representation.

The problem, of course, is that any system with multiple pathways relies on the efficacy of the sorting mechanism used to match cases with appropriate services. Joint representation rests on the premise that individual lawyers, working with prospective clients to discern their interests and objectives, can deploy their trademark professional skills – an understanding of both substantive family law principles and conflicts of interest – to determine when the arrangement would be suitable. Other pathways will turn on decision-making by court staff, guided by some combination of statutory criteria, internal court protocols, and intuition. None of these are going to be perfect, and all of them will face difficult questions about path dependencies and self-fulfilling prophecies. Cases might initially appear to be nonadversarial, but only because some key issue hasn't yet surfaced; the procedural features of the pathway into which the case is routed could then suppress an opportunity to identify and fully resolve the issue in accordance with family law's substantive commitments. These are thorny questions requiring more extensive

[54] Aviel, *supra* note 15, at 1121.

[55] *Id.* at 1121–24. *See also* Dist. of Colo. Bar, *Ethics Op.* 243 (1993). Supposedly in service to this ideal of loyalty, lawyers are channeling clients into arrangements that are considerably worse: where the lawyer represents one of the spouses, and in that posture drafts documents that both spouses will sign.

[56] Aviel, *supra* note 15, at 1143.

treatment than can be provided here. One partial and preliminary answer is to note that the only way to avoid these challenges is to return to a one-size-fits-all approach. Given the demonstrated shortcomings of that model, it is reasonable to press forward in the pursuit of an expanding menu of options, knowing full well how much pressure it places on the development of effective triage mechanisms.

16.3.2 *Offering Advice in a Nonrepresentative Posture*

Just as advice can be unbundled from partisan advocacy, it can be provided in a capacity that is entirely nonrepresentative. Early neutral evaluation, or early neutral assessment as it is sometimes called, does exactly this, offering a model that family law can borrow from other contexts. Descriptions of early neutral evaluation tend to focus on its function as an alternative resolution mechanism – typically for counseled parties – rather than a source of advice for self-represented litigants. The American Bar Association, for example, explains that soon after a case has been filed in court, it may be "referred to an expert, usually an attorney, who is asked to provide a balanced and unbiased evaluation of the dispute."[57] After meeting with parties or reviewing their written comments, the "expert identifies each side's strengths and weaknesses and provides an evaluation of the likely outcome of a trial." This evaluation can assist the parties in assessing their case and may propel them toward a settlement.[58] As this description suggests, early neutral evaluation can be successful as an alternative dispute resolution mechanism precisely because of the expert opinion that evaluators offer to the parties, after applying the governing legal principles to the specific facts of the case.

The insight that parties might obtain from this process, potentially propelling them to settlement, may be particularly valuable for self-represented litigants in family court who have no other access to an expert who can consider their individualized facts and predict how a court is likely to rule. While mediation has been a mainstay of modern divorce for decades now, and has played a substantial role in resolving family disputes with reduced reliance on litigation, early neutral evaluation improves upon some of mediation's recognized shortcomings, including the one we are focused on here: Mediators typically offer divorcing couples just passive facilitation, brokering an agreement without providing the kind of substantive advice that would help the couple contextualize the important choices and trade-offs they may be making.[59]

Family court reformers in Colorado and Minnesota have understood the value of providing more substantive guidance to family court litigants, and both states offer

[57] *Dispute Resolution Processes*, Am. Bar Ass'n, https://www.americanbar.org/groups/dispute_resolution/resources/dispute-resolution-overview/processes (last accessed Feb. 3, 2025) (describing early neutral evaluation).

[58] *Id.*

[59] Aviel, *supra* note 14, at 2285.

voluntary, court-sponsored early neutral evaluation programs that are currently limited to the evaluation of parenting-time disputes.[60] Typical teams are comprised of one lawyer and one mental health professional, with substantive experience in the field of child custody matters. The team draws upon this background to guide the couple in their custody negotiation: After hearing from the parties, the lawyer provides the couple with information about the governing legal framework, while the mental health professional offers insight on child development, attachment theory, and other concepts important for separating parents to understand. The ensuing negotiation is primed to be more successful because the parents have been assisted in developing realistic expectations and have had some expert guidance in developing terms appropriately tailored to the needs of the children in question. This expert guidance is offered early in the process, before parties have dug in on their respective positions, and judges are on hand to convert an ensuing agreement into a decree. This combination has proven to be very effective, allowing parties to resolve their entire parenting-time dispute in a period of three to four hours. As one judge describes the process: "parties can walk into the courthouse for their [early neutral evaluation] session, negotiate a fully comprehensive parenting-time agreement – complete with holidays, transportation issues, and the like – and walk out of the courthouse with a permanent order."[61]

Unsurprisingly, cost is a significant problem in scaling up the program to include more families in its purview. The court-sponsored early neutral evaluation program costs $400 per party,[62] an expenditure that many families either simply can't afford or are unwilling to choose at a juncture that is already financially precarious. At the same time, the cost is minimal compared to traditional representation by an attorney, suggesting that the expansion of such programs should be part of a comprehensive strategy that, as argued here, takes seriously the importance of lawyer assistance in providing meaningful access to justice.

16.3.3 *Allowing Nonlawyers to Offer Advice*

We must think critically and creatively about the various postures in which lawyers can offer legal advice. But as scholars such as Deborah Rhode recognized many decades ago, a comprehensive strategy for enhancing access to advice must also include an expansion of the categories of people who are allowed to provide it.[63] In large part due to her insights and advocacy, the lawyer's monopoly on the

[60] *Id.*

[61] *Id.* at 2286.

[62] Colo. State Cts., *Early Neutral Assessment*, https://www.courts.state.co.us/userfiles/file/Court_Probation/08th_Judicial_District/Larimer/ENA%20Info%20Sheet.pdf (last accessed Feb. 3, 2025).

[63] Nora Freeman Engstrom, *She Stood Up: The Life and Legacy of Deborah L. Rhode*, 74 Stan. L. Rev. Online 1 (2021).

provision of legal advice is finally starting to soften. A small but growing list of states have launched programs that allow trained and licensed professionals who are not lawyers to provide legal services – including the provision of advice – to clients in specified types of cases, including, most prominently, family law.[64] Some of these states offer such programs only in family law,[65] while others include areas such as debt collection and landlord/tenant matters; in the latter group, professionals seeking a license choose the area in which they will specialize.[66] The details of each program vary, but the education, training, and testing requirements to obtain the license are extensive, and the new legal service providers are subject to a disciplinary system that investigates and resolves grievances.[67] A full evaluation of the design considerations in developing and sustaining an alternative legal provider (ALP) program is beyond the scope of what can be covered here, but it is worth noting that data from the existing programs "show that ALPs are making a positive impact in people's lives. Well-trained ALPs are competent, their clients are satisfied with their work product, and they can reach a portion of the population that attorneys are not reaching. Alternative legal providers are providing high-quality legal services at around half the cost of attorneys."[68]

Alternative legal provider programs are an important element of improving access to justice across multiple areas of unmet legal needs, not just family law. But it isn't surprising that several states have made the program available only in family law, or that, even in the jurisdictions with a broader menu of service areas, there's been the most uptake in the family law area.[69] As noted at the outset, family law is often invoked as the paradigm case for the country's shameful justice gap – an area where the vast majority of Americans must navigate legal matters of profound personal

64 Michael Houlberg & Natalie Anne Knowlton, *Allied Legal Professionals: A National Framework for Program Growth*, Inst. for the Advancement of the Am. L. Sys. (June 2023), https://iaals.du.edu/sites/default/files/documents/publications/alp_national_framework.pdf (last accessed Feb. 3, 2025).

65 Colorado, the most recent state to authorize an ALP program, has limited the scope to particular matters within family law, including divorce and the allocation of parental responsibilities. *See* Colo. S. Ct. R. §§ 207-207.14, https://www.courts.state.co.us/userfiles/file/Court_Probation/Supreme_Court/Rule_Changes/2023/Rule%20Change%202023(06).pdf (last accessed Feb. 3, 2025). Washington launched an ALP program in 2012 that was limited to family law; the program was sunset in 2020, purportedly due to cost, but the ninety-one practitioners who had obtained licensure are permitted to continue offering services. *See* Michael Houlberg & Janet Drobinske, *The Landscape of Allied Legal Professional Programs in the United States* 7–8, Inst. for the Advancement of the Am. L. Sys. (Nov. 2022), https://iaals.du.edu/sites/default/files/documents/publications/landscape_allied_legal_professionals.pdf (last accessed Feb. 3, 2025). For additional discussion of the Washington experience, see Jason Solomon & Noelle Smith, *The Surprising Success of Washington State's Limited License Legal Technician Program*, Stan. Ctr. on the L. Pro. (2021) https://law.stanford.edu/wp-content/uploads/2021/04/LLLT-White-Paper-Final-5-4-21.pdf (last accessed Feb. 3, 2025).

66 Houlberg & Drobinske, *supra* note 65, at 8–9, 20–26, and 42–47.

67 *Id.* at 41–49.

68 *Id.* at 28.

69 *Id.* at 21–22.

significance without legal assistance. And as developed throughout this chapter, family law is an area where we might particularly desire alternatives to full-fledged individualized partisan advocacy in the adversarial frame – where what is unaffordable might also be undesirable. The progress that has been made in enhancing self-help support and simplifying divorce procedures is laudable, and considerably more should be done on this front. Given the persistently high cost of legal services, many more couples should be eligible to choose summary dissolution instead of slow and costly judicial proceedings from which they may have little to gain. But ALP programs reflect a growing recognition that in family law and elsewhere, there is a wide gulf between self-help and full-fledged partisan advocacy – perhaps an entire ecosystem, with different levels of service and types of service providers.[70]

16.4 CONCLUSION

As we encourage and foster this proliferation of strategies designed to close the justice gap, we also need to study it: We lack reliable evidence about the effectiveness of these innovations, and experimentation must be accompanied by careful research.[71] Here too, the unique characteristics of family law will require special consideration. As Jim Greiner and Cassandra Wolos Pattanayak observe in their call for additional randomized studies in the provision of legal assistance, "perhaps the highest degree of difficulty in defining desirable outcomes is represented by the area of divorce and child custody."[72] They proceed to note that legal representation may advance important nonpecuniary (and yet measurable) values such as the smooth and efficient operation of the adjudicatory system, "may educate the client as to her best interests or as to what is possible given legal and factual constraints, thereby adjusting the client's goals," and may promote the client's perception of fairness and sense that she was afforded an opportunity to be heard.[73]

We will want to apply the best possible empirical testing to determine whether these essential goals can also be served by the variants on traditional representation considered here: joint representation, early neutral evaluation, representation by an allied legal professional, or an amalgamation of more than one type of innovation.

[70] *Id.* at 28 (explaining that "an ecosystem of legal professionals" is necessary to close the justice gap).

[71] D. James Greiner & Cassandra Wolos Pattanayak, *Randomized Evaluation in Legal Assistance: What Difference Does Representation (Offer and Actual Use) Make?*, 121 YALE L.J. 2118, 2181–82 (2012); *see also* Deborah L. Rhode et al., *Access to Justice through Limited Legal Assistance*, 16 NW. J. HUM RTS. 1, 9 (2018).

[72] Greiner & Pattanayak, *supra* note 71, at 2204 (contrasting divorce and custody matters to disputes over government benefits, where success is easy to define). *See also* Judith G. McMullen & Debra Oswald, *Why Do We Need a Lawyer?: An Empirical Study of Divorce Cases*, 12 J. L. & FAM. STUD. 57, 68 (2010) (noting "a multitude of idiosyncratic custody outcomes which cannot be compared in terms of success or failure").

[73] Greiner & Pattanayak, *supra* note 71, at 2206 (proposing that randomized studies can measure client perception through surveys).

(We could imagine a divorcing couple who, hungry for legal advice but needing to conserve household resources as much as possible, chooses to be jointly represented by an allied legal professional instead of a lawyer.) The first step, as urged herein, is to recognize the continued value of legal advice for family law litigants, and to endeavor to make that advice more affordable and accessible using all the levers at our disposal. We might even be able to anticipate that the entire realm of civil justice could benefit from this very practice: combing through individual areas of law, identifying the precise combination of attributes that might allow us to pry open some space for additional innovation without unmanageable complexity or undue sacrifice of the field's core commitments.

17

Putting Railroad Justice Back on Track*

Samuel Issacharoff and Beverly B. Martin

Between us, we have spent many decades in the upper precincts of American law. One of us went from being a U.S. Attorney to a district court judge to a judge of the Court of Appeals, while the other writes and practices in the heavily resourced domains of complex litigation. We observed and participated in the efforts, not always successful, of federal courts to engage the most pressing demands of our society.

But outside our gaze, and largely without our even really taking notice, the most dramatic transformation of the American legal system was unfolding with astonishing speed and with deep institutional implications. The state court system, in which 95 percent of legal disputes are handled, was being transformed into a massive debt collection operation. No longer the domain of the great common law of torts and property and contract, state courts across the country had been overrun by "assembly line" claimants, executing collection judgments against unrepresented defendants who for the most part have neither the incentive nor the wherewithal to even enter an appearance.[1] These defendants, quite simply, are being railroaded through a legal system characterized by an ever-diminishing pretense of adjudication.

In such courts, a shocking three-quarters of the cases involve an unrepresented party.[2] By contrast, our more familiar domain of federal courts is overwhelmingly populated by represented parties with roughly 70 percent of cases involving representation of both sides of the dispute, and the remaining 30 percent being pro se *plaintiffs* challenging some form of institutional grievance.[3] Even this distinction misses the nature of the transformation of state courts. Many of the unlawyered

* Our deep thanks to Jonathan Goldberg and Matthew Maury for their assistance. We are grateful for the early comments of David Engstrom and Janel Sabel on a draft version of this chapter.

1 Daniel Wilf-Townsend, *Assembly-Line Plaintiffs*, 135 Harv. L. Rev. 1704 (2022).

2 Anna E. Carpenter et al., *Judges in Lawyerless Courts*, 110 Geo. L.J. 509, 511 (2022).

3 United States Courts, *Just the Facts: Trends in Pro Se Civil Litigation from 2000 to 2019* (2021), https://www.uscourts.gov/news/2021/02/11/just-facts-trends-pro-se-civil-litigation-2000-2019 (last accessed Mar. 28, 2024).

disputes involve routine small claims and family law issues.[4] These disputes are generally between parties with comparable resources, familiarity with the legal system, and stakes in the outcome. The problem, then, is not merely that state court litigants lack access to representation. It is that they lack access to representation in domains where the other side commands greater legal resources and strong incentives to press for full judgments.

Asymmetric aggregation, as we shall term this development, is the process of developing mass efficiencies of scale on one side of the "v." in small-stakes disputes. One customarily thinks of aggregate litigation as raising the stakes for all sides, pitting a class action against an institutional defendant or gathering all claims in a multidistrict litigation format. Such aggregate proceedings balance the stakes at play and the potential preclusive effect of litigation across all or large parts of common disputes. Here, by contrast, the asymmetry emerges from the creation of a new species of litigant in cases that, on the surface, still look like the typical A v. B dispute over small amounts of money. This new litigant is a firm, not in the sense of the partnerships that organize lawyers but in the Ronald Coase sense of the firm as an institutional arrangement that provides economic gains from lowering the transaction costs of pursuing an economic objective.[5] But unlike customary aggregate litigation, there are no efficiencies on the other side, as when a class of plaintiffs sues an institutional actor such as a corporation or a government agency.

Under conditions of asymmetric aggregation, there is not a market for the combination of legal interests on the *defense* side of the "v." If we think of the bulk of nominal parties in the state court system, they are small debtors with no common bond, no centralizing prospect for their defenses, and no possibility of joint gain that can be harnessed by an entrepreneurial legal agent, as with a class action plaintiffs' counsel. Ordinarily, one may think of such small-scale debtors as being unlikely to represent a large percentage of the state court caseload because the small-scale creditors on the other side would find the cost of trying to litigate a judgment foreboding. But the inability to recover legitimate debt is not a sustainable position in a mass consumer economy, nor is it a desirable state of affairs.

Enter debt collection firms that can buy up the claims of creditors and who can in turn rationalize the process of enforcing debt obligations. Obviously, this is an area rife with the potential for abuse, memorialized in the cult classic, *Repo Man*. Economies of scale incentivize aggregation of these consumer debt enforcers into a few agencies,[6] including – potentially – third-party collectors outside the scope of

4 John M. Greacen, *Self-Represented Litigants, the Courts, and the Legal Profession: Myths and Realities*, 52 Family Ct. Rev. 662, 664 (Oct. 2014).

5 Ronald Coase, *The Nature of the Firm*, 4 Economica 386 (1937).

6 Agencies can aggregate claims themselves. *See* Sprint Commc'ns Co., L.P. v. APCC Servs., Inc., 554 U.S. 269, 292 (2008) (permitting a private organization to bring suit after others assigned their claims to that organization and recognizing "the assignments were made for ordinary business purposes"). Alternatively, law firms can generate similar economies of scale

formal federal debt collection regulation.[7] Economies of scale also result in downstream efficiencies in the use of form contracts, firms that specialize in litigating claims for the repeat client, and routinized processes for collecting judgments.[8] What is new since the time of *Repo Man* is the ability to capture the state court system as the means of debt collection with mass-produced judgments, rather than the furtive *Repo* collection approach to depriving debtors of their possessions, oftentimes with little regard for the merits of the competing claims.

The rise of "assembly-line plaintiffs," to use Professor Daniel Wilf-Townsend's term, exploits four features: (1) a collection of a few sophisticated and repeat plaintiffs, (2) a large volume of small value claims, (3) a high rate of no-show defendants, and (4) a passive judiciary.[9] Debt collectors and other financial services companies typify the assembly-line plaintiff.[10] Out of 200 possible "top filers"[11] across a sample of states, *ten* debt collectors or financial services corporations were responsible for 84 percent of debt collection filings.[12] In other words, only a few plaintiffs dominate state court dockets.

Pre-litigation forces drive part of this trend. Starting in the late 1990s and early 2000s, this form of aggregation on the plaintiff's side of the "v." became a standard business model for debt collectors.[13] One New Jersey lawyer, for instance, filed more than 69,000 lawsuits in a single year, averaging between 300 and 400 per day.[14] Such economies are crucial to the recent trend in state court litigation. Without them, it would not be profitable to collect on individual debt, which the Federal Trade Commission (FTC) estimates is around $1,600 on average per consumer account.[15]

by building an inventory of plaintiffs. *See* Wilf-Townsend, *supra* note 1, at 1720 (describing law firms that market themselves as providing automated litigation flow and collection systems).

7 *See* Henson v. Santander Consumer USA Inc., 137 S. Ct. 1718, 1721–22 (2017) (holding a party that purchases debt and attempts to collect on it for its benefit is not a debt collector under the Fair Debt Collection Practices Act).

8 Wilf-Townsend, *supra* note 1, at 1718–19.

9 *See id.* at 1717.

10 *See, for example*, Erika Rickard, *How Debt Collectors Are Transforming the Business of State Courts*, Pew Rsch. Ctr. (May 6, 2020), https://www.pewtrusts.org/en/research-and-analysis/reports/2020/05/how-debt-collectors-are-transforming-the-business-of-state-courts (last accessed Feb. 3, 2025).

11 A "top filer" is one of the ten most common plaintiffs in each state. Wilf-Townsend, *supra* note 1, at 1731. "Many companies were top filers in multiple states; only 70 unique companies appeared across the survey." *Id.*

12 *Id.*

13 *Id.* at 1719 (citing Suein Hwang, *Once-Ignored Consumer Debts Are Focus of Booming Industry*, Wall St. J. (Oct. 25, 2004), https://www.wsj.com/articles/SB109865776922954118 (last accessed Feb. 3, 2025) and Paul Kiel, *So Sue Them: What We've Learned About the Debt Collection Lawsuit Machine*, ProPublica (May 5, 2016), https://www.propublica.org/article/so-sue-them-what-weve-learned-about-the-debt-collection-lawsuit-machine (last accessed Feb. 3, 2025)).

14 *See* Kiel, *supra* note 13 (describing the lawyer's workflow, which consisted of multiple screens filed with documents that he briefly reviewed and signed electronically for submission by staff).

15 Fed. Trade Comm'n, The Structure and Practices of the Debt Buying Industry i–ii (2013); *see* Wilf-Townsend, *supra* note 1, at 1720 n.78 ("A total face value of $143 billion divided by 90 million accounts yields an average of $1588.89 per account").

Once the machinery of state courts begins to churn, individual defendants cannot sustain the costs of litigation. Not surprisingly, most of them never appear in court.[16] Figures 17.1 and 17.2 give a sense of the transformation of the state courts into collection agents as contract and other small claims come to dominate the state court docket. The shocking part is not simply the decline of traditional areas of state competence such as torts but the speed with which this transformation occurred.

The result is not just a transformation in the docket but in the nature of how law is practiced. Over the same period of time, the bulk of cases in state courts involve no lawyer on the defense side. Meanwhile, on the plaintiffs' side of the "v.," we see the rise of debt collectors as the single greatest group of litigators.

Not surprisingly, we also see dominant individual firms, the so-called top filers, command a greater and greater part of individual state civil dockets (Figure 17.3).

We engage these legal developments primarily to address potential responses. Returning to the concept of asymmetric aggregation, the problem presented is one of the efficiencies of scale allowing aggregators of debt claims to amortize the costs of legal procedures across mass filings while the debtors themselves remain rationally incapable of hiring counsel, attending court proceedings, and contesting legal arguments. The early proposals for reform address these issues in three characteristic ways.

First, and most evidently, there is the problem that the bulk of defendants are unrepresented. The obvious response is to increase the availability of representation, as with more pro bono offerings or the expansion of law school clinics. There is, in our view, little likelihood of much redress here. The sheer numbers overwhelm any capacity to provide impecunious defendants with volunteer representation. Consequently, more attention is directed to expanding the *concept* of representation by allowing paralegals and paraprofessionals – the legal equivalents of nurse practitioners in medicine – to assume more of the role of qualified legal representatives. We address this as the most significant area for reform through expanding representation.

The second reform approach aims not to provide representation but to lower the cost of individuals representing themselves in order to create systems that can be used with ease by people representing themselves. Many debt collection disputes turn on facts rather than law, such as whether the product actually performed, whether payment was actually made, or whether warranty obligations were actually met – all facts likely known by the debtor. Still another set of claims may be those in which there is a simple defense because the statute of limitations has run, the money has been paid, legal service was not properly done, or the claim has been discharged

[16] Wilf-Townsend, *supra* note 1, at 1721 (citing Peter A. Holland, *Junk Justice: A Statistical Analysis of 4,400 Lawsuits Filed by Debt Buyers*, 26 Loy. Consumer L. Rev. 179 (2014)) ("In the Maryland study, for instance, 85% of defendants who were served with a complaint never filed written response").

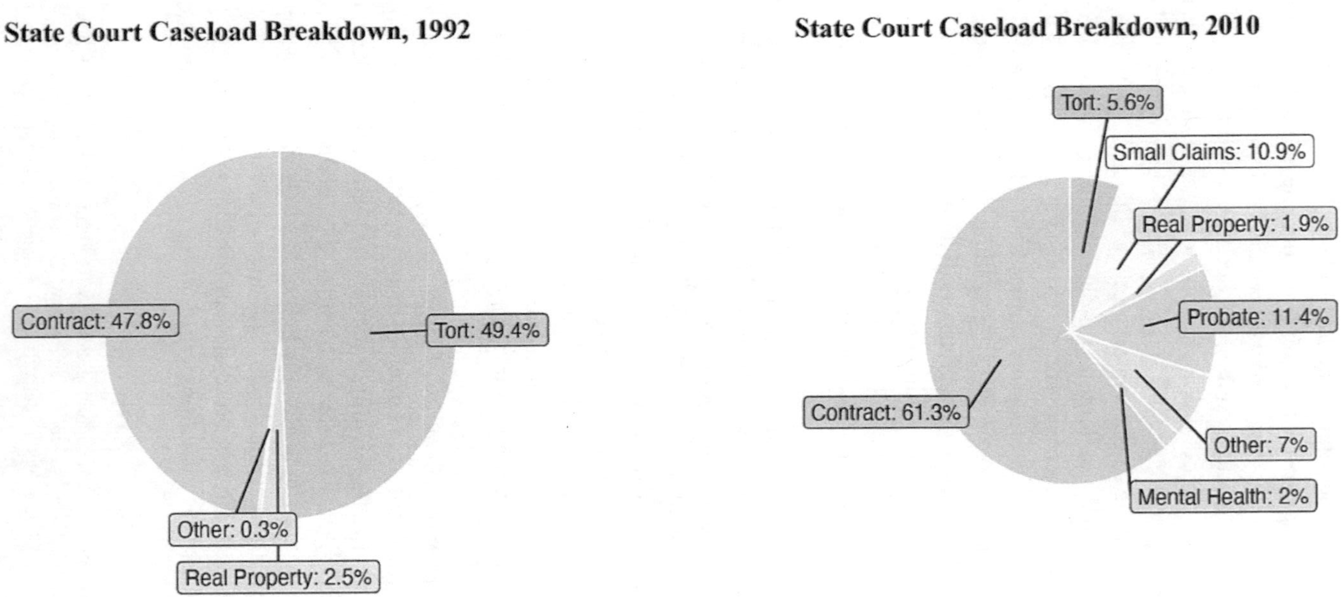

FIGURE 17.1 State court caseload breakdown 1992 versus 2010.
Source: Data from Paula Hannaford-Agor et al., *The Landscape of Civil Litigation in State Courts*, Nat'l Ctr. for State Cts. (2015).

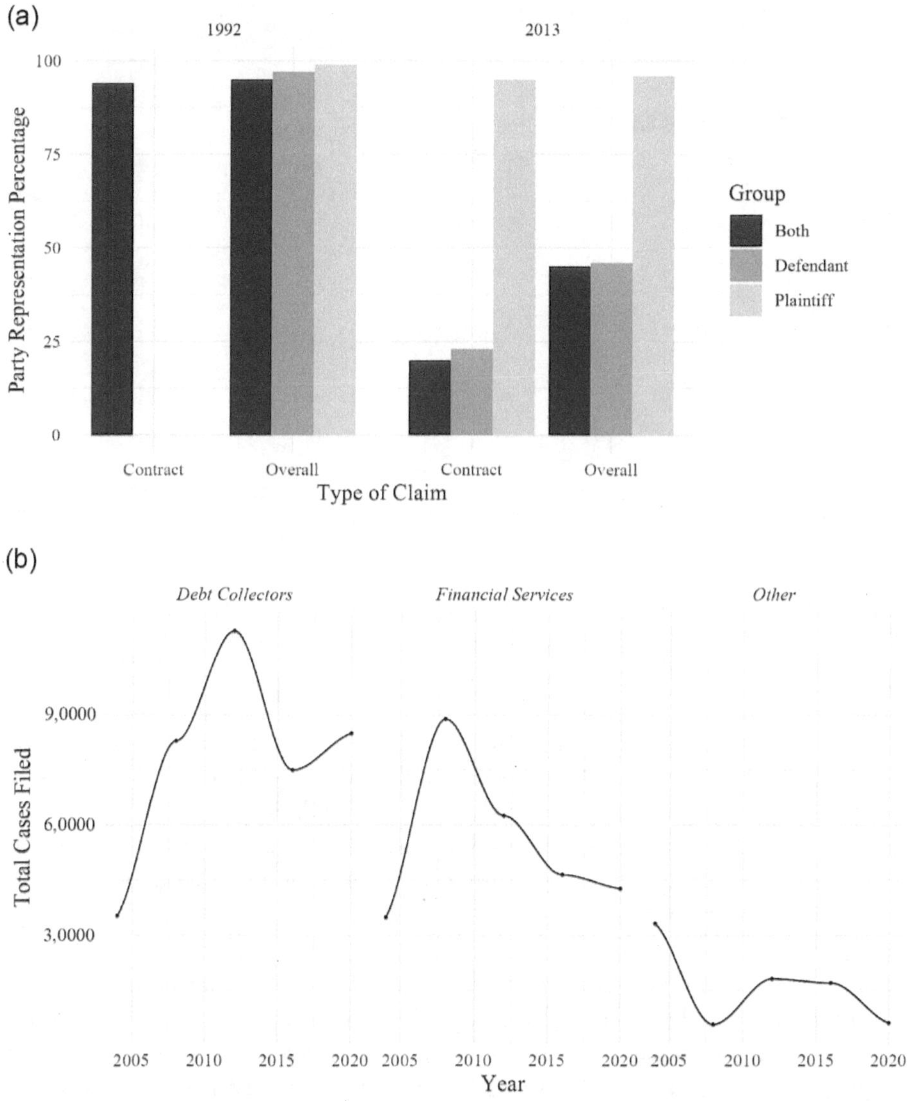

FIGURE 17.2 (a) State court party representation status and (b) identity of top filers in state courts.

Sources: (a) Data from Paula Hannaford-Agor et al., *The Landscape of Civil Litigation in State Courts*, NAT'L CTR. FOR STATE CTS. (2015); (b) Data from Daniel Wilf-Townsend, *Assembly-Line Plaintiffs*, 135 HARV. L. REV. 1704, 1736 (2022).

in bankruptcy. These are not complicated legal issues but may still require some level of legal assistance.

For litigants seeking to defend themselves, a further problem may not be so much the capacity to muster a legal argument but the problem of getting to court. A day off

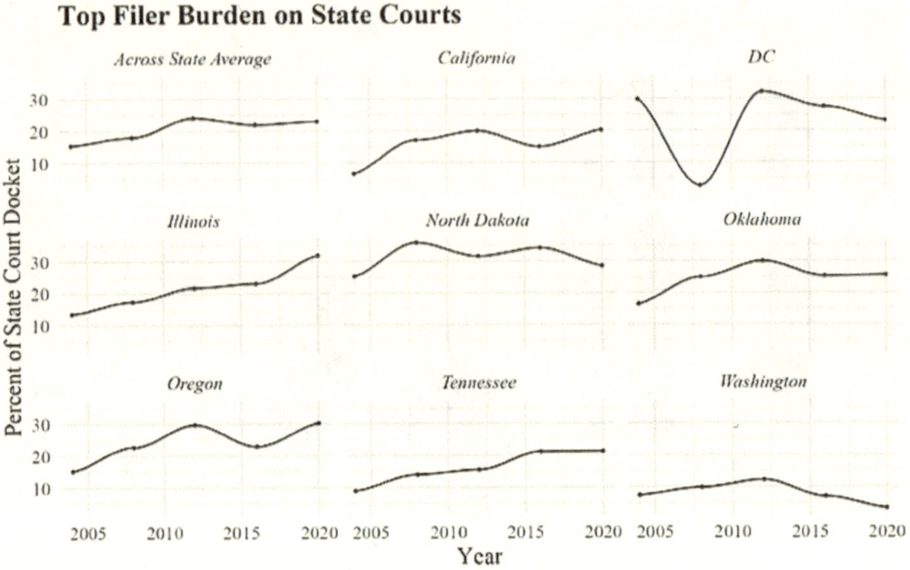

FIGURE 17.3 State-by-state comparison of top filer burden on state courts.
Source: Data from Daniel Wilf-Townsend, *Assembly-Line Plaintiffs*, 135 HARV. L. REV. 1704, 1736 (2022).

of work, the scramble to find child care, or even getting to inaccessible courthouses may put the ability to articulate one's side of the story beyond the reach of working people. One of the fortunate by-products of the COVID pandemic is increased experience and comfort with remote court engagement that, by lowering aggregate costs, may diminish the impact of resource advantages for the debt aggregators. This is also addressed below.

Third, there is the underexamined possibility of direct regulatory oversight. If the problem here is a fundamental asymmetry in stakes that cannot be overcome by aggregation of the debtor (e.g., it is hard to imagine a class action of all consumer debtors), then the problem presents as a species of market failure inviting regulatory response. Two regulatory paths suggest themselves. The first is to rate the repeat filers in terms of the care they have taken to avoid exploiting the vulnerabilities of the debtors. An independent agency – the Consumer Finance Protection Board (CFPB) suggests itself – could require repeat litigants to register the time taken between acquiring debt and filing suit, the number of suits filed against parties who had previously obtained bankruptcy protection, the internal procedures of the firm for verifying whether there are existing complaints or other considerations that should be resolved before executing on the debt, and other such mechanisms of compliance with best practices. Our approach here derives from the literature on responsive regulation and would impose increased prices or limitation on filings for firms that are repeatedly noncompliant.

Alternatively (or perhaps additionally), the regulatory response could come from within the courts themselves. There is no evident reason that the filing of thousands of cases by a single firm, almost invariably yielding default judgments against unrepresented parties, should not attract some institutional scrutiny. Although it is not the custom in American courts, an ombudsman could be appointed to audit some number of claims filed, to investigate complaints about misconduct (such as harassing calls to parties already discharged in bankruptcy or improper service of process), or to secure representation for a sample set of claims. The approach here draws from auditing rather than advocacy and is intended as a regulatory mechanism for quality control.

We discuss these various approaches in turn.

17.1 EXPANDING THE POOL OF REPRESENTATION

If the obstacle to defendants' securing representation is cost, then states could respond by decreasing costs for people to defend their cases. This is the most conventional response, in that it disrupts neither the role of the court nor the way in which any particular litigation is processed through the legal system.

If the problem is identified as the expense of securing adequate representation, then the most obvious solution is to provide free counsel for all defendants. Creating an obligation to provide counsel to all litigants is unlikely to emerge as a litigated rights claim since the Supreme Court has declined requests to extend the 6th Amendment's right to counsel to civil cases,[17] and states have only begun to guarantee access to attorneys in civil cases in limited contexts.[18] But beyond the doctrinal obstacles, the real problem (as in most mass litigation) is simply the sheer size of the challenge. Quite bluntly, it is hard to see the political will for a benefits program of the size required to provide representation in all debt collection cases in state courts.

Where public funds are unlikely to fill the void, private resources may enter the mix. Most often, pro bono representation is part of the expected social return from the highest rungs of the bar, and from the generations of law school entrants to the practice of law. But the scale of the problem outstrips any possible resolution by voluntary representation. One-by-one provision of free or discounted legal services cannot address the scope of the national problem, nor even the yearly filing of one entrepreneurial New Jersey lawyer.

[17] *See* Lassiter v. Dep't of Soc. Servs. of Durham Cnty., N.C., 452 U.S. 18, 25 (1981) ("The pre-eminent generalization that emerges from this Court's precedents on an indigent's right to appointed counsel is that such a right has been recognized to exist only where the litigant may lose his physical liberty if he loses the litigation").

[18] *See* Tonya L. Brito, *The Right to Civil Counsel*, 148 DÆDALUS 56, 57 (2019) (listing examples of states and cities that have begun to fund civil counsel rights in limited contexts, such as housing, child custody, conservatorship, and guardianship cases).

An alternative route is to liberalize access to representation. States can permit paralegals and other certified specialists to represent people who would otherwise lack representation. Some states have already piloted such programs. For instance, Washington developed a program to license nonlawyers in specific areas of the law (Limited Licensed Legal Technicians or "LLLTs").[19] The State of Washington chose to sunset the program but permitted the sixteen active LLLTs to continue practicing. Utah, Oregon, Arizona, and Minnesota have created similar programs.[20]

A big question hanging over these experiments is whether nonlawyer representation works. The most exhaustive research addressing that question comes from several reviews of Social Security benefits cases, where federal law authorizes representation by nonlawyers,[21] creating a rich source of background material. The results indicate that paralegals have proven capable of representing claimants in front of administrative law judges[22] and that "accredited representatives" have been effective before immigration judges.[23]

More supply of legal representation provides a viable means of challenging claims, increasing their likelihood of success and increasing the costs of these debt collection plaintiffs' business model. But it does not address all the issues discussed above. Individuals must receive notice of a claim against them before they can obtain representation, and repeat plaintiffs with resourced attorneys may be able to overwhelm paralegals who will likely be underfunded and overworked.

One should take care to not allow the perfect to be the enemy of the good. Many of the specific abuses that have been identified with mass filers can be picked up by those who are specially trained, even without full legal certification. Known abuses ranging from harassing phone calls to sewer service[24] can be fitted onto a checklist of

[19] *See* Tara Huges & Joyce Reichard, *How States Are Using Limited Licensed Legal Paraprofessionals to Address the Access to Justice Gap*, Am. Bar Ass'n (Sept. 2, 2022), https://www.americanbar.org/groups/paralegals/blog/how-states-are-using-non-lawyers-to-address-the-access-to-justice-gap/ (last accessed Feb. 3, 2025).

[20] *Id.*

[21] 42 U.S.C. §§ 406(a)(1), 1383(d)(2); *see also* 20 C.F.R. § 404.1705(b).

[22] *See* Allan M. Tow, *Teaching Trial Practice and Dramatic Technique*, 13 J. Paralegal Educ. & Prac. 59, 60 (1997) ("One oft-cited study showed that Social Security Administration claimants represented by non-attorneys achieved a success rate very close to that of claimants who were represented by attorneys.").

[23] *Recognition & Accreditation (R&A) Program*, Dep't of Just. (updated May 13, 2024, https://www.justice.gov/eoir/recognition-and-accreditation-program (last accessed July 16, 2023). An "accredited representative" offers immigration legal services to clients appearing before the immigration court through a "recognized organization," *Id.* In turn, a "recognized organization" is an approved nonprofit organization providing immigration-related legal services to indigent or low-income people. 8 C.F.R. § 1292.11(a) (2003). Recognized organizations must apply for an individual to become an accredited representative. *Id.* § 1292.12(a).

[24] Sewer service is the intentional failure to properly serve notice of a complaint on a defendant (often, by a repeat plaintiff), which frequently results in a default judgment against a defendant who had no idea that they had been sued in the first place. *See* Adrian Gottshall, *Solving Sewer Service: Fighting Fraud with Technology*, 70 Ark. L. Rev. 813, 814–17 (2018).

initial inquiries. There may still be a large number of legal issues missed, or the legal implications of conduct underexamined. But for many caught in the debt litigation cycle, this is undoubtedly better than going it alone.

Mostly, our reservations come from the initial framing of the current difficulties as being largely a product of asymmetric aggregation. Expanding representation, even for those capable of securing counsel or its substitute, would still not alter the vast disparity in resources and expertise across the litigation divide. Part of the problem may be addressed by lowering the cost of routine legal advice and expanding the pool of those who may provide less than full legal counsel. The medical profession encountered this with the creation of nurse practitioners and other professionals capable of delivering valuable medical services even without the full training of an MD.[25] While salutary, this approach still puts the burden on the disadvantaged defendant to figure out how to obtain legal services, even at a discount. That advances the ball but is unlikely to be the central answer to the current structural challenges to the courts.

17.2 RECONFIGURING GOING TO COURT

A second approach is to reconfigure what "court" looks like. One path is toward a more inquisitorial model of a supervening court, as opposed to the anything-goes autonomy of an unchecked adversarial model. Professor Jessica Steinberg draws on specialized drug and housing courts to outline a "naming" strategy for altering judicial conduct.[26] States can designate special courts for consumer debt cases that either largely draw upon traditional judicial models or depart significantly – for instance, judges in drug courts generally act as case managers for a rehabilitating party.[27]

Even if state courts were to keep the adjudicatory structure of civil courts intact but develop a specialized bench or procedures for consumer cases, that classification may influence the outcome of many consumer debt cases. Heightened pleading requirements, for instance, might deter fraudulent claims that lack any reliable evidentiary support. Placing the burden on plaintiffs can increase the cost of pursuing claims, especially for claims that only succeed because of the abusive tactics available to plaintiffs in normal state court proceedings. Additionally, in creating special courts, the state redefines the judiciary's nature from a "neutral justice" establishment to a "problem-solving" institution meant to confront the social ill assembly-line plaintiffs perpetuate.[28]

[25] *See* Chapter 8 in this volume.

[26] *See generally* Jessica K. Steinberg, *A Theory of Civil Problem-Solving Courts*, 93 N.Y.U. L. Rev. 1579 (2018).

[27] *See Id.* at 1585–90 (discussing drug courts and their philosophy).

[28] *Id.* at 1607 ("The idea is that, if judges were to view the purpose of the tribunal as, say, improving substandard housing, they would approach their work with an eye toward affording

Perhaps the area of most fertile recent development has been the technological innovations implemented in response to the COVID pandemic. The sudden need to permit remote access to legal proceedings occasioned by the need to avoid interpersonal contact quickly generated readily deployable practices, the simplest being Zoom proceedings that relieve working people and parents of the oftentimes impossible burden of missing work or finding alternative childcare. While remote proceedings would maintain the adversary form of apparent one-to-one litigation, it would transform the process of going to court into something more in keeping with the online exchanges that form the core of the consumer experience. Such experimental court settings will not address the asymmetry in access to information and the knowledge of legal processes between individuals and debt collectors, but they may significantly reduce the transactional barriers that at present serve to deter even meritorious defenses from being aired.

Alternatively, non-technological approaches could provide protection to vulnerable debtors. One government-centric approach would create an ombudsman-like process that would permit plaintiffs to file claims with a state agency, which would then conduct fact-finding from a neutral position. The ombudsman agency would review claims, perhaps collectively adjudicate claims, better understanding a plaintiff's pattern of behavior and adjusting to evidence of fraud, abuse, or meritless claims accordingly.[29] Ombudsmen programs can improve the efficiency of state courts through careful review of systemic problems throughout state courts and by adjusting procedures to ensure access to justice.[30] Though these offices normally do not have final decision-making authority,[31] they can enable rapid response to challenges in alternative adjudicatory systems that states test, or they can begin to alter current practices in state courts of general jurisdiction.[32] Unlike providing legal counsel to indigent individual defendants, or facilitating judges to assume fiduciary-like roles in dealing with unrepresented defendants, an

tenants the benefit of existing substantive and procedural protections – thereby serving as a shield against the dominance of powerful private actors"); *Id.* at 1612 ("One might imagine other areas – principally consumer debt – where a specialized docket might also redefine its mission to confront a social issue that has been impervious to traditional adjudication.").

29 *See id.* at 1769–71.

30 *See* Judith Jones & Alvin W. Cohn, *State Ombudsman Programs*, OFFICE OF JUST. PROGRAMS, U.S. DEP'T OF JUST. 2 (2005), https://www.ojp.gov/library/publications/state-ombudsman-programs (last accessed Feb. 3, 2025) (describing ombudsmen programs generally and explaining most states have ombudsmen for juvenile justice issues).

31 *See, for example*, *Ombudsman Charter*, CONSUMER FIN. PROT. BUREAU (Dec. 8, 2011) https://files.consumerfinance.gov/f/documents/CFPB_Ombudsman_Charter_12-7-11.pdf (last accessed Feb. 3, 2025) (describing the role of the Ombudsman Office as "an independent, impartial, and confidential resource to informally assist consumers, depositories, and nondepositories in addressing issues resulting from the CFPB's regulatory activities").

32 *See* Donald C. Rowat, *Should the State Ombudsmen Supervise the Courts*, 37 INDIAN J. PUB. ADMIN. 162, 166 (1991) (collecting studies of European ombudsmen programs that suggest they resolve claims more efficiently than their court systems do).

ombudsman introduces a nonjudicial actor with oversight review of the entirety of the court process.

No doubt there are other technocratic possibilities looming on the horizon. Firms like eBay and Amazon have used AI tools to create electronic dispute resolution centers. It may be that broad swaths of consumer debt disputes lend themselves to low-cost pattern adjudication that removes human decisionmakers, and their associated costs, with the advent of "online dispute resolution" (ODR) technology. At their most ambitious, ODR proponents aim to "reimagine 'going to court,'"[33] supplanting in-person interactions with judges, prosecutors, and other litigants with "asynchronous" communication, document submission, and dispute resolution, all done from an online user interface.[34] Online dispute resolution enthusiasts intend to "scale" the adjudication of small-dollar disputes,[35] thereby expanding the information garnered from the increasingly routinized nature of collection lawsuits into the adjudicative template for future cases. In some sense, this is a technological advance in the routinization of tort claims at the hands of insurance adjustors and the nascent plaintiffs' tort bar many generations ago.[36]

Online dispute resolution technology originated in online platforms and marketplaces, such as Amazon, eBay, and Alibaba.[37] On those platforms, ODR is the primary venue for adjudicating disputes over, for instance, whether content will remain online, whether a user account will be suspended, whether an online vendor will be delisted,[38] or whether a product delivered to a consumer is as described. These processes have started to make their way to the judiciary with initial uses in Singapore,[39] the Netherlands, Canada, the United Kingdom, and the Hague.[40] Pilot projects in the United States now exist in at least 113 adjudicative tribunals.[41] These

[33] J. J. Prescott, *Improving Access to Justice in State Courts with Platform Technology*, 70 Vand. L. Rev. 1993, 1999 (2017).

[34] *See id.* at 1999–2000.

[35] *See, for example*, *How It Works: Technical*, Matterhorn by Court Innovations, https://web.archive.org/web/20230923151743/https://getmatterhorn.com/tour/how-it-works-tech/ (last accessed Feb. 24, 2025). *See also* Colin Rule, *Online Dispute Resolution and the Future of Justice*, 16 Ann. Rev. L. & Soc. Sci. 277, 281 (2020).

[36] This is the argument elaborated in Samuel Issacharoff & John Fabian Witt, *The Inevitability of Aggregate Settlement: An Institutional Account of American Tort Law*, 57 Vand. L. Rev. 1571 (2004).

[37] *See* Amy J. Schmitz, *Expanding Access to Remedies through E-Court Initiatives*, 67 Buff. L. Rev. 89, 91 (2019).

[38] *See* Rory Van Loo, *Federal Rules of Platform Procedure*, 88 U. Chi. L. Rev. 829, 830–31 (2021).

[39] *See Online Dispute Resolution Moves from E-Commerce to the Courts*, Pew Charitable Tr. (June 4, 2019), https://www.pewtrusts.org/en/research-and-analysis/articles/2019/06/04/online-dispute-resolution-moves-from-e-commerce-to-the-courts.

[40] *See* Ethan Katsch & Orna Rabinovich-Einy, Digital Justice 160 (2017).

[41] *See Courts Using ODR*, Nat'l Ctr. for Tech. & Disp. Resol., https://odr.info/courts-using-odr/ (last accessed June 25, 2023).

experiments with ODR are generally at the local and state levels and use the technology for disputes over taxes, parking fines, and small claims.[42]

The aim of ODR is to "triage the case into an appropriate resolution pathway,"[43] in the inevitable technojargon that one would expect. Most often, the parties can submit confidential "reserve settlements" they would be comfortable paying or accepting. If there is overlap in the reservation prices of the parties, a settlement agreement can be generated through an algorithm. Mediators can also be involved if there is no mutually amenable agreement between parties. If ODR is court-annexed, non-resolution then allows for more conventional court processes to follow. In private settings, as with airlines dealing with claims for lost luggage, the offer is final and, if refused, forces the claimant to initiate legal processes.

One prominent ODR firm describes its product as a "communications platform [that] … implements [a court's] eligibility rules, workflows, and decisions."[44] The firm stresses that its product "offers a neutral place for parties and stakeholders to share information and communicate," and that the product "gives the public their 'day in court' from their own device and from anywhere."[45] But the world is unfortunately not win-win. The benefits of speed and cost may compress legal rights. Streamlined algorithms may discount specific defenses such as the tolling of state statutes of limitations, allegations of identity theft, and invocations of the Truth in Lending Act.[46] Moreover, dispute resolution behavior does not stand still. Facilitating access to rapid resolution of claims may lead to more filings and may allow for process "capture" by deep-pocketed and sophisticated actors.[47]

Early and quite preliminary empirical evidence suggests that ODR does in fact advantage defendants in cases filed by repeat filing plaintiffs. A study of ODR in six states found that ODR reduces the time required to resolve disputes, lowers default rates, and increases disputants' compliance with court-ordered payments.[48] An additional study presents evidence that ODR decreases default rates and allows

[42] *See* Schmitz, *supra* note 37, at 105.

[43] *See* Rule, *supra* note 35, at 284–85.

[44] *What Is Matterhorn?*, Matterhorn by Court Innovations, https://web.archive.org/web/20230530002715/https://getmatterhorn.com/tour/what-is-matterhorn/ (archived page) (last accessed Feb. 4, 2025). Matterhorn's future is uncertain, as it was included in a recent acquisition of public sector software companies. *See Matterhorn Is Now Catalis*, Catalis (undated), https://catalisgov.com/our-story/ (last accessed Jan. 28, 2025); *Our Story*, Catalis (undated), https://catalisgov.com/our-story/ (last accessed Jan. 28, 2025) (describing Catalis's recent acquisition of public sector software companies).

[45] *Id.*

[46] *See* Norman W. Spaulding, Online Dispute Resolution and the End of Adversarial Justice?, *in* Legal Tech and The Future of Civil Justice 251, 267–69 (David Freeman Engstrom ed., 2023).

[47] *See* Robert Condlin, *Online Dispute Resolution: Stinky, Repugnant, or Drab?*, 18 Cardozo J. Conflict Resol. 717, 721–24 (2017).

[48] *See generally* Prescott, *supra* note 33, at 2029–50.

defendants to respond to and engage with disputes outside of business hours.[49] Competing and nuanced evidence on case duration using ODR suggests that ODR reduces case duration when disputants reach an agreement, but in turn *increases* duration when disputes are addressed on the merits, perhaps because the technology's flexibility better allows defendants to vindicate themselves.[50] The jury is still out on how the technology will ultimately play out. Relieving human congestion is no small gain for citizen welfare.

17.3 THE REGULATORY RESPONSE

17.3.1 *Deceleration*

Perhaps the most direct way to control the advantages of aggregators of debt collection is to raise the cost of doing business. Professor Wilf-Townsend, for example, relies on an analogy to congestion pricing.[51] Certain plaintiffs would see their filing fees increase as they file more claims. Such pricing should change the economics for repeat plaintiffs. As their costs increase with the volume of complaints they file, the marginal profit on each additional case decreases, unless their prices go up. At least in theory, and in the absence of overwhelming market concentration, the market equilibrium point would shift to a lower volume, conserving precious judicial resources and protecting some individuals who might otherwise have been sued without the pricing regime.

Even apart from the heroic economic assumptions and the practicalities of such a simple regulatory response,[52] such wholesale deterrence runs up against due process values that encourage open courts. There is nothing unlawful about the aggregation of claims and plaintiffs, even repeat play plaintiffs, are entitled to their "day in court."[53] Such congestion pricing might have the beneficial effect of forcing repeat plaintiffs to internalize the negative externalities their filings create.[54] But the lack of fit between raising the price of admission to the courts and collateral consequences remains a source of concern. More fundamentally, congestion pricing introduces a user-fee approach to public justice. The problem of mass filings does present a vision that reduces the state judiciary from adjudicators to paper pushers. If this is the sole

49 *See* J. J. Prescott & Alexander Sanchez, Platform Procedure: Using Technology to Facilitate (Efficient) Civil Settlement, *in* SELECTION AND DECISION IN JUDICIAL PROCESS AROUND THE WORLD 30, 69–70 (Yun-chien Chang ed., 2019).

50 *See id.* at 58–65.

51 Wilf-Townsend, *supra* note 1, at 1758.

52 *See id.* at 1760–61 (listing other downsides: (1) the easy use of subsidiaries to avoid the fees, (2) increasing cost of consumer credit ex-ante, (3) incentivizing informal methods of debt collection, (4) fees will likely be transferred back to defendants ex-post).

53 Richards v. Jefferson Cnty., Ala., 517 U.S. 793, 798 (1996) (noting our "deep-rooted historic tradition that everyone should have his own day in court" [citation omitted]).

54 Wilf-Townsend, *supra* note 1, at 1758.

concern, then perhaps the best we can do is a system that generates more revenue to expand the state judiciary and distributes the burden of public funding to those who deserve it.[55]

More targeted efforts would look to license debt collection, a move that many states have already made.[56] Licensing begins the process of identifying the players in debt collection activities, the scope of their activities, and the likely areas of potential abuse. By requiring debt collectors to be licensed, states can proactively gain knowledge about who is behind the massive number of debt collection actions filling its courts rather than leaving the courts to merely react to the enormous influx of civil actions filed. As a rule, the licensing statutes prohibit anyone from engaging in the business of debt collection in the state without one.[57] Once licensed, the debt collectors are subject to rules governing their conduct and extensive reporting requirements for their activities in the state.

The licensing statute's standards for conduct seek to address the problems most often encountered by courts on account of bad actors in the debt collection industry.[58] The most common of these problems are (1) suits filed based on inaccurate or insufficient information about the debt, (2) insufficient notice given to the consumer being sued, (3) unacceptably high rates of default judgments being entered against consumers, (4) actions filed or threatened to be filed based on debts that are time-barred, and (5) once a judgment is obtained, improper garnishment of exempt funds. One category of rules established for licensed debt collectors is designed to address these abuses.

Many states are now using licensing requirements to address the risk of abuse in new forms of debt collection.[59] For example, in California, licensed debt collectors are required to comply with all aspects of the Rosenthal Fair Debt Collection

[55] *Id.* at 1759.

[56] Thirty-six states and the District of Columbia license debt collectors. *See* Cons. Fed. of Cal., Addressing Process and Grounds for Granting Debt Collector License Applications 1 n.1 (2021) (noting thirty-four states and D.C. require licenses); Sarah Edwards, *What States Require a Professional Licensing Number for Debt Collectors?*, SoloSuit (Oct. 19, 2022), https://www.solosuit.com/posts/states-require-license-debt-collector (last accessed Feb. 4, 2025) (adding California's and Mississippi's 2022 regulations to that count).

[57] Debt collectors are defined differently under various licensing statutes. Some exempt banks, attorneys, and specifically named businesses that are otherwise regulated. *See, for example,* Cal. Fin. Code § 100001(b)(1) (listing exemptions from California's debt collection licensing requirements). Others include law firms whose predominant business is collecting debt.

[58] Generally, licensing statutes prohibit such misconduct as harassing phone calls and refusal to supply written documentation of the asserted debt. *See, for example,* N.Y. C.A.C. § 20-493.2(a)–(b).

[59] *See, for example,* the cases of Massachusetts, *Apply for a Debt Collector License or Loan Service Registration*, Commonwealth of Mass., https://www.mass.gov/how-to/apply-for-a-debt-collector-license-or-loan-servicer-registration (last accessed Feb. 3, 2025), and Illinois, *Collection Agency*, Ill. Dep't of Fin. & Pro. Regul., https://idfpr.illinois.gov/profs/collections.html (last accessed Feb. 3, 2025).

Practices Act.[60] This statute, which existed before California began licensing debt collectors, prohibits a debt collector from making *any* written statement to a debtor unless it is the sole owner of the debt or is acting on behalf of all owners. Further, any communication must include the debt balance at the time the debt was charged off, together with an explanation of the amount, nature, and reason for all post-charge-off interest and fees, if any, imposed by the charge-off creditor or any subsequent purchasers of the debt. The debtor is also given the name of all parties who have had an interest in the debt being collected and the state registration number of the debt buyer.[61] Once suit is brought against a debtor, the complaint must include this information as well.[62]

California also increased the information necessary to file suit, requiring, for example, that the court receive a copy of the contract from which the debt arose.[63] Also, the debt collector must submit an affidavit attesting to all facts alleged in support of the amount and the ownership of the debt.[64] The statute establishes procedures by which debtors (who have had a default judgment entered against them) can reopen and set aside the judgment based on lack of notice of the suit filed, mistaken identity, or identity theft.[65] The statute establishes rules for collecting debts that may be time-barred or obsolete. And finally, penalties garnish funds that are otherwise exempt from garnishment.

California's Department of Business Oversight existed before the state began licensing debt collectors, but it gained new responsibilities under the licensing scheme. The Commissioner of the Department of Business Oversight is designated as the recipient of the broad range of information required from the licensees. Generally, each California debt collector must now file an annual report disclosing the following information from the previous year: the total number of California debtor accounts purchased or collected on, the total dollar amount of California debtor accounts purchased, the face value dollar amount of the California debtor accounts held in the licensee's portfolio, the total dollar amount of debt collected, the total amount of debt still outstanding, the total dollar amount of proceeds generated by the debtor accounts, and the case number of any action in which the license holder was held liable (by way of final judgment) for failing to meet the conduct requirements imposed by California's Rosenthal Fair Debt Collection Practices Act.[66]

No state receiving the type of information required by the California licensing scheme needs to remain in the dark about who is behind the massive debt collection actions being filed in its courts. While we are aware of no licensing statutes that

60 *See* Cal. Civ. Code §§ 1788.10–1788.185 (defining debt collectors' responsibilities).
61 *Id.* §§ 1788.52(a)(1)–(7).
62 *Id.* § 1788.58.
63 *Id.* § 1788.60.
64 *Id.*
65 *Id.* § 1788.61.
66 Cal. Fin. Code § 100021(a)(1)–(7).

require licensees to report this data to the courts, the courts would benefit from having access to it in aid of the management of debt collection cases. For example, since the California licensing statute requires the licensees to self-report when they have been sanctioned for violating the reporting or collection procedures required by statute, bad actors should be more quickly and easily identified. But for a judge handling a busy docket, information identifying bad actors can take years to become apparent. Even if a single debt collector engages in identical misconduct across numerous dockets assigned to different judges on the same court, there is no established common repository of knowledge reflecting the experience of individual judges. Giving judges access to information gained through the licensing processes can help judges to identify bad actors and thereby expedite either reforming or removing those actors from the marketplace.

17.3.2 *Responsively Regulating*

Another response to the problem of asymmetric aggregation might be to stimulate aggregation on the other side of the "v." Given the dispersed nature of creditors and the small stakes of each disputed claim, private ordering through a defense-side class action does not seem viable.[67] If there were to be a regulatory response instead, it would optimally reflect the nationwide reach of contemporary debt collection actors and would be federal in scope, perhaps lodged in the CFPB. Some academics have proposed mechanisms to police assembly-line plaintiffs. Professor Yonathan Arbel suggests a claim sampling strategy – labeled "adminization" – for debt collection cases.[68] Essentially, a state agency would sample plaintiff filings, audit them for evidence of fraud or abuse, and then penalize plaintiffs with a failing track record.

Certain practices clearly stand out for regulatory response. Start with the brute fact that most defendants never appear in court.[69] Such cases invariably result in a default judgment. The Federal Trade Commission estimated default judgments on debt collection lawsuits occurred at a rate between 60 and 95 percent, and it suggested most jurisdictions trended toward the higher end of that range.[70] This

[67] Several sources discuss defense-side classes in more detail. *See, for example*, Assaf Hamdani & Alon Klement, *The Class Defense*, 93 CALIF. L. REV. 685 (2005); Nelson Rodrigues Netto, *The Optimal Law Enforcement with Mandatory Defendant Class Action*, 33 U. DAYTON L. REV. 59 (2007); Francis X. Shen, *The Overlooked Utility of the Defendant Class Action*, 88 DENV. U. L. REV. 73 (2010); Greg Reilly, *Aggregating Defendants*, 41 FLA. ST. U. L. REV. 1011 (2014).

[68] Yonathan A. Arbel, *Adminization: Gatekeeping Consumer Contracts*, 71 VAND. L. REV. 121 (2018).

[69] Wilf-Townsend, *supra* note 1, at 1721 (citing Holland, *supra* note 16) ("In the Maryland study, for instance, 85% of defendants who were served with a complaint never filed written response.").

[70] Fed. Trade Comm'n, *Repairing a Broken System: Protecting Consumers in Debt Collection Litigation and Arbitration* (July 2010), https://www.ftc.gov/sites/default/files/documents/reports/federal-trade-commission-bureau-consumer-protection-staff-report-repairing-broken-system-protecting/debtcollectionreport.pdf (last accessed Feb. 3, 2025).

high rate of default is not wholly caused by a mass of inattentive individuals. Rather, inadequate notice likely has a significant effect. Debt collectors employ various sewer service tactics to advance collection lawsuits without properly appraising defendants of the action.[71] These include falsifying affidavits for service of process or waivers of notice, which allows creditors to work around normal due process hurdles to swiftly obtain a default judgment. A survey of around 450 New Yorkers who called a hotline to seek advice about debt collection lawsuits discovered that around 70 percent of them had not been served with process or had been served improperly.[72]

Next is the problem of harassing phone calls inviting a debtor to pay only $10 toward an outstanding debt that might be protected by the statute of limitations or by bankruptcy discharge. For example, Georgia limits the debt collection period to six years from the date of the last payment.[73] Yet the renewal of any payment, even for a trivial amount, reopens the collectability of the debt. This invites abuse as sophisticated creditors induce payment of a "good faith" amount from unsophisticated parties with no understanding of the legal implications of their actions.

We believe the problem to be more deep-seated than these specific abuse practices would address. The literature on debt collection issues focuses heavily on the lawyerless aspects of state courts and the passivity of judges in the face of the growing social problem. The core of the problem, though, reflects what Marc Galanter set out in his seminal article, *Why the "Haves" Come out Ahead*.[74] Galanter's insight was to "look through the other end of the telescope" and "think about the different kinds of parties and the effect these differences might have on the way the system works."[75] Galanter concluded, a half century ago, with the need for moving responsibility to the state: "[u]tilizing the criminal law or the administrative process to make it the responsibility of a public officer to press claims that would be unmanageable in the hands of private grievants."[76]

In the intervening period, more subtle regulatory models have fleshed out this picture. John Braithwaite and his colleagues developed the concept of responsive

[71] *See* Gottshall, *supra* note 24, at 814–19; *see also* Robin J. Effron, *The Invisible Circumstances of Notice*, 99 N.C. L. Rev. 1521, 1533, 1545 & n.101 (2021) (discussing "sewer service" and its common constituent practices).

[72] Wilf-Townsend, *supra* note 1, at 1722 (citing The Legal Aid Soc'y Neighborhood, Econ. Dev. Advoc. Project, MFY Legal Servs. & Urb. Just. Ctr., Cmty. Dev. Project, Debt Deception: How Debt Buyers Abust the Legal System to Prey on Lower-Income New Yorkers 9 (2010)).

[73] *See* O.C.G.A. 9-3-24.

[74] Marc Galanter, *Why the "Haves" Come Out Ahead: Speculations on the Limits of Legal Change*, 9 Law & Soc'y Rev. 95 (1973). Galanter's article is consistently one of the most cited of all time. *See* Fred R. Shapiro & Michelle Pearse, *The Most-Cited Law Review Articles of All Time*, 110 Mich. L. Rev. 1483 (2012) (ranking it thirty-seven).

[75] Galanter, *supra* note 74, at 97.

[76] *Id.* at 142.

regulation to help government tune into the differing motives of regulated actors.[77] Some actors – the "good guys" – place an inherent value in rule-following so long as it is economically viable, but others – the "bad guys" – attempt to exploit any opportunity to increase profit and respond only to carrots and sticks.[78] Carrots may be just as important as sticks because a strategy based mostly on punishment fosters resistance to regulation, especially where regulation is incorporated into industry socialization.[79] The core feature is "a minimal sufficiency principle in the deployment of the big and smaller sticks: the more sanctions can be kept in the background, the more regulation can be transacted through moral suasion, the more effective regulation will be."[80]

As applied here, the key is to force repeat-player plaintiffs to disclose information about their activities, providing aggregate statistics and information on individual cases. In some situations, disclosure alone may be sufficient to deter wrongdoing.[81] Yet, as wrongdoing continues, regulators should ratchet up the "stick" side of regulation. When regulators – either some appointed ombudsman or the plaintiffs' bar – discover a pattern and practice of unconscionable collection practices, they file the civil fines and lawsuits that make up the middle of the pyramid. Finally, in the worst cases, the regulator can initiate criminal actions or, more likely, enjoin the debt collector from engaging in further collection activity. In effect, the result would be to experience rate firms based on the quality of their internal process protections and the consequent history of abuse or error.

An administrative ombudsman or other regulators within the state judiciary could enforce the pyramid on the frontlines. They would ideally have access to the information required by licensees and would be enabled to use that information to help the courts manage the massive filings. Such programs can improve the efficiency of state courts through careful review of systemic problems throughout state courts and adjustment of procedures to ensure access to justice.[82] Though these

77 Ian Ayres & John Braithwaite, Responsive Regulation: Transcending the Deregulation Debate 4 (1992).

78 Cynthia Estlund, Regoverning the Workplace 139 (2010) (setting out theory of responsive regulation).

79 Ayers & Braithwaite, *supra* note 77, at 20 ("Punitive enforcement engenders a game of regulatory cat-and-mouse whereby firms defy the spirit of the law by exploiting loopholes, and the state writes more and more specific rules to cover the loopholes").

80 *Id.* at 19.

81 Though not a perfect comparison, research on the opioid epidemic demonstrates the potential deterrent effects of recordkeeping and reporting requirements. *See* Abby Alpert et al., *Origins of the Opioid Crisis and Its Enduring Impacts*, 137 Q.J. Econ. 1139, 1139 (2019) (finding that "OxyContin distribution was more than 50% lower in 'triplicate states' [defined as states that required doctors to keep multiple copies of their prescriptions and send one of them to state regulators] in the years after the drug's launch").

82 *See* Jones & Cohn, *supra* note 30 (describing ombudsmen programs generally and explaining most states have ombudsmen for juvenile justice issues).

offices normally do not have final decision-making authority,[83] they can enable rapid response to challenges in alternative adjudicatory systems that states test or they can begin to alter current practices in state courts of general jurisdiction.[84]

Nationally, the CFPB has been battling the bad actors in the debt collection business as well. However, like judges managing their own busy dockets, the CFPB takes on bad conduct by debt collectors only after receiving and investigating complaints about that conduct. During the delay associated with the complaint process and the investigation that follows, the bad actor is free to continue with the offensive (or illegal) conduct.

The CFPB has authority to investigate and undertake enforcement proceedings.[85] Agency action has been enormously successful in rooting out and punishing bad actors in the debt collection industry, and it plays an important role. Yet, because of the reactive nature of its work in this area, bringing bad actors to justice can be a long and arduous process.

An example of this delay comes with a March 2023 press release explaining the CFPB's enforcement action against a large debt collector based in Virginia. The 2023 complaint describes the widespread and abusive practices engaged in by this debt collector for more than a decade, leading to a consent order in September of 2015.[86] The 2015 consent order was a result of debt-collector misconduct that occurred between July 21, 2011, and the date of the consent order signed on September 9, 2015.[87] Then, a complaint against this same debt collector, filed in March 2023, alleged that after entry of the 2015 consent order the same debt collector "made at least tens of thousands about unsubstantiated debt whose amount or validity a consumer had disputed" without following the procedures it agreed to follow to verify the debt obligations it seeks to collect.[88] And, according to the CFPB complaint, this

83 *See, for example*, *Ombudsman Charter*, *supra* note 31 (describing the role of the Ombudsman Office as "an independent, impartial, and confidential resource to informally assist consumers, depositories, and nondepositories in addressing issues resulting from the CFPB's regulatory activities"). *But see* Robert P. Davidow, *Criminal Procedure Ombudsman Revisited*, 73 CRIM. L. & CRIMINOLOGY 939, 939–40 (1982) (advocating for an independent ombudsman to investigate constitutional rights violations and enter findings of fact to fill the deterrence gaps in the exclusionary rule).

84 *See* Rowat, *supra* note 32, at 166 (collecting studies of European ombudsmen programs that suggest they resolve claims more efficiently than their court systems do).

85 *See* 12 U.S.C. § 5562 (authorizing the CFBP to issue civil investigative demands); *Id.* § 5536(a)(2) (prohibiting any person or entity covered by the CFBP from failing or refusing to permit access to records or providing information to the Bureau); *see also* Consumer Fin. Prot. Bureau v. Heartland Campus Sols., ECSI, 747 F. App'x 44, 50 (3d Cir. 2018) (upholding CFPB's petition to enforce the CID).

86 The misconduct detailed in the prior consent order is shocking. The plaintiff debt collector filed tens of thousands of lawsuits over several short periods, and the firm did not require its attorneys to review any account-level documents prior to filing the lawsuit. Complaint at 12, Consumer Fin. Prot. Bureau v. Portfolio Recovery Assocs., LLC, 2:23-cv-00110 (E.D. Va. Mar. 23, 2023).

87 Portfolio Recovery Assocs., LLC, CFPB No. 2015-CFPB-0023 (Sept. 9, 2015).

88 Complaint at 6, Consumer Fin. Prot. Bureau v. Portfolio Recovery Assocs., LLC, *supra* note 86.

(post-2015 consent order) misconduct took place between March 2016 and September 2020. Thus, while the CFPB has effectively wielded its regulatory power in this area, its process is necessarily reactive and therefore takes years.

In contrast, our proposed licensing regime is more proactive. Placing current and prospective debt collectors on notice of recordkeeping, reporting, and, crucially, disclosure requirements may have an immediate beneficial effect on those considering illicit practices. Annual review of account and complaint-level data provides a more routine outlet for scrutinizing collectors' patterns and practices. And, our suggestion that such information be shared with the courts, specialized ombudsmen, and the public might enable more effective reactionary regulation. Simply, such a regime enlists more guardians in debt collection cases: Judges can readily assess the credibility of a plaintiff's pleadings and enforce the state's heightened pleading requirements; ombudsmen can alert courts of illicit practices, intervene in cases, or levy fines; and an entrepreneurial private bar will quickly bring civil actions against violators of state consumer-protection statutes.

Developing a clear recordkeeping matrix does two things. First, it allows some basis for private enforcement against repeat violators, something akin to the role of regulatory filings with the SEC in the domain of securities fraud. Clear regulatory obligations to disclose debt collector interactions with debtors can help "create the legal conditions that would permit the emergence of an entrepreneurial market in agents willing to ferret out consumer harm."[89] Second, it allows a regulatory agency to relieve good actors of some burdens or regulation and allow them increased market initiatives and, presumably, some competitive advantage against nonconforming competitors. To be effective, such reporting and enforcement practices need to be standard, which probably indicates that the oversight must be federal in scope, most likely through the CFPB.

Again, it is important that the perfect not be the enemy of the good. National-level regulatory response is at best a lumbering creature. Much of the information necessary to demand more certification from miscreant actors and to ease the regulatory burden on rules followers is in the hands of state courts or could be generated through court filing requirements. The courts would then have to create a process of administrative review of specific areas of litigation, wholly independent of who wins or loses in any particular case. This may not be the customary judicial function. But nor should the stamping of endless default judgments against absent and overwhelmed defendants.

17.4 CONCLUSION

For consumers to be able to take advantage of markets, they must be able to contract for themselves and to assume the responsibility of debt. They will no doubt make

[89] Samuel Issacharoff, *Disclosure, Agents, and Consumer Agents*, 167 J. Inst. & Theoretical Econ. 56, 68 (2011).

errors, find themselves more deeply in debt than is reasonable, and face the wrath of bills coming due. Any system that offers credit to consumers has to have some mechanism of collecting on debts; otherwise, the system will collapse. We take all this as a given.

The current debt collection system is not a reasonable mechanism to balance the needs of creditors and debtors in consumer markets. In particular, the discovery of an effective means of asymmetric aggregation leaves the state court system complicit in a process that only resembles legal adjudication. We join the ranks of the concerned and offer some observations as to how to conceptualize possible responses. At the end of the day, it is hard to imagine how the evident current deformities in debt collection "litigation" can be addressed short of a regulatory response, whether generated by administrative action or whether developed from within the courts themselves.

Index

For EU product safety concerns, contact us at Calle de José Abascal, 56–1°, 28003 Madrid, Spain or eugpsr@cambridge.org.

www.ingramcontent.com/pod-product-compliance
Lightning Source LLC
LaVergne TN
LVHW100248210926
848480LV00003B/866
* 9 7 8 1 0 0 9 5 2 8 5 4 2 *